DREAM HOMES

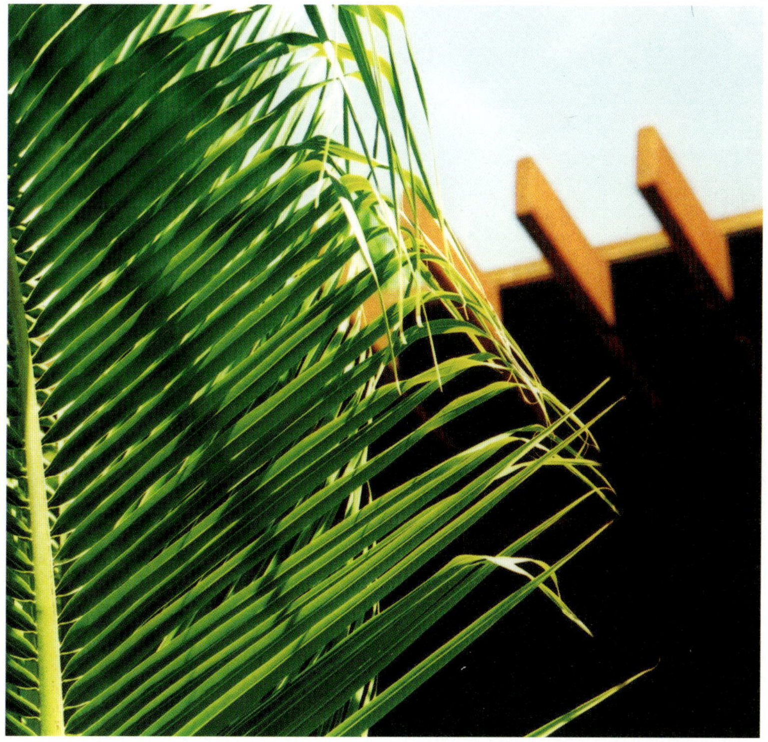

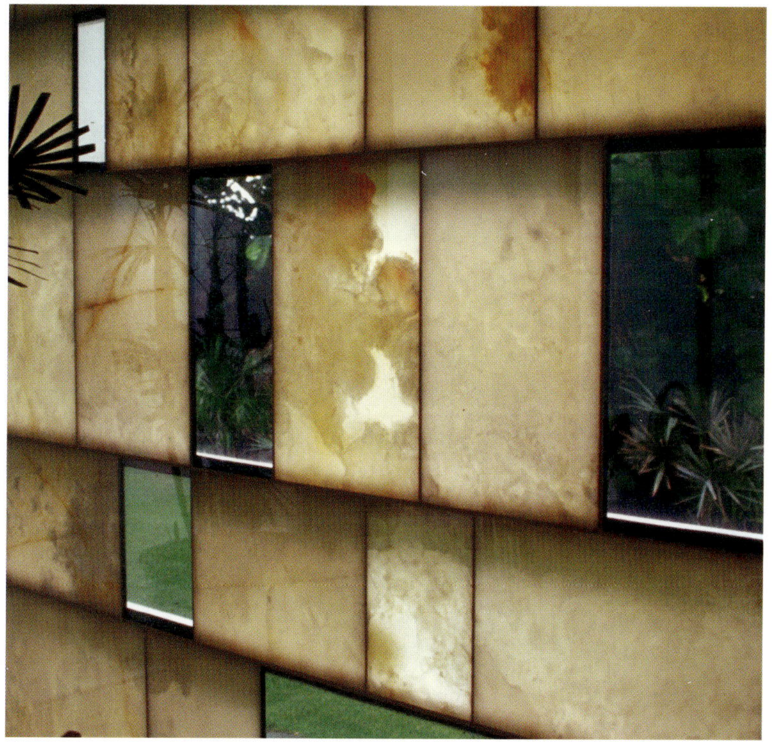

SOUTH FLORIDA

SHOWCASING SOUTH FLORIDA'S FINEST ARCHITECTS, DESIGNERS & BUILDERS

Published by

PANACHE PARTNERS LLC

13747 Montfort Drive, Suite 100
Dallas, Texas 75240
972.661.9884
972.661.2743
www.panache.com

Publishers: Brian G. Carabet and John A. Shand
Executive Publisher: Phil Reavis
Senior Associate Publisher: Beth Benton
Designer: Mary Elizabeth Acree

Printed in China

Distributed by Gibbs Smith, Publisher
800.748.5439

PUBLISHER'S DATA

Dream Homes of South Florida

Library of Congress Control Number: 2005934973

ISBN 13: 978-1-1933415-00-0
ISBN 10: 1-933415-00-2

First Printing 2006

10 9 8 7 6 5 4 3 2 1

Previous Page Left: Max Strang, Max Strang Architecture
See page 173 Photo by Max Strang Architecture

Previous Page Right: René Gonzalez, Rene Gonzalez AIA
See page 109 Photo by René Gonzalez

This Page: Steven Shapiro, Ronnie Pertnoy & Spencer Goliger, Shaprio/Pertnoy Company & SGA Architecture Inc.
See page 69 & 35 Photo by Troy Campbell

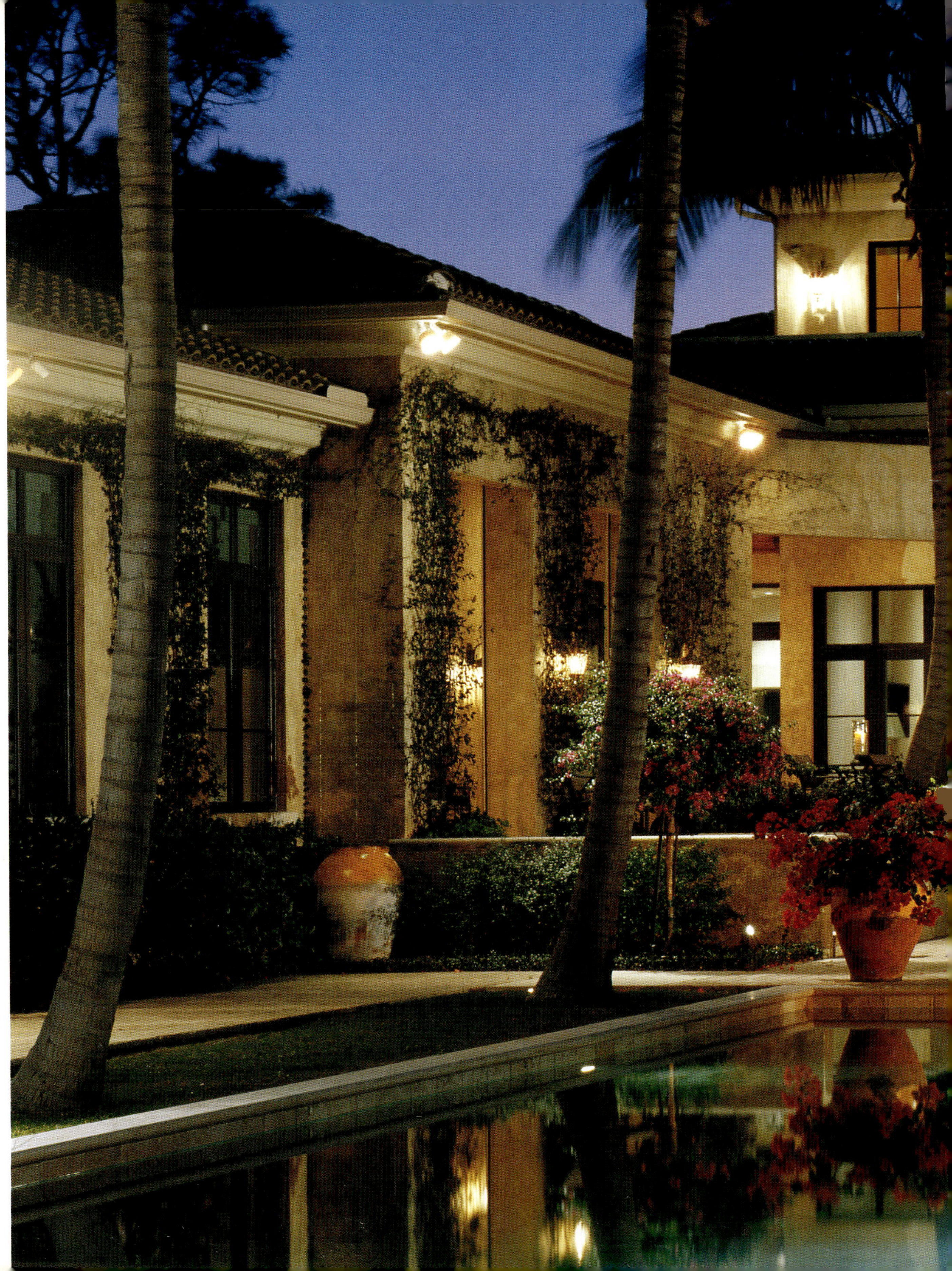

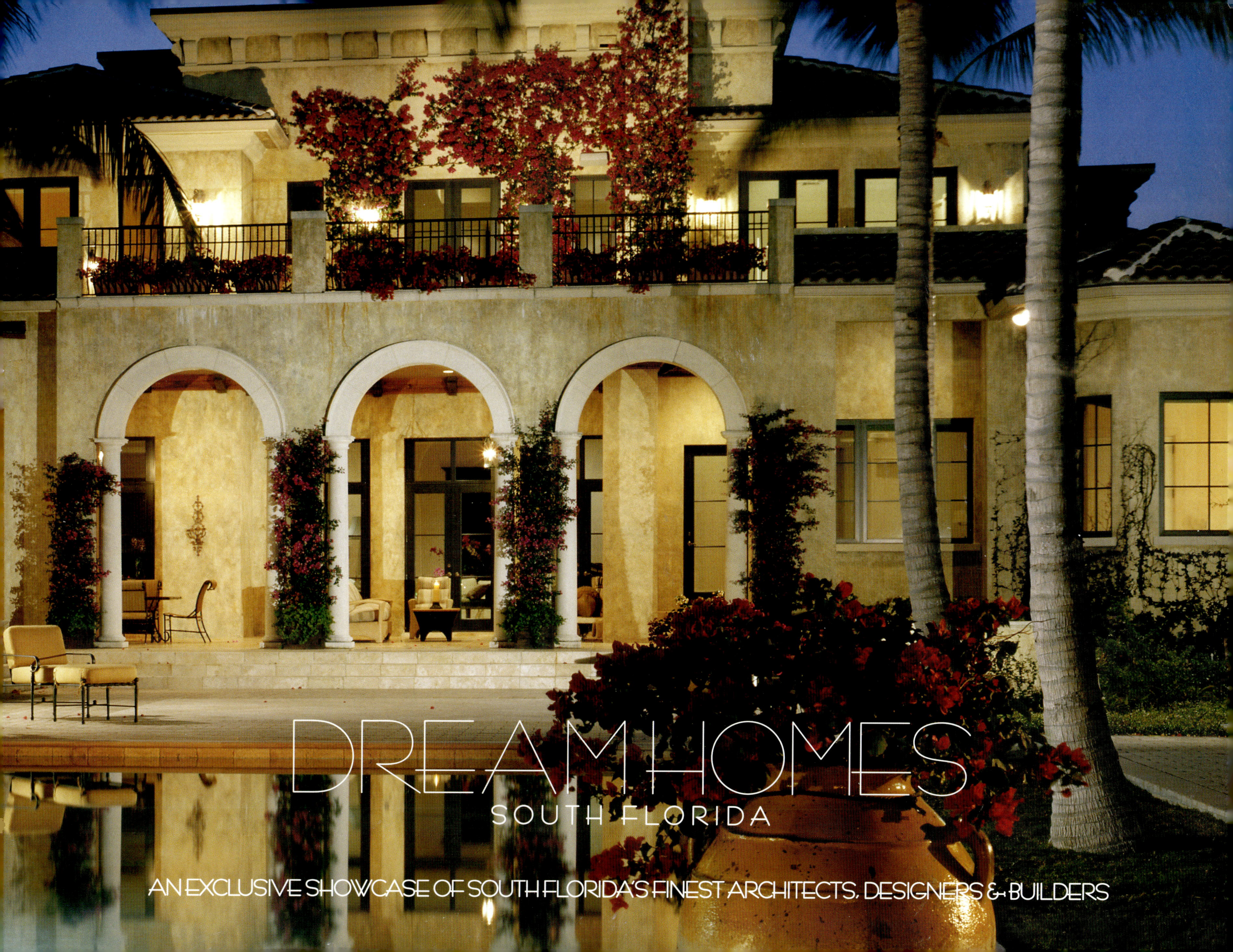
DREAM HOMES
SOUTH FLORIDA
AN EXCLUSIVE SHOWCASE OF SOUTH FLORIDA'S FINEST ARCHITECTS, DESIGNERS & BUILDERS

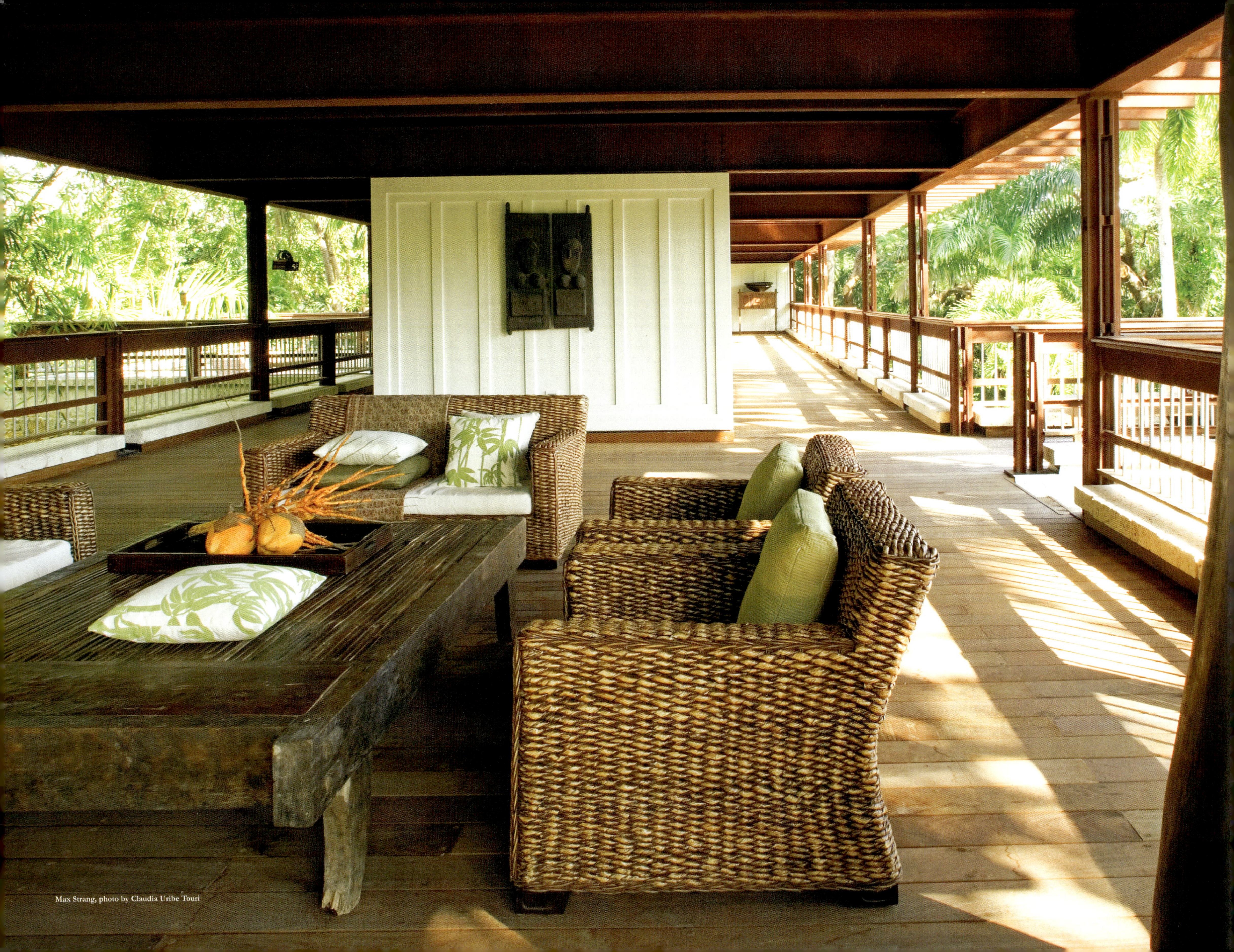

Max Strang, photo by Claudia Uribe Touri

INTRODUCTION

It was a tremendous pleasure to see some of the most incredible examples of a *dream home* in my architectural journey of discovery here in South Florida. It quickly became evident in my journey that despite the broad diversity of what one's interpretation of a dream home may be, there is one constant: the absolute pride and dedication of those who create these unique paradises. This book is about those individuals … the architects and builders who magically transform a concept, a vision, an inspiration, a dream.

The body of work represented by these great visionaries has propelled our own imagination and changed the landscape that surrounds us. This is the gift and accomplishment of these prominent professionals as reflected in the pages that follow.

With the breathtaking natural beauty as the backdrop to these homes, it is the challenge of the architect and builder to elevate their own expertise to the demands of this beauty and the expectations of their clients. The artistic endeavors of each of the individuals featured in this book have more than met these challenges and have far exceeded our expectations.

My thanks to everyone who has been a part of this journey. My sincere appreciation to our production team for your passion and commitment to making this exceptional book. And finally, my personal gratitude to Elle, Peter and John who inspire me to not only to love, but love what I do.

We exist only to discover beauty; all else is a form of waiting.

--Kahlil Gibran

Beth Benton

Senior Publisher

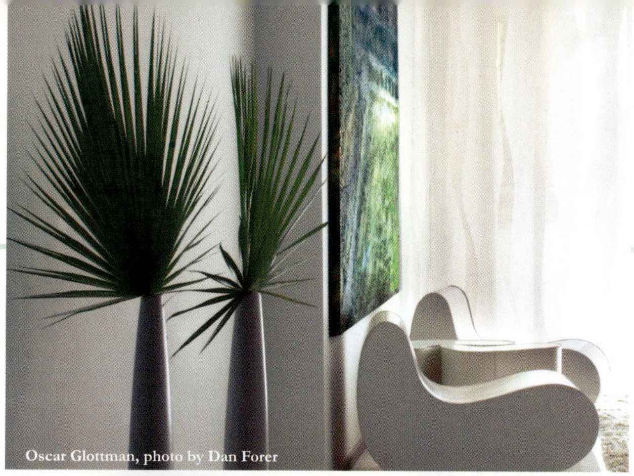

Oscar Glottman, photo by Dan Forer

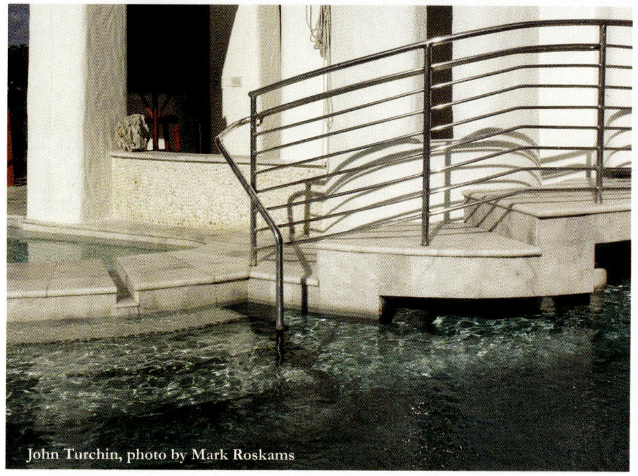

John Turchin, photo by Mark Roskams

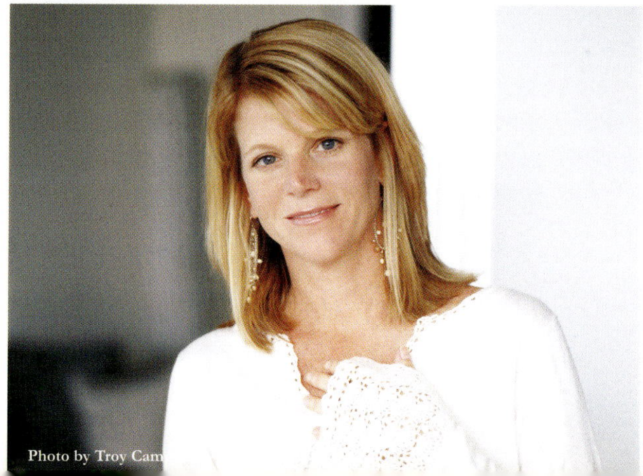

Photo by Troy Cam

Zeb Jarosz, photo by Troy Campbell

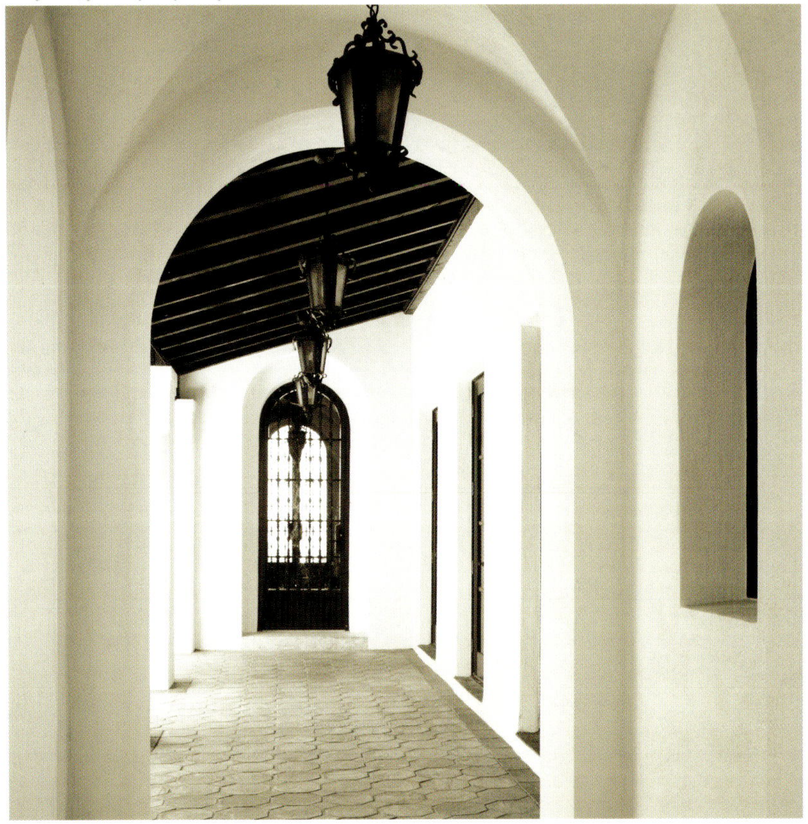

Ramon Pacheco, photo by George Cott

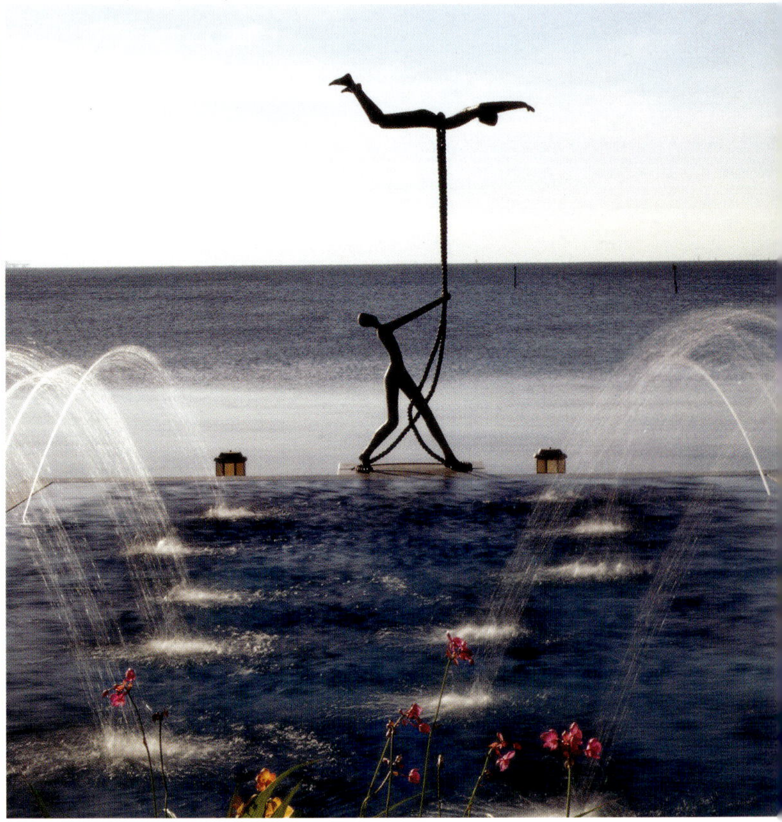

PALM BEACH

CONTENTS

Randall Stofft, photo by Troy Campbell

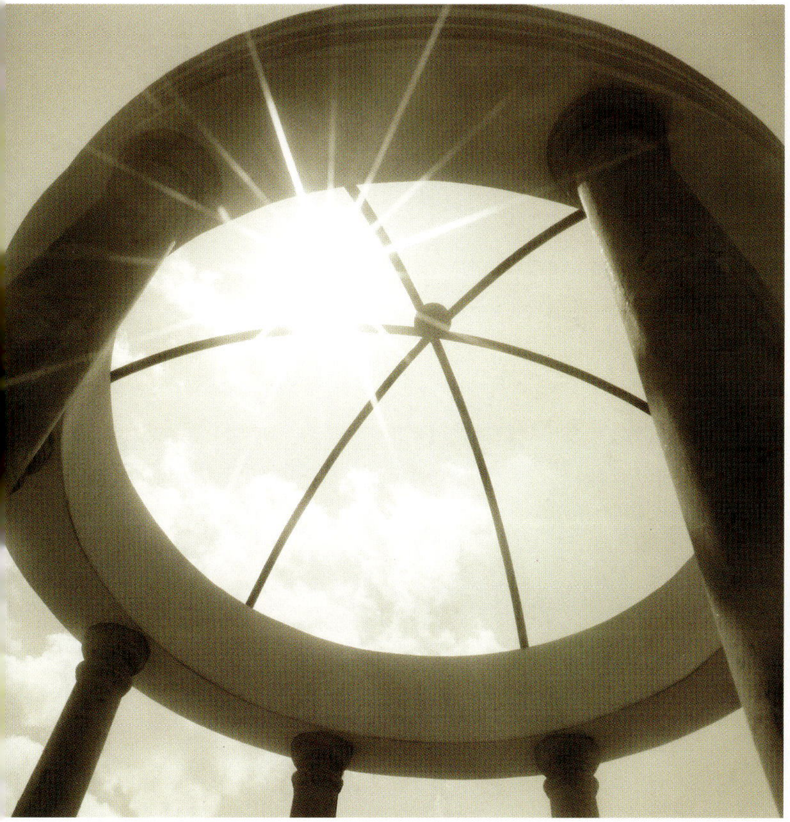

Randall Stofft, photo by Troy Campbell

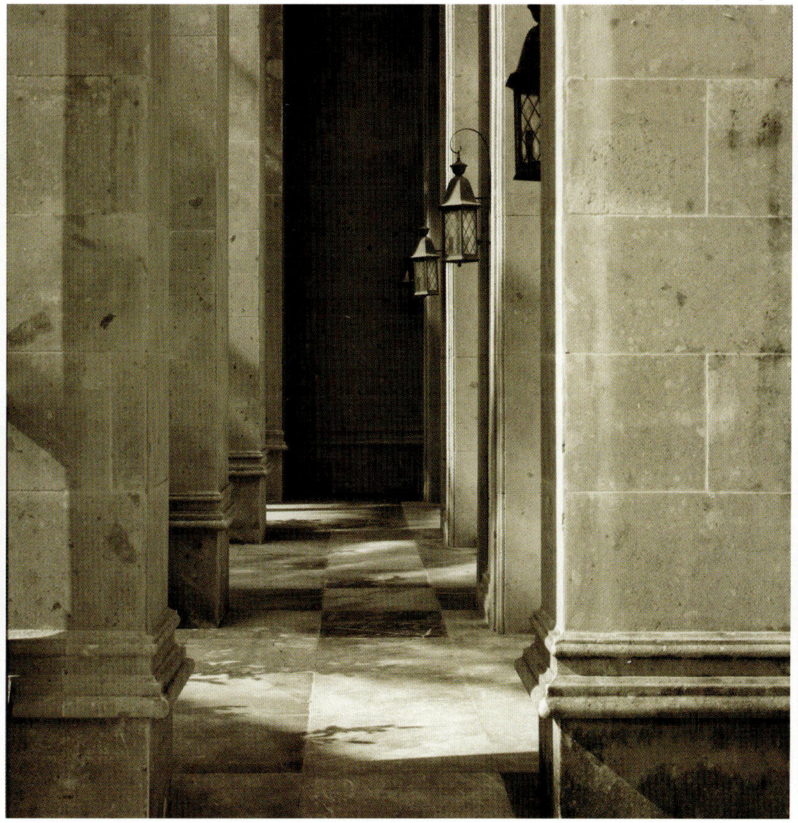

Oscar Glottman, photo by Dan Forer

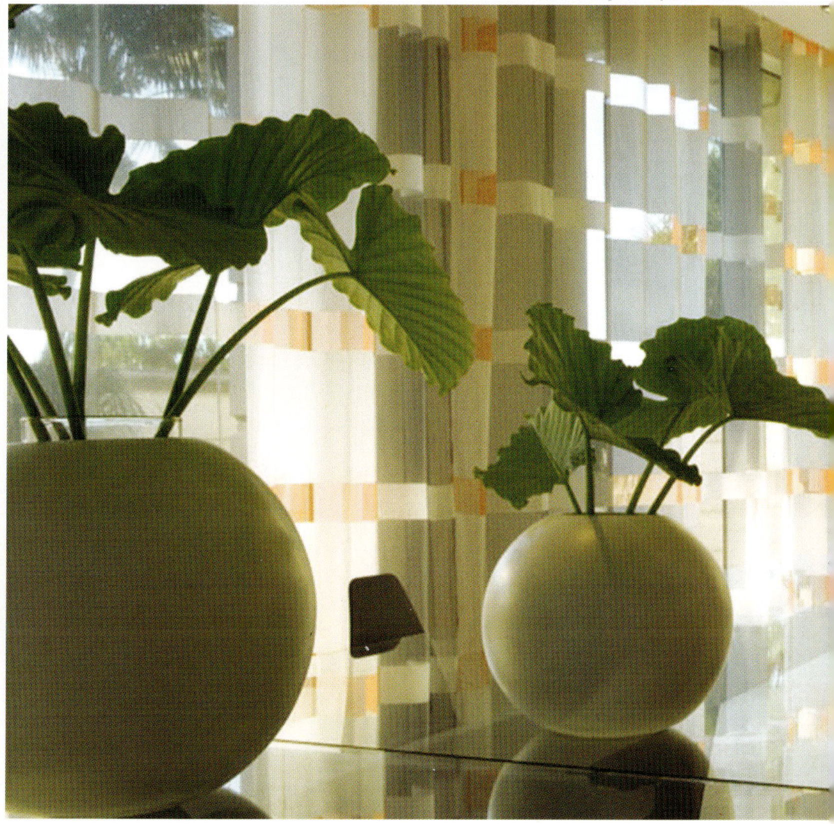

MIAMI DADE

A PERSPECTIVE

In a region where, historically, affluence is in abundance, residents who have the unabashed means to live anywhere in the world consider South Florida the closest thing to paradise on Earth. Architecturally rich and inviting, exciting and hip, the lore of South Florida beckons all who seek to live the lifestyle at heights of which others can only dream.

It is no surprise that much of South Florida pays homage to its Spanish ancestral roots. Upon closer inspection, one will find a spread of diverse architecture unlike any in the United States with a history filled with as much glitz and glamour as the people who live there. Celebrating and inviting the diversity of taste and culture, Florida boasts a history as rich as her land.

The Gilded Age, which historically lasted from the late 1800s to about 1935, is often credited with an everlasting architectural legacy in Florida. Many of the most influential architects of today still look to the structures of the ground-breaking designers and benefactors of that period. While visiting the state, Henry Flagler, cofounder of Standard Oil, noticed an absence in luxury hotel and travel accommodations, the likes of which he was accustomed. Recognizing this golden opportunity, he financed and built his East Coast

Randall Stofft, photo by Troy Campbell

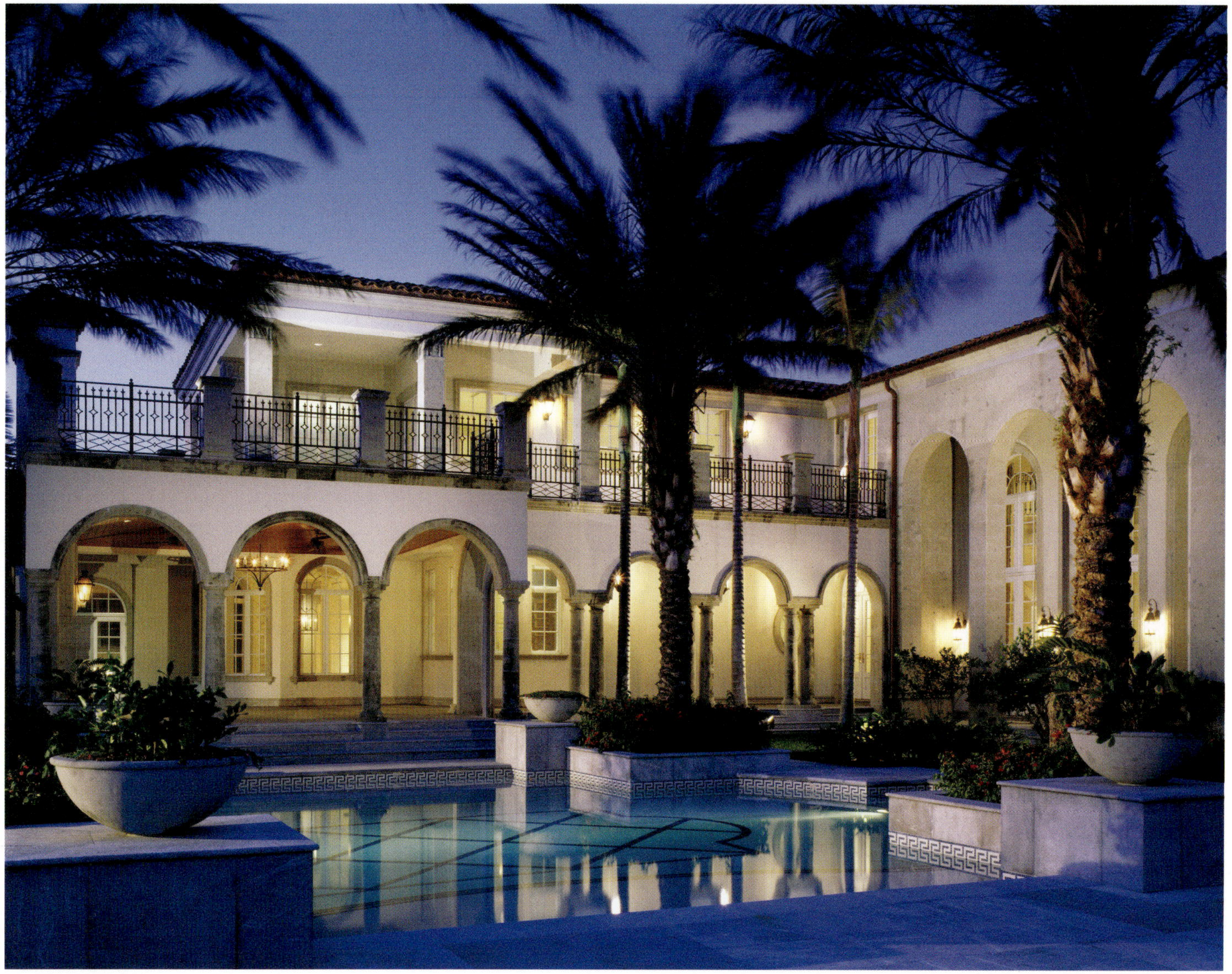

Jose Luis Hernandez, photo by Carlos Domenech

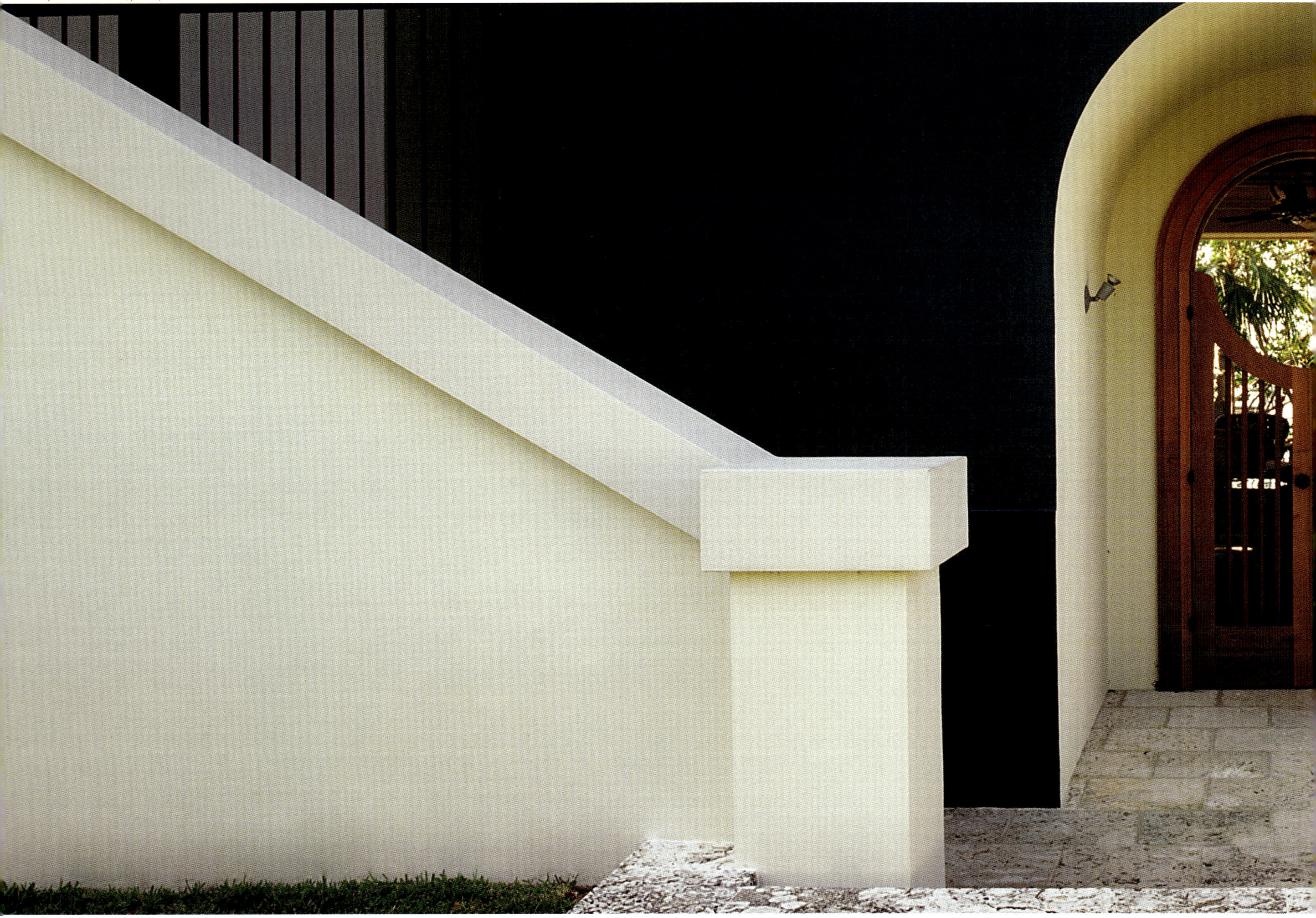

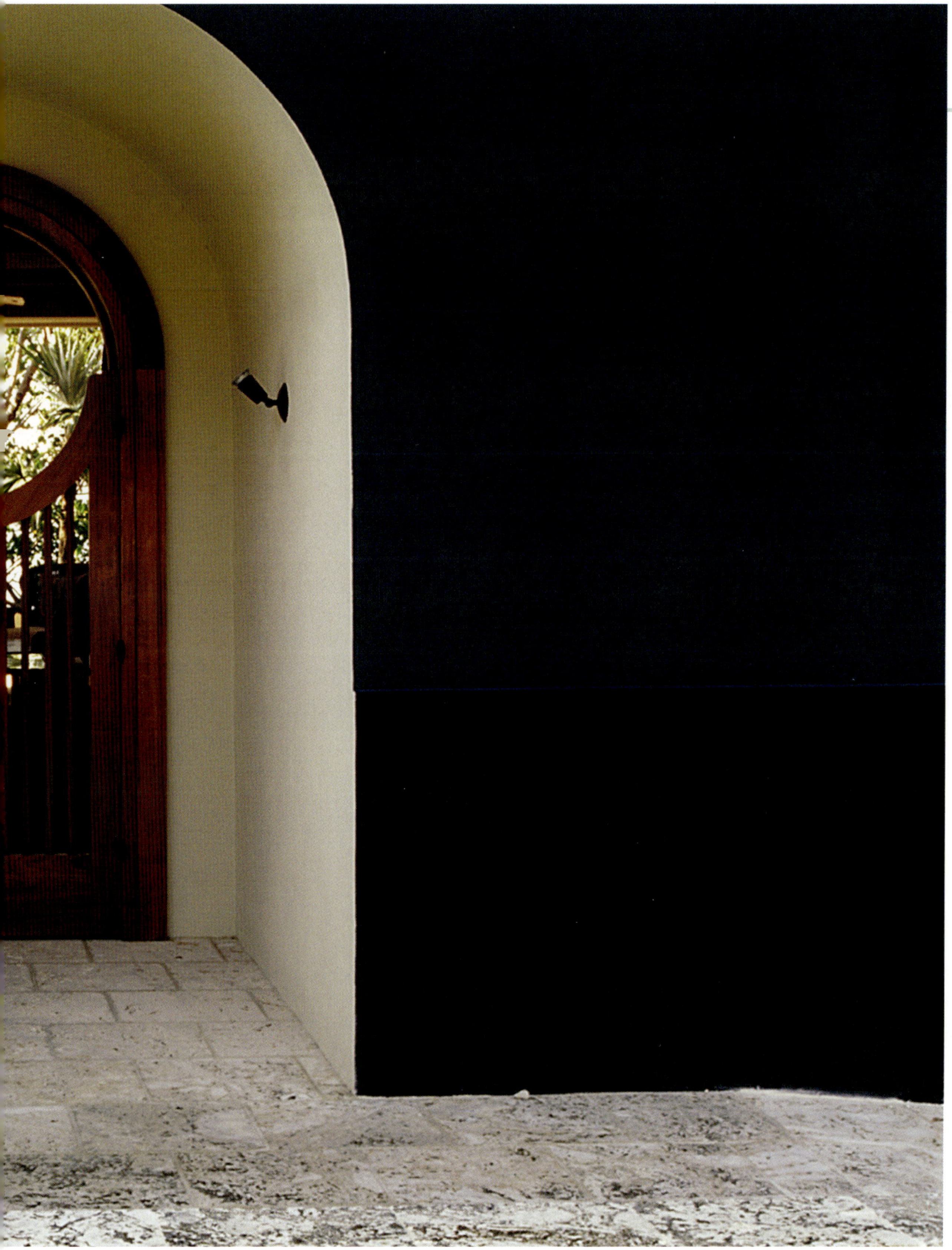

Railway, leaving a chain of luxury hotels, train depots and houses from the northeast down to Key West. As a result, the railway provided the perfect opportunity for trade with Cuba and Latin America and increased trade with the Panama Canal. Thus, the door was opened for more Latin influence.

One of the most notable Flagler buildings is the luxurious Palm Beach Italian-Renaissance manor-style Breakers Hotel. Designed by John Carrere and Thomas Hastings and completed in 1896, its stately and opulent splendor continues its solid hold as one the most desirable places to stay in South Florida.

It was Flagler and his third wife who solidified Palm Beach as the winter retreat for the rich and famous. His breathtaking 60,000-square-foot Classic Revival mansion, Whitehall (now a public museum) remains as a reminder of the Gilded Age and the man who helped finance it.

When one thinks of South Florida, Addison Mizner almost immediately comes to mind as the man who single-handedly began an architectural

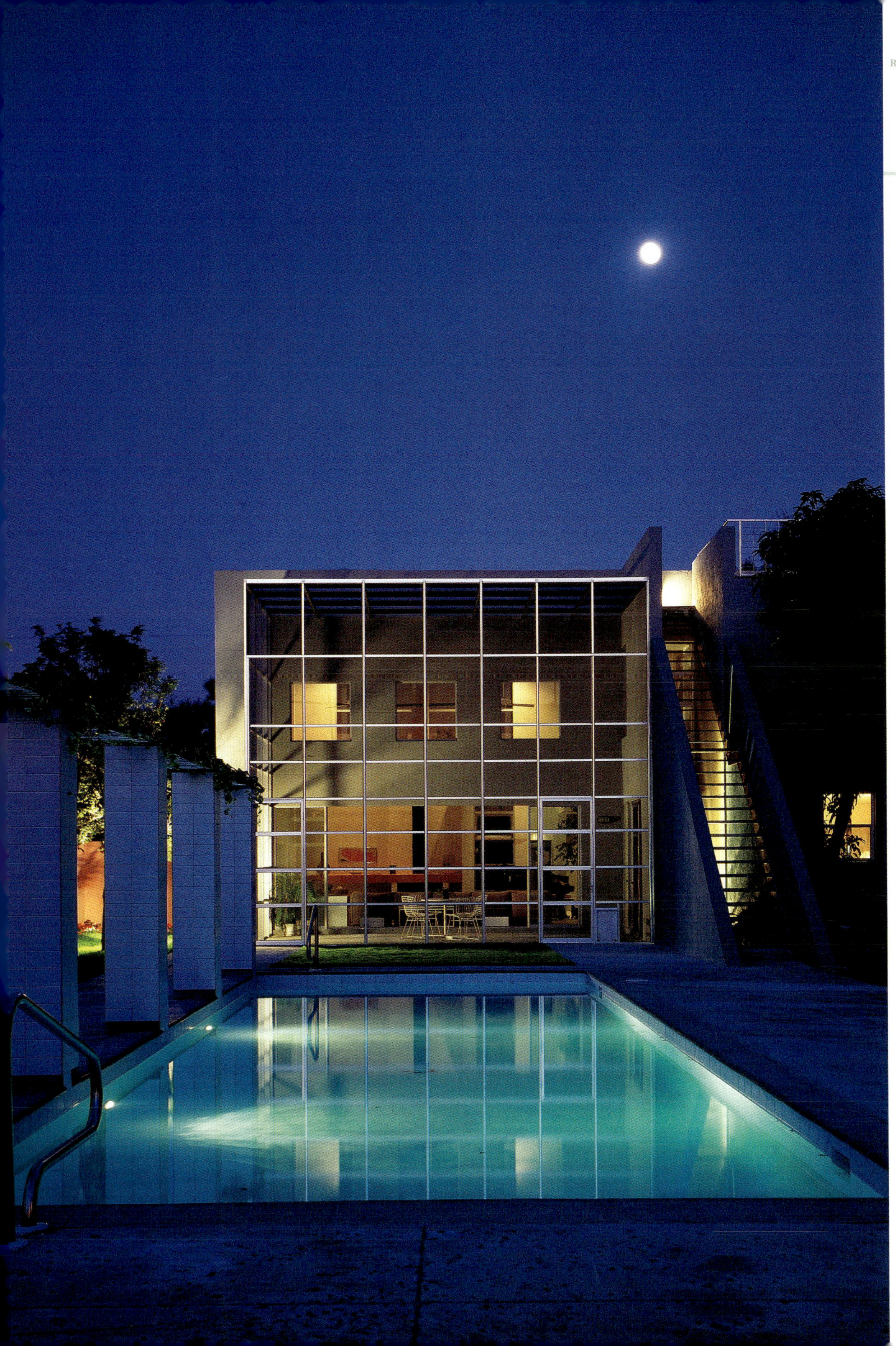

Roney Mateu, photo by Troy Campbell

movement. Aspiring to transform the small town of Boca Raton into a posh community on a grand scale, he infused it with his signature blend of Mediterranean Revival architecture. The self-taught designer was influenced by the legendary New York architect Sanford White, whose success aspired to and attained.

The elements that herald "Mizner" are so commonly viewed throughout South Florida, that without the cream stucco, red tiles roofs, arches and lush courtyards, the face of South Florida would be indiscernible, save for the tropical climate and beautiful topography.

While these recognized movements were taking shape in South Florida, there was an undercurrent in Miami. As recently as 1998, the name MiMo, meaning Miami Modern, was coined as a promotional term to garner public support for preserving structures built after World War II through the mid 1960s. Long overshadowed by the drama of the earlier and popular Art Deco movement, MiMo has been given fresh life.

Kobi Karp, photo by Troy Campbell

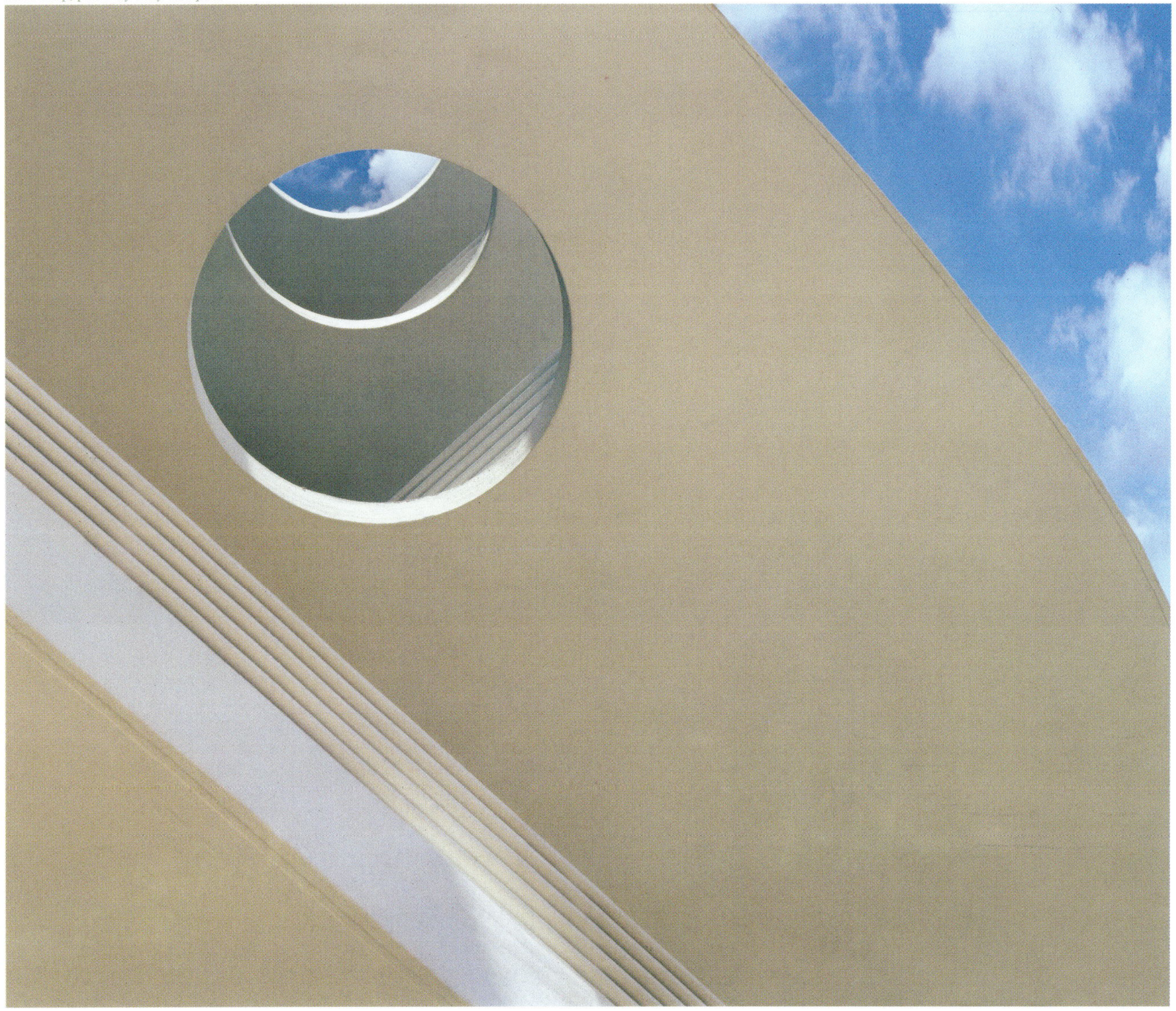

Suzanne Martinson, photo by Troy Campbell

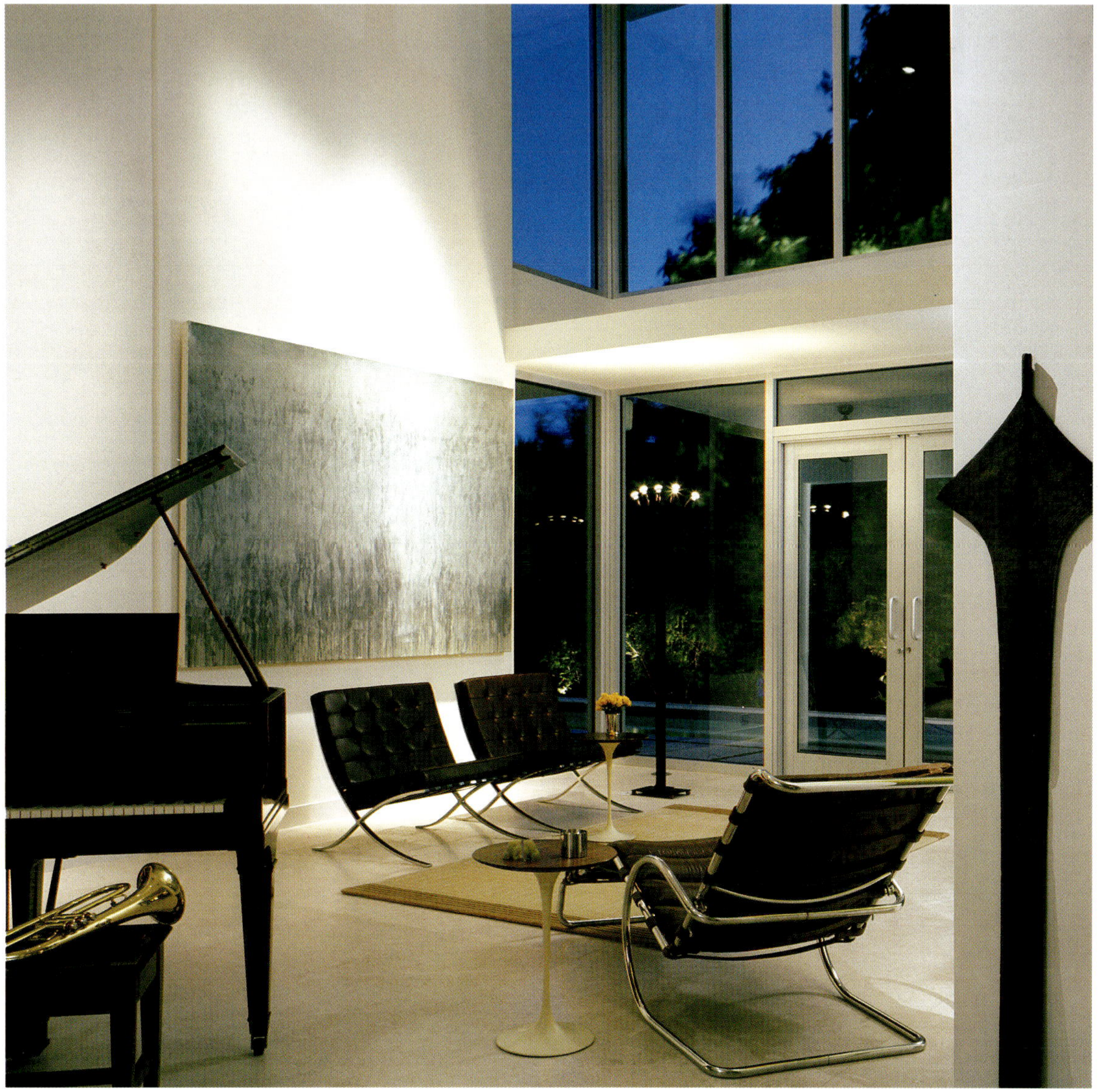

Zeb Jarosz, photo by Troy Campbell

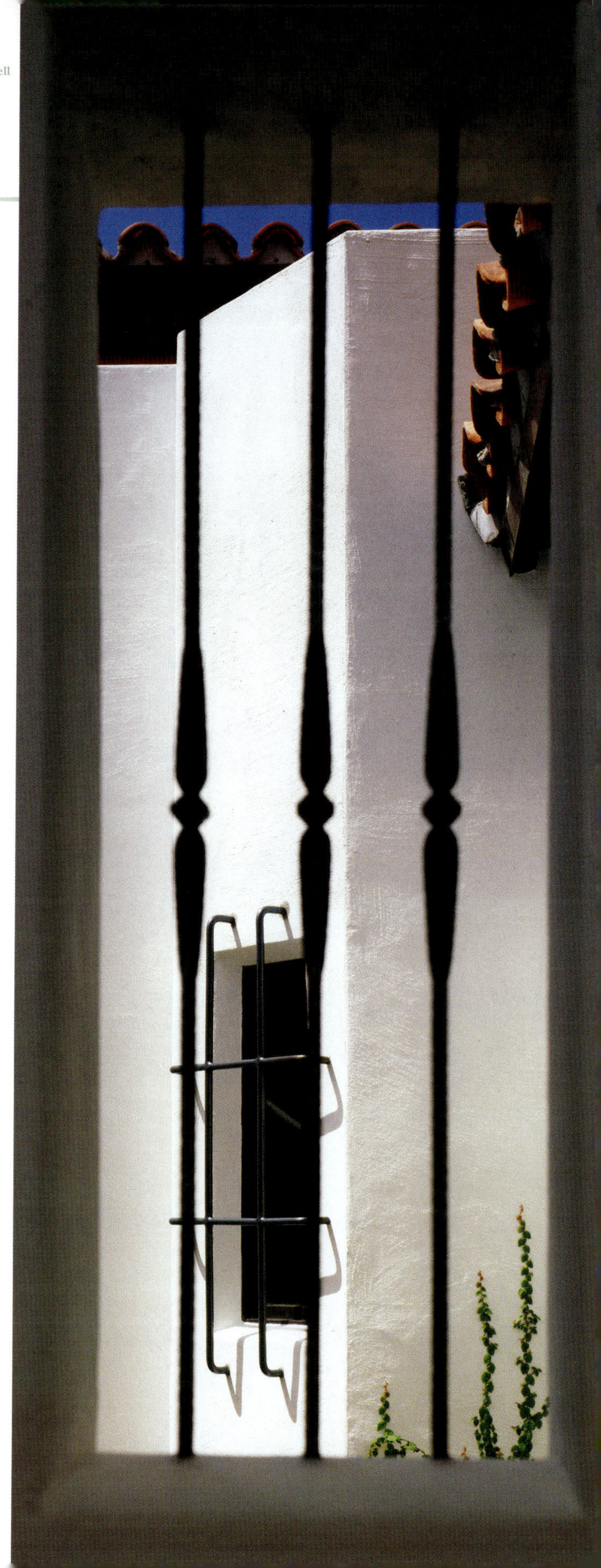

While most architects of the time were embracing the Bauhaus ethic of "less is more," architects in Miami were taking their cues from the bustling and vibrant city. Adding a spin on the modernist aesthetic with stunning colors, concrete Frank Lloyd Wright-influenced cantilevers and surprising cut-out patterns in walls, these unassuming designers were never properly recognized. Architects such as Lapidus, Norman M. Giller, Igor B. Polevitzky, Melvin Grossman and Kenneth Triester designed these residences, hotels and commercial buildings in many parts of the city, namely in North Miami Beach, from 63rd Street to 87th Terrace.

Today, South Florida's architecture has taken on many different faces—from the broadness of "modern" style to the details that define a modern design's style as minimalist, deconstructionist or even new urbanism. All styles—from classic to modern—are represented and met with open arms and minds.

A scenic ride along Ocean Drive with its sprawling mansions, and famous estates and high-rise cities has caused more census shuffling than any other road in America. So many have responded to that beauty by architecturally cultivating and enhancing it, including history's most notable architectural figures who each added their own visions to Florida's "architectural melting pot."

Kelly Yates & Dennis Rainho, photo by Daniel Newcomb

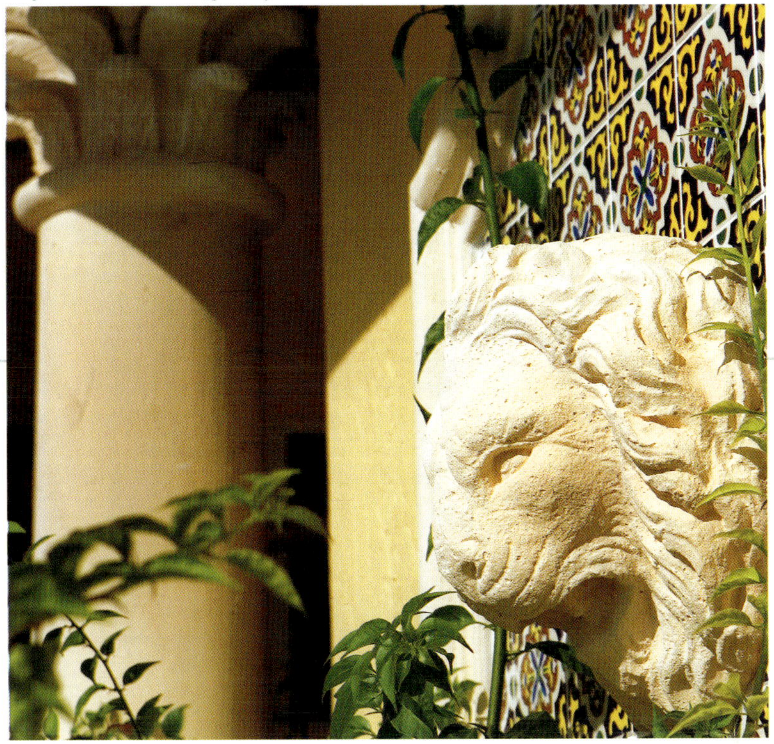

Pat Segraves, photo by Robert + Carmel Brantley

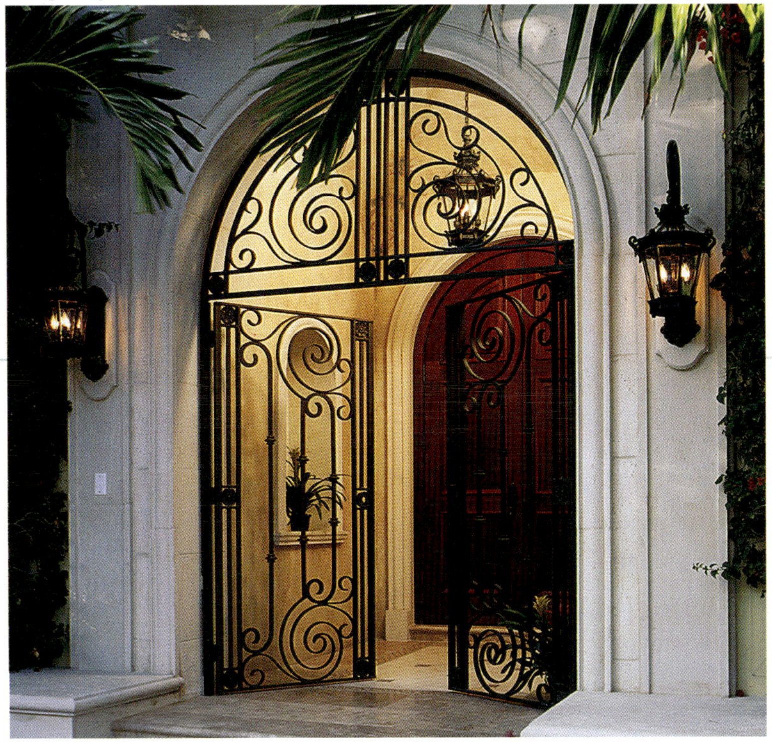

Carlos Martin, photo by Kim Sargent Architectural Photography

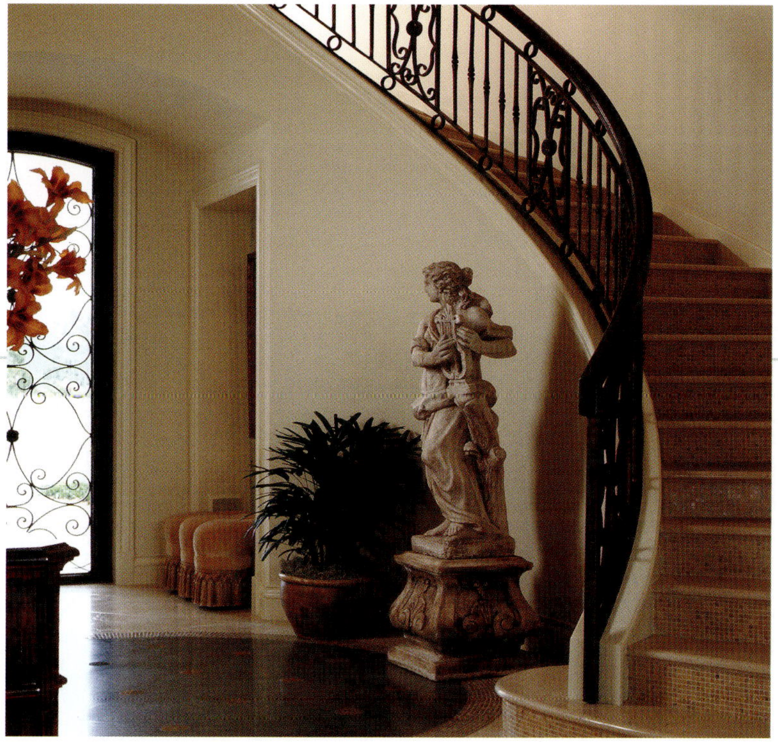

CHAPTER ONE

PALM BEACH

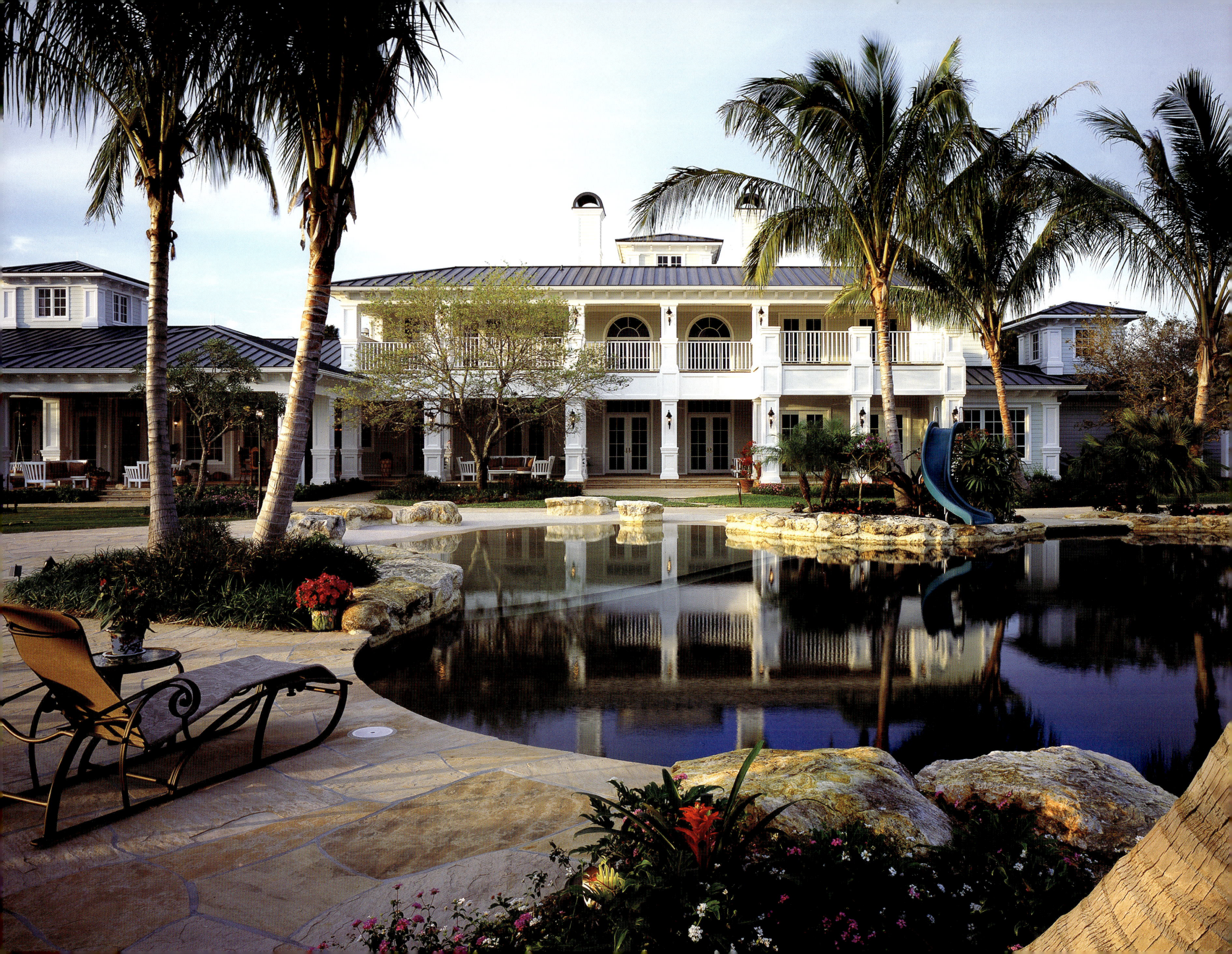

RENÉ ALONSO

Alonso & Associates

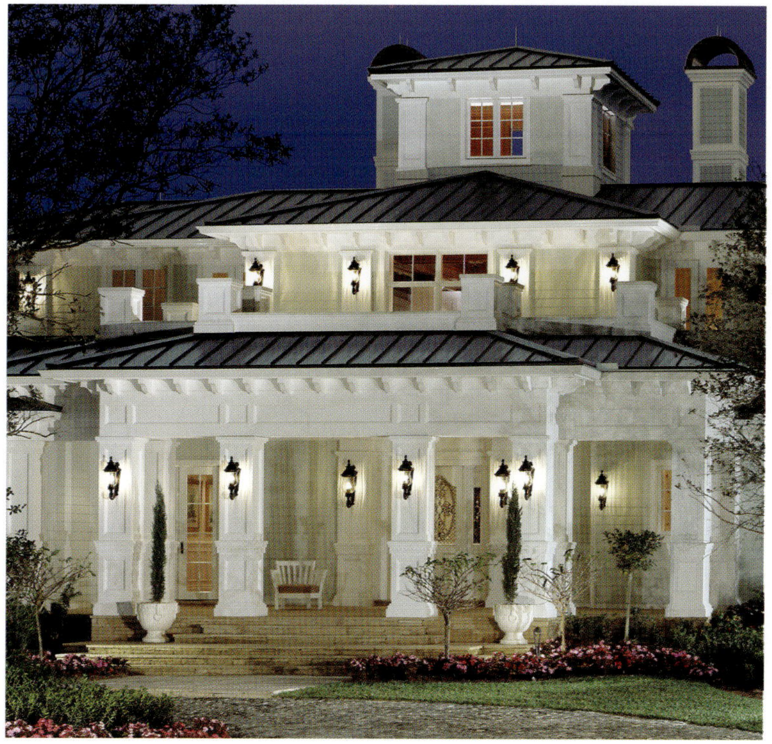

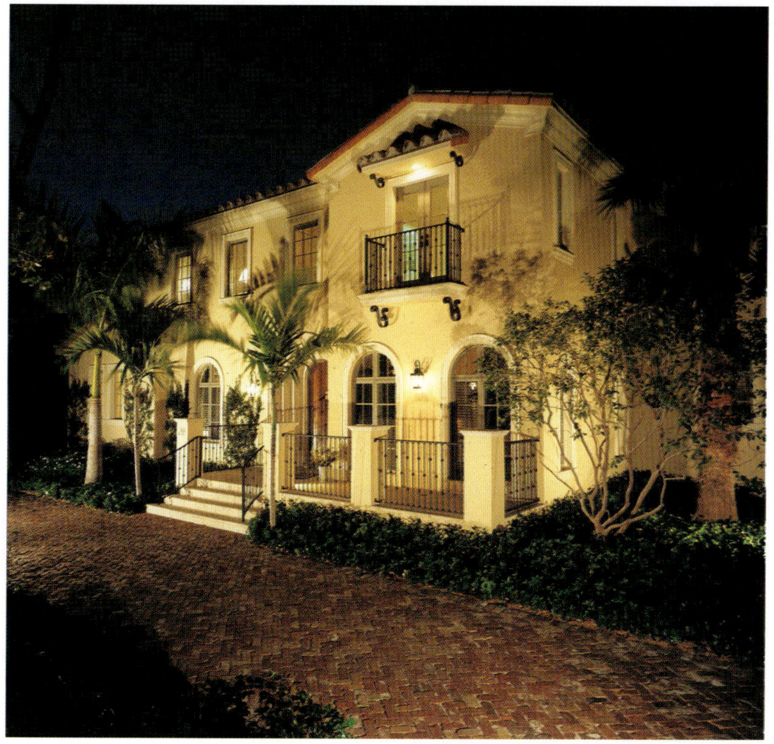

René Alonso was always destined to do his own thing. He arrived in Miami from his native Cuba at eight years old and from then on he began achieving his life goals at a young age. After ten years of working with architects, starting right after high school and through college, René decided that his true calling was building. The hands-on nature of being out in the field appealed to him far more than being inside all day and so he began preparing to take his general contractor's exam and launch his own business.

He got his big break when the plans for a house he had collaborated on but had never been built was given the green light by a prominent Ft. Lauderdale businessman. One day René got a fortunate call from him. "He said, 'I was told you did most of the drawings for the house and I want to get the project going.' I went to see him and told him I was now building. He said, 'Well, why don't you just build it?'"

That started things moving for René and today he is at the helm of Alonso & Associates, which has been building luxury homes from Palm Beach to Miami Beach and the surrounding areas for nearly 30 years. The company has built two houses on the prestigious Indian Creek Island.

ABOVE LEFT: Entrance to house on preceding page.
Photograph by Liz Ordoñez

ABOVE RIGHT: Palm Beach residence. Mediterranean Revival.
Photograph by Liz Ordoñez

LEFT: Rear of 15,000-square-foot residence in one of Palm Beach County's most exclusive communities. Lagoon pool has a "walk-in" edge. Pool deck is sand stone from Arizona.
Photograph by Liz Ordoñez

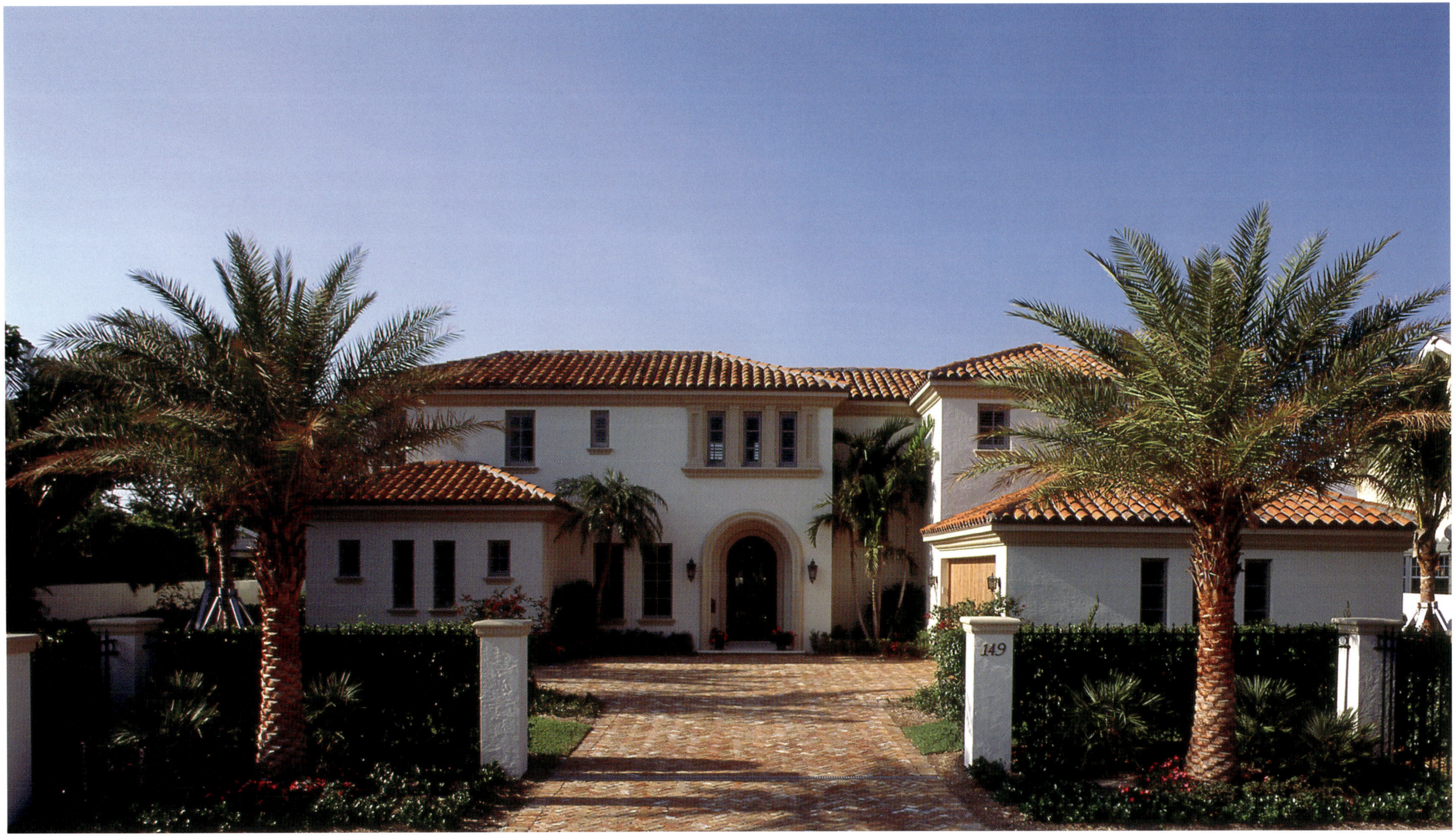

René discovered early on that it is key to appeal to the client—not one's own tastes—when building and that is the premise on which he does business to this day. His favorite aspect of the professional process is working closely with the client and the architect to come up with an innovative and inspired design that appeals to the client's needs, desires and lifestyle, yet repects the architect's design.

His architectural background gives René the advantage of foresight in that he can view a set of plans and determine where potential problems might lie, then fix them before they ever come to pass. He prides himself on the fact that in 26 years of doing business, he has never had to back charge for omissions because of his keen ability to problem-solve. In fact, problem-solving is as integral a part of his job as designing homes.

Though building is his first love, René is inspired by good architecture. He collects books on the subject and appreciates everything from classic to contemporary. "Good architecture captures my eye and I'm attracted," he says. "I've been fortunate that I've been able to build a lot of houses that are architecturally beautiful and architecturally correct."

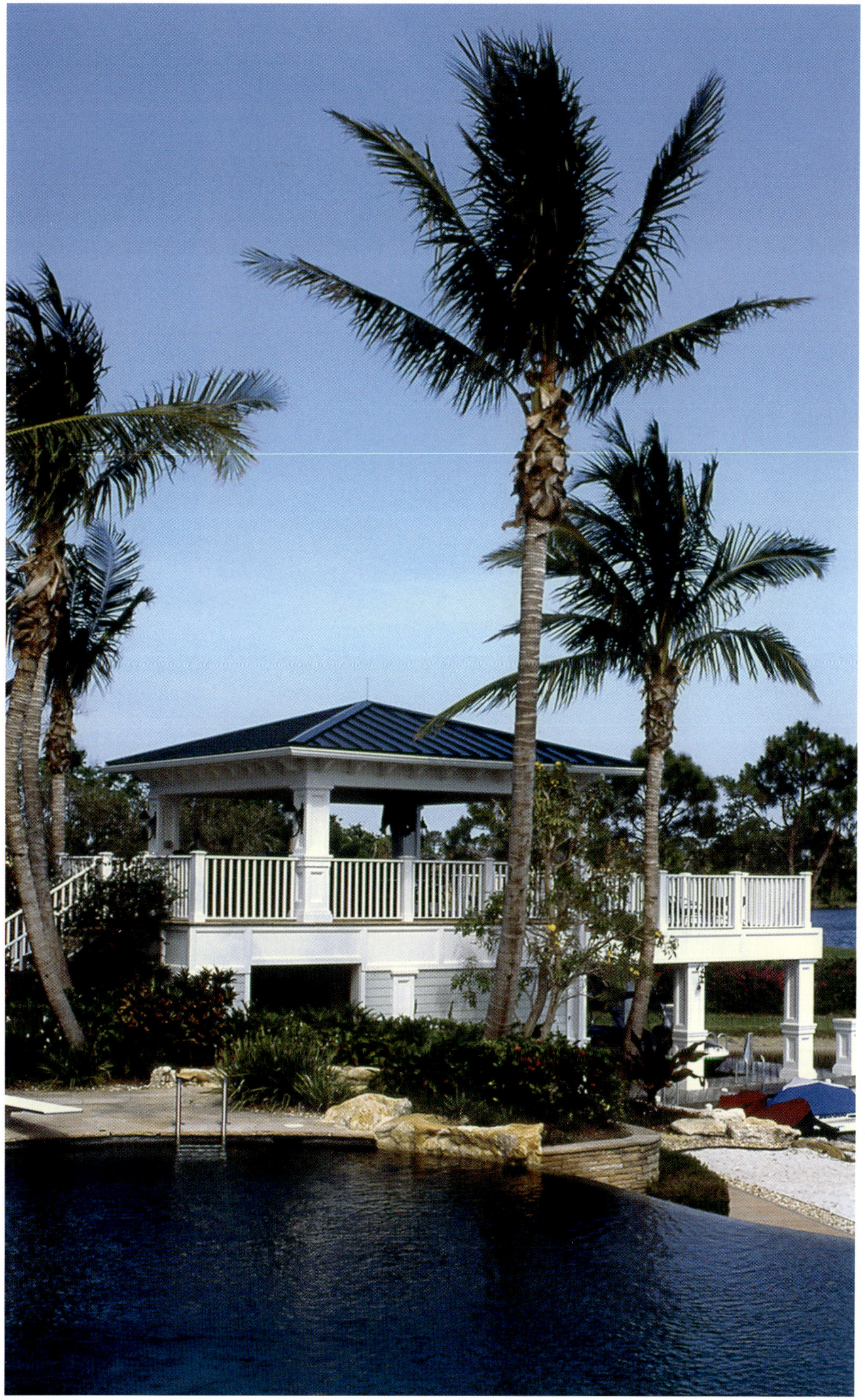

Q&A
more about rené...

WHAT PERSONAL INDULGENCE DO YOU SPEND THE MOST MONEY ON?

Golf trips, when I can get away from work.

WHAT COLOR BEST DESCRIBES YOU AND WHY?

Blue—I consider myself conservative and loyal.

WHAT BOOK HAS HAD THE GREATEST IMPACT ON YOU?

How To Stop Worrying and Start Living by Dale Carnegie.

WHAT IS THE HIGHEST COMPLIMENT YOU'VE RECEIVED PROFESSIONALLY?

When I'm introduced as "my builder and my good friend."

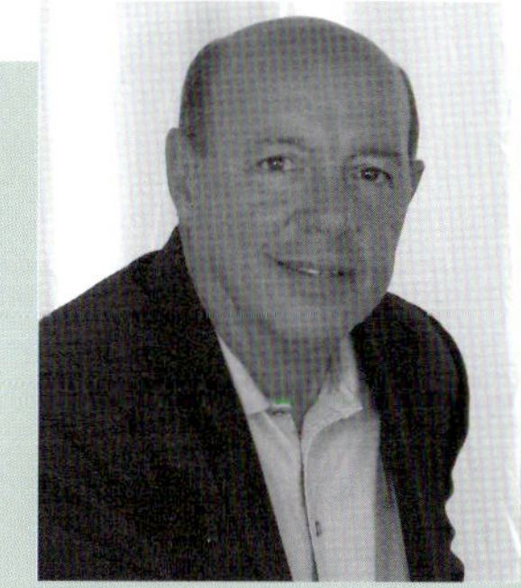

ALONSO & ASSOCIATES
René Alonso
361 South County Road, Suite F
Palm Beach, FL 33480
561.837.2820
Fax 561.837.9830

LEFT: Boathouse on lower level and outdoor kitchen on upper level overlooking lake, beach and lagoon pool.
Photograph by Von Kantor, Inc.

FACING PAGE: Palm Beach residence. Mediterranean Revival. "Simple elegance."
Photograph by Von Kantor, Inc.

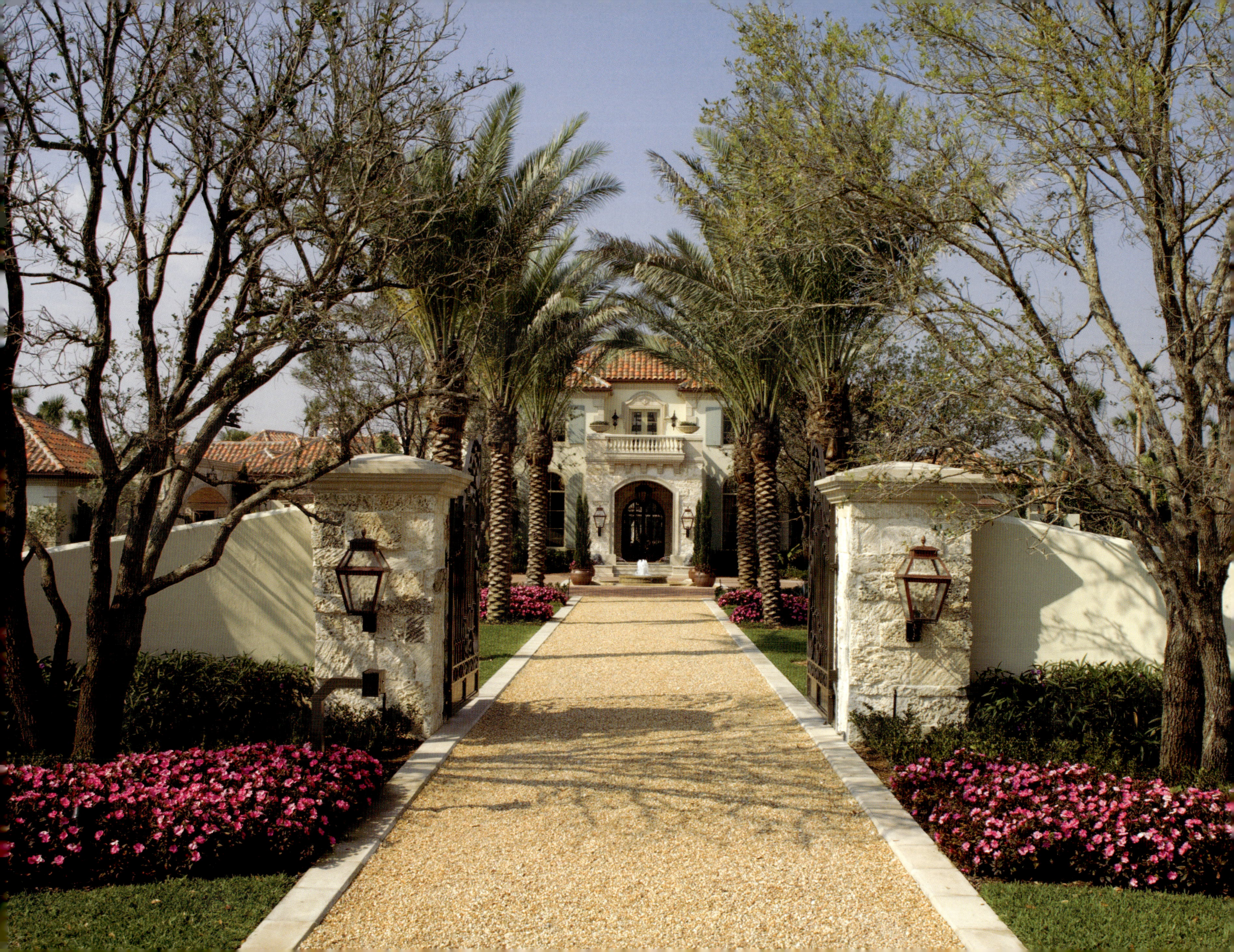

SHANE AMES

Ames Design International

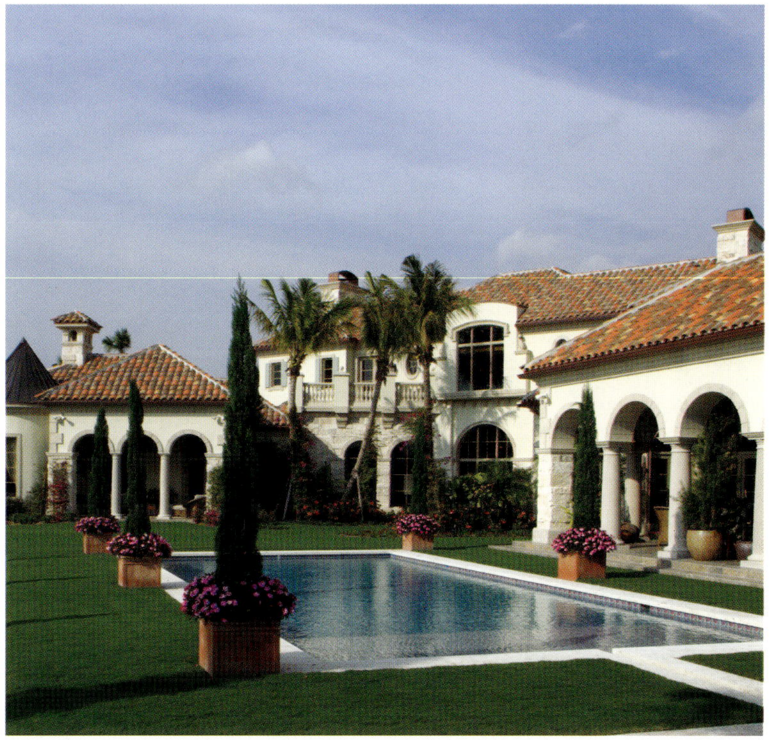

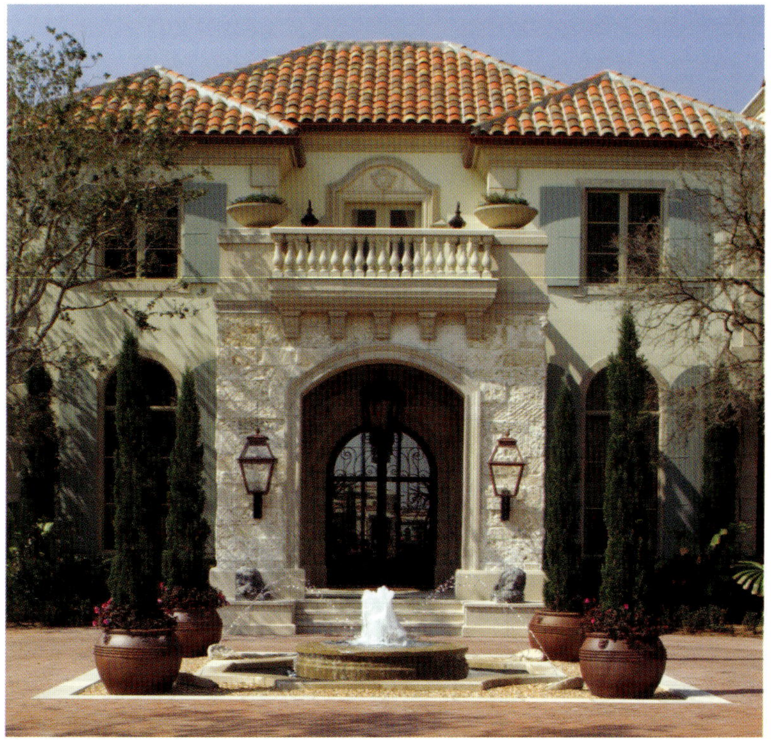

Shane Ames grew up in South Florida and he says he's been an architect since he was three years old. "I started out with Legos and Lincoln Logs," he explains, "As an only child, I had a lot of time on my hands."

He knew his calling from that early age, and after studying at the University of Cincinnati, he worked in California and Florida, participating in a six-year baccalaureate work/study program that allowed him to experience his profession by taking jobs around the country. Having moved there as a child, Florida was his final destination because "anywhere you went to high school is home." In 1985, after eight years of working for other firms, he opened Ames Design International. He already had quite a following who appreciated his work and since that time, his client base has steadily grown.

With 1,200 people moving to the state of Florida each day, Shane says there's so much building going on that his workflow remains steady and interesting all the time. He attributes this in part to the beautiful Florida sunshine. "Everybody wants to be here," he says. "With this weather you're not cooped up inside a house six months a year like you are up North. You can live in a quiet community, but be blocks from a cosmopolitan area at the same time."

Ames Design International has a staff of approximately 18 and projects from as far south as Queenstown, New Zealand, and Johannesburg, South Africa, as far north as Toronto, Canada, and throughout the Unites States, although his work is primarily in South Florida. The company specializes

ABOVE LEFT: Rear view integrating water features and landscape to verandas enhance the outdoor living experience.
Photograph by Kim Sargent, Sargent Architectural Photography

ABOVE RIGHT: Main entry courtyard featuring a simple fountain to add sonic pleasure to arriving guests. Painted shutters add ambiance and visual contrast.
Photograph by Kim Sargent, Sargent Architectural Photography

LEFT: Stately entrance featuring gas lights on stone piers and gravel drive to make you slow down and enjoy the view.
Photograph by Kim Sargent, Sargent Architectural Photography

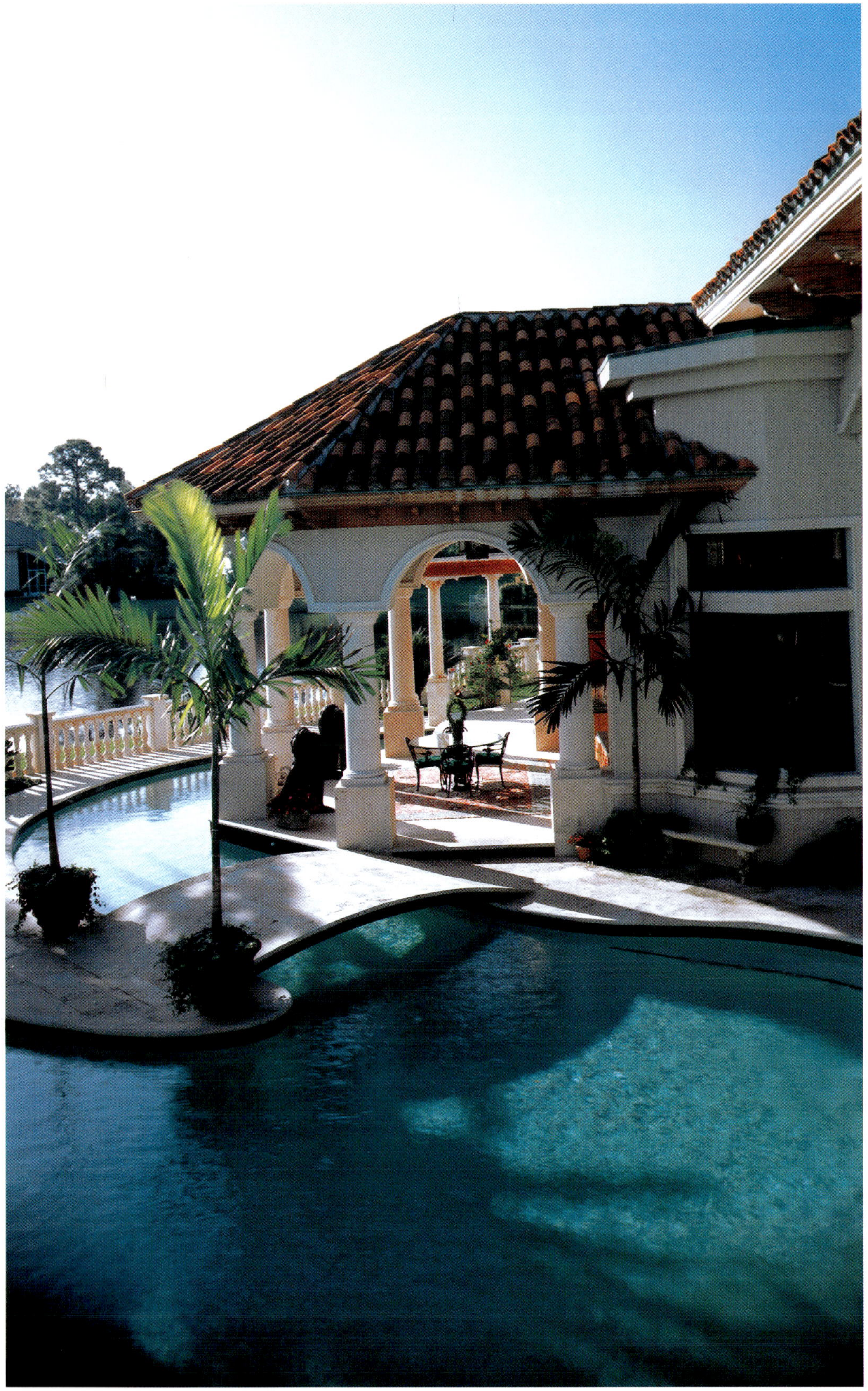

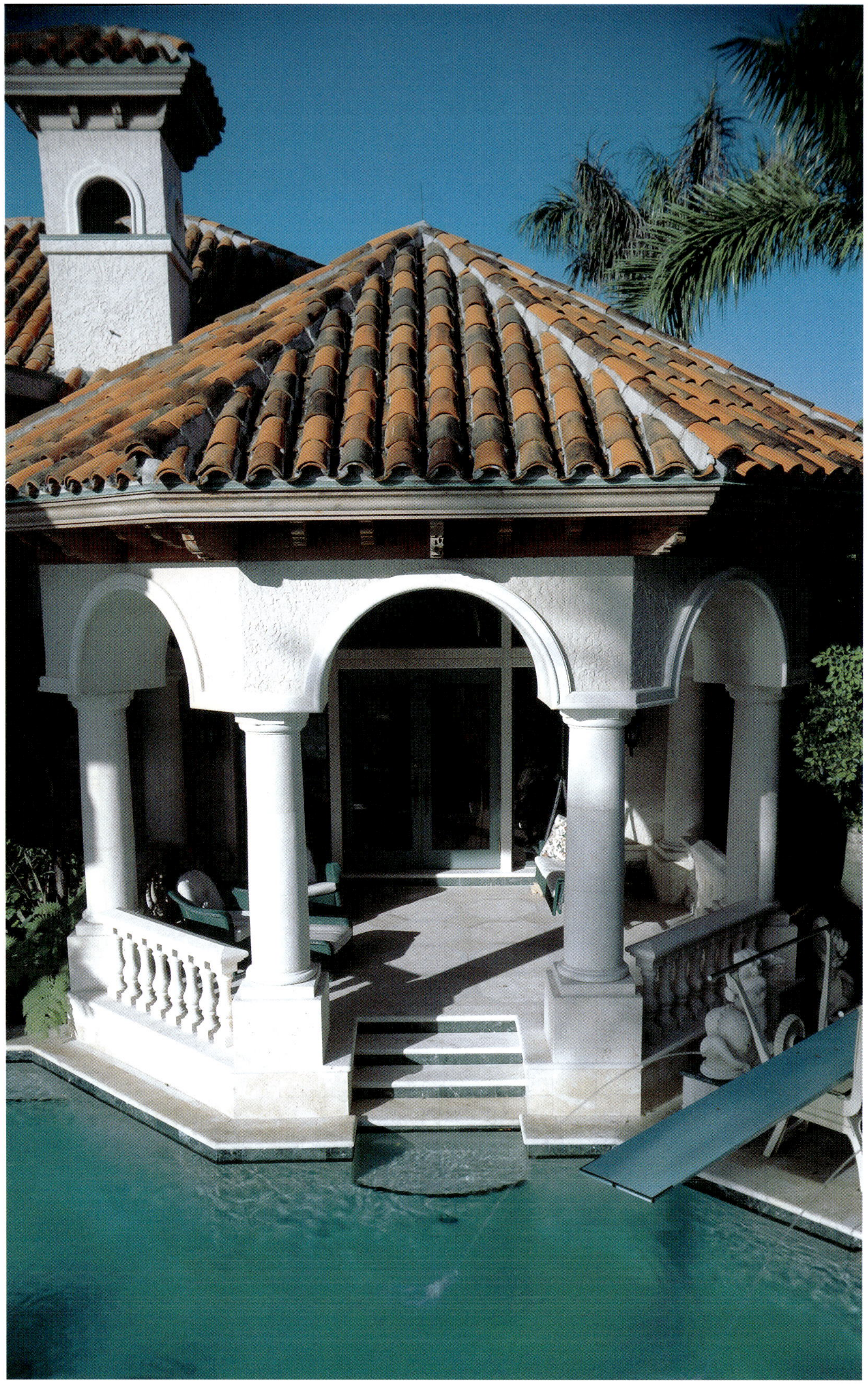

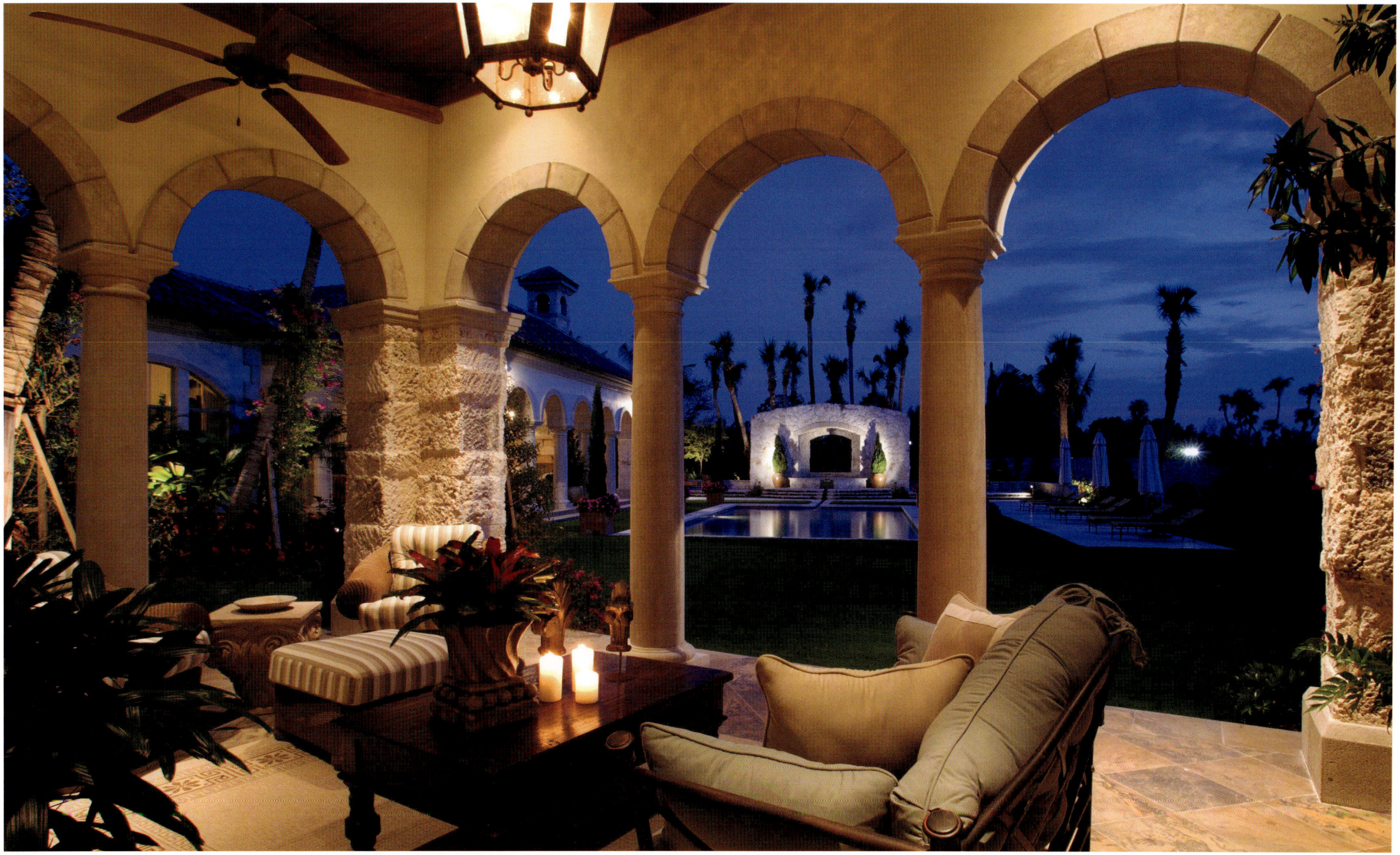

in luxury custom residences as well as developing corporate identities and other commercial projects including shopping centers, apartment building, warehouses, doctors' offices and retail stores—basically "anything interesting." These interesting projects often come by way of his existing clients, many of them Fortune 500 listers interested in doing design projects other than homes. Such projects have included a custom garage for a prized-possession automobile collection, specially designed amenities for a spoiled four-legged family member or even helping arrange a home according to the principles of Feng Shui.

ABOVE: Warm and inviting master retreat, exterior lounge viewing featured landscape backdrop.
Photograph by Kim Sargent, Sargent Architectural Photography

FACING PAGE LEFT: Total integration of swimming pool and outdoor entertainment areas with wrap around pool and access bridges so you can always have a seat on the waters edge.
Photograph courtesy of Ames Design International

FACING PAGE RIGHT: Master retreat loggia with direct access to pool.
Photograph courtesy of Ames Design International

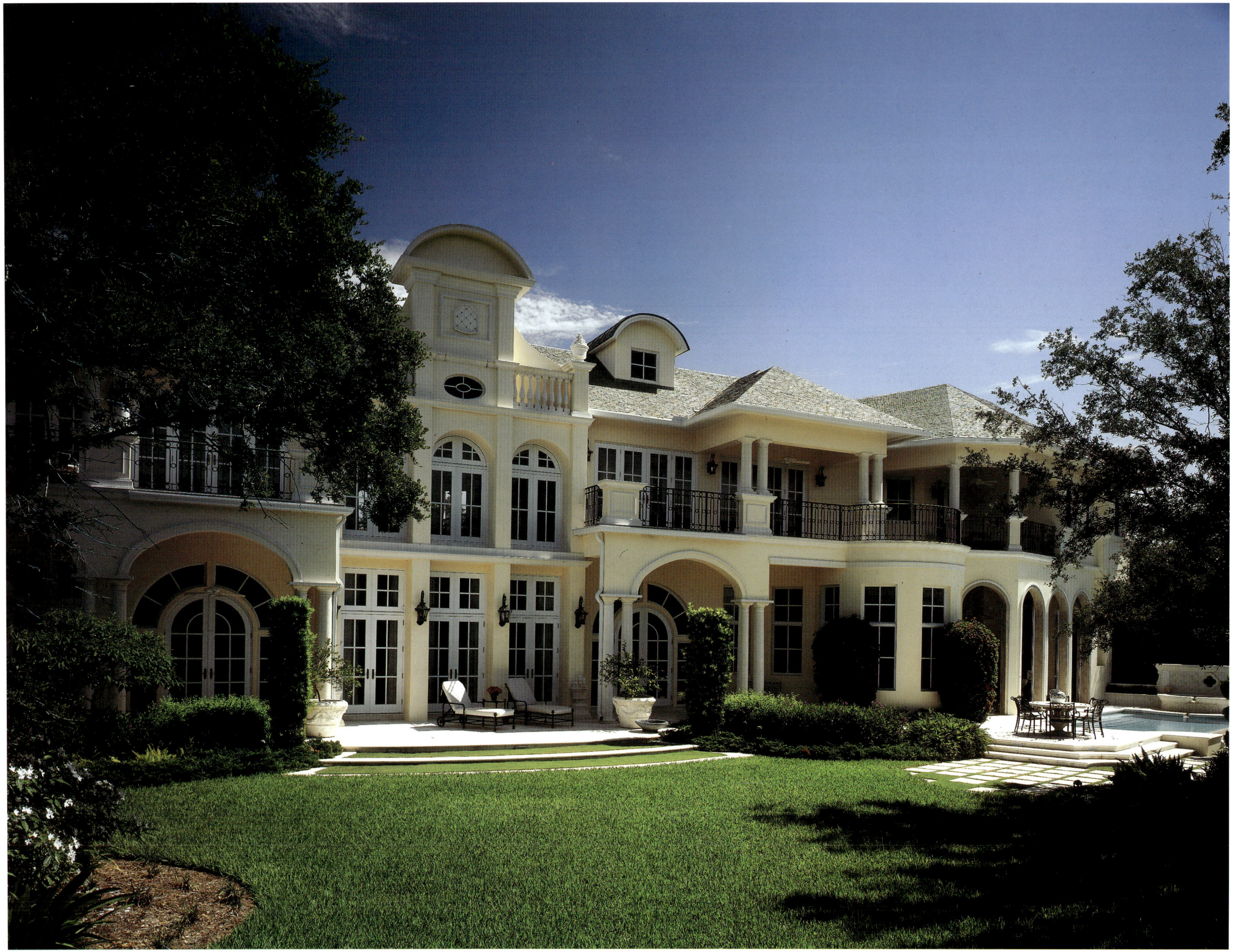

Ames Design's hallmark is the personal touch it places on every one of the firm's projects. Shane says that while talking to his clients over a period of two hours or so, he comes up with their house plans then and there. He believes it is a tremendous advantage when one considers the time factor. It also enthuses and excites the clients because they feel part of the birth.

The process of design begins with the site and its specifics: view, orientation, elevation and surroundings. Taking this information, Shane then creates something to fulfill the particulars with consideration to the functionality of a house and how a client wants it to function. Usually, the dazzling outcome is a 180 degree difference from what the client initially thought it would be; a fact that delights Shane.

To get the process going in a positive forward motion, Shane designs three or four options in front of the client instead of taking a bunch of notes and coming back two weeks later with something they don't necessarily like, then inevitably having to start the process all over again. He walks his clients through his 3-D sketches to ensure they fully understand every minute detail of the project; only then does it go to the CAD for efficiency.

The talented principal of Ames Design International revels in the use of lighting, both natural and indoor. His approach leans towards theatrical in feeling. He also suggests his clients illuminate and prominently display their collectibles. If they don't have a collection of any sort, Shane tries to help them start one or discover one they didn't know they had.

Not restricted to buildings, Shane's scope of talent also extends to hardscape design including swimming pools, gardens, driveways and walkways. His approach is always the same inside and out: create interesting lines or lines of sight that aim toward a certain view and always keep a balance.

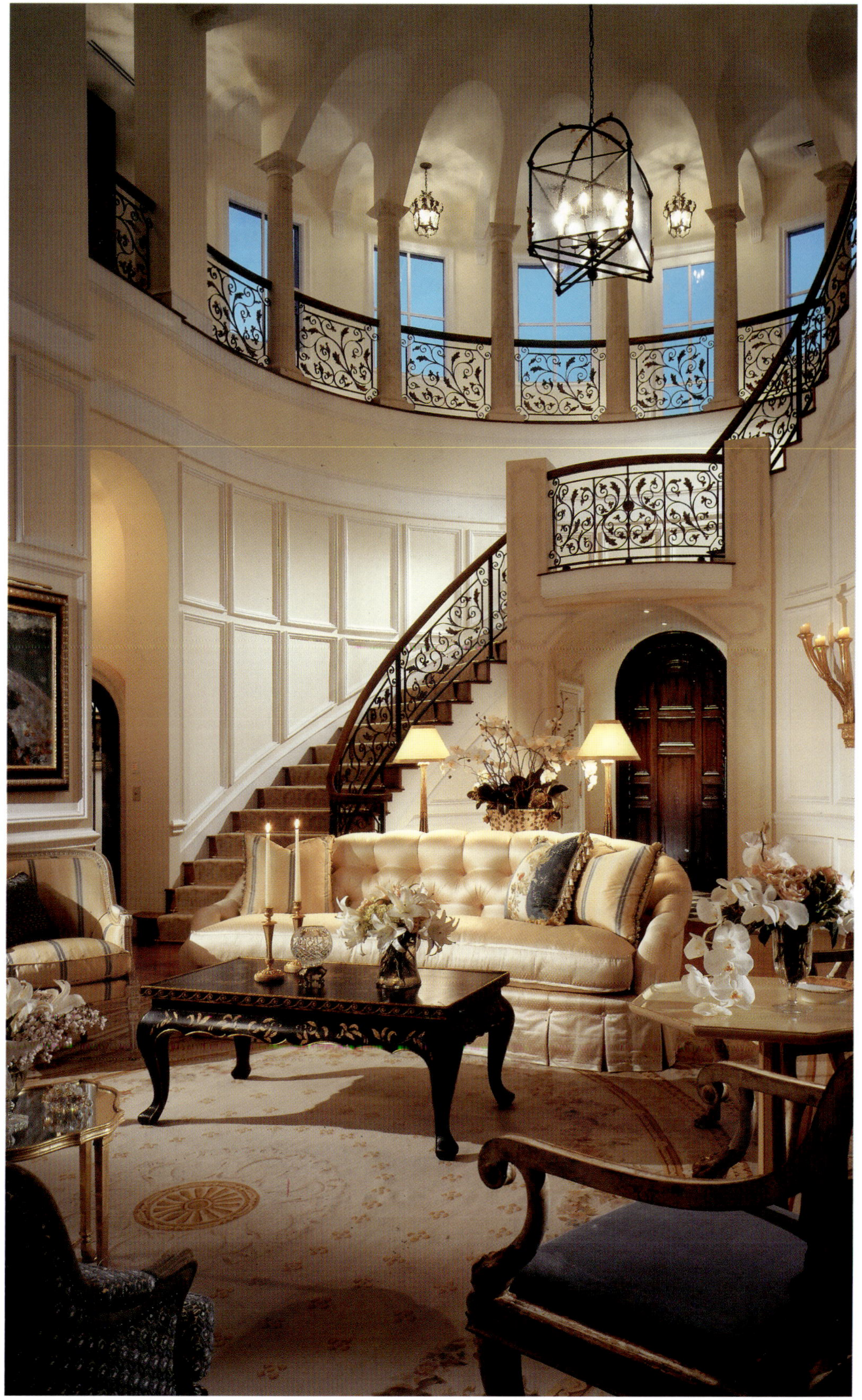

RIGHT: Spectacular curving stair with Romeo and Juliet balcony with intricate groin vaulted gallery above.
Photograph by Kim Sargent, Sargent Architectural Photography

FACING PAGE: Formal rear entertainment area on this baronial estate villa.
Photograph by Kim Sargent, Sargent Architectural Photography

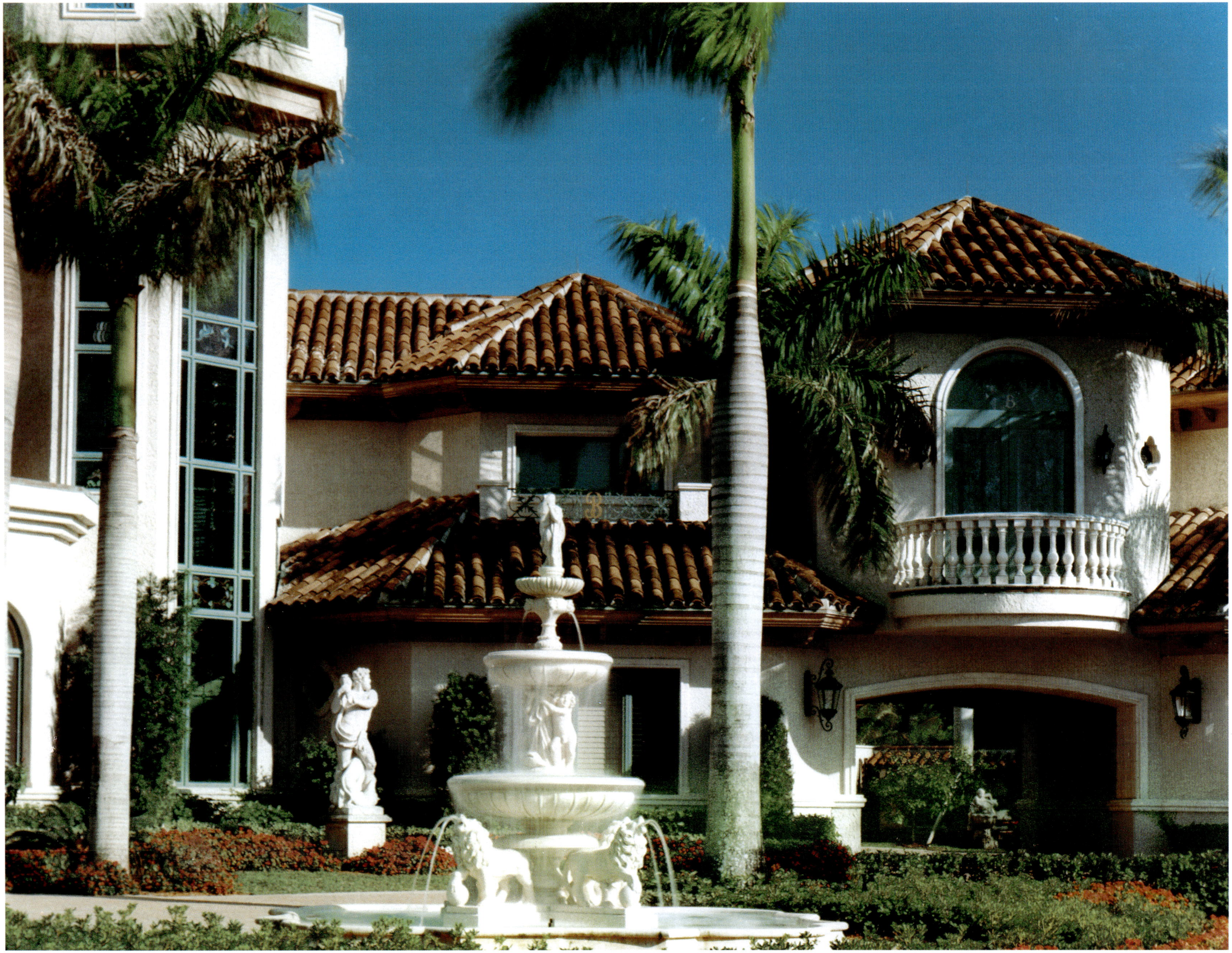

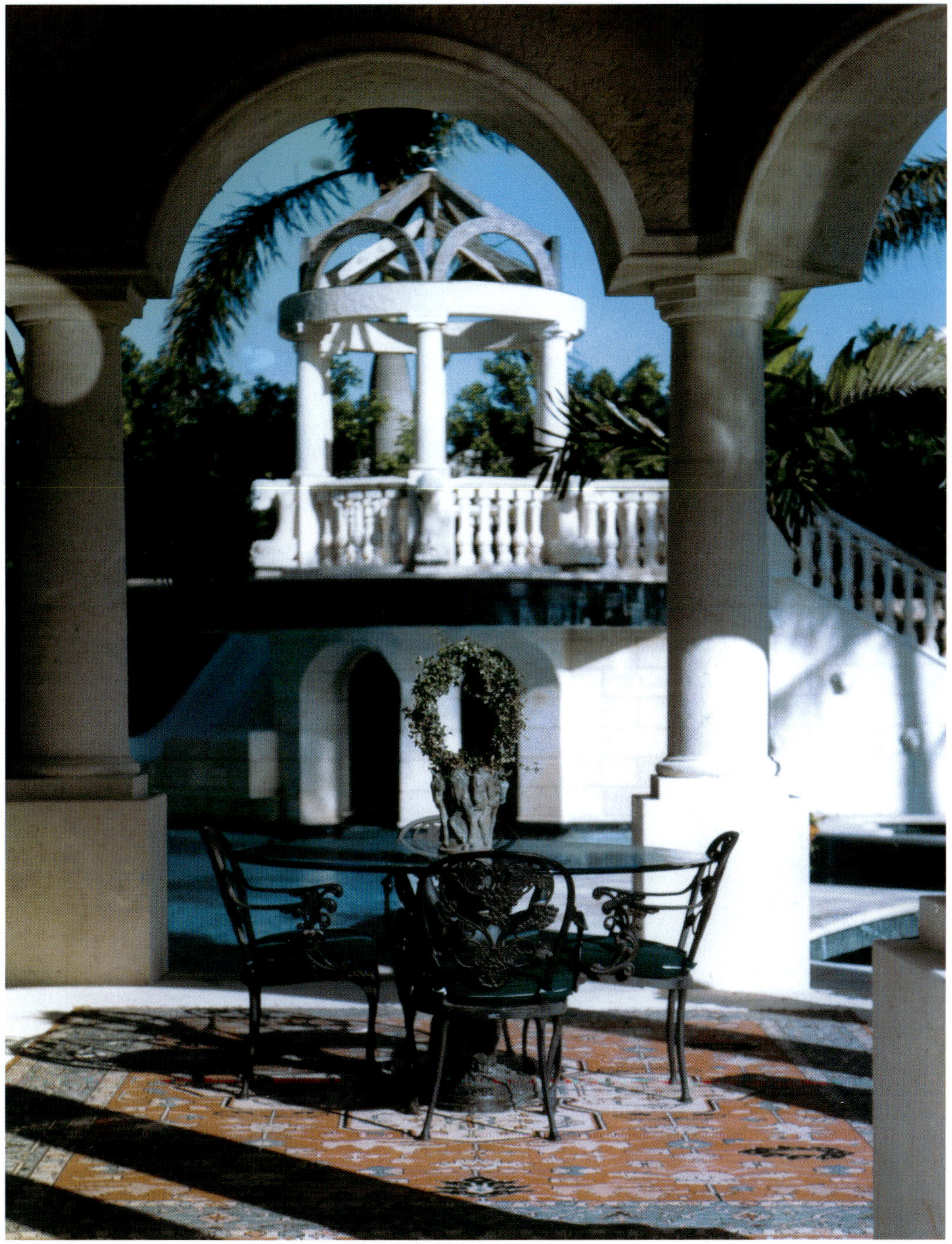

Running his firm with a mix of "psychology, sociology and understanding," Shane asserts that his job is to interpret his clients' speech, inflections and body language to direct and steer them into the design of their project without involving ego. In the end, he knows it's not his house, it's theirs. And that is why his clients consider him a rare talent and keep him busy through repeat and referral business. The proof? In 20 years, Shane has never advertised and he's never had a lull in business.

Q&A more about shane...

WHAT PERSONAL INDULGENCE DO YOU SPEND THE MOST MONEY ON?

My exotic auto collection: I own ten exotic cars.

WHAT IS THE BEST PART OF BEING AN ARCHITECT?

The rush I get walking through the finished product; it is instantly gratifying. The worst part is that I can't turn it off and am continually analyzing every building.

WHAT IS ONE OF THE MOST IMPRESSIVE PROJECTS YOU HAVE WORKED ON?

I am currently working on a historical preservation project on St. Croix. It is the restoration of a hotel that was once the main house of a 17th century sugar plantation. I was commissioned by a client whose house he was designing in South Florida.

WHAT IS THE HIGHEST COMPLIMENT YOU HAVE RECEIVED PROFESSIONALLY?

I want you to work on my next house/building/project!

WHAT IS ONE THING YOU WOULD DO TO BRING A DULL HOUSE TO LIFE?

I would go into the home and rearrange the existing furniture to take advantage of certain lines of sight. Amazing transformations can be made with what the client already has.

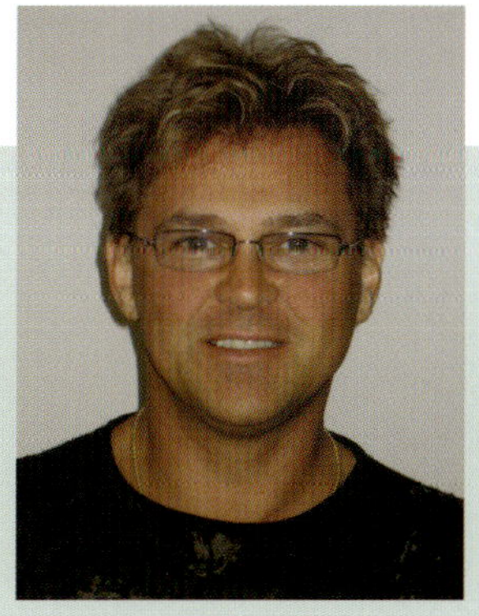

AMES DESIGN INTERNATIONAL

Shane Ames

203 Dixie Boulevard

Delray Beach, FL 33444

561.274.6444

Fax 561.274.6449

LEFT: The best seat in the house viewing the sky gazebo and grotto.
Photograph courtesy of Ames Design International

FACING PAGE: Mediterranean estate with stair tower, drive through and custom fountain.
Photograph courtesy of Ames Design International

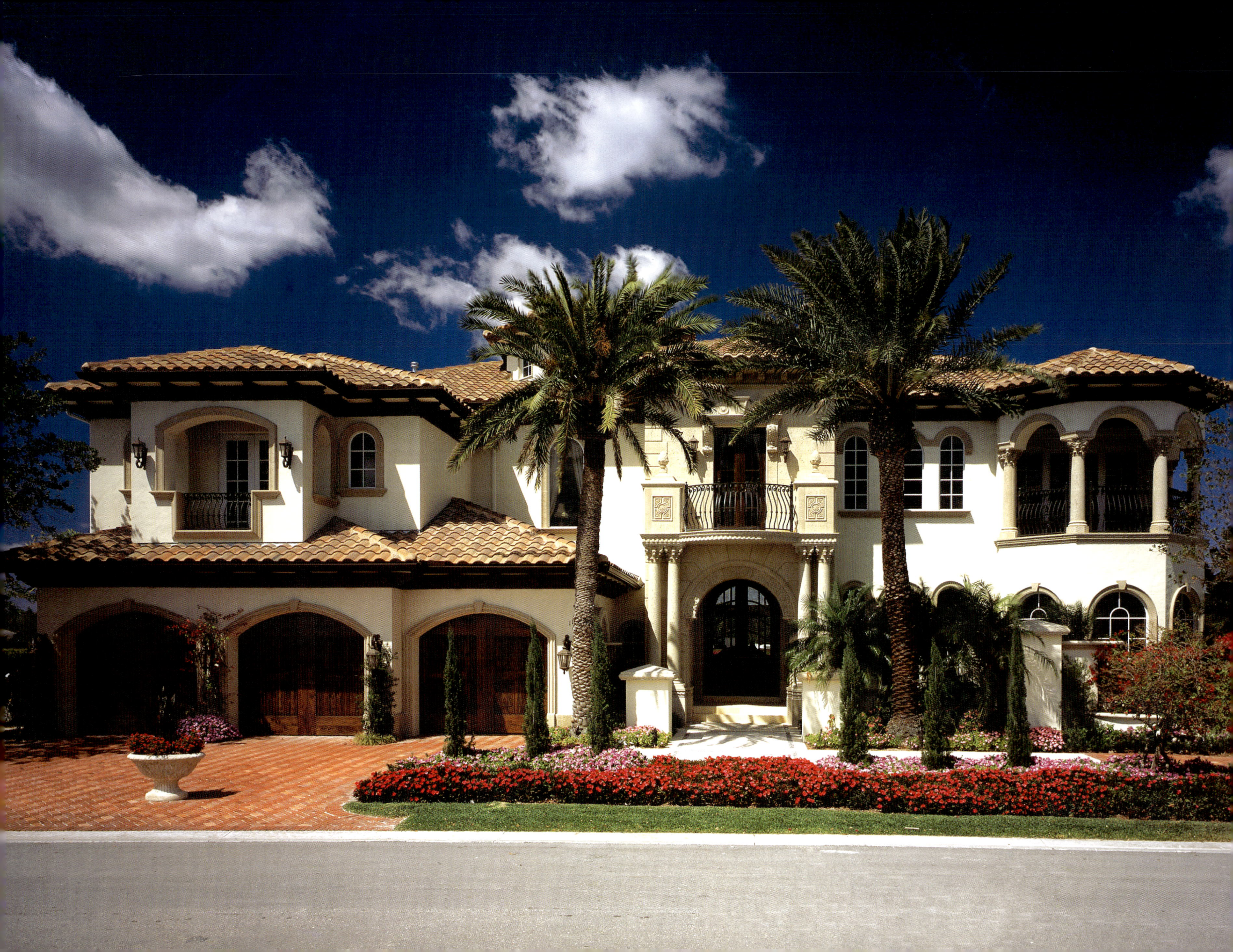

LAWRENCE FRANKEL

Frankel Estate Homes, Inc.

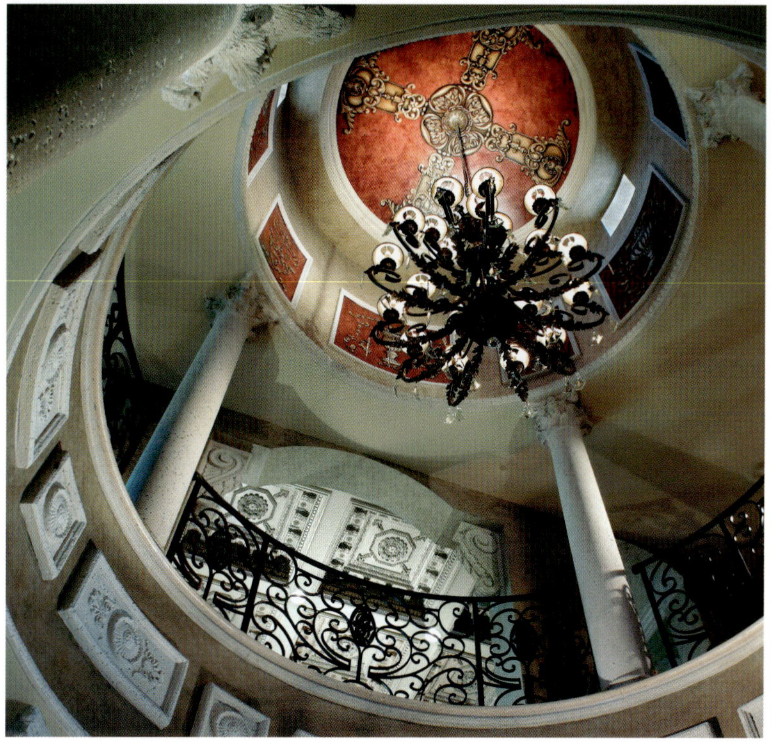

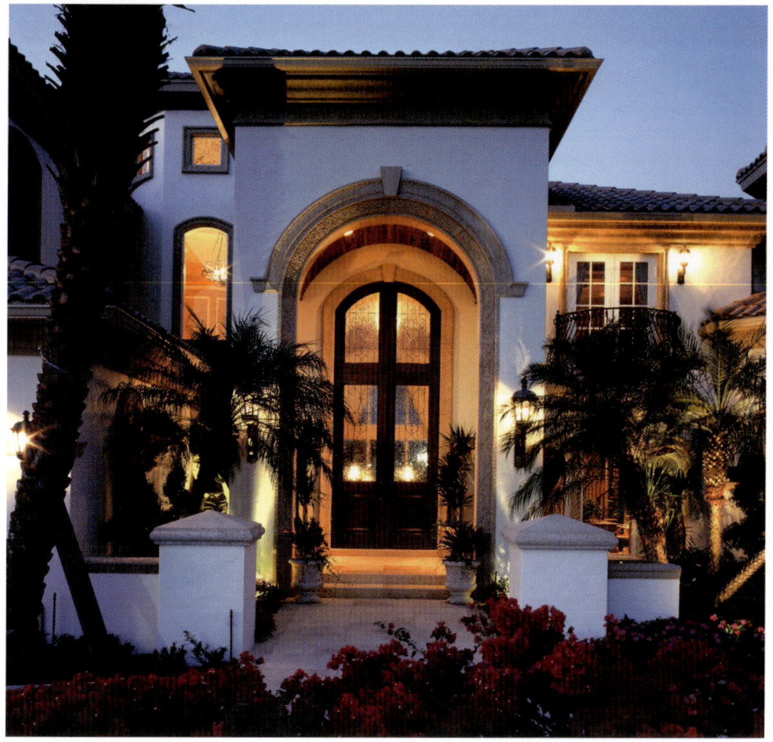

As young as 13 years of age Lawrence "Larry" Frankel worked for his father's custom home building company. This early education paved the way for the young man to grow up and follow in his father's foot steps into the family business.

Frankel Estate Homes was founded 26 years ago by Larry's father, Victor, after leaving a successful commercial building business in New York City to move to Florida. They tried to steer Larry into another line of business, but it was inevitable that he would follow in his father's footsteps. As Larry said, "it was a natural progression."

Larry went to school at Boston University, where he met his wife and started his own real estate business before heading back to Florida to work with his father. When he started working for his family, it helped take the pressure off of his father who was then, after years of hard work, able to relinquish control over the business.

Over time, Larry's role in the family business grew and along the way he learned all aspects of the industry. He started as a superintendent, moved on to project manager, then to president and he is now the owner.

ABOVE LEFT: This photo captures the essence of the foyer vestibule of our Suspiro model. We wanted a very dramatic circular foyer with hand-painted dome ceiling, custom wrought iron railings and stone columns and appliqués.
Photograph by Lapeyra Photography

ABOVE RIGHT: The Villa Castellina was a breakthrough home for us. It was one of the first homes in which we tried to raise the bar by providing finishes and details that were beyond our homeowner's expectations for a home of this caliber.
Photograph by Robert Brantley

LEFT: Front elevation of the Ravello model. We wanted to bring some authenticity to this model home by employing classic Mediterranean details such as a two-story stone cladded entry, Pecky Cypress garage doors, outriggers and custom antiqued wood front door.
Photograph by Kim Sargent, Sargent Architectural Photography

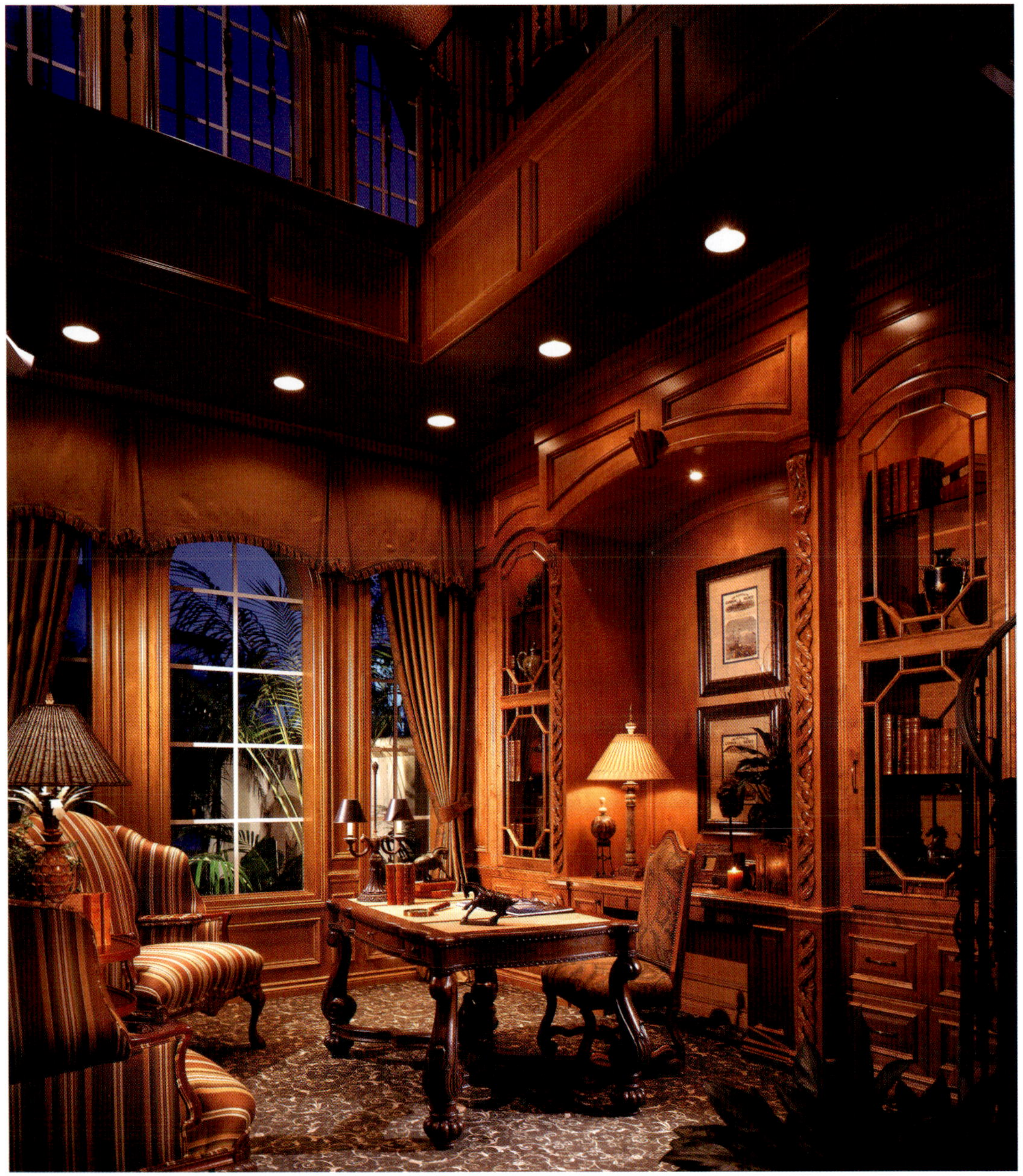

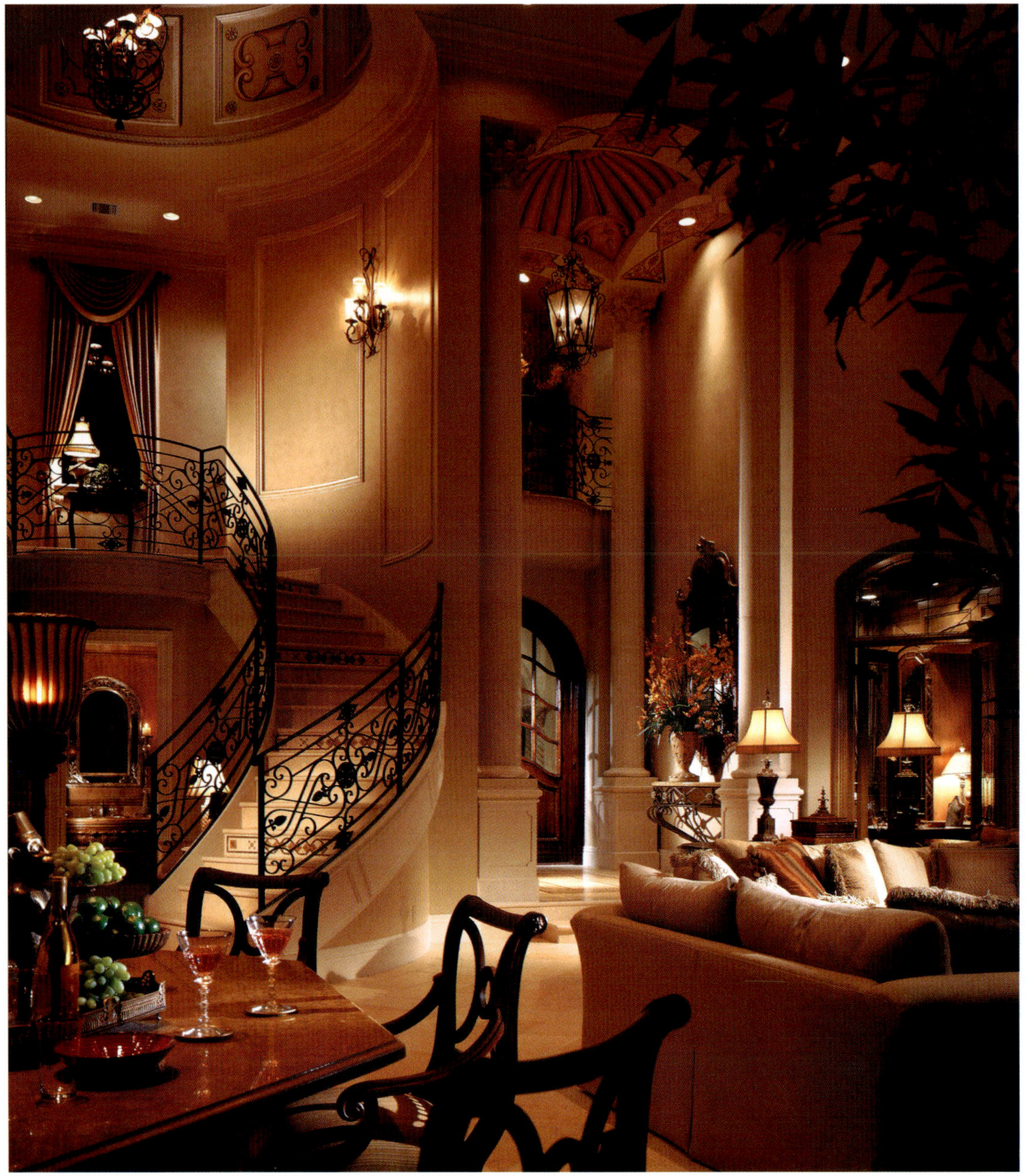

Today, Frankel Estate Homes operates exactly on the principles that it was founded. They design homes to fit their customers' needs and lifestyles, doing whatever it takes to make clients happy. If a project requires it, Larry assembles a team of designers, architects and landscape experts to help make his clients' dreams realities. This second generation custom homebuilder says that he enjoys building true custom homes. In the end, when the projects come together, he feels a sense of pride in what he has accomplished: something original and beautiful.

In an era of big developers that can mass produce homes, Larry feels he has a niche market that fills his sophisticated clients' needs. The niche market that Frankel Estate Homes has established itself in is a market where they build homes that are very complicated and difficult—Larry feels he will always have work because his clientele demands a true custom home experience.

Being open minded, flexible and finding ways to evolve are Larry and Co.'s greatest assets as home builders, but the number one priority is satisfying the client. "Besides being really flexible, I do whatever it takes to make our homeowners happy. You can never do too much for your customer and you can never work too hard. Our success stems from just being willing to do whatever it takes to satisfy our clients. We continually adapt and evolve to our customers' requests and needs."

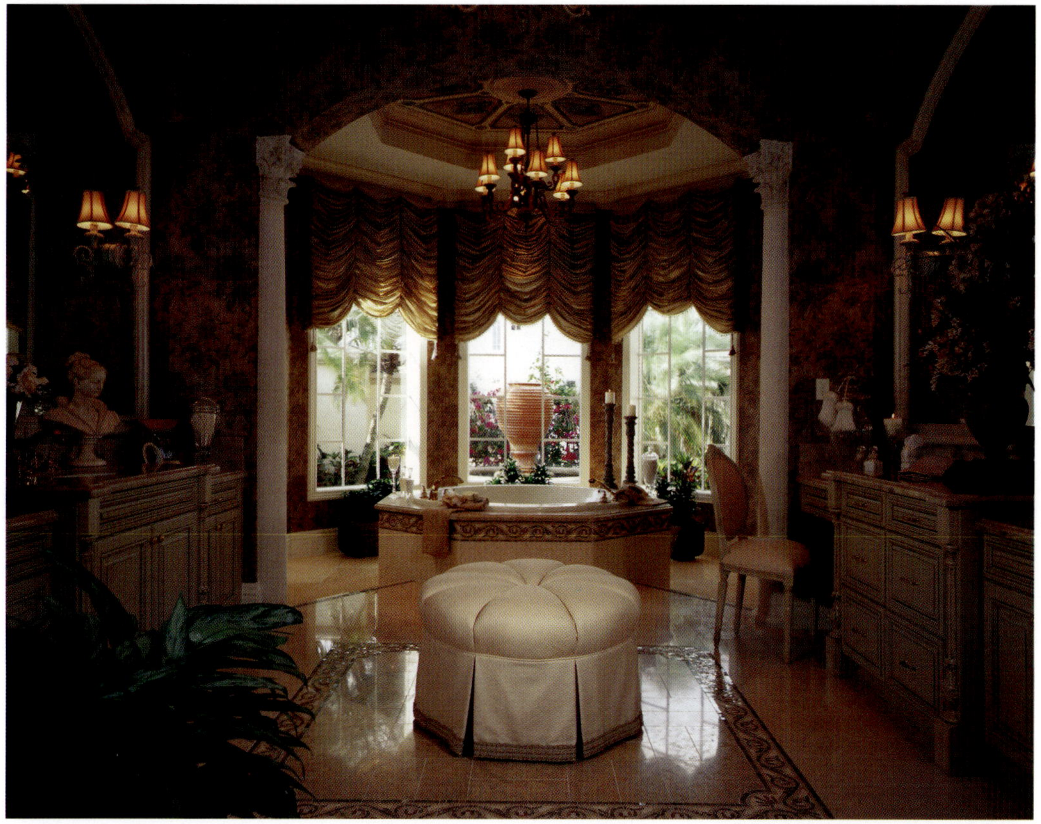

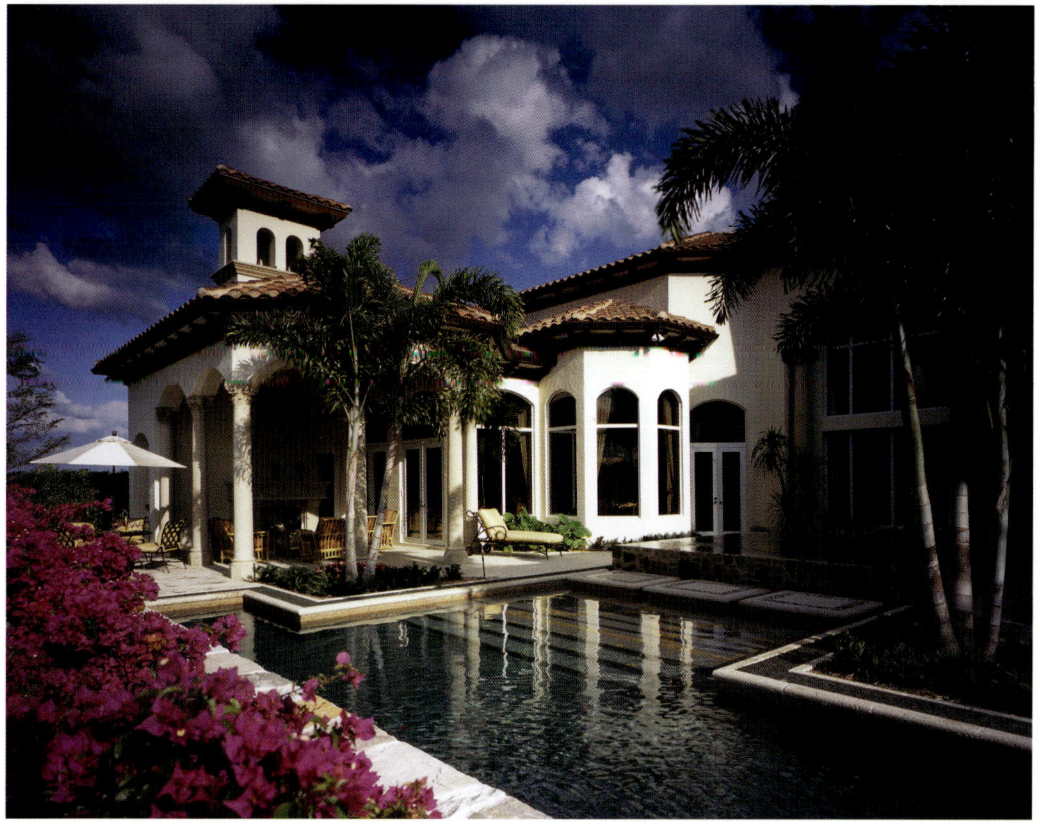

Q&A more about larry...

WHAT ARE YOU MOST PROUD OF?

In an era where the world is dominated by big business and mass production, I'm so proud that I can call myself a true custom home builder. I truly enjoy the ability to create original work. I enjoy the relationship that I develop with each client. I believe that quality, passion and integrity are everything in this business and in life. I love the fact that my wife and children are so proud of who I am and what I do for a living.

WHEN I'M NOT WORKING YOU CAN FIND ME ...

With my wife and kids either swimming in the pool, playing in the park, eating out together or just playing at home.

WHAT COLOR BEST DESCRIBES YOU?

Blue. It is so versatile. It can be strong, subtle, soothing, deep and elegant. It can be almost anything.

WHAT PERSONAL INDULGENCE DO YOU SPEND THE MOST MONEY ON?

Good food and good wine.

FRANKEL ESTATE HOMES, INC.
Lawrence Frankel
1200 Clint Moore Road
Boca Raton, FL 33487
561.994.6443
Fax 561.994.6030

TOP: The intention behind this master bathroom was to create a special retreat just for her. Details include mosaic floor inlays, hand-painted ceiling, gracious vanities, floating tub deck and water feature in master bath privacy wall area.
Photograph by Kim Sargent, Sargent Architectural Photography

BOTTOM: We wanted to create an original pool for this home. We felt that we achieved this with details such as a brimming spa that sits within a brimming reflecting pool, Pennsylvania Limestone cladding, floating step-stones with mosaic inlays and cast bronze trench-grate. We felt that this pool complemented the homes' architecture and helped maintain a feeling of warmth at the rear elevation, covered loggia and pool deck.
Photograph by Kim Sargent, Sargent Architectural Photography

FACING PAGE LEFT: We wanted to create a signature piece for this home. We felt that a paneled two-story library with billiard/club room above would satisfy even the most particular of our clients.
Photograph by Kim Sargent, Sargent Architectural Photography

FACING PAGE RIGHT: This photo showcases the architecture, design and detailing that we try to incorporate in every home we build.
Photograph by Kim Sargent, Sargent Architectural Photography

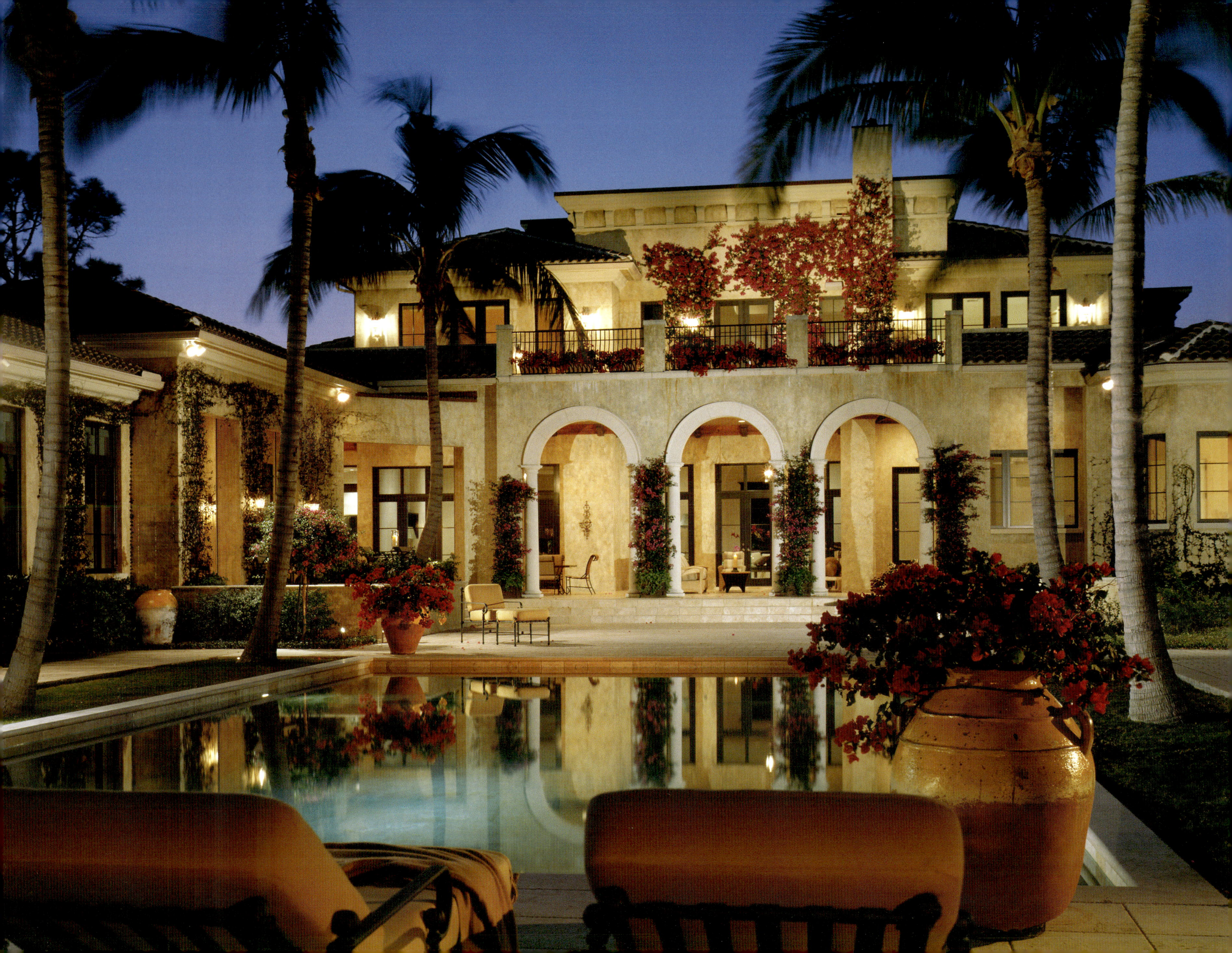

SPENCER GOLIGER

SGA Architecture, Inc.

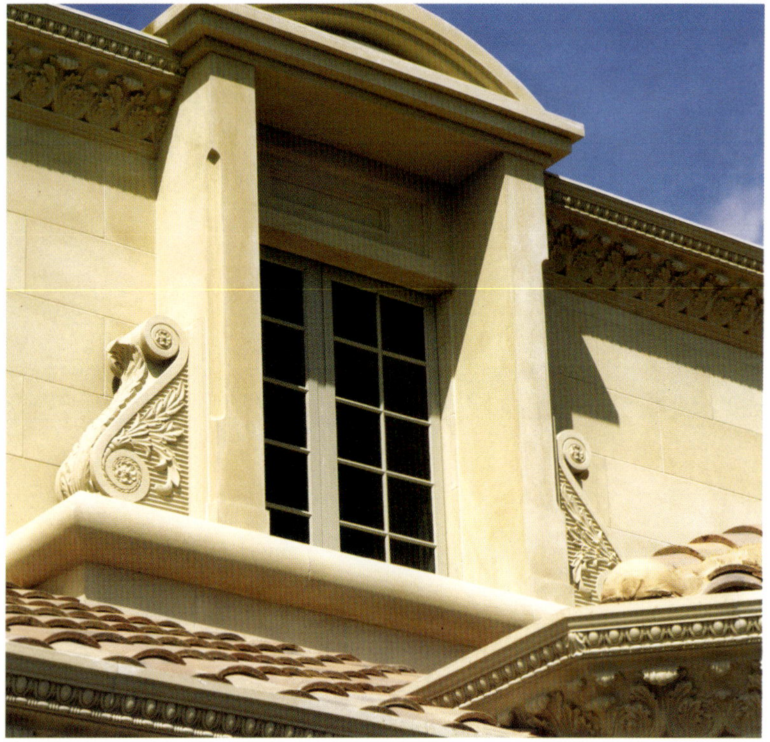

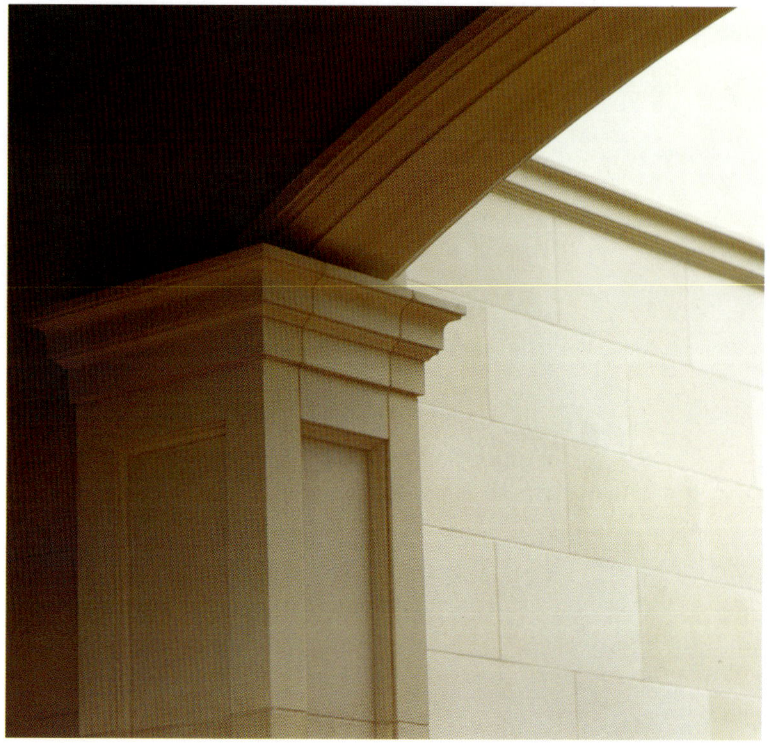

The "moment of truth" is a magical moment for Spencer Goliger, his company, SGA Architecture, Inc., and his clients. When a new home is unveiled and creates amazement within his client, then and only then does Spencer enjoy the sense of a job well done. Spencer knows this feeling well. For many years he has been creating beautiful homes for discriminating clients throughout South Florida and the United States.

Spencer's interest in the field of design was apparent from a very young age. He began to develop and hone his artistic talent before starting his formal education and after extensive travels through Europe. He ultimately made his way back to Southern California, securing a job with a prestigious architectural firm. Several years later he transferred to Florida, where he headed that company's design branch until he started his own business in Boca Raton, finally settling in Palm Beach.

His clients are referred via word-of-mouth for his one-of-a-kind designs. Spencer's design approach is not limited to a particular style; instead he has developed a proactive interview style that challenges his clients to think beyond their wants and desires and focus on creating a home that reflects their lifestyle. Guiding and suggesting, revising and sharpening, Spencer hones the client's image into a shared vision. The entire creative process exposes different ideas and concepts and weaves them into the ultimate design.

ABOVE LEFT: Beautiful stone elements accentuate this deep framed window, supported by carved stone scrolls, topped by an arched stone ledge, highlighted by decorative stone roof details.
Photograph by Troy Campbell

ABOVE RIGHT: The simplicity and grandeur of stone block is expressed in this simple wall, and handsome column, topped by an arched stone element.
Photograph by Troy Campbell

LEFT: The covered outdoor living terrace features arched columned access to the pool. Bronze framed windows accent soft gold walls, highlighted by a profusion of colorful bougainvillea.
Photograph by Troy Campbell

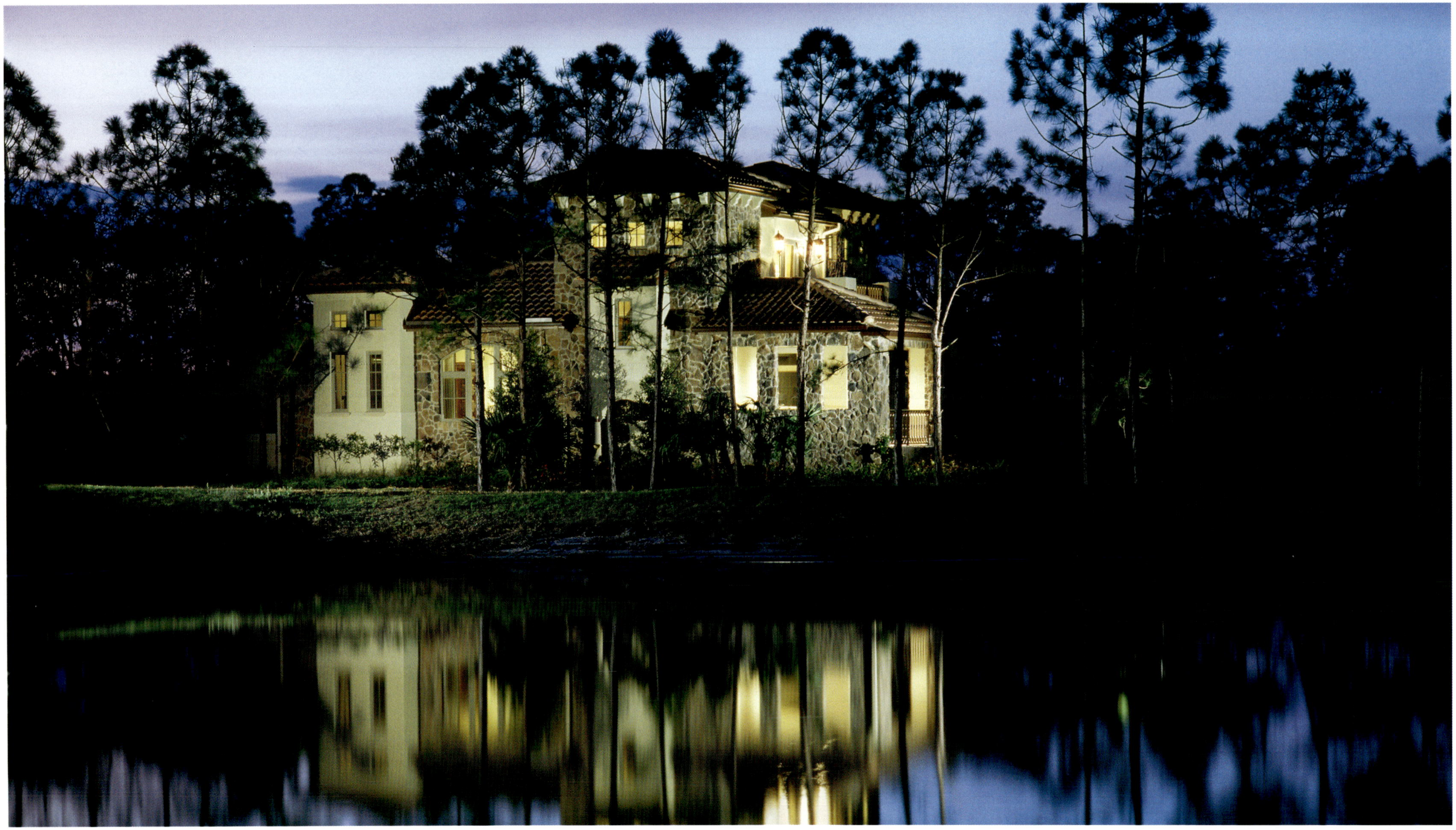

Although Spencer's designs impart a historic language, they are developed without a preconceived idea of what they should be. His designs are truly an evolution of ideas into a vision, then into a tangible reality. His clients tend to be more sophisticated and better informed. Most are well traveled and have collected ideas and concepts of design that form the core of their wants and needs.

If they want an Italian or Tuscan style home, many of them have traveled to these places and have returned with all kinds of ideas that can help Spencer and his team develop unique environments for these clients. "It's really more like a collaboration in terms of the whole architecture, including interiors and the landscape," Spencer said, describing an important element of the design process that he and his team never overlook. "It's how the house lives—in terms of what the owners are looking for, whether or not this is a primary residence, a second home or whether they entertain a lot. Each home should reflect its intended use."

Of all the aspects of being a designer, which includes building relationships with clients, selecting materials and ultimately putting pencil to paper, Spencer believes that the design is the most rewarding part of the process for his clients and for him. Part of their success is that Spencer and his staff truly look after their clients by really listening to them and through continuing close communication. Clients come to Spencer for his creative designs and for the language that speaks to them of "the lofty ideas of beauty and truth that make each project unique—the potential beauty of function."

Traveling helps Spencer with design because it exposes him to different lifestyles and gives him the opportunity to have different dialogues with a variety of people. European and U.S. cities with old hotels, are exciting for Spencer. He is inspired by the communal environments created in hotels, how these spaces are presented to visitors and how people relate to each other and to the spaces.

Spencer's designs are of the highest quality for clients who will settle for nothing less. A philosophy of personal service, fine design and a steadfast adherence to quality have earned him the complete respect and admiration of his clients and peers, resulting in an ever-increasing client base.

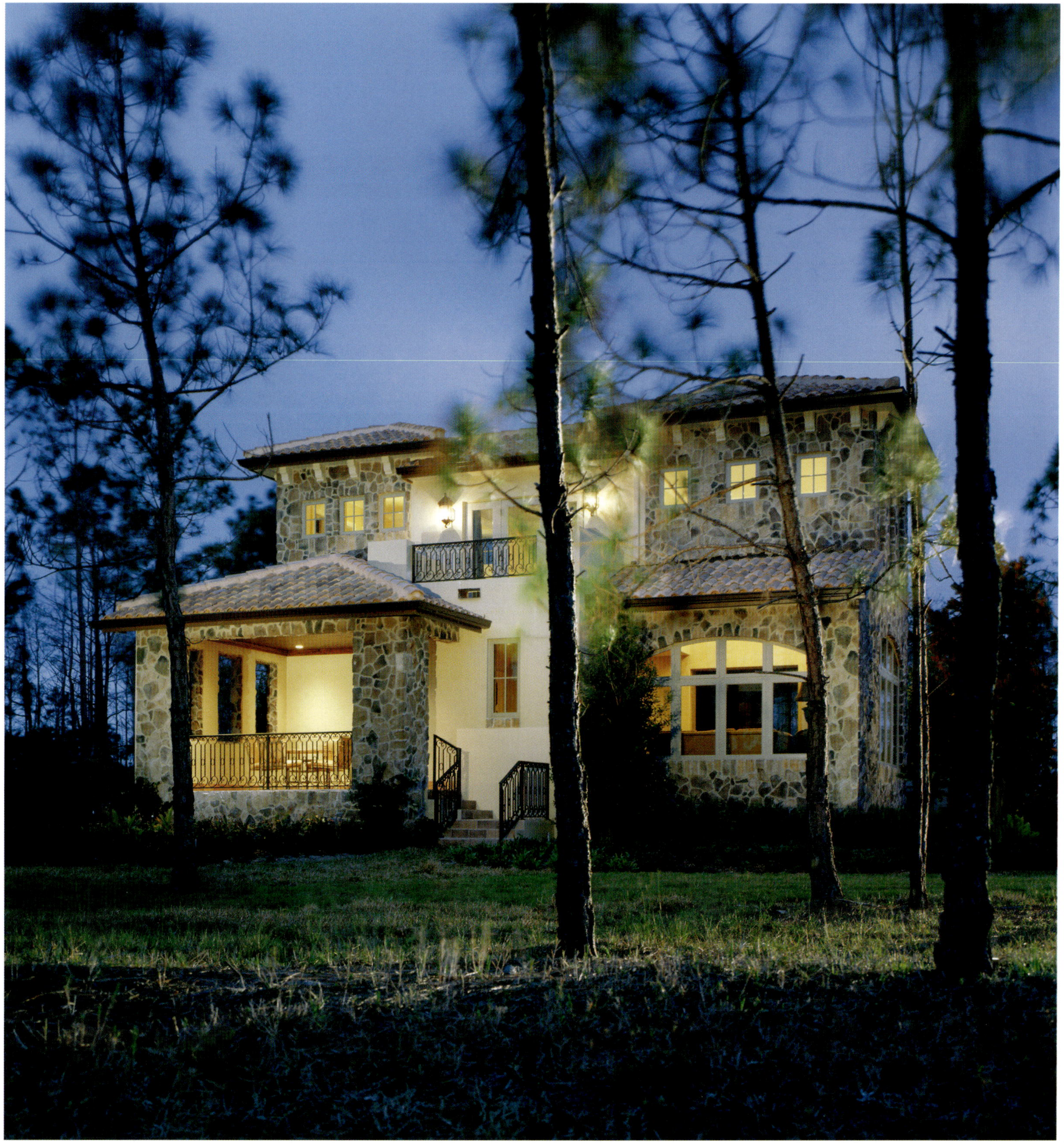

RIGHT: Hand set natural stone walls complement smooth stucco walls, highlighted by elegant yet simple wrought iron balustrades and decorative ledgers at the roofline.
Photograph by Troy Campbell

FACING PAGE: Softly illuminated at dusk and reflected in the lake, this dramatic home is clad in natural stone with smooth stucco highlights, topped by a barrel tile roof.
Photograph by Troy Campbell

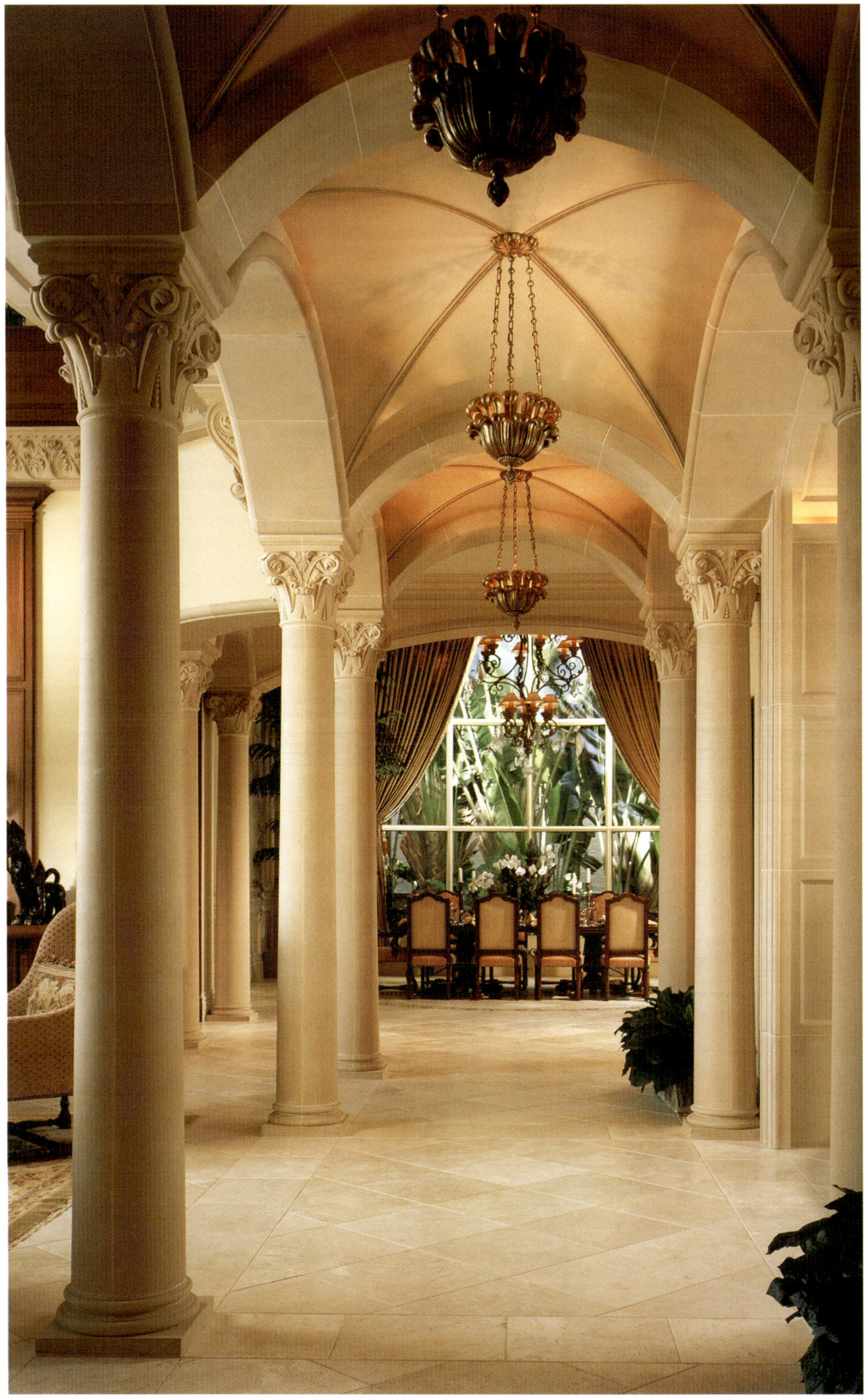

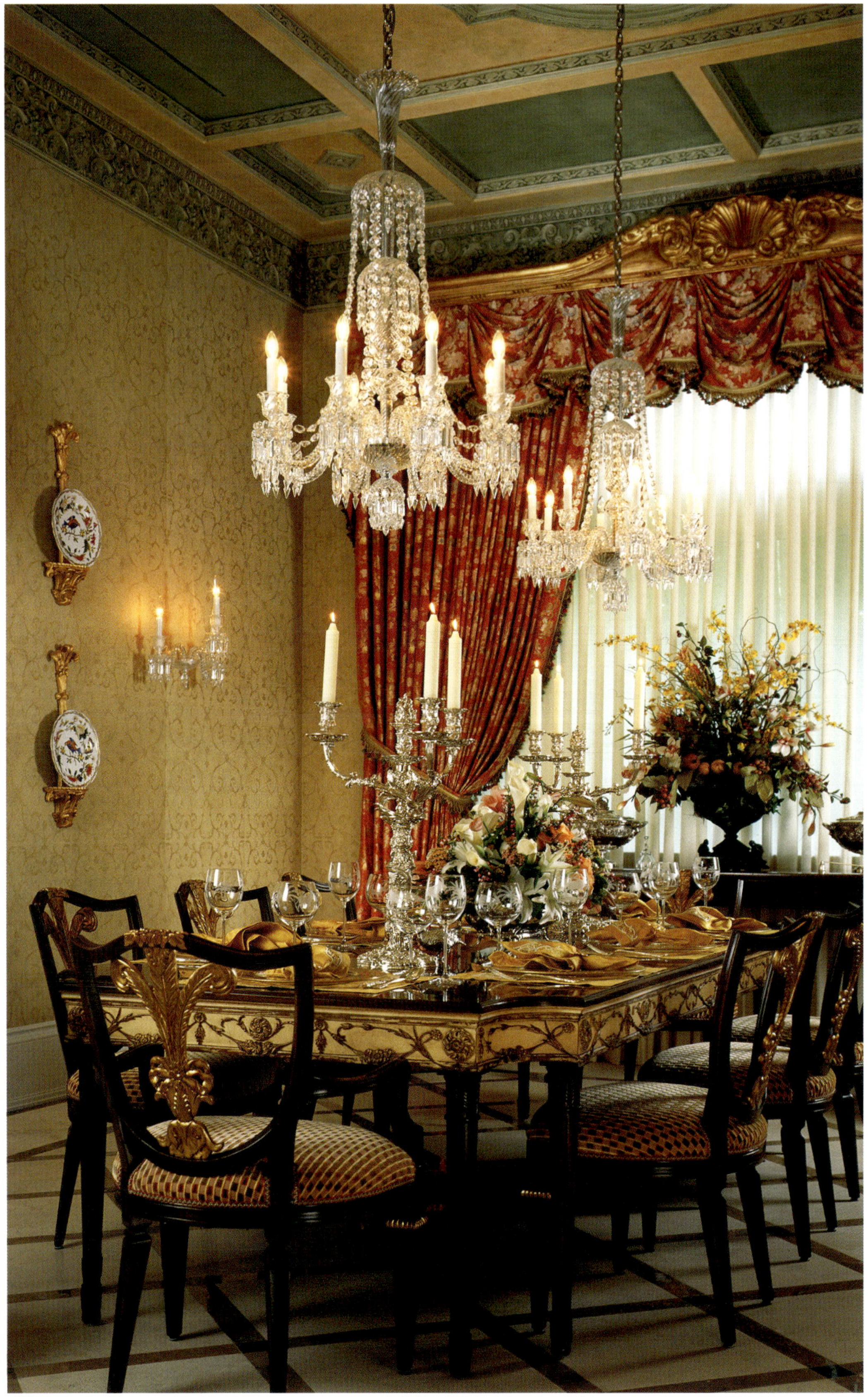

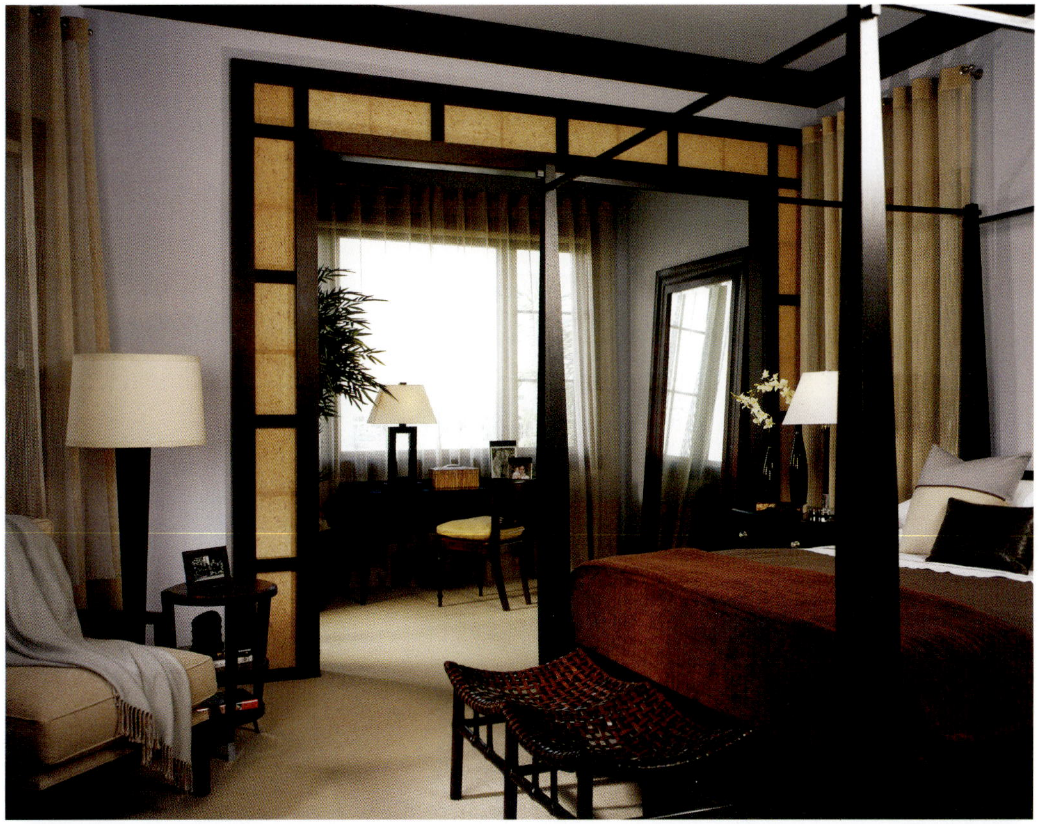

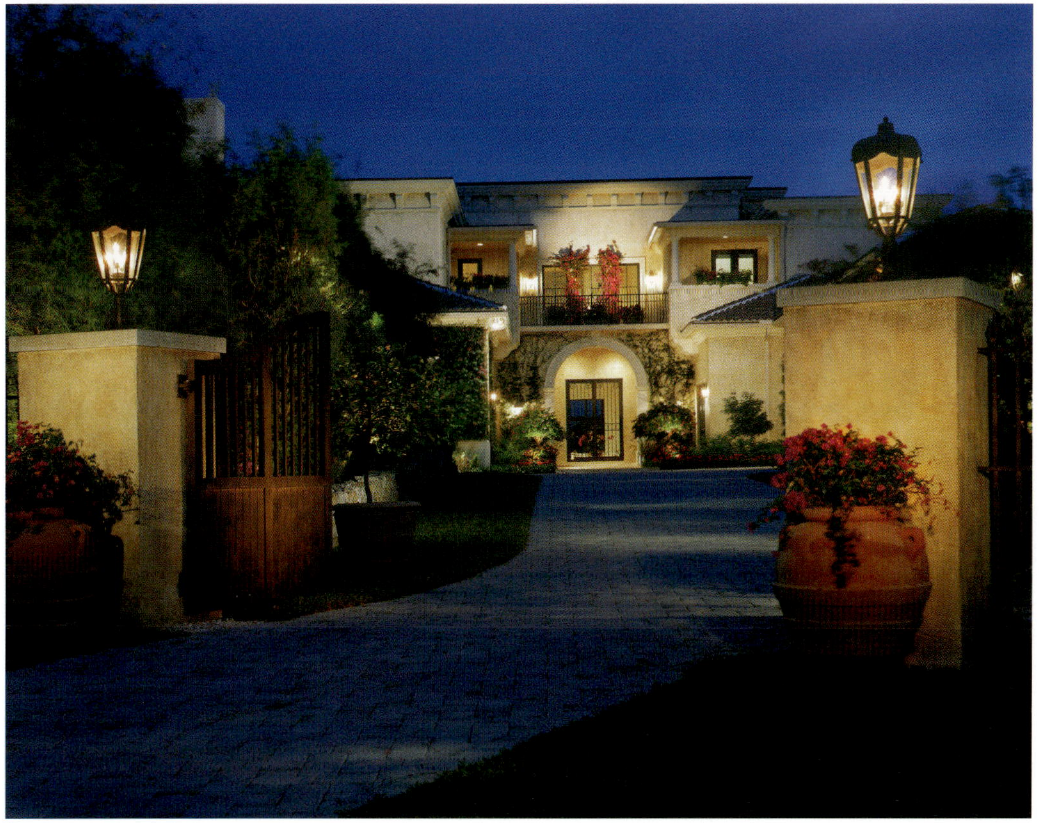

Q&A

more about spencer...

IF YOU COULD ELIMINATE ONE STYLE FROM THE WORLD, WHAT WOULD IT BE?

It's not so much about eliminating a style as it is keeping it fresh and up to date. I feel passionate about design and believe that good design will always be in vogue.

WHAT SEPARATES YOU FROM YOUR COMPETITION?

My charisma and my designs.

WHAT DO YOU LIKE MOST ABOUT DOING BUSINESS IN YOUR LOCALE?

Southern Florida is a melting pot of people. It is a dynamic place to live and work with lots of different cultures to interact with.

WHAT IS THE HIGHEST COMPLIMENT YOU'VE RECEIVED PROFESSIONALLY?

Knowing that I have created an environment that is a living piece of art, with sculptured forms and spaces where one can relax and enjoy life. Of course the awards for design are nice as well.

SGA ARCHITECTURE, INC., FL AA26000808
Spencer Goliger, President
Harry Morris, Architect VP, FL AR0005147
251 Royal Palm Way, Suite 300A
Palm Beach, FL 33480
561.832.1883
Fax 561.832.1433

TOP: Rich, dark wood crown molding highlights the ceiling and frames the translucent panels at the entrance to the dressing area of this gracious contemporary bedroom.
Photograph by Kim Sargent, Sargent Architectural Photography

BOTTOM: Carriage lights top the columns at the gated entry to this Tuscan-style villa. Limed yellow-gold stucco walls topped by stone ledgers create an Old World ambiance.
Photograph by Troy Campbell

FACING PAGE LEFT: The corridor between the master wing and the dining room is architecturally appealing, flanked by Corinthian capped columns and converging arched ceiling with exquisite chandeliers.
Photograph by Kim Sargent, Sargent Architectural Photography

FACING PAGE RIGHT: A diamond patterned inlaid marble floor, an intricately painted box tray ceiling and lavishly draped tall windows set the stage for this elegant, formal dining room.
Photograph by Kim Sargent, Sargent Architectural Photography

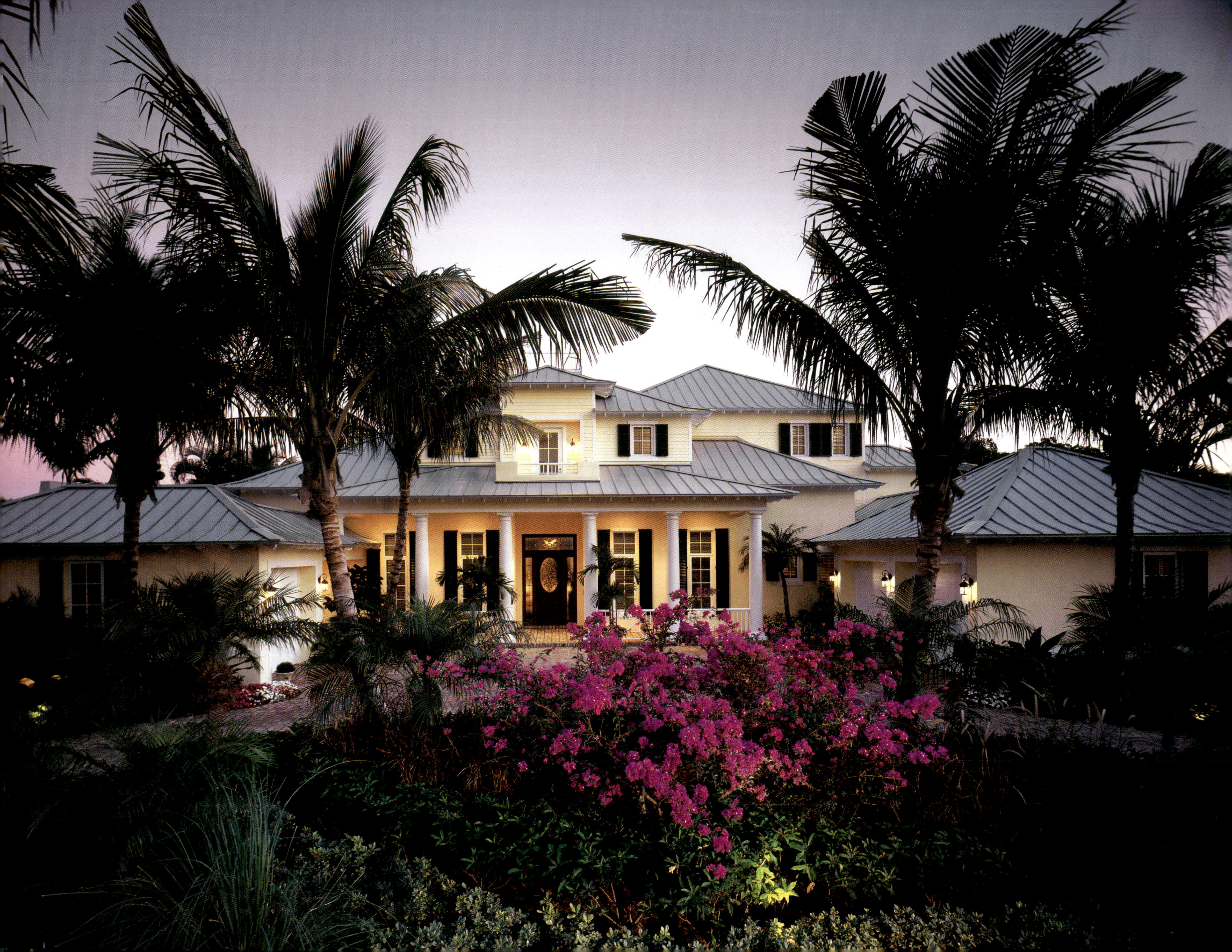

BILL HASEY

Bloomfield Construction, Inc.

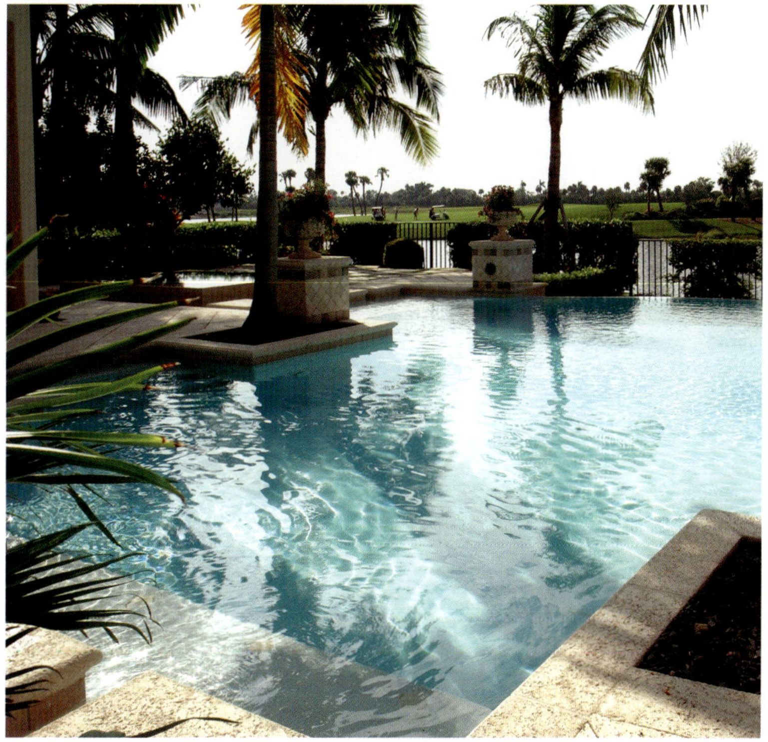

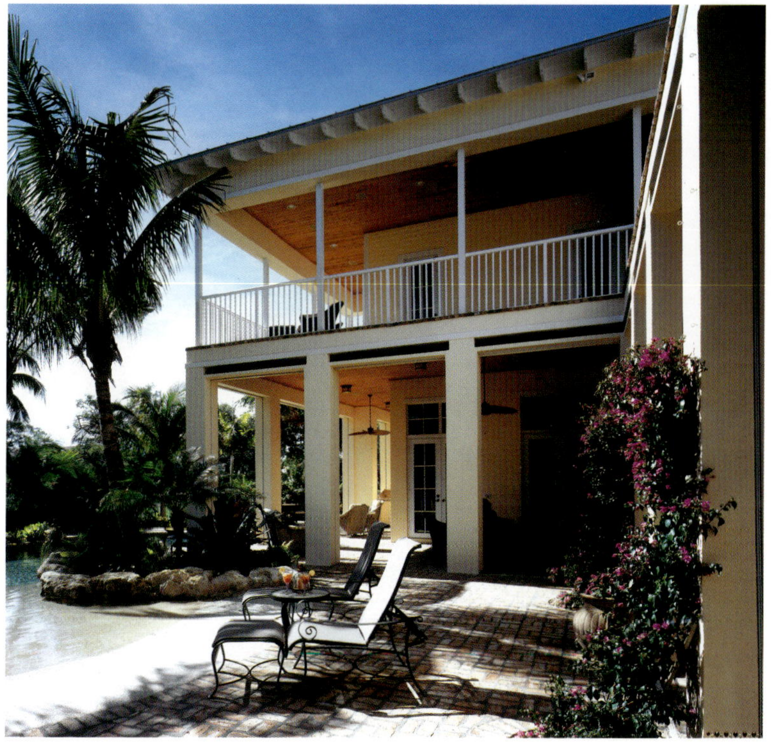

For over 25 years, Bloomfield Construction Inc.'s staunch commitment to delivering truly exceptional homes, to even the most discerning clientele, has resulted in an impeccable reputation revered by architects and elated clients alike. Owner and president, Bill Hasey, a White Plains, New York native, lived for 26 years in Bloomfield, Michigan, from whence his company earned its name. During the 1970s, Bill gained an invaluable business perspective while working in sales for IBM, and later, his father's pharmaceutical company, Meyer Laboratories (Glaxo). Eventually, as Vice-President of Sales for Glaxo (United States), Bill's position brought him to Boca Raton.

Upon arriving in Boca Raton, Bill sensed the amazing real estate opportunity that presented itself in the area's beautiful land. He formed a real estate investment and property management firm in the early 1980s and, eventually, began constructing homes.

Over two decades later, Bloomfield commands a strong presence in the building world of South Florida. Bill operates his company with the business savoir-faire gained from his past and present "lives" in two seemingly unrelated fields, which actually have everything to do with his firm's formula for success today: focus on the client, give exhaustive attention to detail, and seek the best of everything. Bloomfield only draws upon the most qualified contractors, the highest quality materials and the most proficient management team to help accomplish this formula. The proof? A simple tour inside

ABOVE: *Photographs courtesy of Bloomfield Construction, Inc.*

LEFT: *Photograph courtesy of Bloomfield Construction, Inc.*

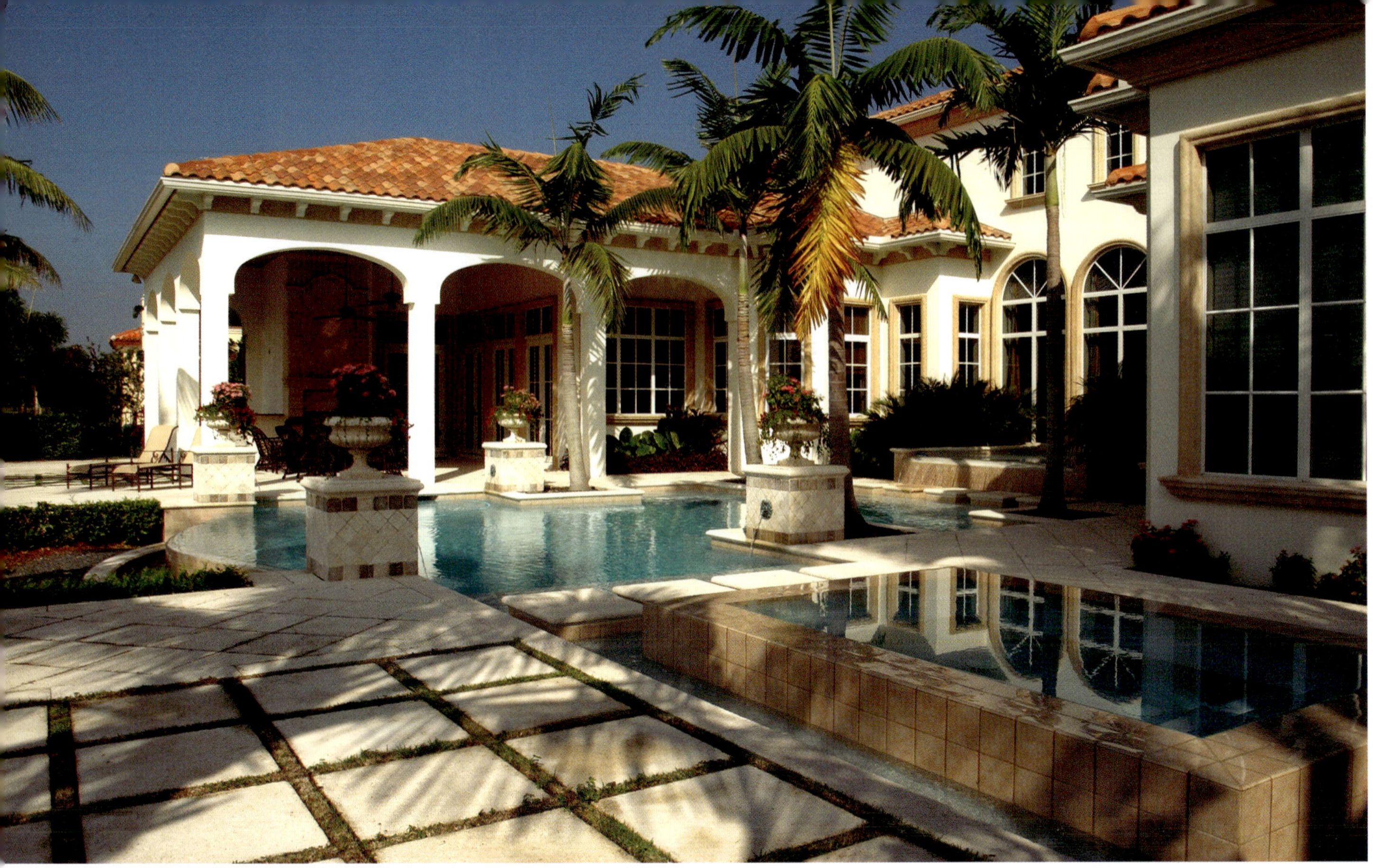

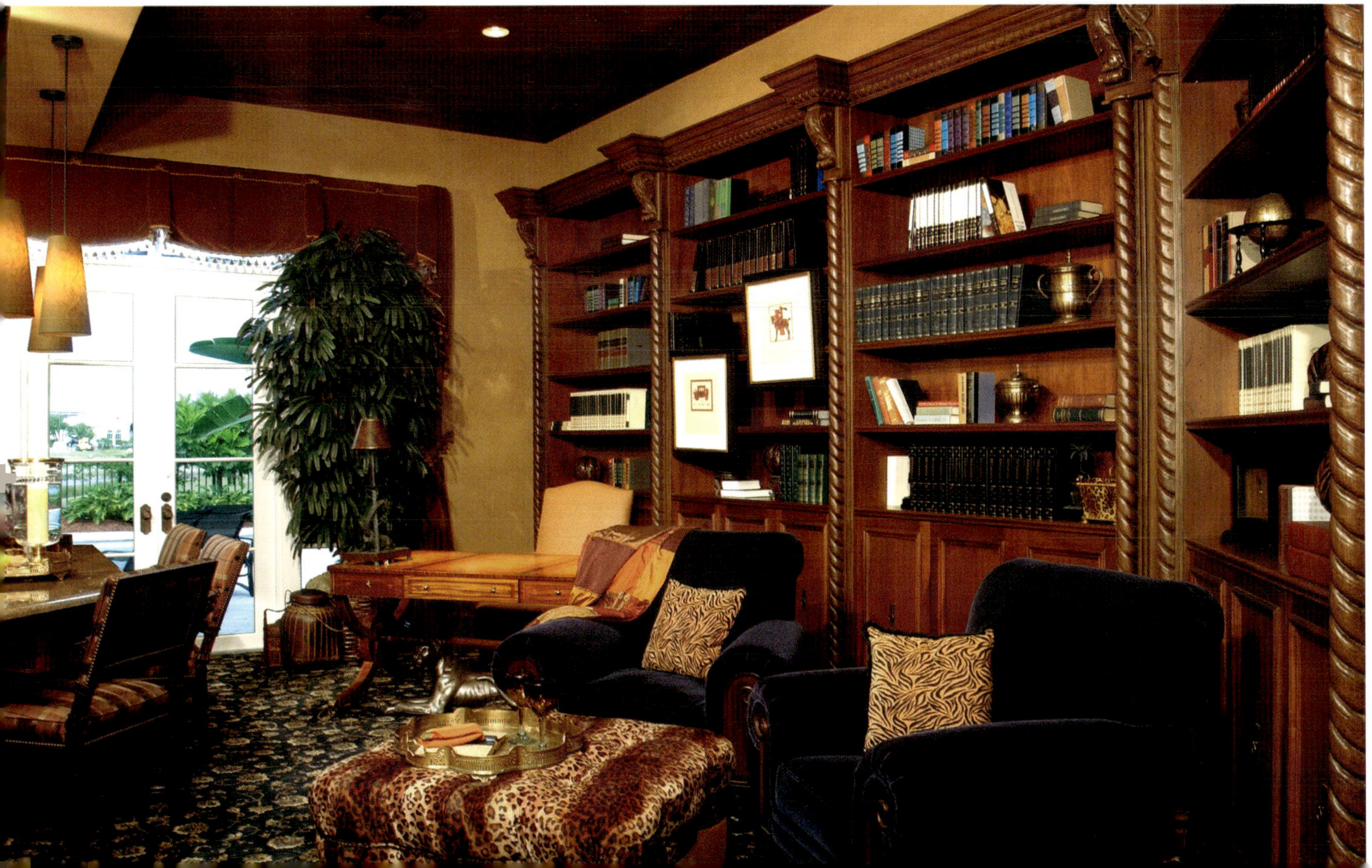

and outside any one of Bill's innovative, timeless homes is all one needs as confirmation.

South Florida's luxury home buyers are savvy… and they can be; the area is a haven for lavish new home construction. Limiting his practice to about 10-15 single family home projects a year, Bill is able to give his clients the kind of attention they merit, and his homes, the level of craftsmanship for which his company is widely reputed. The majority of Bill's clients are from the Northeast, nearing or at retirement, and desire a dream home to entertain family and friends while enjoying the Palm Beach lifestyle they have worked their whole lives to attain. Bill understands and appreciates the gravity of this responsibility.

Bloomfield's average home is about 7,000-square-feet which requires about four months of conception and about 12 months devoted to its superior construction. Prompted by a glowing reputation, clients seek Bill to construct their homes and in turn, he guides them through the process suggesting an architect in harmony with their style preferences. He believes that critical to the entire process is the ability of the design team—comprised of the architect, interior designer, landscape architect and himself—to work together seamlessly from the start.

Building dream homes is, creatively, one of the most satisfying jobs. In the end, Bill is able to see his company's hard work pay off—and in breath-taking form. From spectacular French Mediterranean to West Indies/Key West homes, Bill delivers the homes of people's dreams. Bloomfield Construction Inc. has won numerous awards, including the coveted PRISM Award and a Custom Residence award for a stand-out West Indies-style home and has been heralded in a variety of publications including *Builder/Architect* and *Boca Raton News*.

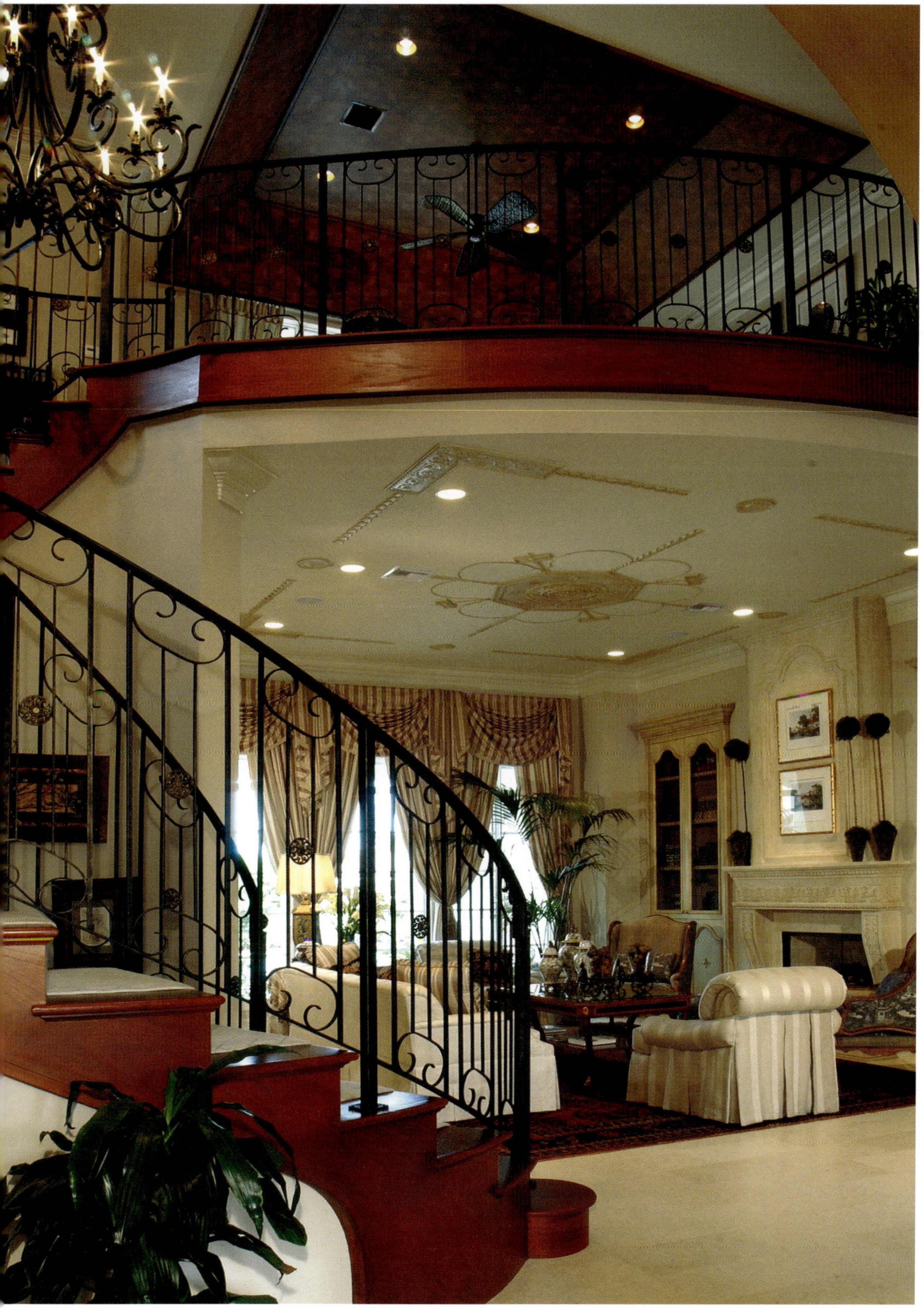

Q&A more about bill...

WHAT COLOR BEST DESCRIBES YOU AND WHY?

Blue, because it is calm.

WHAT ELEMENT OF STYLE OR PHILOSOPHY HAVE YOU STUCK WITH FOR YEARS THAT STILL WORKS TODAY?

Tell the truth.

WHO HAS HAD THE BIGGEST INFLUENCE ON YOUR CAREER?

My father.

DESCRIBE YOUR STYLE OR DESIGN PREFERENCES.

They are as varied as my clients: from Mediterranean to Key West.

BLOOMFIELD CONSTRUCTION, INC.
Bill Hasey
1877 South Federal Highway, Suite 202
Boca Raton, FL 33432
561.368.5521
www.bloomfieldconstructioninc.com

LEFT: *Photograph courtesy of Bloomfield Construction, Inc.*

FACING PAGE: *Photographs courtesy of Bloomfield Construction, Inc.*

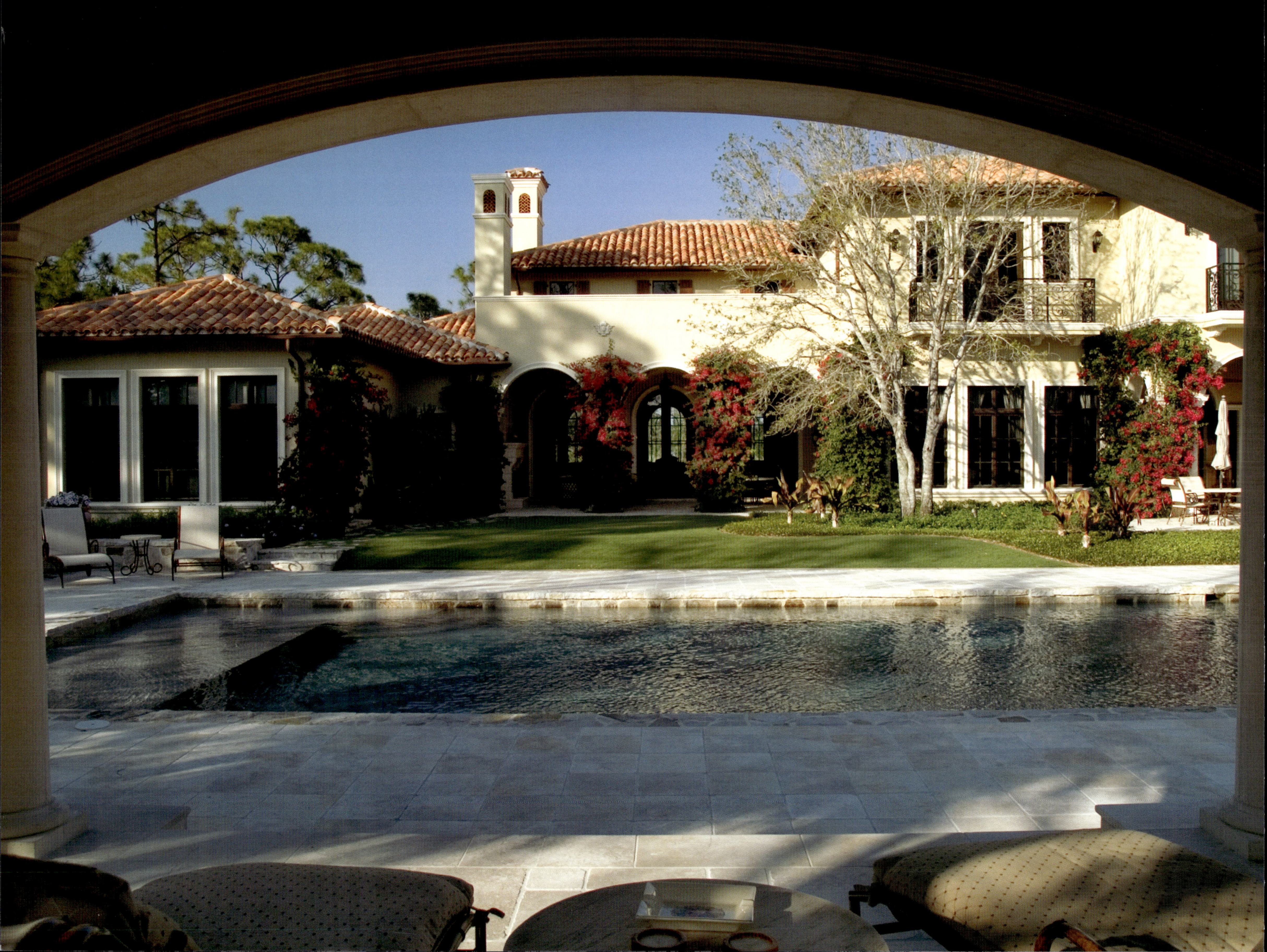

MARTIN HASEY

Pinetree Homes, Inc.

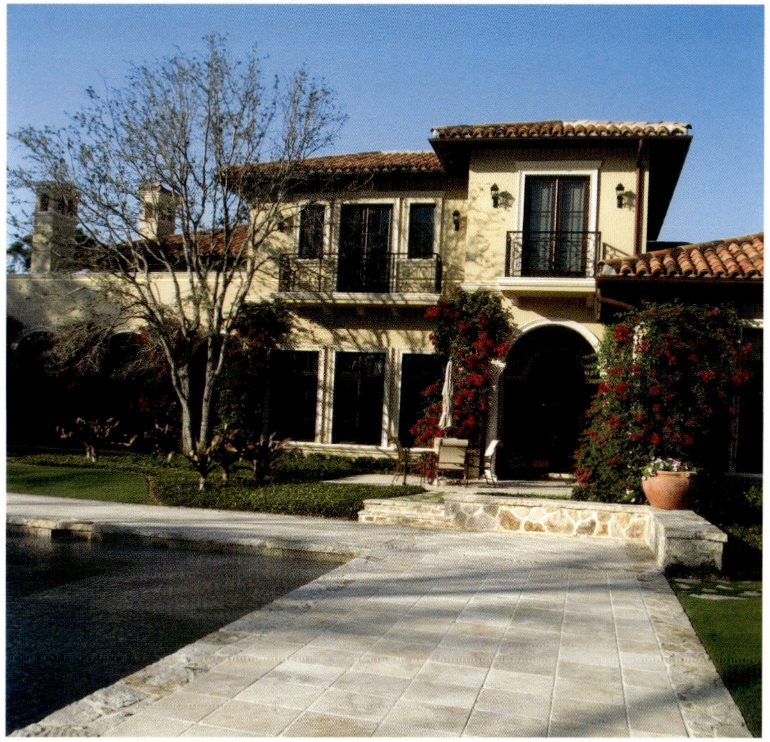

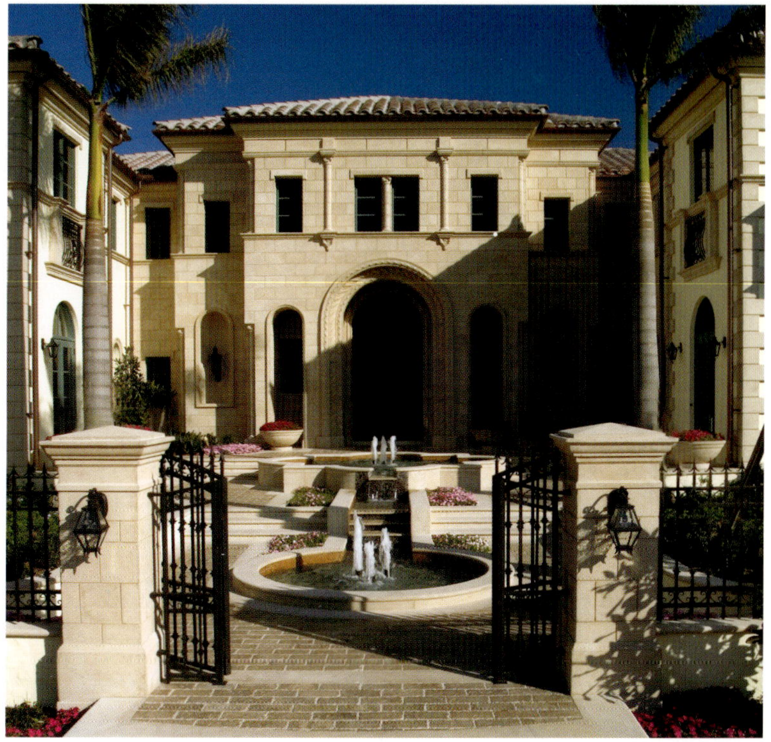

Since its founding nearly 26 years ago, Pinetree Homes has proven that solid business standards, the highest quality craftsmanship, and breathtaking excellence will certainly earn a reputation and the success to match.

Founder and principal Marty Hasey is passionate about his clients and the level of service they receive. The company's structure is proof of this customer-oriented philosophy: each home is assigned a general contractor acting under Vice-President Barry Ratner who has been with the company since 1992. Before each project, the construction team painstakingly reviews the plans to ensure there is no room for misinterpretation or error. Committed to providing their clients with the knowledge required to be an integral member of the team, Pinetree outlines all the design and technological choices available so nothing is overlooked or compromised. Marty maintains intimate knowledge and is active in each project.

A well-known presence primarily in Palm Beach County, Pinetree Homes is distinguished as the only builder in all three of the most prestigious country club communities in the Palm Beach Gardens and Jupiter area.

Future homeowners seek the company based on referral and often firsthand knowledge. With over 500 remarkable custom homes to their credit, many of the most celebrated and luxurious homes in Palm Beach County boast "Pinetree Homes built."

ABOVE RIGHT: The welcoming front elevation of an 11,000-square-foot, two-story Mediterranean home which features a lovely fountain.
Photograph by Sue Buxton

ABOVE LEFT & FACING PAGE: Two magnificent rear elevation perspectives of a 10,000-square-foot, two-story home taken from the pool cabana.
Photographs by Sue Buxton

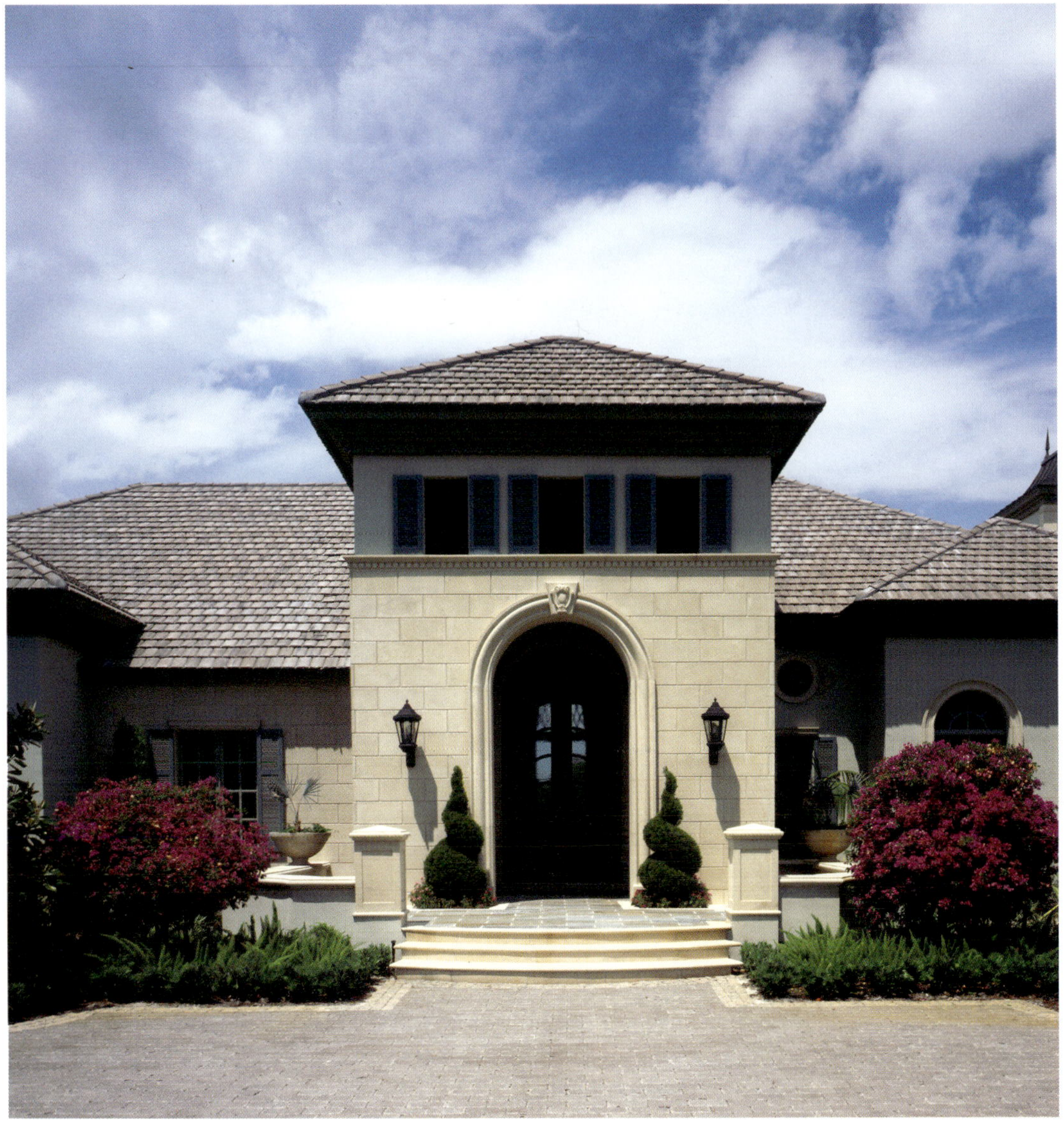

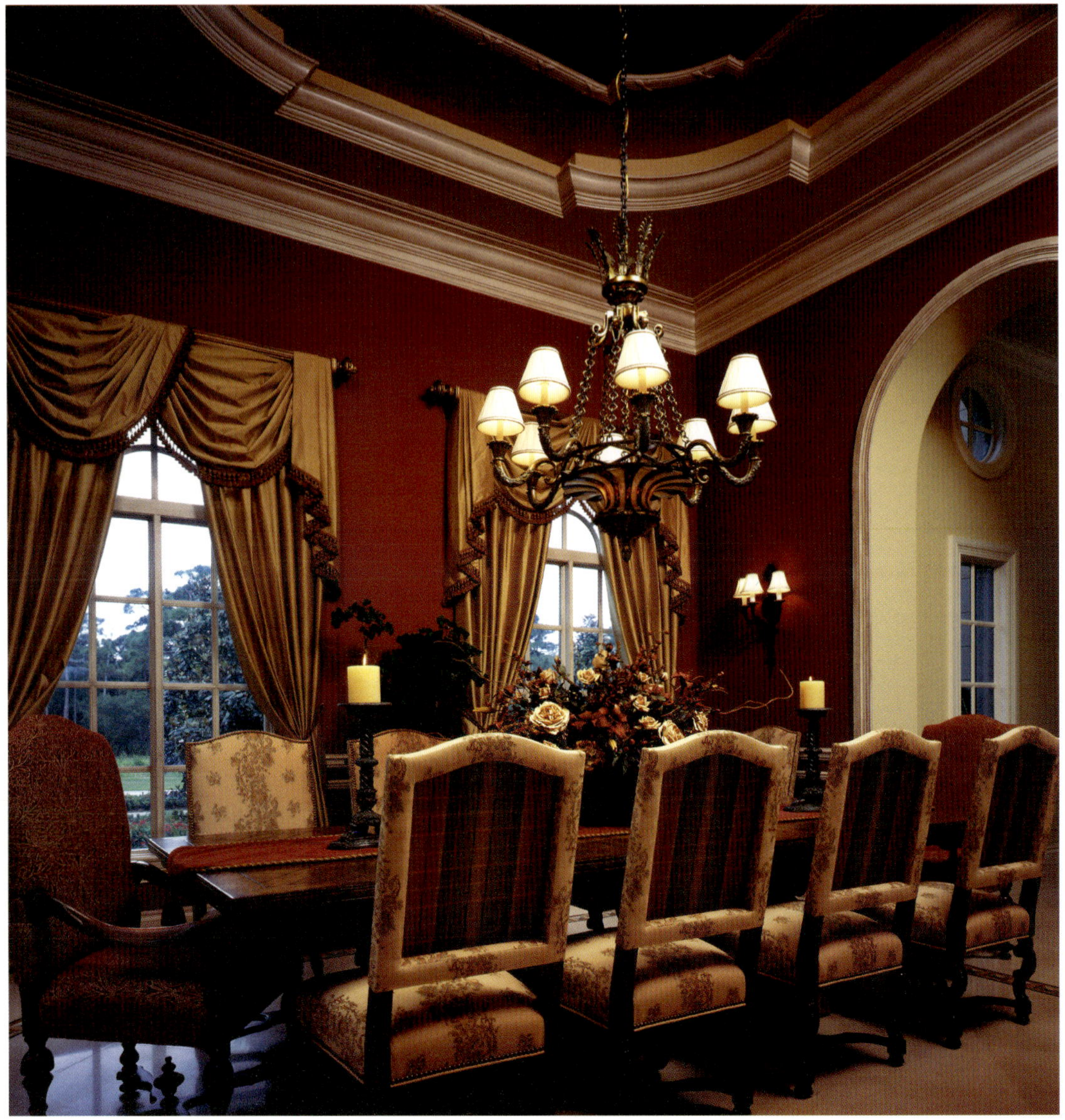

Known for superior craftsmanship and an inherent sense of the natural site elements, Pinetree uses only the highest quality materials and subcontractors, many of whom Marty has worked with for 15-20 years. Although it is ultimately the client whose personal tastes determine their home's style, Pinetree can accommodate any genre from ultra contemporary to Art Deco to Mizner and everything in between. Outstanding quality will always remain timeless.

Although the company has been larger in the past, they have intentionally chosen to pare down with six to eight extraordinary projects a year. This affords each employee the availability to give the client the undivided attention and guidance they deserve. The team approaches each project as a challenge, giving it meticulous thought and effort. No matter the budget, value and timeliness is of the utmost, and through vigilant practices, Pinetree always exceeds expectation.

A memorable and recent commission involved a well-known South Florida interior designer. The extraordinary 16,000-square-foot very contemporary home now rests on ten acres in Boca Raton. It was quite an honor and testament to Pinetree's reputation to build the home of one whose creative career dictated that no design detail—from leather to terrazzo flooring—be overlooked and that nothing be "ordinary."

Accolades aside, and there are many, Marty delights in what matters most: his company's legacy in South Florida. To that end, son W.J. has recently come on board after graduating with a degree in construction and Marty looks forward to sharing his wisdom and gaining a fresh perspective as well.

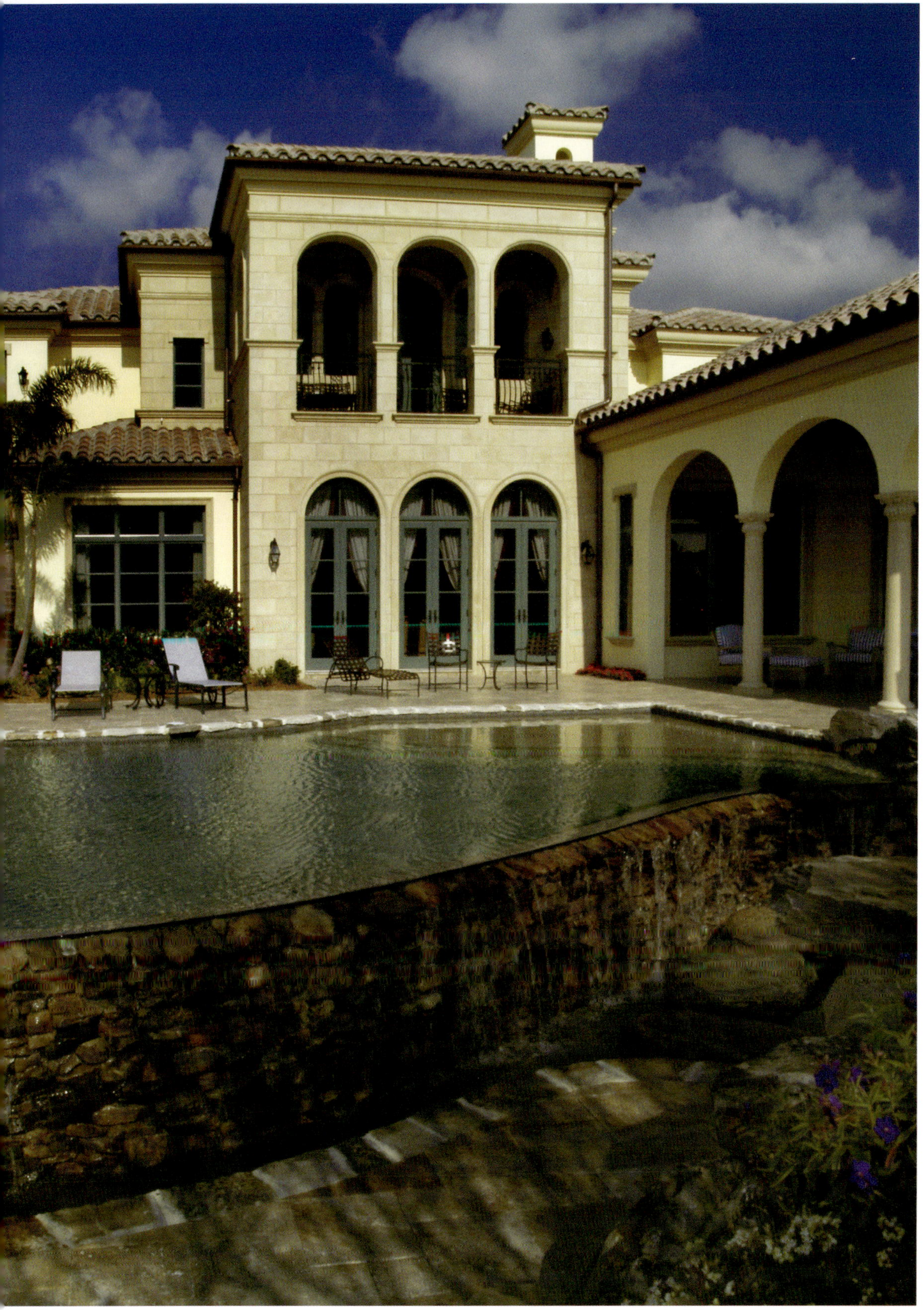

Q&A

more about martin...

HOW LONG HAVE YOU BEEN A BUILDER?

The company is completing its 25th year. I founded Pinetree Homes in 1980.

WHAT IS THE MOST UNUSUAL/EXPENSIVE/DIFFICULT DESIGN OR TECHNIQUE YOU'VE USED IN ONE OF YOUR PROJECTS?

A pool/spa area on a home that we just completed. The pool had everything imaginable—a beach entry, waterfalls, spa waterfalls, vanishing edges.

WHAT ONE ELEMENT OF STYLE OR PHILOSOPHY HAVE YOU STUCK WITH FOR YEARS STILL WORKS FOR YOU TODAY?

Regardless of the home's price point, try to give the clients a gorgeous house with a great value.

WHAT'S THE BEST PART ABOUT BEING A BUILDER?

The reward of seeing the finished product and a family enjoying your efforts for years to come.

IF YOU COULD ELIMINATE ONE DESIGN/ARCHITECTURAL BUILDING TECHNIQUE OR STYLE FROM THE WORLD, WHAT WOULD IT BE?

None. One of our strengths is being able to produce what our clients' interests and design preferences are.

PINETREE HOMES, INC.
Martin Hasey
42 North Swinton Avenue, Suite II
Delray Beach, FL 33444
561.274.6187

LEFT: A perspective of the same Mediterranean home on page 45 (shown above right) from the vanishing-edge pool. The serene beauty of the pool area blended with the charm of this elegant rear elevation makes it an exquisite outdoor living space.
Photograph by Sue Buxton

FACING PAGE LEFT & RIGHT: The front elevation of an 8,000-square-foot single family residence. This elevation is more French Provincial than Mediterranean. Rich millwork is beautifully highlighted in the dining room of the same home.
Photographs by Robert Brantley

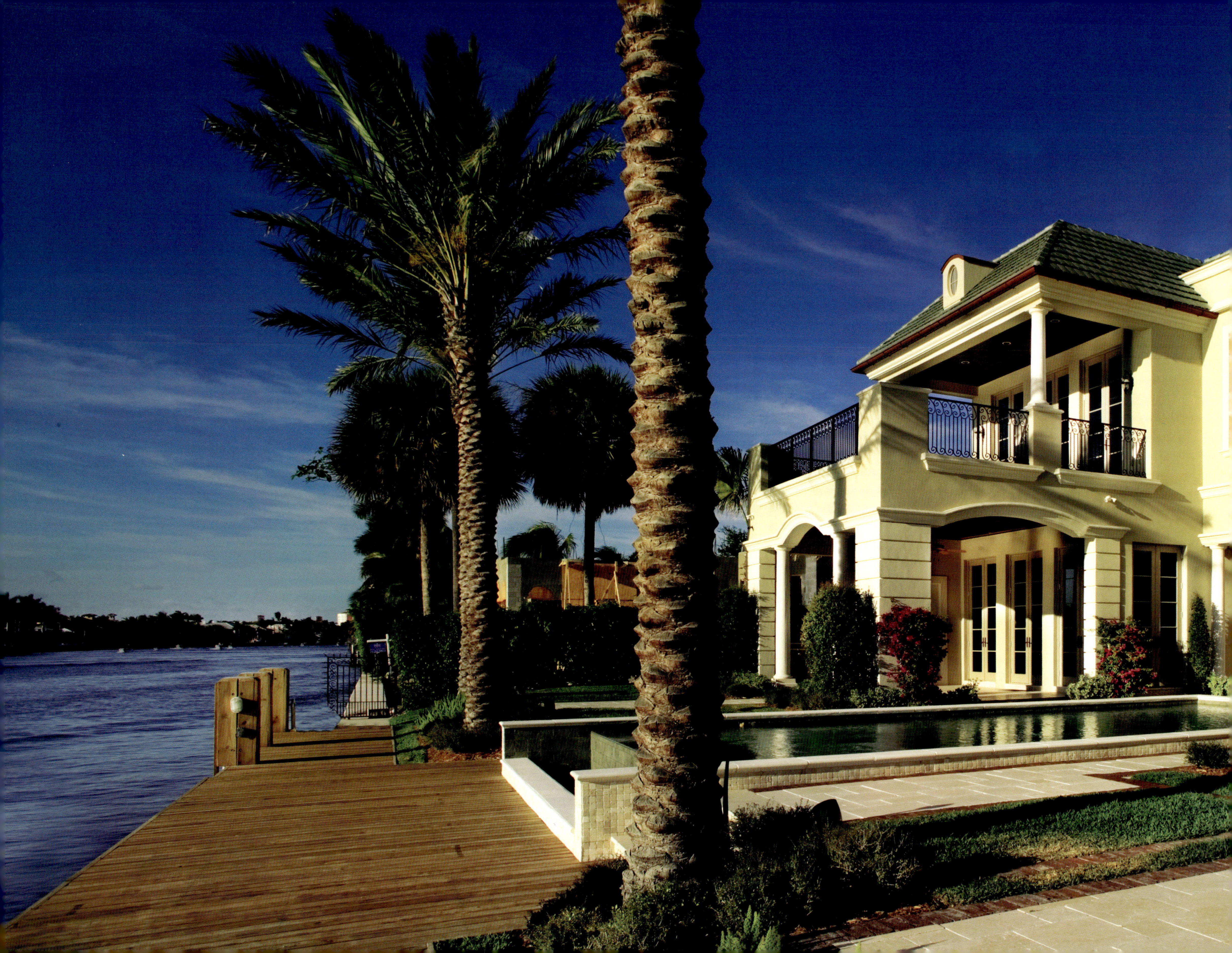

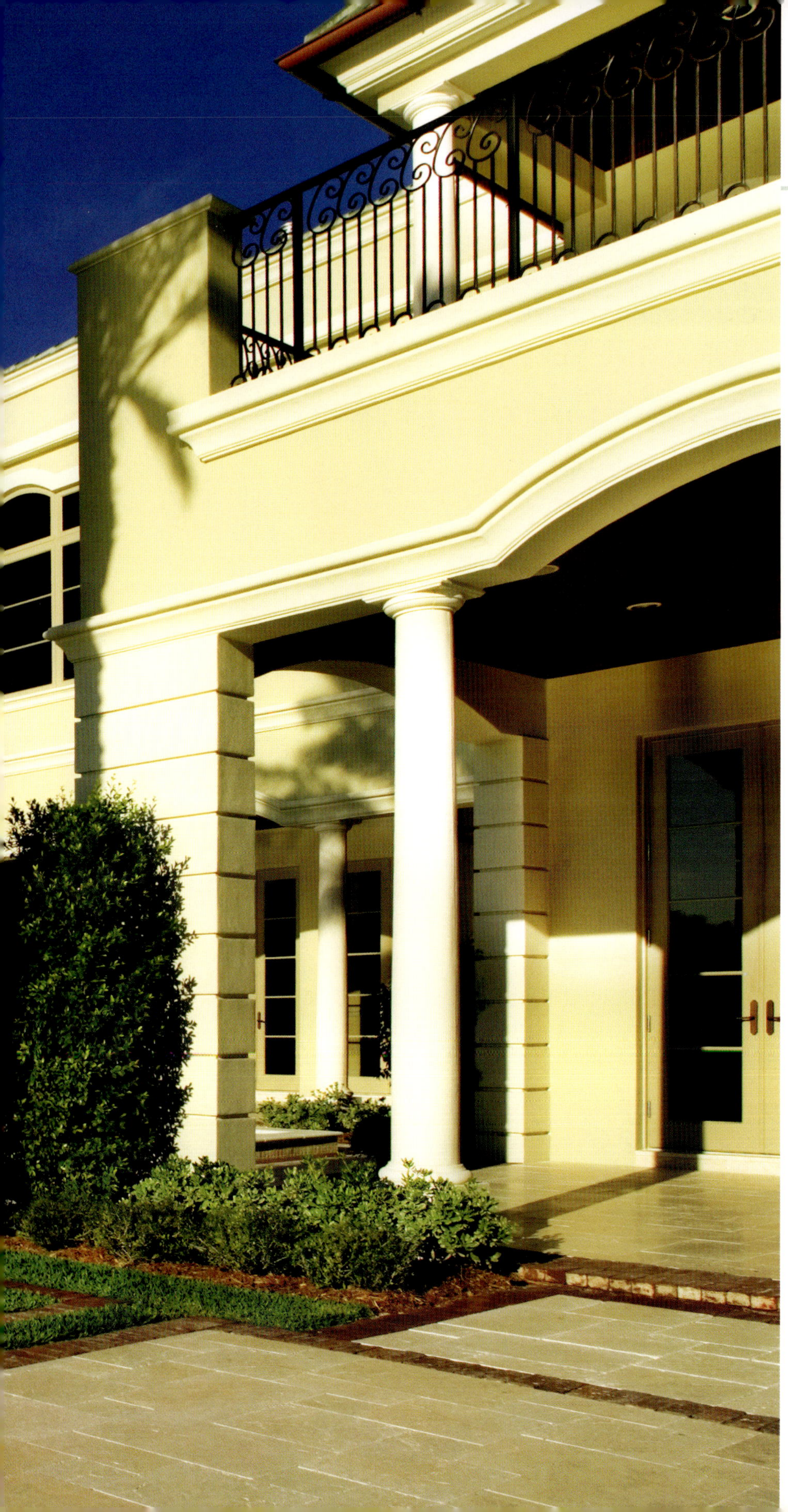

CARLOS A. MARTIN

Carlos Martin Architects, Inc.

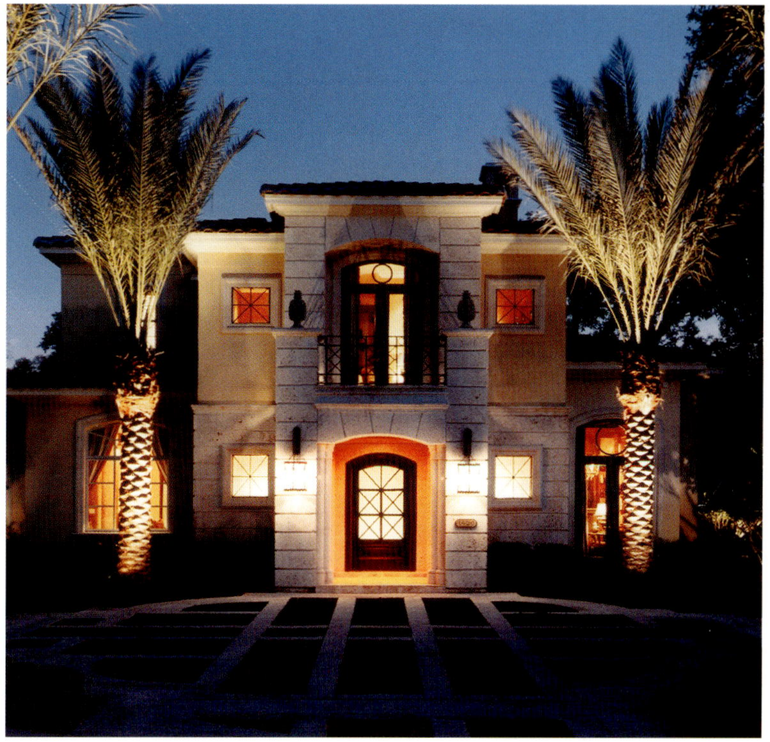

Carlos A. Martin likens the challenges of being an architect to those of a fashion designer. Never one to repeat the same design, Carlos' approach is always to work within the times to achieve something newer and better. Adding to that challenge is the fact that building a luxury home often takes up to two years, so the architect needs to be ahead of the game and create a design that will still be fresh at that point in time—and be timeless at the end. "I always try to push the envelope, not be afraid and work with eclectic forms. It's been very successful for me."

A native of Caracas, Venezuela, Carlos earned his Master's in architecture in Texas and worked there for a period of time before deciding to relocate to Florida. After several years of working for other firms in Fort

ABOVE: Natural coquina stone fully clad the front entry and exceptional arrival court for this elegant and private Neo-Classical and Mediterranean residence.
Photograph by Kim Sargent, Sargent Architectural Photography

LEFT: Classical French Regency-inspired estate with symmetrical outdoor living spaces and open decks surrounding an infinity-edge pool maximize the beauty of the waterfront backdrop.
Photograph by Red Square Photography

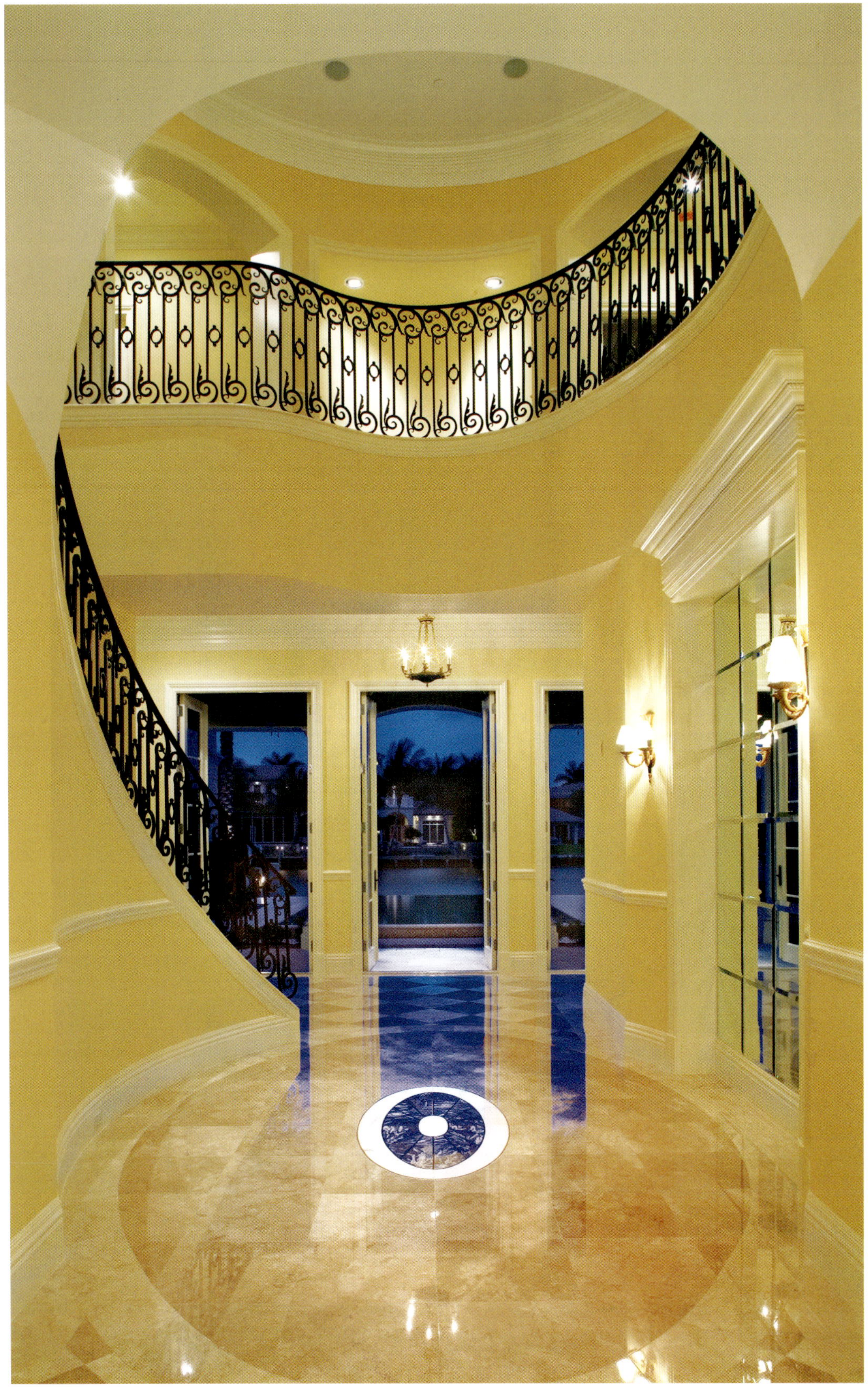

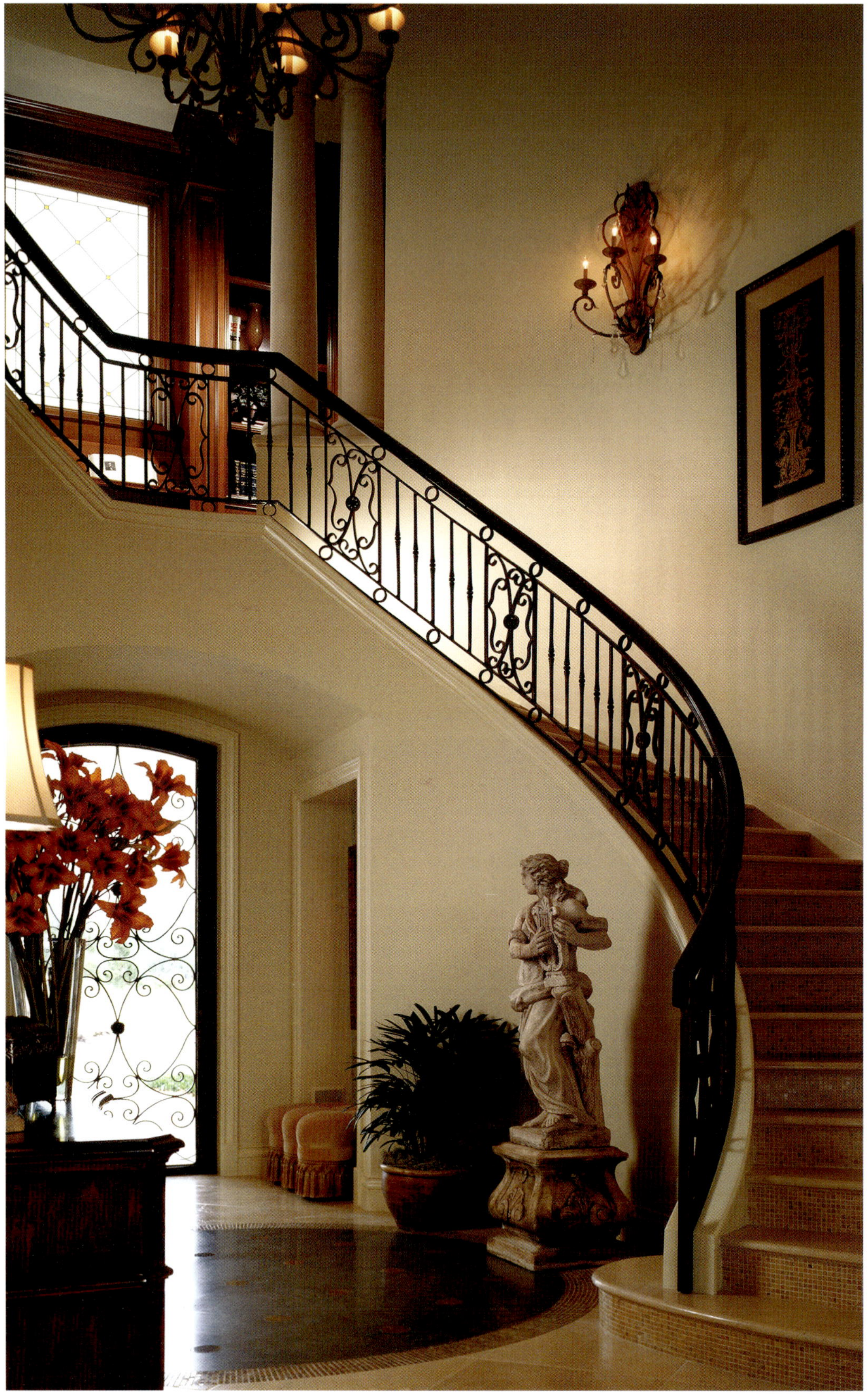

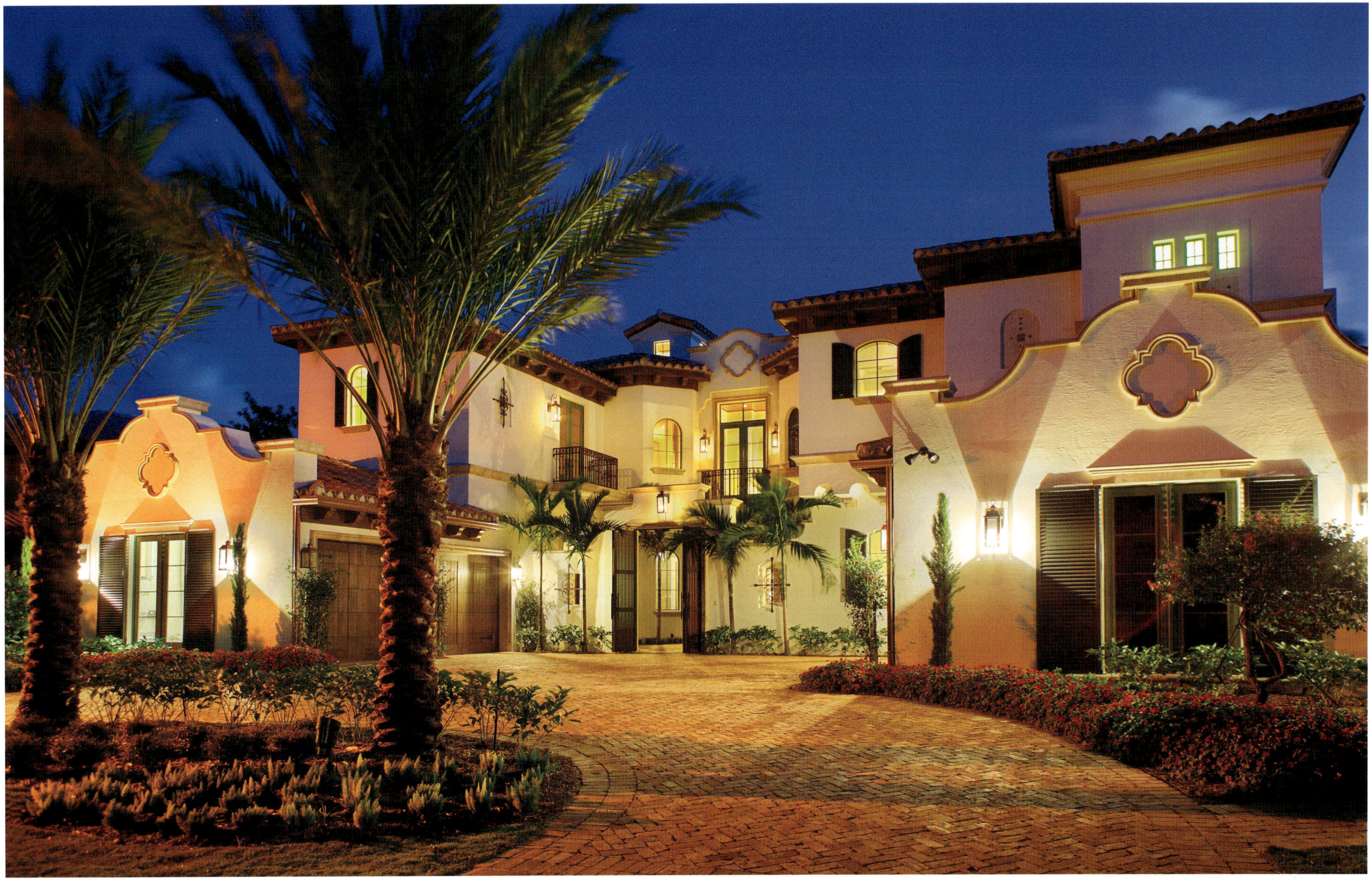

ABOVE: Evoking the great Mediterranean villas of Portugal and Spain, this Portuguese manor courtyard estate is showcased as a serene and sumptuous indoor and outdoor waterfront retreat.
Photograph by Red Square Photography

FACING PAGE LEFT: Direct water views bring to light the soaring elliptical foyer, framed by stately galleries presenting the principal living areas appointed with an inlaid marble floor.
Photograph by Red Square Photography

FACING PAGE RIGHT: The petite bibliothèque overlooking the elegant and classical grand circular stairs and entry foyer sweeping over the elegant front entry iron and glass door.
Photograph by Kim Sargent, Sargent Architectural Photography

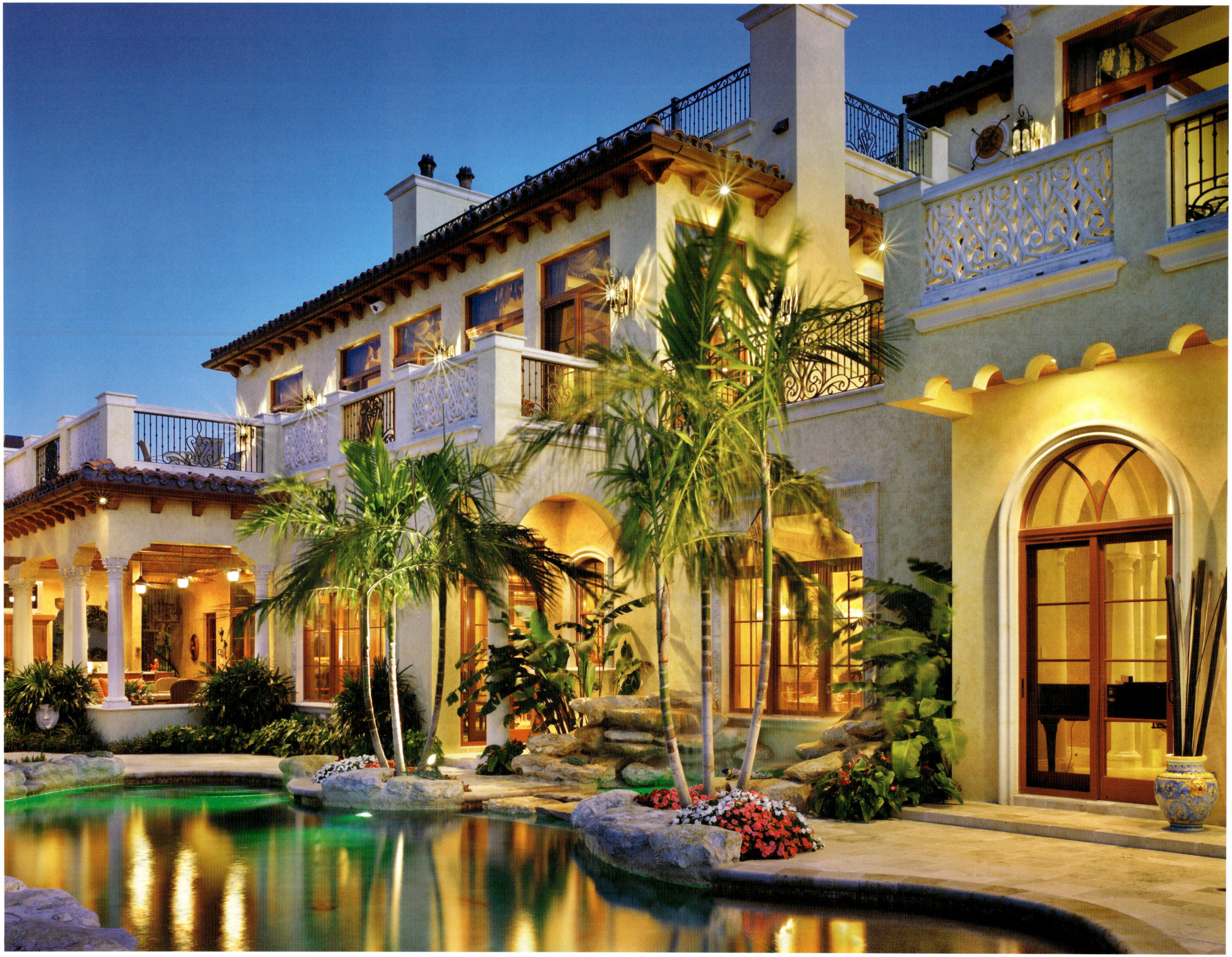

Lauderdale, Deerfield Beach and Palm Beach, he decided to venture out on his own. Almost immediately he had many high-end residential projects under his belt, including upscale locations such as Naples, Palm Beach, Winter Park, Celebration, Coral Gables, Jupiter and Boca Raton.

Carlos cites attention to detail as the key to making a home authentic and unique and strives each time to create spectacular one-of-a-kind architecture. Because his clientele is well traveled, they often come to him having recently stayed in a resort in Bali, a country house in the south of France, a villa in Italy or a palace in the Andalusian region, which has inspired unique desires for their new home. Whether it's ironwork spotted in a door, a fireplace they admired or a courtyard they have experienced, in some way, they want to capture that image and translate it in their home. In this way, Carlos recognizes and appreciates the importance of his clients' visual and stylistic preferences.

Growing up, Carlos idolized Mexican architect Luis Barragán and admired the contemporary clean-lined style of Mies van der Rohe. Later on, his designs were more influenced from George Washington Smith, Wallace Neff, Marion Sims Wyeth and Robert A. M. Stern. "There was a magical time in the 1920s and 30s when the architecture exploded with great designs, where craftsmanship and styles are still represented as the best in a historical and contemporary context until today."

As a youngster, Carlos traveled to Spain, Italy and the Canary Islands, then while in college, he took a trip back to Italy. It was a serendipitous point in his life because the

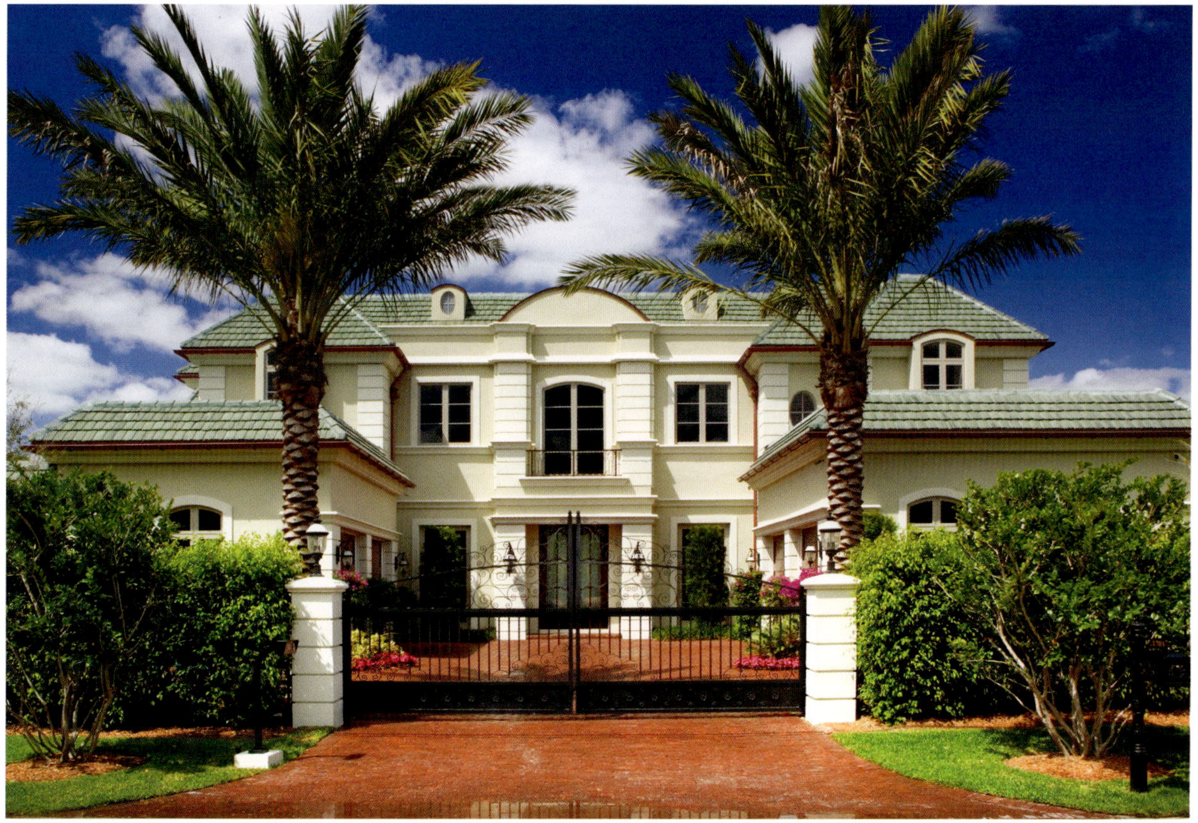

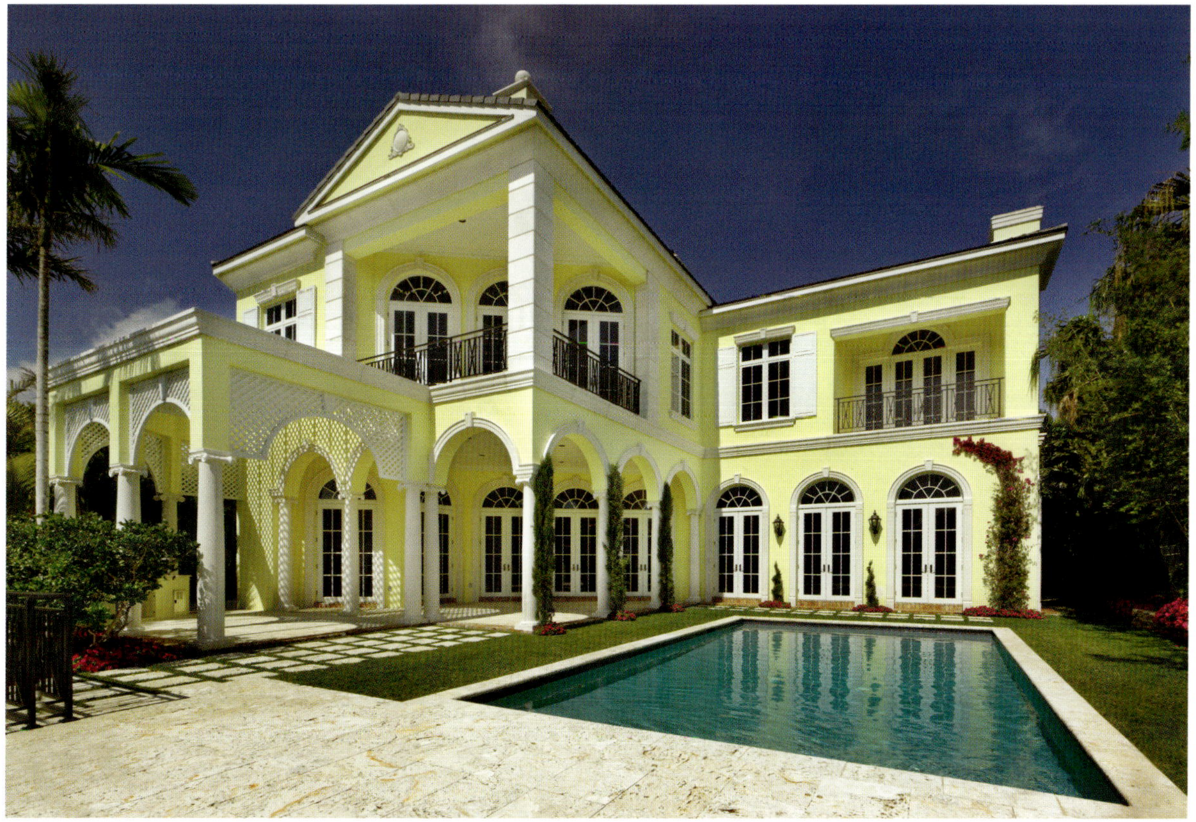

TOP: In the classical symmetry of a courtyard design, this French Regency-inspired estate is flanked with timeless ambiance.
Photograph by Red Square Photography

BOTTOM: Classical elegance and serene outdoor settings proclaim this Palm Beach Georgian-inspired residence.
Photograph by Red Square Photography

FACING PAGE: This beautiful island style pool, with appointed waterfalls and tropical landscaping is surrounded by a magnificent Italian-style waterfront estate.
Photograph by Red Square Photography

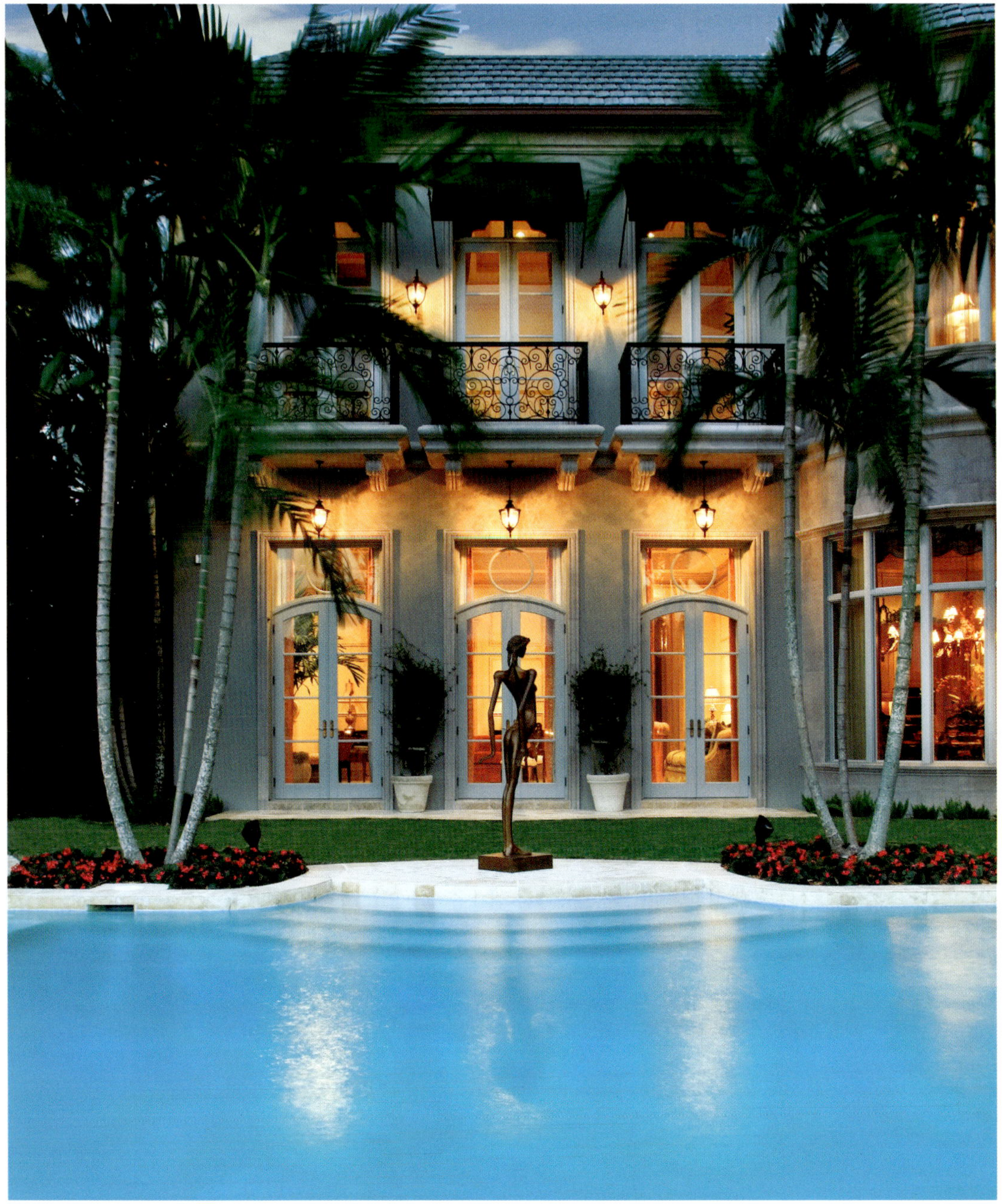

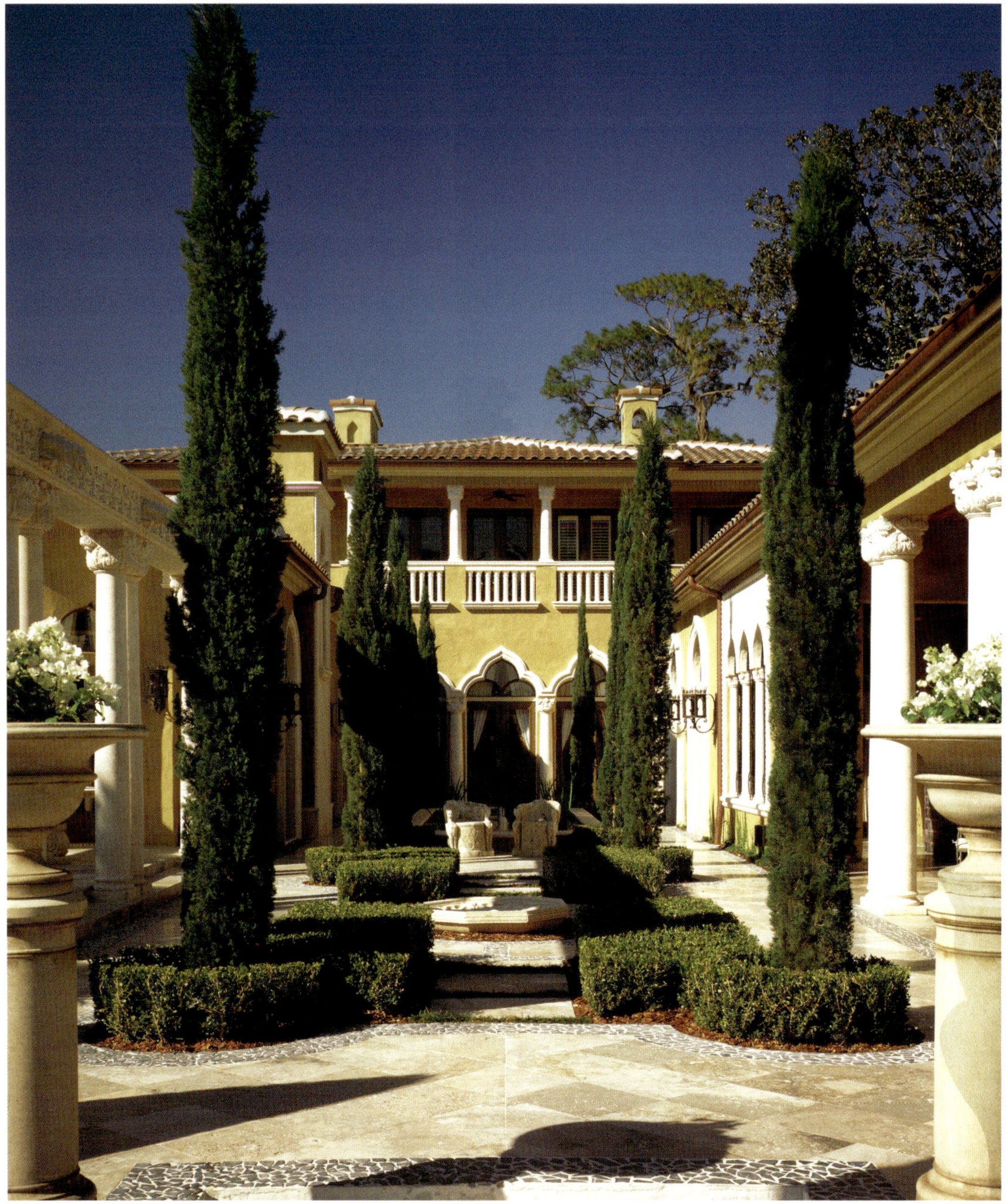

incredible experience had a lasting effect on him. The exposure to classical lines stayed with him and has inspired him throughout his career.

As for his own personal preference, Carlos favors the Mediterranean Spanish Revival and the Classical look. It fits so well into this marketplace, which he also enjoys for a myriad of reasons: the weather, the water, the people, the music and the food. He is sure to point out that "it is the first stop from Europe and South America."

South Florida has always been a hot market and now it caters to a more exclusive crowd—artists, glamorous people, athletes and some of the richest in the nation. It is this hip factor that continually changes the face of modern architecture. While addressing the modern needs of his clientele, Carlos Martin Architects, Inc. never loses sight of the quest for a result that far exceeds the level of design found in residential construction today.

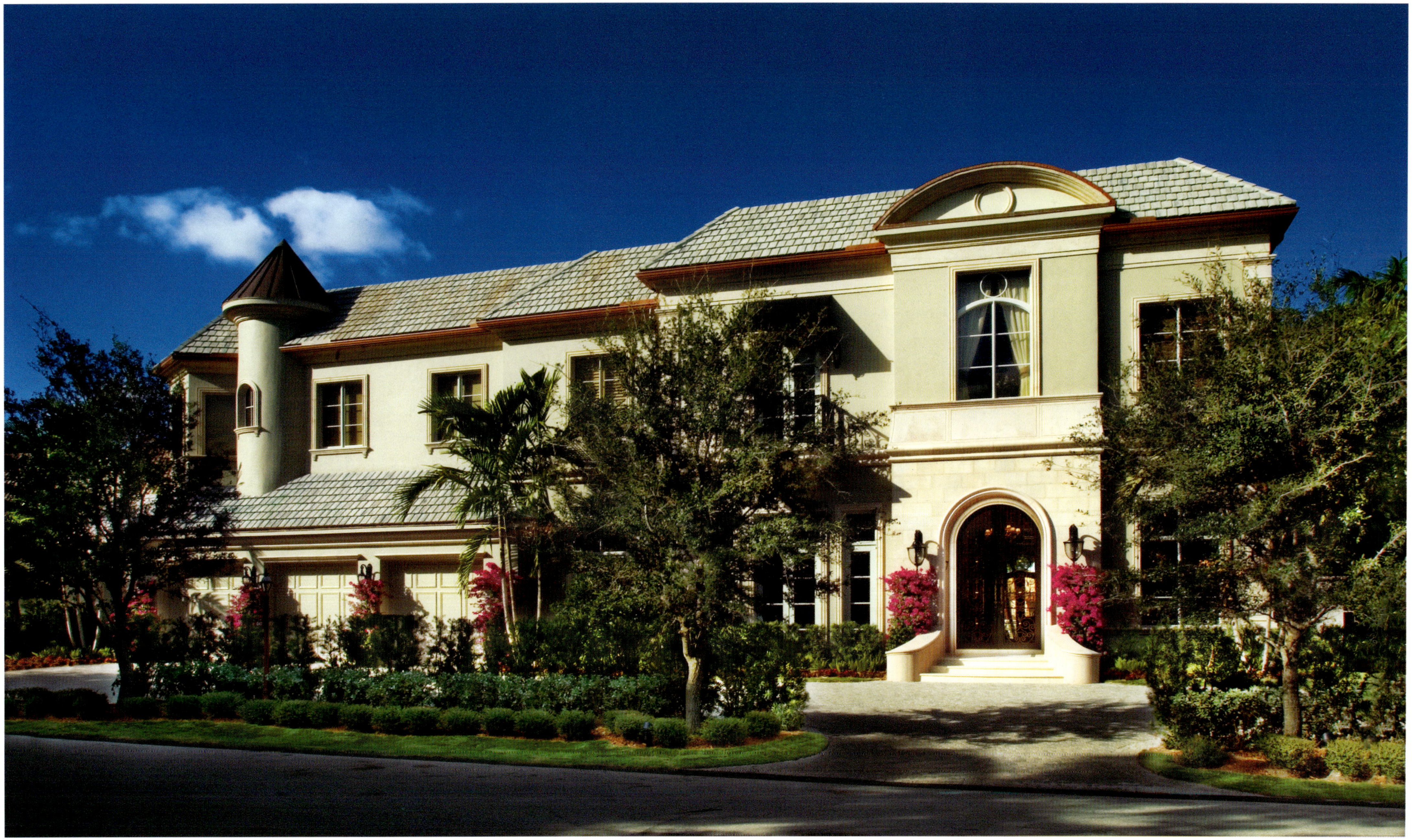

ABOVE: The regal elegance of this lavish French Chateau estate presides over majestic tropical grounds introduced by a formal court of tumbled cobblestone and limestone details.
Photograph by Red Square Photography

FACING PAGE LEFT: Bel Air elegance and regal romance, the Grand Salon French doors and the suite's elaborate iron balconies frame the resplendent resort-style pool and gardens.
Photograph by Red Square Photography

FACING PAGE RIGHT: Classical Venetian-Gothic style palazzo enriched by a manicured koi pond courtyard with flanking Italian cypresses, outdoor living spaces and an elegant swimming pool.
Photograph by Kim Sargent, Sargent Architectural Photography

CARLOS MARTIN ARCHITECTS, INC.
Carlos A. Martin, AIA
5100 West Copans Road
Suite 700
Margate, FL 33063
954.979.2650
Fax 954.979.2850

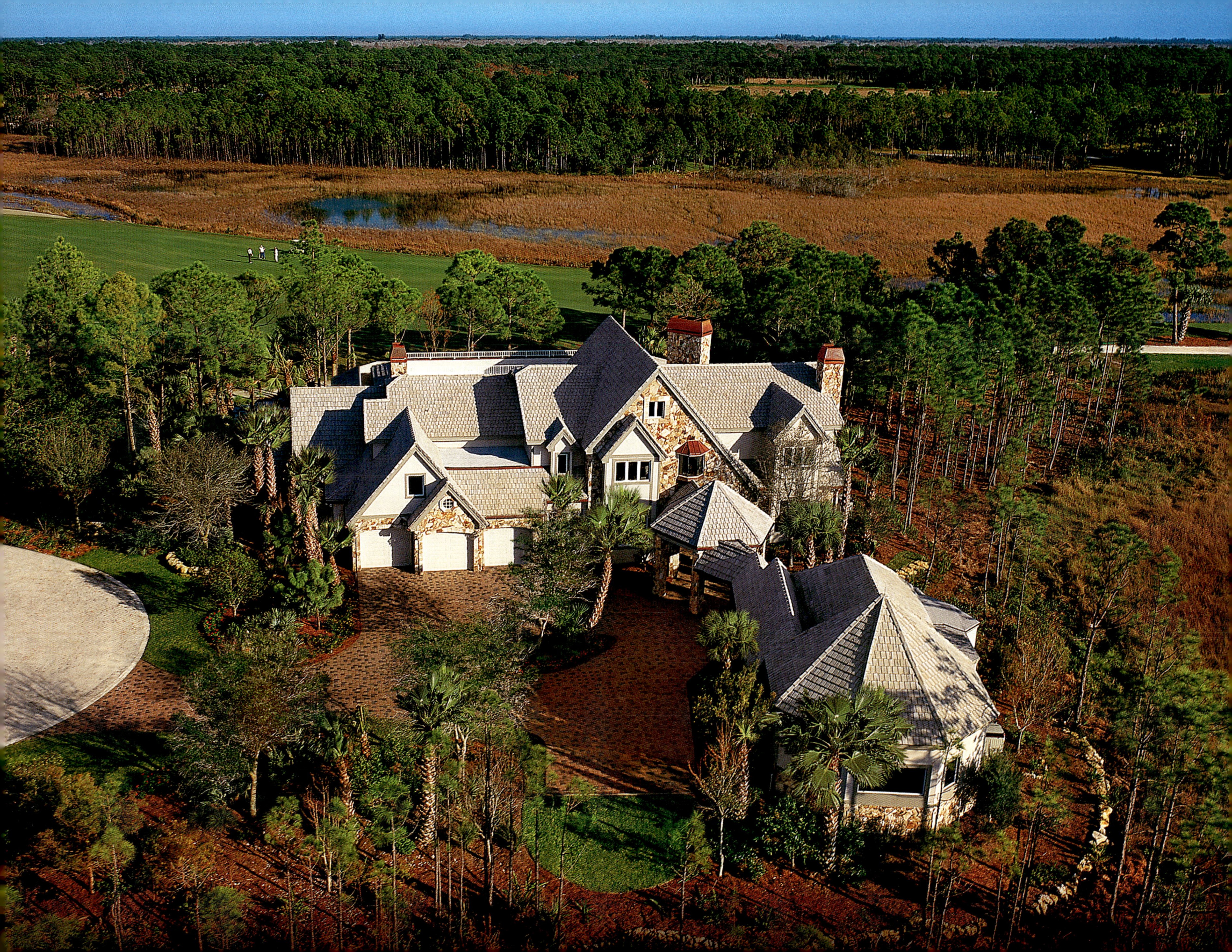

GREGORY C. MIKLOS & QUINN I. MIKLOS

Miklos & Associates

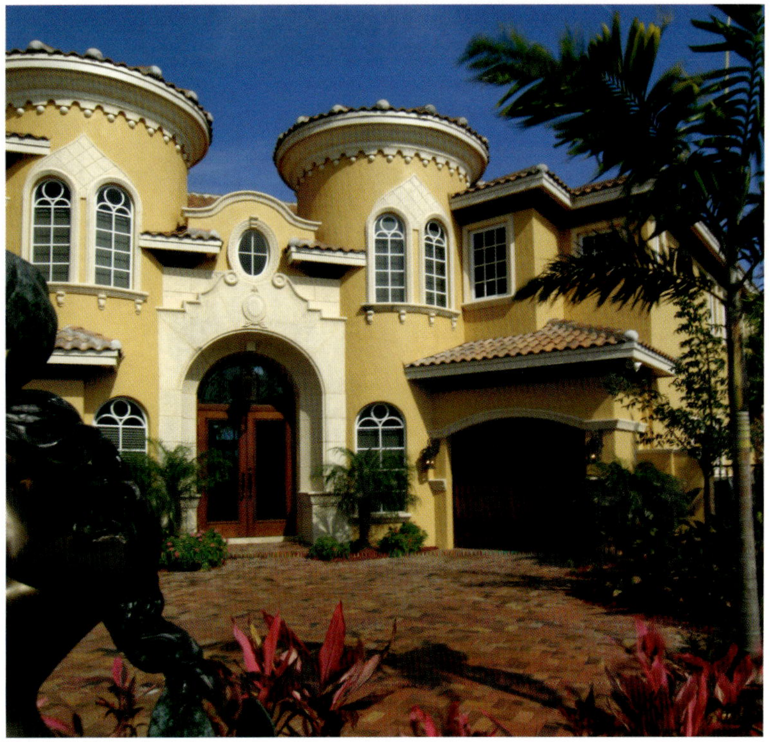

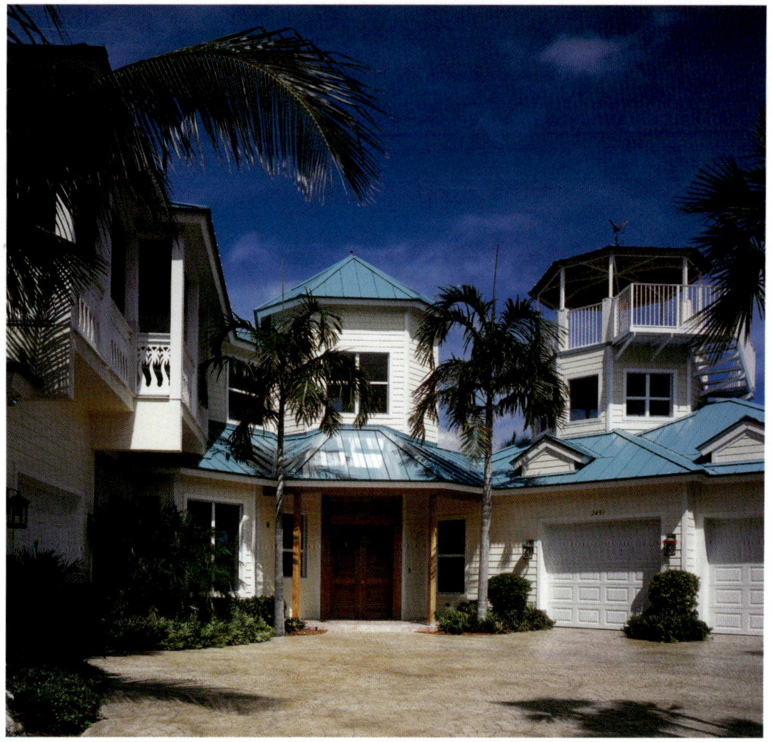

ABOVE LEFT: Mediterranean estate and formal motor court with statue.
Photograph by Quinn Miklos

ABOVE RIGHT: Tropical Florida vernacular home located on the water, complete with a tree house.
Photograph by Matt Silk

LEFT: Located on a beautiful lot overlooking the marsh and one of Florida's most prestigious golf courses, Old Marsh Golf Course, Palm Beach Gardens, Florida.
Photograph by Venue Advertising and provided by Old Marsh G.C. Sales

Architecture is a Miklos family tradition. Their architectural heritage extends back six generations to Europe where their great-great-great-grandfather designed churches and other public buildings. Founded in 1983 by Gregory C. Miklos, Miklos and Associates has developed a reputation for being custom architects dedicated to highly creative design solutions for individuals, corporations and municipalities.

Together with his architect son Quinn, Gregory has built their family business to national prominence, with their work appearing in national magazines and network television.

A unique, in-depth level of understanding architecture is what sets Miklos & Associates apart from their competition. They love architecture on a grand scale—for them it is a public art form where they are designing buildings that enhance the visual environment.

Quinn maintains a respect for each project by asking a series of highly important questions, "Okay, it looks pretty on paper, but can it be built, will it be on budget, will it last and does the client like it?"

Whether it is a custom home for an art dealer, one of the largest mausoleums in the world or a car dealership, Quinn and his team of architects take a hands-on approach to designing and building structures that are functional, stylish and that stand the test of time. They put an importance on a design standard that will look good in this decade and decades to come.

MIKLOS & ASSOCIATES
Gregory C. Miklos, AIA
Quinn I. Miklos, RA
2263 Northwest Boca Raton Boulevard, Suite 112
Boca Raton, FL 33431
561.392.6762
Fax 561.750.8465
www.miklosarchitecture.com

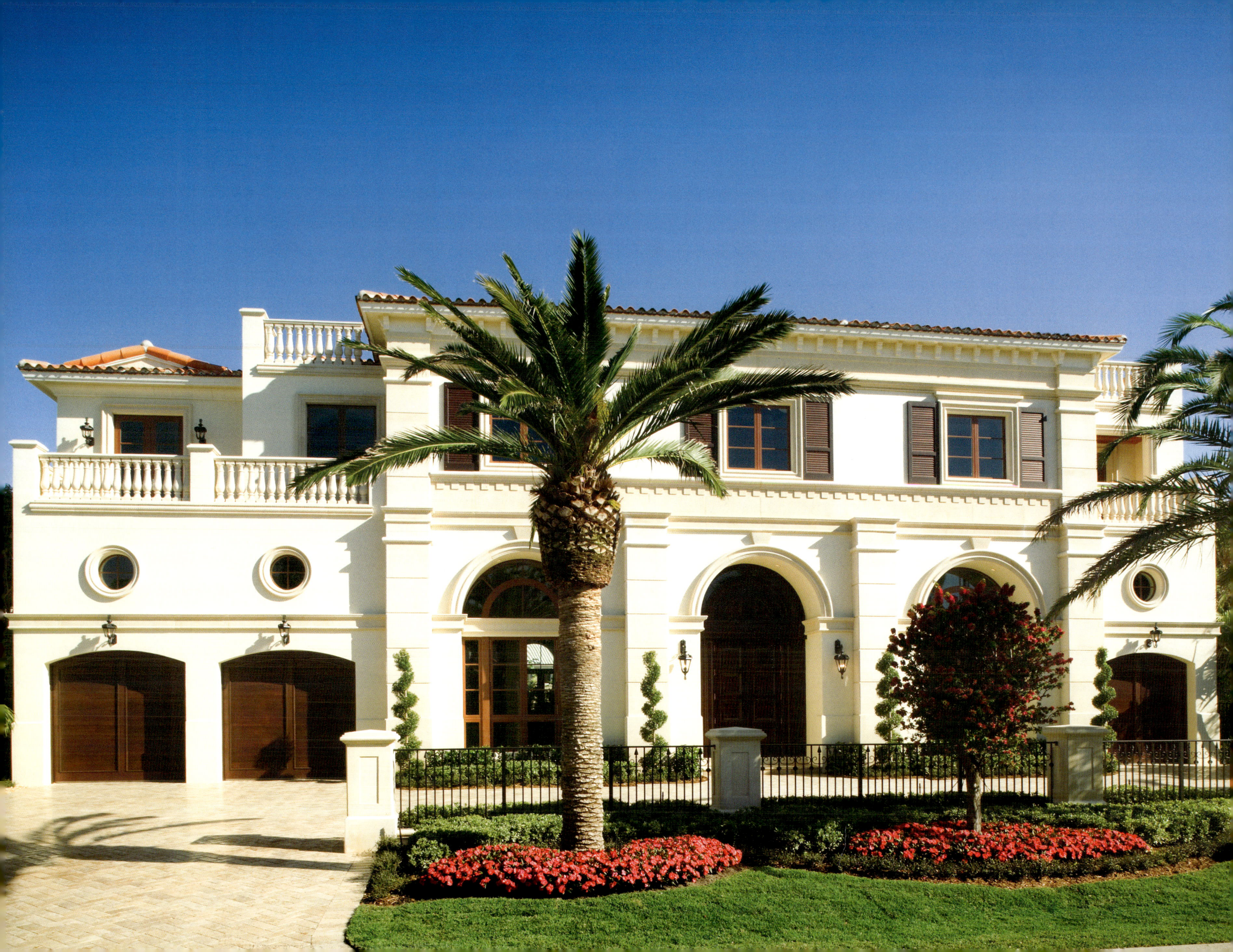

RICK PFENDLER

National Custom Homes

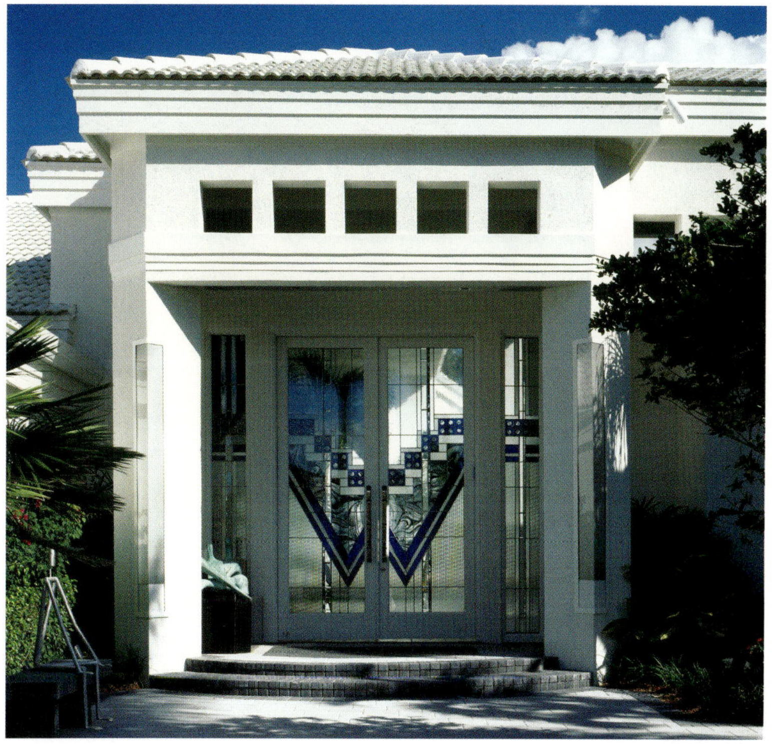

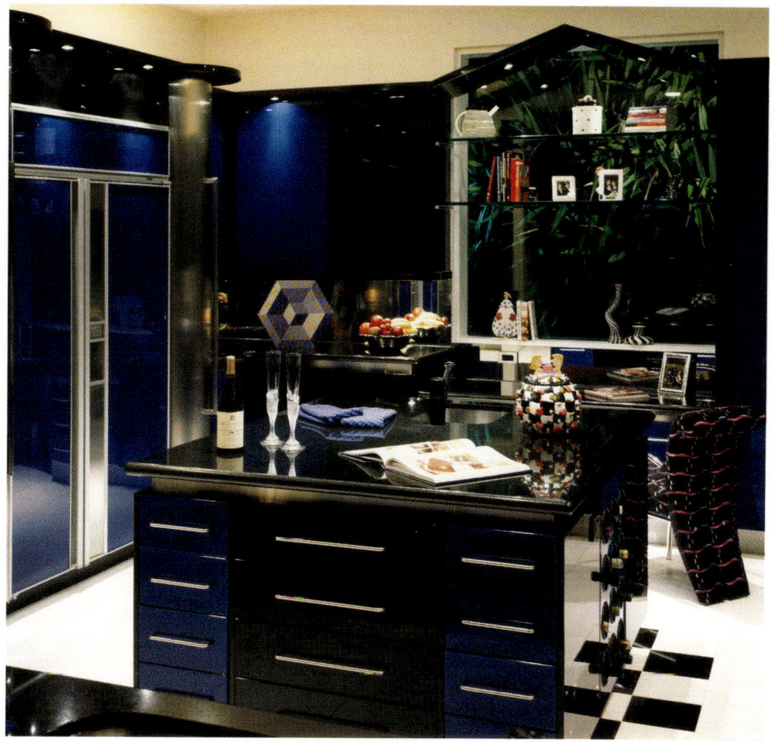

Without having met Rick Pfendler, owner of National Custom Homes, one is still able to get a sense of him from the hundreds of thank-you letters received from past clients. One meeting with Rick is all it takes for potential clients to become current clients: his integrity, the devotion and high regard with which he holds his clients appeals to the most seasoned home buyers. Although South Florida is a highly competitive market for custom home building, Rick's accountability and impeccable reputation has been demonstrated in the over 3,000 superiorly crafted homes built during his 40-year career.

In the late 1960s Rick got his start as a day laborer after serving his country in Vietnam. Decorated with four Purple Hearts, a Gold Star and Vietnamese Cross of Gallantry, he credits this overwhelming experience with teaching him that a person's character is everything and that "tough" is a relative term. Learning from the ground up, Rick worked tirelessly to absorb the lessons only experience could teach, and from that, developed a skill set rivaled by few in the industry. To this day, Rick continues to be hands on, preferring to be right out there "in the dirt" with his sub-contractors, a practise that has earned the respect of his clients and team.

Catering to clients usually on their third or fourth custom home, National Custom Homes consistently surpasses their level of expectation. The company primarily builds in the multi-million dollar areas of Boca Raton, Deerfield, Delray and Palm Beach, but has also built in Colorado.

ABOVE LEFT & RIGHT: This contemporary home is located in the Vintage Oaks subdivision of the Polo Club of Boca Raton and boasts the ultimate designer kitchen in keeping with the same style genre.
Photographs by Brantley Photography

LEFT: This magnificent 9,600-square-foot Tuscan-style custom spec home displays the luxury of a tropical environment and of superior craftsmanship. The Sanctuary model is listed at $10 million. Rex Nichols, Architect.
Photograph by Brantley Photography

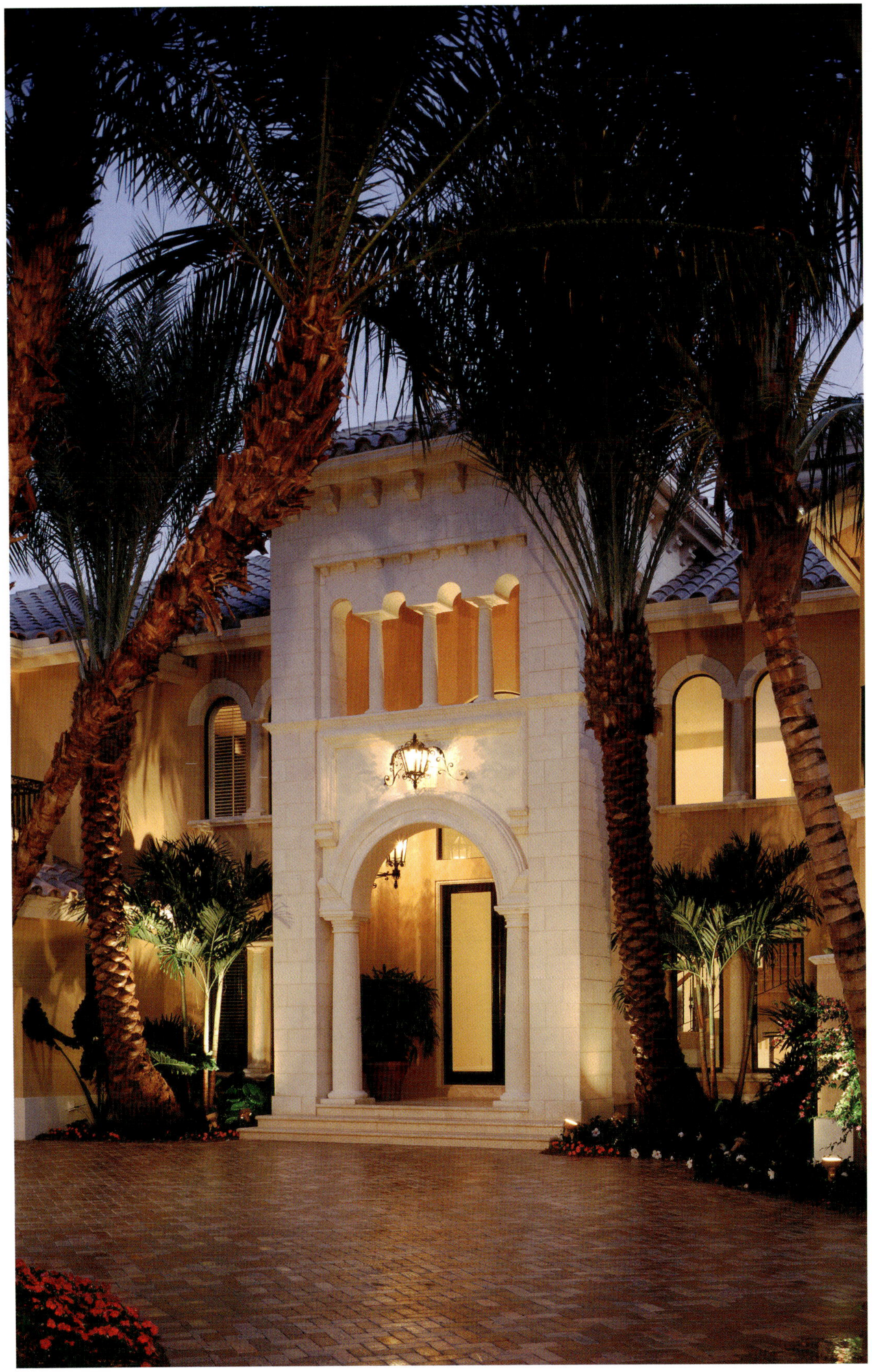

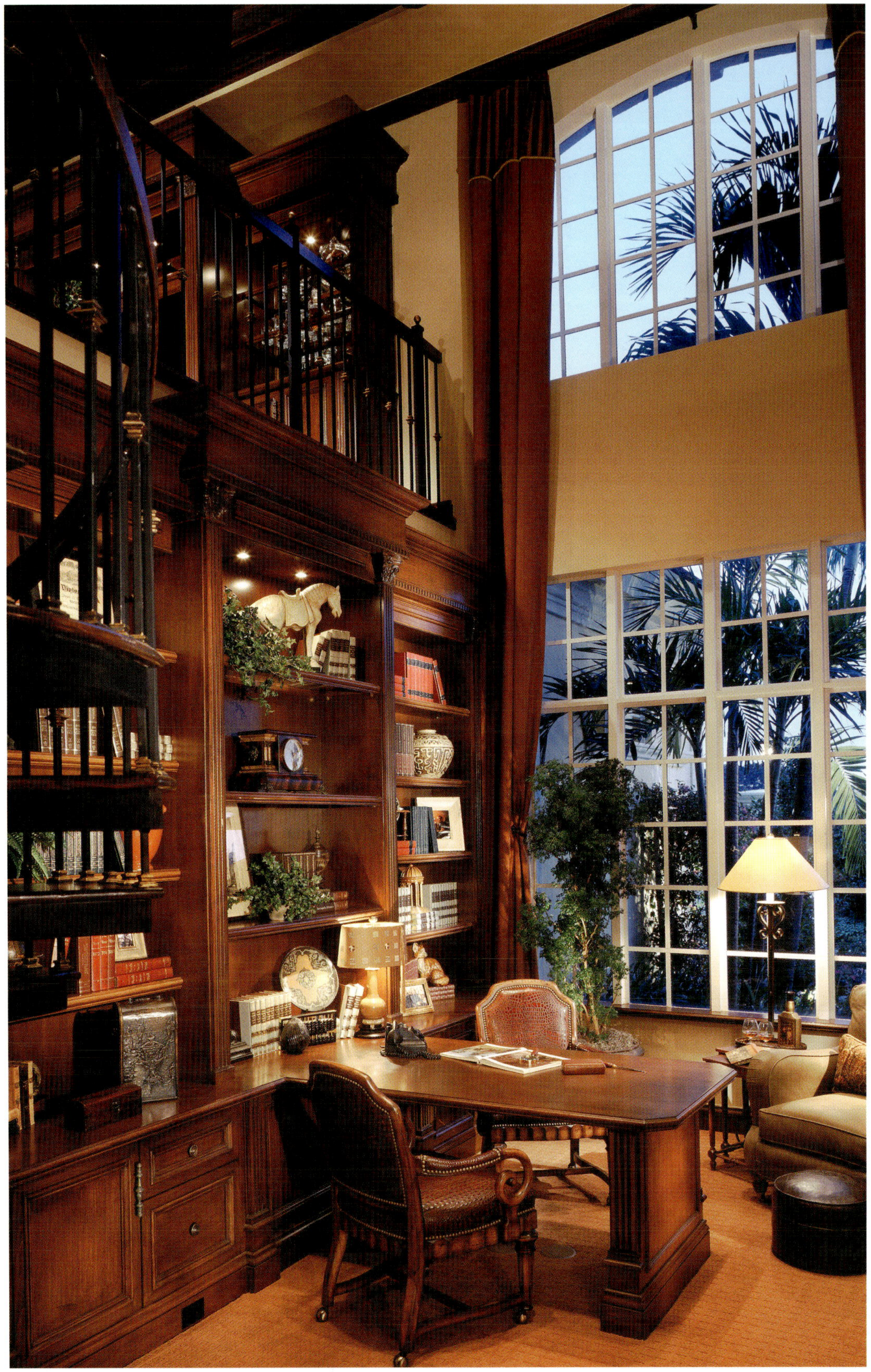

The rich millwork, opulent detail and outstanding craftsmanship found in every home built by National Custom Homes may temporarily render one speechless, but once speech is restored people never fail to ask, "Who built this home?" Rick chooses only the highest quality materials, never ever cutting corners. Subscribing to the belief that "homes should be built right," Rick uses high quality concrete construction rather than wood on the exterior of all of his homes.

Many clients are shocked that such a masterpiece may be achieved under the projected time allotment, but Rick's homes often do. He has never missed a closing date. This is simply because Rick offers realistic projections and does not overextend his project list. The "small" company does about four to twelve jobs a year, opting for quality over quantity with a strong commitment to personal client attention.

Before beginning a home, Rick meets with his clients to complete a check-list (which will give a realistic approximation of cost and timing), and views the site. Rick even suggests an architect whom he believes will fit with the desired style. Because each project presents its own set of challenges including staunch community restrictions and rigid building

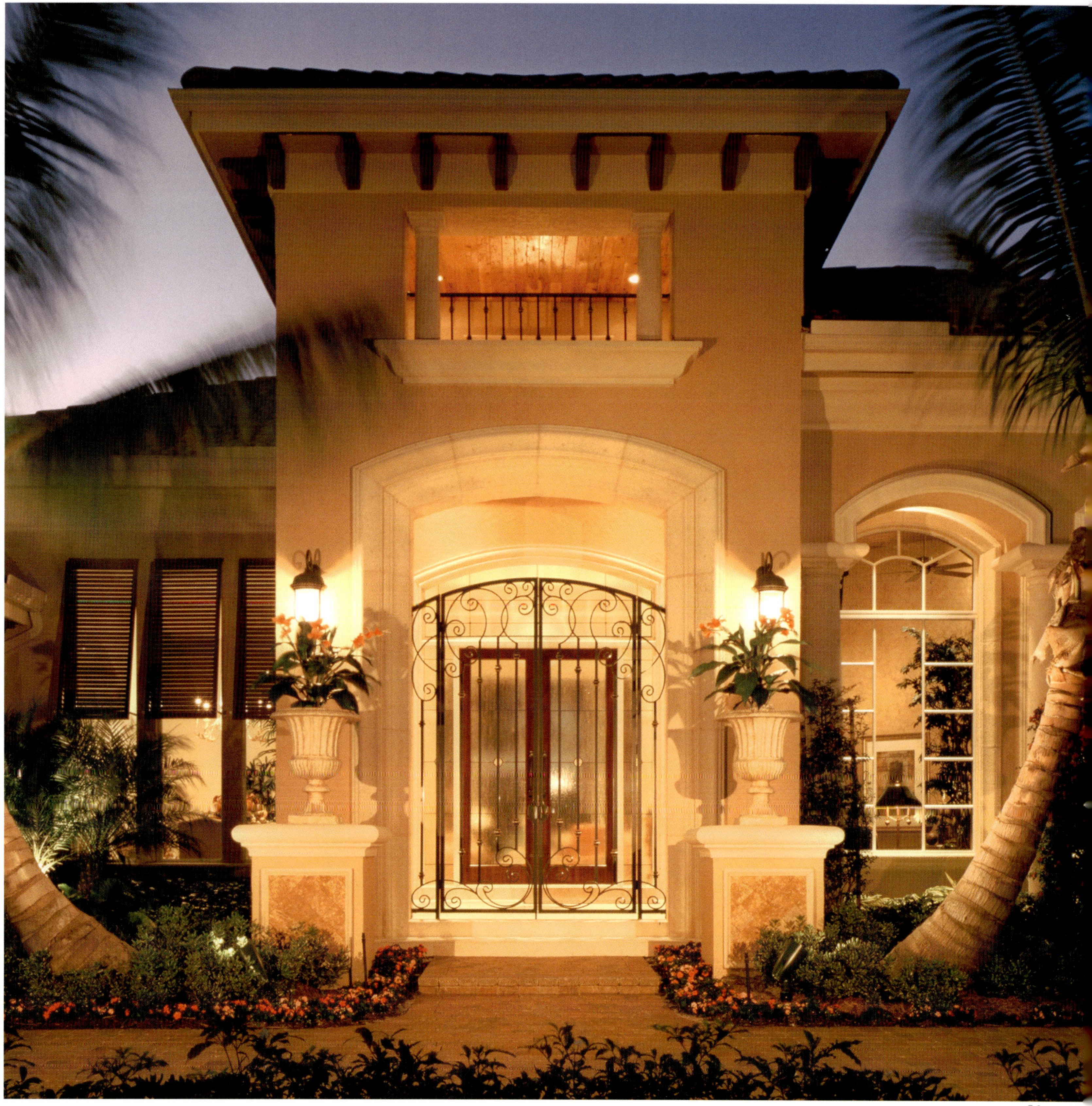

RIGHT: The Martinique model, an expansive Tuscan "villa" in the Vintage Oaks subdivision of the Polo Club of Boca Raton.
Photograph by Brantley Photography

FACING PAGE LEFT: Located in the Vintage Oaks subdivision of the Polo Club of Boca Raton, a dramatic arched exterior entryway sets the tone to into this home's grand entrance. Bau-Tech Design, Architect.
Photograph by Kim Sargent, Sargent Architectural Photography

FACING PAGE RIGHT: The rich two-story library in this Le Rivage estate features a handsome winding staircase and spacious windows.
Photograph by Brantley Photography

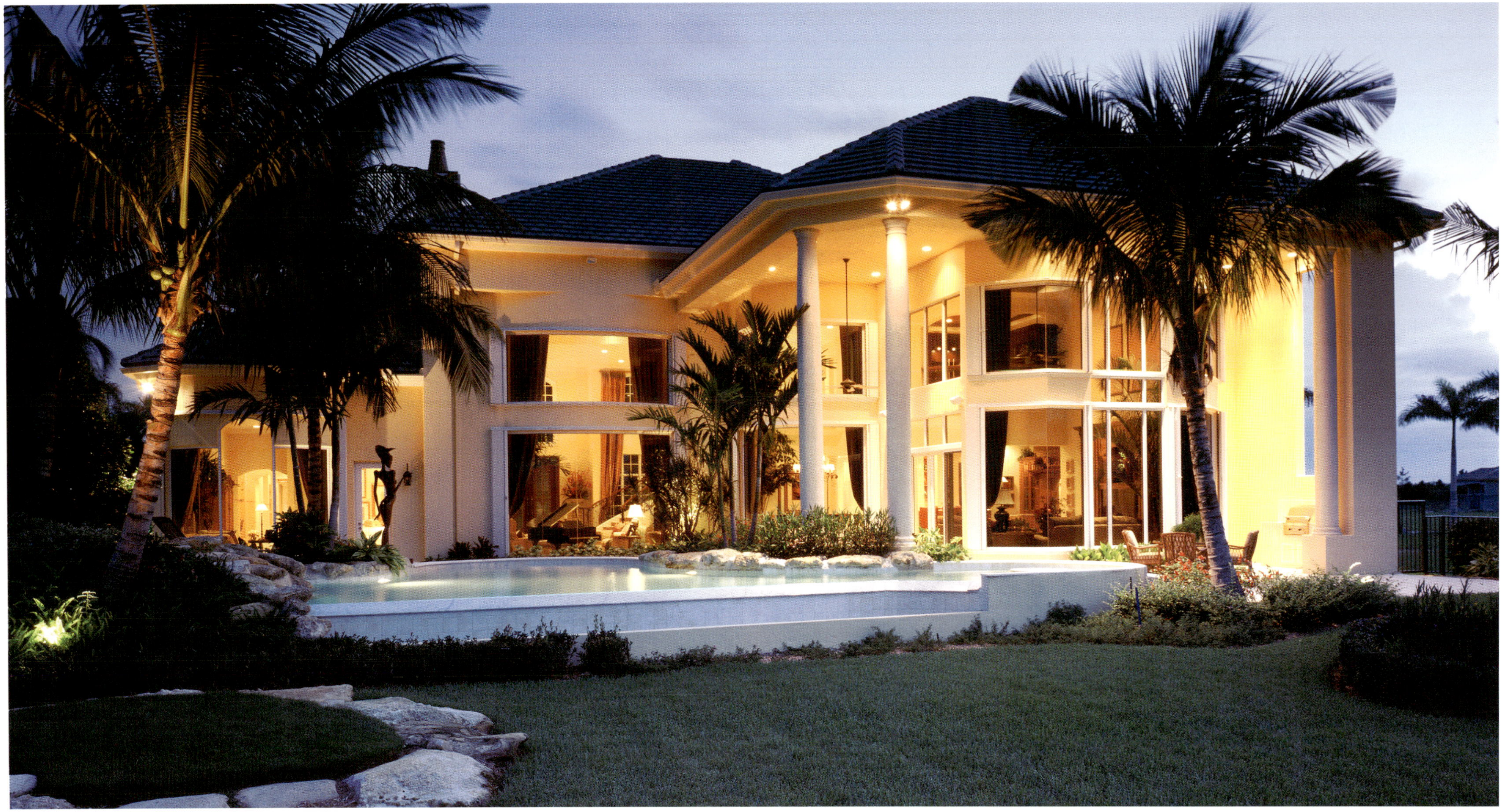

codes—especially for waterfront homes—Rick relies on a collaborative relationship with each home's unique design team of architect, interior designer and landscape architect.

Relationships are important to Rick. Many of his subcontractors have worked for him for over 20 years and counting. So close to his heart is his business, that his family is vitally involved as well. His wife, Sandra, who had a 32-year career as an interior designer of high end custom homes, helps clients design their homes or simply makes helpful suggestions. Proudly, his son Scott joined the company, making it a true family business.

Rick and his staff treat each one of their homes as if it were their own. From the gracious office staff, professional superintendents to the finest subcontractors in the industry, the team at National Custom Homes appreciates the great responsibility to build the homes of clients' dreams. Rick makes himself available to clients 24/7, from a simple call of assurance to a client's idea which may require a total redesign; he welcomes the opportunity to be a different kind of builder.

Rick's favorite part of the job comes when the lights go on at a job's completion and he can see the firsthand look of admiration and delight in his clients' eyes. It can be summed up in one client's note, "My wife sat up straight in bed at 6 a.m. and said, 'I love this house.'" Only then does Rick consider his job a success.

National Custom Homes has been featured in *Florida Design Magazine, Builder/Architecture* and *Architectural Digest.*

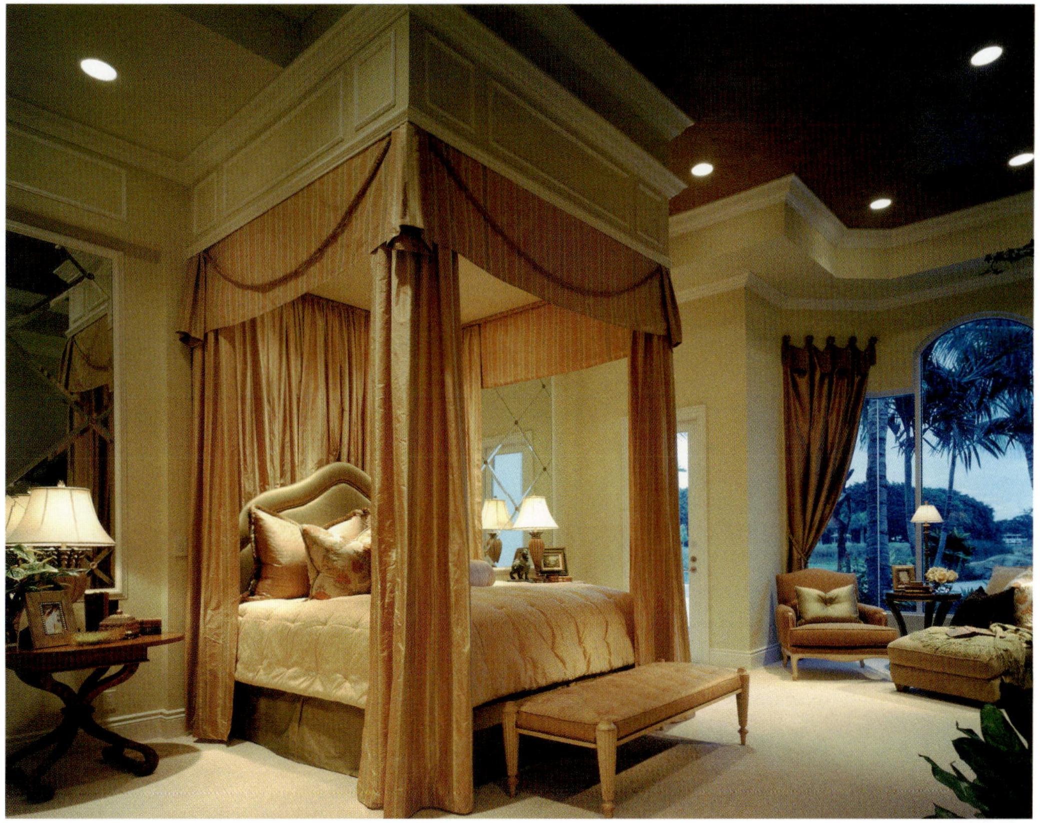

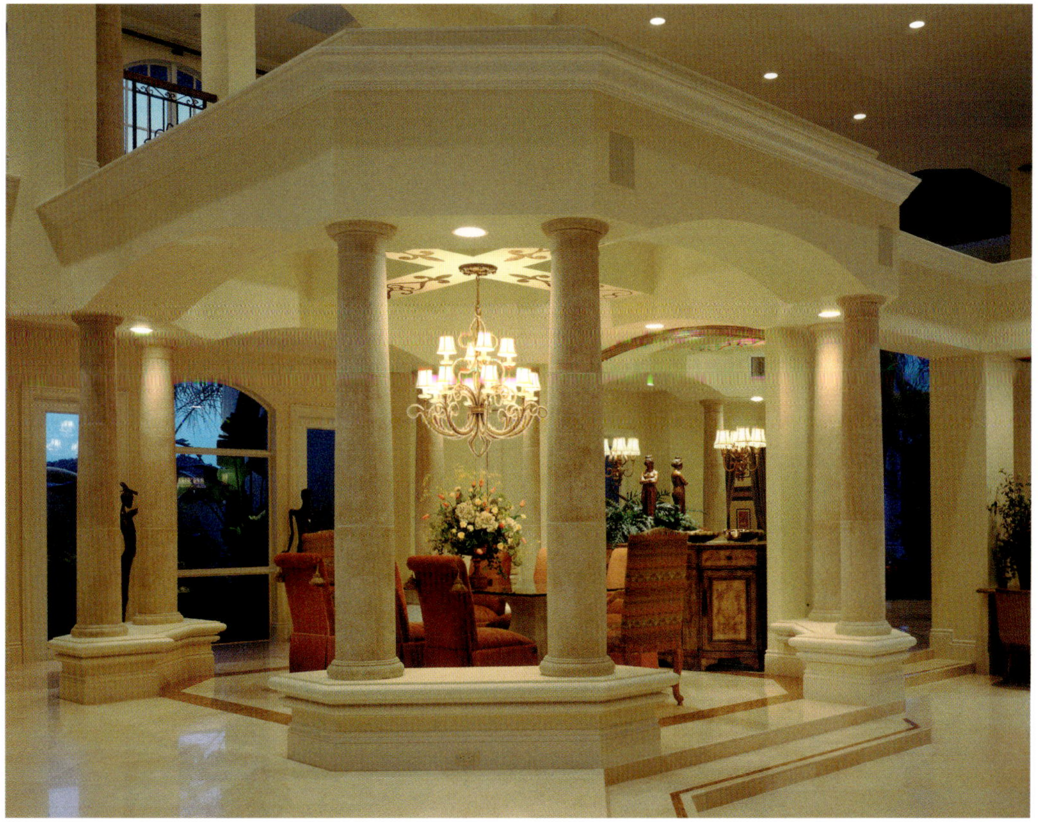

Q&A more about rick...

DESCRIBE YOUR DESIGN PREFERENCES.

I do not have just one style. Every new project excites and challenges me in new ways. There is no limit to quality and imagination.

WHAT IS THE HIGHEST COMPLIMENT YOU'VE RECEIVED PROFESSIONALLY?

A customer, who was also a builder from up north and a former president of the National Home Builders Association, said I built his house better than he could do himself.

WHAT IS THE MOST IMPRESSIVE/UNIQUE/BEAUTIFUL HOME YOU'VE SEEN? WHY?

My own … my wife and I put our heart and soul into every detail to make it a place we are truly "at home" in. I have done hundreds of homes over the years and every one of them has given me great satisfaction while giving clients their dreams homes. The most rewarding thing is they are happy to refer me.

WHAT COLOR BEST DESCRIBES YOU AND WHY?

Black and white—there are no gray areas. I tell it like it is.

NATIONAL CUSTOM HOMES

Rick Pfendler

1181 South Rogers Circle, #31

Boca Raton, FL 33487

561.495.0309

Fax 561.495.0553

TOP & BOTTOM: The Calais model, in Le Rivage, Boca Raton, features a master bedroom with a brilliant view of the lake. The home's dining room is an elegant focal point in perfect juxtaposition to the sunken living room.
Photographs by Brantley Photography

FACING PAGE: Le Rivage, Boca Raton features 18 custom homes on one-acre home sites. This Mediterranean style home's rear elevation, replete with large windows, makes the most of its private lot with views toward the infinity-edge pool.
Photograph by Brantley Photography

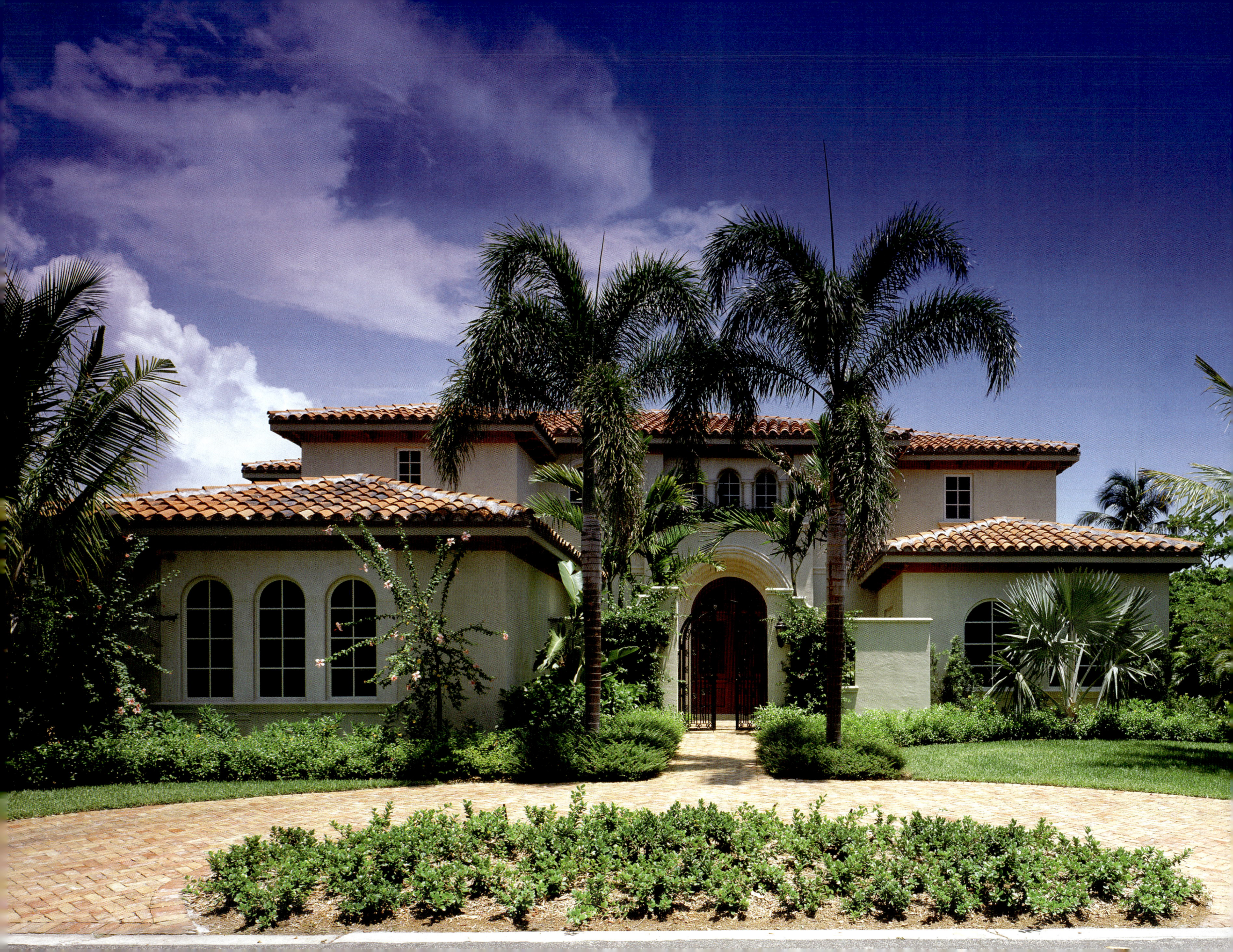

PATRICK SEGRAVES

SKA Architect & Planner

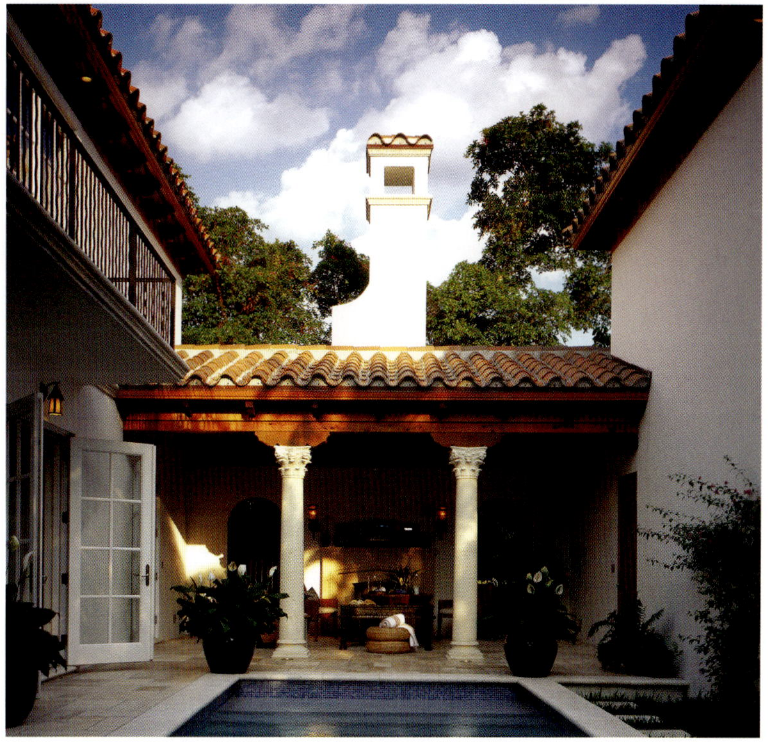

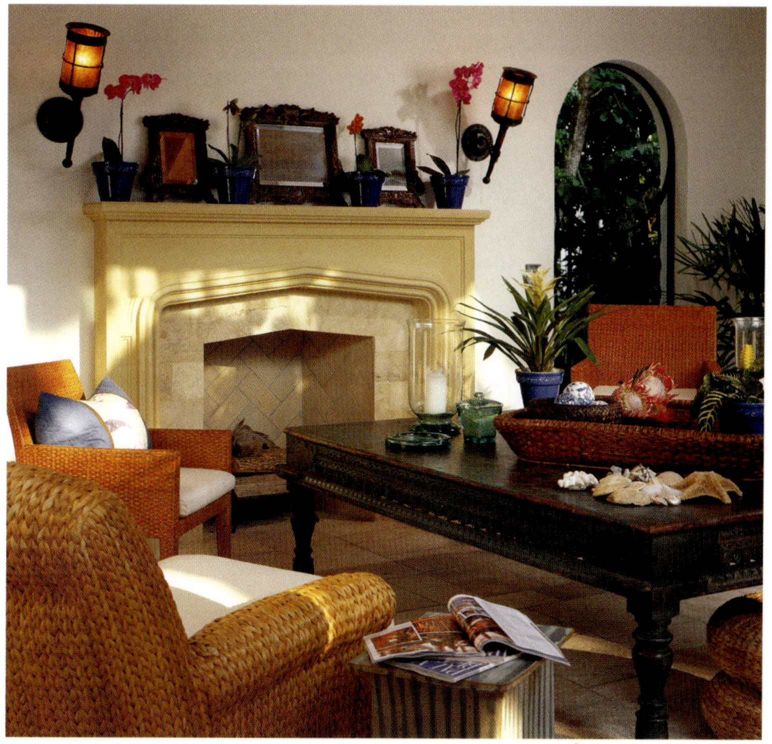

It's a typical day in South Florida. Patrick is standing outside one of his signature Mediterranean homes and he's a happy man.

Pat's made a career designing these beautiful homes for clients who adore the culture of the sun.

As a young man, Pat's father, also an architect, encouraged him to study architecture. Pat is now glad of this because architecture and designing homes has become something that he loves to do. He wouldn't change a thing.

Pat says when taking on a new project, he listens to his clients ideas and desires and tries to accommodate them. Ninety percent of his firm's work is referred via word-of-mouth and many of his new clients have seen his Mediterranean and Island Style homes and want something within those genres. He says, "No problem; it's a tropical environment and you should live in a home that complements that life style."

Although Pat loves going to his office every day, meeting with clients and designing new structures, he also has a few other passions. First, he loves to travel and find inspiration from the different cultures, environments, and architectures. For this reason, he travels as much as he can, wherever he

ABOVE LEFT: Loggia and pool. Mediterranean Revival home in the older area of smaller properties in Palm Beach.
Photograph by Kim Sargent, Sargent Architectural Photography

ABOVE RIGHT: Outdoor fireplace in outdoor loggia creates outdoor room.
Photograph by Kim Sargent, Sargent Architectural Photography

LEFT: Mediterranean Revival Home, Palm Beach
Photograph by Robert + Carmel Brantley

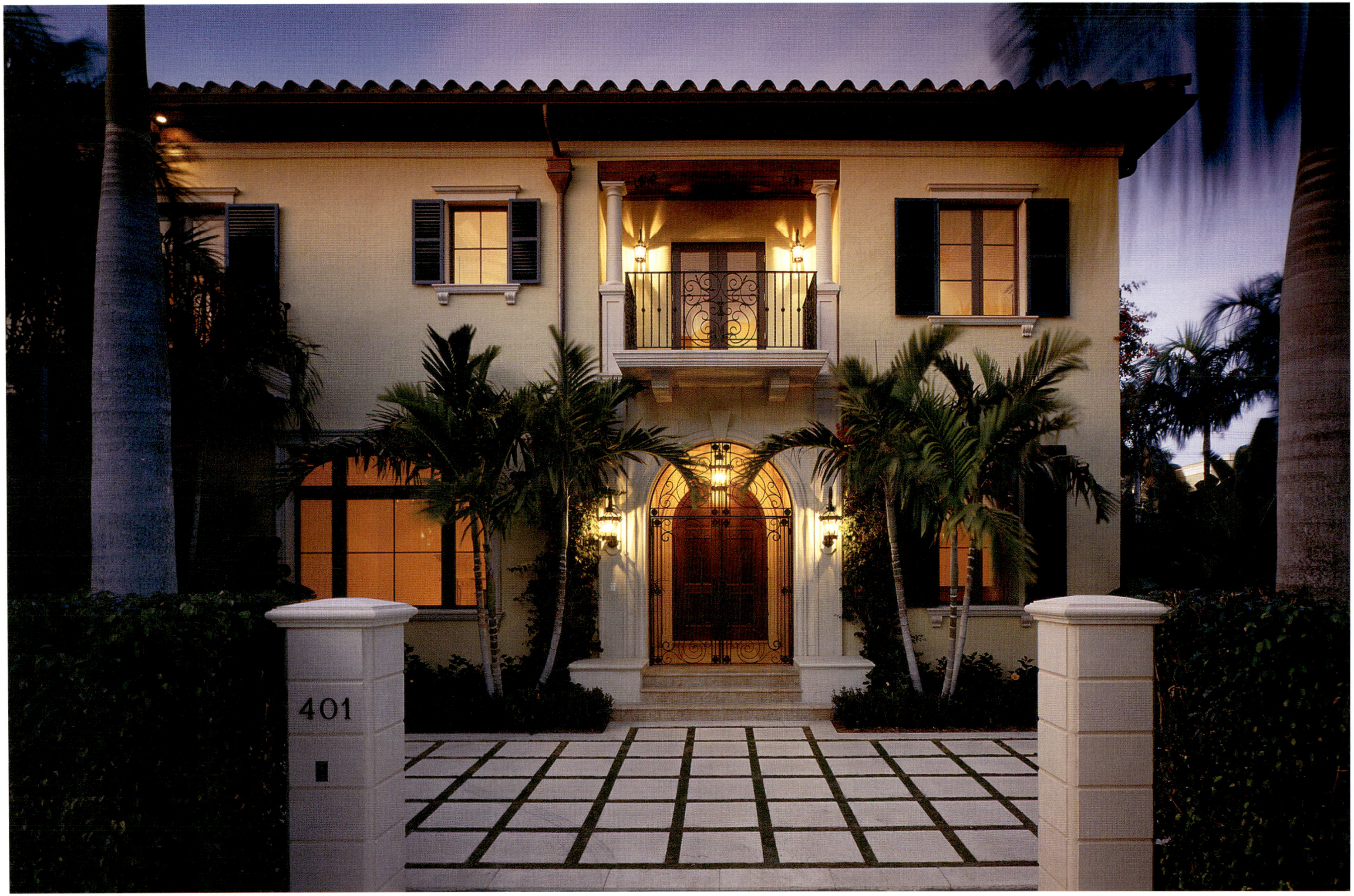

can. His only limitations on traveling are his clients and his work load in Southern Florida. Second, he absolutely loves to be on his sailboat, Tonic, off the coast of Florida. He says everything is more beautiful and clean when he's sailing.

SKA Architects & Planners pride themselves on being very personable and hands-on, and the secret to their success is that hands-on approach. Pat does all the design work himself and he says that when a client hires him to design their home it won't be farmed out to some architect who that client doesn't even know. "When they hire me to be the architect they are going to get me doing the work."

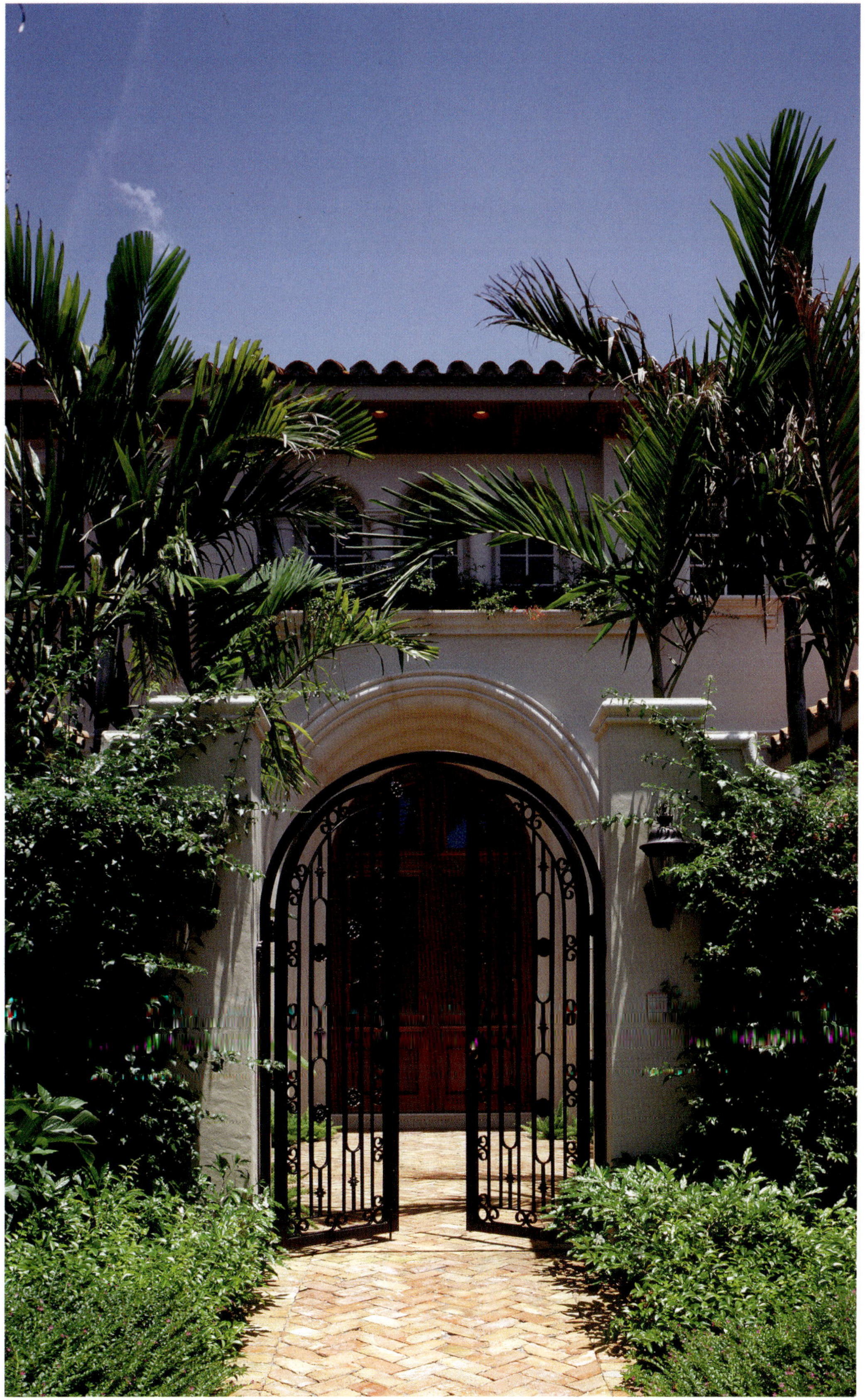

Q&A more about patrick...

WHAT SEPARATES YOU FROM YOUR COMPETITION?

As a small boutique firm, I am able to provide individual attention and do all the design.

DESCRIBE YOUR DESIGN PREFERENCES.

Island style, British Colonial and Mediterranean Revival.

WHAT IS YOUR COMPANY'S SPECIALTY?

We are a small architectural firm that specializes in residences in Palm Beach and coastal areas around Palm Beach.

SKA ARCHITECT & PLANNER
Patrick Segraves AIA, Principal
204 Phipps Plaza
Palm Beach, FL 33480
561.655.1116
Fax 561.832.7828
www.skaarchitect.com

LEFT: Iron gate at entry of a home in Palm Beach.
Photograph by Robert + Carmel Brantley

FACING PAGE: Italian Mediterranean home in Palm Beach with stone and grass motorcourt.
Photograph by Robert + Carmel Brantley

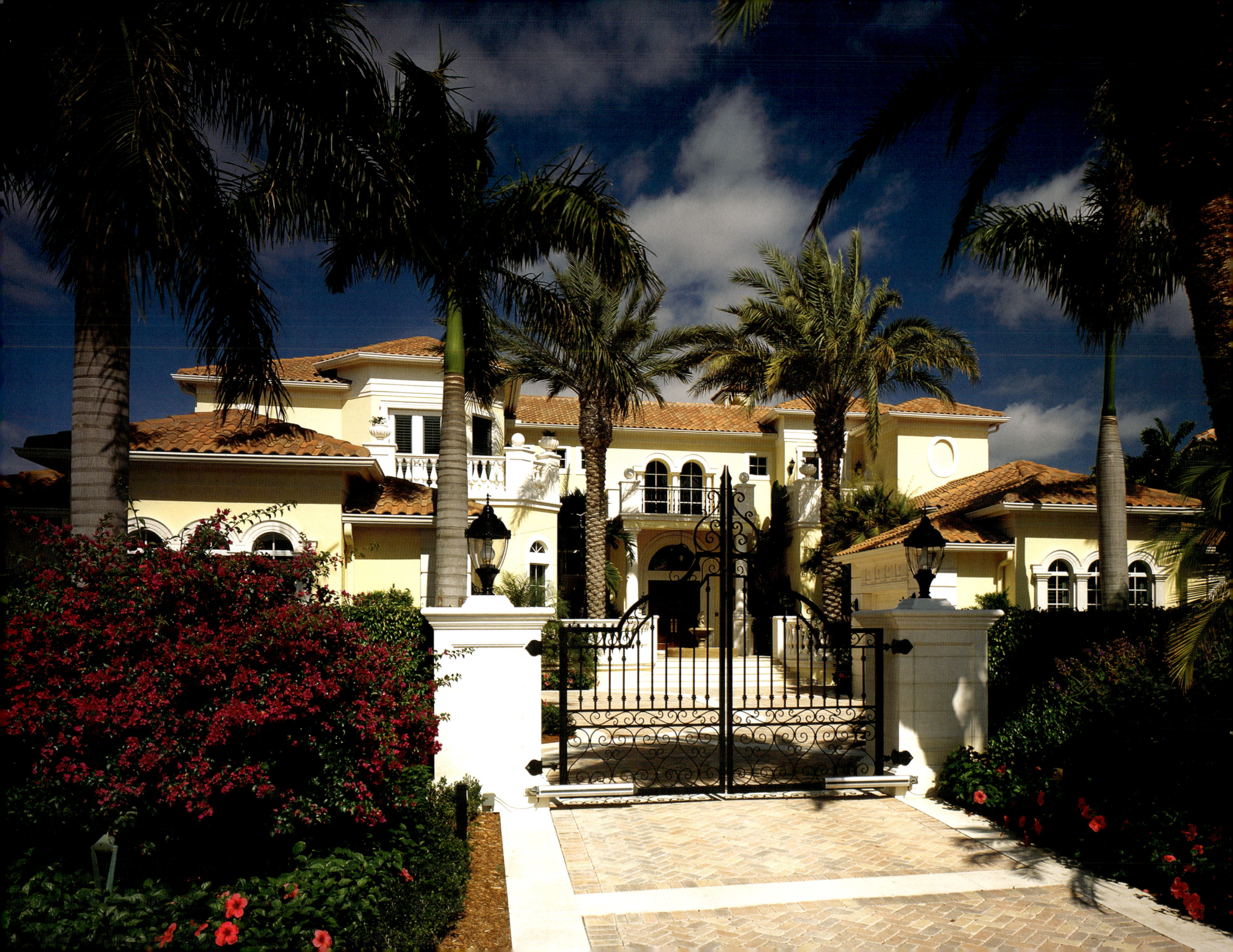

STEVEN SHAPIRO & RONNIE PERTNOY

Shapiro/Pertnoy Companies

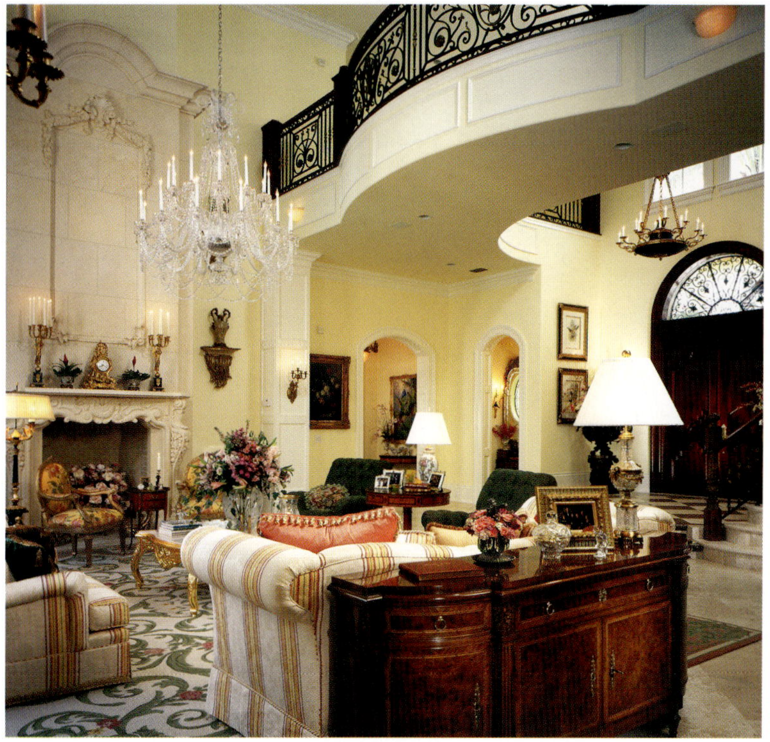

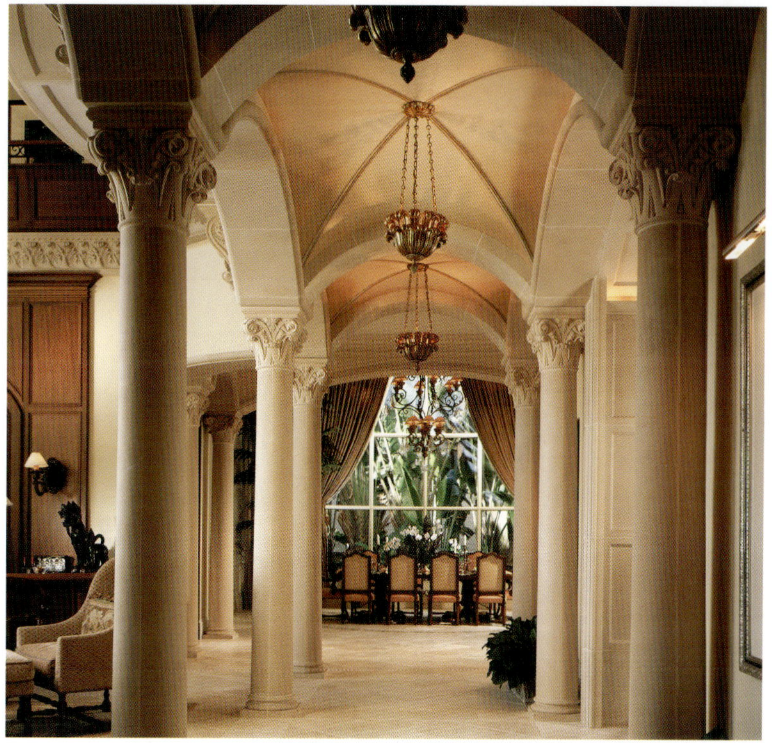

While growing up in Miami, cousins Steven Shapiro and Ronnie Pertnoy received a practical, or rather, serendipitous education in the retail men's clothing stores run by their fathers, who were also uncle and nephew. From the beginning, the pair was immersed in learning the necessity of quality in a product and experienced the true reward of conducting business with high principles and integrity. They also learned the importance of all relationships—the ones originating from inside the business to the ones extending outside. Although one may not immediately connect retail business to home building, the core similarities are undeniable: deliver the best, highest quality product possible, treat clients like "family," offer terrific value and conduct business according to the mantra, "the customer is always right."

In the mid-1970s Steven, having just sold his TV commercial production company, visited his cousin, Ronnie, who had just started his own homebuilding firm after working his way up the corporate ladder at one of South Florida's largest construction companies. Ronnie's natural affinity and love for the homebuilding process was enough to convince Steven that the two should join forces to build a business together. After all, it was in their genes and they had once worked well together in a popular hippie clothing store associated with their fathers' stores. The Shapiro/Pertnoy Companies were born.

ABOVE LEFT: Ornamental bridge floats over formal living room.
Photograph by Kim Sargent, Sargent Architectural Photography

ABOVE RIGHT: Gallery with Venetian plaster groin vault ceiling.
Photograph by Kim Sargent, Sargent Architectural Photography

LEFT: Private residence in Jupiter, Florida.
Photograph by Kim Sargent, Sargent Architectural Photography

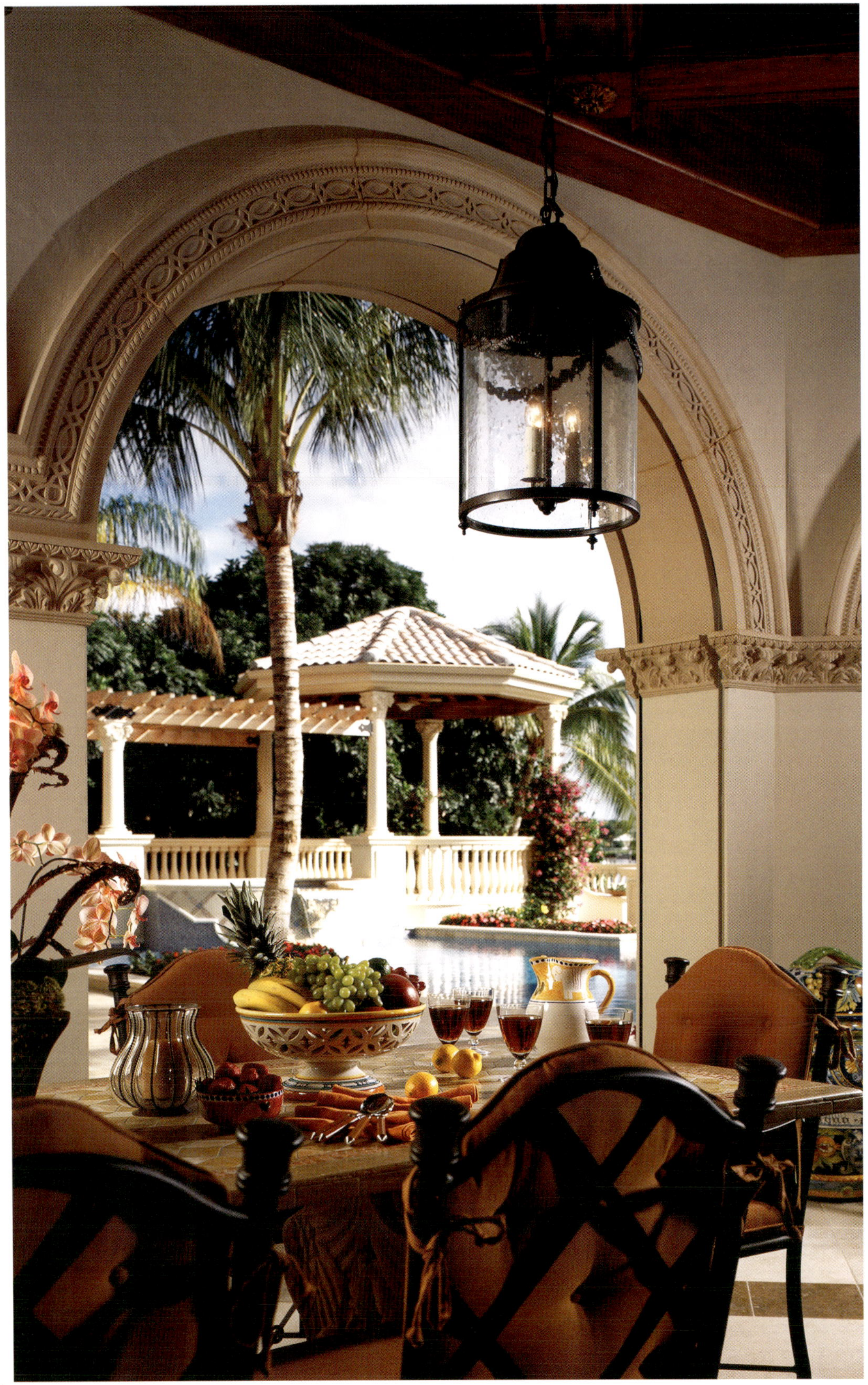

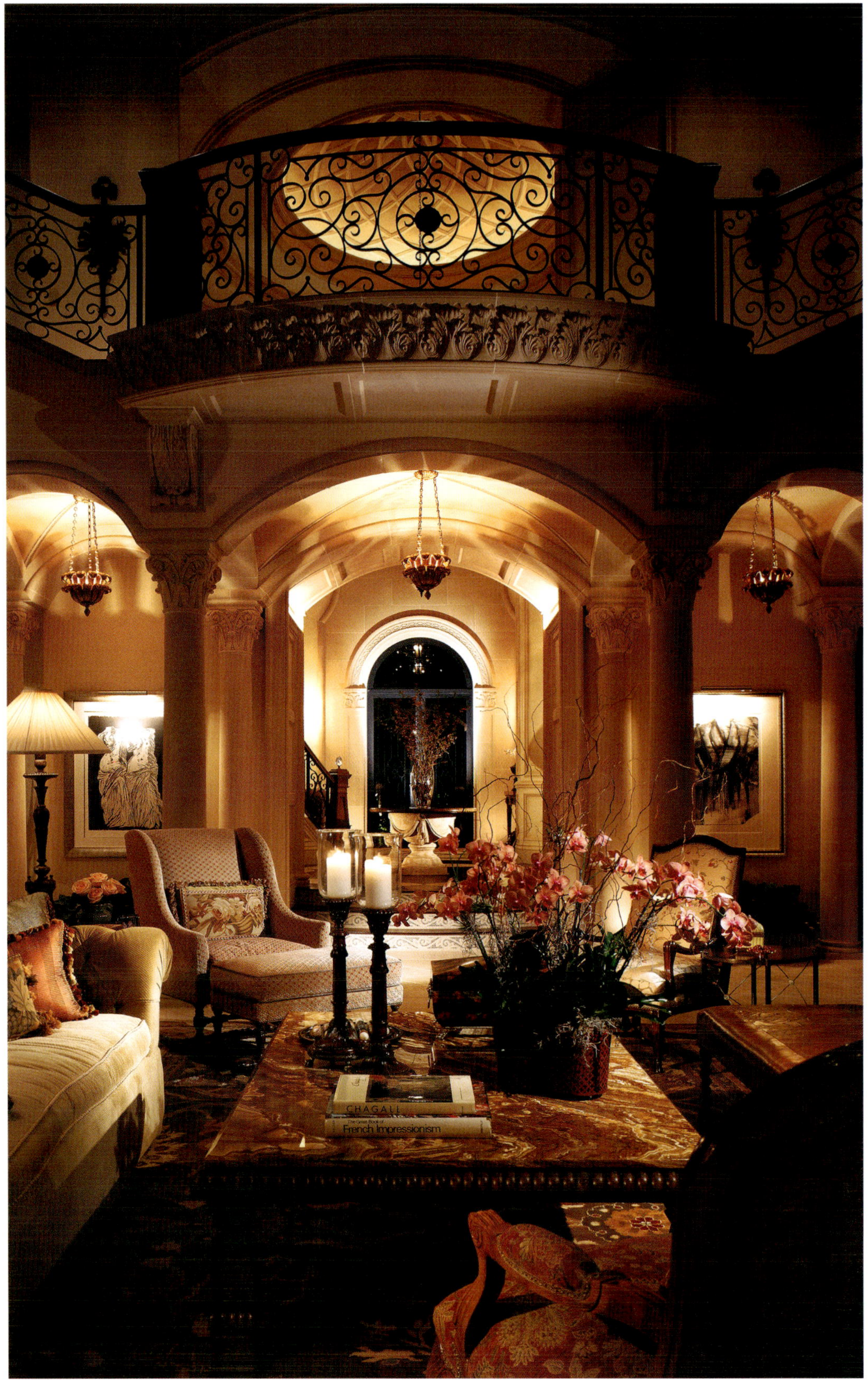
CHAGALL
French Impressionism

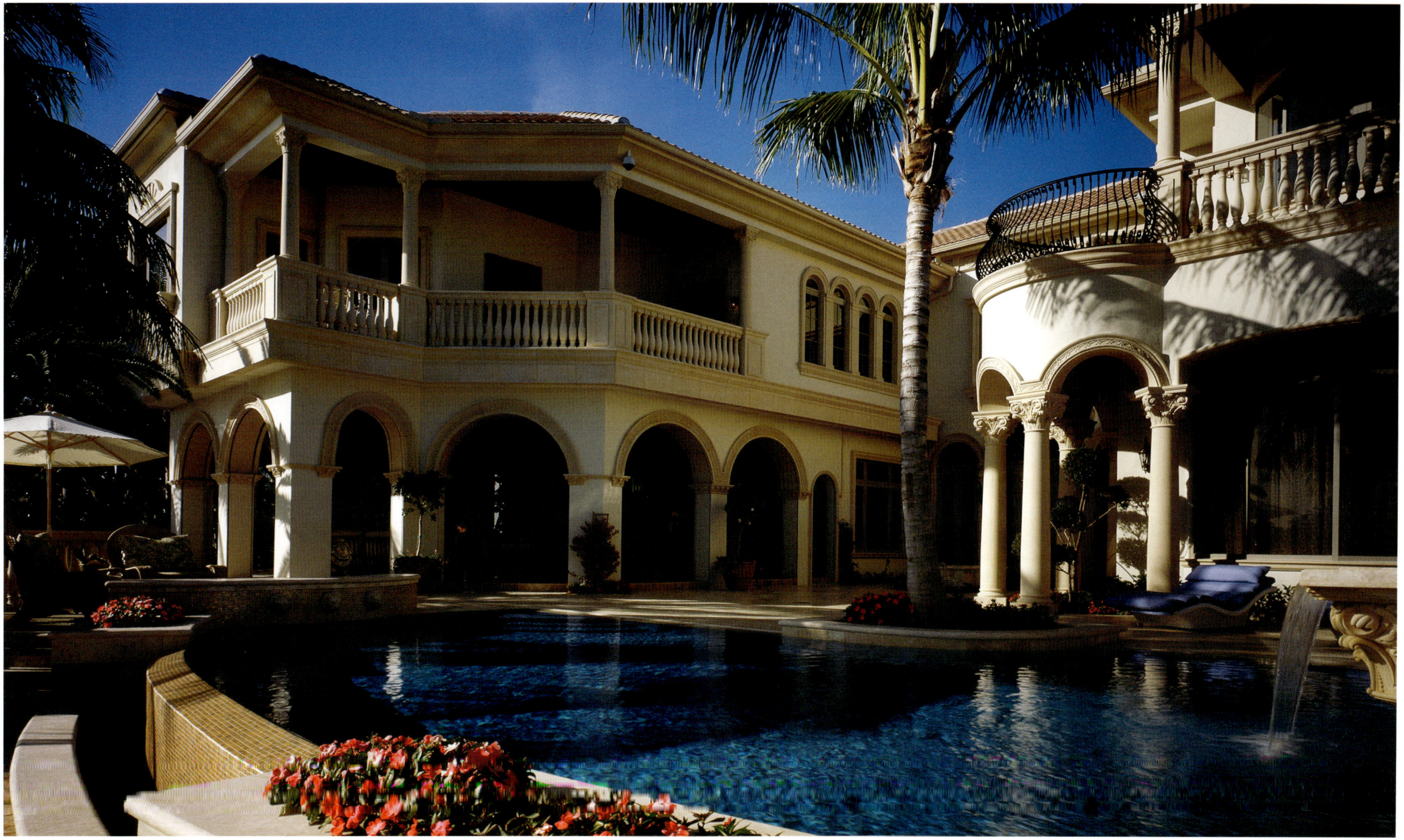

Although they enjoy the fruits of their labor today, from the company's inception in 1978, their business has always involved long hours and hard work. Fortunately for them, what they do brings sufficient gratification that it never seems like work anyway. At the outset of their vision, Pertnoy recalls waking his children up in the middle of the night because that was the only time he could see them. Likewise, Shapiro has not forgotten about 24-hour work days which have since proved well worth the effort. Shapiro/Pertnoy is one of the leading custom home builders in the Southeast and the premier of South Florida.

ABOVE: Infinity-edge pool amongst entertainment decks and patios.
Photograph by Kim Sargent, Sargent Architectural Photography

FACING PAGE LEFT: Covered loggia overlooks rear entertainment area.
Photograph by Kim Sargent, Sargent Architectural Photography

FACING PAGE RIGHT: Symmetry provides ideal balance of architectural elements.
Photograph by Kim Sargent, Sargent Architectural Photography

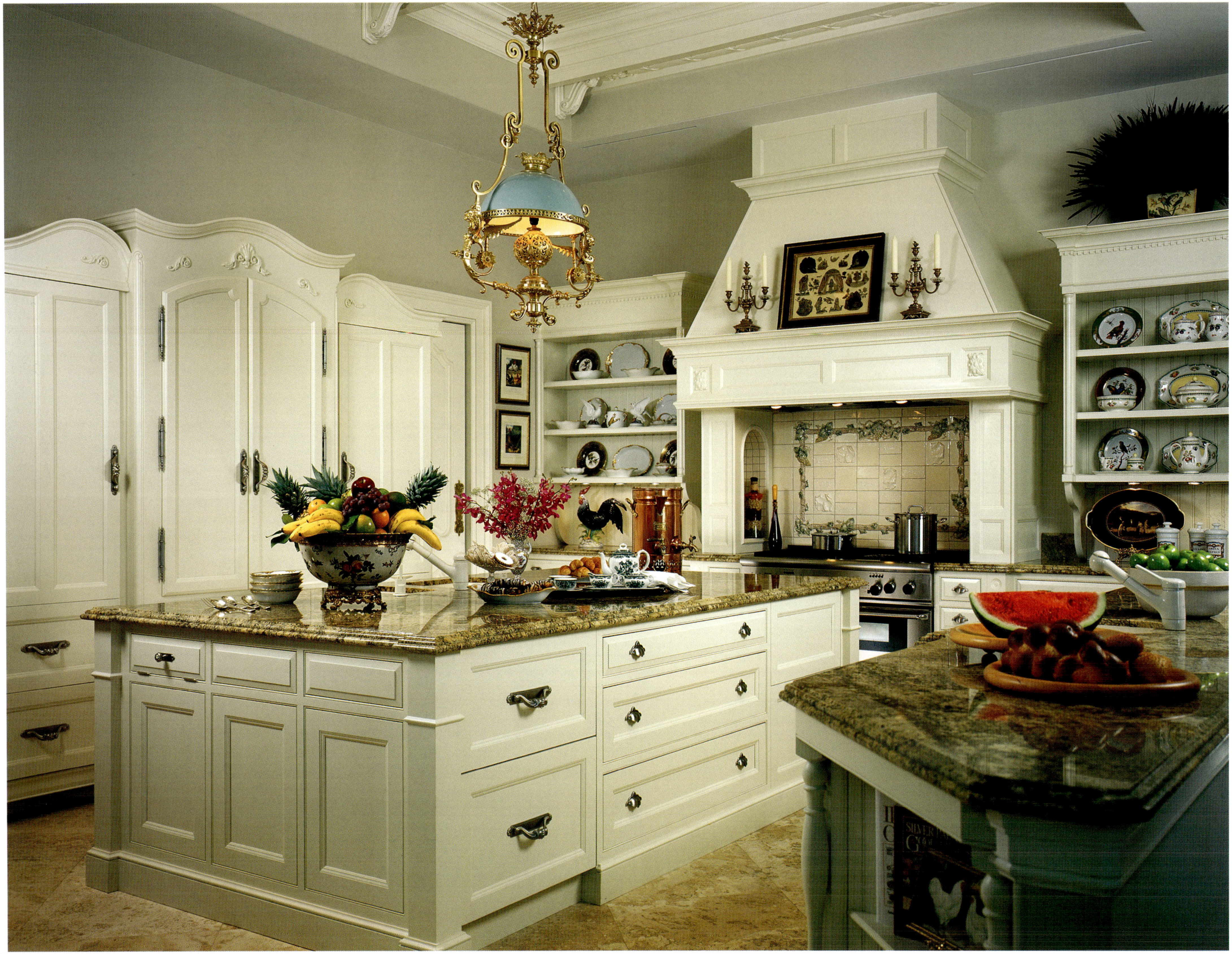

Steven and Ronnie built Shapiro/Pertnoy—and an impressive reputation—based on quality, precision and the work ethic of true artisans. They specialize in luxury residential properties, but have extensive experience with retail, office and industrial development. Customer service is first, because Shapiro/Pertnoy does not just build homes, they build their clients' dreams.

Wellington will always be home. In fact, when Ronnie Pertnoy "discovered" this planned community it was considered "the boondocks" by some. Both Wellington and Shapiro/Pertnoy have expanded considerably since those days. In the late 1970s, they were thrilled to sell a home there for $109,000. Now, it is not unusual to find several Shapiro/Pertnoy homes under construction with price tags over $10 million. One of the largest residences they have been commissioned to build is an impressive 30,000-square-foot nearly completed residence, located in Jupiter.

Although their clients may be among the more affluent, Shapiro/Pertnoy understands that even this clientele seeks value for their money. Construction agreements are based on the actual builder's cost, plus a fee. "Because of the sheer volume of work we produce, our actual cost can be quite a bit less than the average homebuilder. We pass these savings on to our clients."

Steven and Ronnie's clients have come to appreciate the firm's treatment of their affairs with tremendous discretion and respect. Most of their clients are able to surround themselves with the best of everything, and they consider Shapiro/Pertnoy to be the best at what they do—building extraordinary homes.

Shapiro/Pertnoy strives to provide an ideal experience to each client through timely and thorough communications, friendly service and only the highest quality of materials. The family-owned company has a talented staff of 30 employees and countless qualified contractors. Shapiro and Pertnoy have tremendous confidence in their team, and enjoy escaping for the occasional fishing vacation—and even then, clients can always reach them.

One of the keys to Shapiro/Pertnoy's success is the diversity of their business interests. Ronnie credits these investments from a little tip he got from his dad, "He told me to get myself a candy store,

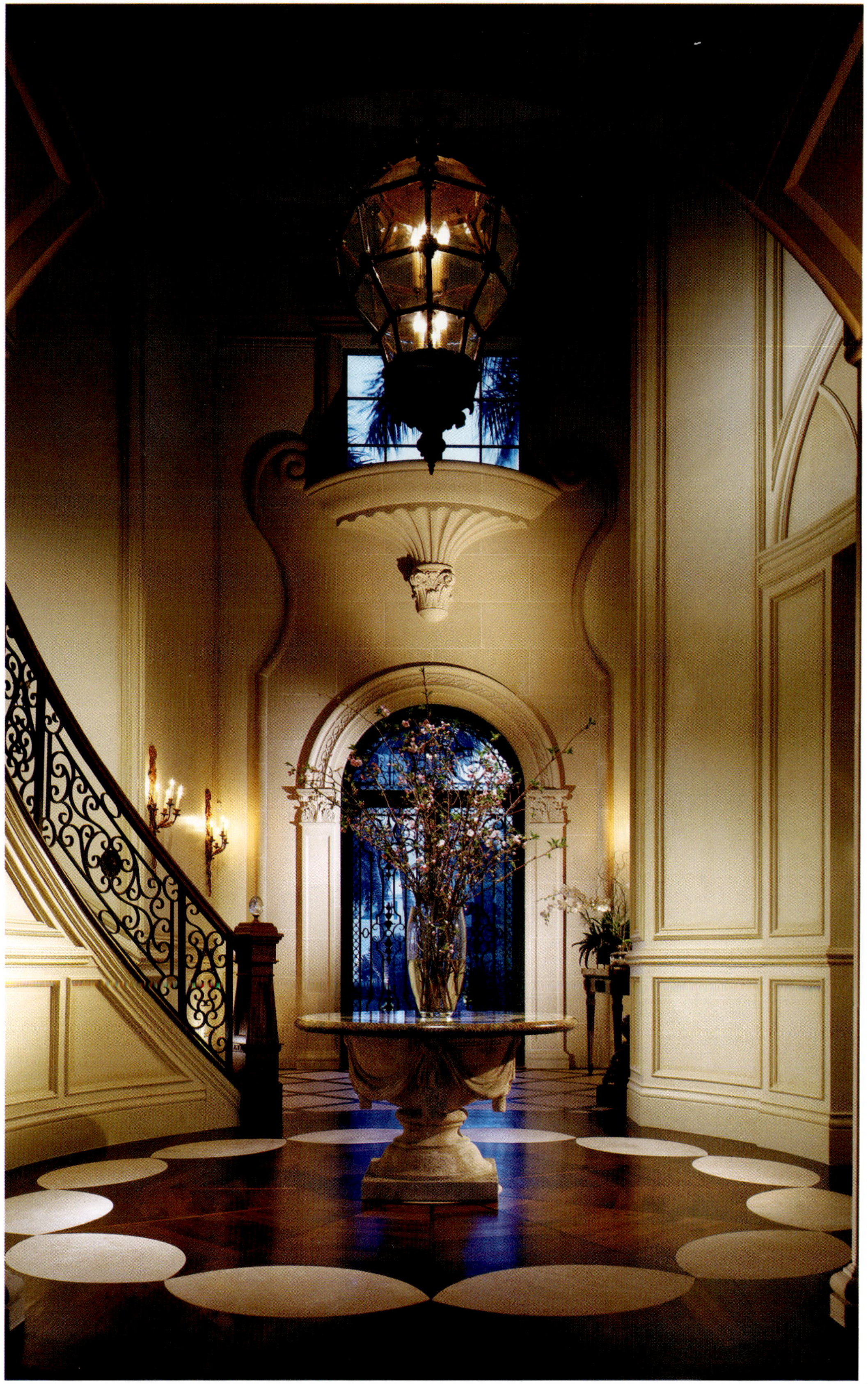

RIGHT: Marble inlays, paneled walls, intricate iron work and artisan stonework create this foyer's character.
Photograph by Kim Sargent, Sargent Architectural Photography

FACING PAGE: This highly functional kitchen is also beautiful and elegant.
Photograph by Kim Sargent, Sargent Architectural Photography

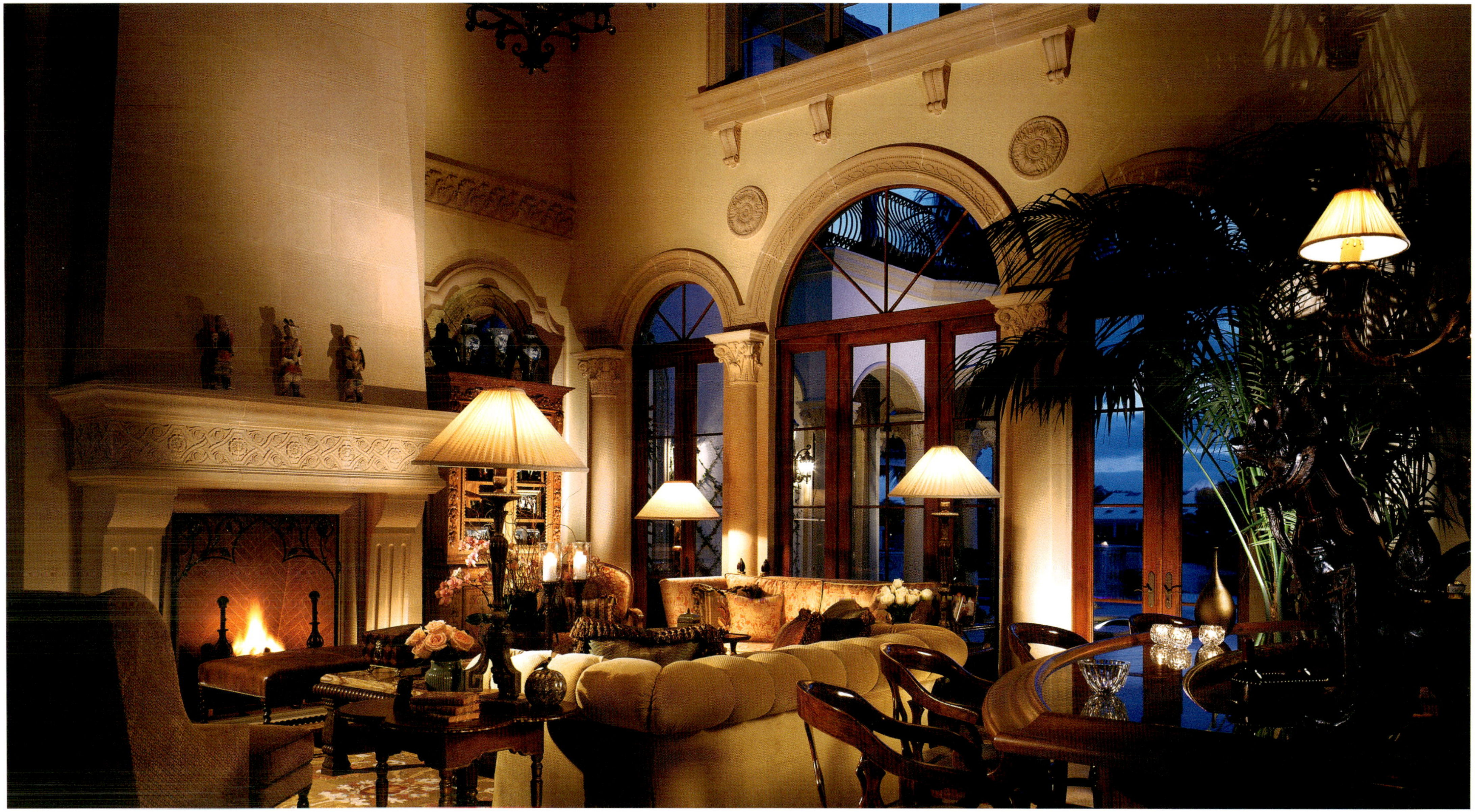

which is our housing business, while developing the occasional commercial project for eventual retirement. As it turns out we became pretty good at running the candy store." Not only do they develop and build tremendous structures including many well-known office and industrial parks, they also manage their commercial properties and offer brokerage and lending services. Also, the partners' skills are quite complementary, with Steven's emphasis on marketing/sales and administration and Ronnie's focus on acquiring properties and managing construction.

Shapiro/Pertnoy has been recognized in countless publications, some of which include: *Architectural Digest, Florida Designs*, and *Arts & Antiques*. They are the recipient of the Best in State Award and have also received recognition through Aurora and Prism Awards. Their highest compliments come from clients who have experienced their expertise and recognize the quality behind which Shapiro/Pertnoy stands. Many former clients still consider Ronnie and Steven cherished friends.

Steven and Ronnie have a family history of entrepreneurship and are thrilled that their enterprising sons have taken active roles in the company. Values of hard work and quality work have been instilled in the young men since birth, so the fathers have every confidence in their sons' abilities. Above all, relationships are valued at Shapiro/Pertnoy and even though the company has grown tremendously since its inception, the partners still enjoy the process of building special relationships with their clients and helping them build their dreams into realities.

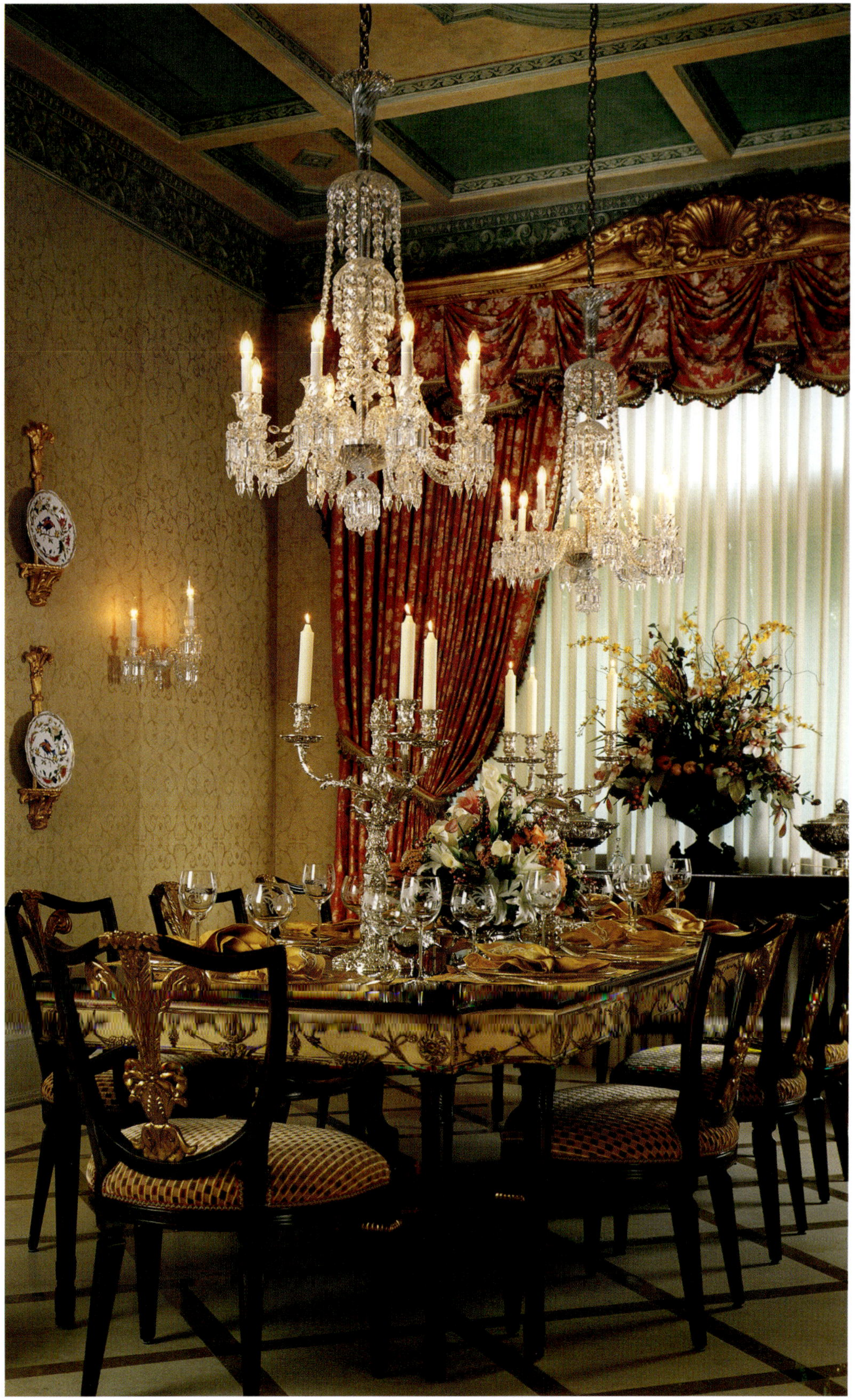

Q&A

more about steven & ronnie...

MY FRIENDS WOULD TELL YOU I WAS...

Ronnie says his friends would tell you he is very caring, respectful and passionate person. He is also the toughest and fairest business person.

NAME ONE THING MOST PEOPLE DON'T KNOW ABOUT EITHER OF YOU.

Ronnie spends much of his 18-hour days working on numerous charitable projects. As for Steven, not many know he is an inventor who patented his invention, the Plantag, an organizational tool for blueprints and maps.

WHAT IS THE HIGHEST COMPLIMENT YOU'VE RECEIVED PROFESSIONALLY?

Steven says it is when his clients say, "I want you and Ronnie to build my next house!"

WHAT ONE ELEMENT OF STYLE OR PHILOSOPHY HAVE YOU STUCK WITH FOR YEARS THAT STILL WORKS FOR YOU TODAY?

Treat the customer with respect; that means reaching beyond their expectations on all levels.

WHO HAS HAD THE BIGGEST INFLUENCE ON YOUR CAREER?

Our fathers.

SHAPIRO/PERTNOY COMPANIES
Steven Shapiro
Ronnie Pertnoy
3111 Fortune Way, Suite B-18
West Palm Beach, FL 33414
561.793.2003
www.shapiropertnoy.com

LEFT: Dining in style!
Photograph by Kim Sargent, Sargent Architectural Photography

FACING PAGE: Family room warmth with views of the waterway.
Photograph by Kim Sargent, Sargent Architectural Photography

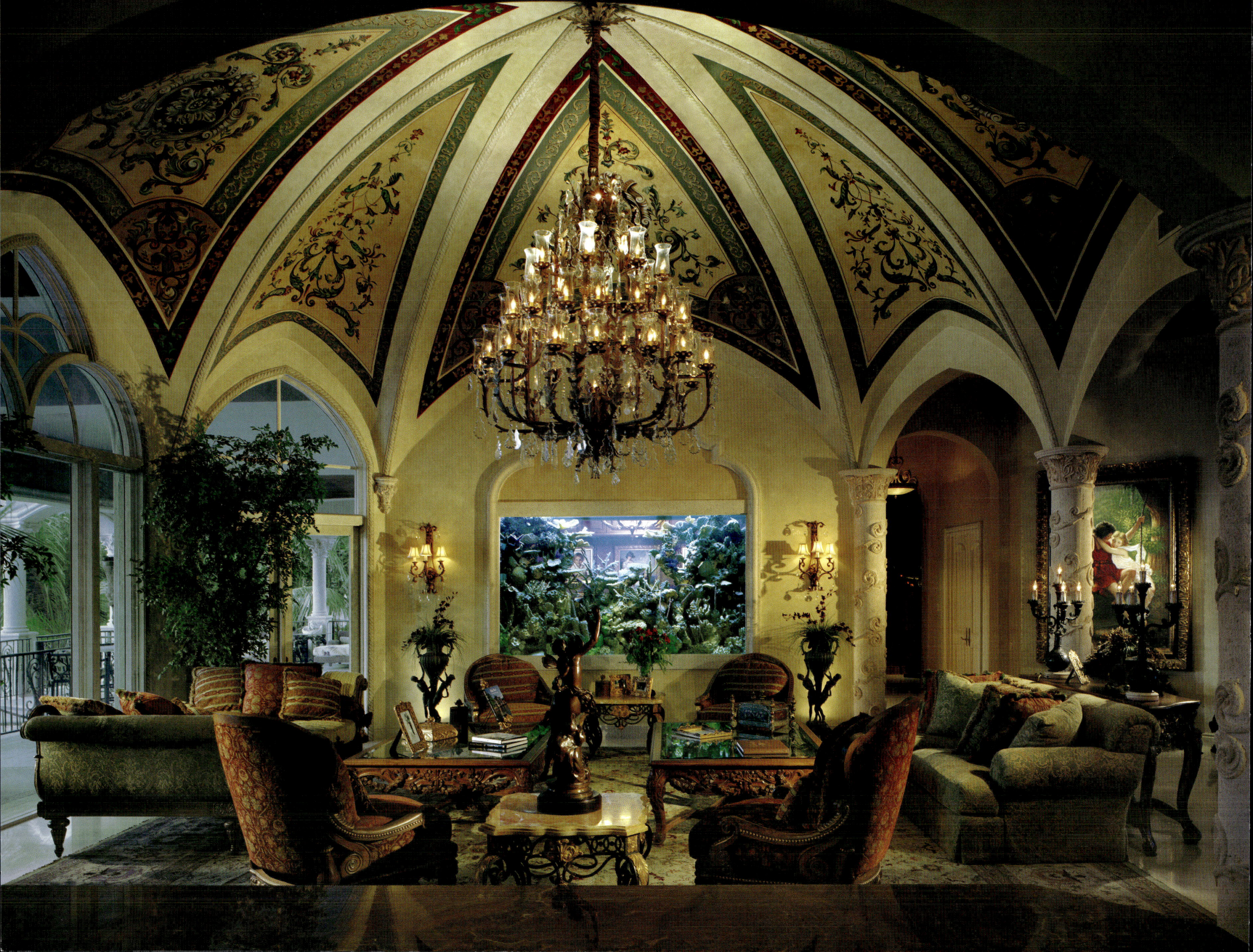

LAUREE SIMMONS & JULIE LUXTON

Simmons & Saray Interiors Group, Inc.

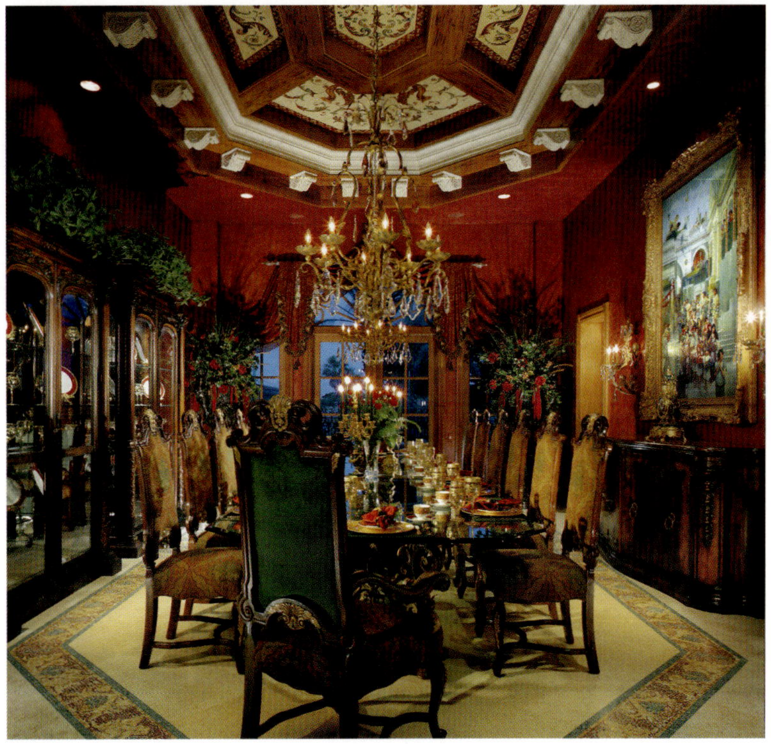

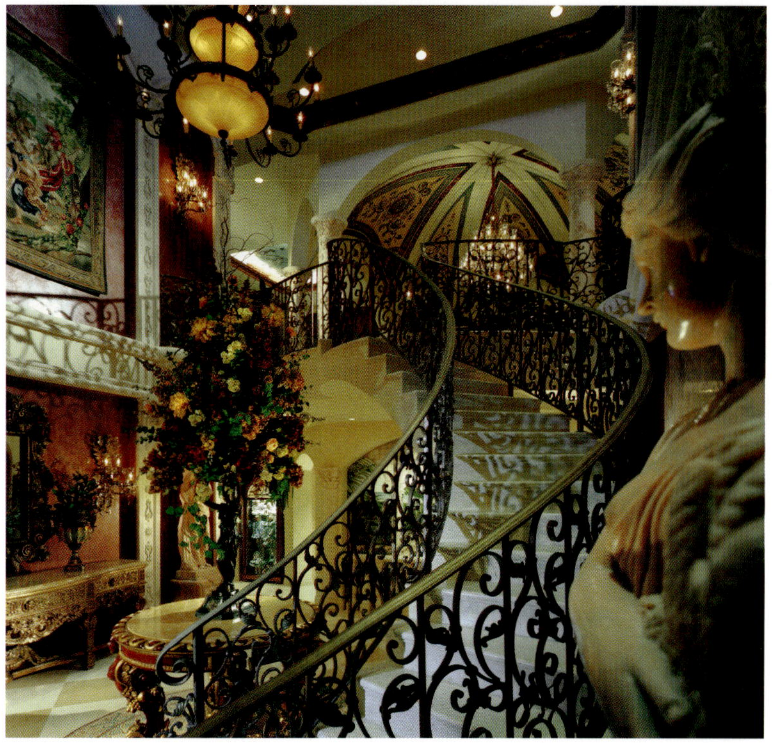

The beauty of the relationship between Lauree Simmons and Julie Luxton is that it is a relationship between complementary core design strengths and a shared vision setting the standard for excellence and gracious character. Committed to excellence, together they work in tandem to create the most unique and dynamic homes in Florida today.

Simmons and Saray Interiors Group, Inc., the interior design firm Julie and Lauree partnered to create, was founded in 1998. Together they often work hand-in-hand with Simmons Building Corporation, a national award-winning construction company founded by both Lauree and her husband, Bob Simmons. Throughout the entire design and building process, Lauree and Julie deliver sophisticated awe-inspiring homes that meld together architecture and the interiors into a progression of beauty that has enriched the landscape of beautiful sunny southern Florida.

Peerless for almost a decade while residing in one of the wealthiest counties per capita in the nation, Simmons and Saray Interiors Group produces high-end interior design in homes that range from 10,000 to 30,000-square-feet—homes that live up to clients' expectations of the designers unique vision and exceptional talent.

ABOVE LEFT: A luxurious dining room comprised of rich russet tones, elegant carved wood chairs and custom mosaic floor inlays combine beneath a glorious ceiling design.
Photograph by Dan Forer

ABOVE RIGHT: The grand foyer, complete with custom iron railings, decorative precast columns and lavish hand-carved custom furnishings, leads a pathway to the second floor living room.
Photograph by Dan Forer

LEFT: Eight sided groin vault arch, hand-painted with old Mediterranean motifs hangs above large living room with two sided custom fish tank.
Photograph by Dan Forer

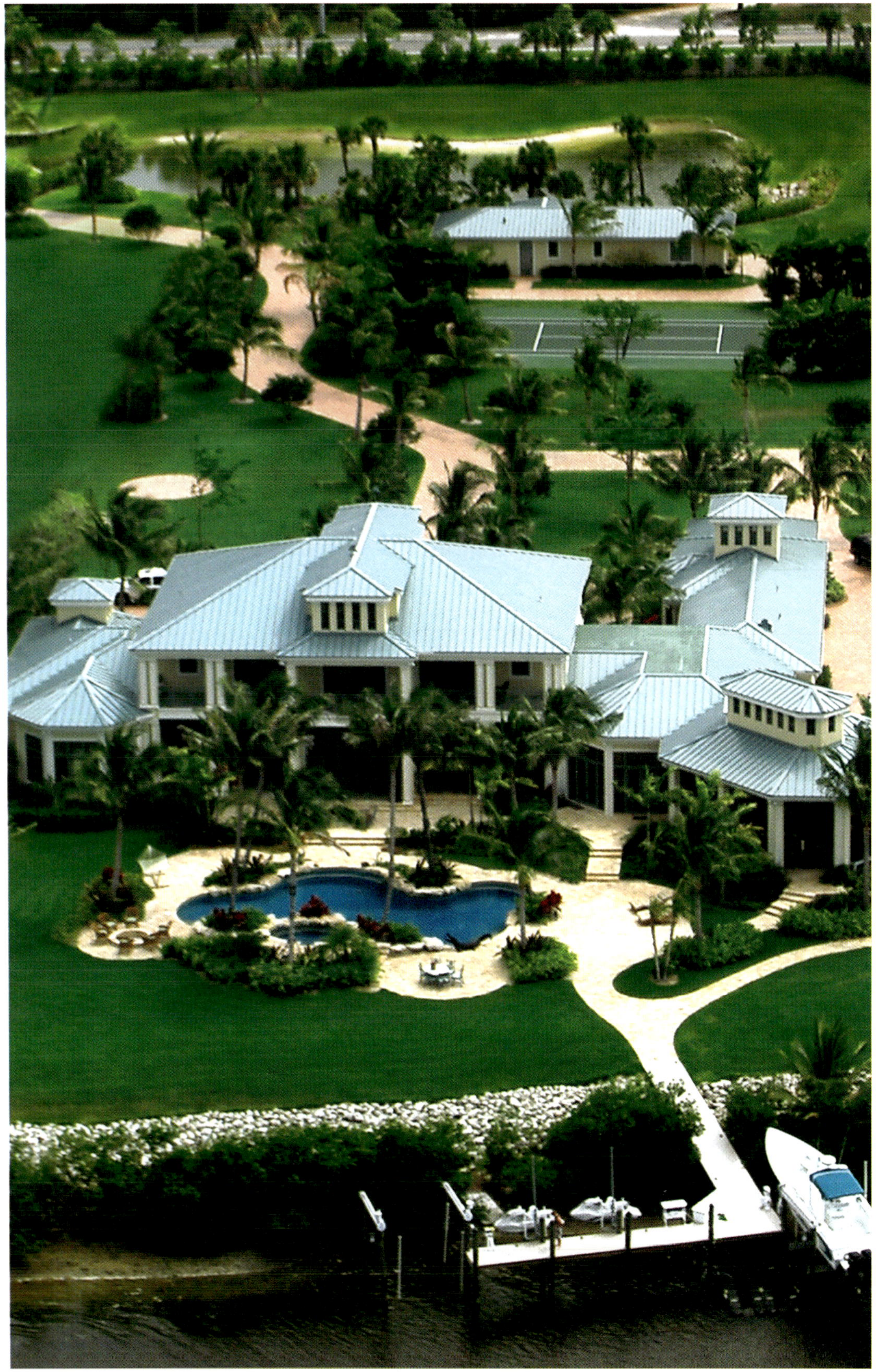

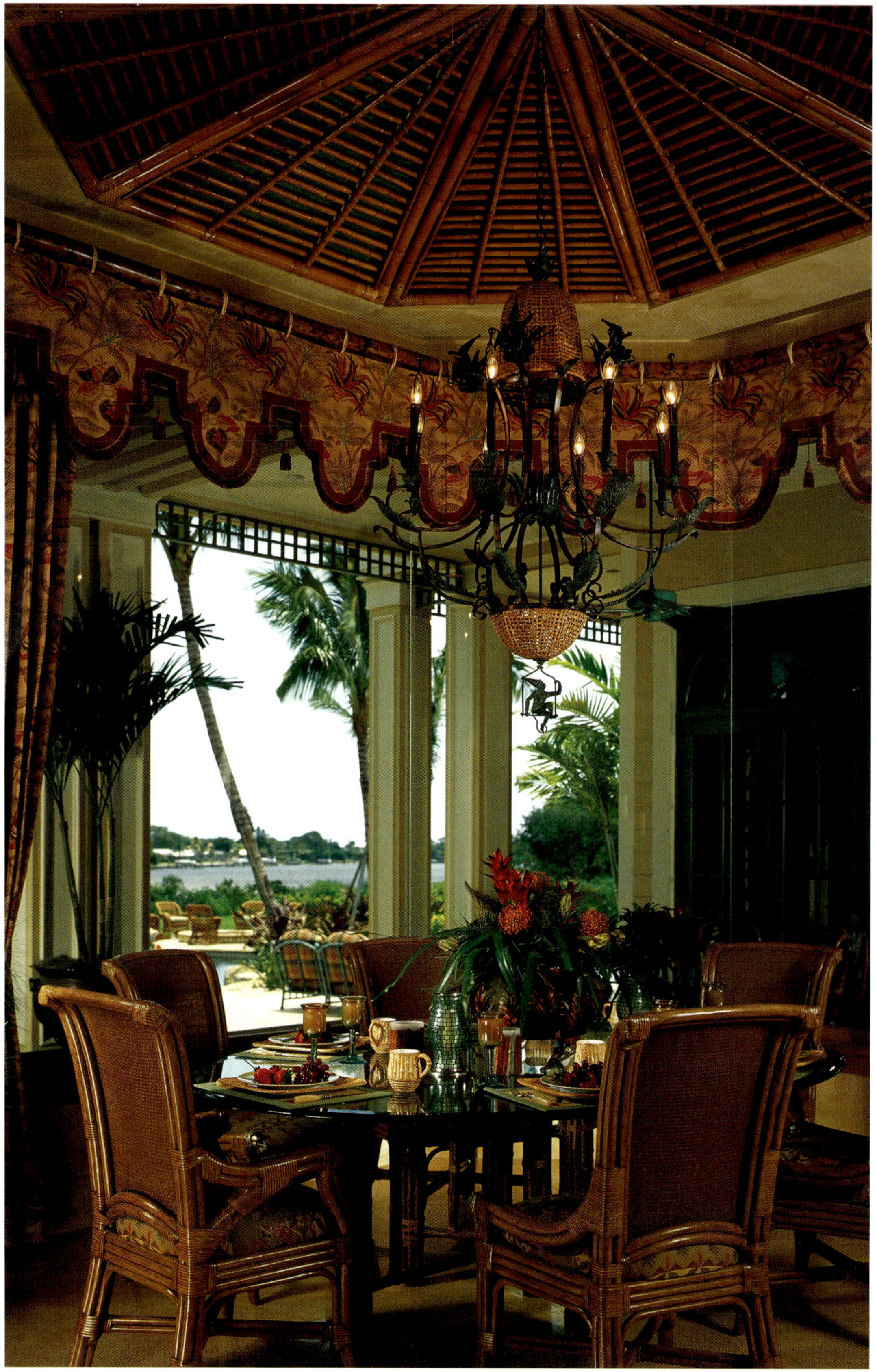

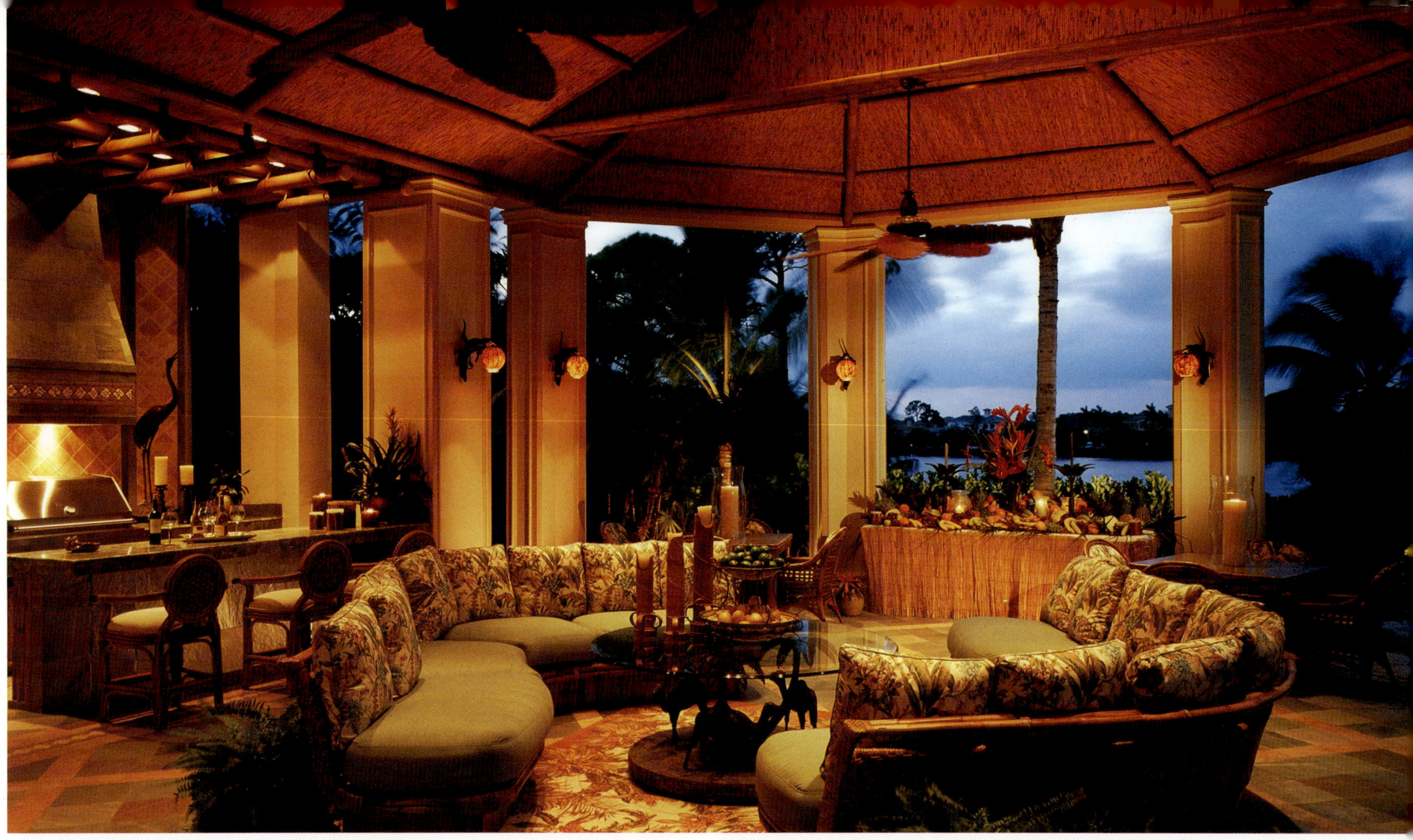

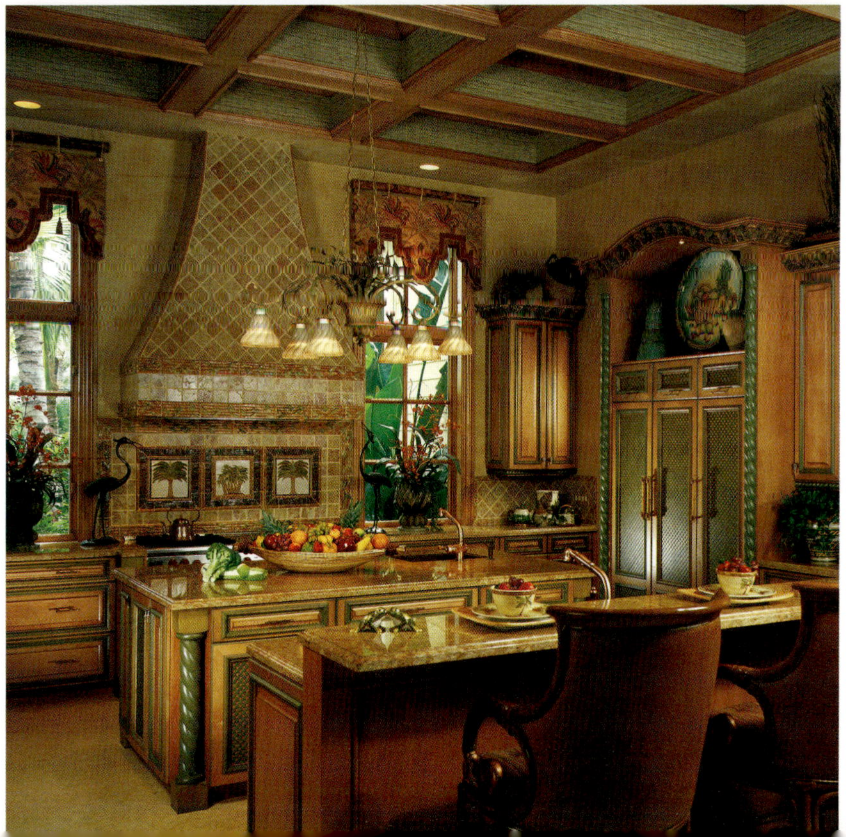

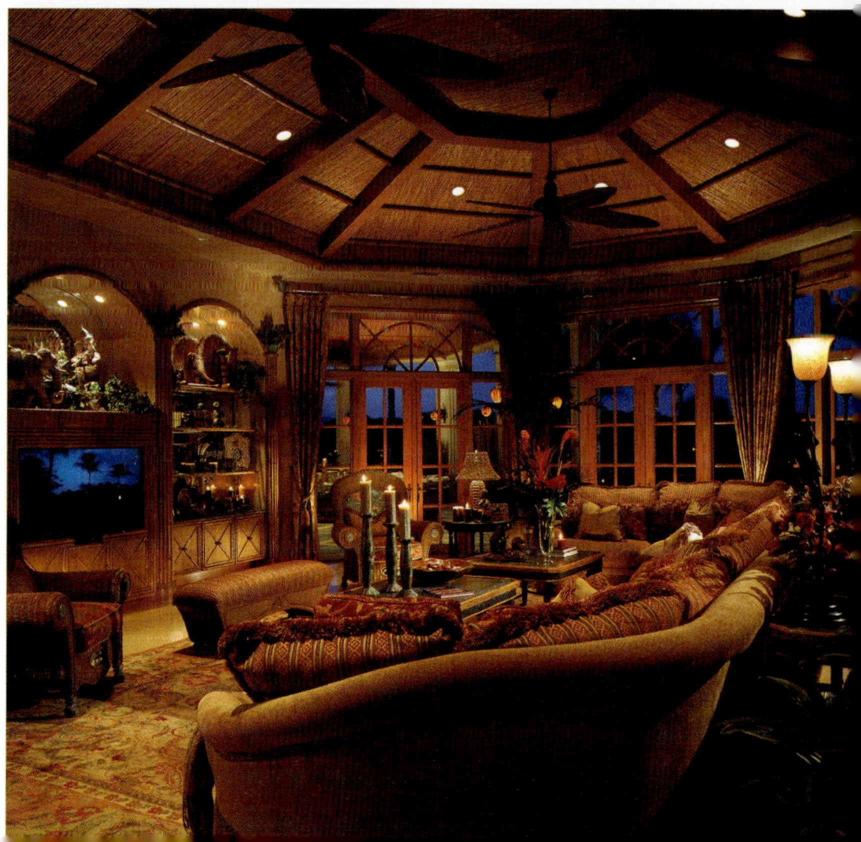

TOP: Outside living at its finest, the ceilings are covered in split bamboo with elegant outdoor furnishings situated below.
Photograph by Kim Sargent, Sargent Architectural Photography

BOTTOM LEFT: Warm and inviting, this island-style kitchen showcases lattice work on the cabinetry and grass cloth on the coffered ceilings. Perfect for both cooking and entertaining.
Photograph by Kim Sargent, Sargent Architectural Photography

BOTTOM RIGHT: Luxurious fabrics in combination with bamboo ceilings and a custom bamboo tropical-themed built-in set a warm and inviting mood in this family room.
Photograph by Kim Sargent, Sargent Architectural Photography

FACING PAGE LEFT: A bird's eye view of the palatial tropical plantation, showcasing Florida style living at its best with a beautiful free form pool and lush landscaping.
Photograph by Bob Simmons

FACING PAGE RIGHT: Bringing the outside in, this breakfast room exudes all things tropical. An octagonal bamboo vaulted ceiling hangs above a monkey chandelier and tropical themed furnishings.
Photograph by Kim Sargent, Sargent Architectural Photography

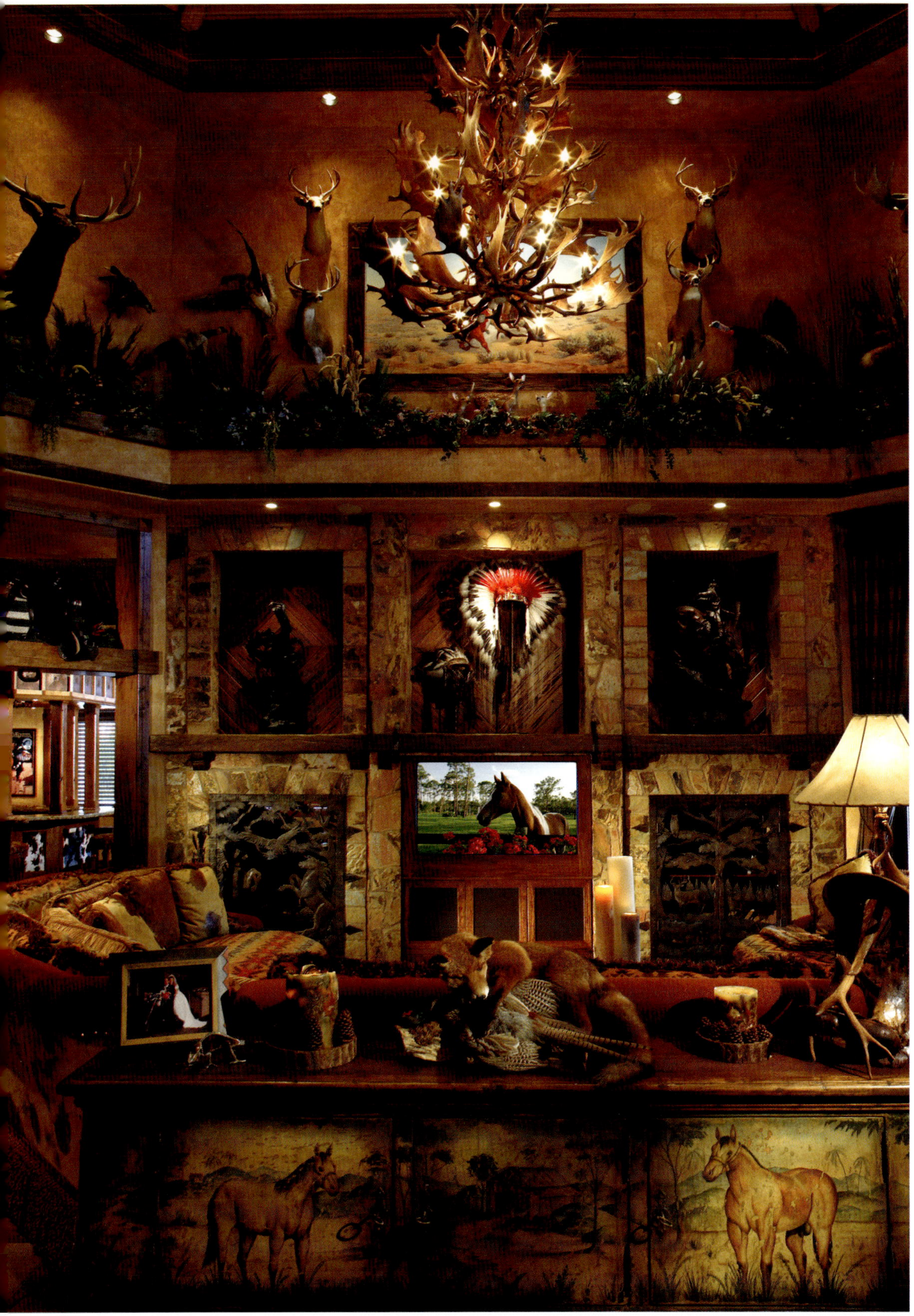

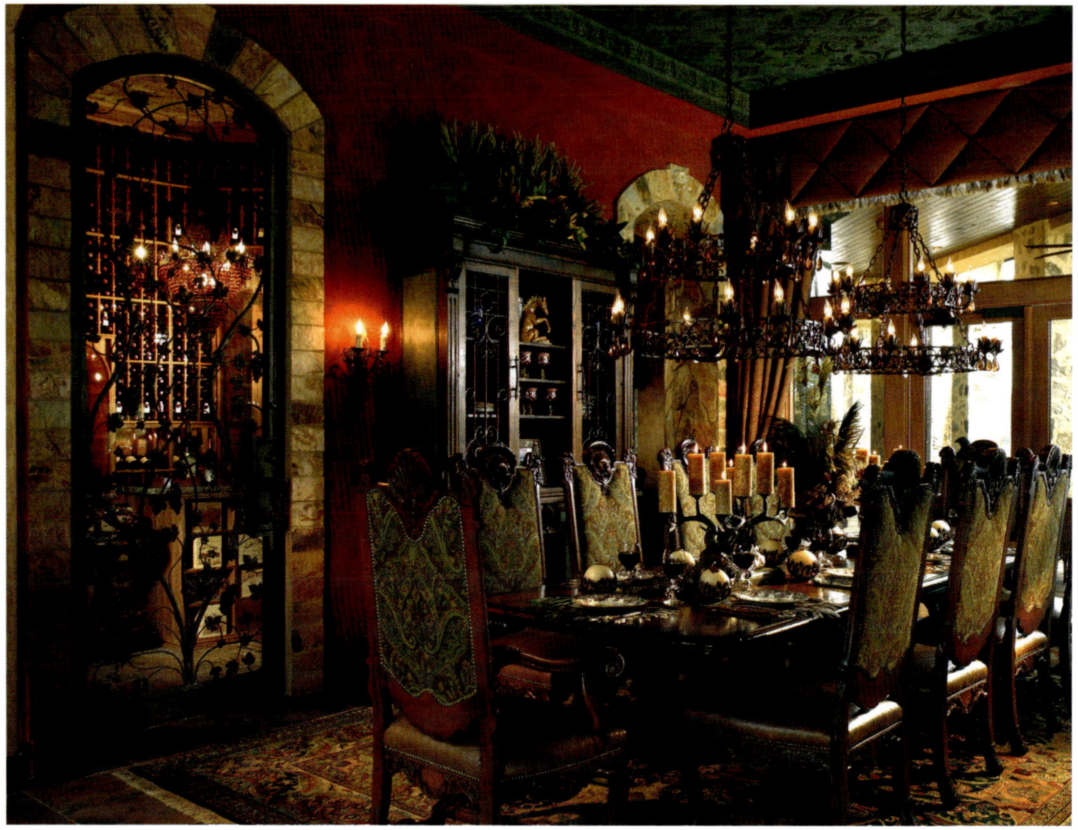

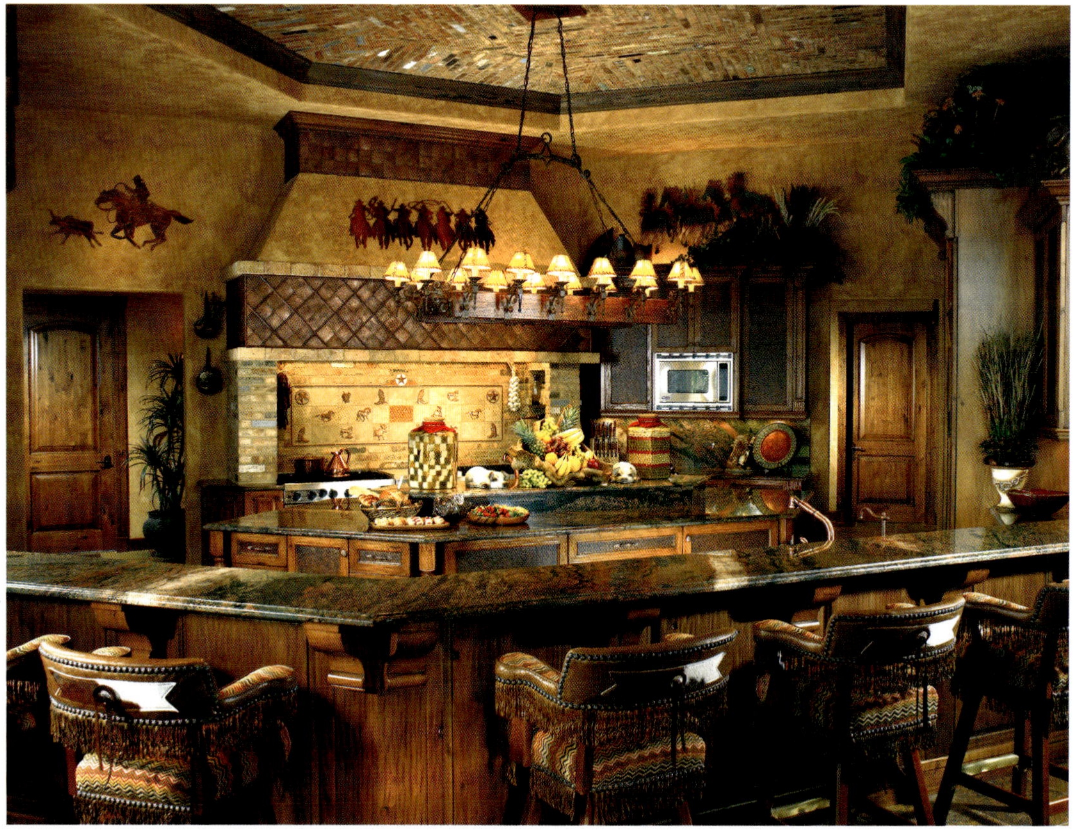

Because of their national and regional reputations, Simmons and Saray Interiors Group has been a widely acknowledged leader clients have turned to again and again. From delivering sophisticated turn-key homes from blueprint to completion, Lauree and Julie like to create an aesthetic that is warm and inviting, in essence, timeless. Often found in Florida are nuances of Old World Mediterranean architecture. Simmons Building Corp. follows suit with stately homes of Tuscan, Spanish and even Old English influences. The interiors always follow the architectural lead. "Our designs are always a complement to the architecture from beginning to end." Julie says.

Lauree and Julie are very passionate about their work. The duo are fiercely creative and not just about selling furniture and getting projects done, but refusing to compromise the vision of what their homes are supposed to look like when built. At the end of the day, being proud of a job well done is the ultimate satisfaction for them.

Both Simmons Building Corp. and Simmons and Saray Interiors Group work beautifully together because they steer their projects through a complete design and building process. Starting with the architecture, they work with their clients through every detail of construction coinciding with the interior design; which includes exquisite architectural details, furnishings, faux finishes, cabinetry and sumptuous window treatments. "You have the same team of people with the same concept from the architecture to the final inception of the project. It really makes for a nice cohesive project for the client, by having fewer people to deal with because we're all on the same page," Lauree says.

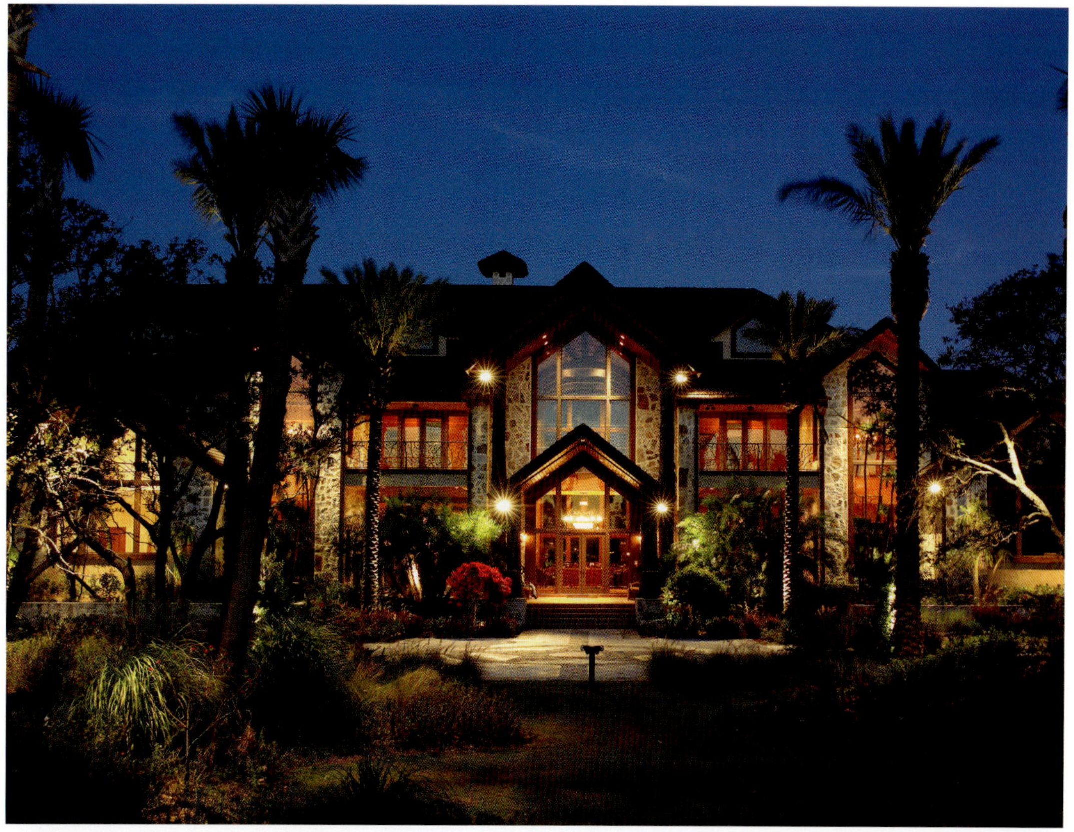

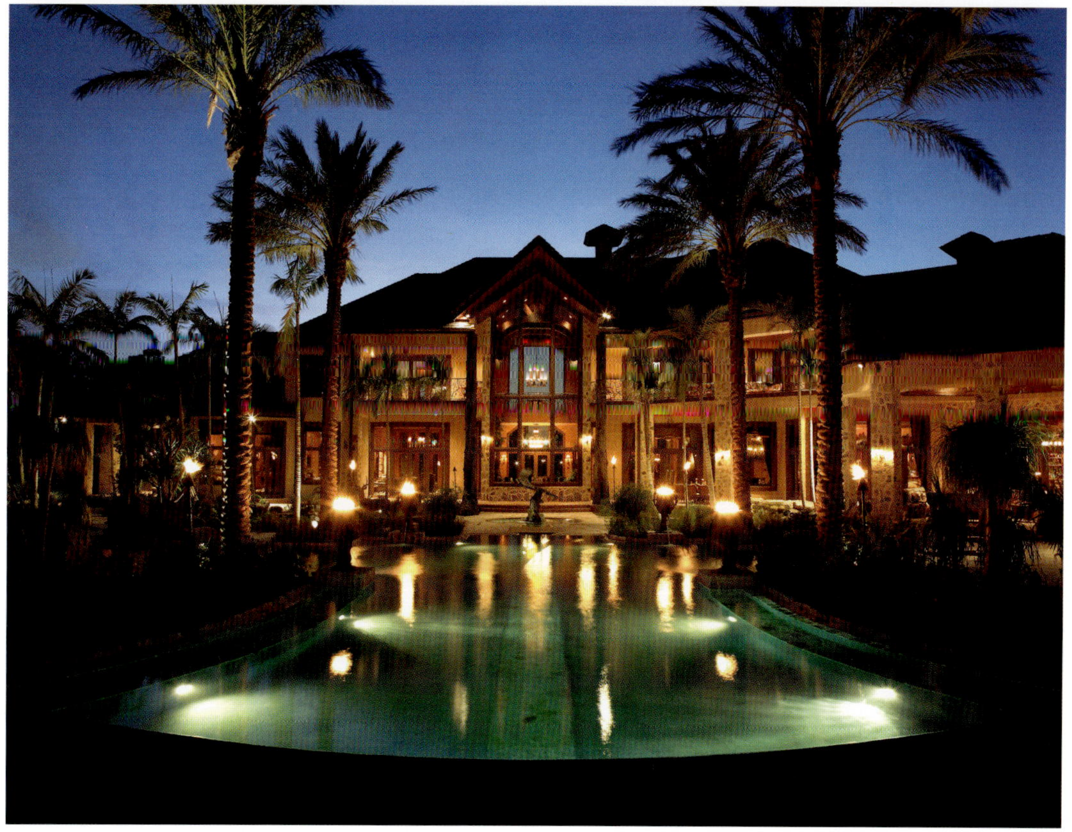

TOP: A paradox of western lodge architecture and natural Florida landscaping create a unique and distinctive facade for this one-of-a-kind Florida ranch home.
Photograph by Kim Sargent, Sargent Architectural Photography

BOTTOM: Sitting poolside at this Florida lodge style residence, the palms elegantly sway over the custom designed horizon edge pool with bronze deer head spitters and flame torches.
Photograph by Kim Sargent, Sargent Architectural Photography

FACING PAGE LEFT: "Cowboy Chic" sets the tone for this Florida ranch-style two-story family room showcasing Indian artifacts, animal mounts and a stunning stone surround fireplace.
Photograph by Kim Sargent, Sargent Architectural Photography

FACING PAGE TOP: Formal elegance meets western ways in this unique dining room with its stone and iron wine room entrance and double iron chandeliers.
Photograph by Kim Sargent, Sargent Architectural Photography

FACING PAGE BOTTOM: The heart of any home, this kitchen represents western warmth with an oversized copper and stone range hood complemented by fine hand-hewn alder cabinetry with copper inlays.
Photograph by Kim Sargent, Sargent Architectural Photography

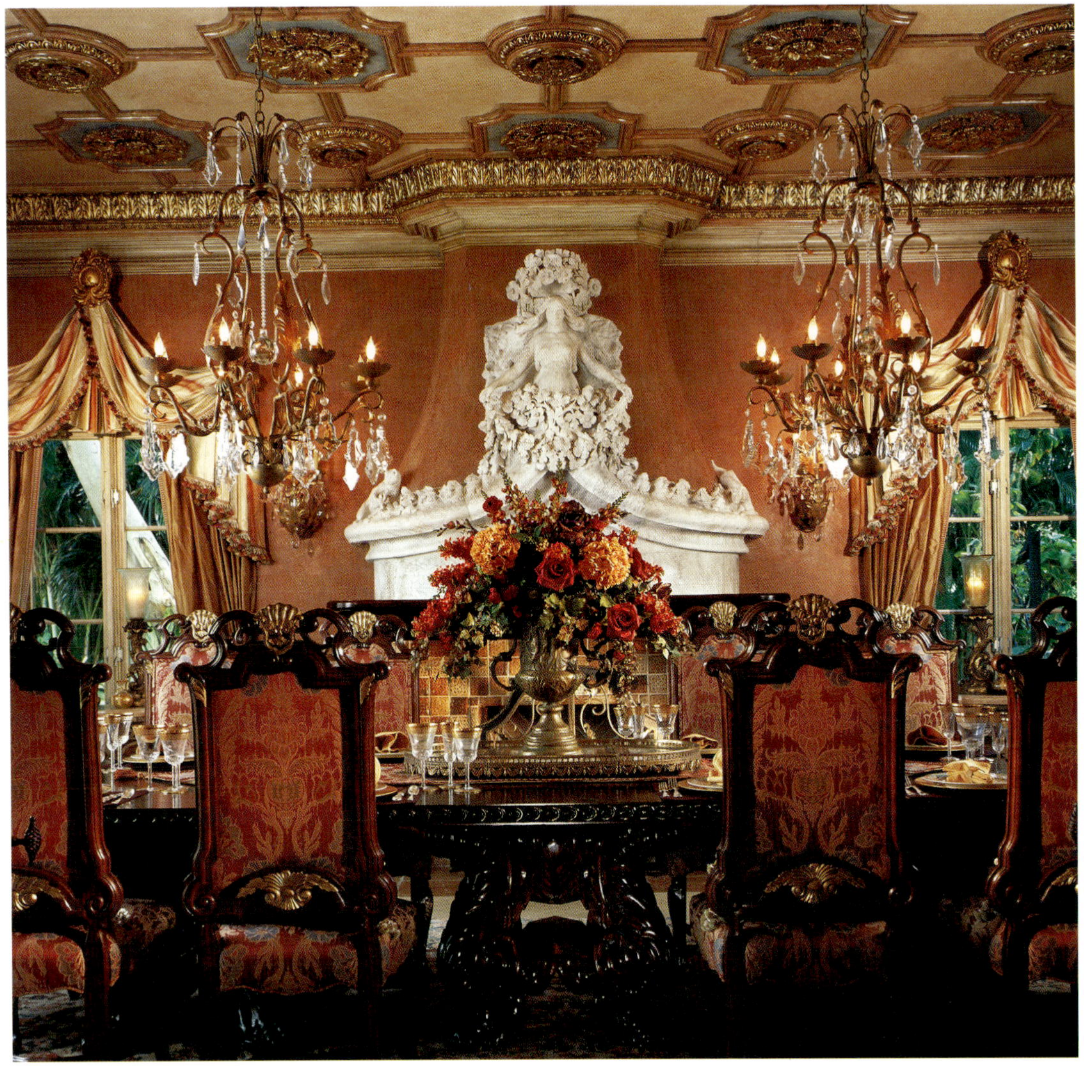

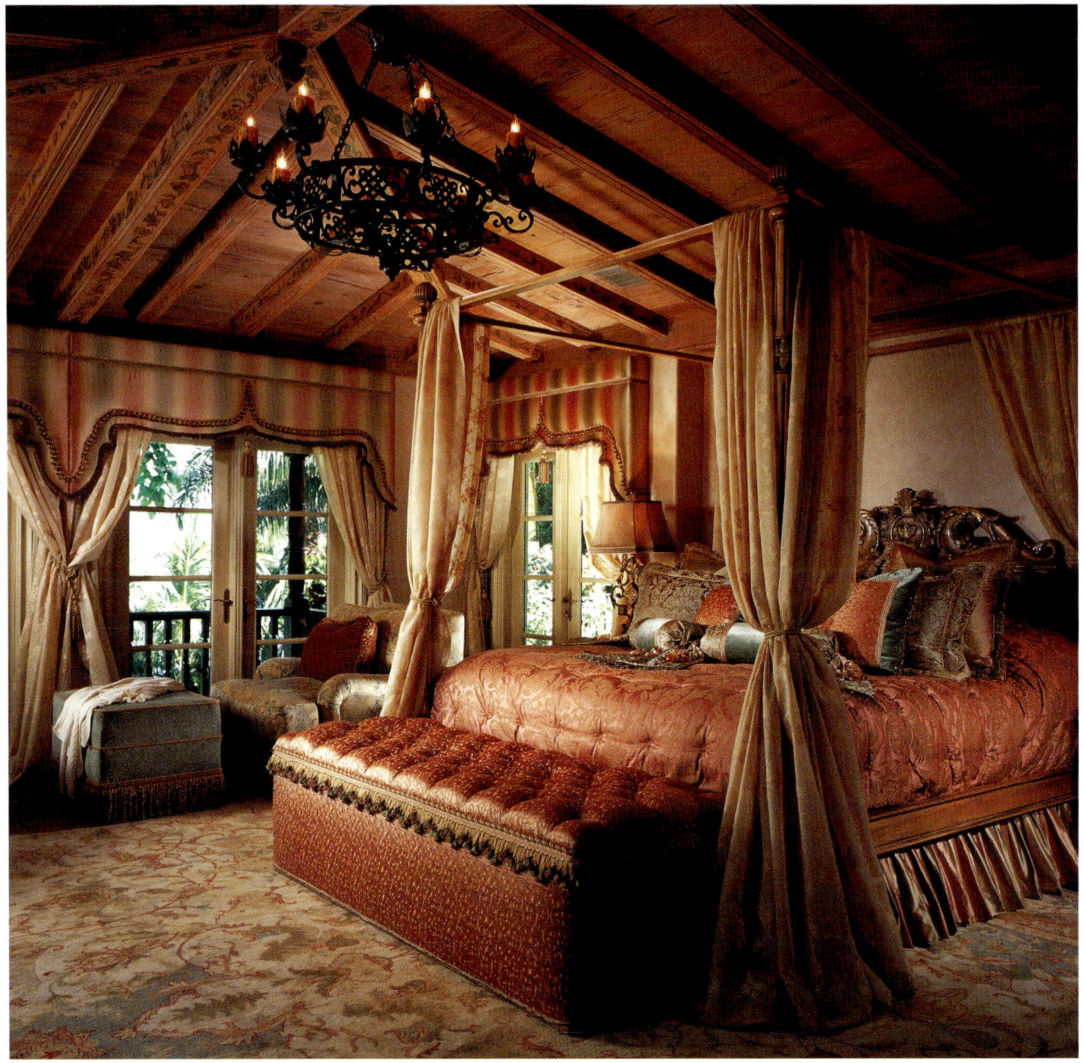

The two designers work very interestingly together in the execution of their interior designs. Their partnership is unique in that Lauree is a general contractor and she is more involved with the building side of interior design, while Julie is more involved with the soft goods, such as the furniture and the window treatments. "Her fortés are my weakness and my fortés are her weaknesses. Lauree is more involved with the front end of projects in dealing with the architectural detailing such as cabinetry, ceiling details and flooring. I come in, we meet in the middle and make selections of primary furniture pieces. My forte is more the softer side of design such as furniture, fabrics, window treatments, art and lighting—yet we're both working together side by side throughout the process."

The Perfect Piece, their 12,000-square-foot furniture showroom helps give them another level of customer service that most competition can't compete with. Julie and Lauree help with every aspect of a project. They not only help pick out furniture and appliances, they'll even help clients find the right property to build on as well.

Simmons and Saray have a very close connection with their clients. They have a relationship that is completely different from any other association with other professionals because of intimate knowledge of their clients' lives. Julie says her goal is to help people make wise aesthetic choices that they feel comfortable with, which is one of the reasons she and Lauree work as much as they do.

Working six or seven days a week, they both admit they are work-aholics, but love what they're doing. They get extremely excited about each new project and they very much enjoy the relationships built with their clients. Ultimately for Lauree and Julie, it is all about having a product at the end that they can be proud of and is exquisite and timeless.

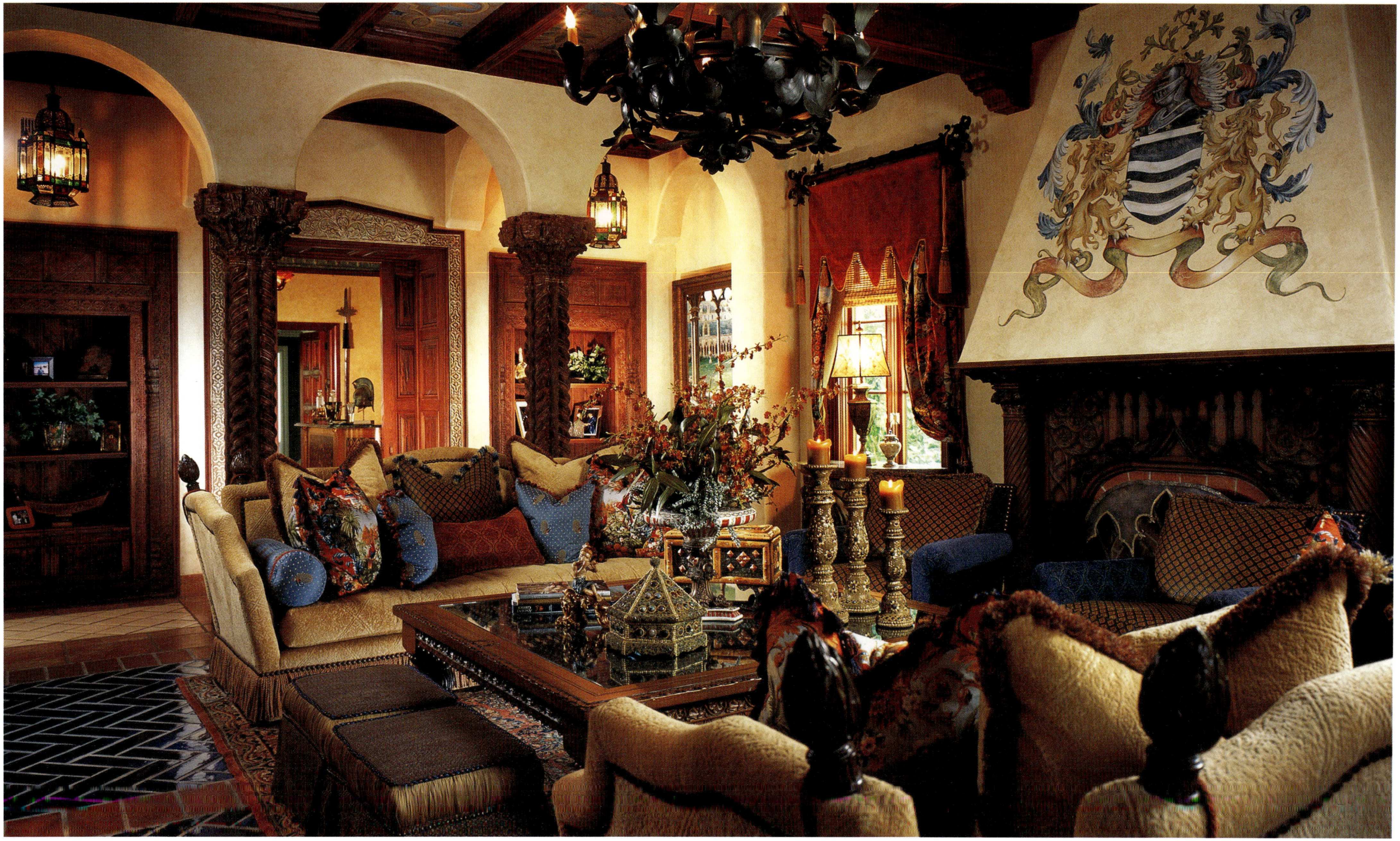

ABOVE: Old World Mediterranean architecture with Spanish influences combined with heavy chenille and jewel toned fabrics, create a warm and sophisticated living room complete with family crest.
Photograph by Kim Sargent, Sargent Architectural Photography

FACING PAGE LEFT: Old World Mediterranean elegance is showcased by a one-of-a-kind marble fireplace mantel, intricately designed and gilded ceiling mouldings and heavily hand-carved furnishings.
Photograph by Kim Sargent, Sargent Architectural Photography

FACING PAGE RIGHT: Pecky cypress ceilings above a four poster bed of luxurious silk fabrics, sumptuous window treatments and Mediterranean influence combine to create a beautiful mater bedroom suite.
Photograph by Kim Sargent, Sargent Architectural Photography

SIMMONS & SARAY INTERIORS GROUP, INC.
Lauree Simmons, President
Julie Luxton, ASID, Vice President
1090 Jupiter Park Drive
Jupiter, FL 33458
561.747.9099
Fax 561.747.9059

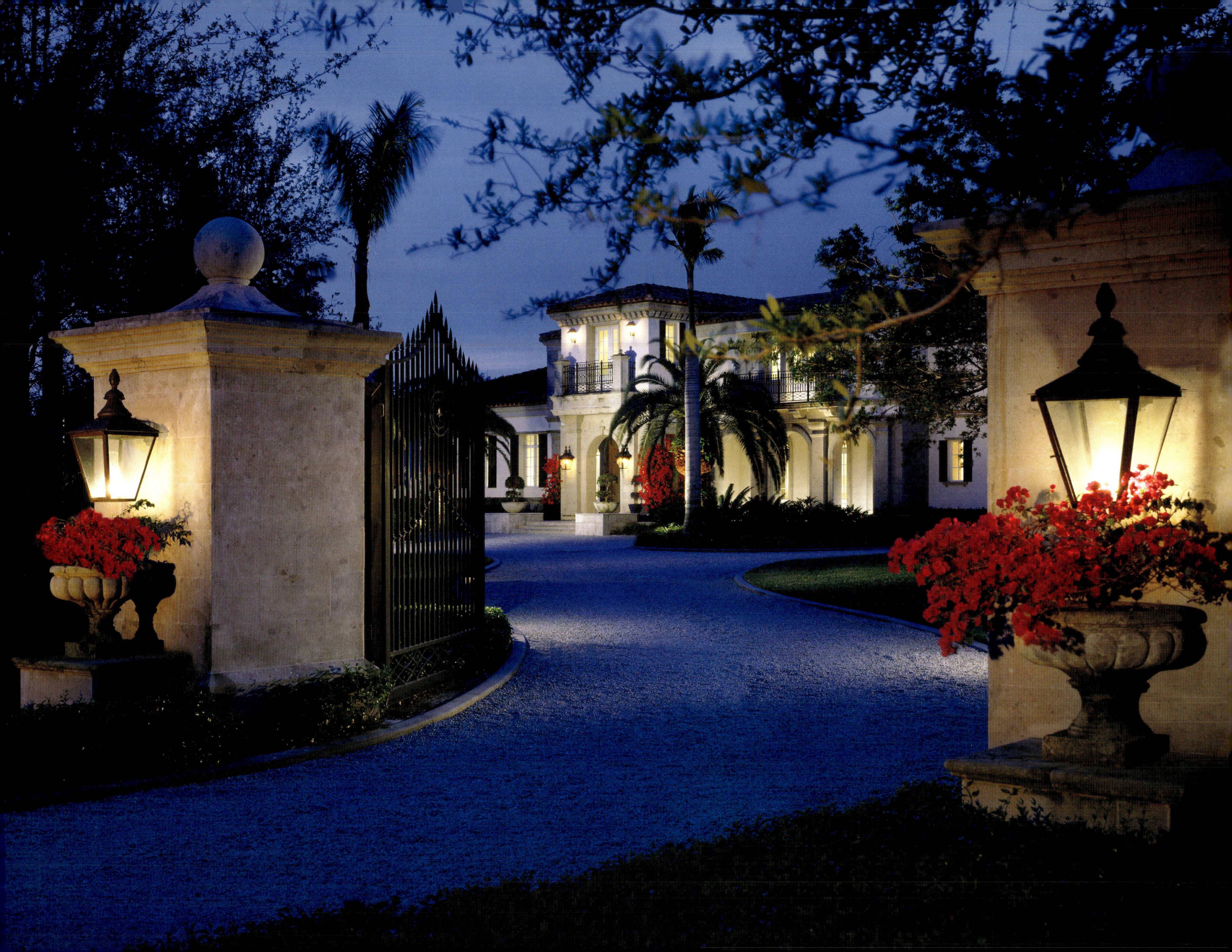

RANDALL STOFFT

Randall E. Stofft Architects PA

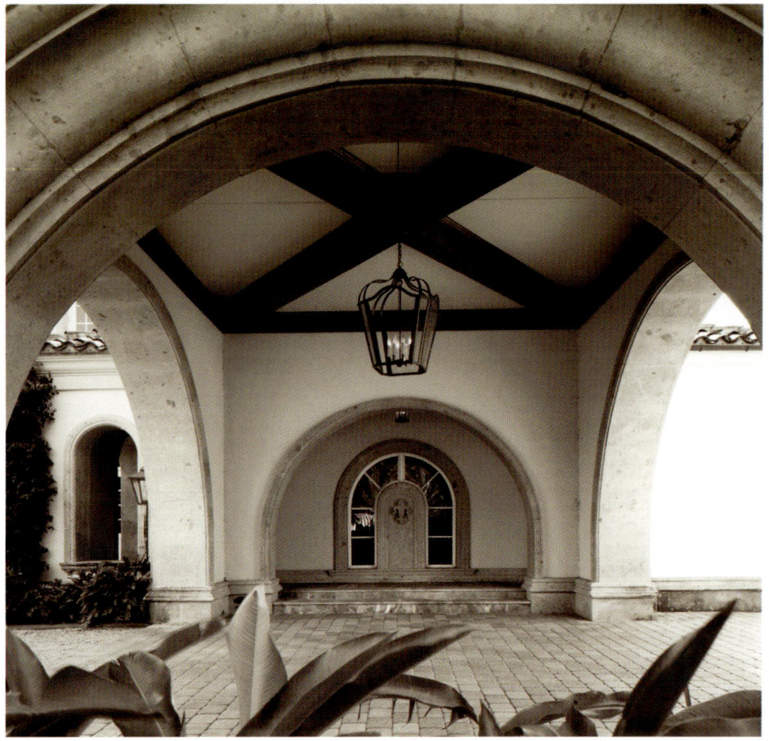

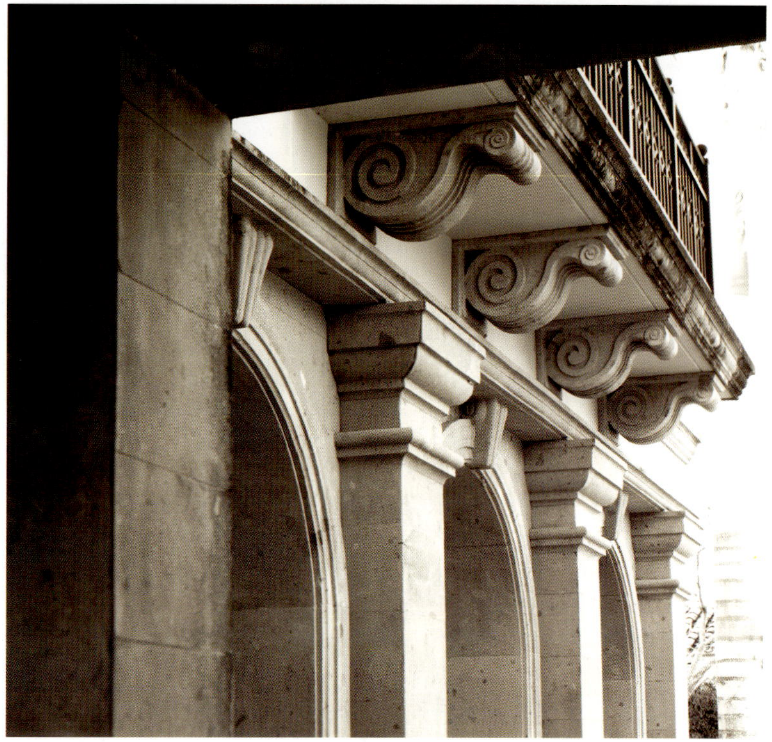

Without even stepping foot in his office, one need only experience a handful of Randall Stofft's brilliantly designed homes in order to grasp the magnitude of his design philosophies and awe-inspiring talent. One of the most influential and celebrated architects in Florida and the Southeast, Randall's work reflects the melding of his life experiences, his client's dreams and his dynamic design solutions.

While growing up on Chicago's North Side, Randall was surrounded by wonderful residences, including some by his earliest inspiration, Frank Lloyd Wright. Though he dreamed of being an artist, he was "guided" into pursuing the more lucrative art form of architecture. Randall was formally educated and trained in Arizona where he was further influenced by Wright's Taliesin Winter Camp. Upon graduation, he returned home to Chicago and while there, gained practical knowledge at the prestigious firm of Skidmore Owings & Merrill. In 1983, opting for a change of scenery, he relocated to the Sunshine State and opened his own firm, Randall E. Stofft Architects, in Boca Raton. Since that time, tremendous success, 50 employees, four offices—in Delray Beach, Naples, Vero Beach and Cleveland, Ohio—and countless clients have followed.

ABOVE LEFT: Side porte cochere separates the motor court, guesthouse and tennis court.
Photograph by Troy Campbell, Troy Campbell Photography

ABOVE RIGHT: Weathered cantera detailing with whitewashed stucco and black iron railings highlight this classical European residence.
Photograph by Troy Campbell, Troy Campbell Photography

LEFT: Weathered gray cantera stone pilasters and a granite chip driveway frame the entry to this French revival residence.
Photograph by Troy Campbell, Troy Campbell Photography

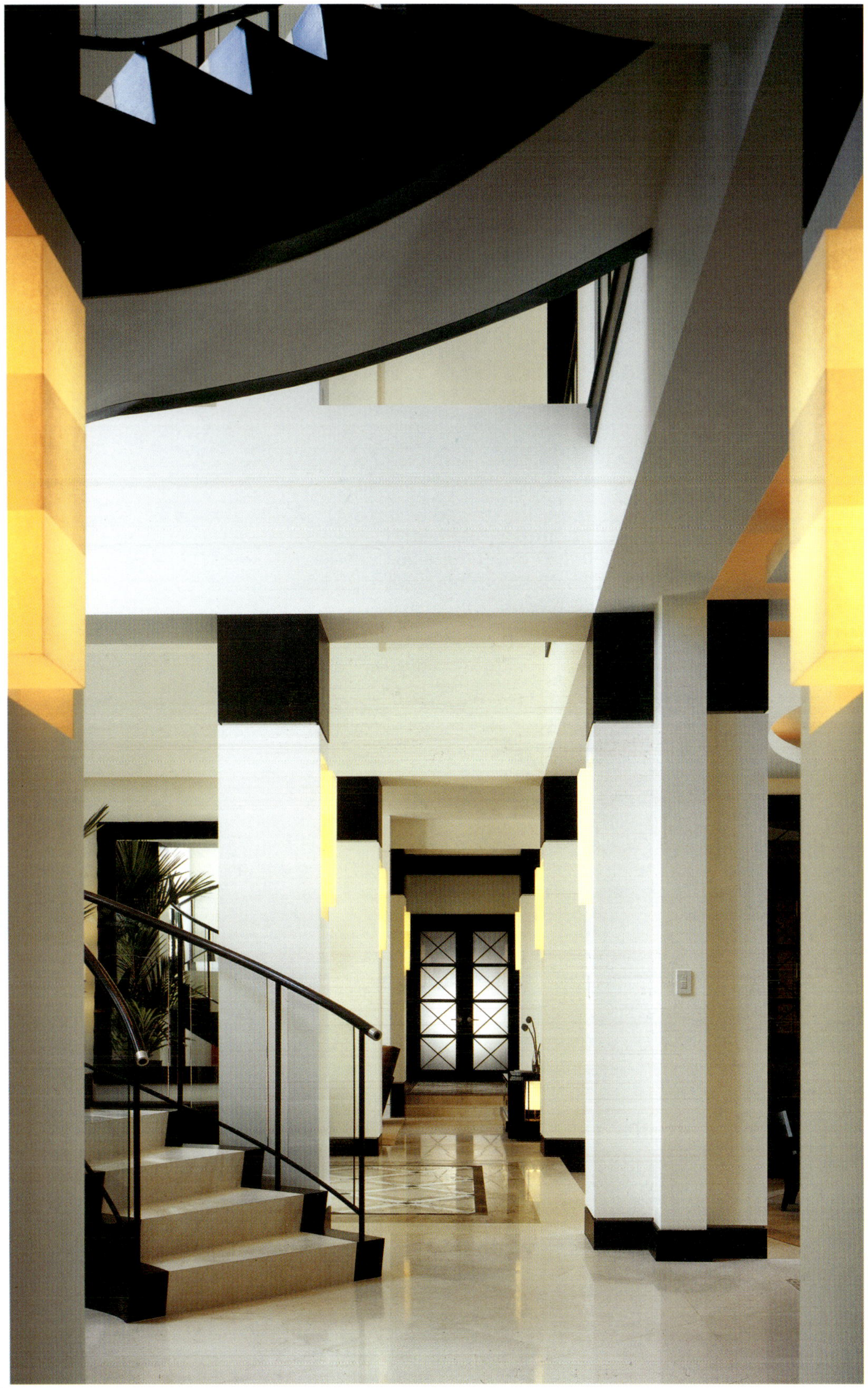

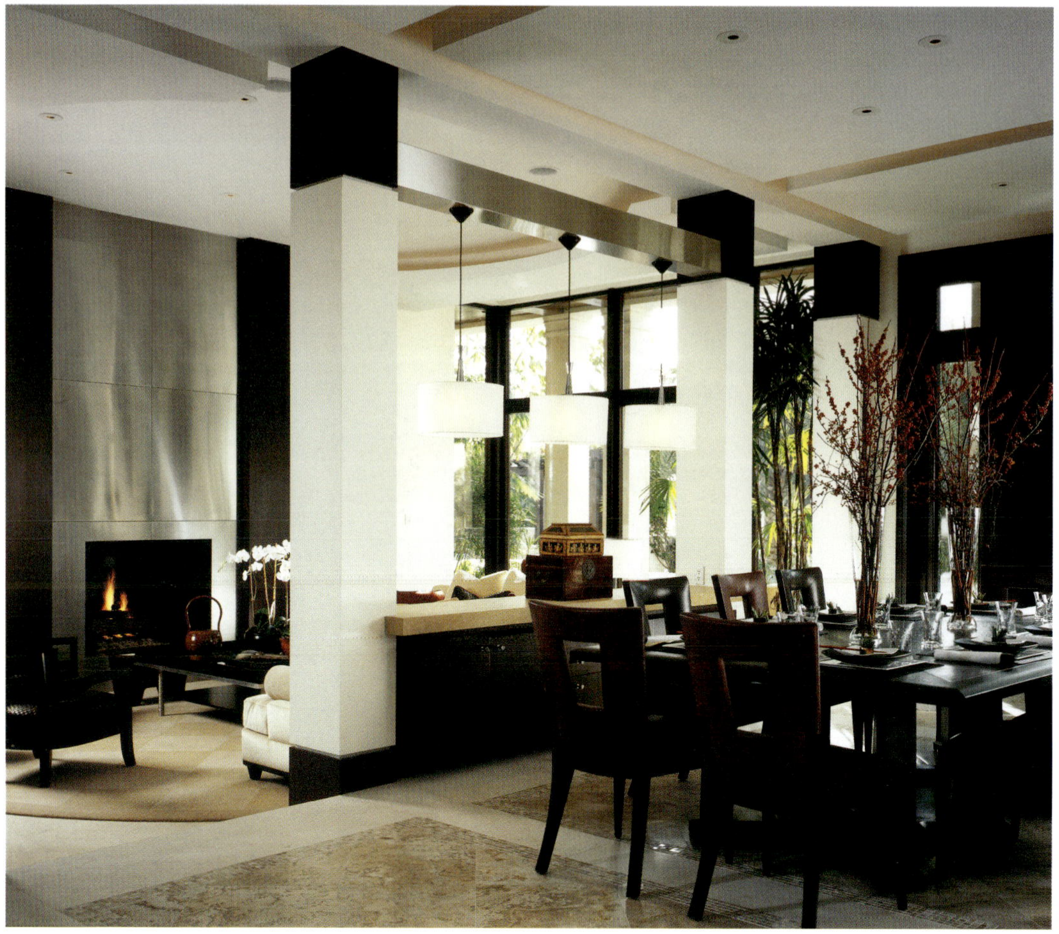

Randall describes his style as "classical tropical," noting that all details are based on classical proportions and lines. His scope of work reaches well beyond that genre to reveal influences from the most emulated, diverse styles throughout history. These styles include Palladian, Mediterranean, Craftsman, Modern and what he has termed "Old Florida Revisionist," a return to the old tin-roofed, colonial outpost look, most popular in the islands decades ago.

Throughout his professional career, Randall has designed distinctive and elegant resorts, hotels and residences for some of the world's wealthiest, most high-profile clients including celebrities,

ABOVE: The living room and dining room while delineated with pilasters, counter and level change still work spatially together and create a light-filled great energy space.
Photograph by Kim Sargent, Sargent Architectural Photography

LEFT: The contemporary Asian feel of this residence is evident in the rhythm of this gallery.
Photograph by Kim Sargent, Sargent Architectural Photography

FACING PAGE: Classic symmetrical geometry, mahogany windows, crisp limestone details and an authentic Ludowici barrel tile roof are the framework for this residence.
Photograph by Kim Sargent, Sargent Architectural Photography

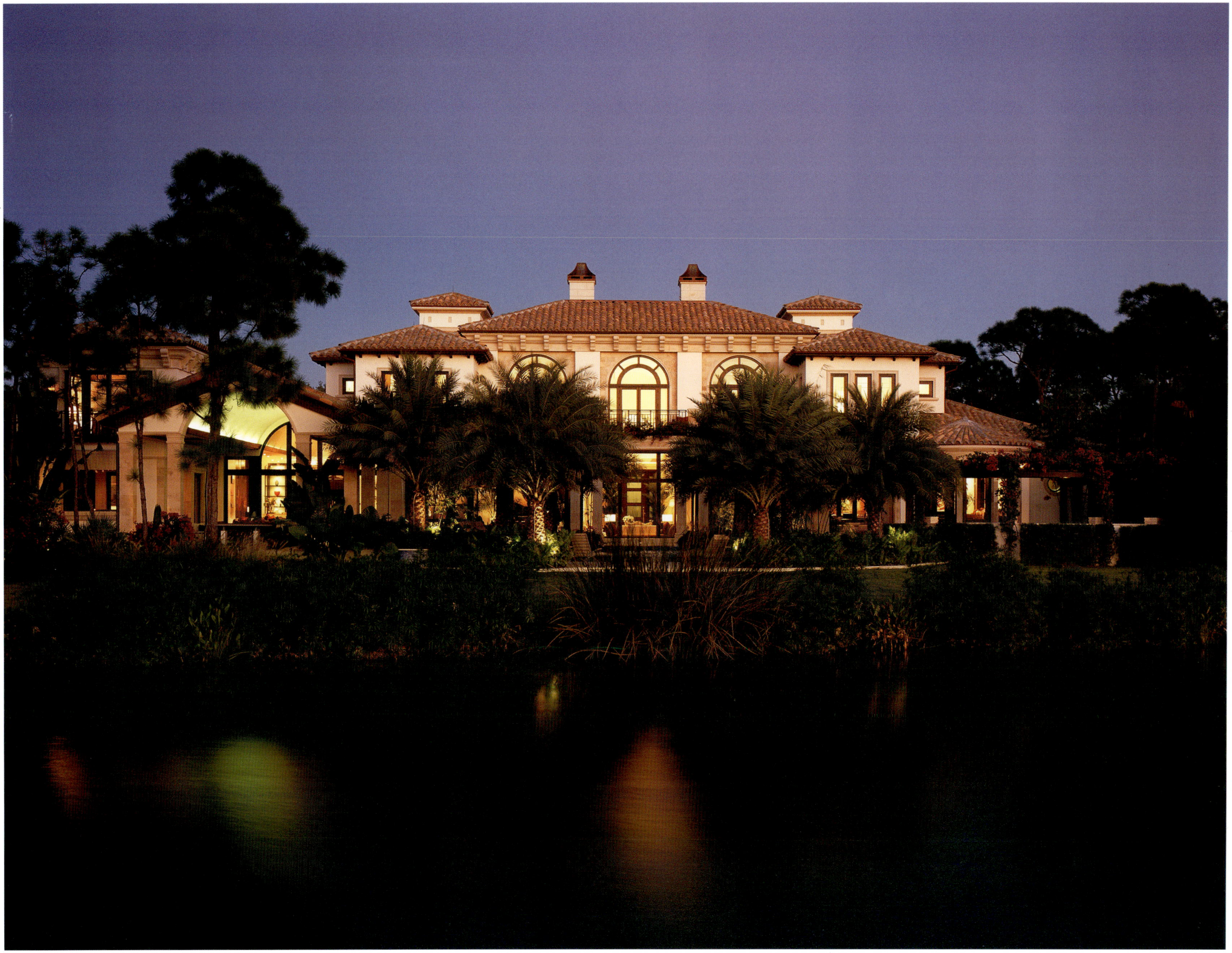

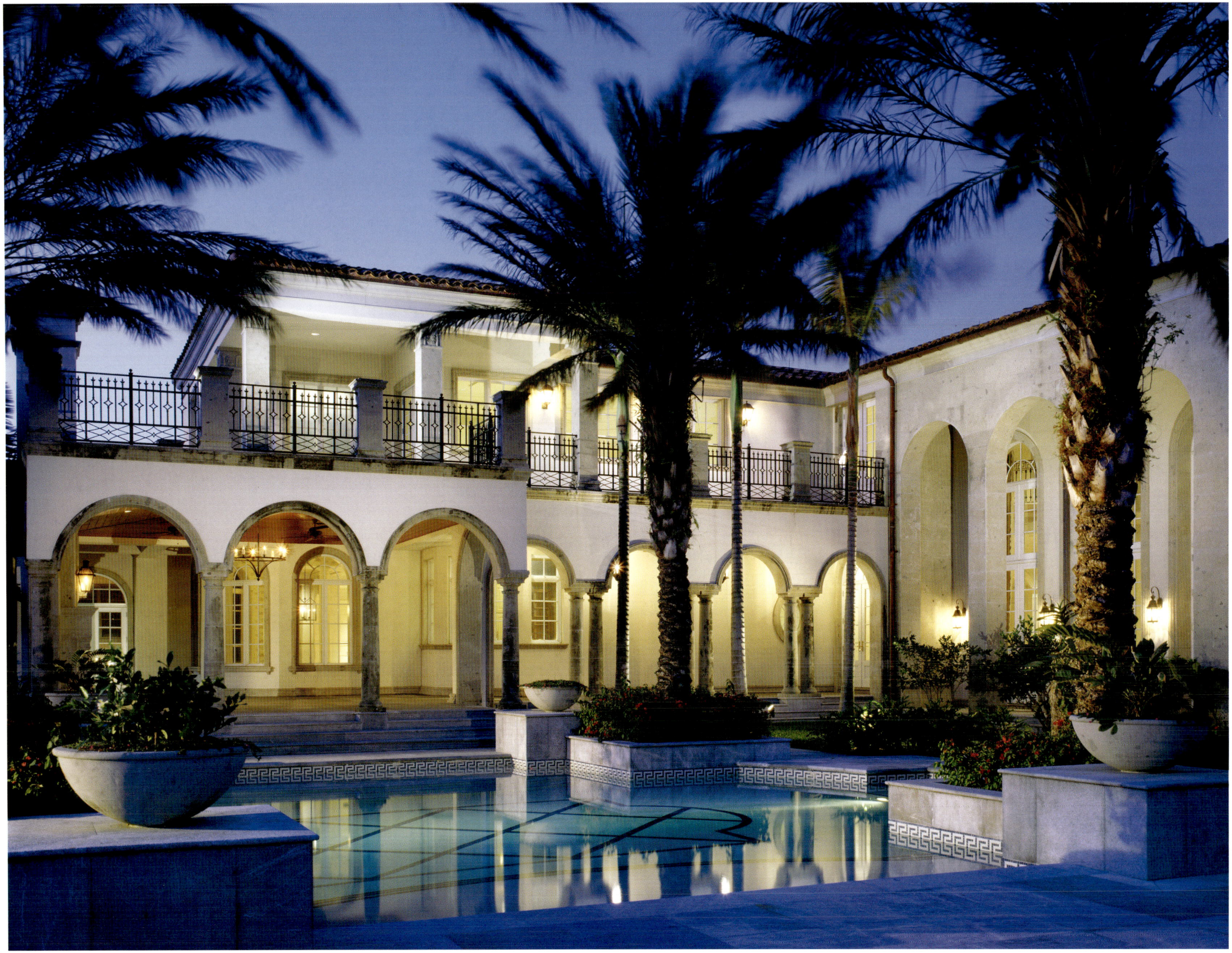

sports stars, entrepreneurs and CEOs. With an early arrival in the high-end country club communities including Boca Raton's prestigious Le Lac, Bay Colony and others, Randall helped set the bar and continues to hold a commanding presence in the architectural face of South Florida.

His homes average in the 6,000-7,000-square-foot range, though a recent "tour de force" in Manalapan encompassed design of a palatial 60,000-square-foot personal residence. Although Randall appreciates the creative freedoms allowed in designing homes of this magnitude, he has a particular fondness for smaller homes. While the majority of his designs are located in Florida, the breadth of his client base extends much further—from the western United States to the Caribbean to Eastern Europe.

Even though his tropical designs encompass a flavor indigenous to its locale, oftentimes Randall's homes are a testament to his innate ability to embrace a particular style or clients' desired feeling for their future home and create magic. In essence, Randall does not rely on the safety of one "look." In one recent residential project, the client wanted a contemporary Asian interior coupled with practicality. Randall expertly blended the two with a synthesis of classical and relaxed Asian elements that also keep the home in a careful juxtaposition with its environment. Having beautifully accommodated his clients' wishes within the home, Randall also accommodated the wishes of the community which called for its home elevations to be Mediterranean style. Although the home is of grandiose stature, the overall feeling is as intended—relaxed, warm and unimposing. "Our work is historical but not rigid," he says.

The diversity of Randall's work is extraordinary: from sensual, tropical casitas in the Bahamas to a blend of Italianate amid tropical Jamaican influences in the Dominican Republic. In one spectacular project Randall captured the essence of a charming, traditional Connecticut estate reinterpreting it into a sprawling oceanfront Jupiter compound replete with shutters, brackets and clapboard.

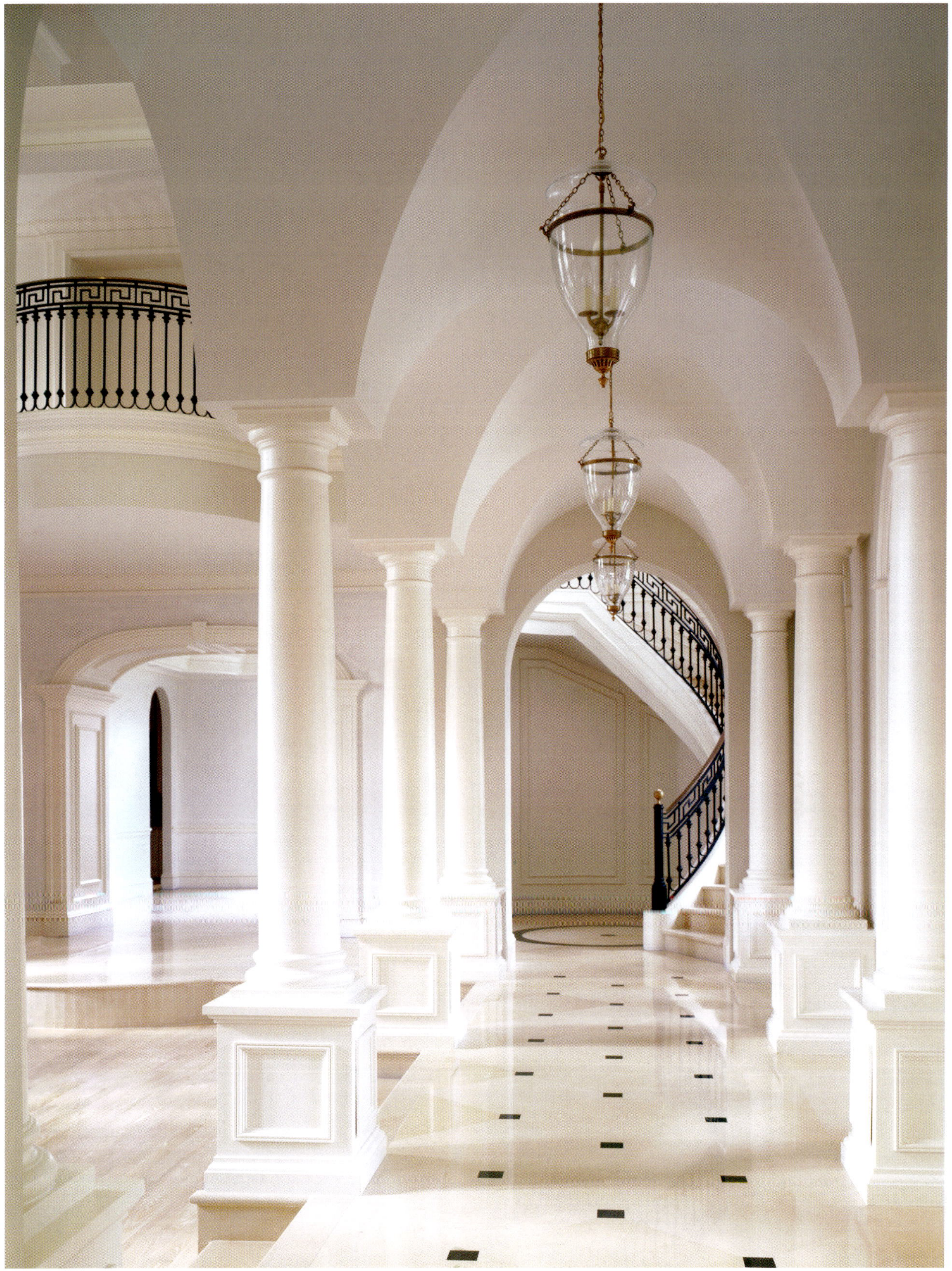

RIGHT: This clean groin vaulted gallery is terminated by the simple classic staircase.
Photograph by Troy Campbell, Troy Campbell Photography

FACING PAGE: The rhythm of the loggia set against the classic pool form a wonderful outdoor environment.
Photograph by Troy Campbell, Troy Campbell Photography

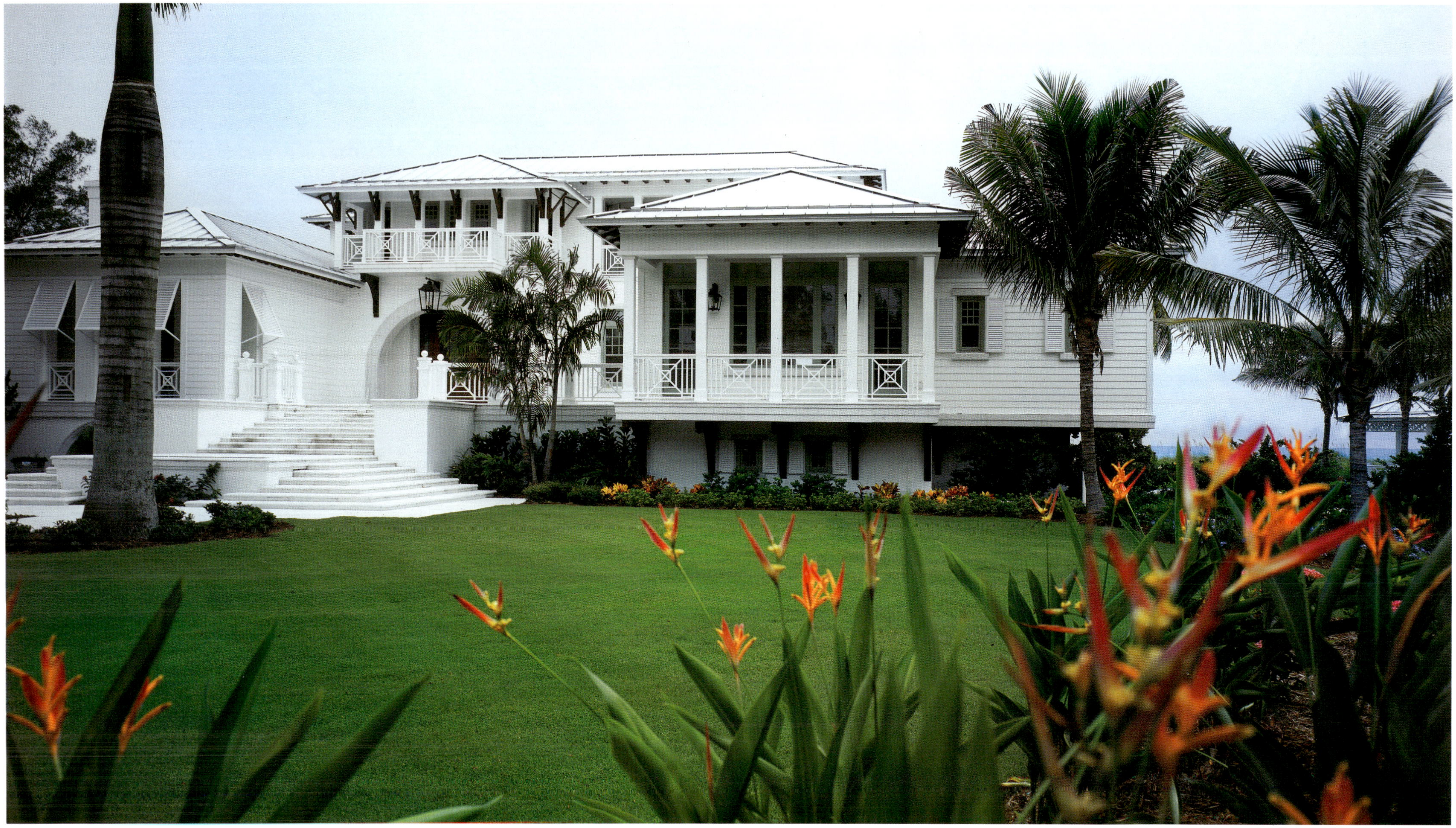

In another home, a client wanted a Beaux Arts influence so Randall placed large areas of glass behind exterior pilasters to keep the Beaux Arts façade and proportions, yet skillfully took advantage of the spectacular ocean views through the glass reaches. Before he even embarked on the design, he did his homework thoroughly, as he always does. He traveled to St. Louis, known for its imposing Beaux-Arts-style homes, built at the time of the 1908 World's Fair, near the city's Frederick Law Olmsted designed park.

In yet another very tropical home on Florida's Captiva Island, Randall used cantilevered balconies to let the home "hover" above the dune. "You feel like you are in a boat in paradise," he explains.

There are still countless other homes that reflect his creative eye and architectural skill. He's learned from the past and adds his own larger-than-life imagination. While infusing what he sees around him through his frequent travels, he delves deep to fulfill his clients' needs, always considering the idiosyncrasies of the site, always blending the indoors with the outdoors, including its views, light or climate—or all of the above.

Passion for the craft will always remain the catalyst that drives him and will forever be reflected in his work. Randall's work has appeared regularly in magazines, books and articles, including *Florida Architecture, Florida Design* and *Architectural Digest.*

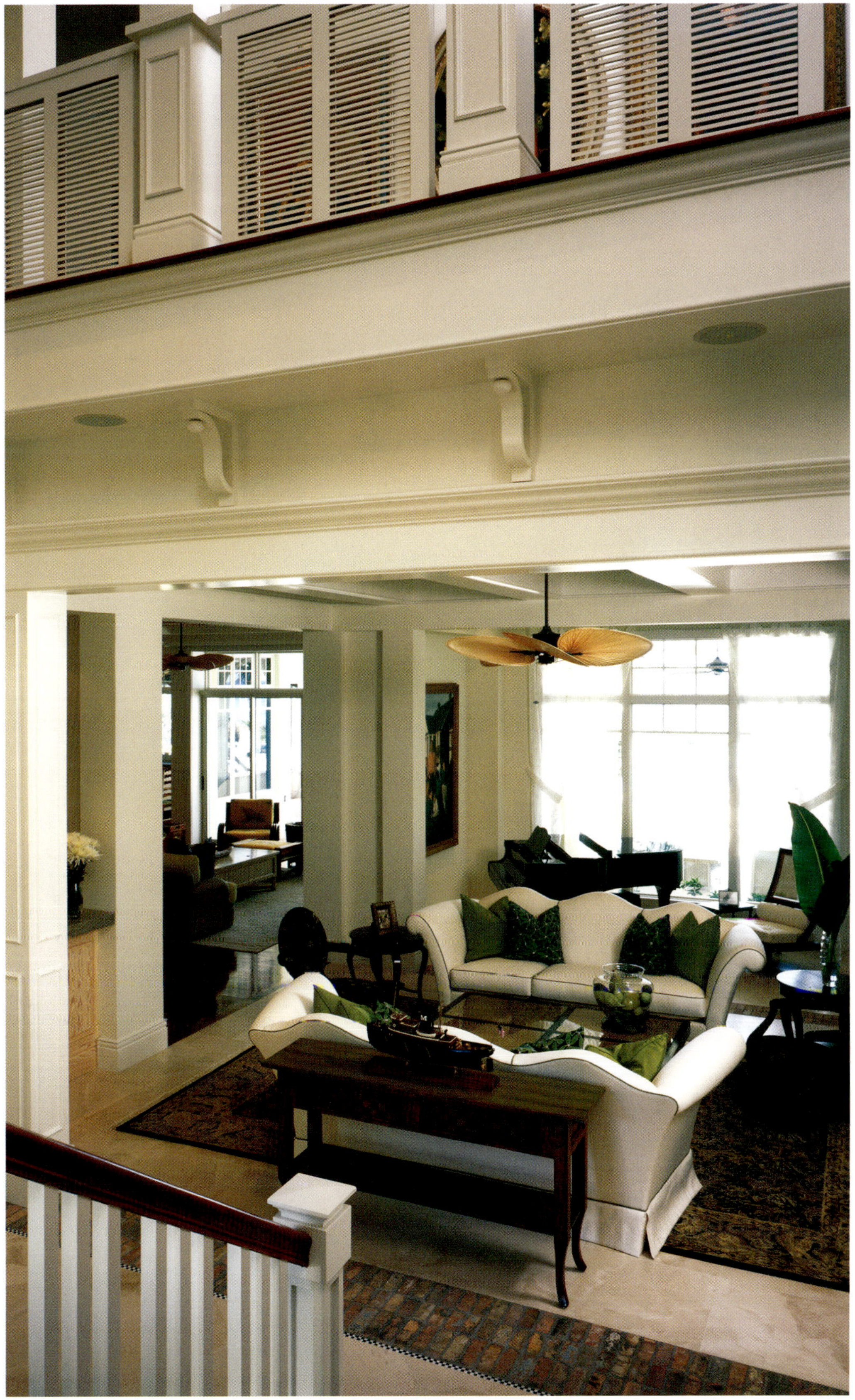

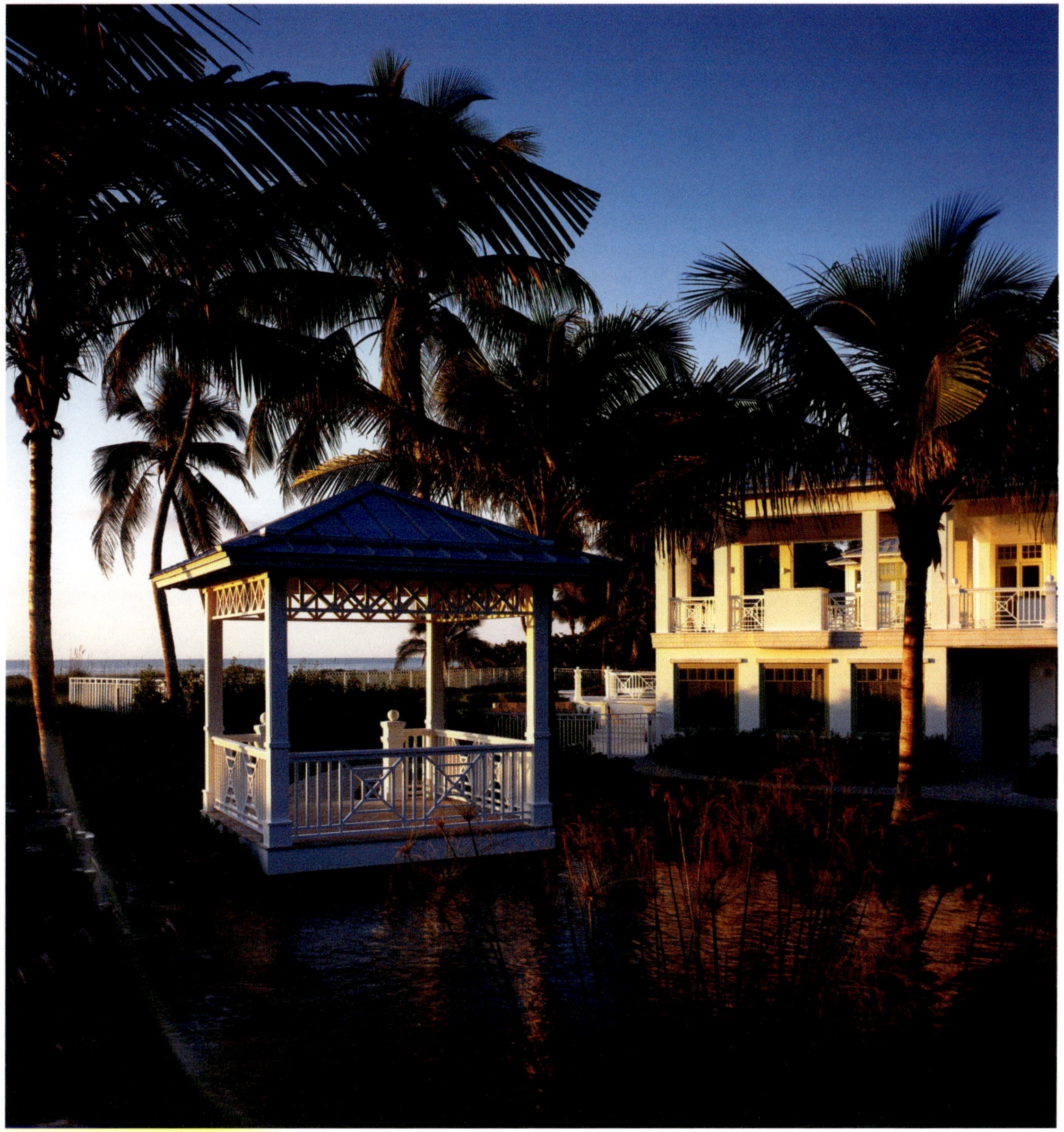

ABOVE: The "floating" pavilion creates a great escape from the main house and forms a nice framework to the ocean view from the back property and guesthouse.
Photograph by Hamilton Photography

LEFT: This entry foyer and staircase features a view through the parlor and family room. These kinds of interior vistas and views to the ocean are prevalent in Stofft's work.
Photograph by Carmel Brantley, Brantley Photography

FACING PAGE: This tropical Caribbean influenced residence appears to "hover" over the dune due to extensive bracketed cantilevers.
Photograph by Carmel Brantley, Brantley Photography

RANDALL E. STOFFT ARCHITECTS PA

Randall Stofft

42 North Swinton Avenue

Delray Beach, FL 33444

561.243.0799

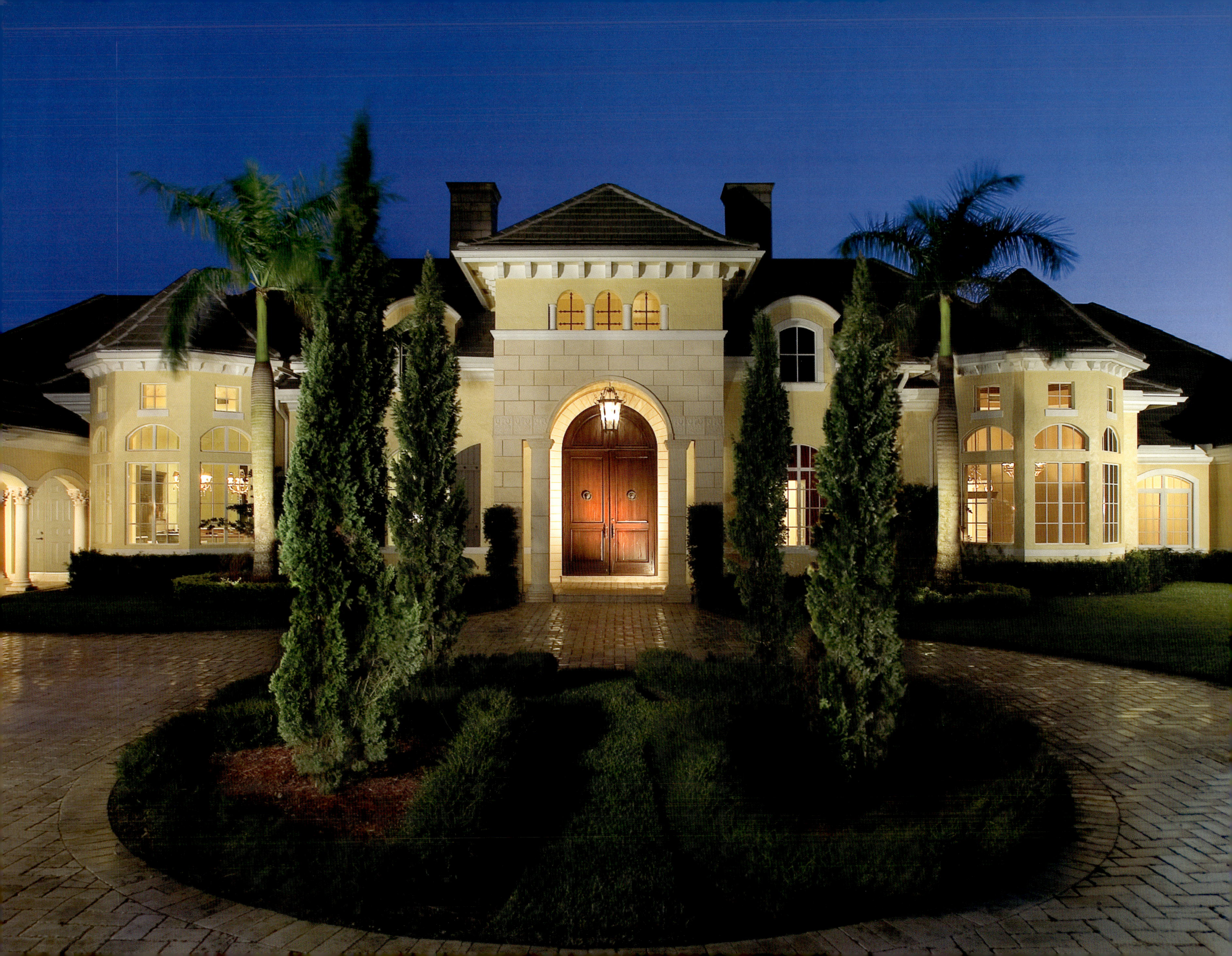

KELLY YATES & DENNIS RAINHO

Yates Rainho Architects, Inc.

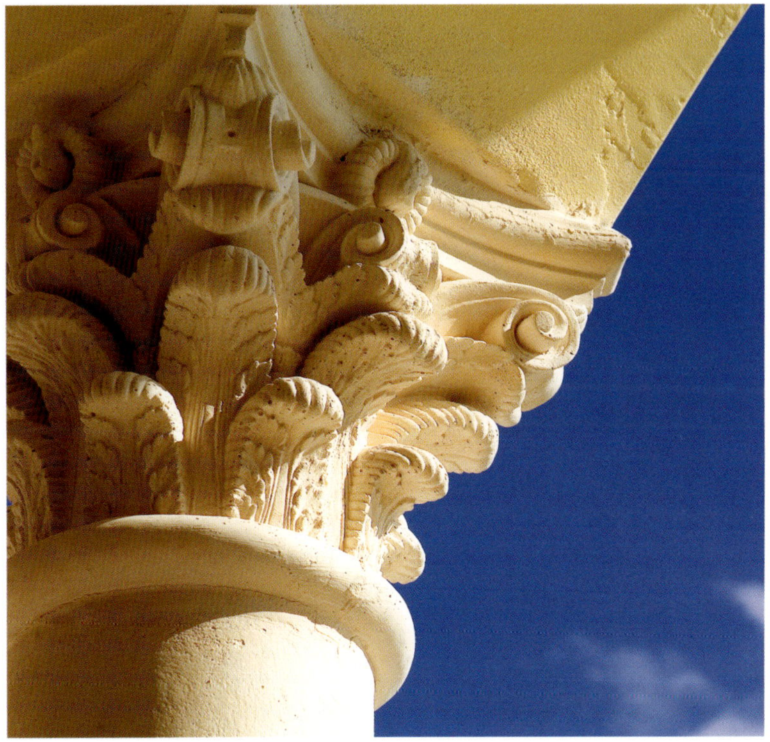

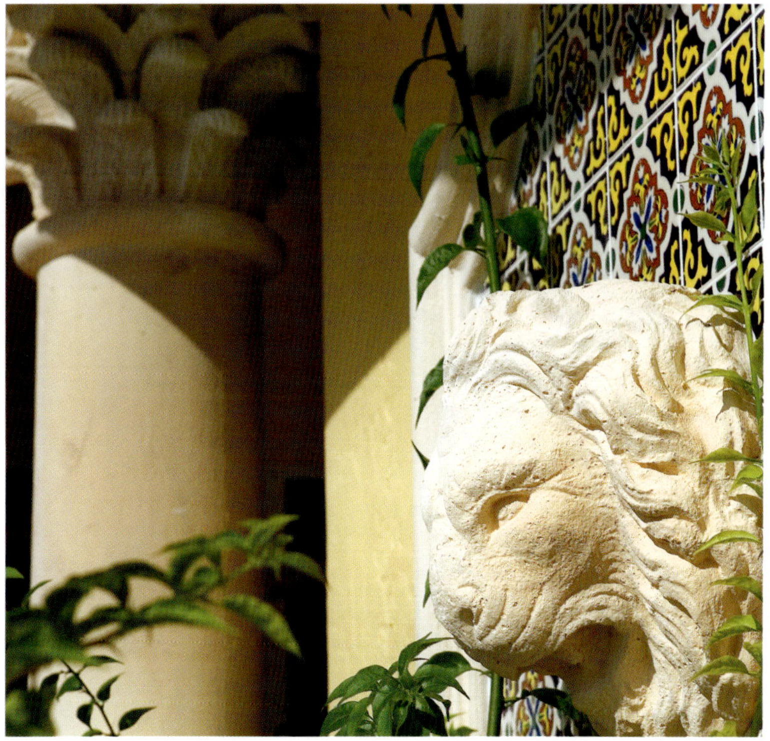

ABOVE LEFT: The use of design elements such as Corinthian columns defines the elegance of Classical Mediterranean style.
Photograph by Daniel Newcomb

ABOVE RIGHT: Incorporating numerous Old World elements allow for the embellishment of the exterior facades. Here, the combination of a lion's head and floral mosaics express a Spanish Mediterranean vernacular.
Photograph by Daniel Newcomb

LEFT: Designed with balance, the architectural vernacular of French-Mediterranean is reflected with dormers, roof pitch and a sculptured formal entry.
Photograph by Daniel Newcomb

Dennis Rainho, a native of Portugal educated in New York and Florida and Kelly Yates, Texas native who arrived in Florida in 1987, have been working together successfully for over 14 years. Their combined talent makes up Yates Rainho Architects, Inc.

Dennis' strength is in project management and design while Kelly is extremely knowledgeable with construction, site planning and project design; each plays off and complements the other's abilities and focuses on his own particular strengths. Since the duo began working together in 1992, South Florida has gone through a lucrative real estate boom. "During the recent growth in land development, Kelly and I have enjoyed a diversity of projects which allow us to strengthen our talents and challenge our design capabilities while always keeping up with the technology of today," remarked Dennis Rainho.

Dennis and Kelly characterize their specialty as luxury custom architecture; the majority of their work is comprised of residential projects while the remaining projects are commercial, such as executive offices and restaurants. Theirs is a boutique firm that over the past three years has received the prestigious PRISM award and been honored with at least a dozen awards from industry-related organizations, including the Gold Coast Builders

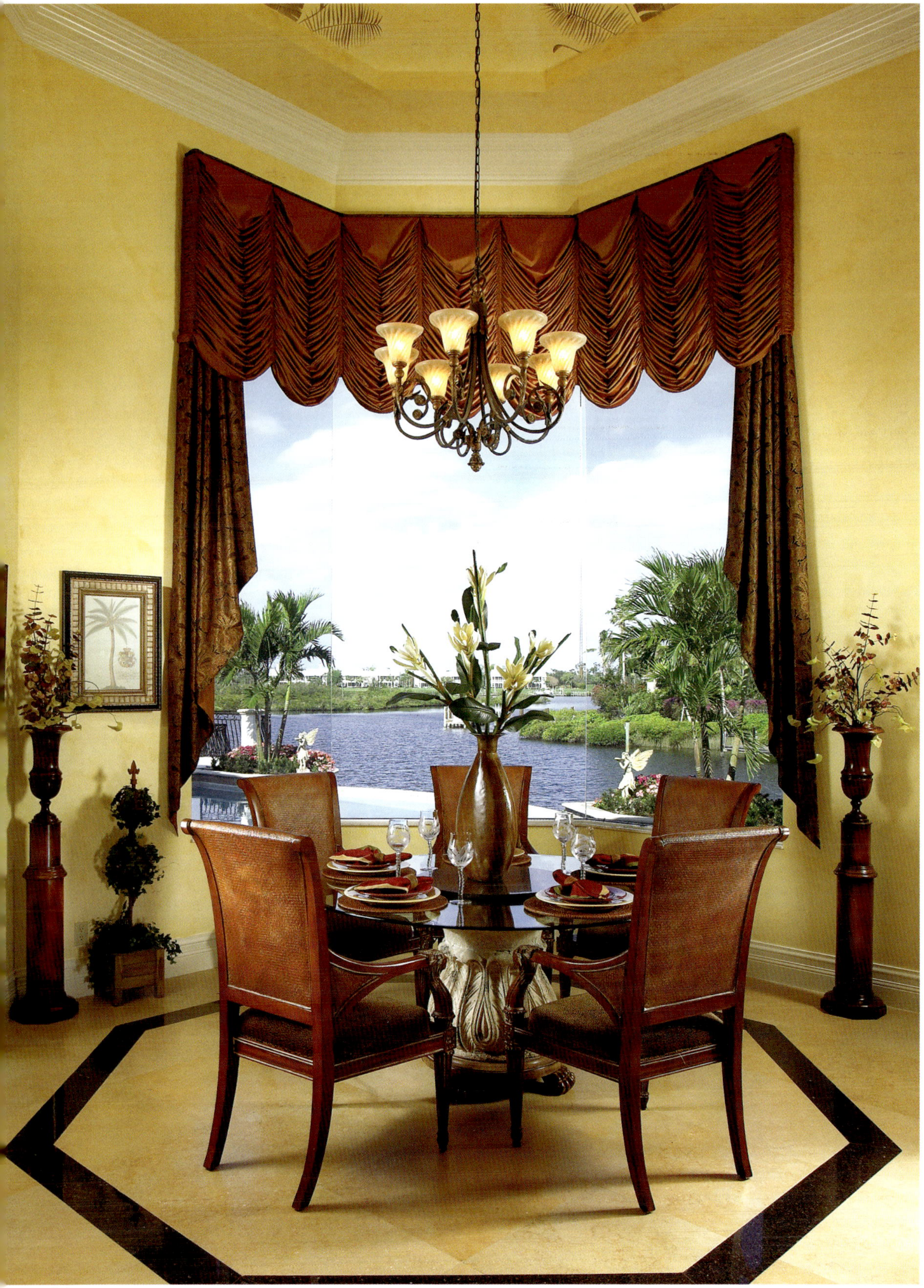

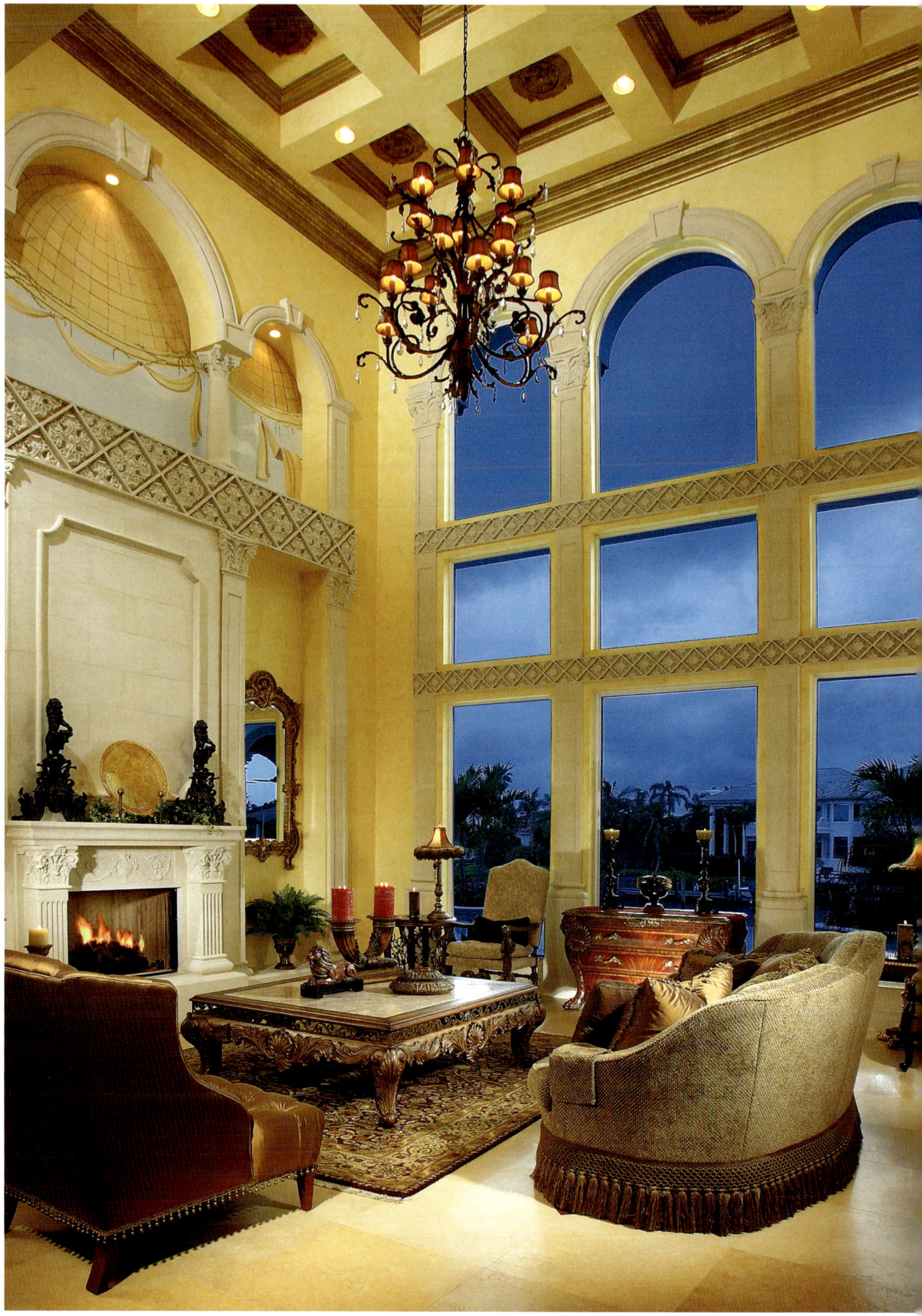

Association. Dennis and Kelly are members of the National Association of Home Builders and the local chapter Gold Coast Builders Association.

Putting awards aside, Dennis and Kelly take great pride in giving their clients the one-on-one time they are entitled to. After getting familiar with the needs, desires and dreams of the client, they work together through the entire project.

Dennis compares a business partnership to a marriage, "If the chemistry isn't just right, it is doomed from the beginning."

Yates Rainho Architects focuses on interior flow from space to space and they believe exteriors should match the gracefulness of their interiors. It is a continuous proportionality that "just makes sense." One naturally occurring element the firm capitalizes on is the abundant Florida sunshine. Their homes invite the warm sunlight, with spaces designed to play off and play up that light. Their talent is evident in

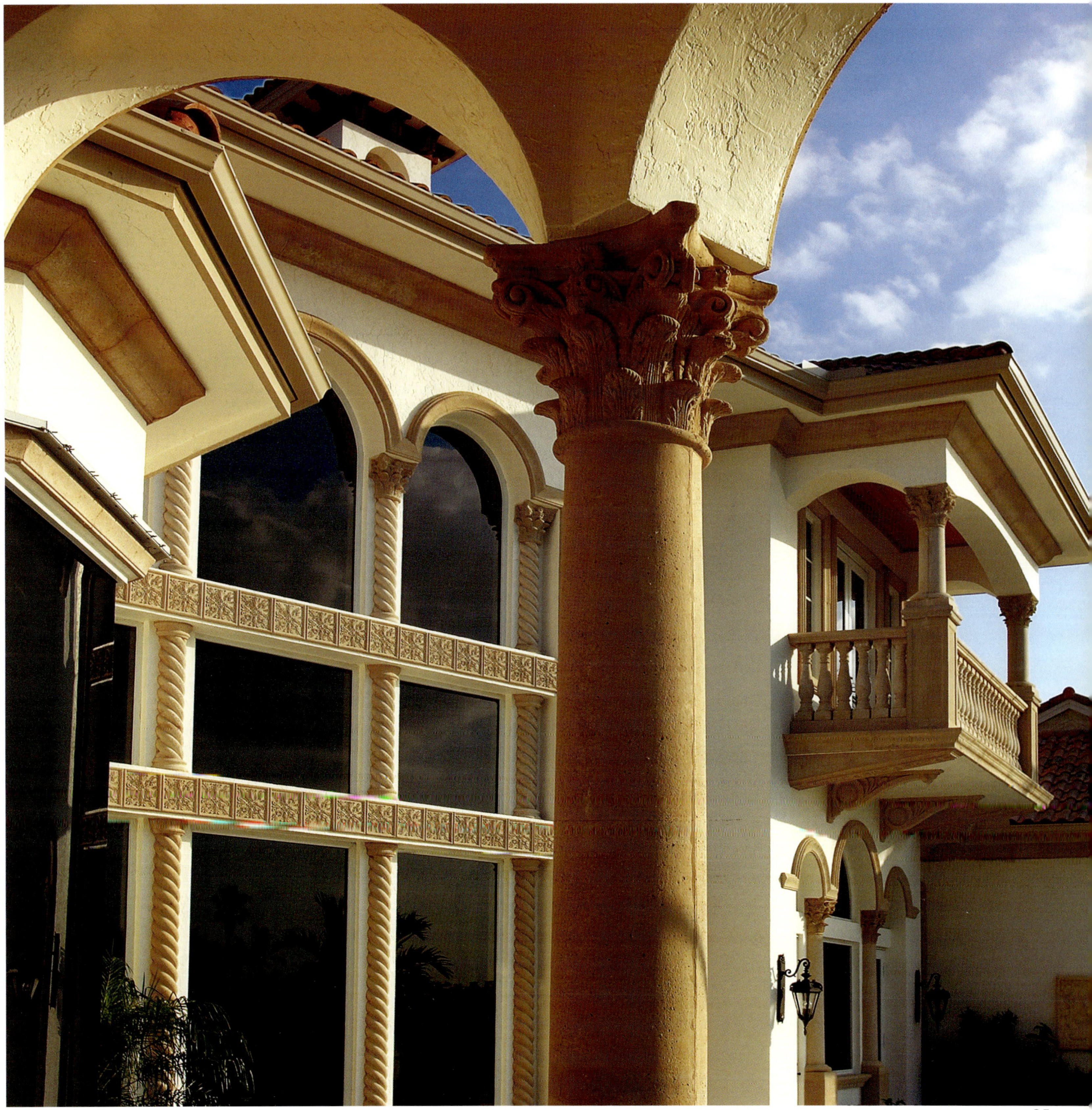

RIGHT: Both classical and playful, the architectural ingenuity of combining elements adds aesthetic and visual dimension. The juxtaposition of rustic and contemporary elements adds vitality to a façade.
Photograph by Daniel Newcomb

FACING PAGE LEFT: Boundaries are blurred between the indoor and outdoor spaces through the use of fenestration. Vistas are extended beyond the living space.
Photograph by Daniel Newcomb

FACING PAGE RIGHT: Accentuating spatial volume, sculpted windows and the abundance of light announce the grandeur of a formal living room.
Photograph by Daniel Newcomb

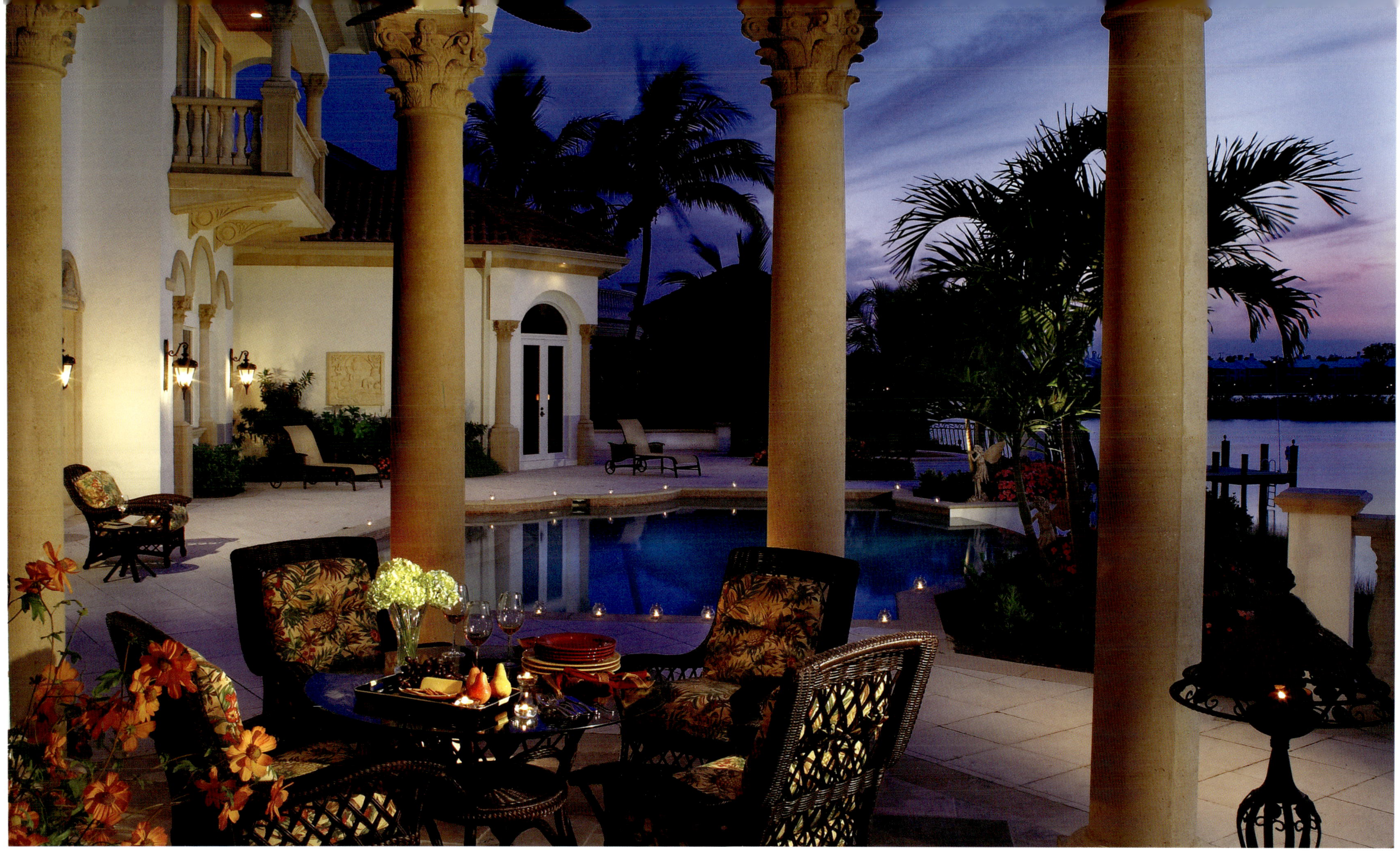

the methods and designs which meet and exceed the building code requirements. Old-fashioned in their approach, they sketch their designs by hand because they are still "soft" designs made to be improved and changed. Once perfected, the designs move onto CAD for efficiency.

Because they do custom work, their goal is to make sure clients get what they are looking for, whether it is Mizner-style, French provincial or Mediterranean/Spanish. Also included among their repertoire are British-Colonial and Key West style projects. The key message is not that they are not trying to label themselves as specialist in any one style, but that the eclectic diversity of their talent enables Yates Rainho Architects to satisfy every palette.

Their full-service office also assists in easing the process for their clients by coordinating consultant services including interior design, electrical, landscaping and mechanical design. They work with a select group of contractors whom they have come to trust and admire for their high quality of work. Accessibility also sets them apart from other firms—a client can always get Dennis or Kelly on the phone personally.

For the principals of Yates Rainho Architects, service does not end the day the job is completed—it continues even after their clients move in. They understand their clients have full lives and work within those busy schedules to achieve the same spectacular result every time.

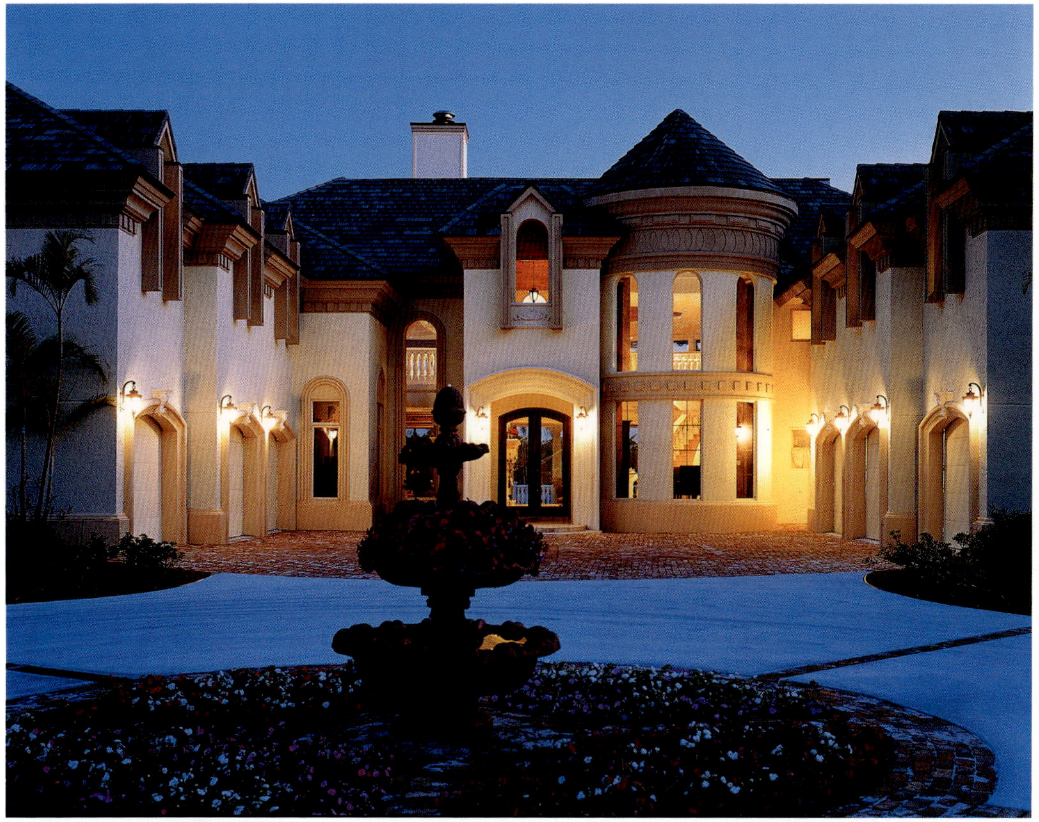

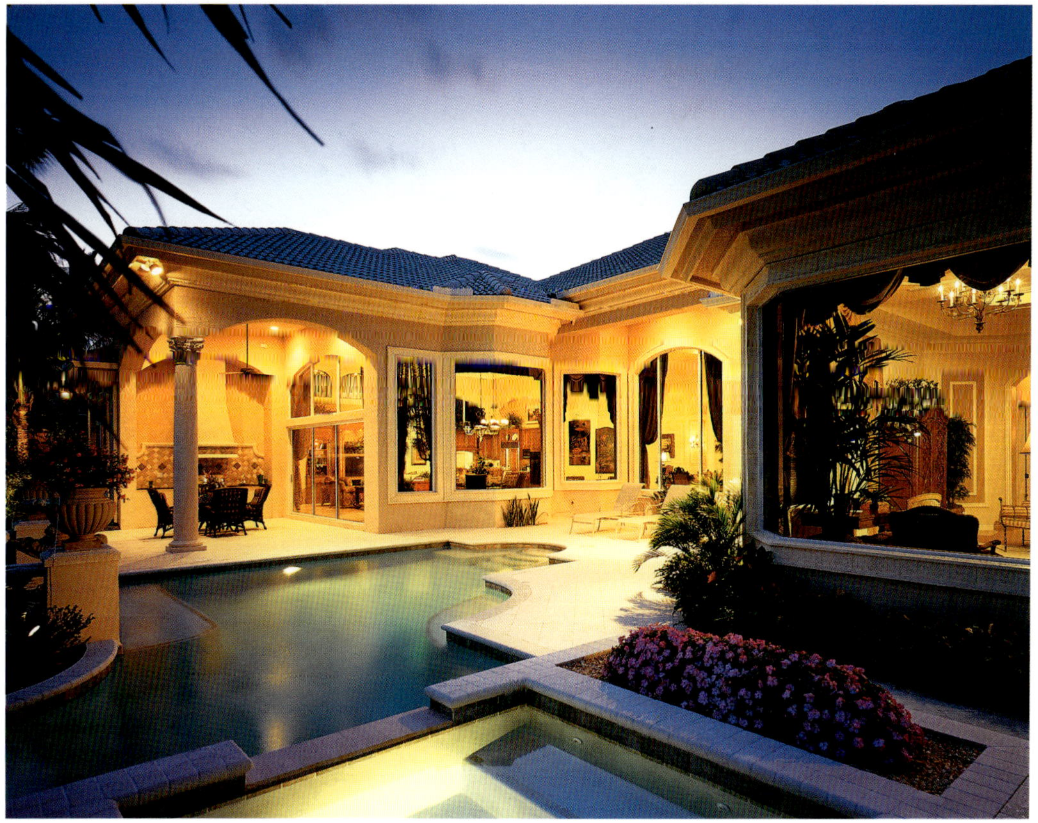

Q&A

more about kelly & dennis...

WHAT IS THE BEST PART OF BEING AN ARCHITECT?

The emotional process of seeing an idea transform to a physical reality, while experiencing the most tangible process of that transformation: the groundwork to final building construction.

WHAT IS THE HIGHEST COMPLIMENT YOU'VE RECEIVED PROFESSIONALLY?

Being recognized by our peers through the GCBA Prism awards for the past three years. We also relish the complimentary words of our clients and friends regarding the quality of our work.

WHO HAS HAD THE BIGGEST INFLUENCE ON YOUR CAREER?

There have been so many it is hard to name just one. Our favorite architects that have influenced our style would be Addison Mizner, Maurice Fatio, Marion Simms Wyeth, Le Corbusier and Richard Meier.

WHAT IS ONE PHILOSOPHY YOU HAVE STUCK WITH FOR YEARS THAT STILL WORKS FOR YOU TODAY?

The one philosophy that still guides us today is that of personal service. Styles change over the years, but our personal service will not.

YATES RAINHO ARCHITECTS INC.
Kelly Yates
Dennis Rainho
5707 South Dixie Highway, Suite 8
West Palm Beach, FL 33405
561.493.1500
Fax 561.493.1560
www.yra-design.com

TOP: Sculpted roof lines, circular elements and punctuated windows create a gracious Neo-French Classical estate elevation.
Photograph by Michael Forester

BOTTOM: Boundaries are erased when exterior and interior space form a harmonious living environment.
Photograph by Brantley Photography

FACING PAGE: Defined by a gently arched colonnade of cast columns which form a perimeter, outdoor living interacts with nature.
Photograph by Daniel Newcomb

Max Strang, photo by Claudia Uribe Touri

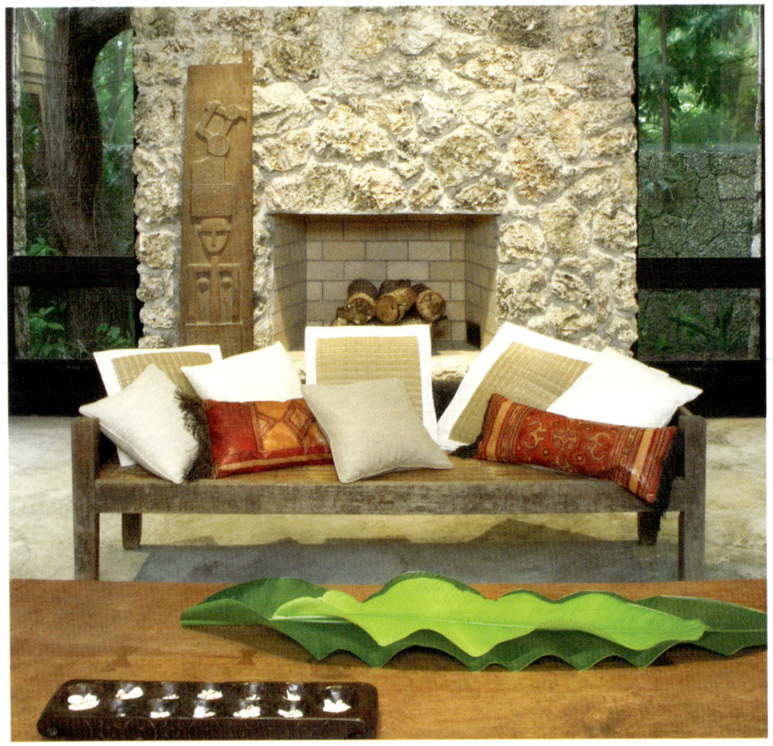

Ramon Pacheco, photo by George Cott

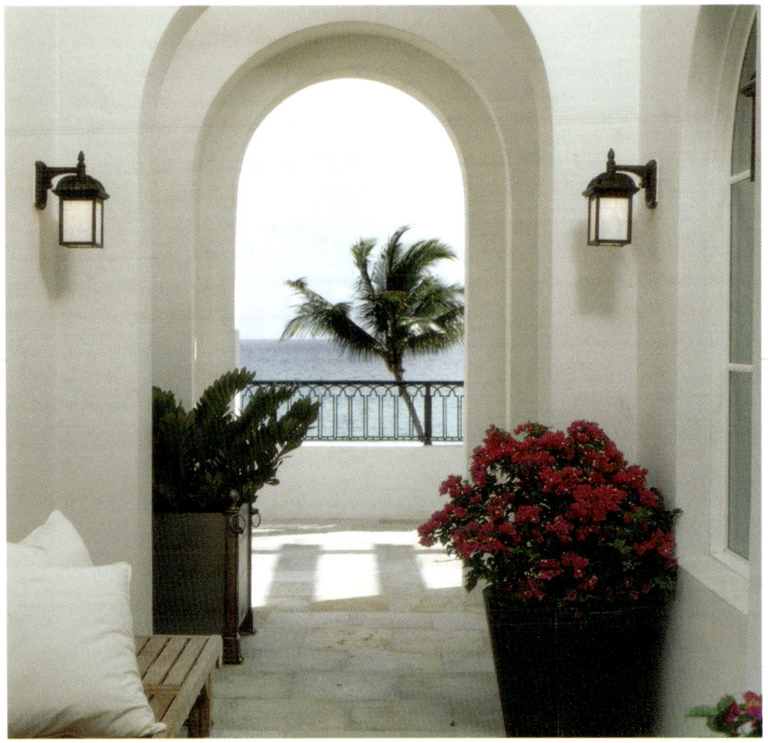

Roney Mateu, photo by Troy Campbell

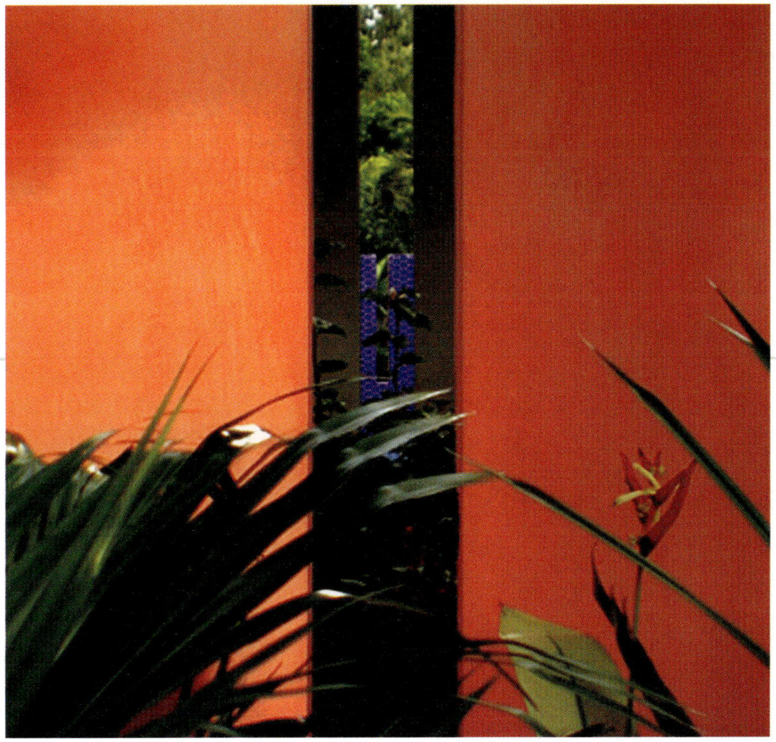

CHAPTER TWO

MIAMI-DADE

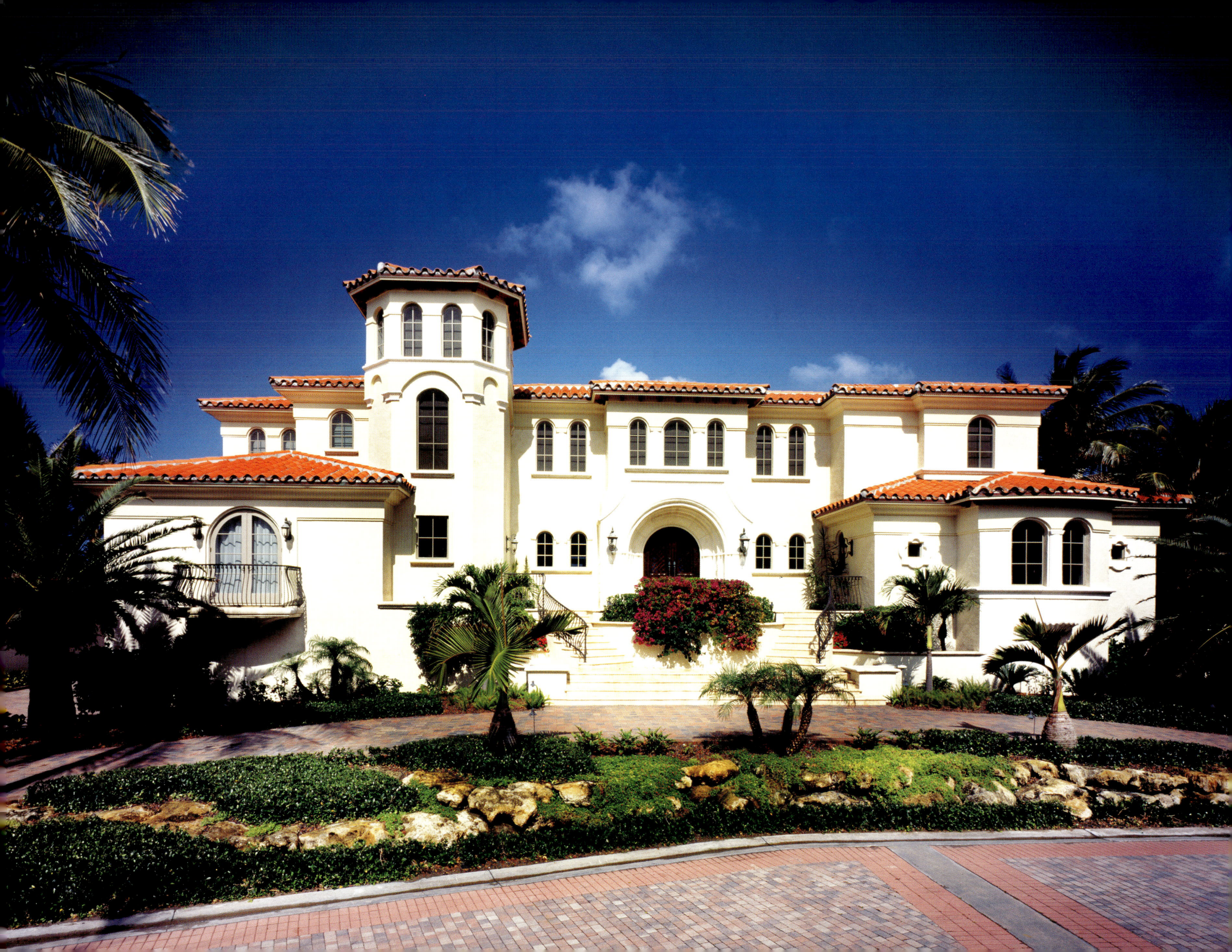

MANUEL ANGLES

Angles Architect, LLC

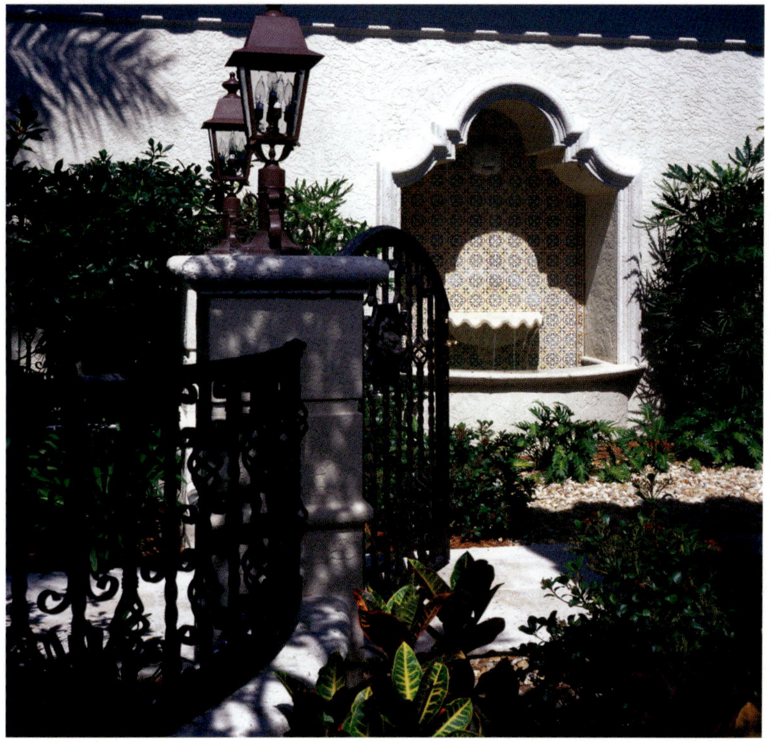

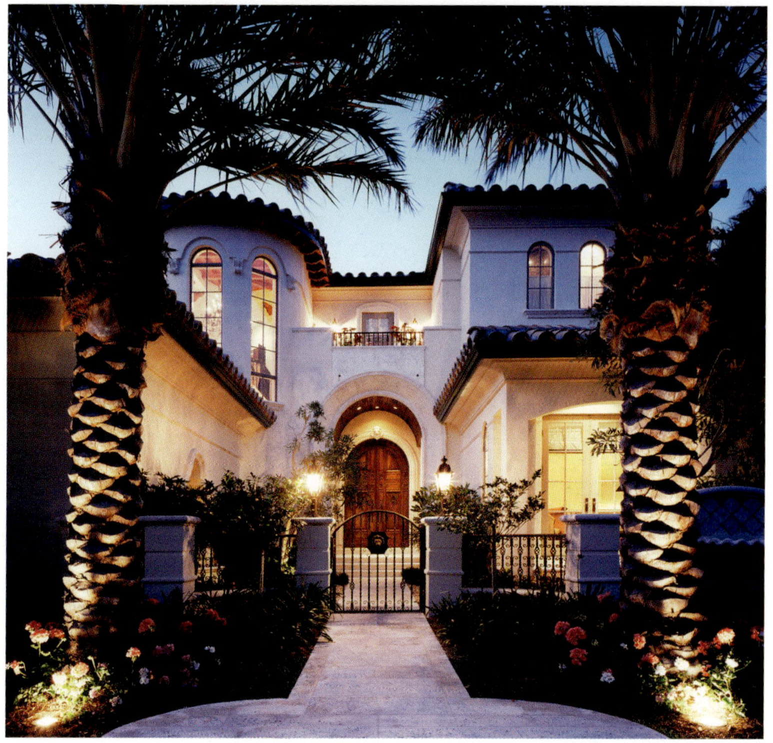

The day 10th grader Manuel Angles walked into the architectural firm nearest to his high school, little did he know his life had forever changed. He hoped that he might secure a job as an office boy, gaining exposure to the architectural business, but instead he was immediately immersed into a model shop where he learned the miniature basics of architectural design. Later he would find this fated opportunity was in fact a true blessing in disguise.

While working towards a degree in architecture at the University of Miami, Manuel started a freelance business that allowed him to work with different architectural firms on many amazing and diverse projects, including both commercial and residential. The experience proved invaluable and he received his bachelor of architecture degree in 1978.

Having worked in the commercial field on both private and governmental projects, Manuel quickly found he liked working with residential clients more than commercial. He then focused on designing residential homes exclusively. Slowly, he built a business out of designing high-end private homes doing both the architectural and interior designs.

ABOVE LEFT: An entry courtyard serves as a transitional space. It foretells of the commencement of tranquility and refuge.
Photograph by Robert Stein Studios

ABOVE RIGHT: The major design factor for this home was to incorporate views from every angle. The home features views of a harbor at the rear, rolling greens of a golf course at the front and vistas even from the stairs.
Photograph by Robert Stein Studios

LEFT: This home is sited to overlook the Atlantic Ocean and was inspired by the great villas of the early 1920s in West Palm Beach.
Photograph by Robert Stein Studios

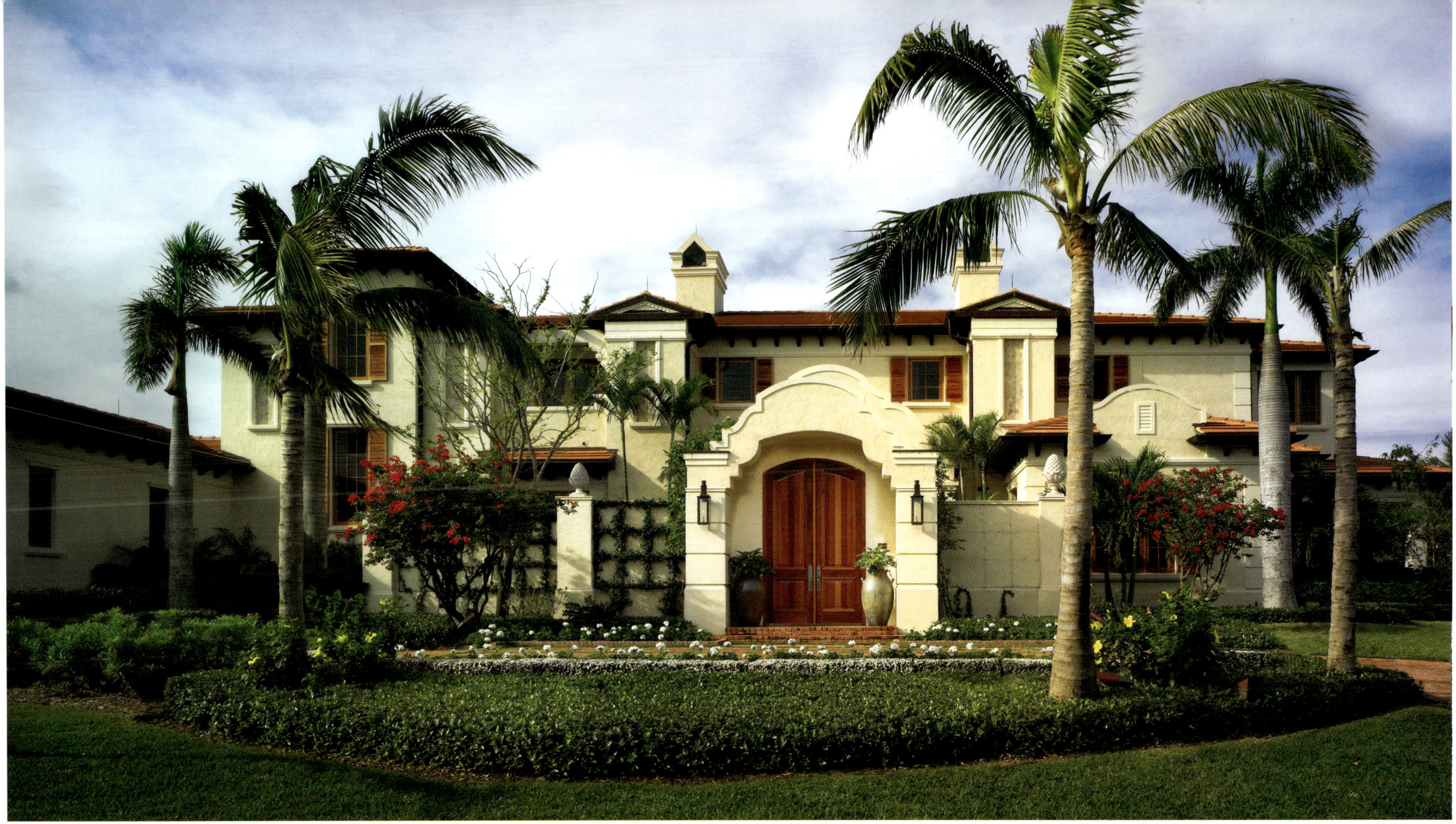

The manner in which the homeowner lives and in what capacities their home functions is critical for Manuel when approaching a design for a client's new home. He says that he doesn't care for fads in architecture because before too long they date a structure, which is why a sense of timelessness is crucial for each of his designs. He believes this timelessness keeps a home's value economically viable, while fads tend to devalue a home over time.

Eero Saarinen, the architect who designed the TWA Terminal #5 at JFK Airport and the Gateway Arch in St. Louis, Missouri, was known for his diversified design solutions to architectural problems. Like Eero Saarinen, Manuel believes that personal style shouldn't be forced, that style should lie within the parameters of the client's needs without compromising "your own architectural beliefs."

Visiting all of his job sites on a weekly basis is one of the ways that Manuel keeps a close hands-on approach to his projects. He says that every one of his projects are based upon an integrated design and that nothing is left to chance.

As projects progress, he walks clients through the whole process, much like an architectural shepherd and in the end there are not any surprises. "The best compliment paid to me was when I was walking through a house with the owner, upon its completion. The homeowner looked at me and said 'You know what? There are no surprises. It looks exactly the way I expected it to.' I was pleased because I felt the same way."

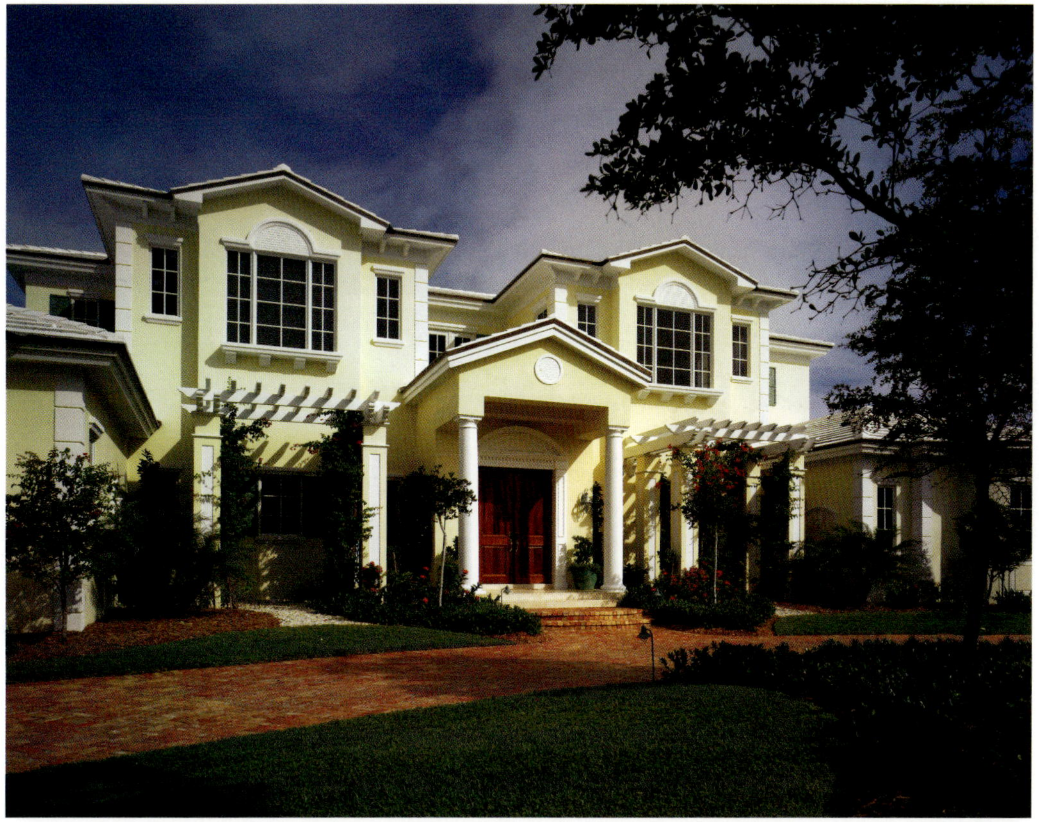

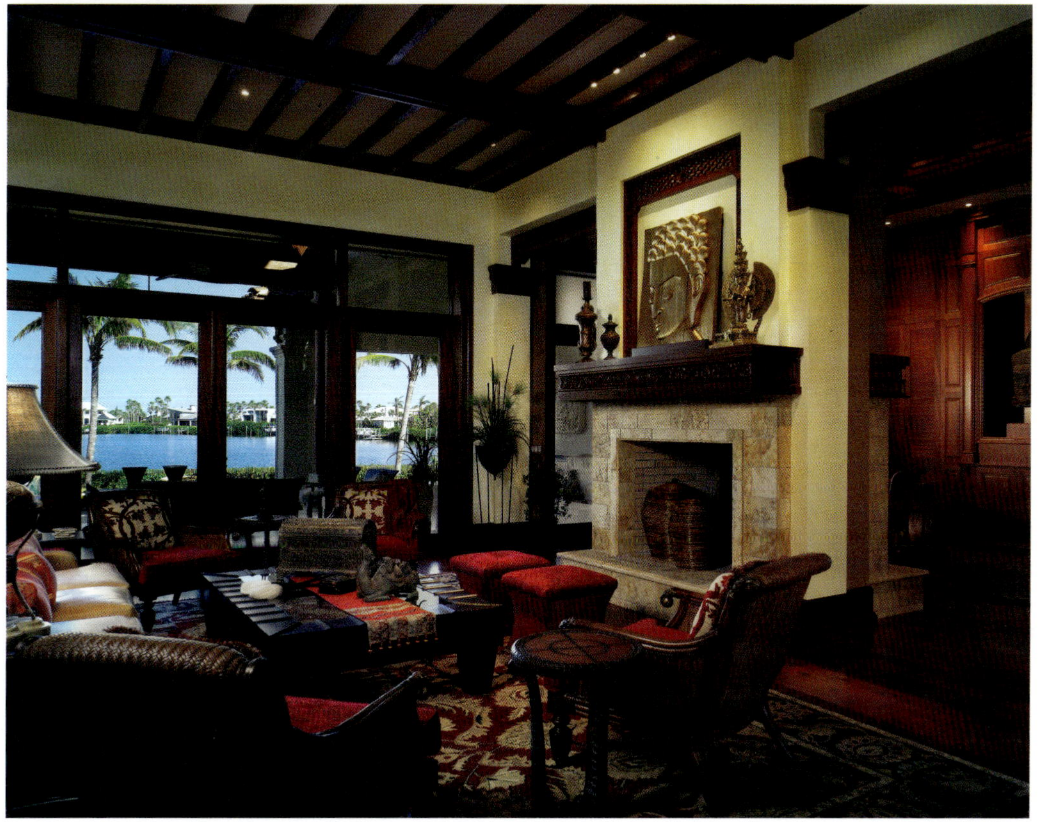

more about manuel...

Q&A

IF YOU COULD ELIMINATE ONE ARCHITECTURAL STYLE FROM THE WORLD, WOULD YOU?

I would not; each preceding style, technique or design has had an influence on successive design movements. We always learn more from the past failures than triumphs.

WHAT IS YOUR FAVORITE COLOR AND WHY?

Blue, because it reminds me of the sky and ocean.

NAME ONE THING MOST PEOPLE DON'T KNOW ABOUT YOU.

I'm moody.

WHAT IS THE BEST PART OF BEING AN ARCHITECT?

The creative processes and interacting with talented people.

ANGLES ARCHITECT, LLC
Manuel Angles, NCARB, AIA
3148 Southeast Gran Parkway
Stuart, FL 34997
772.221.0297
Fax 772.221.0299

TOP: Classicism with tropical island flair. Classical and traditional elements were the client's requirements while maintaining a casual ambiance.
Photograph by Robert Stein Studios

BOTTOM: My client's extensive collection of Thai and Balinese art influenced the interior architectural details and extensive use of stone and wood carvings.
Photograph by Robert Stein Studios

FACING PAGE: Inspired by homes in the West Indies, this home overlooks the St. Lucie Inlet. Once you enter the courtyard, every room has a view of the inlet and nature preserve.
Photograph by Robert Stein Studios

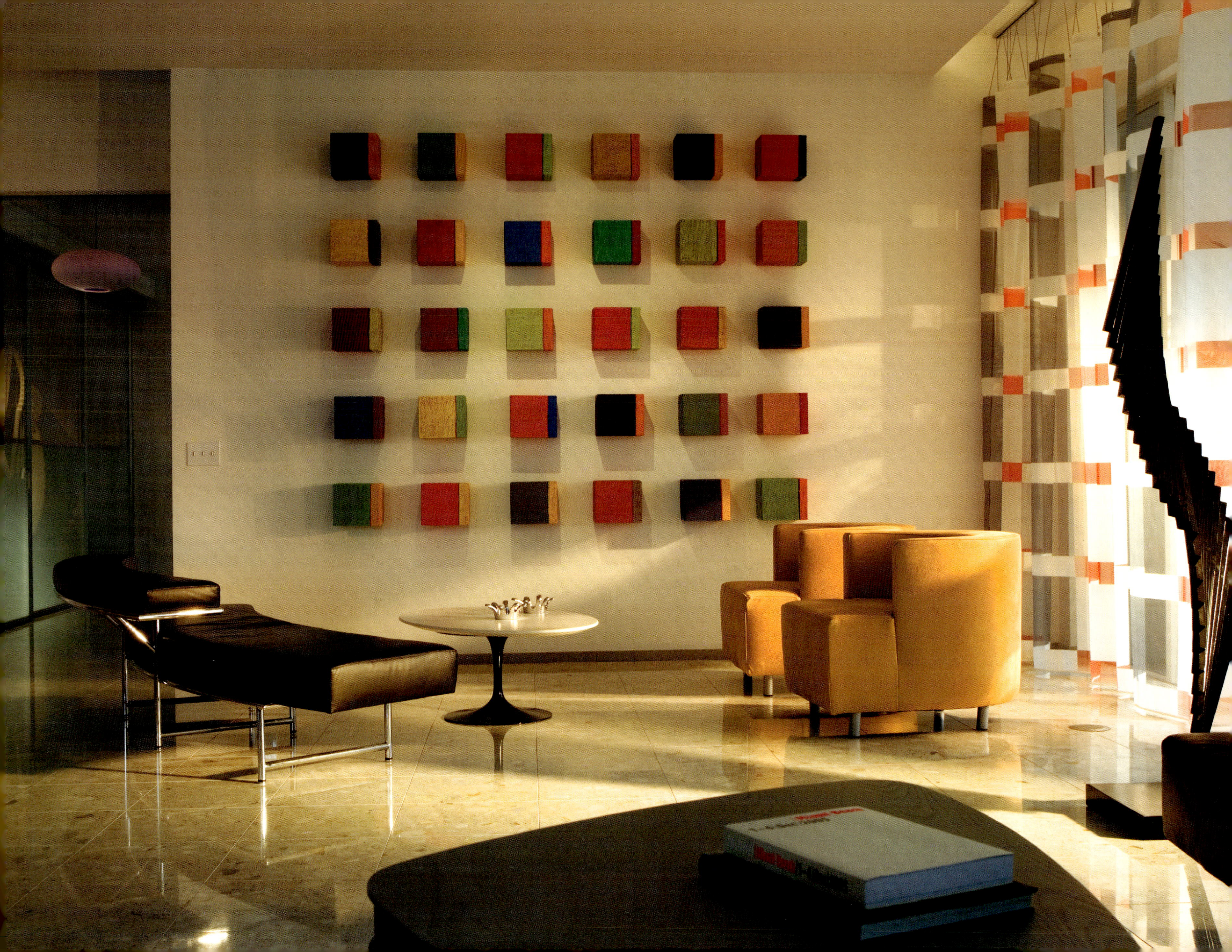

OSCAR GLOTTMAN

Glottman Architecture

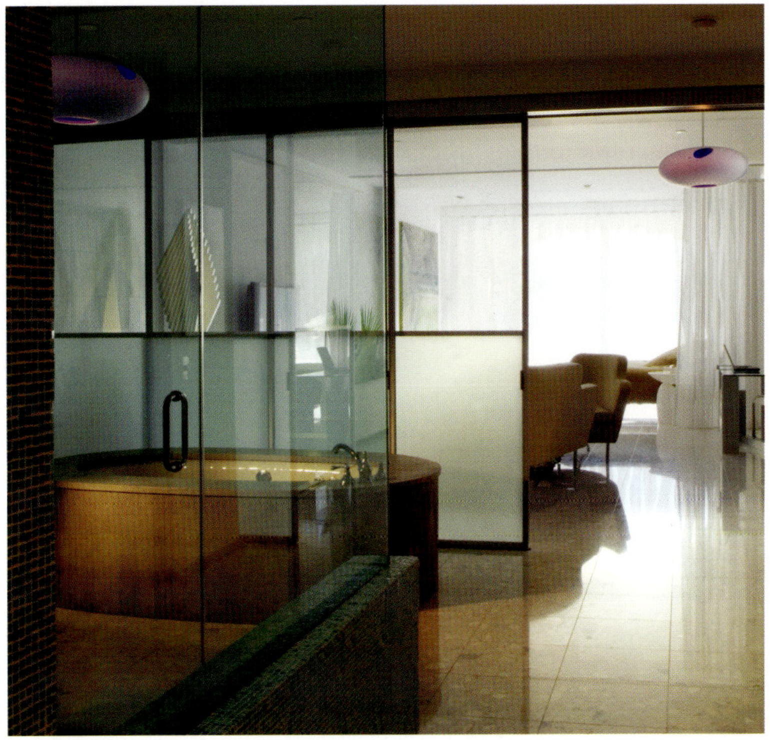

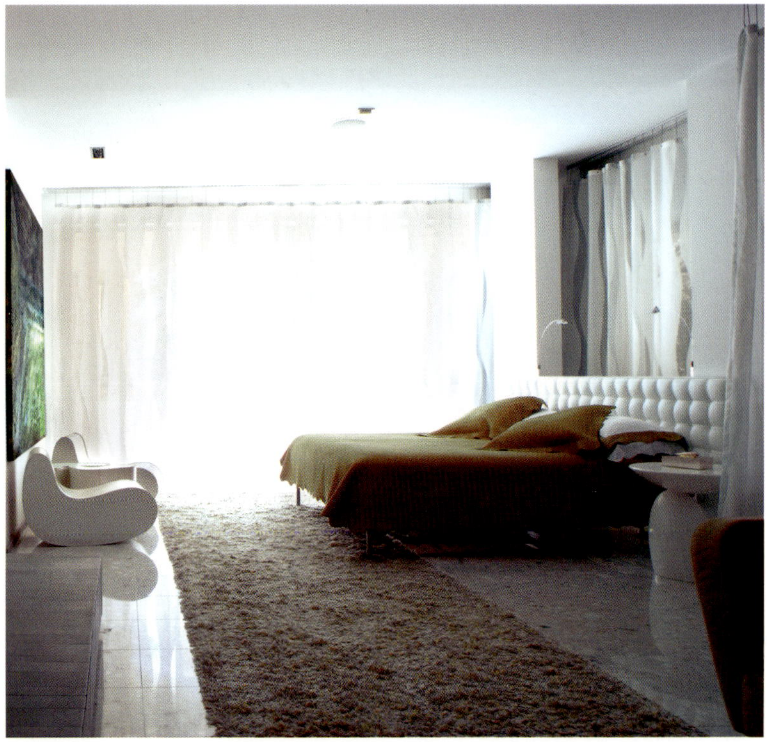

For most architects, the intimate aspects of a project are typically among its final elements. For Oscar Glottman, they are the starting point. Working from the inside-out, Oscar inverts the traditional approach to architectural design by beginning with the most personal details and allowing the form to progress in an organic regeneration of space. Program, in Oscar's hands, is as much an emotive issue as a pragmatic one. "I am as much concerned with how the inhabitants of a room will experience light as I am with how appropriately the architecture suits the geographic region," he says. "In fact, I could as easily begin the design process with the selection of knife and fork as with the architectural elements. My impetus is that personal." This sensitivity triggered by a curiosity for current ideas and technologies and a particular talent for forging strong relationships with his clients are the driving forces behind unique projects that maintain a common contemporary clarity. As he moves from concept to context, then to topography, Oscar exposes his process via materials, sophisticated construction systems and tectonic patterns. This is as evident in his commercial projects as in the residential ones, his recent focus.

Featured among these pages is an interior architecture project on Fisher Island, a residential island development in Miami. Oscar created architecture out of a vacuous, generic, developer's interior to embody his clients' progressive lifestyle and fulfill their wish for a contemporary home that incorporates South Florida's natural elements. The assignment was further enriched by the family's request for a family-friendly environment within a setting that displays an extensive art collection.

ABOVE LEFT: The expansive master bath forms part of the open plan of the master bedroom. Sliding panels with clear glass on the top panes frame the oceanfront views and bring in natural light all the way to the back of the space.
Photograph by Dan Forer

ABOVE RIGHT: In the bedroom, a series of built-in architectural forms, including a bench, columns and wall dividers creates a landscape of horizontal and vertical planes. Movable fabric partitions and layered window treatments provide for various levels of privacy and light.
Photograph by Dan Forer

LEFT: The door opens to the master suite in a continuity of spaces that can be divided at will. The somewhat formal living room illustrates Glottman's choreography of a tight relationship between furniture and adjacent art.
Photograph by Dan Forer

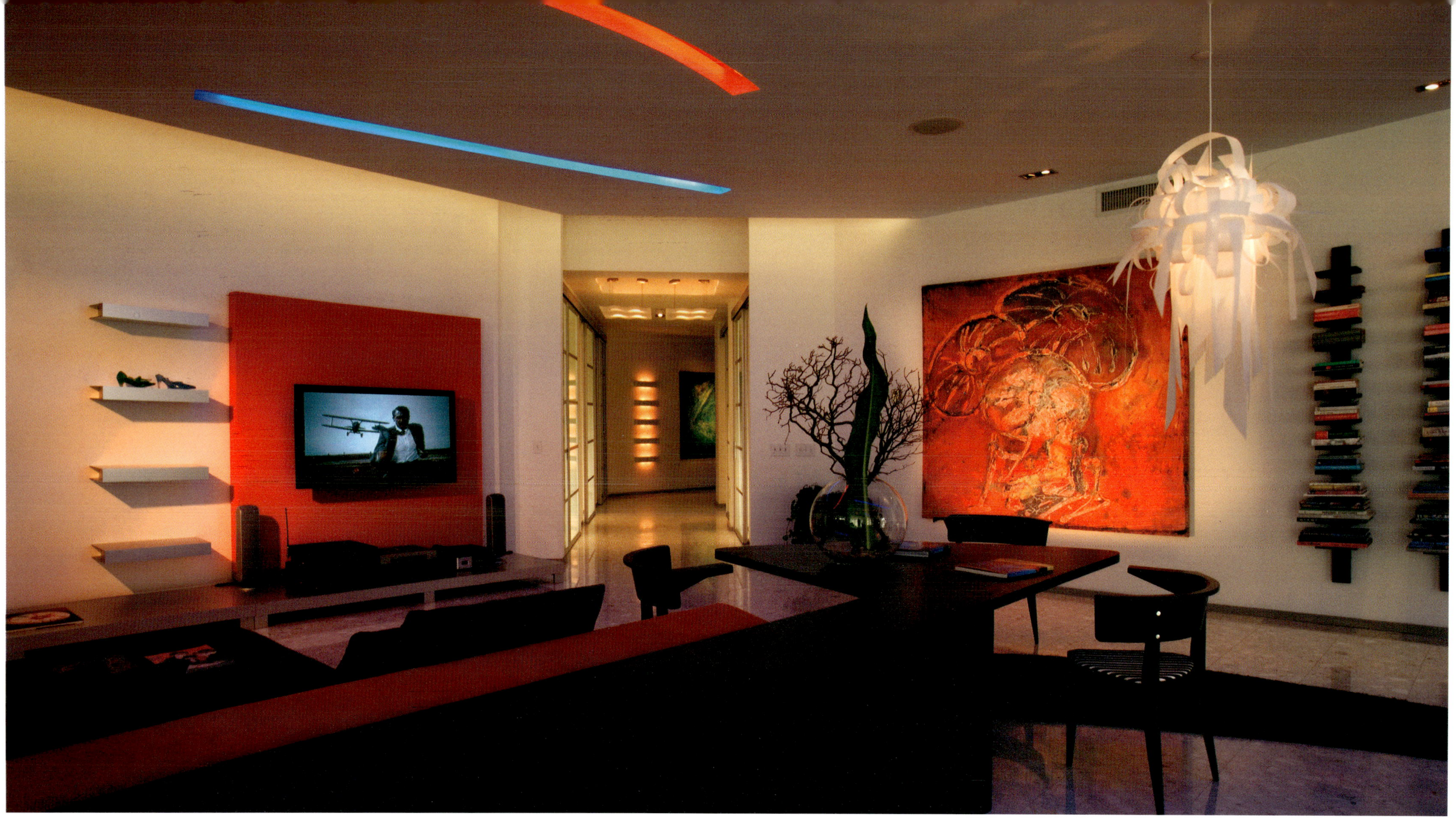

Oscar first considered the project in terms of the universal requirements of function, circulation, comfort, natural light patterns and materiality. The project diagram features a bipolar arrangement subdivided by a circulation spine that practically defines two homes within one. A sequence of material and visual layers provide the family of seven with the ability to congregate and separate with ease, as well as to entertain while maintaining their privacy. Sliding panels and curtains divide the space within rooms and from their bounding central corridor. Oscar created paths and spatial relationships through the use of screens, art, lighting, furniture, and the built elements. Departing from the obvious solution of providing for independent gallery space, the paintings and sculpture are incorporated equally into all areas of the home blurring the boundaries between life and the display of art, which was the theme of the project. Interplay of concealed functional lighting, suprematist compositions of colored cathode bulbs and some sculptural decorative fixtures reveal a thoughtful lighting design project. The furniture is also a function of the architecture, with pieces selected not only for their own design integrity, but also choreographed to play an active role in the invocation of design patterns. A series of architectural elements, including built in furniture, columns, floating ceiling planes and carved out ceiling crevices, create a landscape of horizontal, vertical, diagonal and sweeping planes. The final result is an elegant spatial organization ruled by flexible functionality that celebrates South Florida's natural light and sea. Oscar Glottman's creative approach includes concept development, architecture and interior architecture, as well as lighting, furniture and sound design. Having two firms, he is unusually equipped to fulfill this one vision/one source approach: Glottman Architectural Corporation has been providing architectural services since 1988. Glottman ADF, with a lifestyle showroom in the Miami Design District, offers creative construction systems like modular walls and untraditional doors along with design furniture, kitchens, closets, lighting and accessories, strongly represented by European lines.

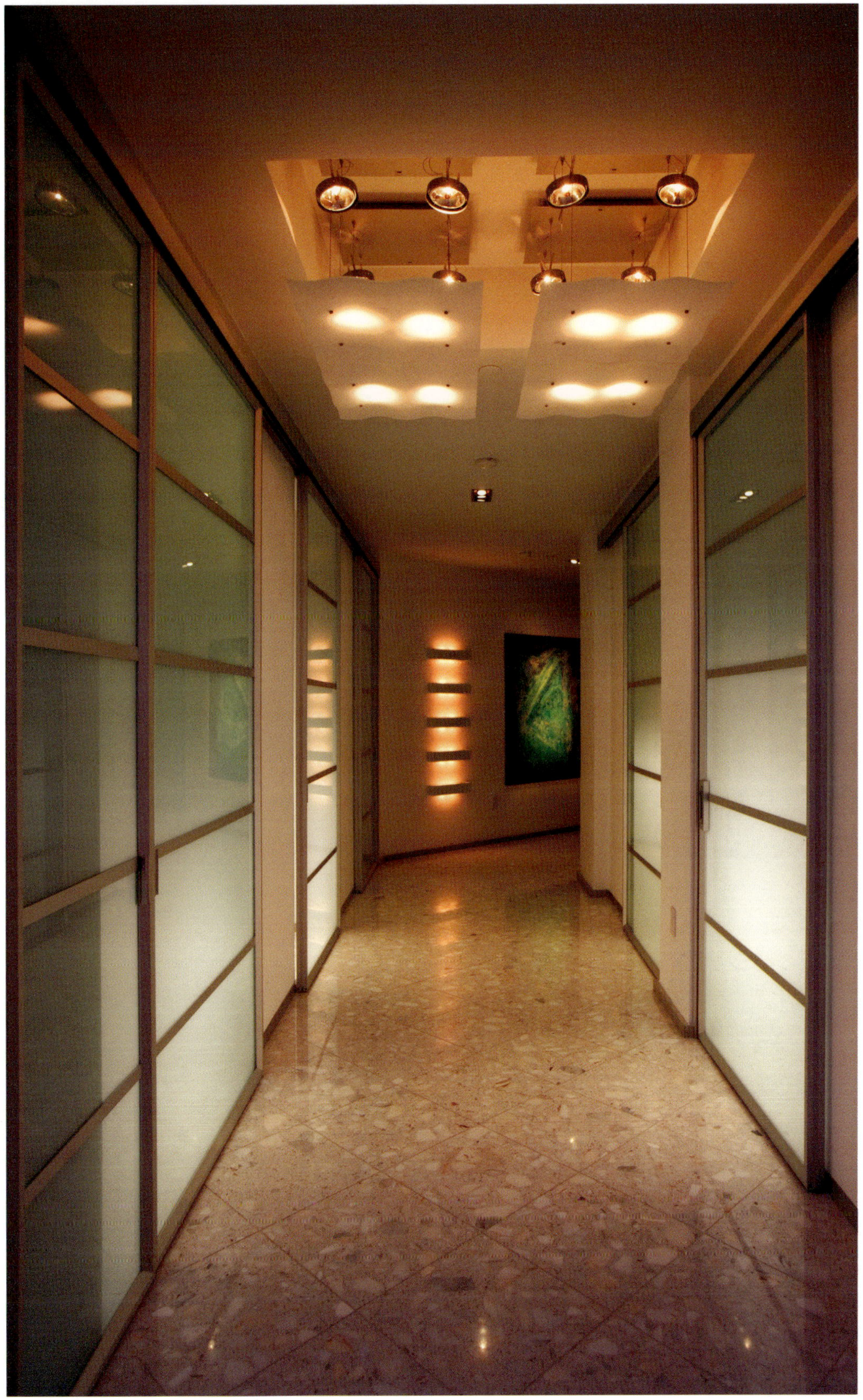

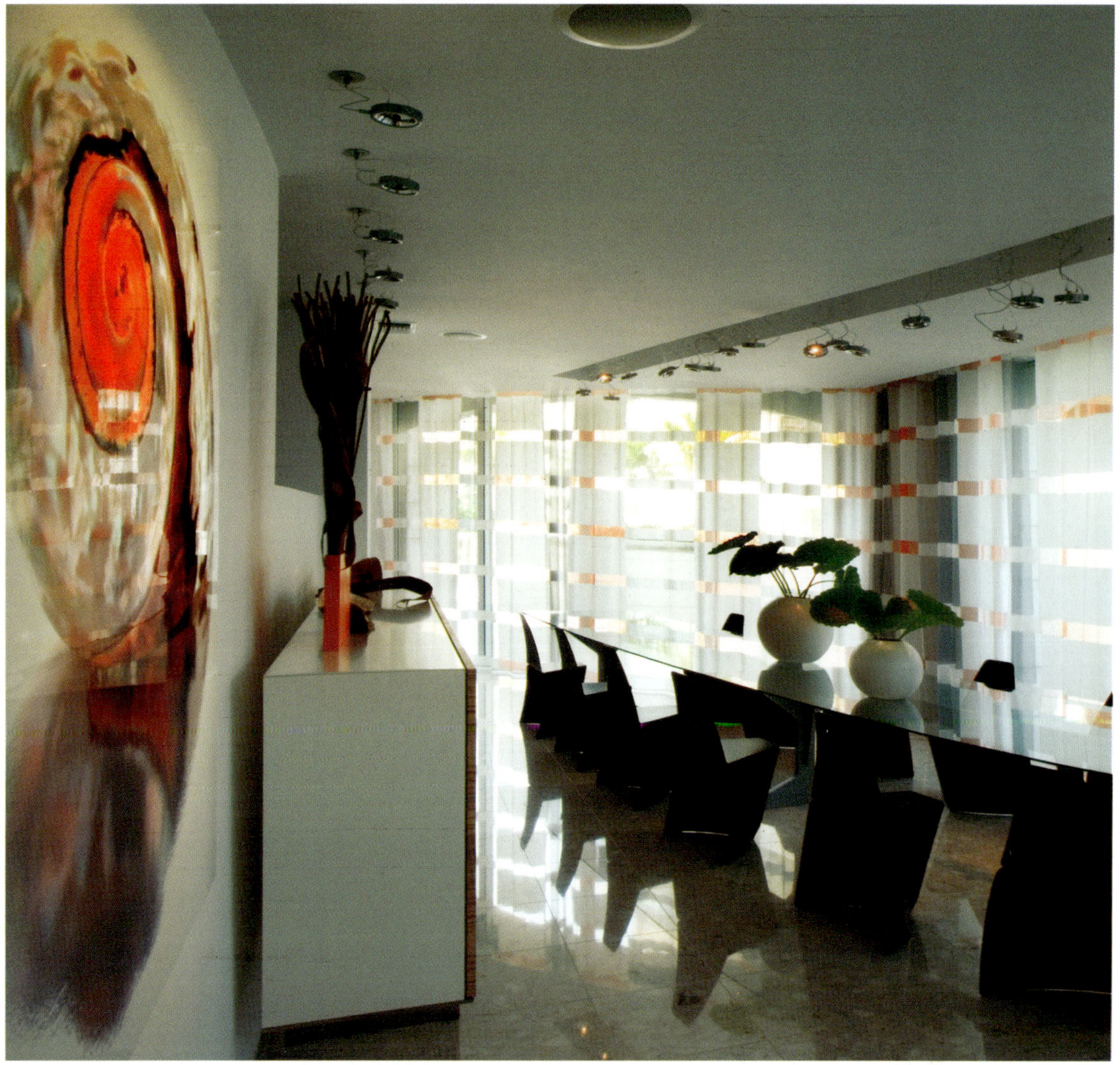

ABOVE: The dining room is a composition of diagonal, curving and rectilinear planes that capitalize on the room's sweeping lines and complement the suprematist inspired lighting and furniture composition in the living room.
Photograph by Dan Forer

LEFT: The original entry corridor is the spine of the home, defining the children's quarters on one side and the master suite on the other. The space is purposefully designed with lighting to feature the art, be featured as art and celebrate the transparency of unusual sliding glass panel walls.
Photograph by Dan Forer

FACING PAGE: The entry sequence terminates in the media room with a sweep of kinetic space. Architecture has been subtly carved out of an otherwise ordinary horizontal space.
Photograph by Dan Forer

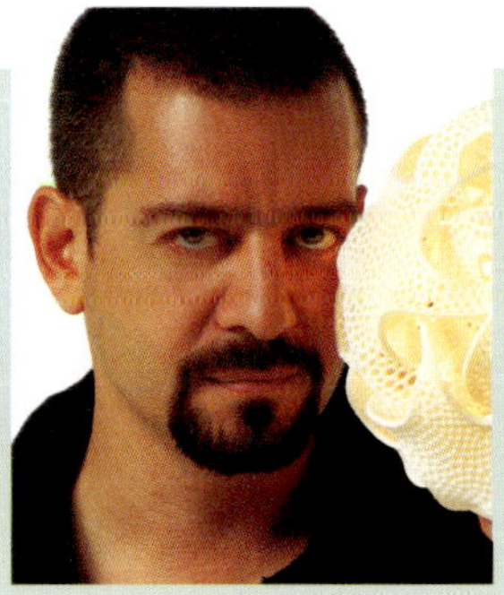

Glottman Architecture
Oscar Glottman
270 Northeast 39th Street
Miami, FL 33137
305.438.3711
Fax 305.438.3713
www.glottman.com

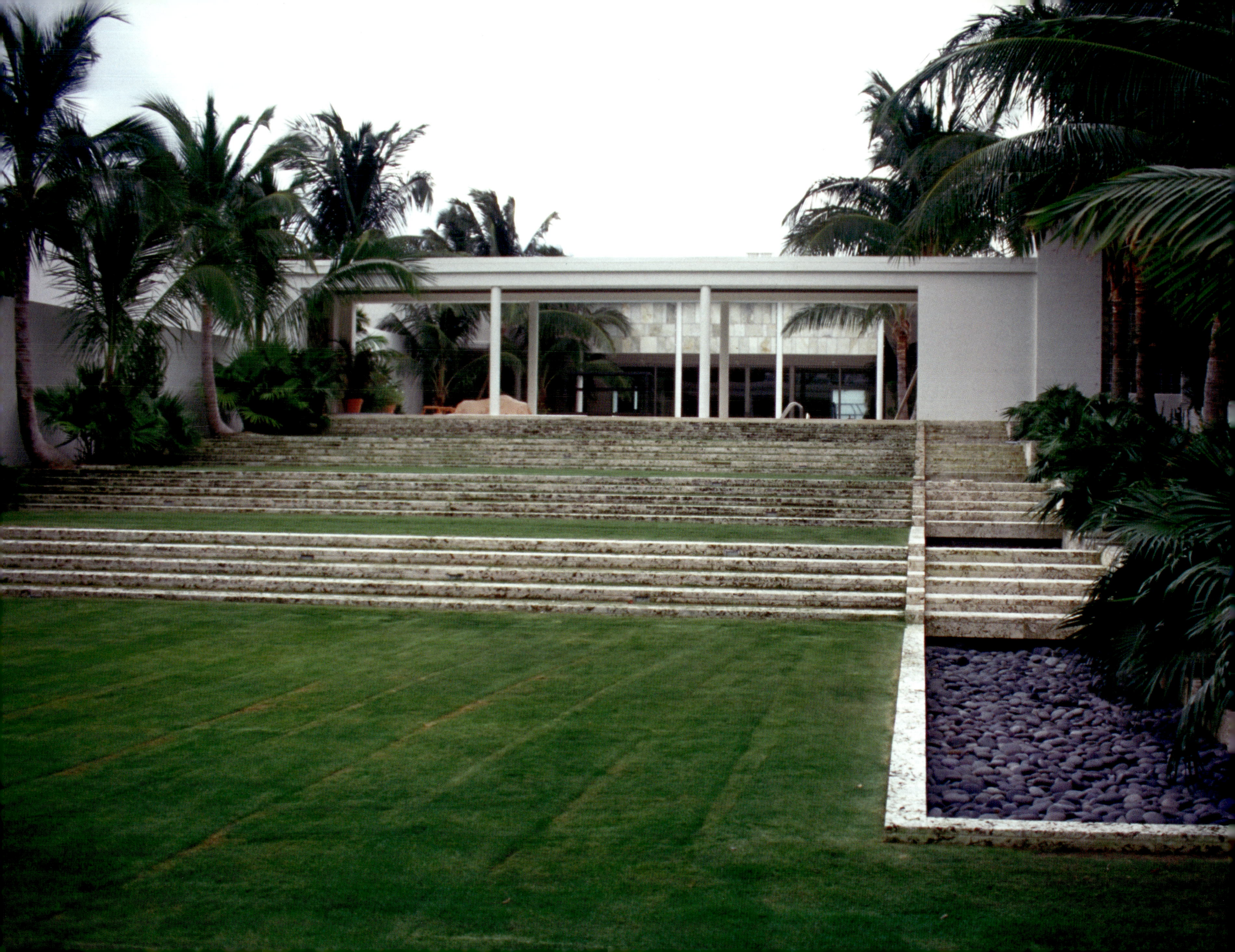

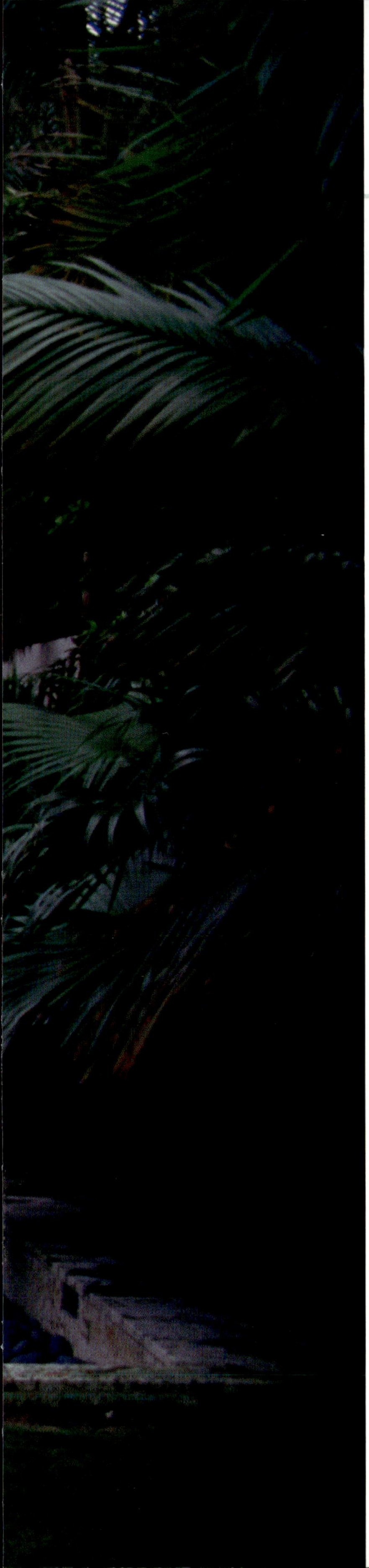

RENE GONZALEZ

Rene Gonzalez

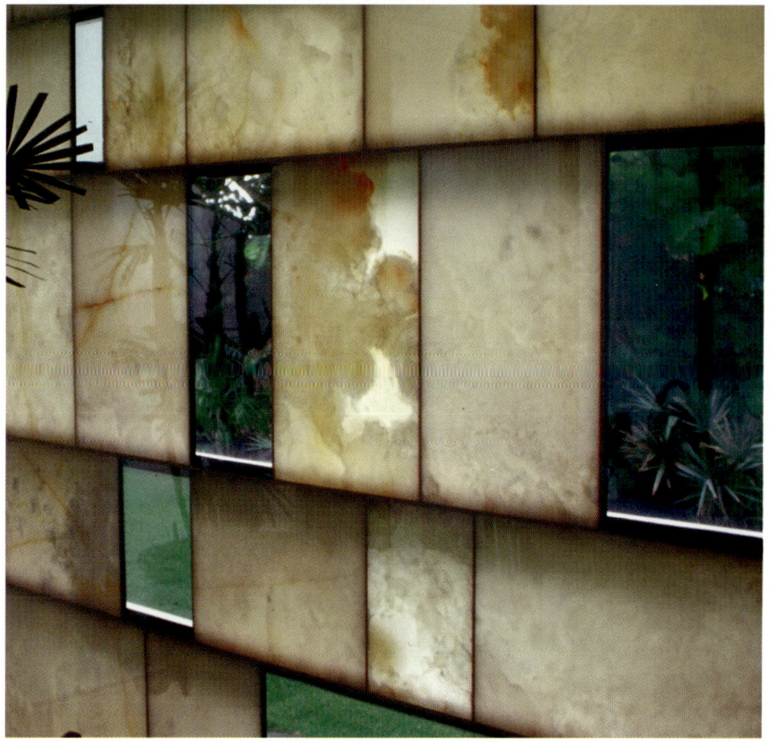

Many architects believe themselves to possess style, but few exude an architectural stylishness quite like Rene Gonzalez. Rene started his career as a project designer with the architect Richard Meier working on the Getty Museum and Center in Los Angeles before returning to Florida and starting his own firm in 1997.

A highly intensive design office, Rene has created structures including homes, museums, office buildings, art installations and structures for municipalities.

An opportunity to create a holistic experience with his architecture is what Rene strives for with each new project he undertakes. He loves working on projects which allow him to develop the interior and the landscape designs to seamlessly integrate themselves into a flowing, inspired environment.

ABOVE: Detail of ocean pavilion's onyx wall.
Photograph by Rene Gonzalez

LEFT: Terraced garden that creates a grand scale stage to entertain guests at ocean front house in Palm Beach, Florida.
Photograph by Rene Gonzalez

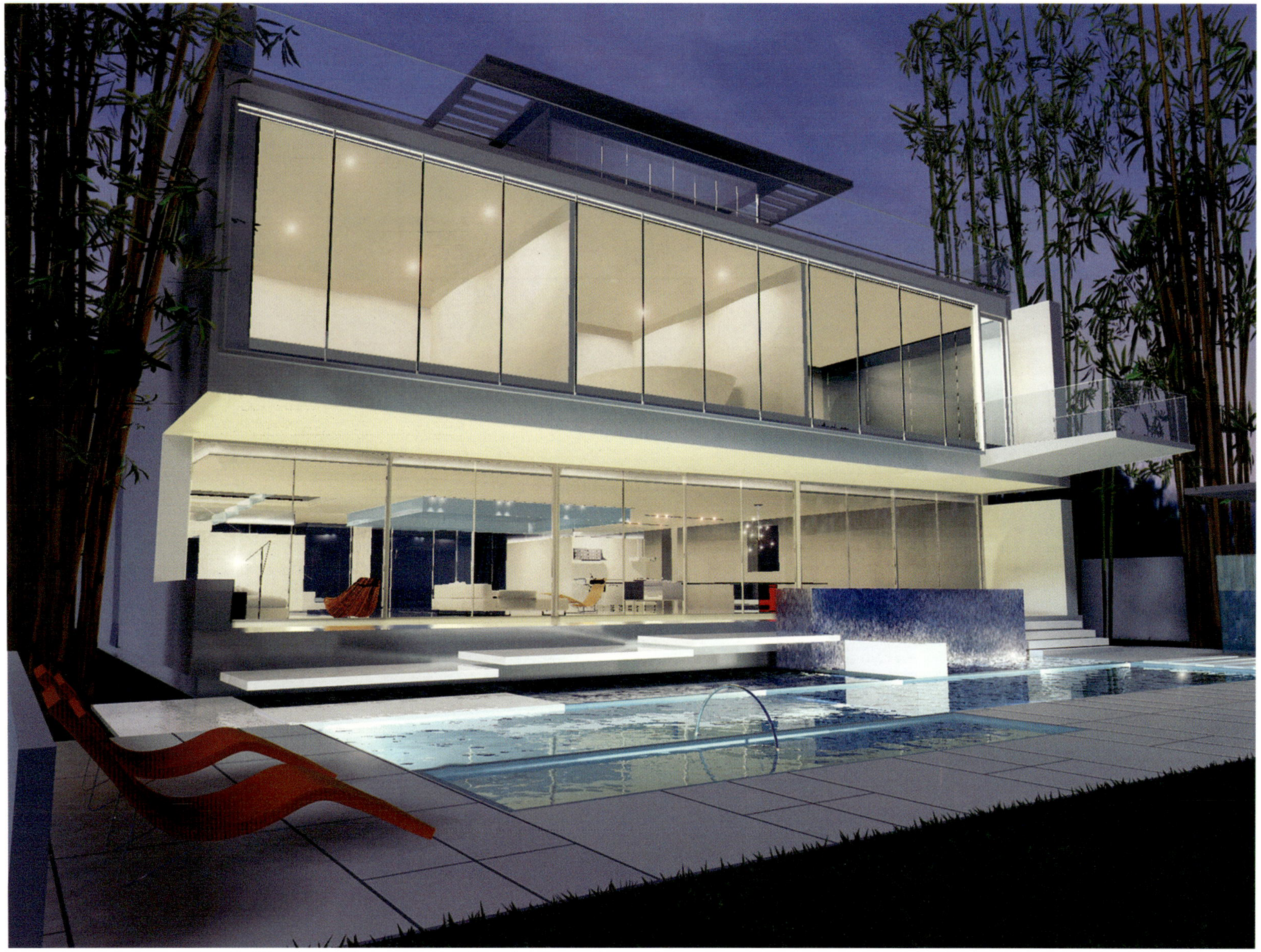

Influenced by architects like Mark Hampton and John Launter, amongst others, Rene is interested in the development of houses which connect themselves spatially to the landscape, he says that his style of architectural development is "contemporary, connected to the environment and light."

Usually, he tries to create structures that are in tune with the surrounding environment and respondent to a location. As was the case when he designed a museum in downtown Miami where he strived to bring nature into an austere warehouse district in Miami in which the neutral elements of the concrete and steel surrounded the building site. "We covered the whole building with an image of a jungle because we wanted to contrast the rough qualities of the surroundings and instill this greenery that didn't exist in the area."

Striving to discover and utilize new materials is a priority for Rene, however he says, it is important to utilize those new materials within reasonable parameters and in doing so an architect has to understand their limitations.

Rene says, his clients come to him with an understanding of the type of architecture that he creates. It is not about the scale of the project or the type of project to be designed; his goals are developing projects for clients that are interested in the contemporary-holistic type of structures which he creates.

He has designed museums, gallery installations and residential projects for art collectors. Among them are the new Museum for the Cisneros Fontanals Art Foundation, the lobby and installations at the Museum of Contemporary Art in Miami and installations at the Miami Art Museum.

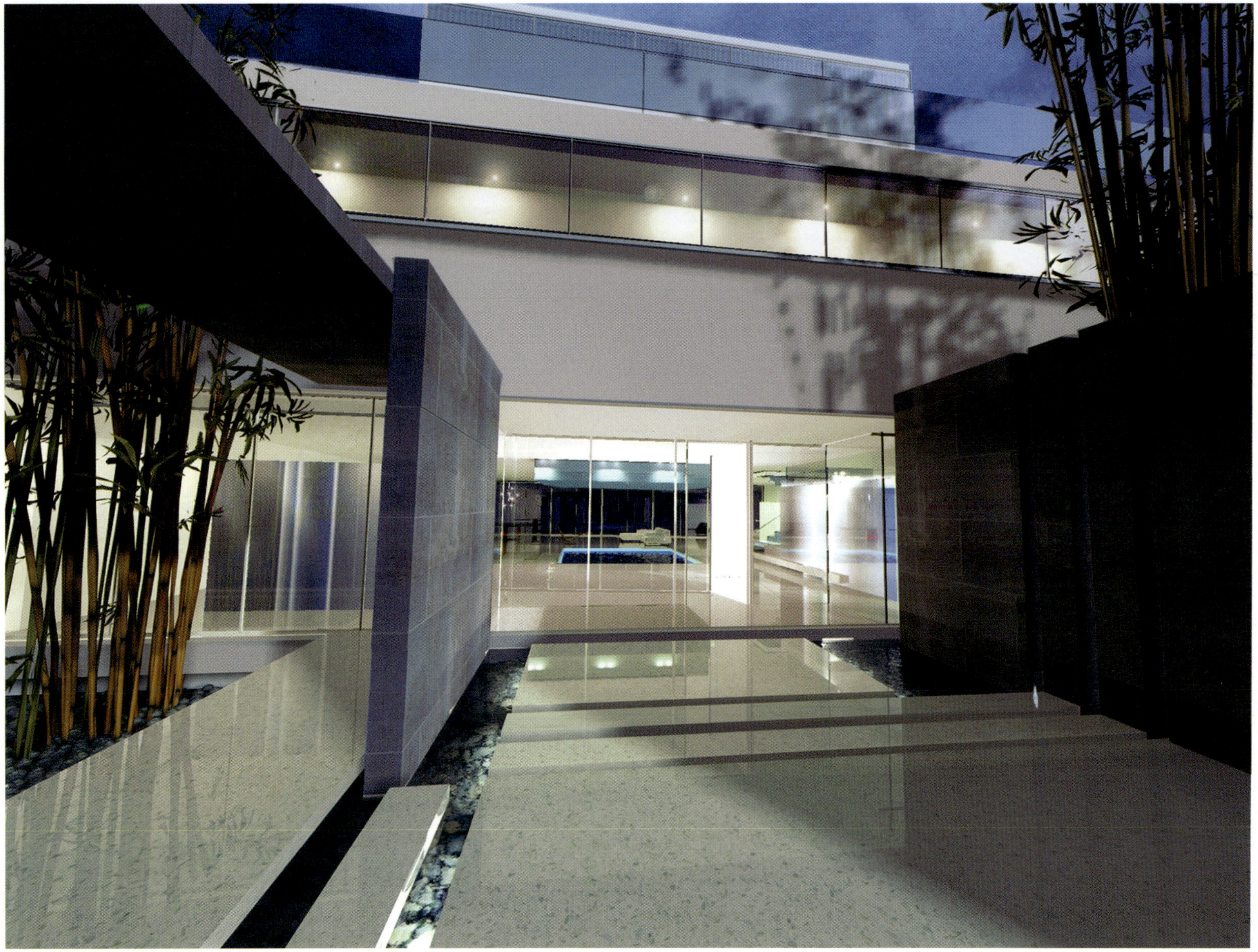

ABOVE: View of entry garden, reflecting pool and steps of Key Biscayne waterfront house.
Photograph by Zero Fractal

RIGHT: Portrait of Rene Gonzalez at the Cisneros Fontanals Art Foundation's "jungle" mosaic façade.
Photograph by Robert Melee

FACING PAGE: View of rear terrace and pool of Key Biscayne waterfront house.
Photograph by Zero Fractal

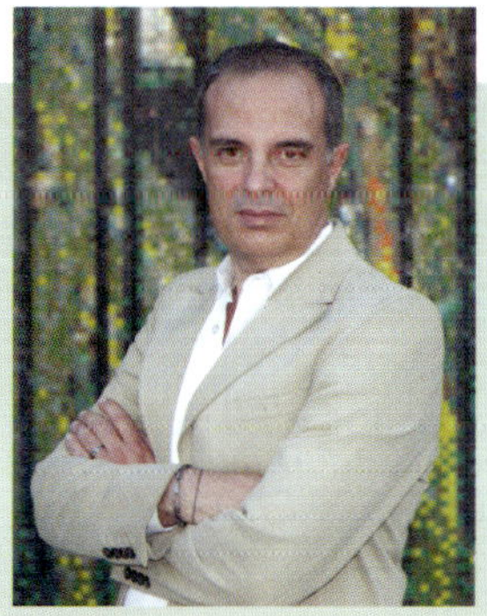

RENE GONZALEZ

Rene Gonzalez

670 Northeast 50 Terrace

Miami, FL 33137

305.762.5895

Fax 305.762.5893

www.renegonzalezarchitect.com

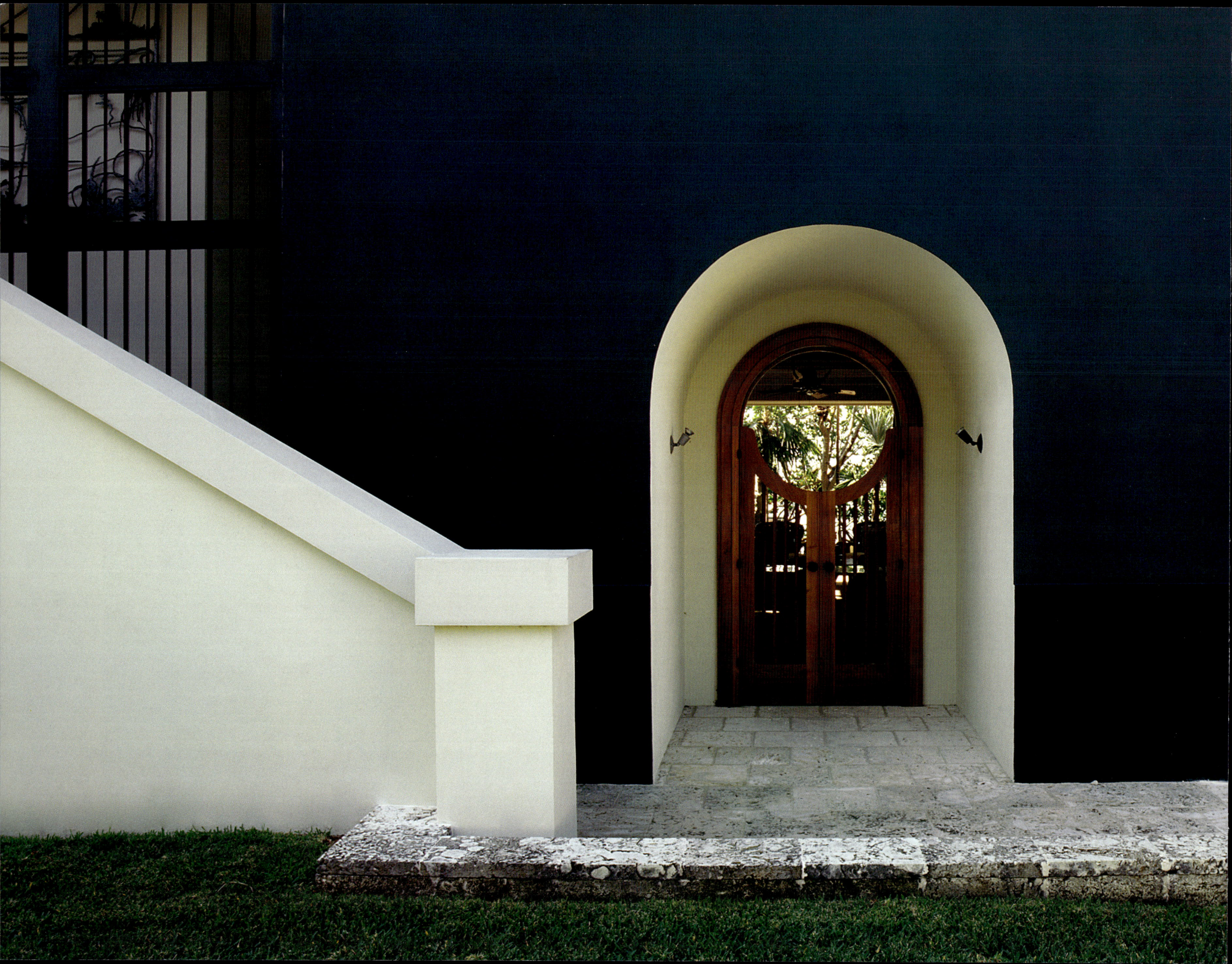

JORGE L. HERNANDEZ

Jorge L. Hernandez Architect

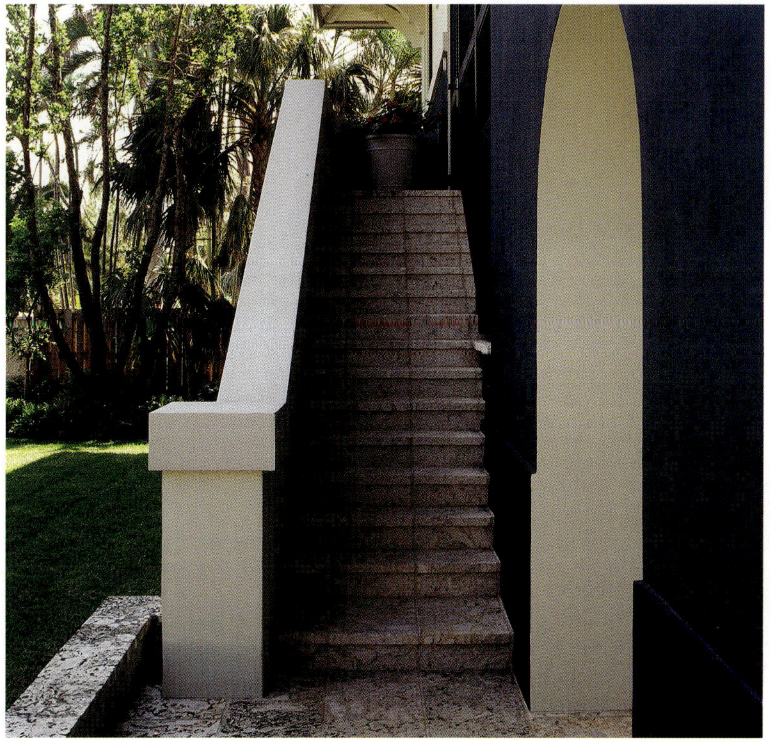

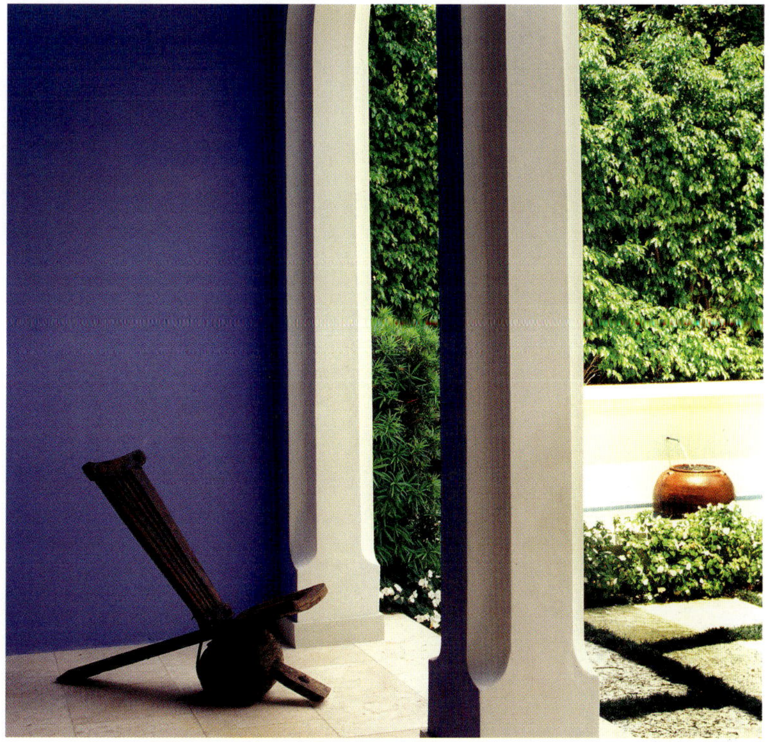

Jorge L. Hernandez is one of those rare breeds of professionals who not only teaches; he practices as well. Architecture has infiltrated his sensibility from a young age. Even today, he vividly remembers the old Bauhaus building in Havana where he lived when he was only five years old. "I have childhood memories of sitting on the projecting balconies with their metal pipe columns, terrazzo floors and lots of glass," he says. "Those are my earliest memories of my environment."

Environments have continued to make an impact on Jorge L. Hernandez and he has made it his life's work to create them for the benefit of others. He majored in architecture at the University of Miami and subsequently taught there; he remains a professor of architecture there today. "I've never done one without the other," he says of practicing architecture and teaching it. One year after graduating, he designed a dental office in Palm Beach that was published in the *Architectural Record*, a major achievement for such a young professional.

ABOVE LEFT: Matheson Residence, Key Biscayne, Florida. Entry stair.
Photograph by Carlos Domenech

ABOVE RIGHT: Alter Residence, Miami Beach, Florida. Entry portico.
Photograph by Carlos Domenech

LEFT: Matheson Residence, Key Biscayne, Florida. Ground floor entry gate.
Photograph by Carlos Domenech

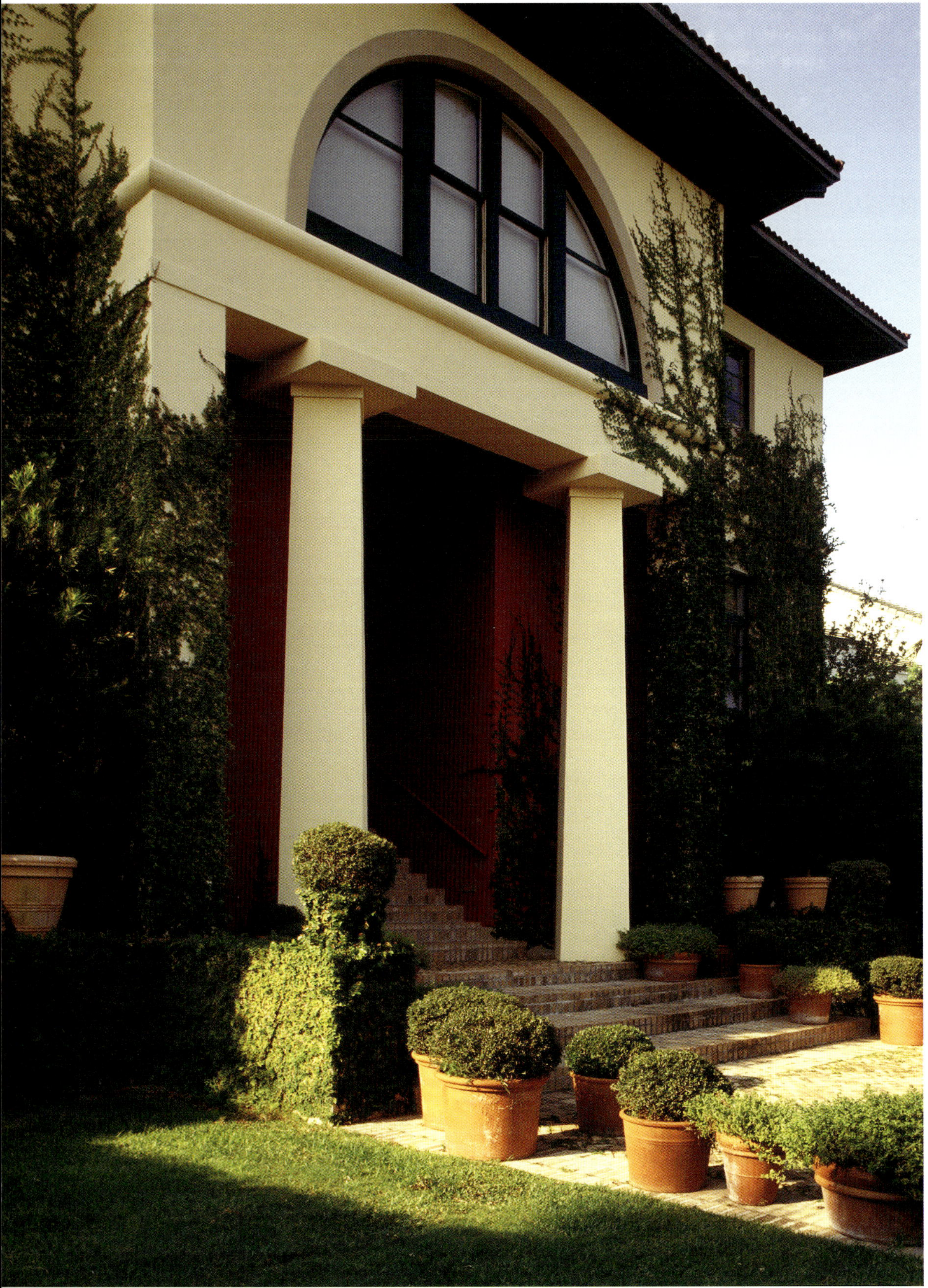

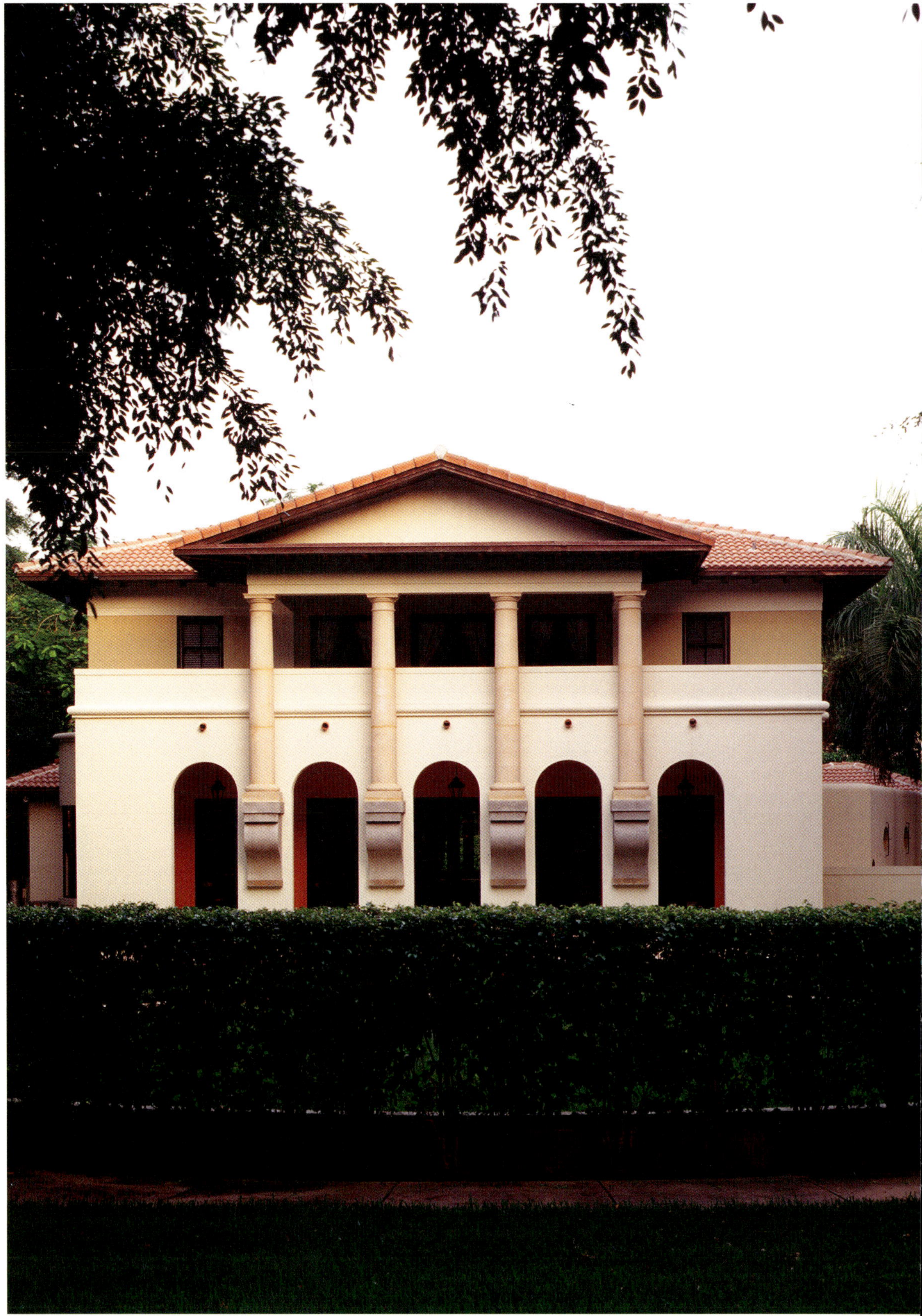

Today Jorge L. Hernandez runs a boutique firm of ten employees, including his wife, who is the company's business manager. He selects projects very carefully—only about six homes per year—because of the great deal of attention that is devoted to each one. Jorge is directly involved with all of them, which are primarily luxury homes with some civic and commercial projects sprinkled in. Because he is heavily involved in preservation—he is the former chairman of the Florida Historical Commission, the most significant volunteer position in the state in the preservation arena—he does a lot of architectural planning in historic and environmentally sensitive contexts.

Jorge loves working in Miami, a city to which he says he is still attracted, even after living in it almost his entire life. "It's a town that is multifaceted; a lot of it is rustic, archaic and intriguing," he says. "It has a very interesting character, much of which is tied to its landscape, but it is still young and building itself out."

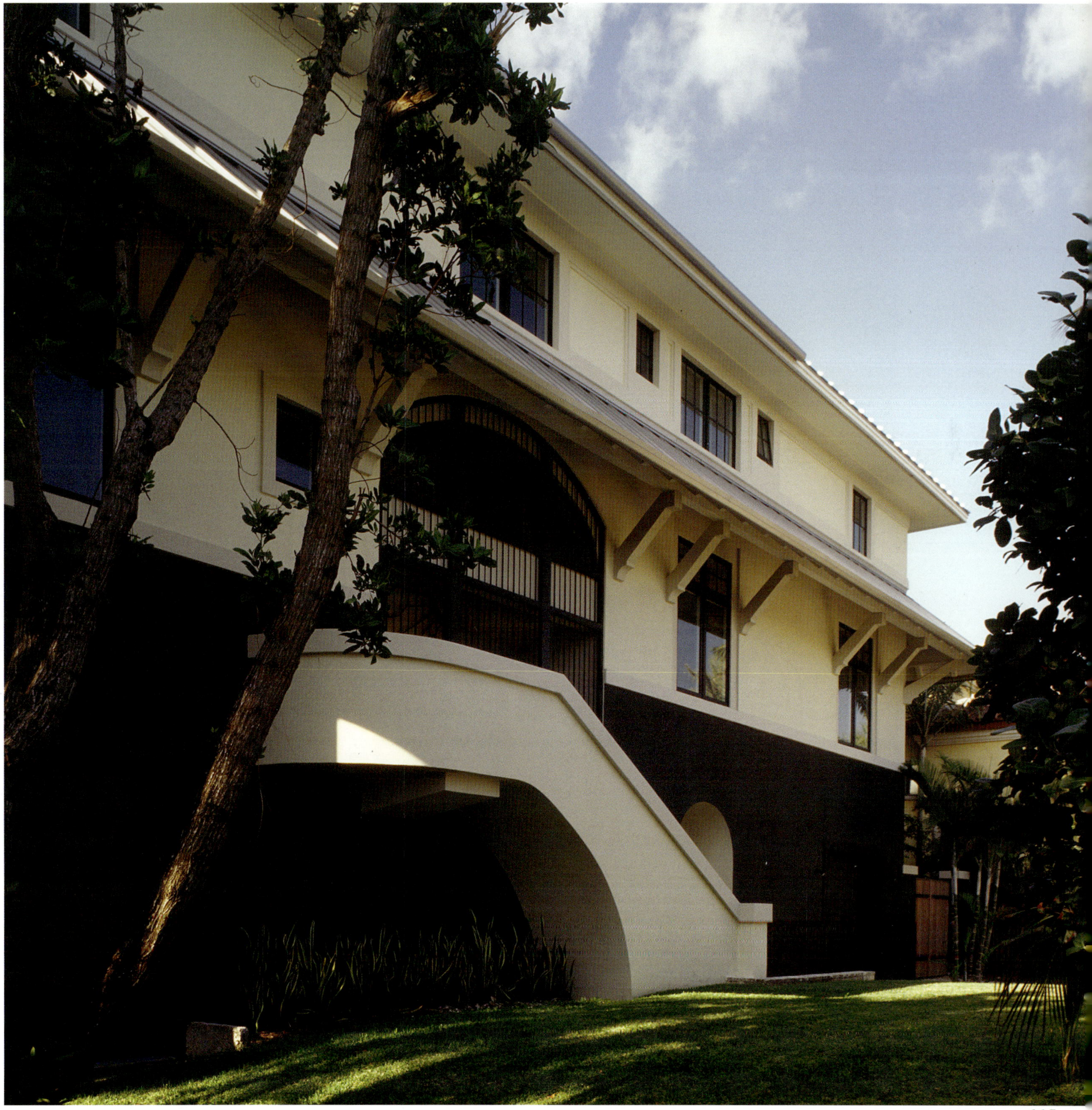

RIGHT: Matheson Residence, Key Biscayne, Florida. Main exterior stair.
Photograph by Carlos Domenech

FACING PAGE LEFT: Gutierrez Residence, Coral Gables, Florida. Front entry.
Photograph by Carlos Domenech

FACING PAGE RIGHT: Hidalgo Residence, Coral Gables, Florida. Front facade.
Photograph by Carlos Domenech

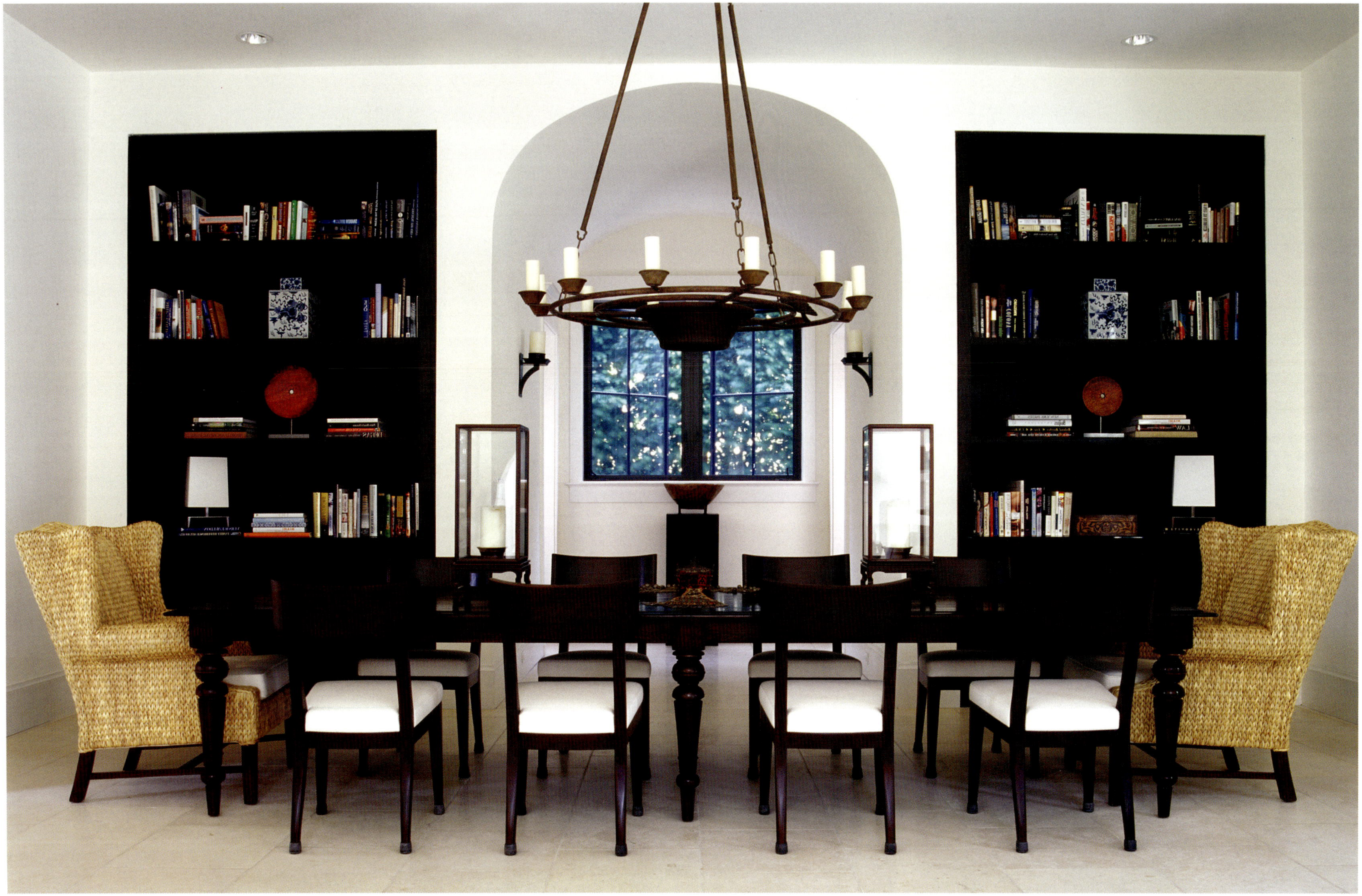

Jorge lives and works in Coral Gables, a historic area, where he is currently designing the Coral Gables Museum with walls made from solid slabs of coral stone. But it is designing personal environments—homes—that most inspires this architect. His first step in designing each one is studying the land, the light and the lot in order to marry the architecture with the earth on which the home will be built. "It's very rewarding because it is different every time," he says. "You talk to the clients who will live there about the quality of their life and their travels and you extract an aesthetic from their story. We make a script and then we make a design. That is what makes architecture a form of portraiture." And it is what makes Jorge L. Hernandez a true artist as well as an architect.

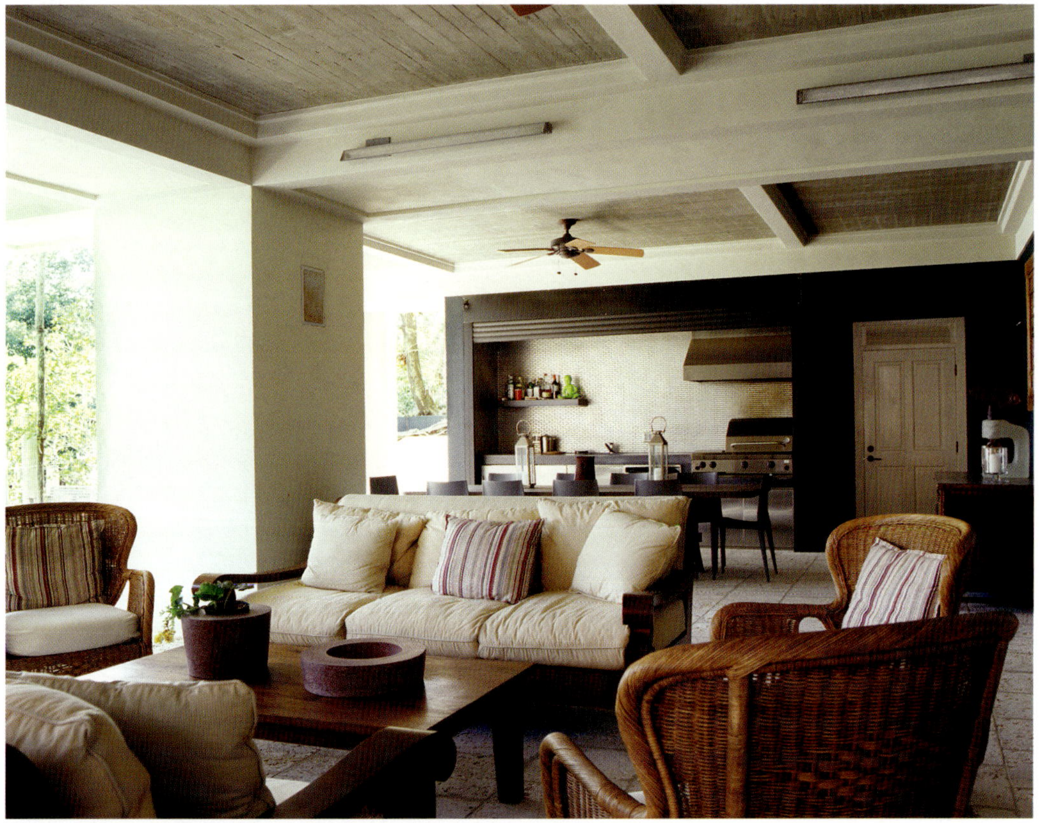

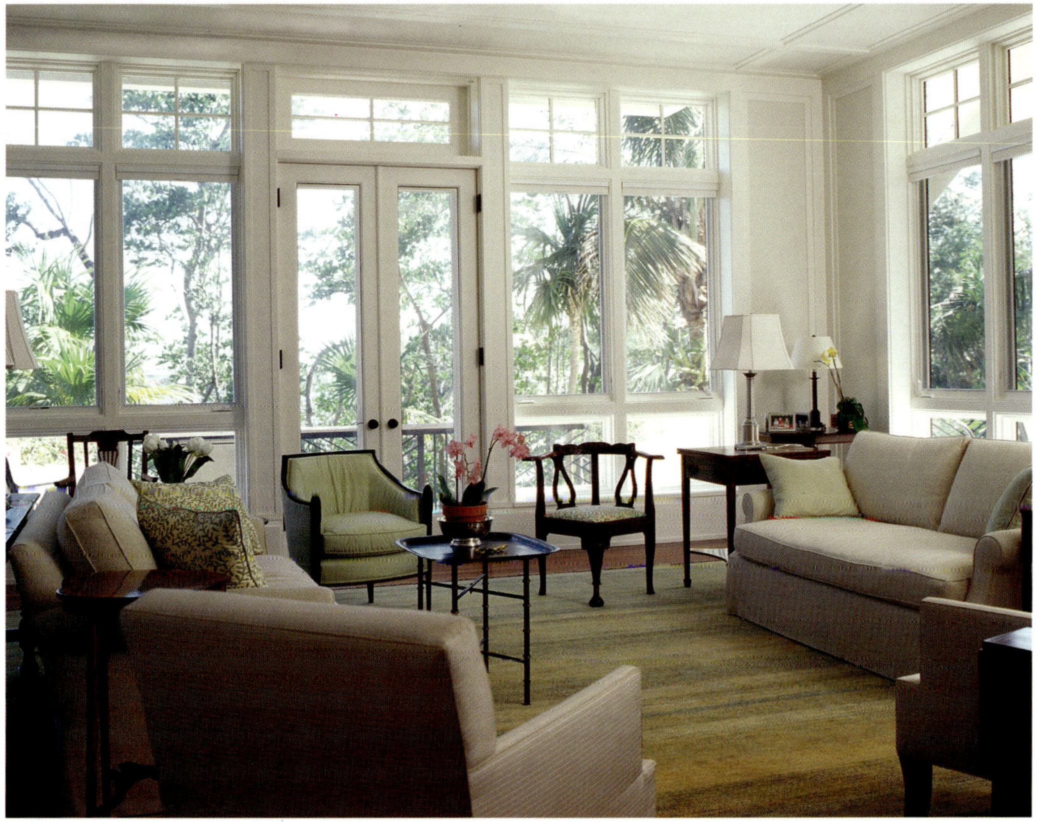

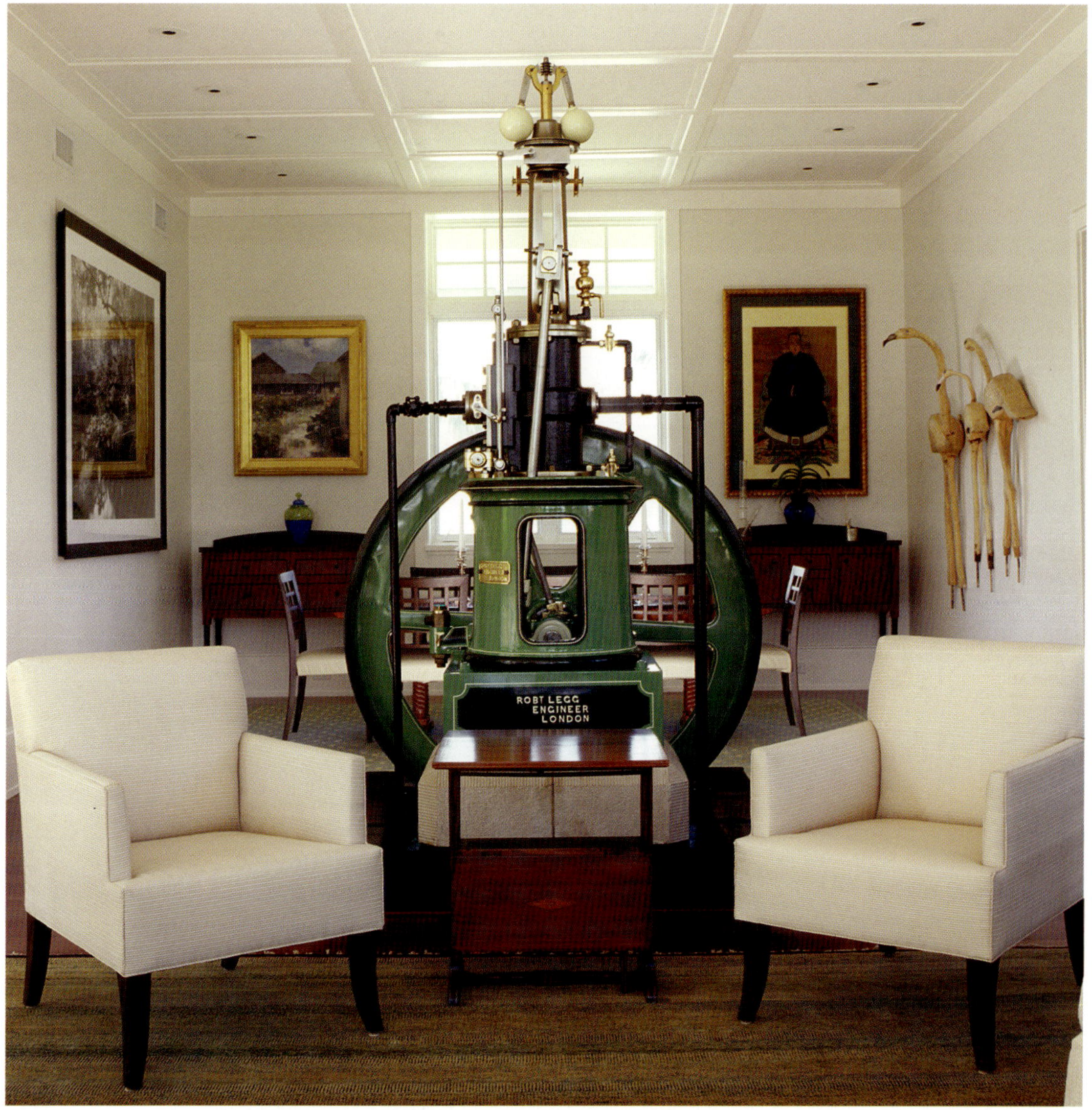

JORGE L. HERNANDEZ ARCHITECT

Jorge L. Hernandez

337 Palermo Avenue

Coral Gables, FL 33134

305.774.0022

Fax 305.774.0055

ABOVE: Matheson Residence, Key Biscayne, Florida. Living room/dining room.
Photograph by Carlos Domenech

TOP LEFT: Matheson Residence, Key Biscayne, Florida. Summer kitchen.
Photograph by Carlos Domenech

BOTTOM LEFT: Matheson Residence, Key Biscayne, Florida. Living room.
Photograph by Carlos Domenech

FACING PAGE: Alter Residence, Miami Beach, Florida. Dining room.
Photograph by Carlos Domenech

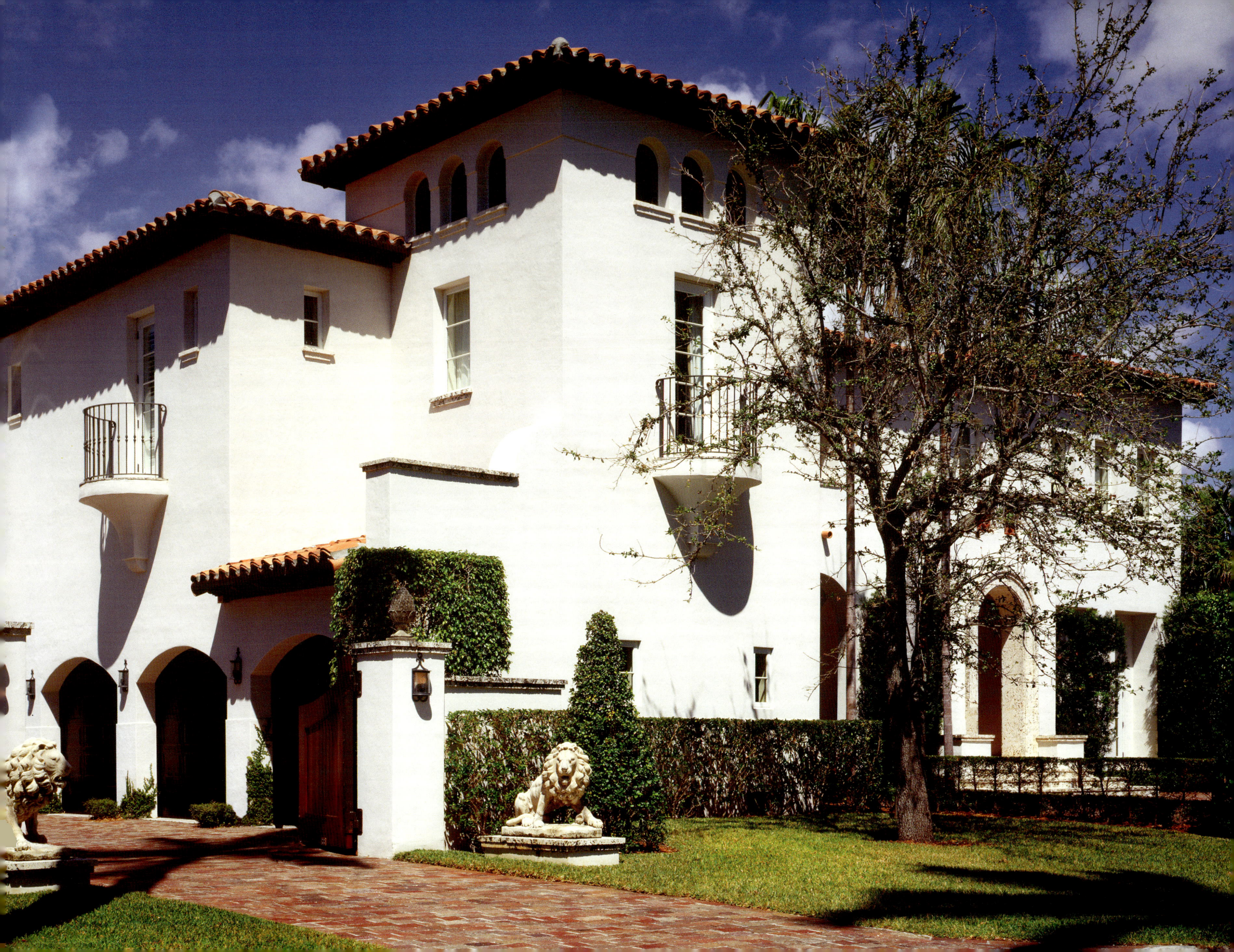

ZBIGNIEW "ZEB" JAROSZ

Z. W. Jarosz Architect, PA

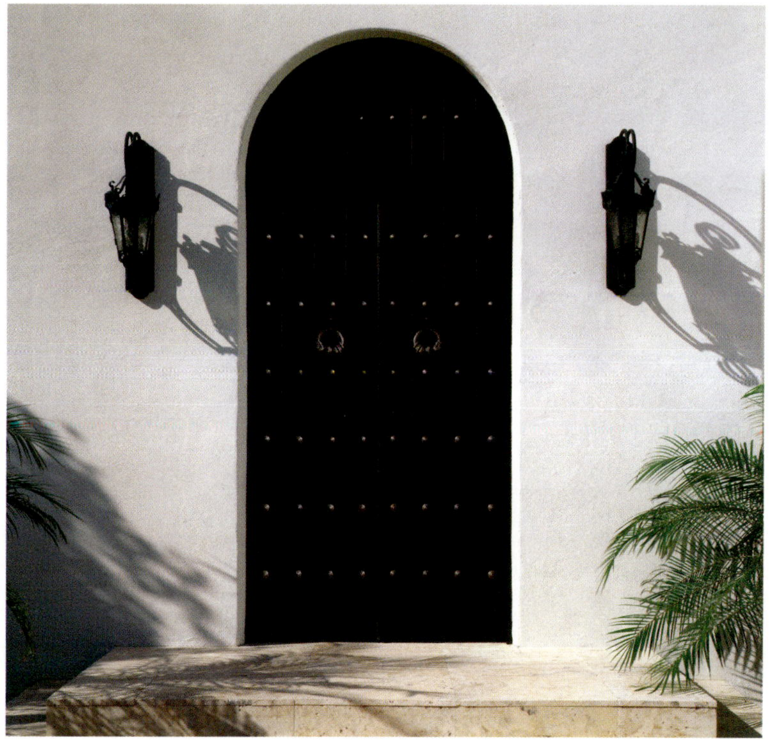

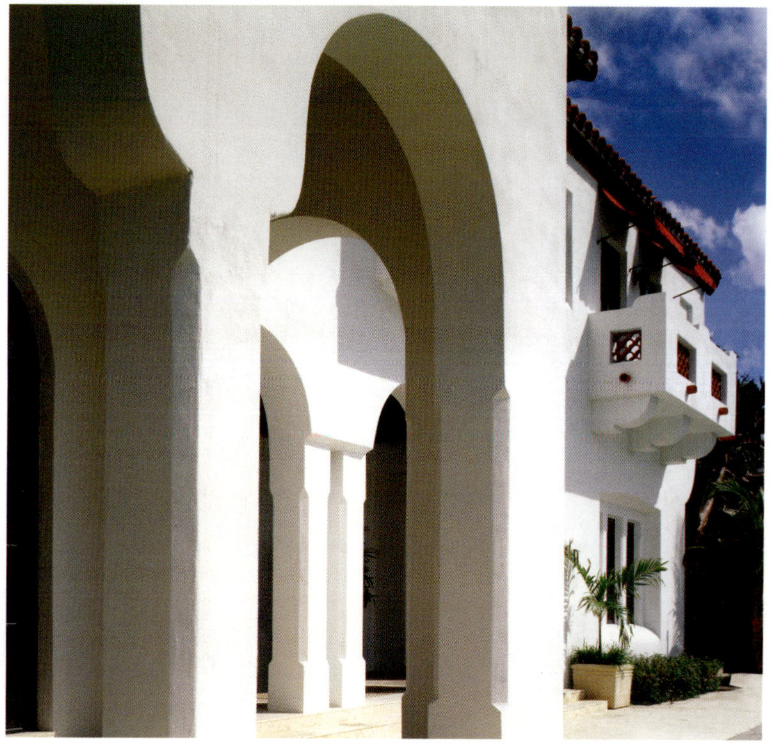

Stepping off his boat, "Blue Waters," on to a shady waterfront on the Florida coast, one would never know that "Captain Zeb" is one of the premier luxury home architects in the world.

Zbigniew "Zeb" Jarosz was born in Poland and in 1971 he graduated from Krakow University with a master's degree in architecture and engineering. Immediately after graduation he worked on reconstruction and preservation of a number of historical buildings in Poland. In 1975, he came to the United States for a one month vacation and one thing led to another. He sailed around the Caribbean and the Bahamas, married and after passing the Florida board exam for architects, he opened his own practice in 1979 where he has been working in Florida ever since.

Raised in a family full of sailors and sea going captains, Zeb always wanted to be a sailor, but was forced into architecture by his father who knew the hardships of life at sea. However, after he started his architectural studies, he discovered that he excelled at the craft and eventually realized he could only truly express himself by sitting behind a drafting board and drawing.

ABOVE LEFT & RIGHT: Bay front residence, Miami Beach, FL.
Photographs by Troy Campbell

LEFT: Residence on La Gorce Island, Miami Beach, FL.
Photograph by Troy Campbell

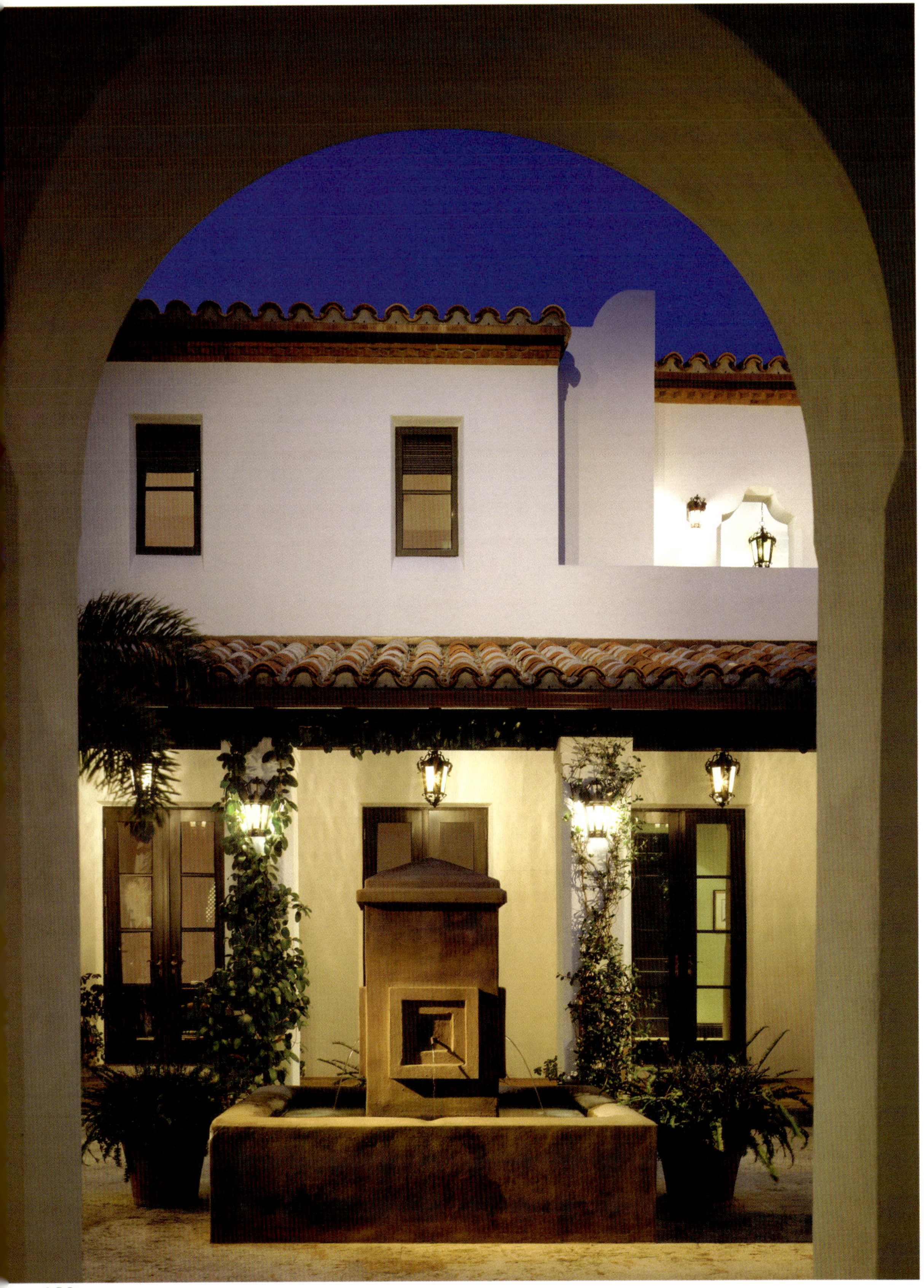
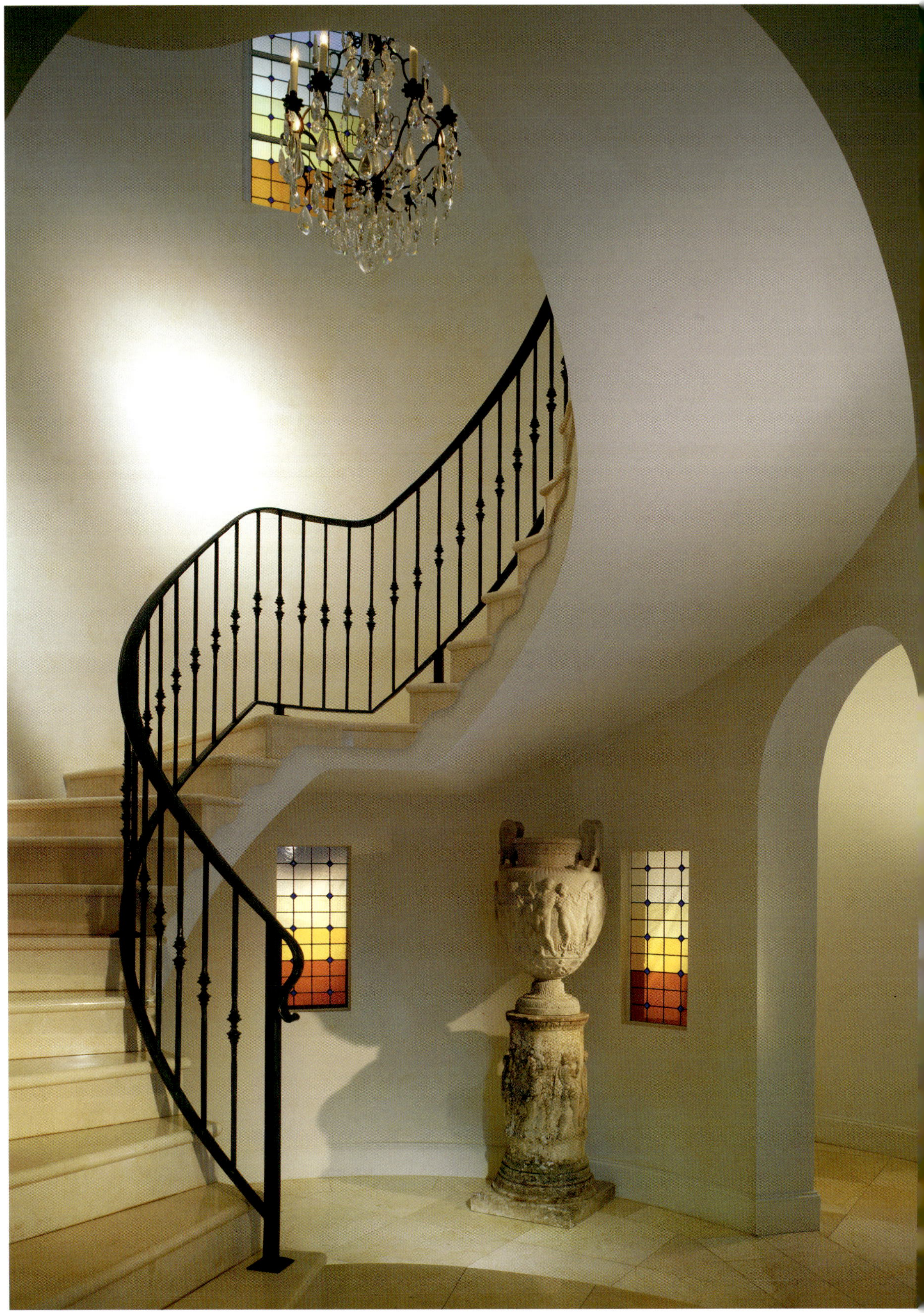

In 1984, after being frustrated with the translation of his design into realty, Zeb expanded his business to encompass construction as well. He wanted control of his projects from beginning to end to maintain control and be able to fine tune his projects up until completion.

Admitting that he posses an alter ego, Zeb has a U.S. Coast Guard Merchant Marine's license and runs a small yacht charter company where he occasionally skippers his boat for clients. In some parts of Florida, Zeb says no one knows he's an architect and some of his buddies only know him as "Captain Zeb."

Zeb grew up in Poland around some wonderful buildings and architecture which he says really effected his aesthetics and sense of style. Working with historical reconstruction and preservation of historical buildings has very much influenced his sensibilities as it pertains to design and his sense of order and proportion. He says he has an understanding for the reasons things have happened a certain way throughout architectural history. He has a comprehension of underlying purpose, whether it is related to actual spatial and aesthetic arrangements or social and historical dynamics and influences.

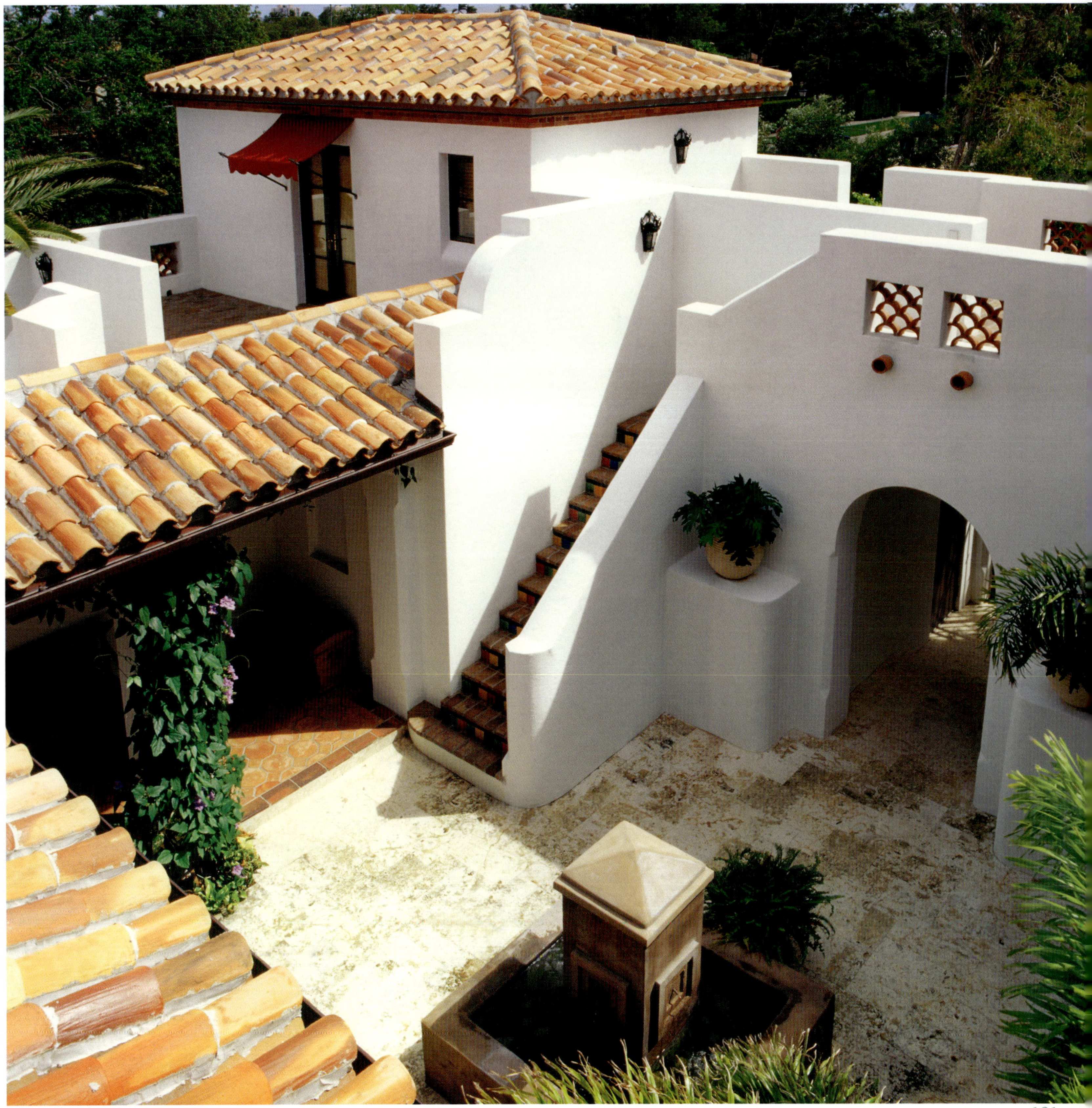

RIGHT: Bay Front residence, Miami Beach, FL.
Photograph by Troy Campbell

FACING PAGE LEFT: Bay Front Residence, Miami Beach, FL.
Photograph by Troy Campbell

FACING PAGE RIGHT: Residence on La Gorce Island, Miami Beach, FL.
Photograph by Troy Campbell

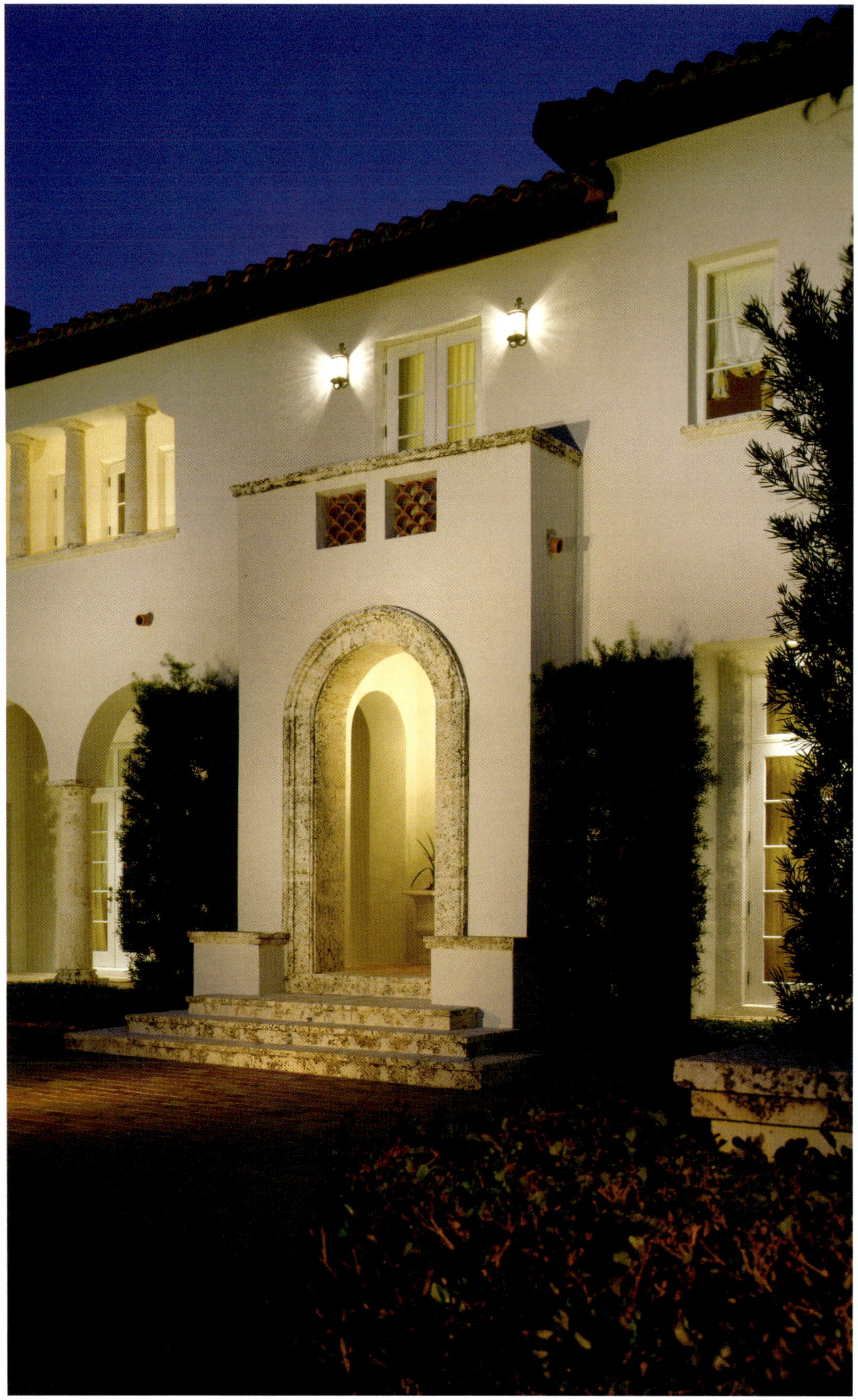

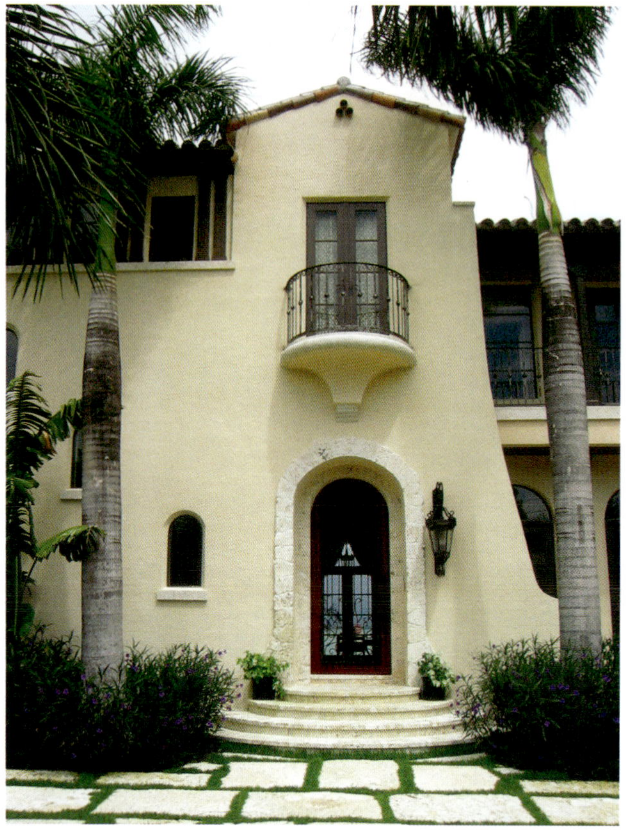

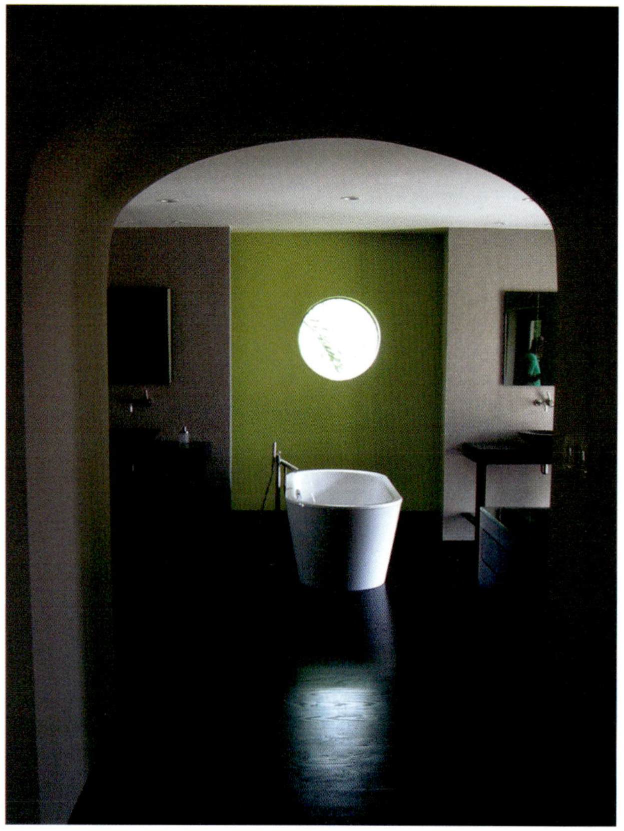

LEFT: Residence on La Gorce Island, Miami Beach, FL.
Photograph by Troy Campbell

TOP: Bay Front Residence, Miami Beach, FL.
Photograph by Zeb Jarosz

BOTTOM: Residence for Actor Matt Damon, Miami Beach, FL.
Photograph by Zeb Jarosz

FACING PAGE: Residence Journeys End, Coral Gables, FL.
Photograph by Zeb Jarosz

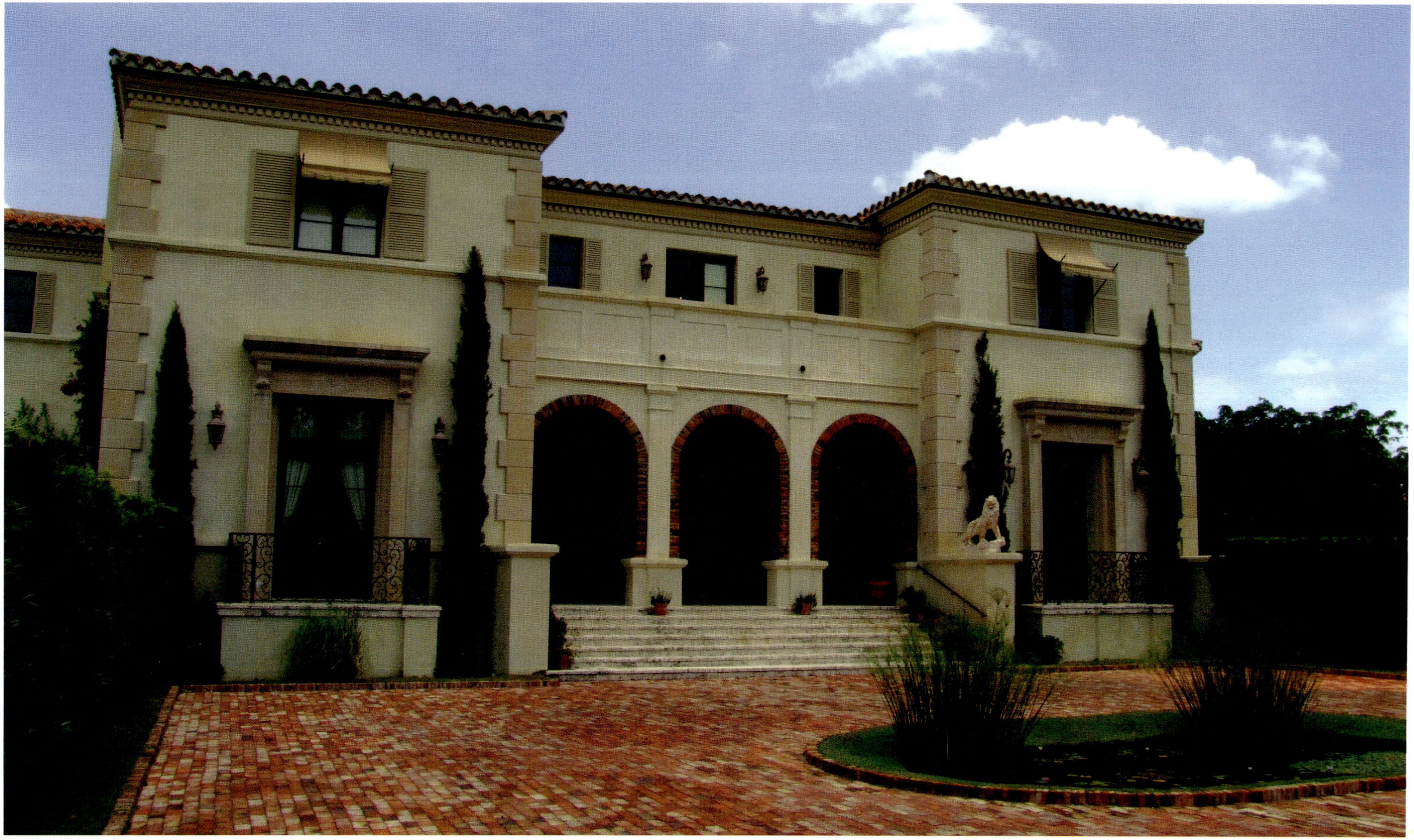

A following is hard to come by, but Zeb says that his clients seek him out for his style. His clients come to him because they have already seen some of his work, which is rooted in historical precedence, but at the same time is somewhat simplified. He tries to produce something that is authentic, but he also puts his own personal imprint on it. He relies on memories of spaces, massing and proportions for the detailing of his work and his clients respond very positively.

Zeb's architectural aesthetic relies very much on the Classical and the Neo-classical in the sense of spatial organization. He says he has tried to learn from the very basic premise of western culture, which has roots leading back to Greek and Roman architecture and re-incorporates these elements into his work.

His greatest lesson has come in acquiring a certain level of confidence, which has come relatively late into his career. Zeb says he has been his worst critic, but he is gradually finding pleasure in his finished projects. In the future, Zeb still wants to improve his work and says, "Life is a never ending process of searching and learning."

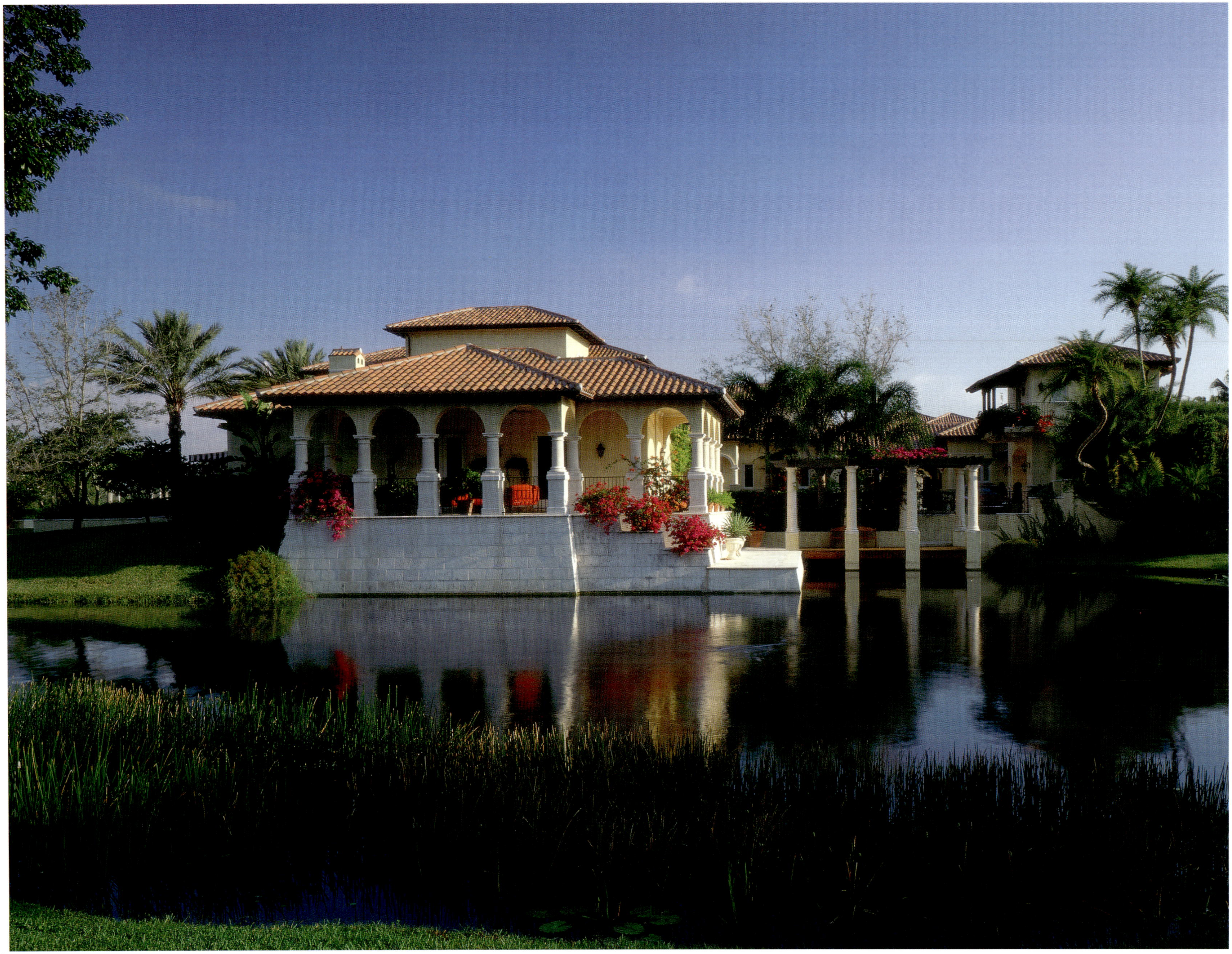

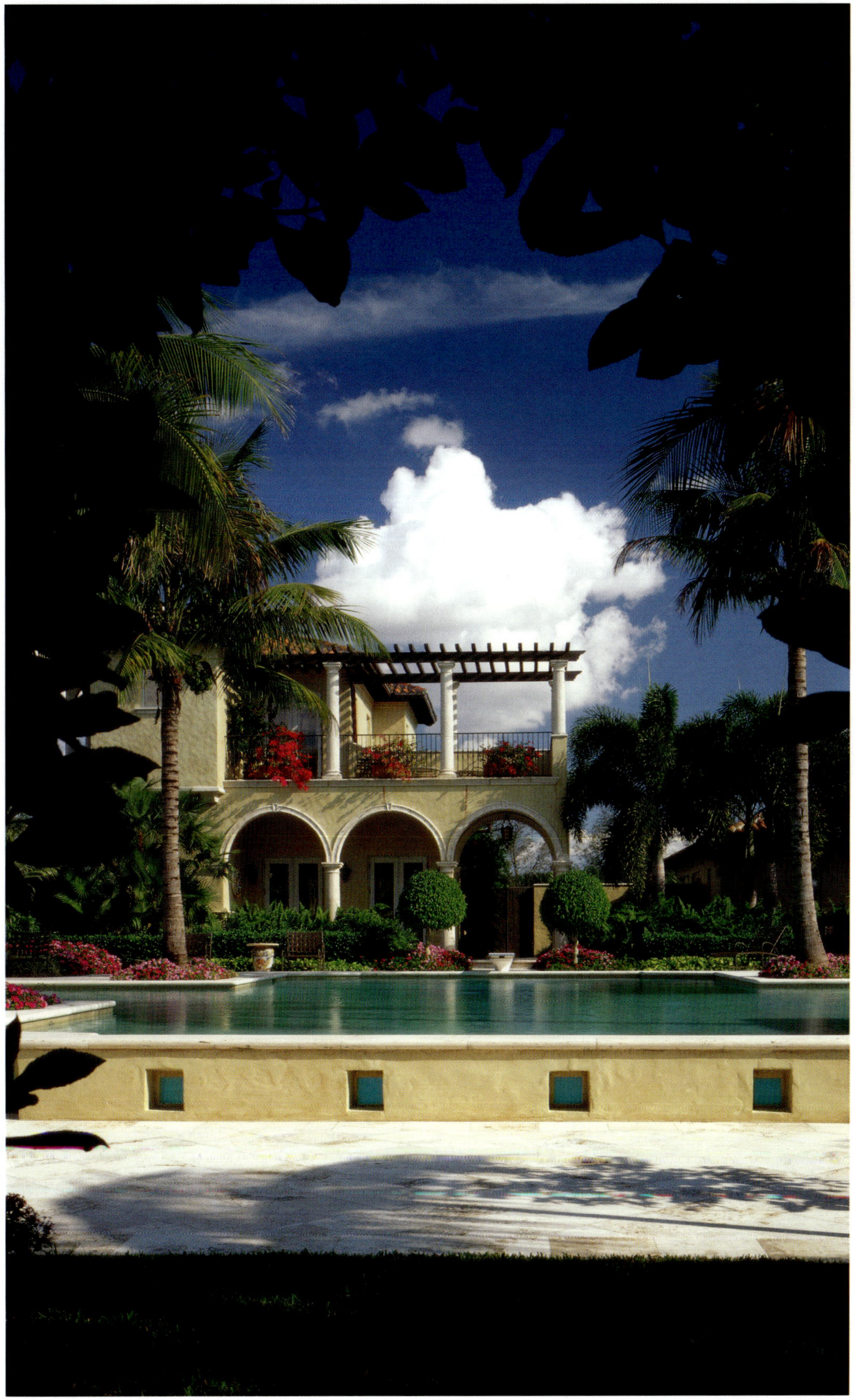

Q&A more about zeb...

NAME ONE THING MOST PEOPLE DON'T KNOW ABOUT YOU.

I was a merchant marine captain.

YOU WOULDN'T KNOW IT, BUT MY FRIENDS WOULD TELL YOU I AM ...

Addicted to road cycling.

WHAT IS A SINGLE THING YOU WOULD DO TO BRING A DULL HOUSE TO LIFE?

A bulldozer—I do recommend a bulldozer to my clients most of the time. It is not only based in humor, it is based in the reality of construction. Very often the numbers just do not add up with remodeling and really very often it is much easier and cost effective to level it and start from scratch.

Z.W. JAROSZ ARCHITECT, PA
JAROSZ DEVELOPMENT CORPORATION
Zbigniew "Zeb" Jarosz, President, AIA, RIBA
3326 Mary Street Suite 500
Miami, FL 33133
305.446.0888
Fax 305.447.1177
www.jaroszarch.com

LEFT & FACING PAGE: Residence for Miami Dolphins Dan Marino, Weston, FL.
Photographs by George Cott

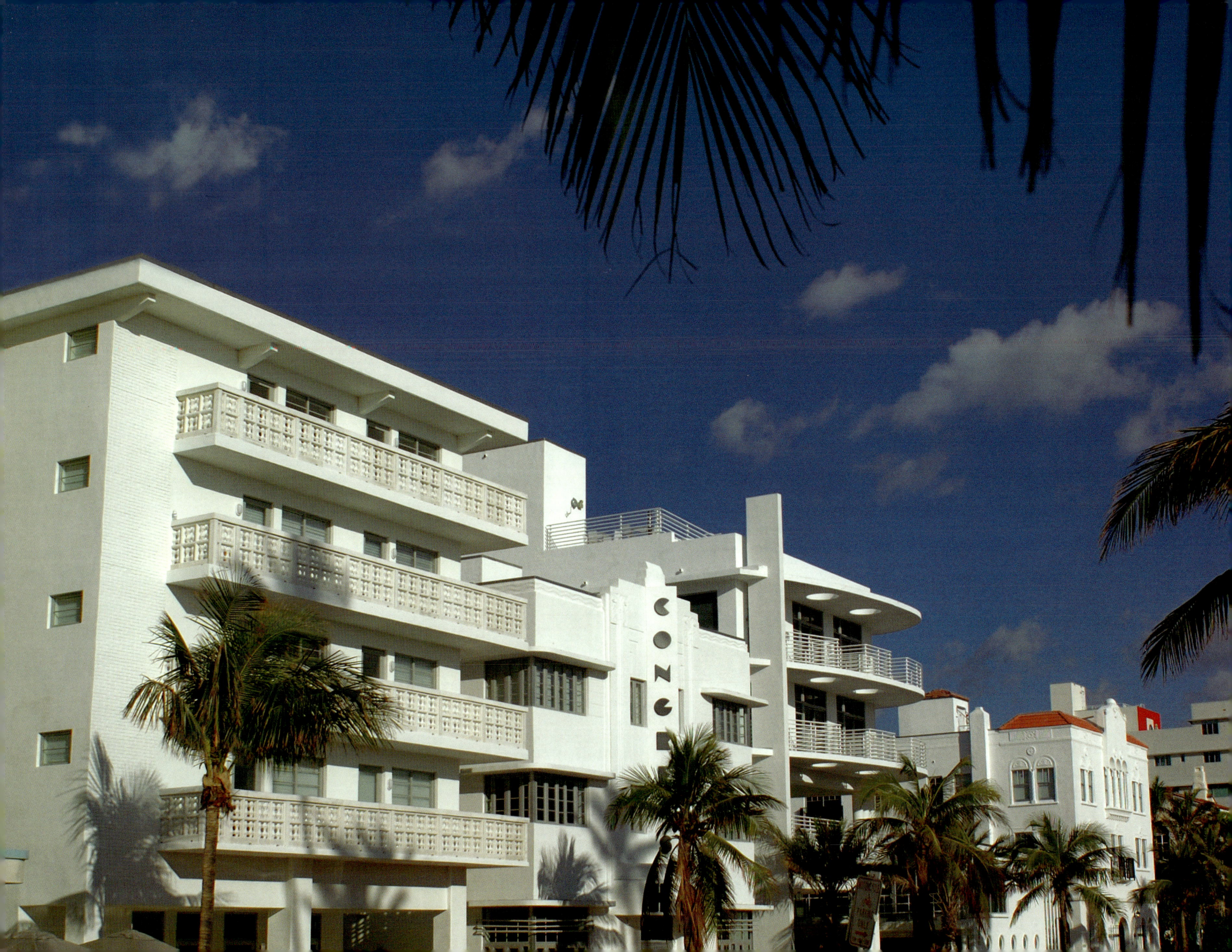
CONG

KOBI KARP

Kobi Karp Architecture & Interior Design

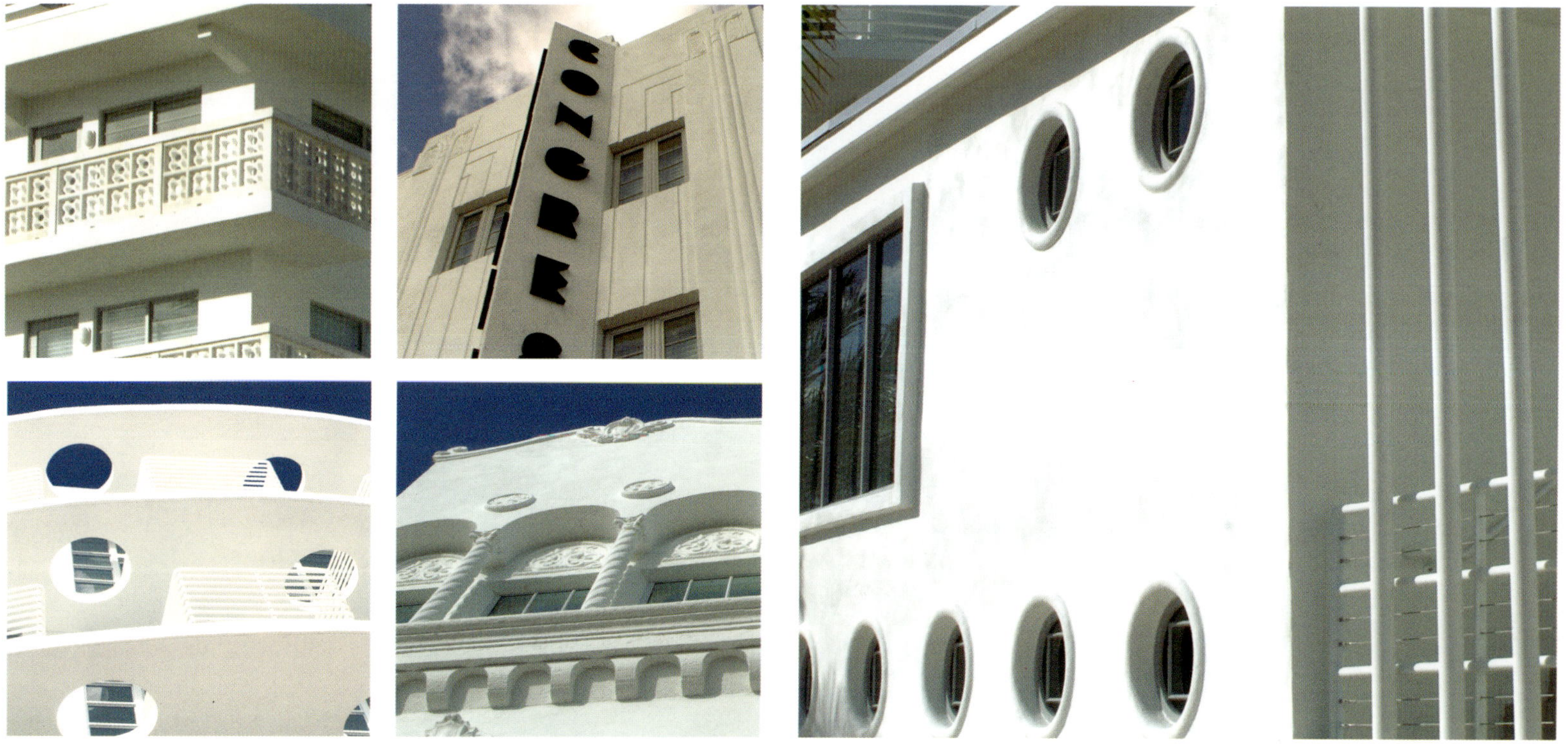

Kobi Karp creates intelligent buildings. Smart, in the fact that within each neighborhood where his structures stand they connect with the past and develop the present. But most importantly, for this architect, a Karp creation sets the tone for future architects by showing them that buildings need to be thoughtfully humanistic and artistically balanced with the surrounding environment. "When designing, it is important to have balance in every way," says Mr. Karp. "I maintain a clear state-of-mind with each endeavor and then balance out client needs, my thoughts and what surrounds the project. I thrive on harmony."

Although a listener, Karp's work is highly tuned to that of 21st century Modern architecture. It is just the angles, heights and lines that change for clients. One thing that has not changed is Karp's influence by architect Frank Lloyd Wright, whose design emphasis on how buildings relate to their existing environment is part of Mr. Karp's sphere of influence. Having attended The Prairie School, part of University of Minnesota's Institute of Technology where Mr. Karp earned degrees in both Architecture and Environmental Design, as well as an education in real-life, where throughout the mid-west Mr. Karp visited Wright's work. But to be solely tied to the past is not part of Mr. Karp's agenda.

ABOVE: Architectural details from the unique buildings that comprise The Strand. Each photo captures a different time in Miami Architecture.
Photographs by Al Ricketts

LEFT: A north view of Kobi Karp's restoration project The Strand in the Historic Deco District of Miami Beach's Ocean Drive. The four buildings reflect four different architectural styles of Miami Modern, Art Deco, Contemporary and Mediterranean Revival.
Photograph by Al Ricketts

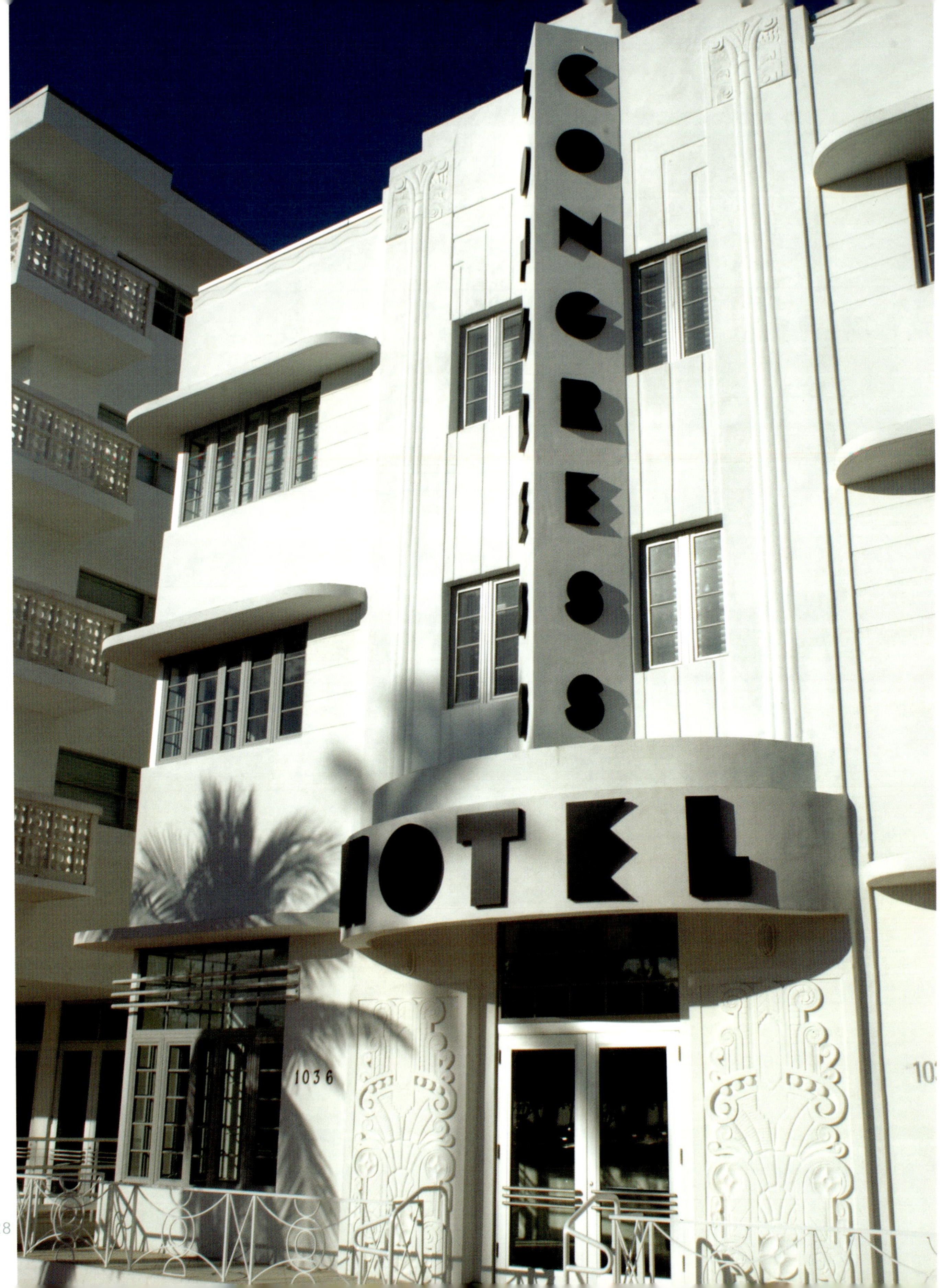

"Design is not static; design is dynamic which means it is continuously evolving," notes Mr. Karp. "I see design as being fluid, but at certain points, the design process has to cease so the structure can be built." And when it is built, people talk. In 2006, Mr. Karps' Miami based firm, Kobi Karp Architecture & Interior Design (KKAID) was presented with the Norman Giller Award from the North Beach Development Corporation. Coveted and high profile, Mr. Karp's work was called "pure genius" by community and civic leaders.

It is accolades like these that in less than a decade has led KKAID to design much of Miami's skyline, redefine resort living in the Caribbean and continue to allow occupants of his dwellings to rejoice in their living space. "Seeing people enjoy their habitat after completion is the highest honor for me," says Mr. Karp.

And heights are something Mr. Karp likes, especially ones that involve the environment. Although Mr. Karp acknowledges new methods of living and new necessities of architecture and the use of the newly invented or newly perfected materials, which enable the designer to meet these necessities, nature must always remain the same. "In cities such as New York, you walk out of your unit and you look up or down and see gardens up in the air," Mr. Karp says. "I like seeing that in all of my projects. I like for people from other buildings to look out and not just see cement and windows, but to see life."

Like his work, Mr. Karp's life is not over stylized. His home is unique, but comfortable. His family is cultured, brilliant and gracious. Mr.Karp, always surveying his surrounding environment wearing jeans and a button-down and for those that know him, the wheels of design and its' evolution always spinning.

LEFT: The Congress Hotel's original Art Deco glamour was brought back to life by Karp who preserved the original details of its grand façade.
Photograph by Al Ricketts

FACING PAGE: Rooftop minimalism and modernism allows for an open appreciation of the breathtaking views of Miami Beach—one of Karp's primary considerations when bringing the 1052 building to life.
Photograph by Troy Campbell

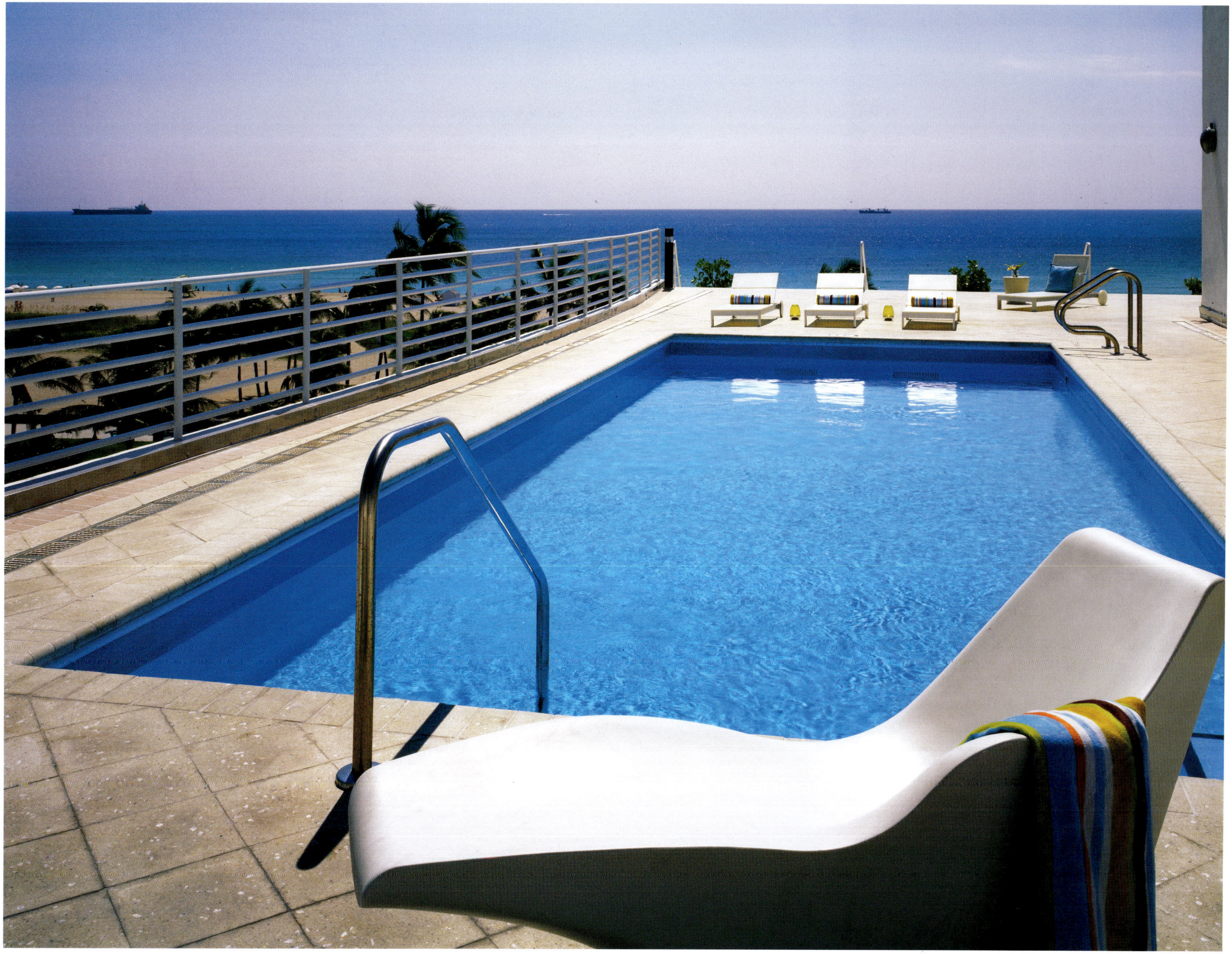

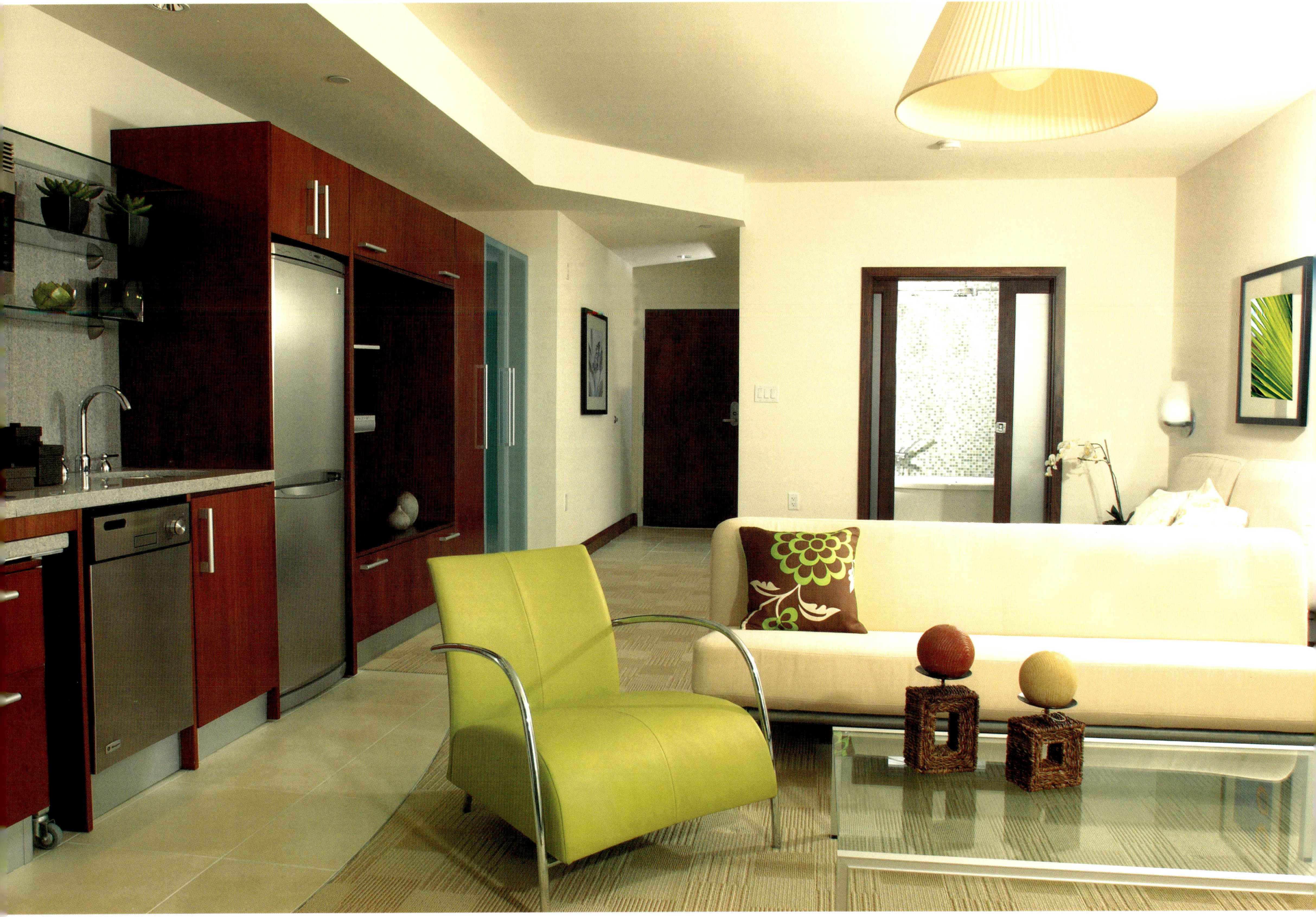

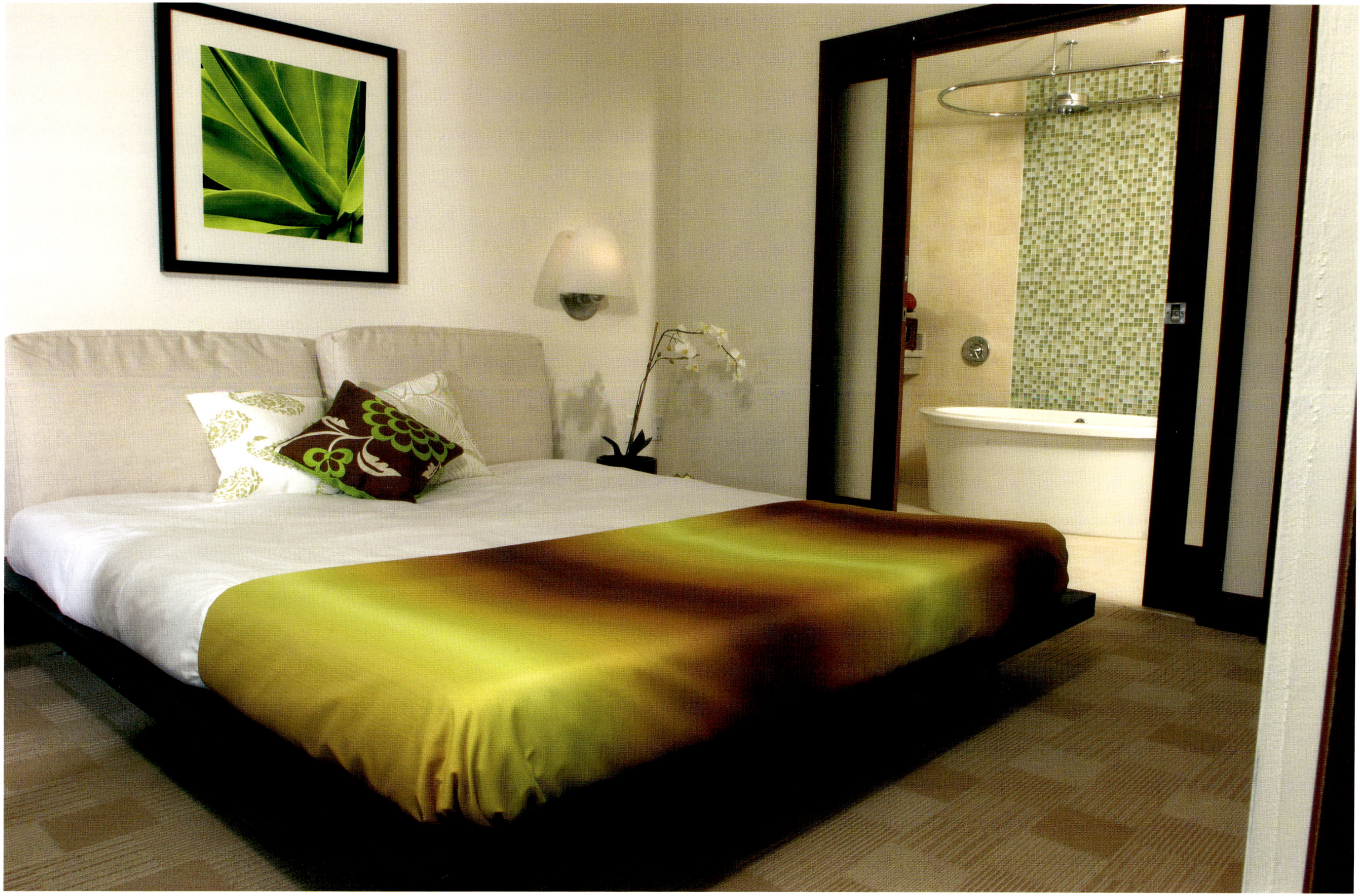

ABOVE & FACING PAGE: Sleek modern interiors and unit designs were incorporated into The Strand providing contemporary luxury living, functionality and comfort a specialization of Kobi Karp.
Photographs by Al Ricketts

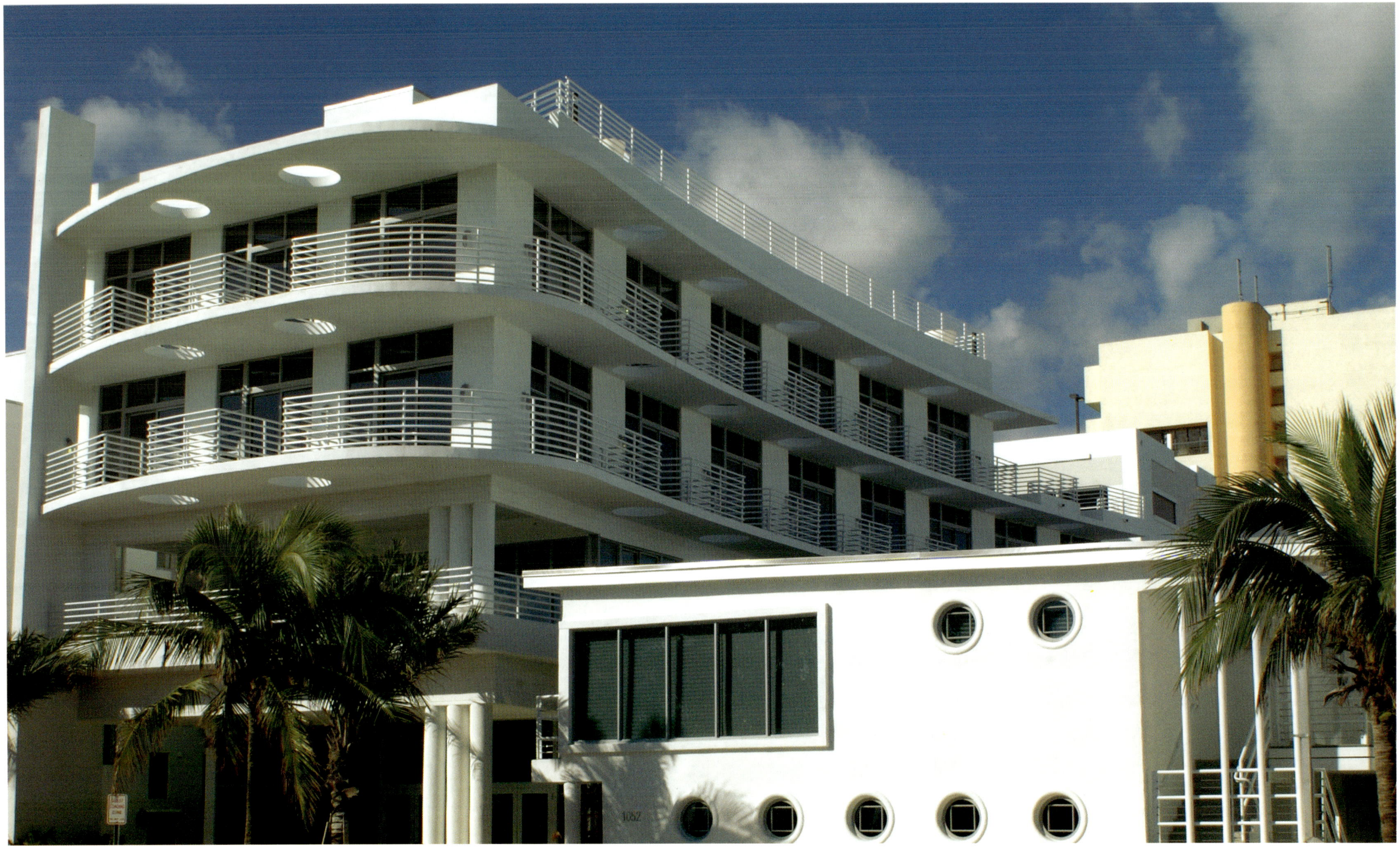

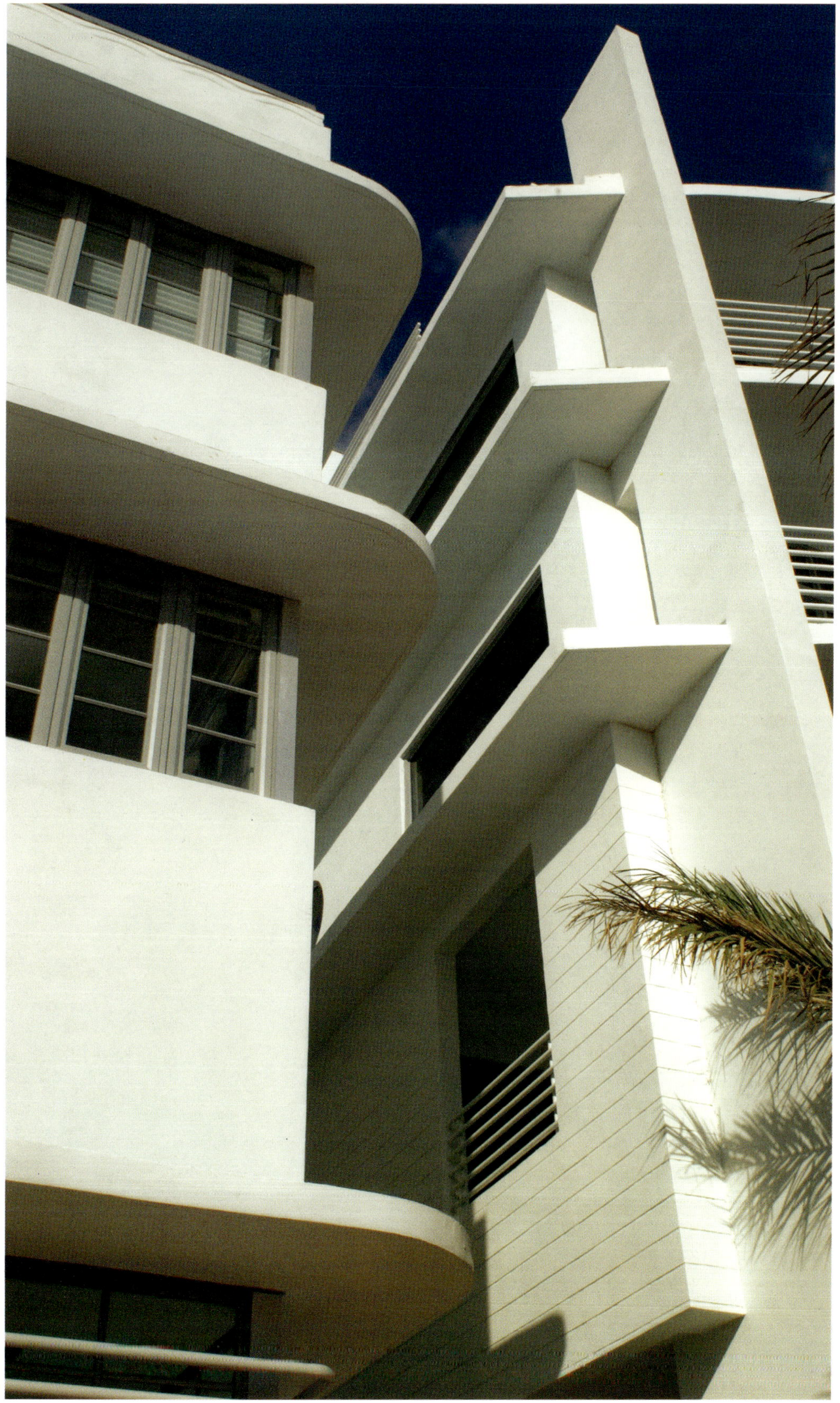

Q&A more about kobi...

WHAT SEPARATES YOU FROM YOUR COMPETITION?

Our business experience and understanding of the economic markets allow us to implement realistic design solutions that result in the feasibility of projects from design to the construction process. In summary, our firm specializes in the creation of modern, constructible design.

DESCRIBE YOUR STYLE.

We adhere to the vernacular, the context and the cultural influences of each project and community. Our style morphs as we progress through our challenges and experiences.

WHAT PERSONAL INDULGENCE DO YOU SPEND THE MOST MONEY ON?

My two children whom I adore.

KOBI KARP ARCHITECTURE & INTERIOR DESIGN
Kobi Karp, AIA
2915 Biscayne Boulevard, Suite 200
Miami, FL 33137
305.573.1818
Fax 305.573.3766
www.kobikarp.com

LEFT: Karp's preservation of The Strand's contrasting architectural styles are shown in this photo of the 1036 and 1052 Ocean Drive building.
Photograph by Al Ricketts

FACING PAGE: The 1052 Ocean Drive building embodies modernism and historic preservation with its design inclusion of architectural characteristics derived from its original, Miami Modern Architecture building.
Photograph by Al Ricketts

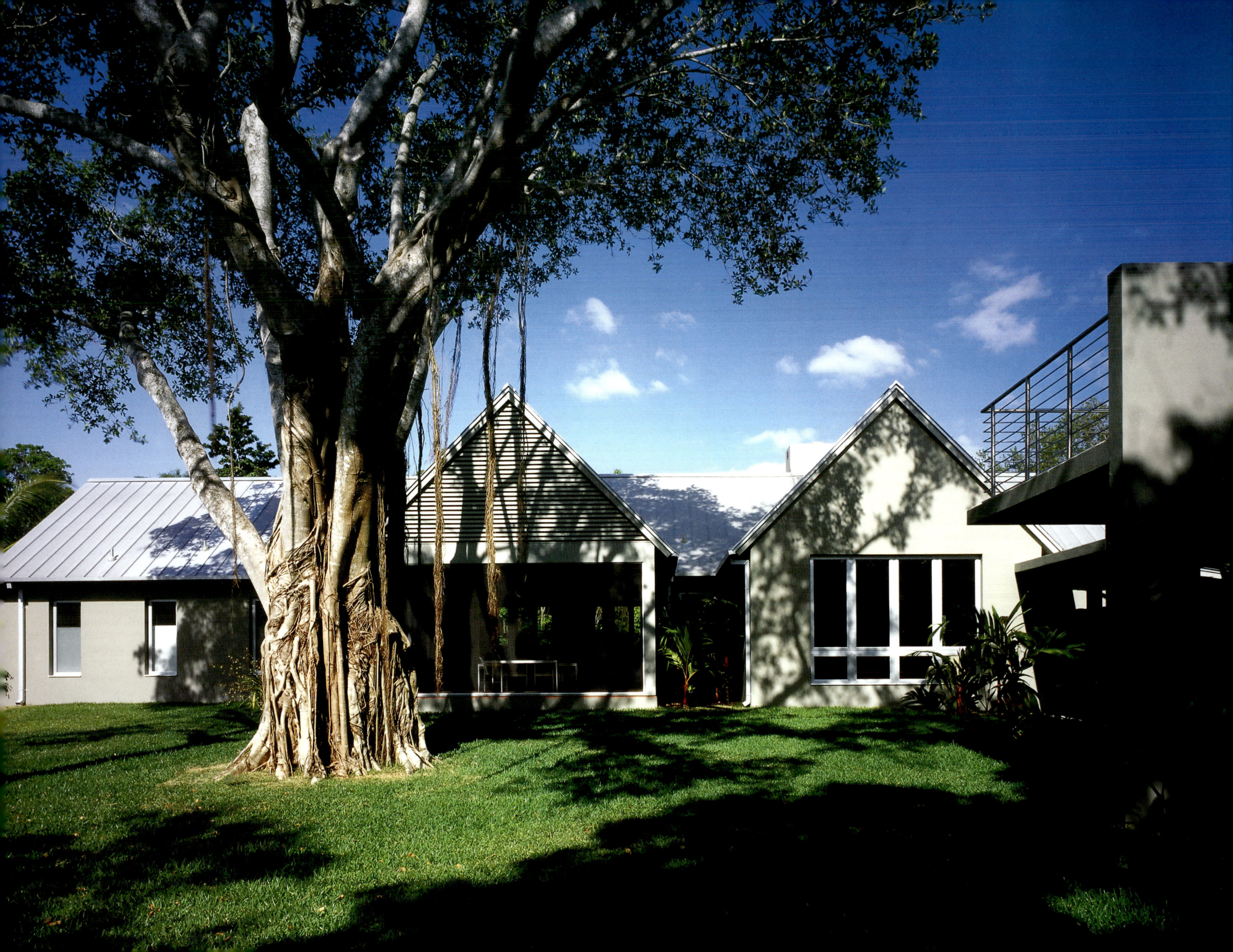

SUZANNE MARTINSON

Suzanne Martinson Architects, Inc.

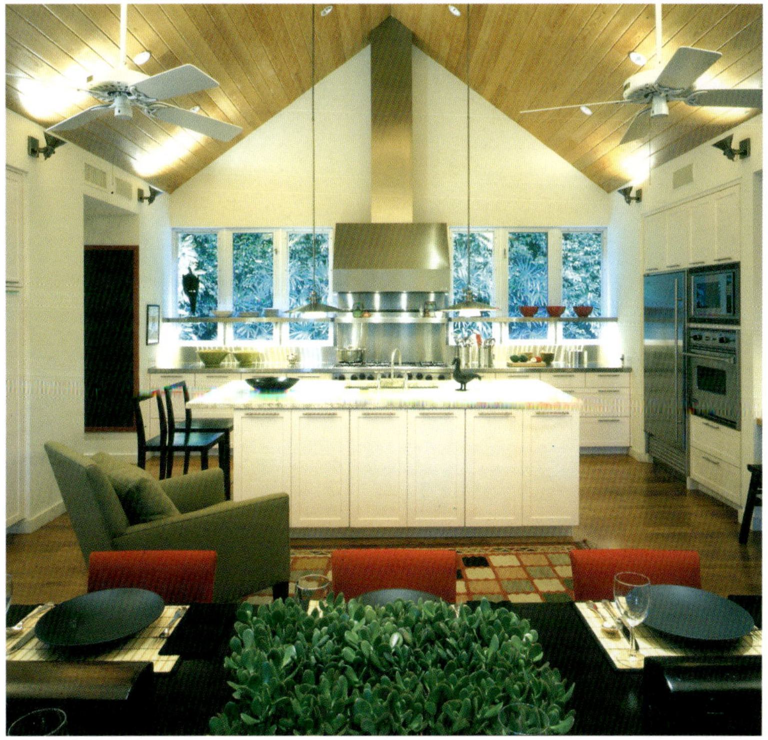

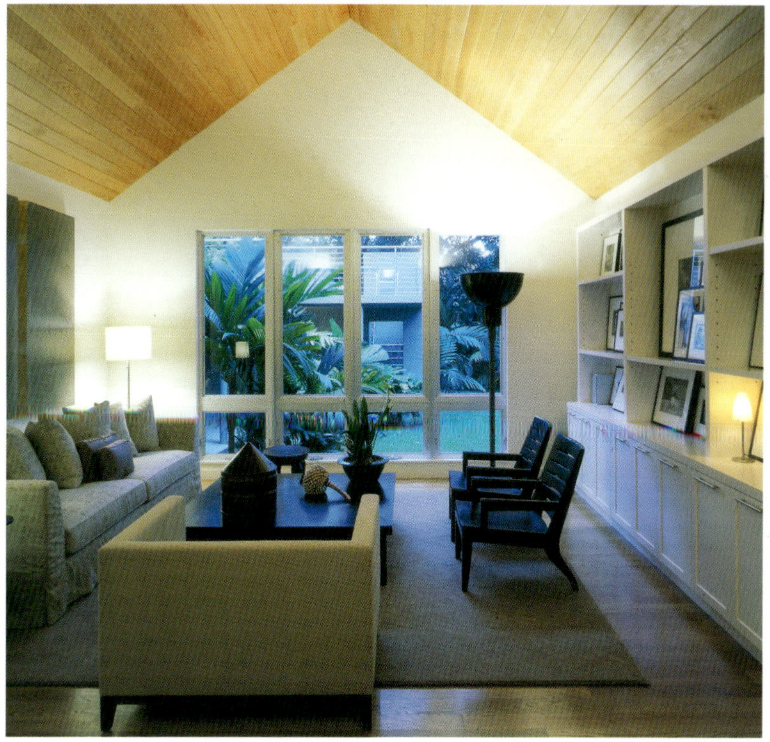

Suzanne Martinson's architectural practice is founded on the early Modernist philosophy that homes are "machines for living." Consequently, she makes each of her designs as functionally beautiful as possible.

Born in the Midwest, Suzanne has spent most of her life in South Florida. She received her interior design degree from the University of Florida and practiced for six years. She then attended the University of Miami and Columbia University for her degrees in architecture. Suzanne wanted to design not only the interiors but also the structural framework for those interiors. She sought to control the scale and proportions of the spaces, the circulation, the views, and, ultimately, how people experienced their homes.

Suzanne strives to produce "green" houses that are environmentally friendly and highly functional. She considers homes to be the interface between the natural environment and our technologically controlled environment. A true Modernist, Suzanne is excited about the technological advances in architecture and their promise for the future of residential design.

ABOVE LEFT: The Ellison Residence kitchen features meticulously crafted custom cabinetry, a wood ceiling, and floor and marble counters.
Photograph by Steven Brooke

ABOVE RIGHT: The Ellison Residence living room, oriented to the garden, features exacting proportions that provide a sense of both grandeur and intimacy.
Photograph by Steven Brooke

LEFT: The rear elevation of the Ellison Residence features steep sloped roofs that define the volumes of the living room, kitchen/dining area and screened porch.
Photograph by Steven Brooke

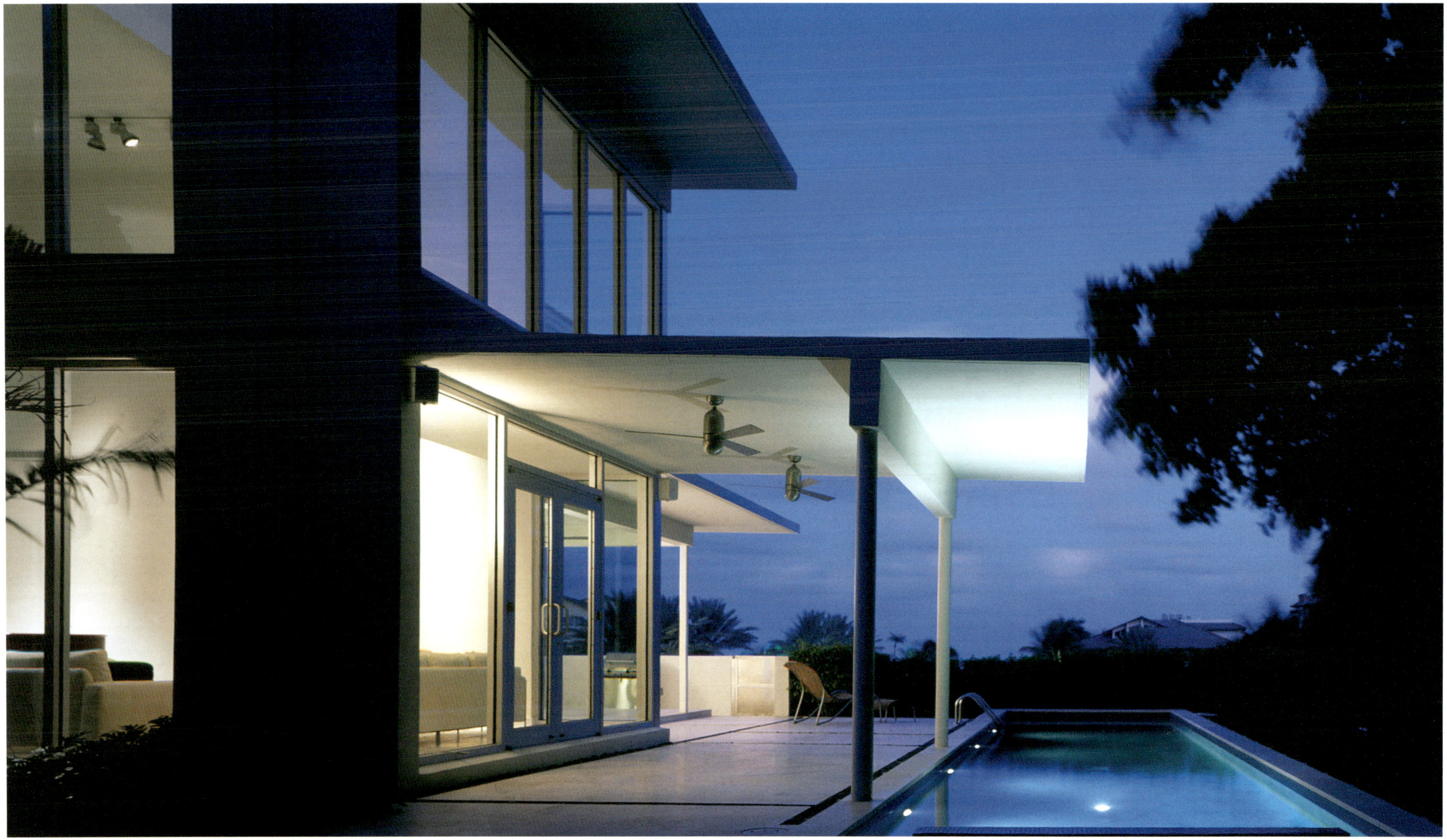

Historically, Suzanne believes that appearance of our buildings speaks volumes about the society in which we live. She feels that society has a responsibility to protect the environment and to conserve our precious natural resources, especially in design of residential architecture. She believes that development of alternative energy sources for our homes is a must, and that in the near future it will be absolutely required. She is optimistic that those requirements will inspire the creation of very exciting architectural components. Suzanne embraces these advances and will continue to incorporate these new technologies into her architecture.

Besides being on the cutting edge of innovation and culture, Suzanne enjoys exploring the relationship between the outdoors and the indoors in her designs. The South Florida landscape with its exotic botany is crucial to her work. Capitalizing on the tropical nature of the climate adds uniqueness to her architecture. "Seeing green" for Suzanne isn't a form of envy on her part; it is her very personal response to the beautiful tropical land that is her home and her inspiration.

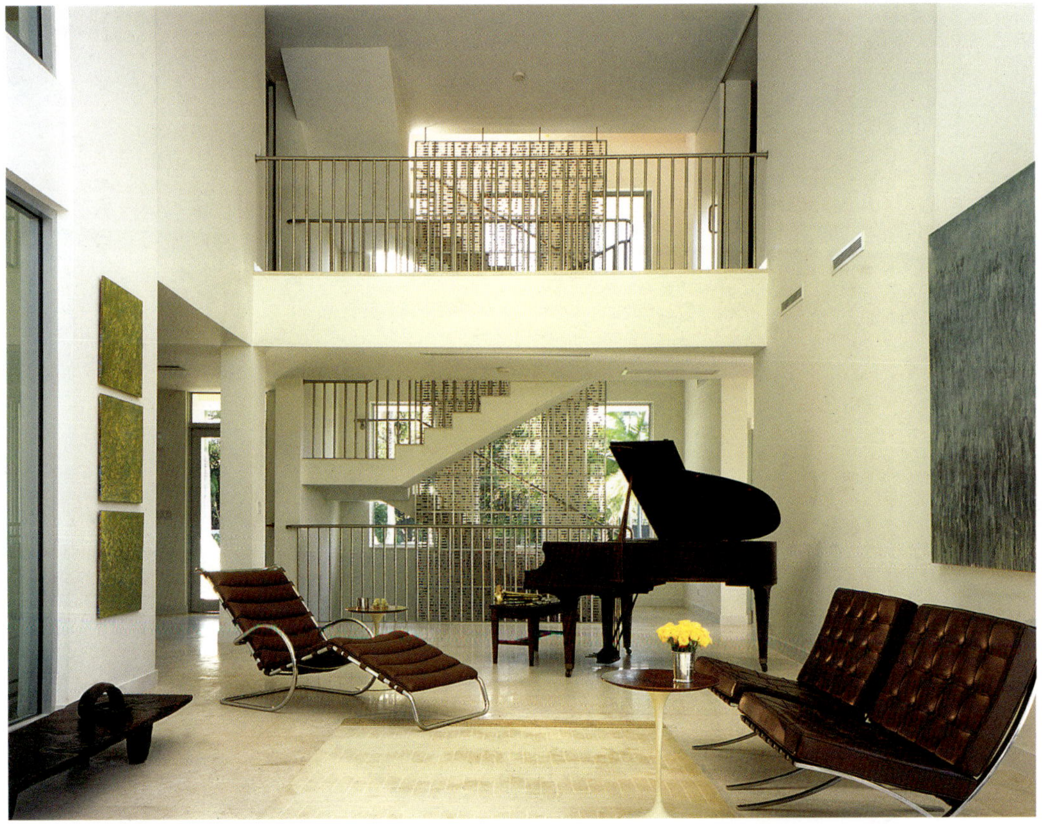

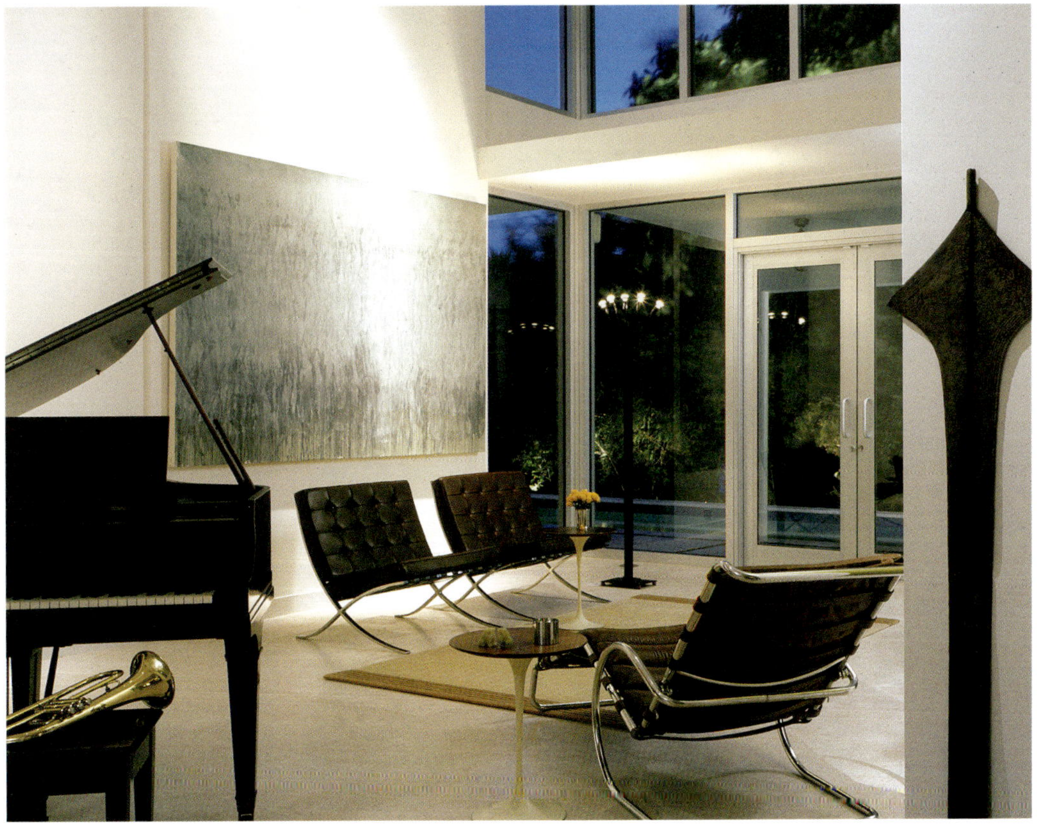

Q&A

more about suzanne...

WHAT SEPARATES YOU FROM YOUR COMPETITION?

My attention to detail and structure. I seek to produce well-proportioned, uncluttered, flowing spaces with magnificent views to the landscape.

DESCRIBE YOUR STYLE OR DESIGN PREFERENCES?

Tropical Modern/ Romantic Modern. My style incorporates aspects of architectural history without being the least bit nostalgic. It is grounded in modernist principles but embraces the uniqueness of the tropical environment.

WHAT IS THE BEST PART OF BEING AN ARCHITECT?

Creating a framework from which my clients may best view the world and enjoy their lives.

SUZANNE MARTINSON ARCHITECTS, INC.
Suzanne Martinson, AIA
7911 Southwest 55th Avenue
Miami, FL 33143
305.667.3944
Fax 305.663.0405

TOP: Cross Residence living room. A sculpture by Stephen Dean punctuates the scissors stairs in the double-volume living room.
Photograph by Steven Brooke

BOTTOM: Cross Residence living room. The Cross's collection of contemporary art and classic furniture complements the minimalist interior.
Photograph by Steven Brooke

FACING PAGE: A cantilevered slab pierces the rear wall of the Cross Residence forming a porch that overhangs the lap pool.
Photograph by Steven Brooke

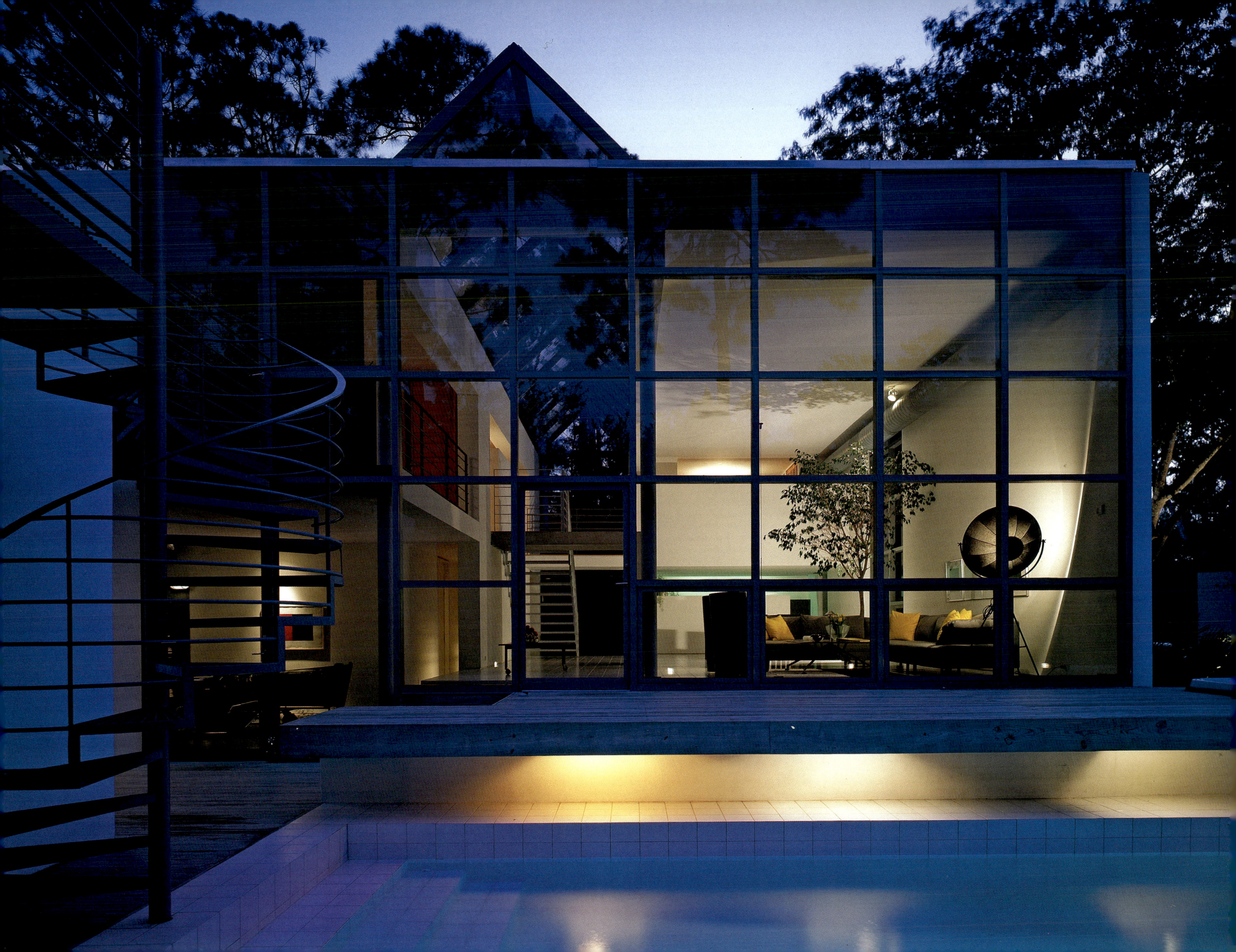

RONEY J. MATEU

Mateu Architecture Incorporated

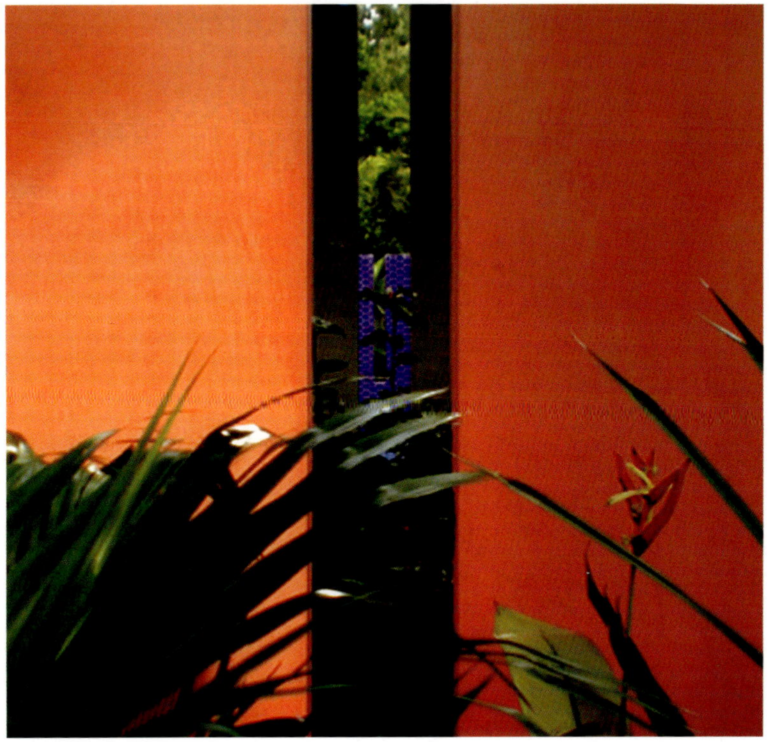

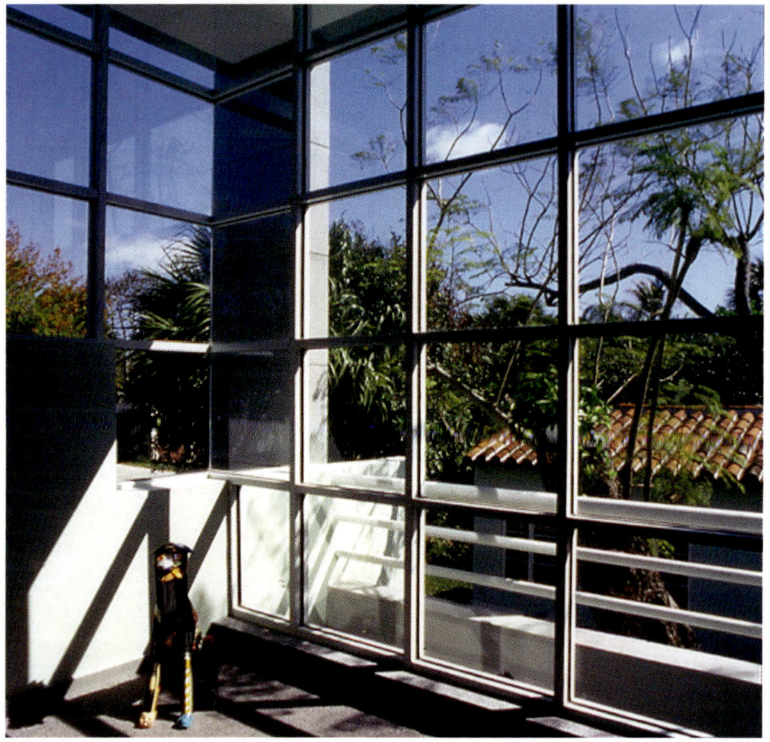

From the time that Roney Mateu could draw he's been drawing houses. It should come as very little surprise that he would grow up to become a premier, award-winning architect of modern structures in Florida and the Caribbean.

Originally from Cuba, he moved to the United States with his parents at the age of eight, attended the University of Florida and then graduated from the University of Miami with an architectural degree in 1976. After graduation there wasn't much work for the flowering architect, and as a result, he purchased a lot on Old Cutler Road in south Miami-Dade County and proceeded to build his first home there.

In the meantime he secured a job working for an architectural firm in Coconut Grove, where he declared that he would either become a partner there or start his own firm. Almost two years to the date from his start, he got a call from a church needing a new church building, which was right up his alley as he had completed his thesis based on a dynamic church building. Seeing this phone call as a sign from above, he put in his letter of resignation. Upon telling his wife of the good news, she had some news of her own—she was pregnant with their first child, all during the construction of their second home in Coconut Grove. Roney considered the whole adventure as a leap of faith and continued forward on his chosen path.

ABOVE LEFT: Color pops on this entrance wall with charming detail.
Casa Solana, Coconut Grove, Florida.
Photograph by Carlos Domenech

ABOVE RIGHT: Master bedroom addition to Addison Mizner house.
Old Floresta, Boca Raton, Florida.
Photograph by Kate Zari

LEFT: A spectacular view is had from inside this home to the outside pool patio. Lighted in the evening, it offers a dramatic effect.
Snapper Creek Lakes, Florida.
Photograph by Carlos Domenech

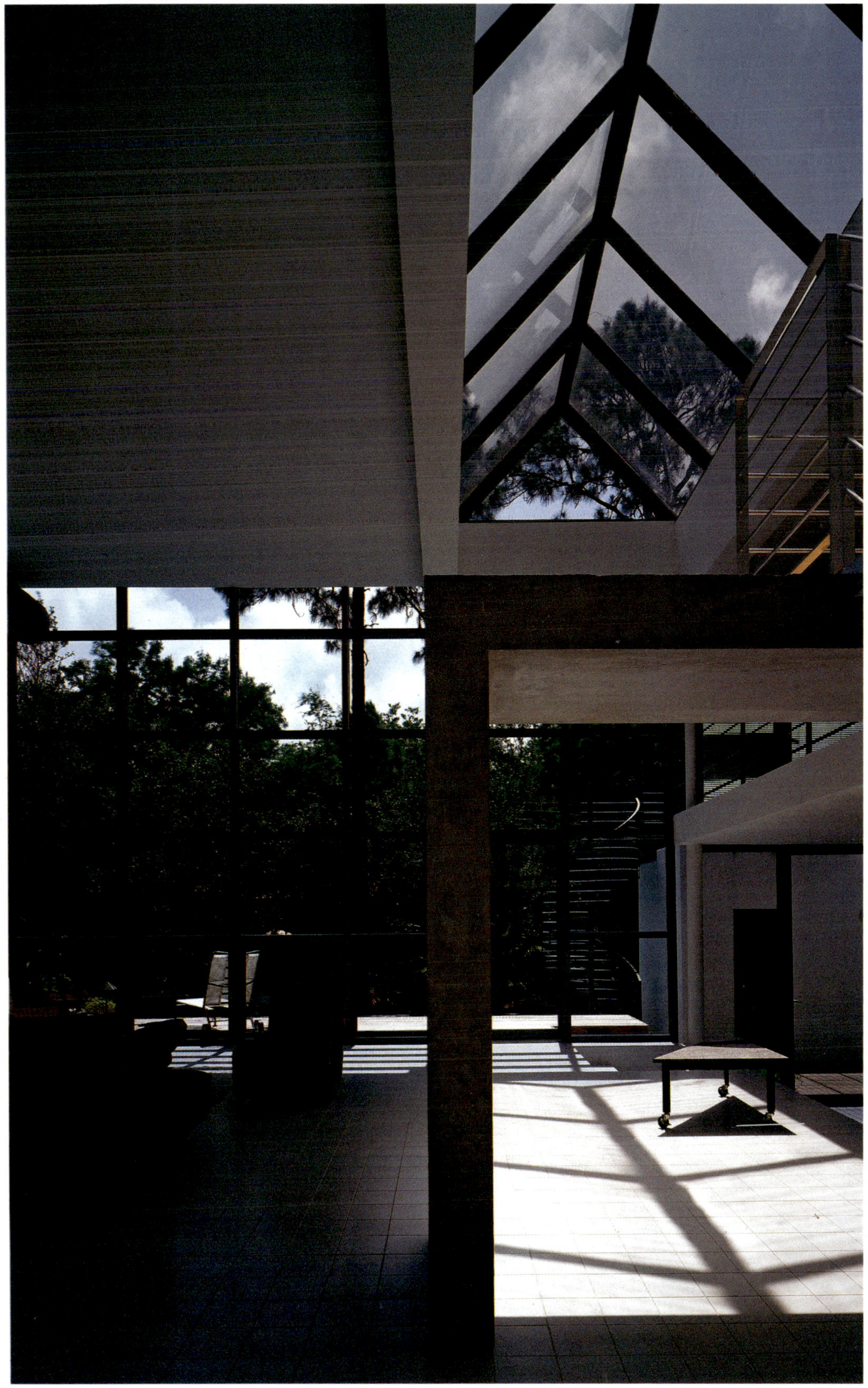
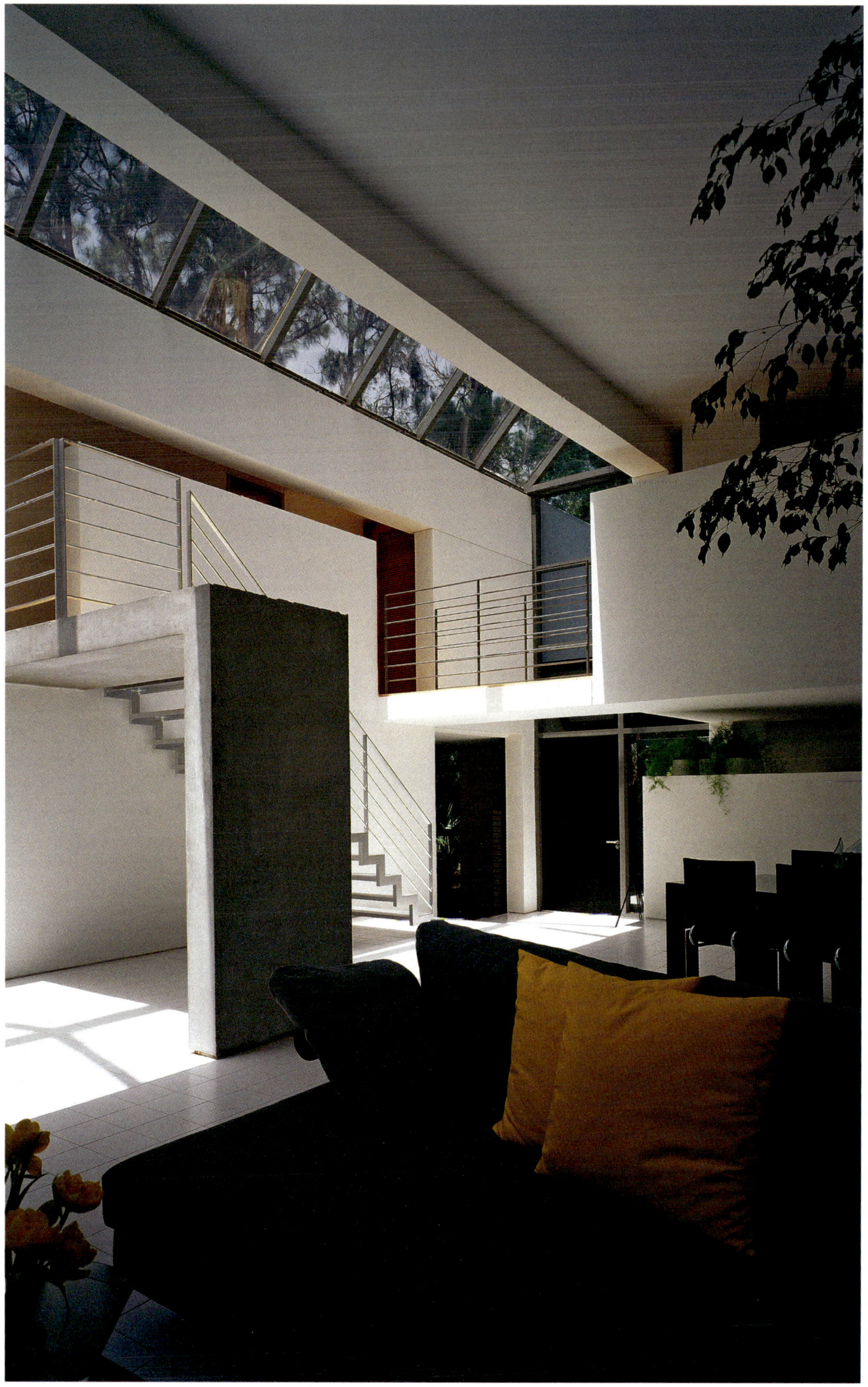

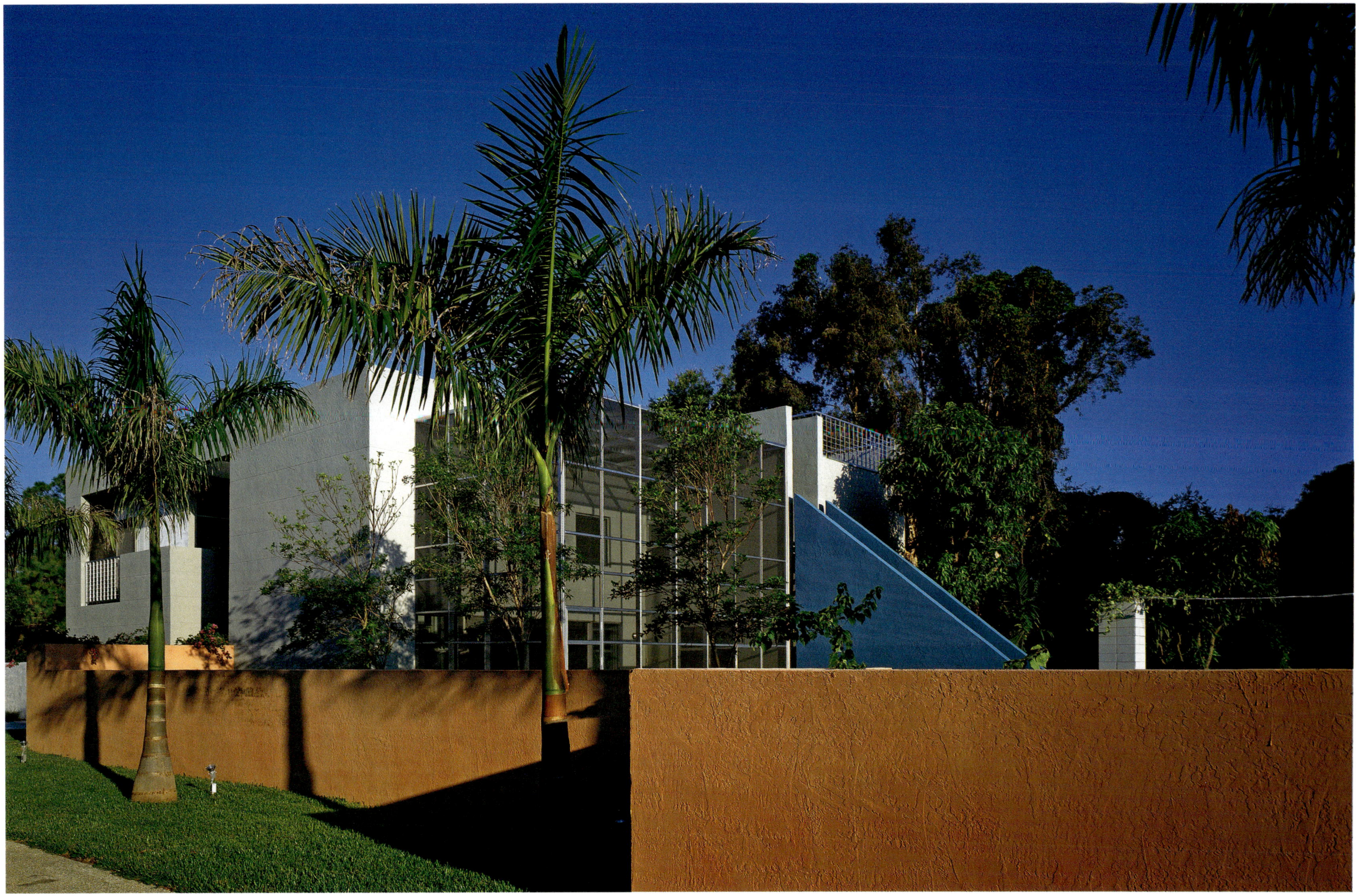

ABOVE: Main House, Mateu Family Compound, Pinecrest, Florida.
Photograph by Carlos Domenech

FACING PAGE LEFT: An interesting view from the entryway of this private residence. Snapper Creek Lakes, Florida.
Photograph by Carlos Domenech

FACING PAGE RIGHT: The main living room of a private residence. Snapper Creek Lakes, Florida.
Photograph by Carlos Domenech

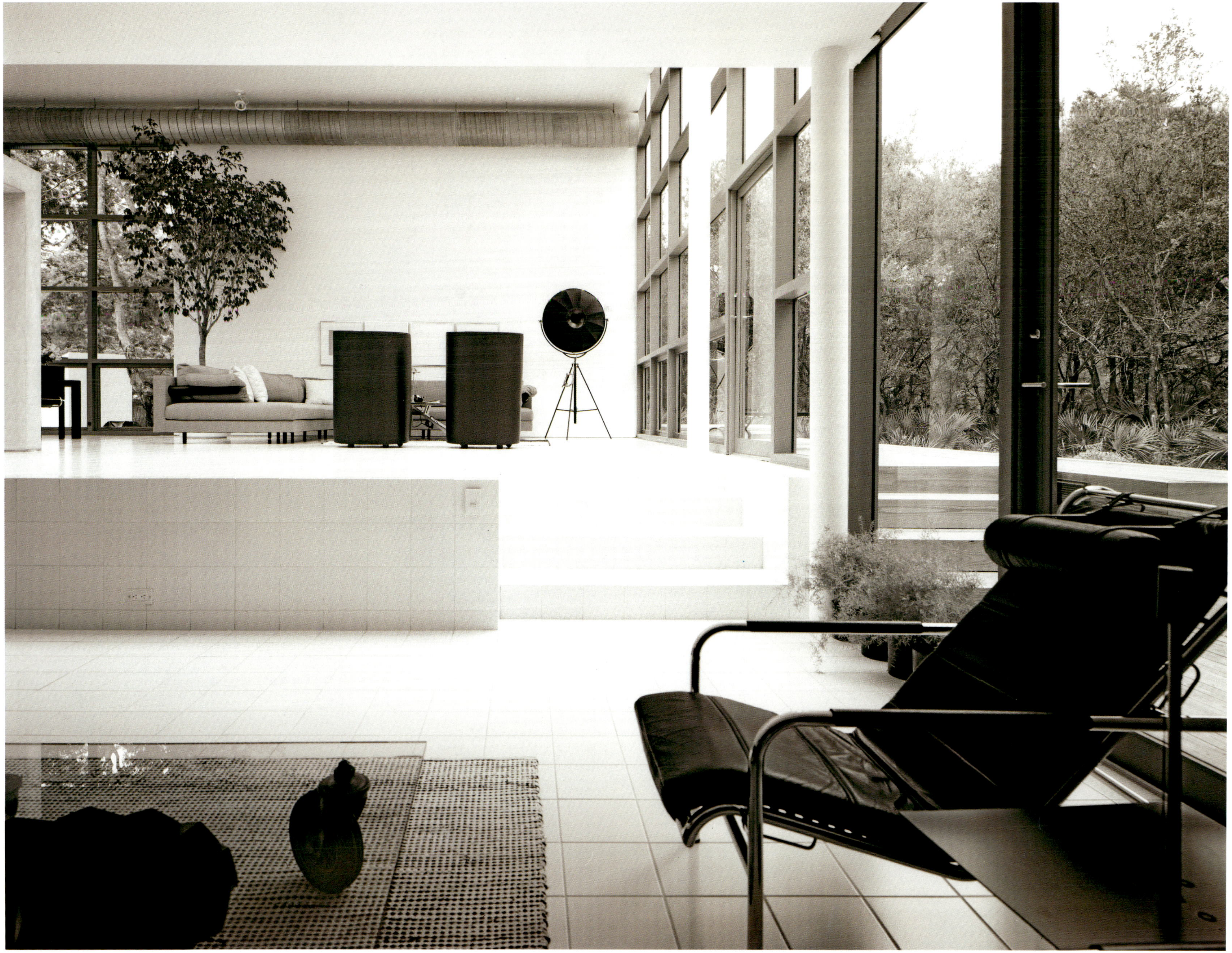

The church was never built, but his own office was now open and business came streaming through the door.

Today, Roney's firm has designed everything from an airport terminal, to home additions and everything in between. The thread of consistency between each of his projects is that they are all highly modern structures; there is never a discussion of his firm's stylistic preference or convictions. Simply put, they are firmly rooted in pushing the envelope of highly modern design. "Our aesthetic is one of function, straight forwardness, minimalism, simplified and efficient architecture. Our designs are appropriate for their place and time. They are always respectful of context. Everything that we do is unique for the program, for the client and for the site."

The materials Roney uses for his modern structures are available at any home improvement store, however widely available he doesn't use construction materials in a conventional way. His firm digs to the roots of design and space and allows the design to be a canvas for the homeowners or the business.

In the past Roney hasn't traveled much because he's been too busy satisfying his clients, but in the past few years he's been able to travel to places he's never been. In turn, he has been inspired by the ancient structures of the Old World. He says that traveling, particularly to the older cities in Ireland and Italy, have actually inspired him to create even more modern architecture because even when those old structures were being built they were truly on the cutting edge of modern design, which is what Roney strives to achieve with each project—a truly modern and timeless design.

In 1992, Roney's forward-thinking design won him the highest architectural design award that one can receive in the state of Florida. It was The Award of Honor for Design from the American

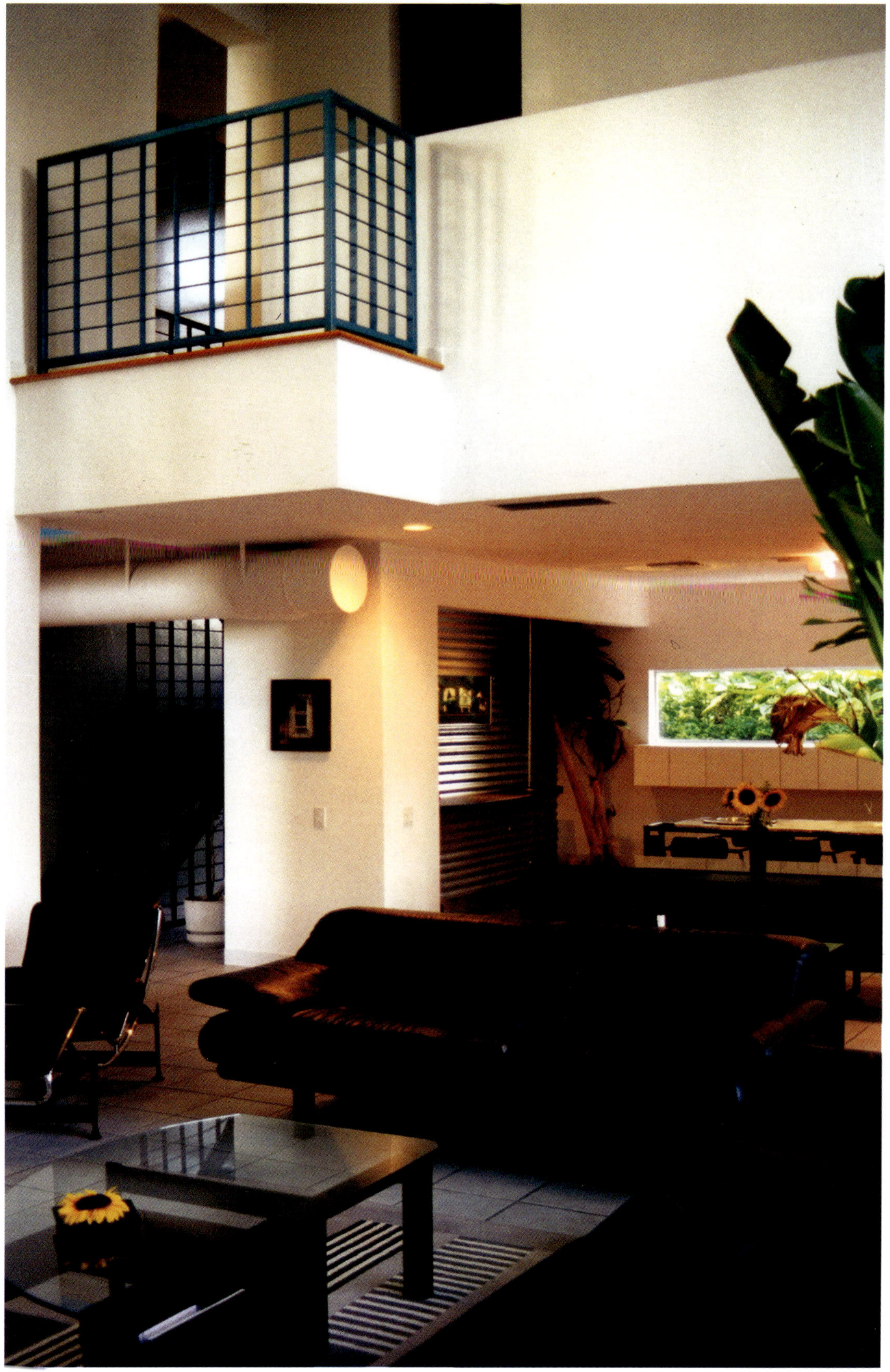

RIGHT; Living room area of the main house, Mateu Family Compound, Pinecrest, Florida.
Photograph by Roney J. Mateu

FACING PAGE: View from den to main living room. Private residence, Snapper Creek Lakes, Florida
Photograph by Carlos Domenech

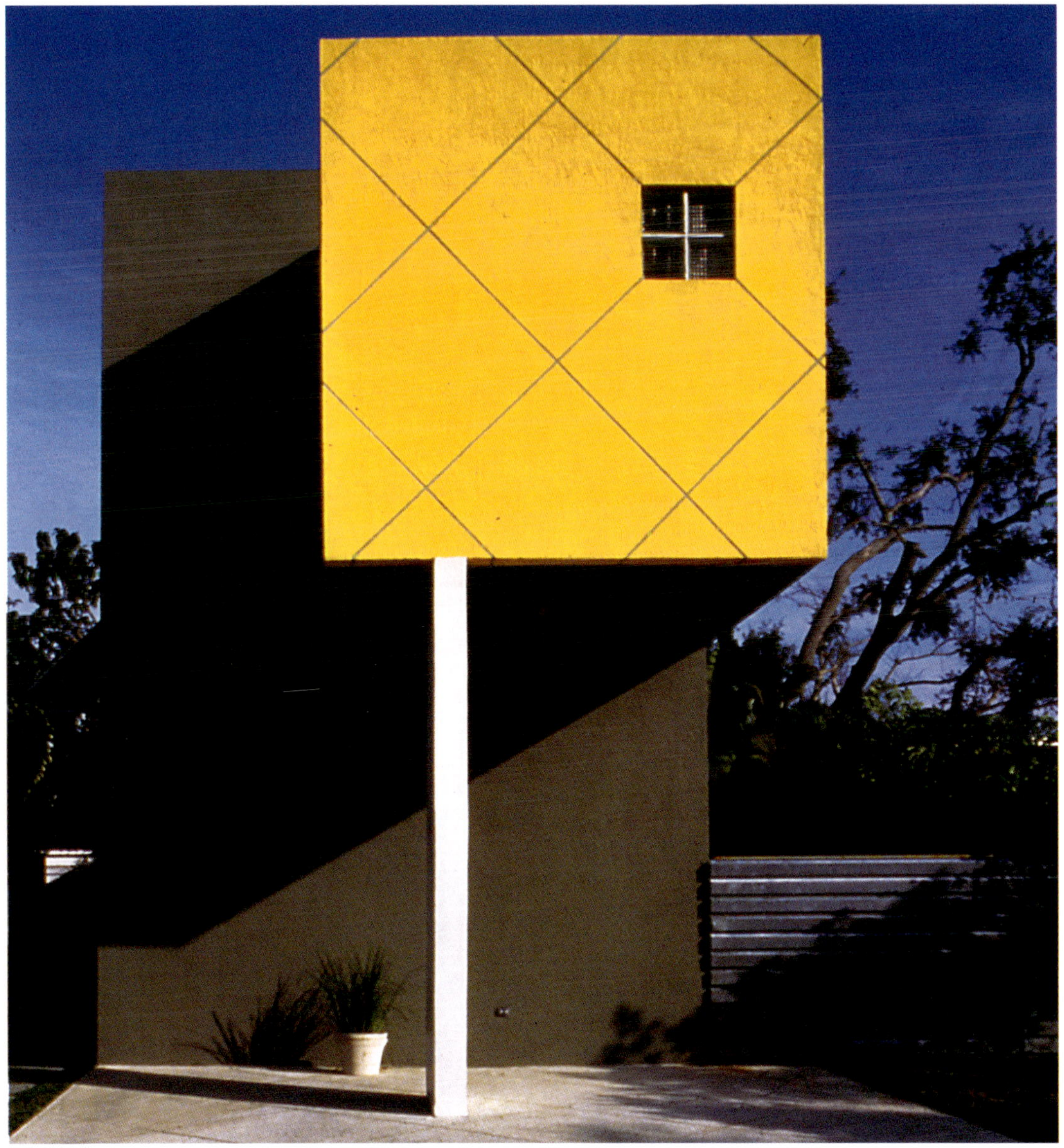

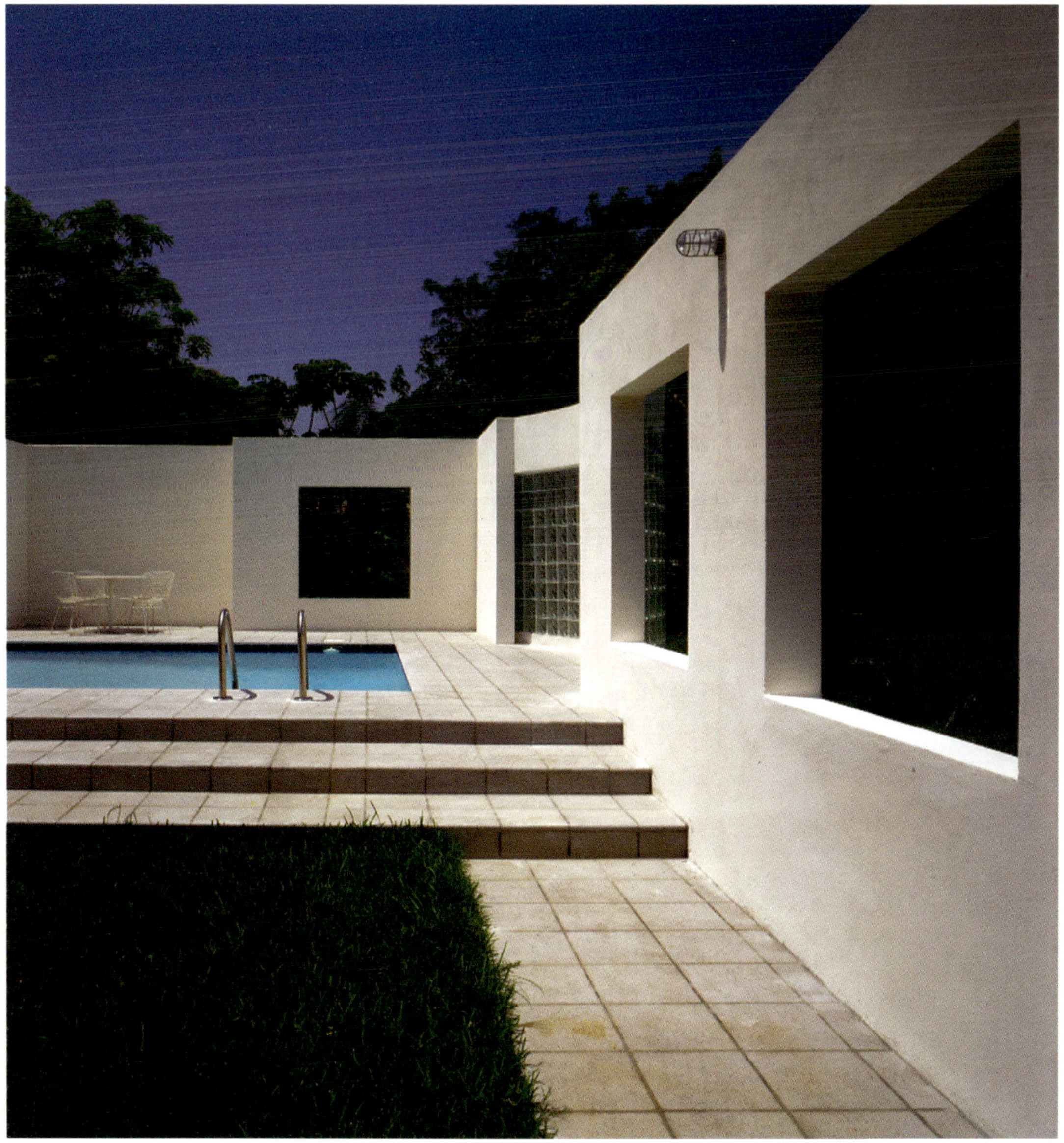

Institute of Architects. He's the youngest architect ever to receive this award in its history. To apply for the award a variety of projects must be submitted to the judges. Included in the list of projects he submitted was a picture of his kids. "The best project I've ever created has been my children, in collaboration with my wife."

Mateu claims that the most exciting and rewarding project that his firm has created, even though not the largest, was the Mateu Family Compound where Roney now lives. It's a two-house compound for his family and his parents (now deceased) separated by a pool area that symbolically details the story of the Mateu family. Through architectural expression he's told the story of his family, the generational differences and similarities between them, their cultural values and the impact of coming over from Cuba which is represented by the water in between the two houses. "When my parents used to look out their living room towards our house they saw the future," he said. "When we look out of our house towards theirs we see the past. Architecturally all of this was put together very subtly, not overtly, but very gently and I believe very successfully."

In the future, Roney says he will continue to push the architectural envelope, but ever so slightly, and his firm will continue their commitment to designs that are appropriate for the place, the site and the time. "We'll always experiment with materials and ideas and continue to pursue a timeless body of work."

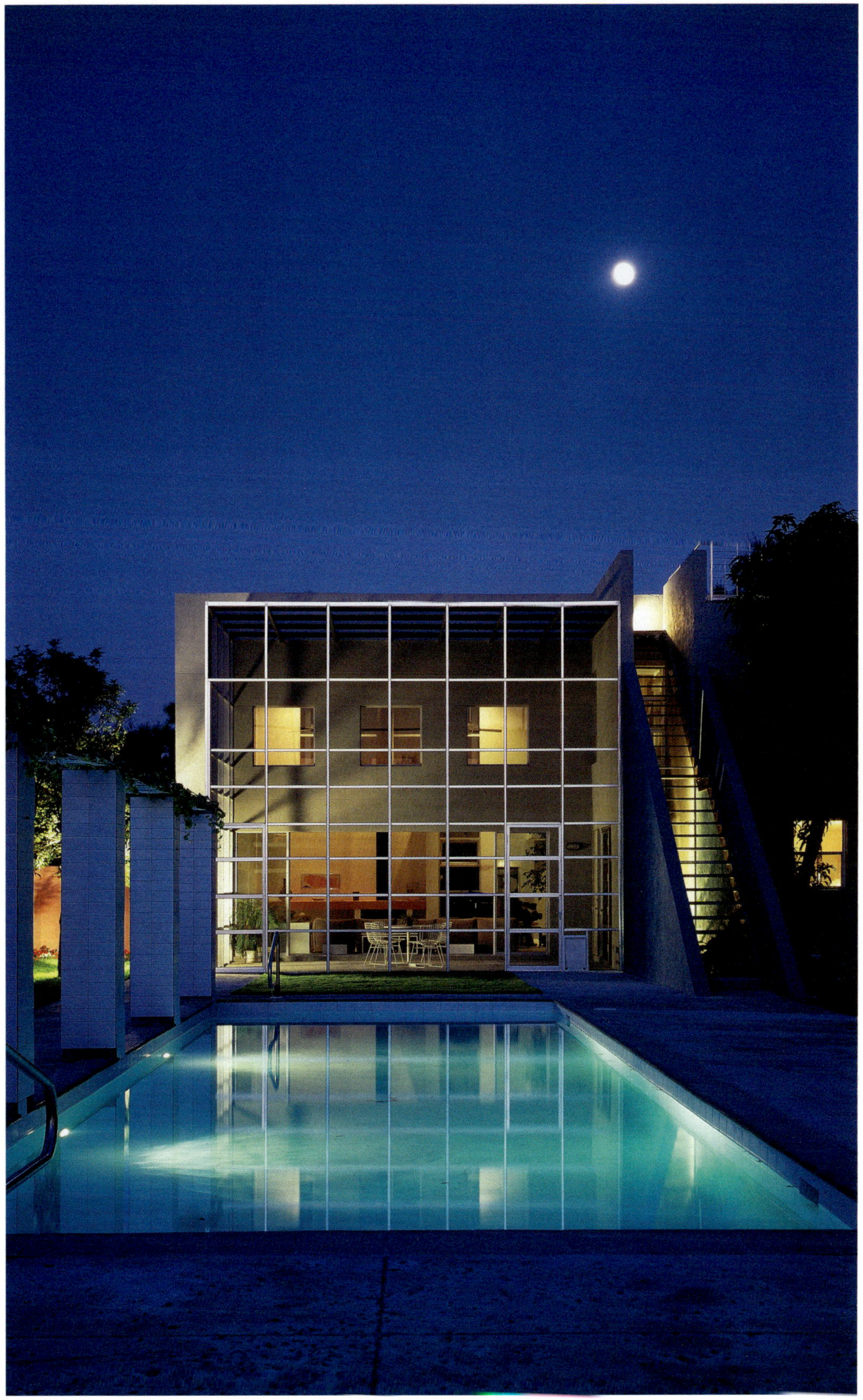

Q&A more about roney...

YOU CAN TELL I LIVE IN THIS LOCALE BECAUSE I ...

I drive a convertible and wear Tommy Bahamas clothing.

WHAT SINGLE THING WOULD YOU DO TO BRING A DULL HOUSE TO LIFE?

Call in the bulldozers.

NAME ONE THING MOST PEOPLE DON'T KNOW ABOUT YOU.

I used to race Go-Karts.

MATEU ARCHITECTURE INCORPORATED
Roney J. Mateu AIA, President
Palmetto Bay Village Center
18001 Old Cutler Road, Suite 550
Palmetto Bay, FL 33157
305.233.3304
Fax 305.233.3326
www.mateuarchitecture.com

LEFT: Outdoor living room, Mateu Family Compound, Pinecrest, Florida.
Photograph by Carlos Domenech

FACING PAGE LEFT: House on a 25-foot-wide lot, Coconut Grove, Florida.
Photograph by Carlos Domenech

FACING PAGE RIGHT: Pool patio, private residence on 53rd Avenue, Miami Dade County, Florida.
Photograph by Steven Brooke

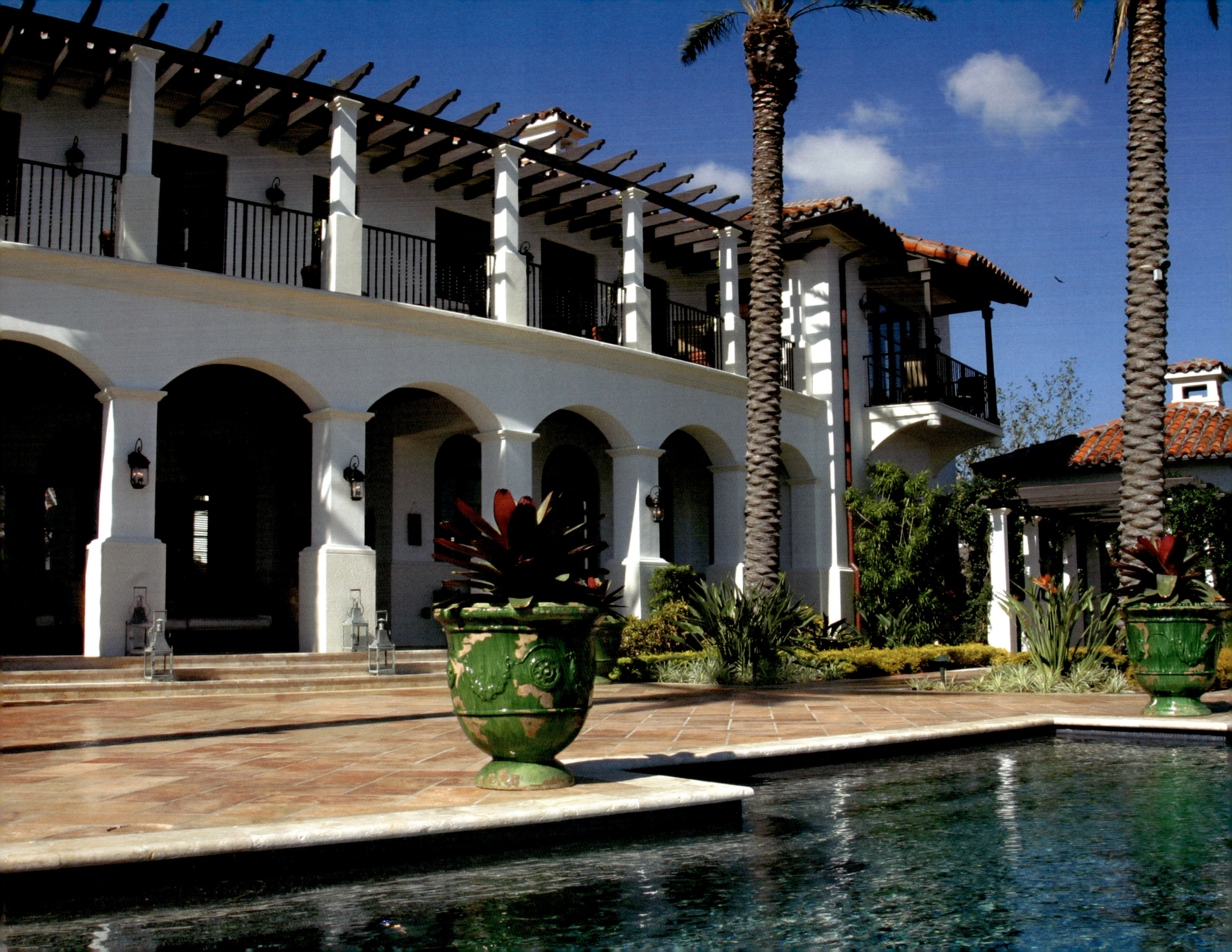

CESAR MOLINA & JODEL NARCISSE

Molina & Narcisse, Inc.

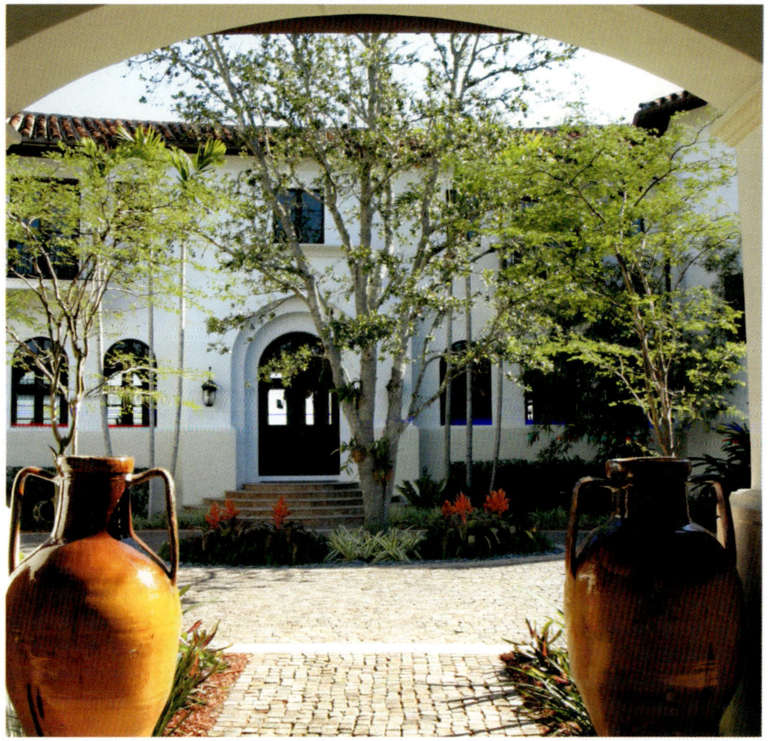

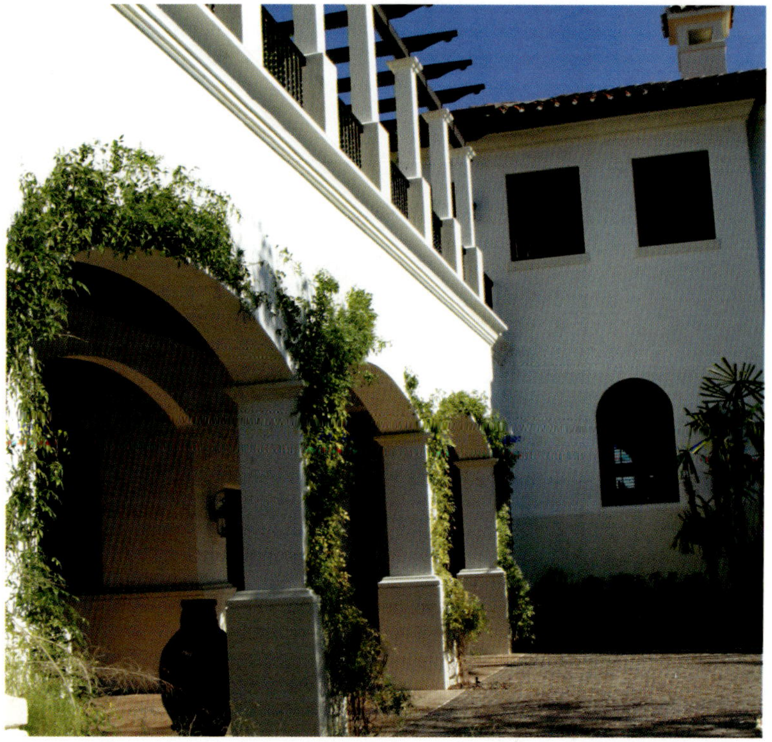

In 1992, while students at the University of Miami School of Architecture, Cesar Molina and Jodel Narcisse spent hours together in the studio, discussing their projects and working late into the night. As Cesar says, "We were usually there most of the time, often pulling all-nighters." After graduation, they became colleagues, working at the same firm on commercial and institutional buildings. When Cesar was commissioned to design his first house, he decided to open his own practice and asked Jodel to join him.

Fourteen years later, the friendship established as students has evolved into a fruitful professional partnership. Today, Cesar and Jodel run a successful boutique architectural firm focusing primarily on the design of custom luxury residential and resort properties throughout South Florida and the Caribbean. The high-energy duo and their team of 10 young architects and designers possess a passion for design and engage clients who share in their enthusiasm. "We want this to be a fun process, for them and for us," says Cesar.

Inspired by the vernacular and modern architecture of the Caribbean, West Indies and Asia, Cesar and Jodel's work is defined by the use of natural materials, quality craftsmanship and restrained detailing. Reluctant to assign a particular label to their designs, Jodel points out that "our architecture is less about style than quality of space. We try to design responsible interpretations of whichever aesthetic we are engaging." The point of departure for the design is its geographic and cultural context, imbuing the final product with a character appropriate to its location.

ABOVE LEFT: The residence is organized around a central courtyard, a transitional outdoor private space. The entry is marked by an oak tree which, once mature, will offer protective shade.
Photograph by Hanna Bared

ABOVE RIGHT: The architectural elements are detailed in simple materials and softened by creeping vines.
Photograph by Hanna Bared

LEFT: The fan-shaped plan corresponds to the configuration of the property and affords expansive water views, sinuous loggias and distinct pool side spaces for relaxation.
Photograph by Hanna Bared

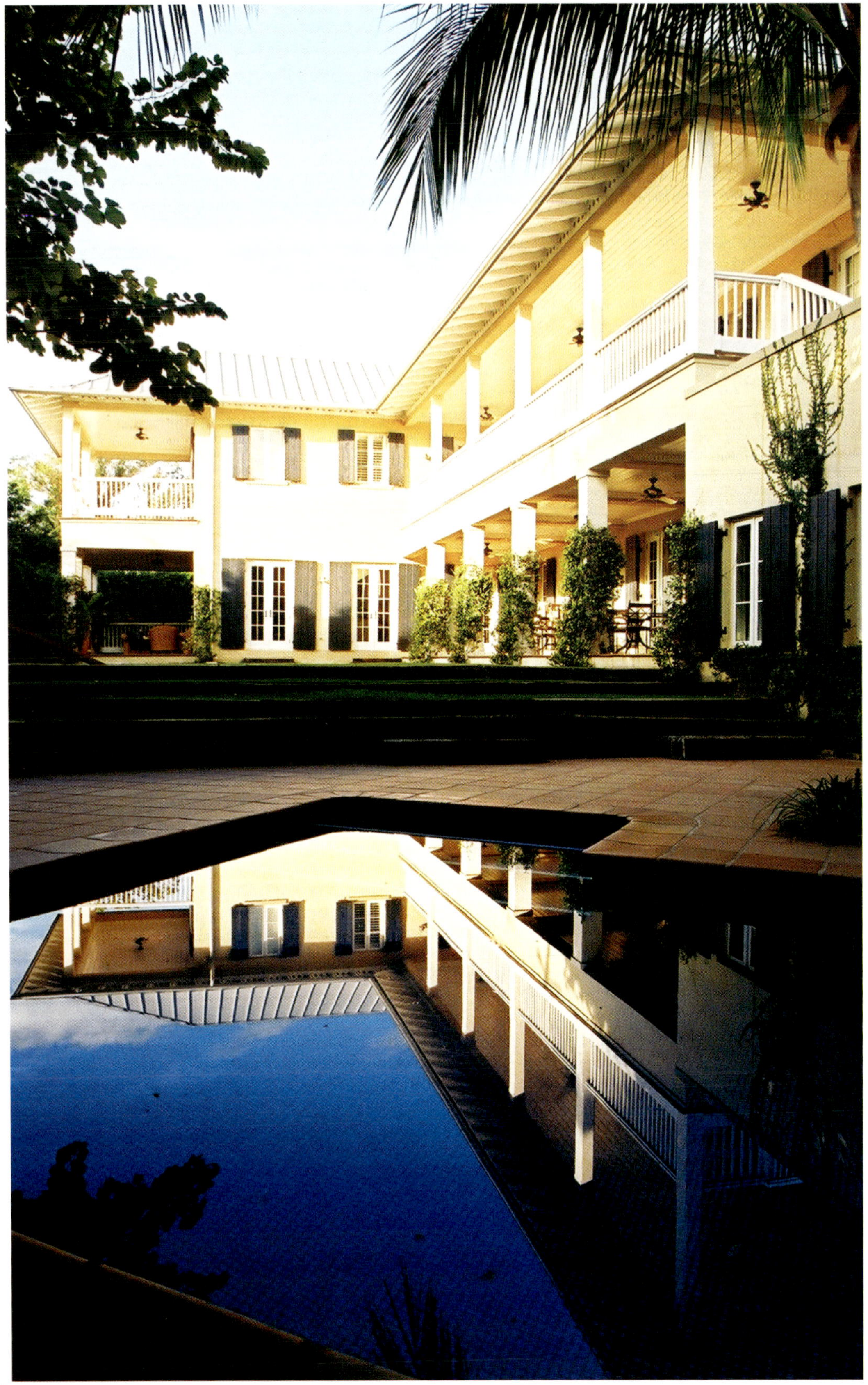

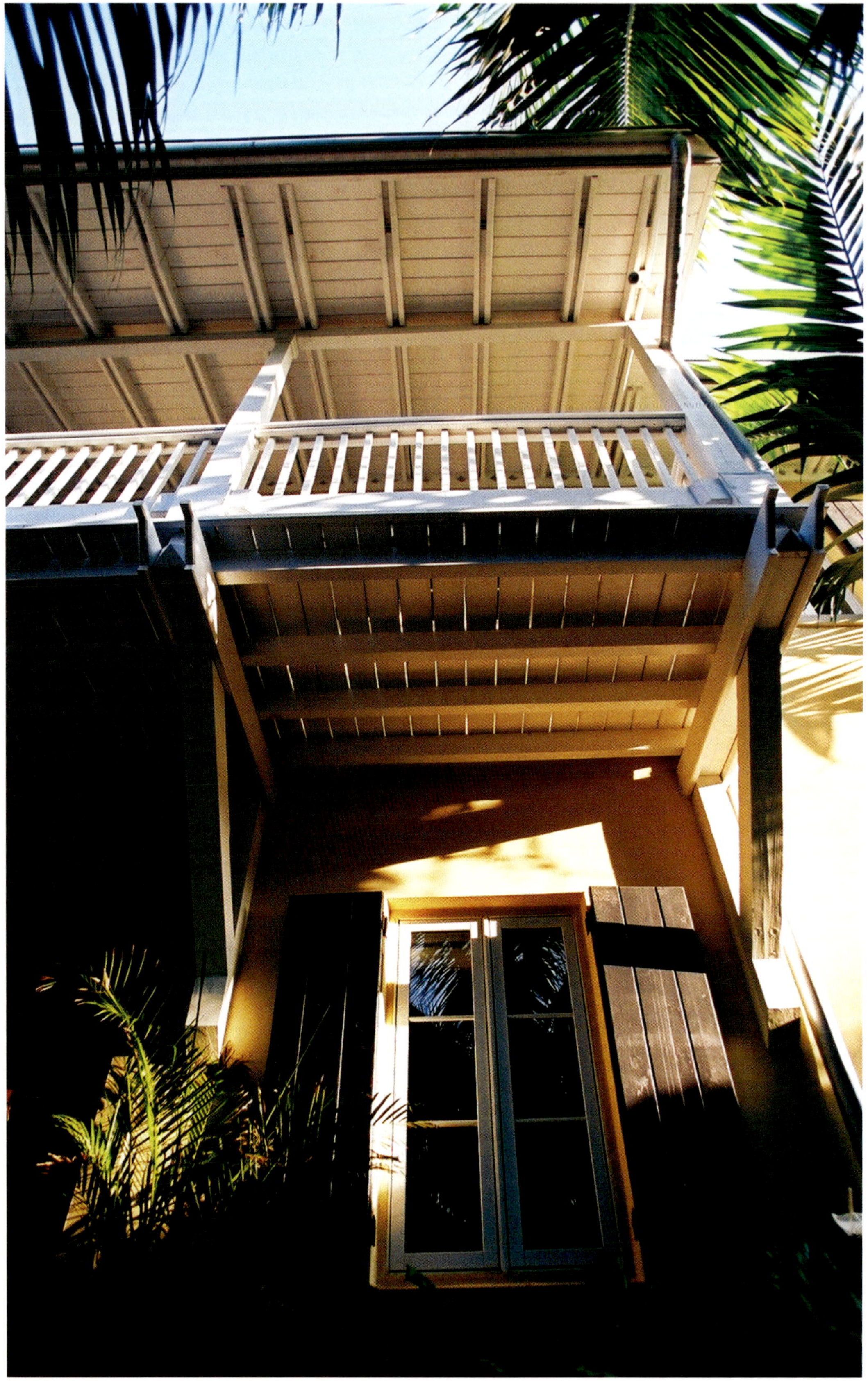

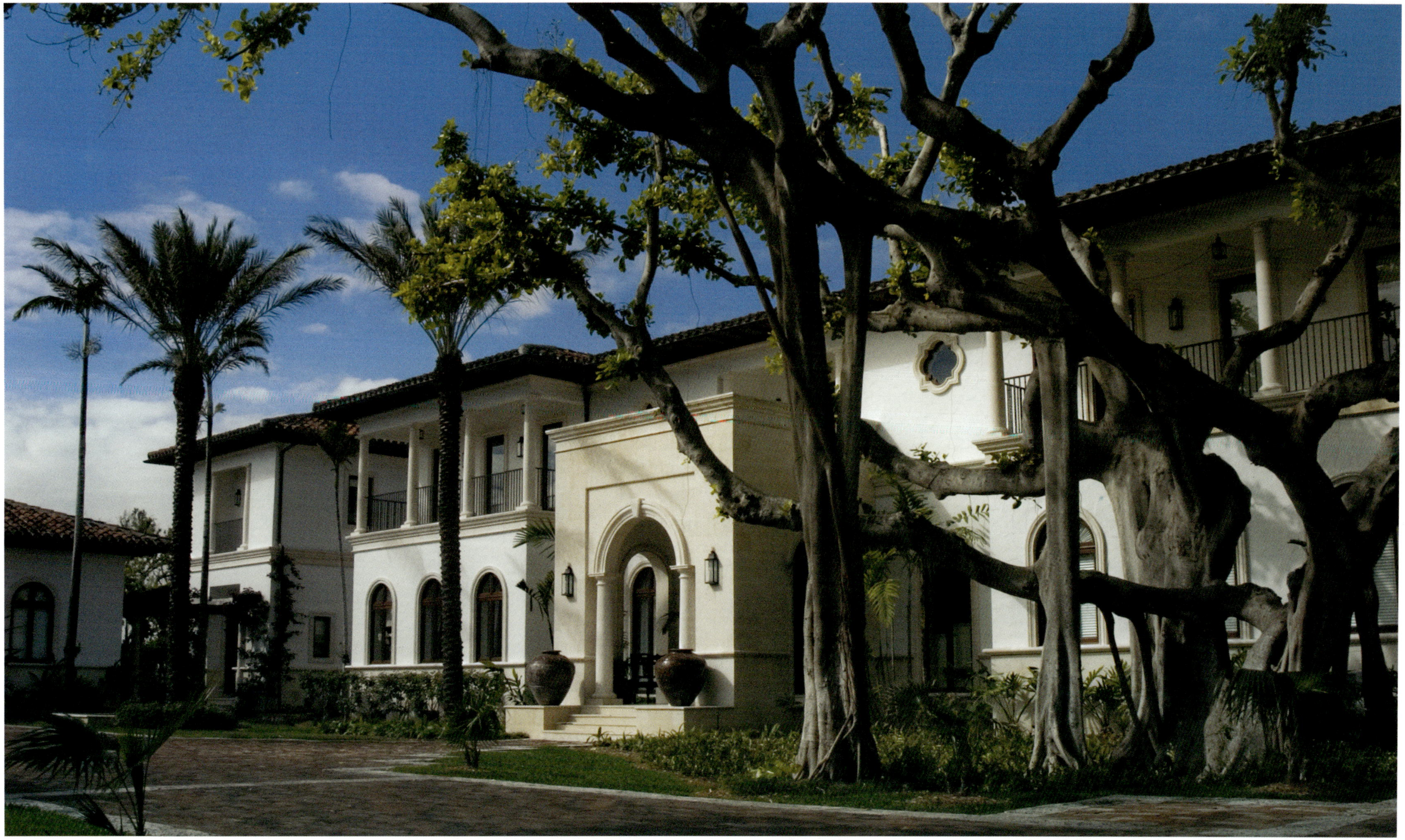

ABOVE: The formality of this Palm Beach inspired home is accented by Mexican coquina stone facing and classical details.
Photograph by Hanna Bared

FACING PAGE LEFT: The terraced lawn and remote location of the pool afford ample space for entertaining.
Photograph by Robin Hill

FACING PAGE RIGHT: The wood board shutters, balconies and railings are typical of the vernacular architecture of St. Augustine, Florida, which inspired the design of this home.
Photograph by Robin Hill

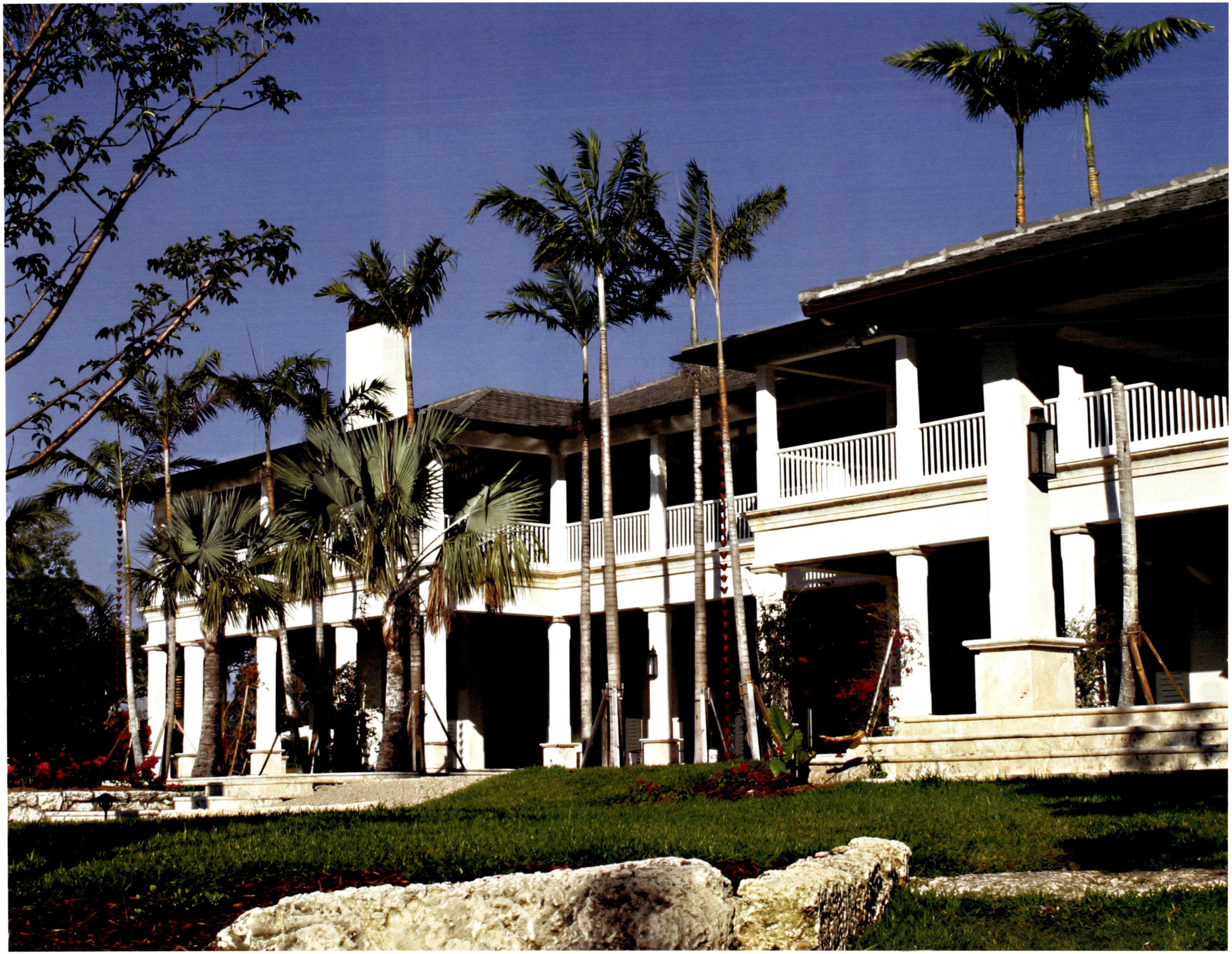

Central to their practice is the belief that the client is at the heart of a successful design team. They see themselves as architectural guides, mindful of incorporating as much of a client's wish list as possible within the framework of a stylistically responsible building. "You have to listen carefully to what your client wants because at the end of the day, although you want to be proud of your work, you need to remember that this is a house that somebody else is going to live in," Cesar notes. "I think much of our success stems from the fact that we are open minded and strive to offer a high level of service."

To that end, Cesar and Jodel have branched out into the related fields of construction, interior and furniture design. "We have had many requests for a fully-integrated project, one in which the house and interiors were conceived simultaneously," says Jodel. The result of that type of holistic approach is a highly personal and cohesive design, bearing the unique imprint of its owners.

The project on which they have been most able to explore the possibilities of symbiotic design is on a 22-acre private island near Antigua in the West Indies. 12 distinct pavilions connected by lushly landscaped grounds comprise the residence and offer a full spectrum of spatial experience, from the rustic open air bar pavilion to the 60-foot high lighthouse guest room. The design for the island required sensitive integration of Old World style with state-of-the-art technology—two equally important components for the owner. "Because we were commissioned to design everything from the door knobs to the buildings to the furnishings to the security system, we were able to ensure that all elements were fully customized and thoughtfully incorporated," says Jodel. Cesar adds, "While the island is a very special case, the lessons learned are applicable to projects of any scale."

With 28 active projects currently on the drawing board, there is ample opportunity to put those lessons to use. Nonetheless, Cesar and Jodel continually seek out new challenges. "It's important for us to push ourselves, to try new things and keep learning. We want to explore different aspects of design and

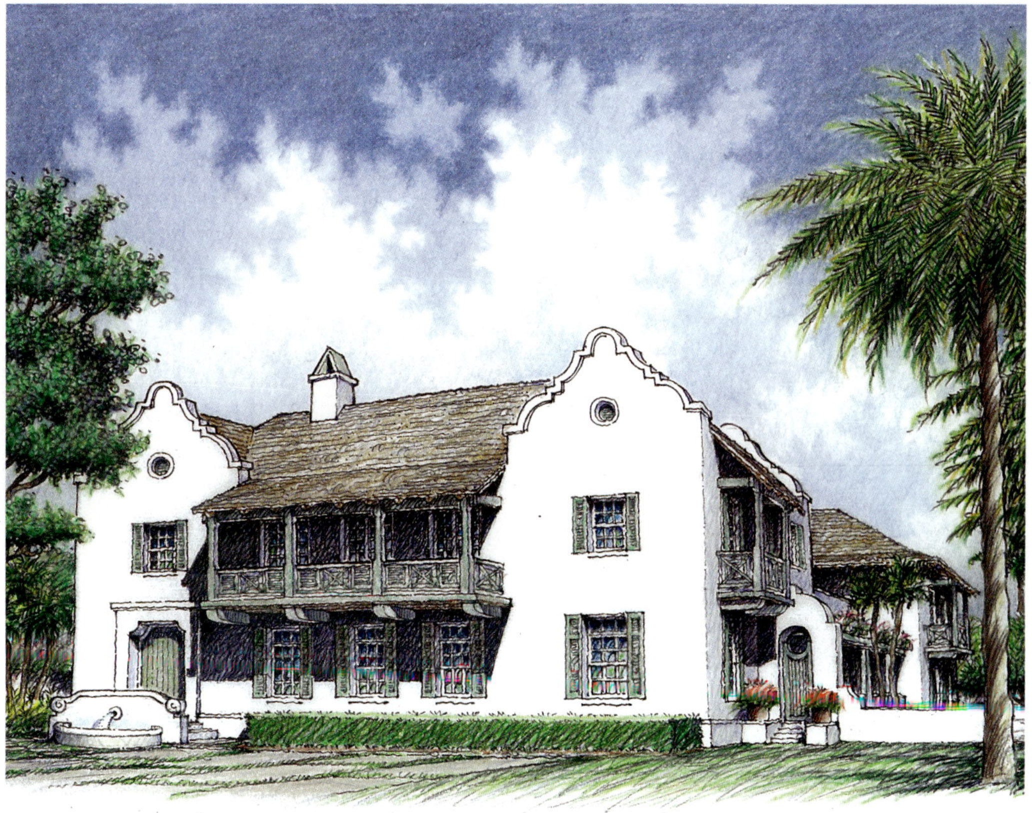

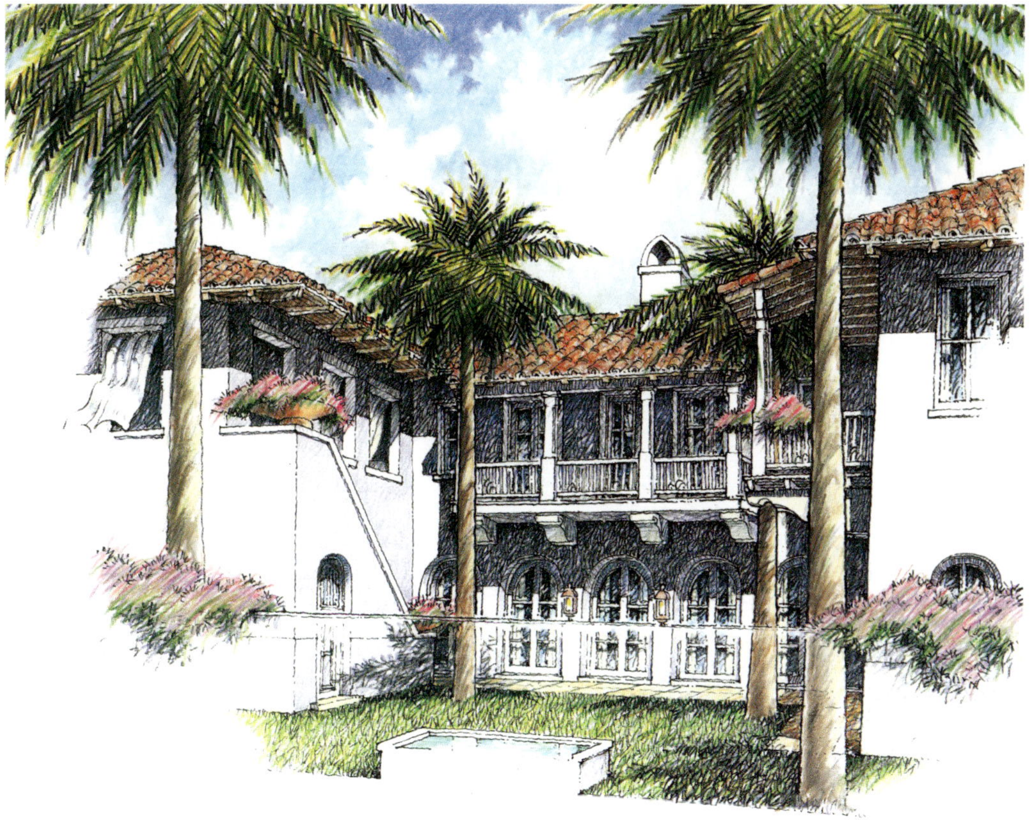

TOP: The design for this Dutch Caribbean home pays tribute to one of the many distinct colonial architectural traditions evident in South Florida.
Rendering by Molina & Narcisse, Inc.

BOTTOM: Proposed for a narrow interior lot, the design for this Miami Beach residence is conceived as a series of rooms arranged around a central courtyard.
Rendering by Molina & Narcisse, Inc.

FACING PAGE: Deep porches and overhangs typify the Anglo-Caribbean architecture of this Coral Gables residence.
Photograph by Hanna Bared

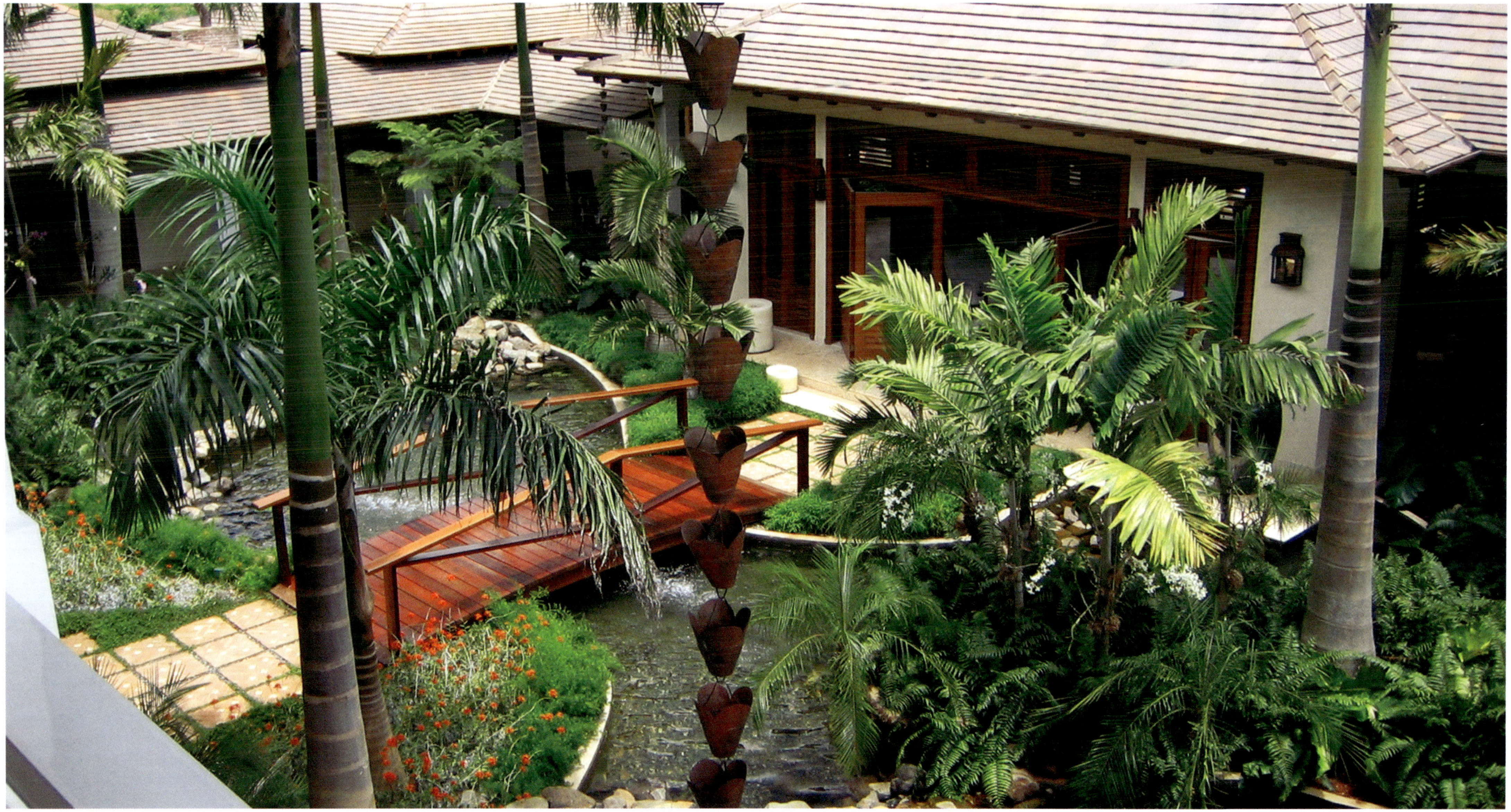

we don't want to feel that our work has become stagnant," confesses Jodel. To that end, they recently expanded their scope of work to include multi-family residential design, including an 80-unit town house development as well as a mid-rise loft condominium on the Miami River. "The challenge for us in those projects is giving our clients the well planned and detailed spaces they have come to expect from our luxury single family homes in an entirely different type of space," says Cesar. "It's a balancing act but one we welcome."

The foundation of the firm remains single-family residential work. From a 30,000-square-foot beach house in the Dominican Republic of South Pacific inspiration to a 5,000-square-foot Dutch Caribbean home in Miami, the process is the same. "We enjoy getting to know our clients and translating their ideas into a physical space, into a home," shares Jodel. "It is always a collaborative effort, between the client, us and our team."

Cesar and Jodel hope that they will continue to have the opportunity to work with their clients in creating unique projects. "There is a positive energy evident in our studio because we love what we are doing," Cesar said. "Our goal is to create places where people feel comfortable. We are less interested in winning awards than in seeing our clients happy in their homes."

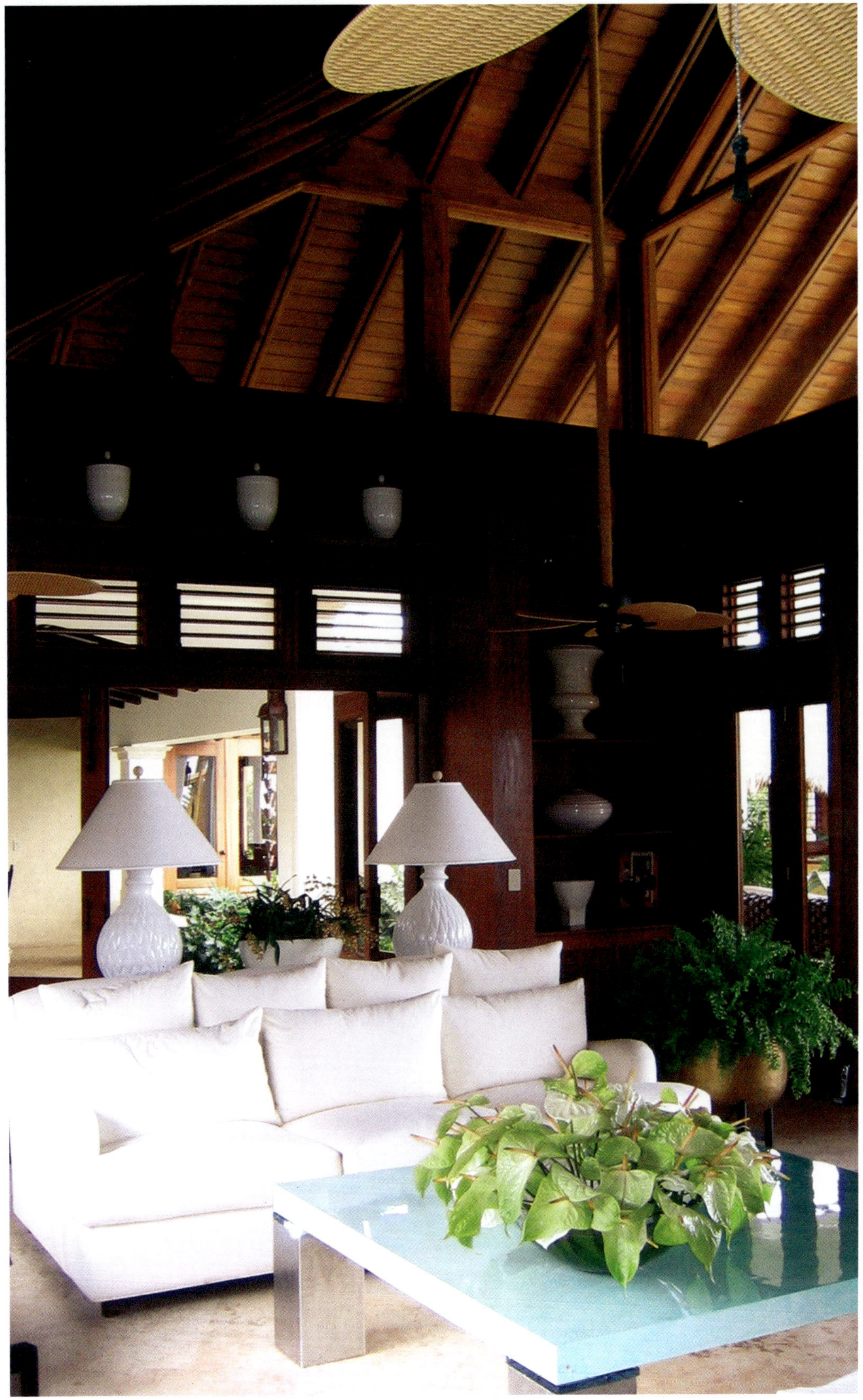

Q&A

more about cesar & jodel...

WHAT IS THE BEST PART OF BEING AN ARCHITECT?

Seeing a project develop from drawings to a real building. It is always exciting.

WHAT IS THE SINGLE THING YOU WOULD DO TO BRING A DULL HOUSE TO LIFE?

Paint the walls clean white, change the lighting and add great art.

WHAT ONE PHILOSOPHY HAVE YOU STUCK WITH FOR YEARS THAT STILL WORKS FOR YOU TODAY?

Always be prepared to take advantage of an opportunity when it presents itself.

WHAT IS THE HIGHEST COMPLIMENT YOU'VE RECEIVED PROFESSIONALLY?

Hearing a client say: "This is exactly what I wanted!"

MOLINA & NARCISSE, INC.
Cesar Molina, Principal
Jodel Narcisse, Principal
232 Andalusia Avenue, Suite 101
Coral Gables, FL 33134
305.448.4200
Fax 305.448.4215
www.mnarchitects.com

LEFT: Tailored white furniture and a cool blue glass coffee table are juxtaposed against a mahogany backdrop in the living room of this Dominican Republic vacation home.
Photograph by Cesar Molina

FACING PAGE: The rooms of this Dominican Republic home are arranged around a lushly landscaped courtyard accented by copper chain rain gutters and a wooden footbridge, both the work of local artisans.
Photograph by Cesar Molina

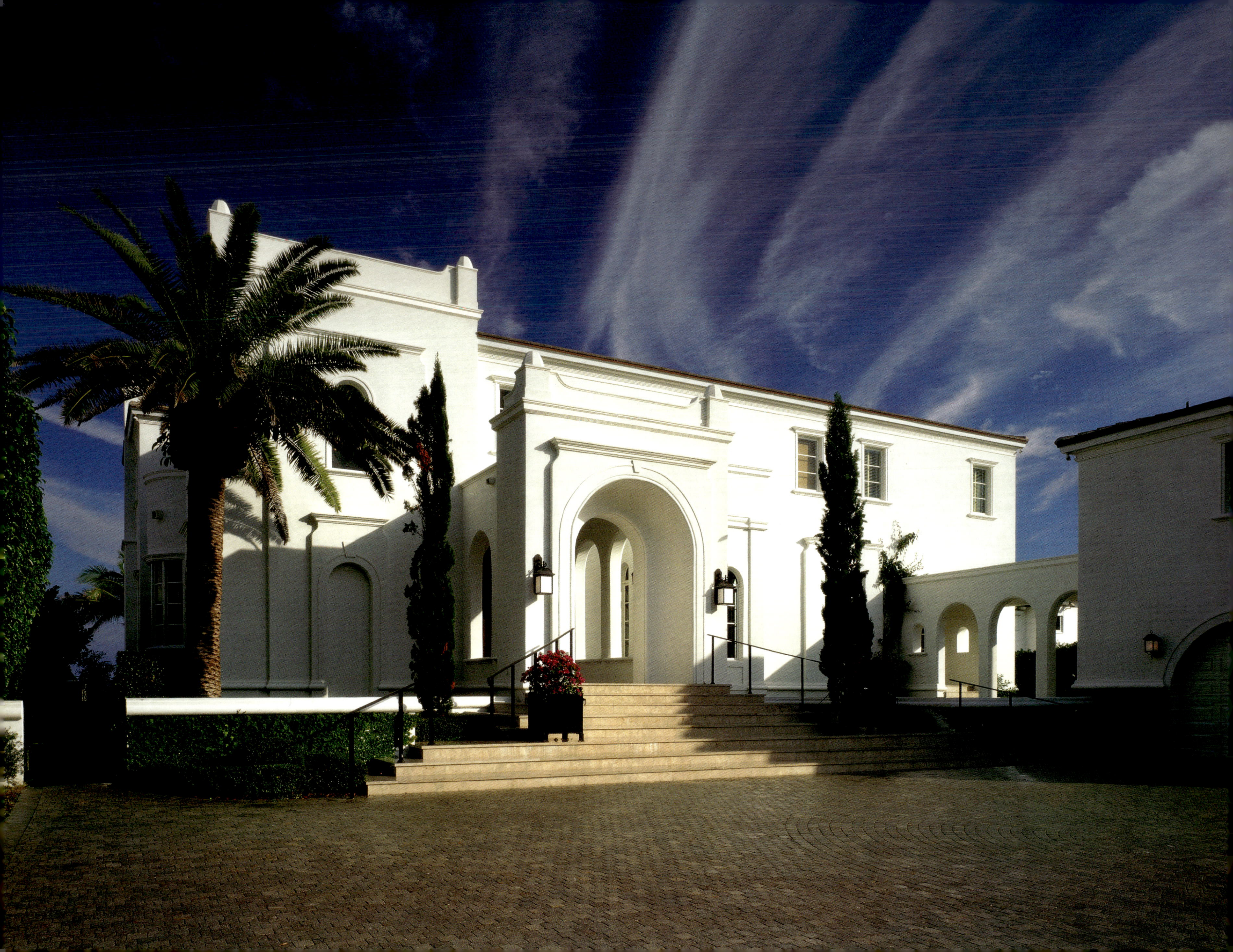

RAMON PACHECO

Ramon Pacheco & Associates, Inc.

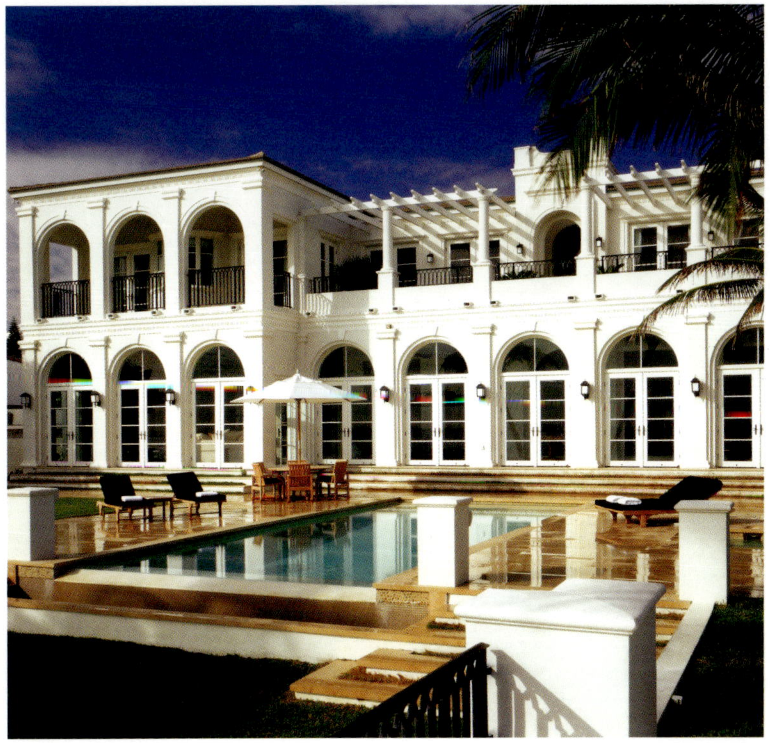

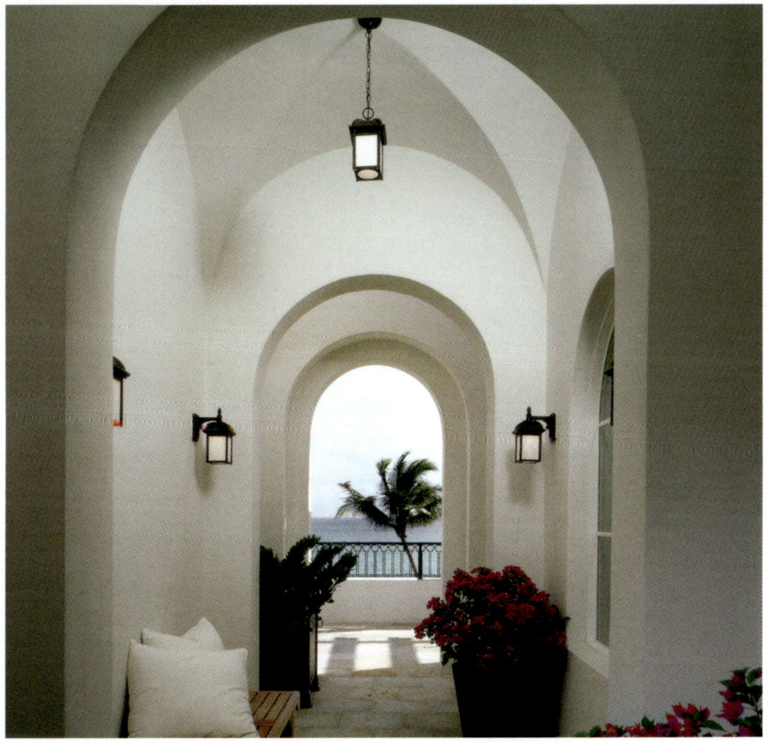

"Not only am I an architect, but I have a passion for art." "As an artist, my designs are an expression of my love of art," Ramon Pacheco, "The Architect to the Stars" said from his office in Miami.

Originally from Cuba, Ramon immigrated to the United States at the age of 17. He finished high school and graduated from the University of Florida. He then traveled around the world enjoying and studying architecture before establishing his reputation as one of the premier architects of the Western Hemisphere.

Ramon has a larger-than-life client list that includes actor Michael Caine, Latin musician Gloria Estefan, Cristina Saralegui also known as "The Oprah of Latin America" and Mario Kreutzberger known as Don Francisco of Sabado Gigante.

Specializing in private commercial, institutional, and high-end residential luxury homes, Ramon says that he has tremendous satisfaction designing homes because of the intimacy and scale of the projects and the friendships that he develops with his clients.

Over the years, Ramon's style has evolved. As a student, he was influenced by the modernism of Le Corbusier and Louis Kahn, the modern pioneers of his youth. On his journeys to Italy and other parts of Europe, he has been inspired by the architecture of Andrea Palladio, who has long been considered

ABOVE LEFT: Golden Beach Residence: The rear of this residence, an indoor/outdoor family room, faces a wild dune and beyond the Atlantic Ocean. The quietly striking architecture of this home expresses clean detail and repetitive arches throughout.
Photograph by George Cott, Chroma Inc.

ABOVE RIGHT: Golden Beach Residence: Through these full arches, one can see an amazing view of the Atlantic Ocean. The simplicity of groin vault ceilings makes this view spectacular.
Photograph by George Cott, Chroma Inc.

LEFT: Golden Beach Residence: This house represents a contemporary interpretation of Neo-Traditional Architecture.
Photograph by George Cott, Chroma Inc.

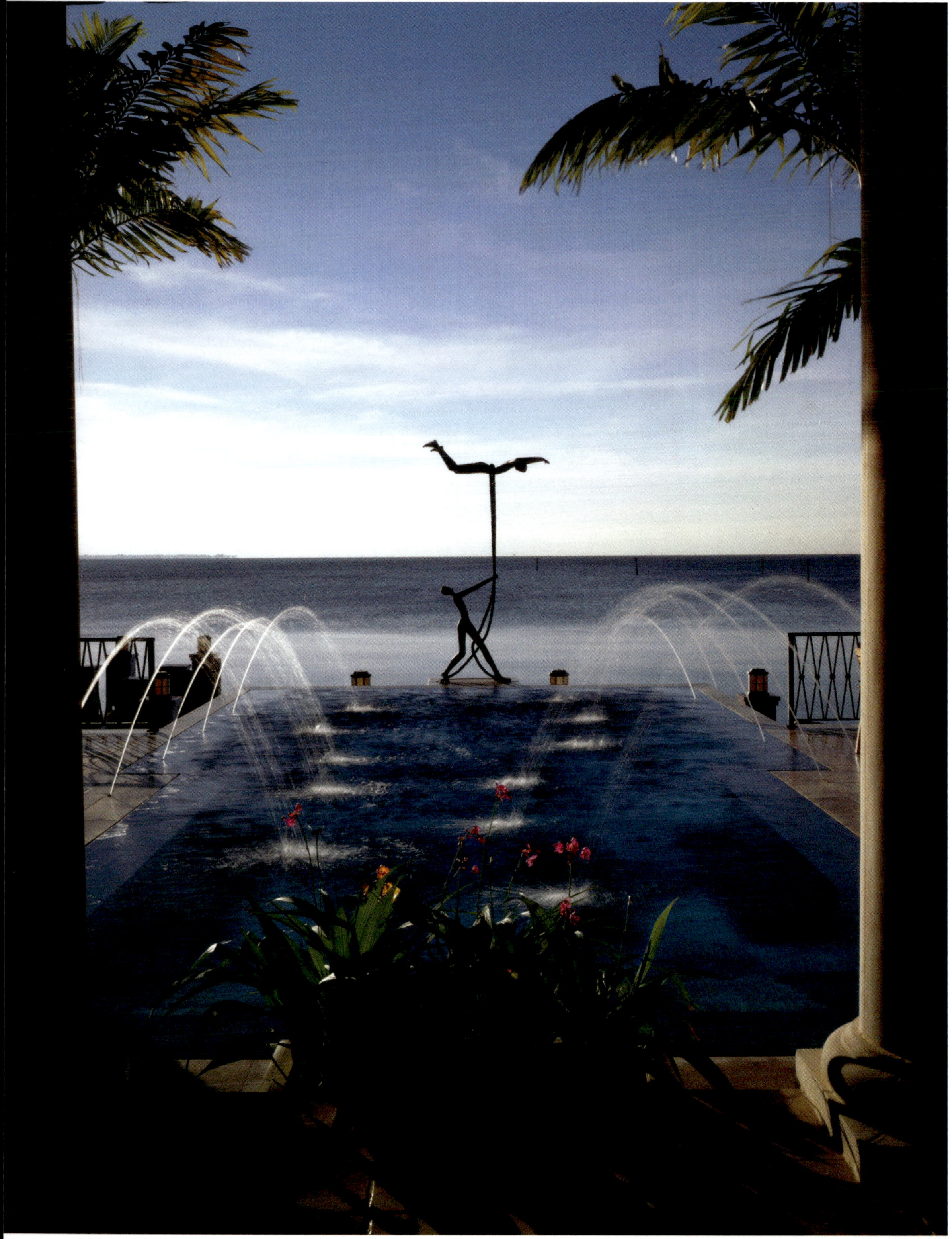

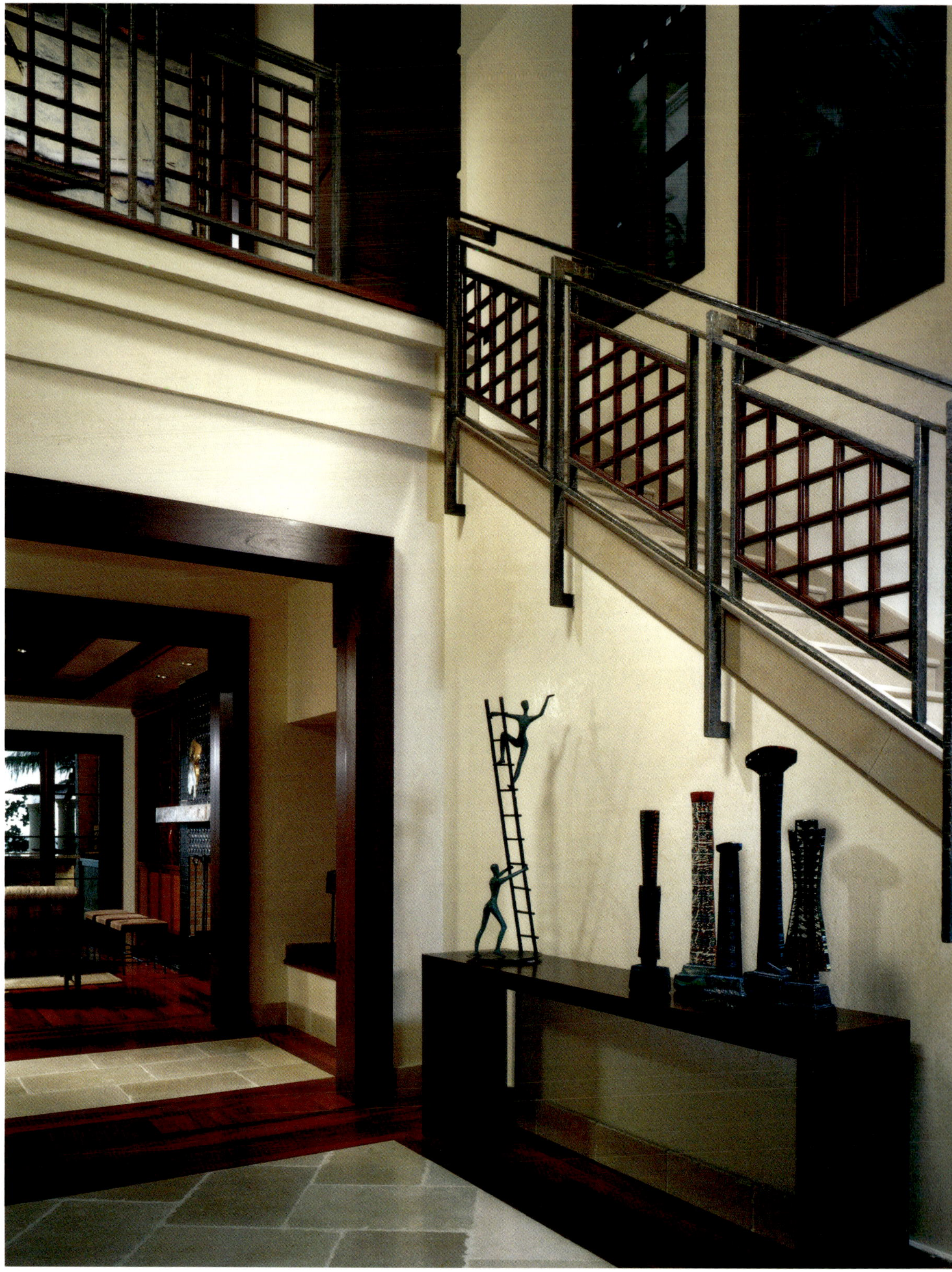

the father of classicism. He's carried Palladio's influence from Europe to North and South America and especially in Florida where he practices, and incorporates classical elements to some of his own architectural work.

With over 500 homes under his belt in the Southern Florida region, Ramon gets 90 percent of his work via referral. Some of his new clients get referred by not only one client, but sometimes as many as four. They say, "You have to talk with Ramon because he is the best." Why? Because as he tells his daughters, who are also in the family architectural business, bad things spread in one second—good things take a long time.

Ramon loves his client base because he's built a reputation that allows him to pick and choose which projects he really wants to work on. He tries to choose clients that are appreciative of what he does and that work with him on an even level. He works with his clients on a basis of mutual respect.

What makes Ramon successful is his ability to listen to his clients and understand the essence of what they are envisioning for their home to be. He says that not listening to clients and doing whatever you want, is a recipe for failure.

When working on a project, Ramon's main concern is listening to his clients' desires and then, developing a concept that will be successful. He

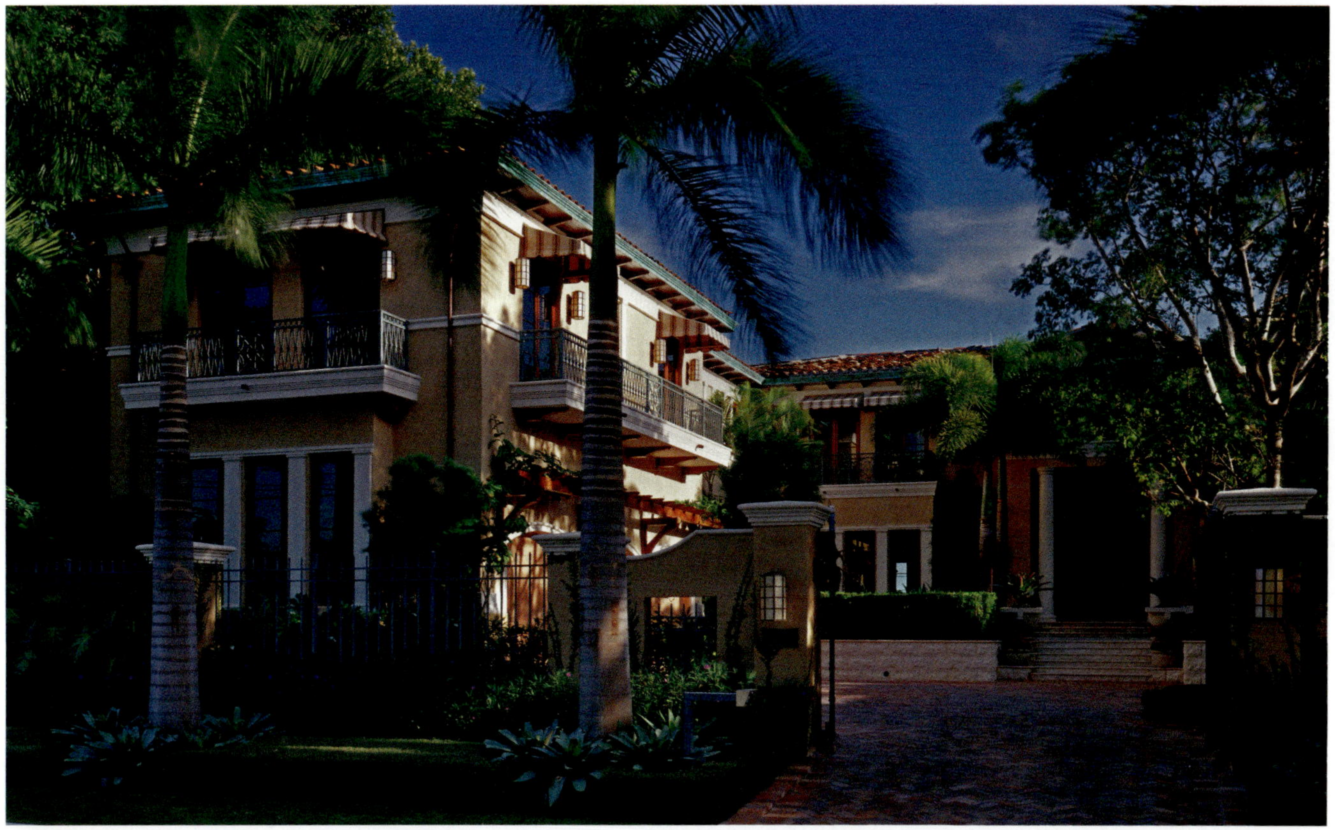

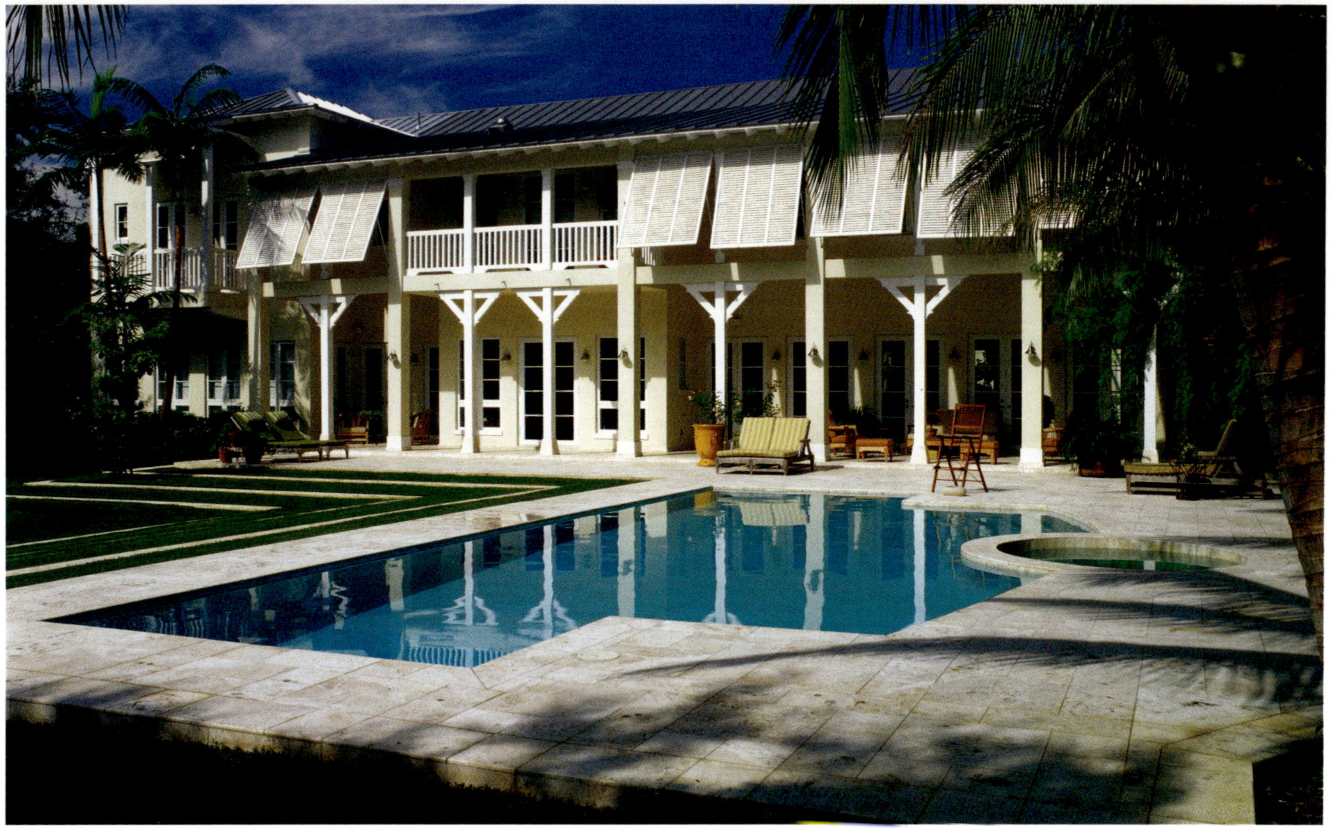

TOP: Coconut Grove Residence: This contemporary Palladian residence is situated on a 70-foot wide lot by 200-feet of depth facing a breathtaking view of Biscayne Bay. The goal was to have the major living spaces look toward the water, which was accomplished by creating an inviting courtyard at the entry.
Photograph by George Cott, Chroma Inc.

BOTTOM: South Dade Residence: This home will take you away to paradise with its Bermuda/Key West-inspired architecture nestled among lush tropical gardens.
Photograph by Christian Zitzmann

FACING PAGE LEFT: Coconut Grove Residence: Using an enclosed space, Ramon was able to give a feel of the pool "opening-up" into the Biscayne Bay. The infinity pool blends with the view of the bay, like out of a dream; this view extends beyond imagination.
Photograph by George Cott, Chroma Inc.

FACING PAGE RIGHT: Coconut Grove Residence: This Grandeur staircase is a modern Art Deco inspired décor. The sophistication of the interior is based on straight lines and simple geometry.
Photograph by George Cott, Chroma Inc.

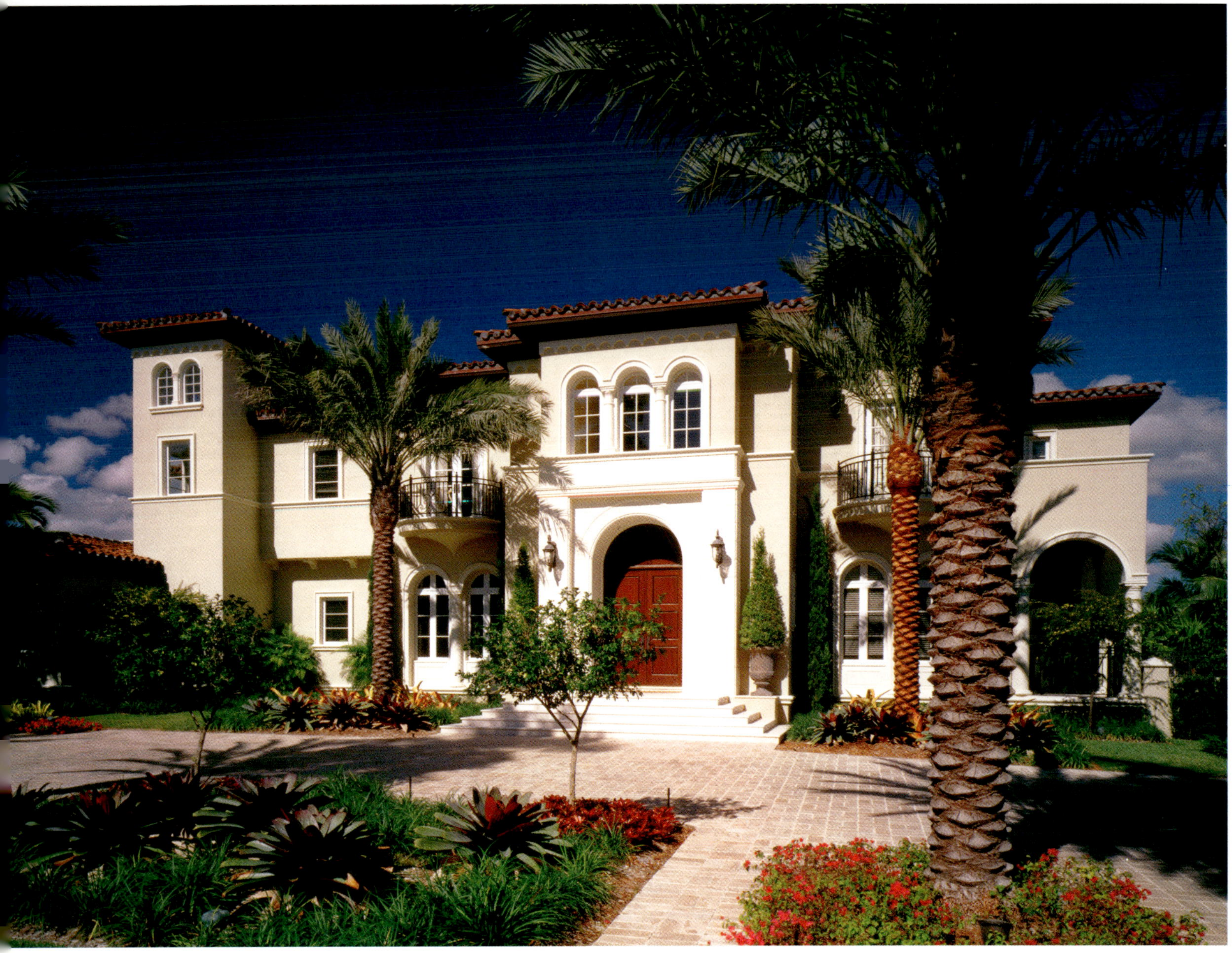

visits the site where the new home is to be built and weighs the pros and cons of the land. He tries to orient the new structure according to the environment and then he conceptualizes a three-dimensional structure in a rough sketch. Sometimes, he says, he draws out his idea on restaurant napkins over lunch or dinner. Ramon says that when there is a solid concept behind a project everything comes out with both strength and beauty. He says he is thankful for the impressive architect team that assists him and together, have produced and designed very successful projects.

After 35 years of working as an architect, Ramon says that he's not ready to retire. His hobby is architecture and the thought of sitting at home bores him to tears. What he enjoys most is going to his office every day, solving problems and making a living at what he loves. "I don't know what the word 'retire' means."

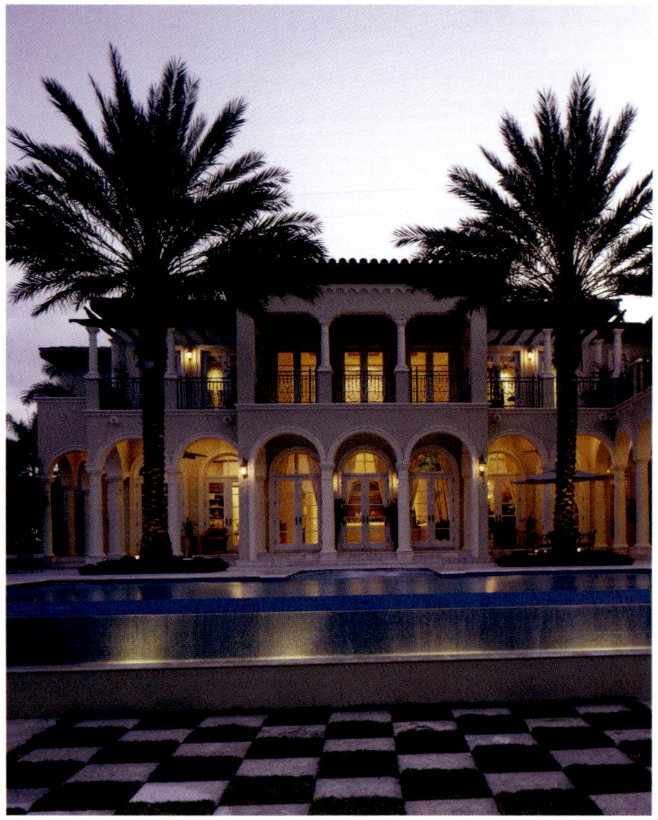

ABOVE: Gables Estates Residence: This residence represents classical Mediterranean architecture with its colonnades, high ceilings, and arched windows with grand views. This home is a lavish rendition of Ramon's unique style.
Photograph by Christian Zitzmann

RIGHT: Gables Estates Residence: This elegant formal, yet warm, rear elevation has an arched veranda framed by two huge date palms. The infinity edge pool and checkerboard patio create a rear focal point for the home.
Photograph by George Cott, Chroma Inc.

FACING PAGE LEFT: Coral Gables Residence: A brushed nickel staircase leads upward to gallery space above overlooking the foyer where a display of this home's art greets guests. An undulant shape was introduced to contrast with the straight lines.
Photograph by George Cott, Chroma Inc.

FACING PAGE TOP: Coral Gables Residence: This residence expresses a character of sovereignty reinforced by the symmetrical Palladian approach of ideal proportion. The front of this home has two large Macedonian stone columns articulated at the entry with clean concrete molding throughout and a flat gray cement roof tile.
Photograph by George Cott, Chroma Inc.

FACING PAGE BOTTOM: Coral Gables Residence: Light and views of this home's Coral Gales waterway are captured along the entire back wall of this house with large French doors framed in Wingate wood. The fireplace acts as a sculptural focal piece providing transparency between the living room and the entry sitting area at the library.
Photograph by George Cott, Chroma Inc.

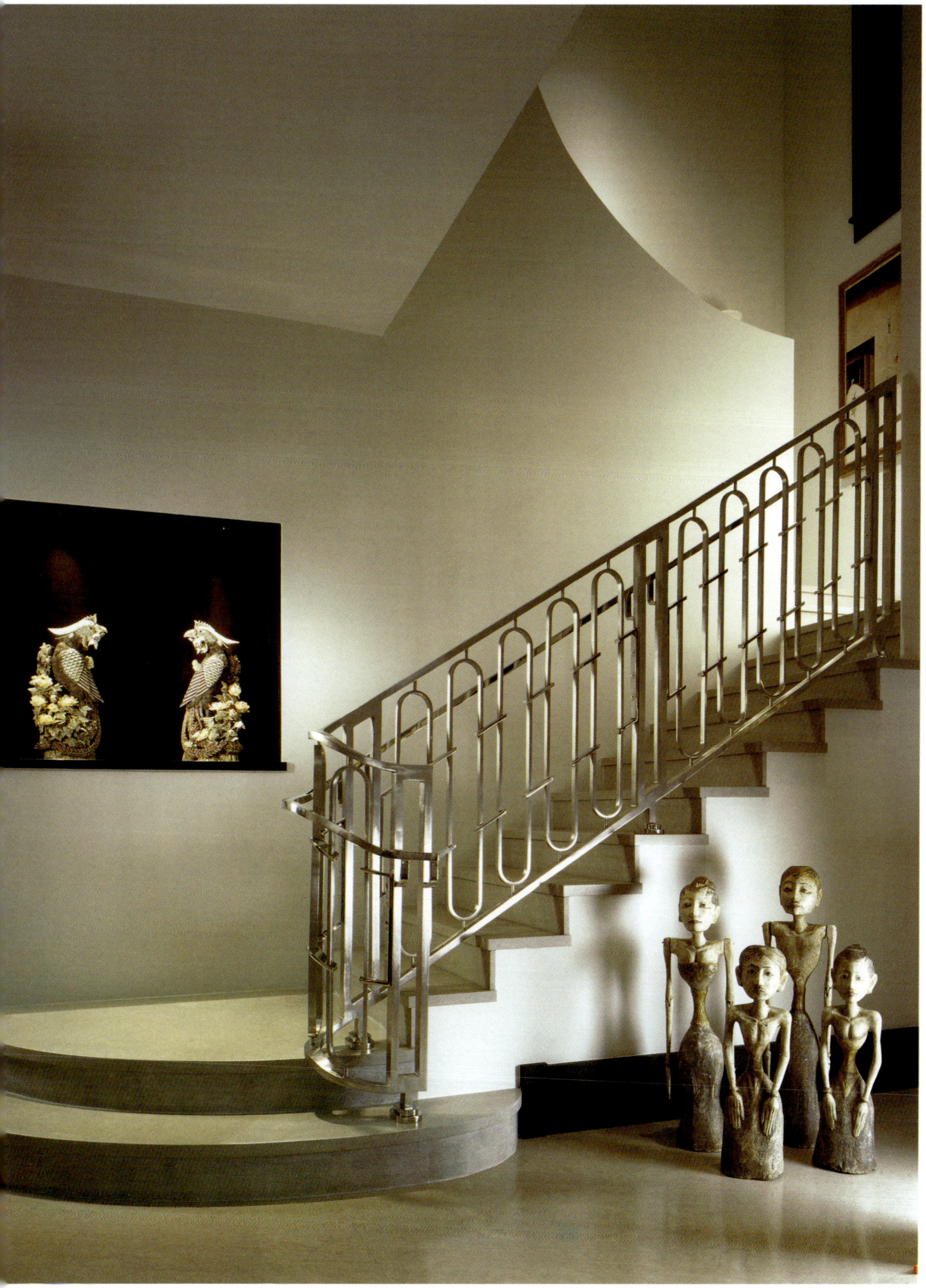

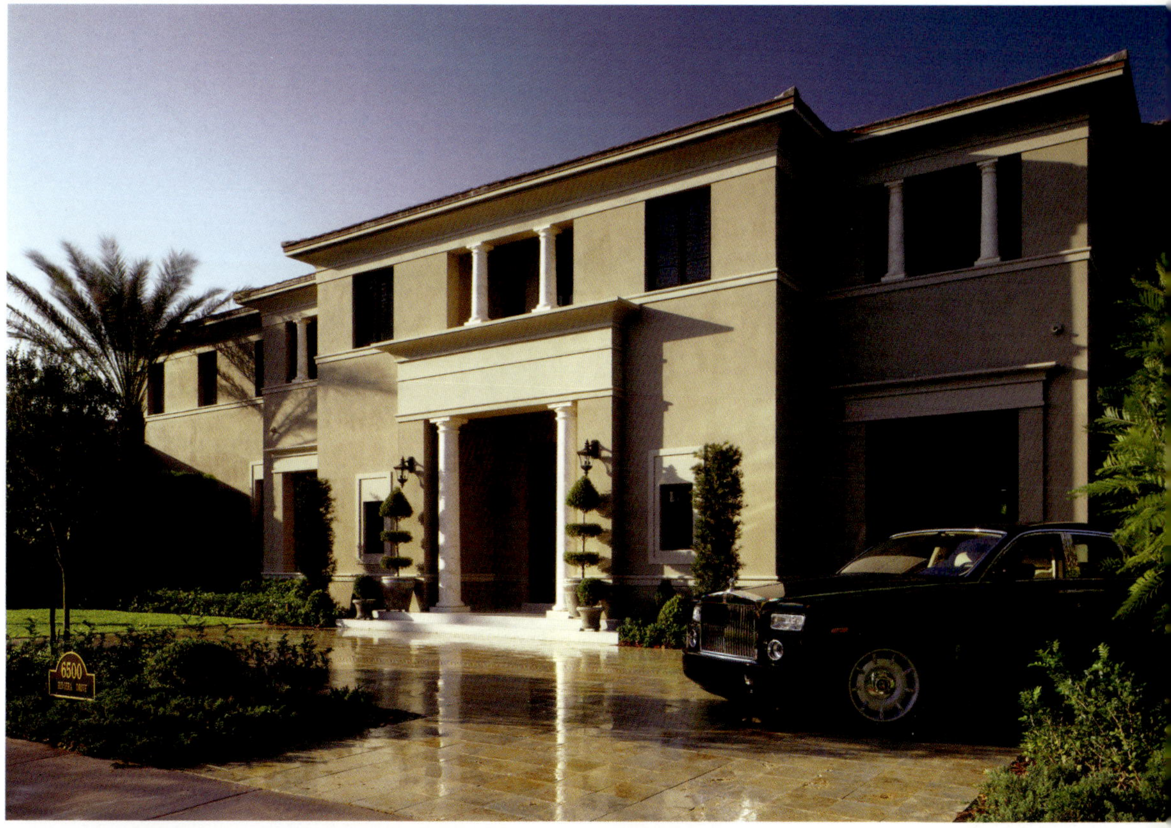
6500

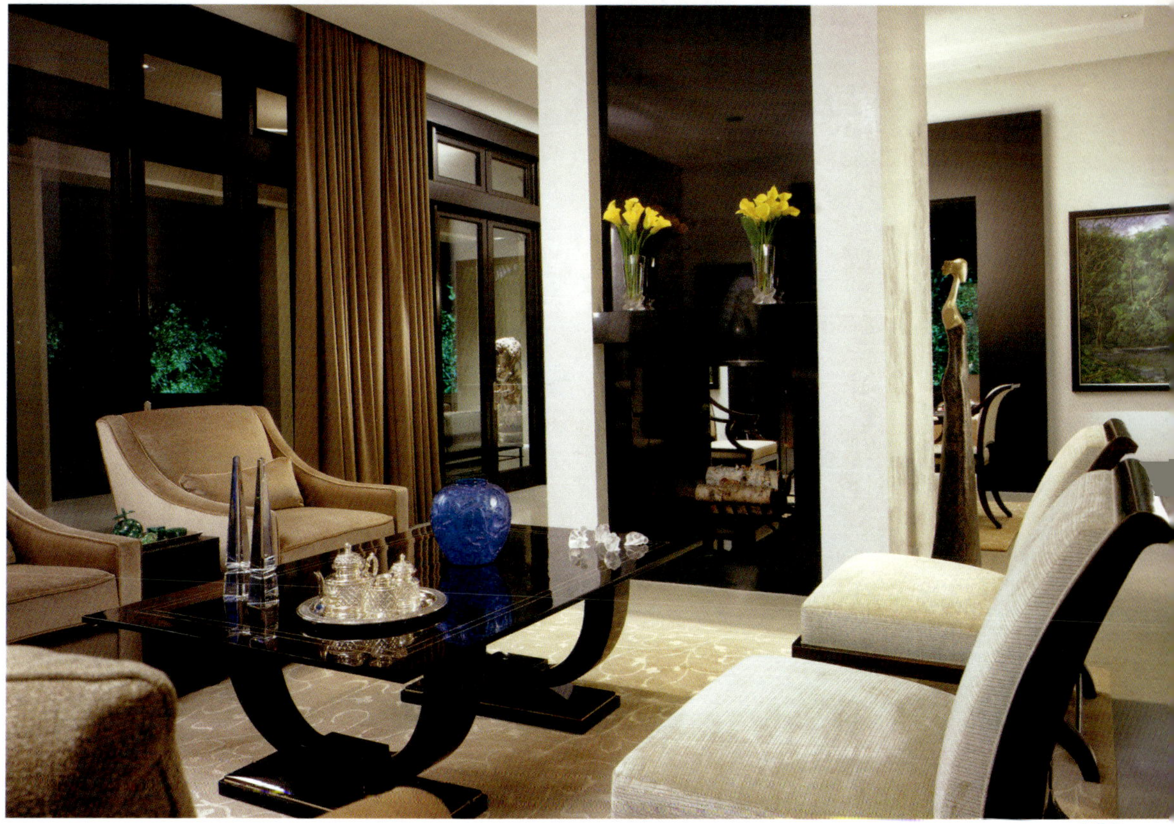

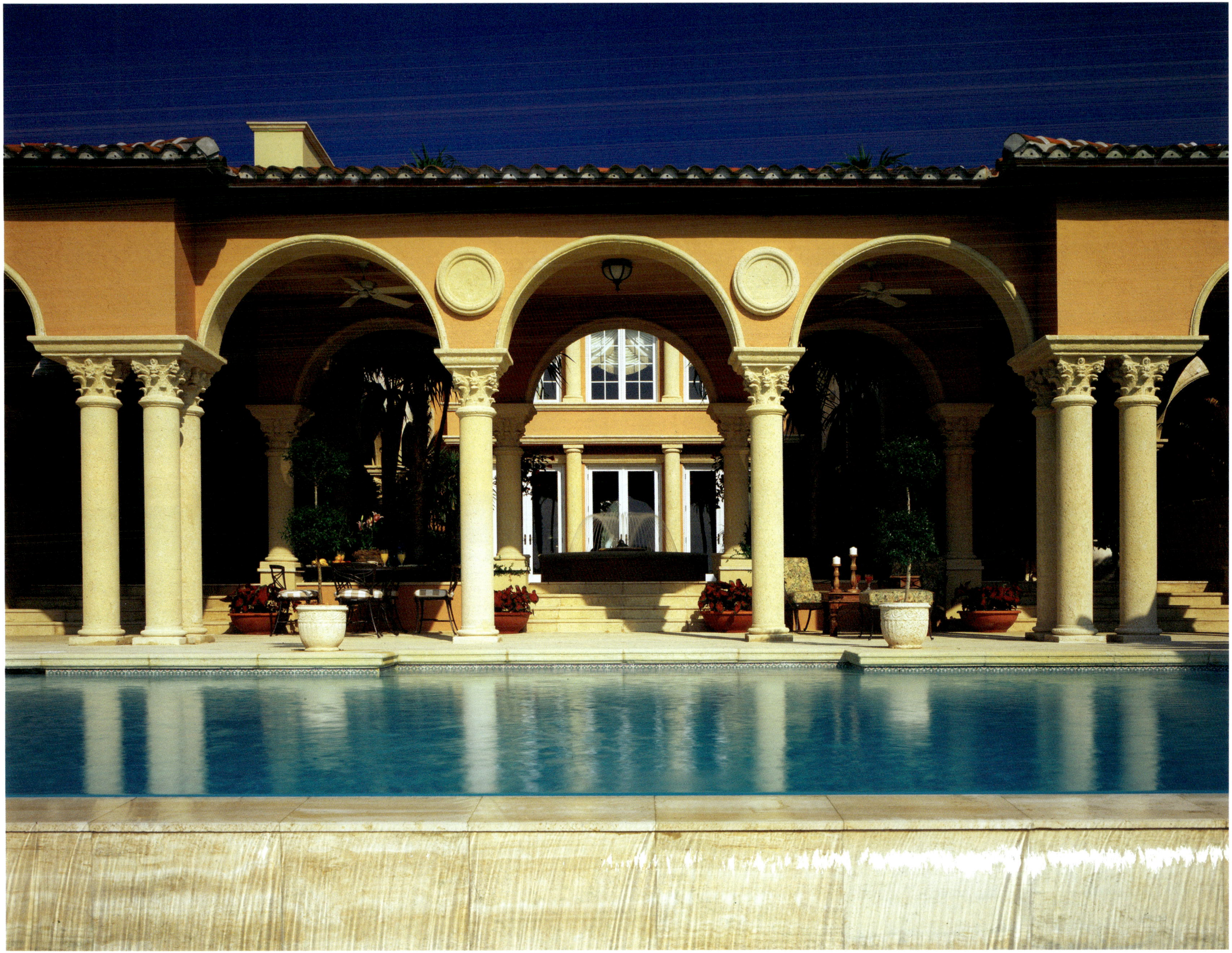

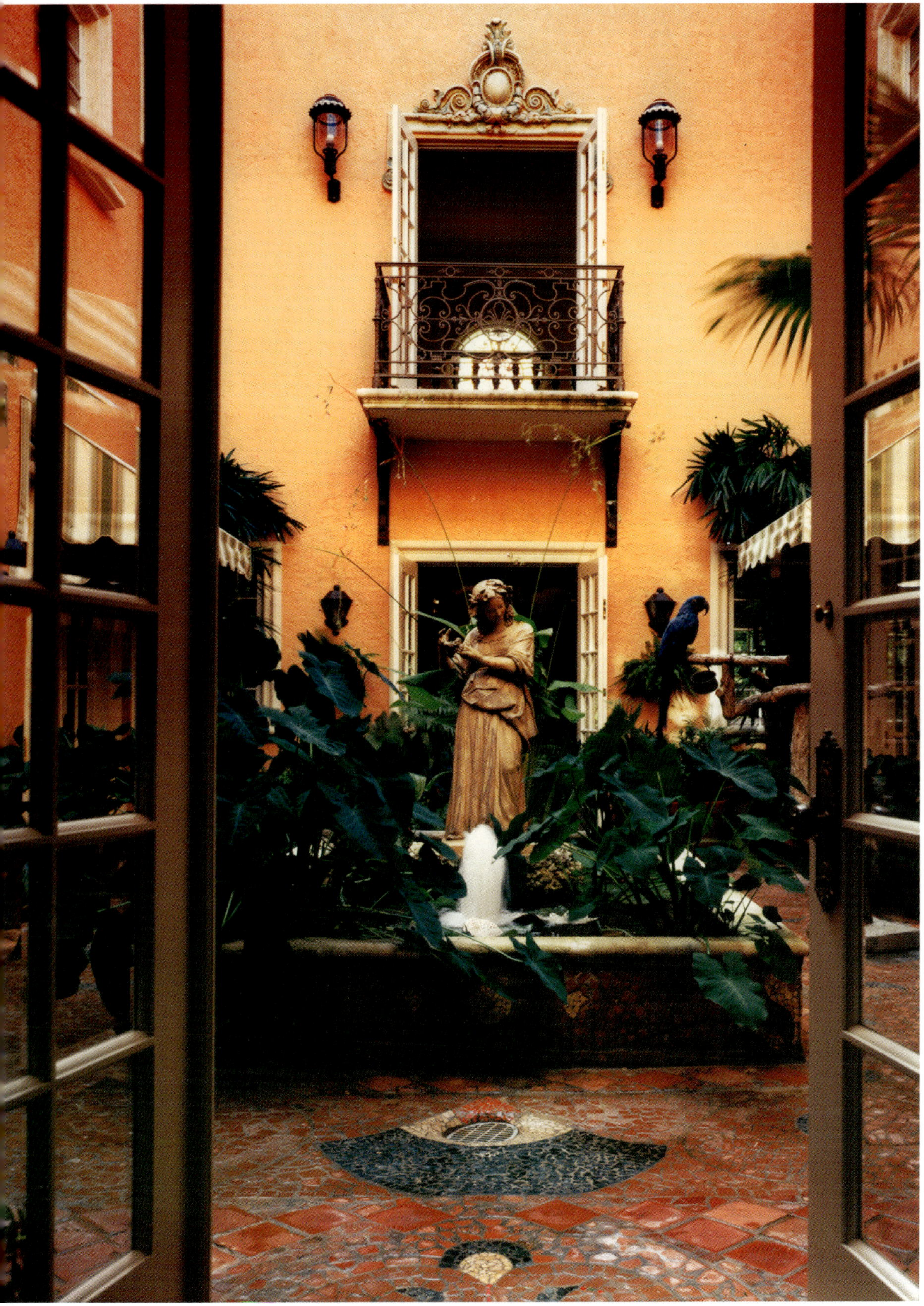

Q&A more about ramon...

WHAT SEPARATES YOU FROM YOUR COMPETITION?

The tremendous dedication and passion I have for each of my projects and through it all, I still maintain patience and serenity.

WHAT IS THE BEST PART OF BEING AN ARCHITECT?

The creative process, continuously creating a new and different style of living.

WHAT IS THE HIGHEST COMPLIMENT YOU'VE RECEIVED PROFESSIONALLY?

The satisfaction I receive from clients after the completion of a project.

WHAT PERSONAL INDULGENCE DO YOU SPEND THE MOST MONEY ON?

My personal indulgence would have to be buying architectural books and plants for my garden. I also have a love for landscape architecture, which I incorporate in all of my designs. When I'm not at the office, you can find me hidden in my private garden.

WHAT IS THE MOST BEAUTIFUL HOME YOU'VE SEEN?

It would have to be the Villa Capra or La Rotunda by Andrea Palladio; it is my favorite example of classical architecture.

RAMON PACHECO & ASSOCIATES, INC.
Ramon Pacheco, AIA
4990 Southwest 72 Avenue, Suite 101
Miami, FL 33155
305.666.2573
Fax 305.666.3871
www.pachecoarch.com

LEFT: Tahiti Beach, Coral Gables Residence: French doors open up to this home's center courtyard of tropical serenity. A balcony looks down to a display of an artist's palette, a mosaic floor pattern.
Photograph by Carlos Domenech

FACING PAGE: Tahiti Beach, Coral Gables Residence: Located on the private island of Tahiti Beach, this classical Italian residence gives a Pallatial feel with Corinthian columns and Roman arches.
Photograph by George Cott, Chroma Inc.

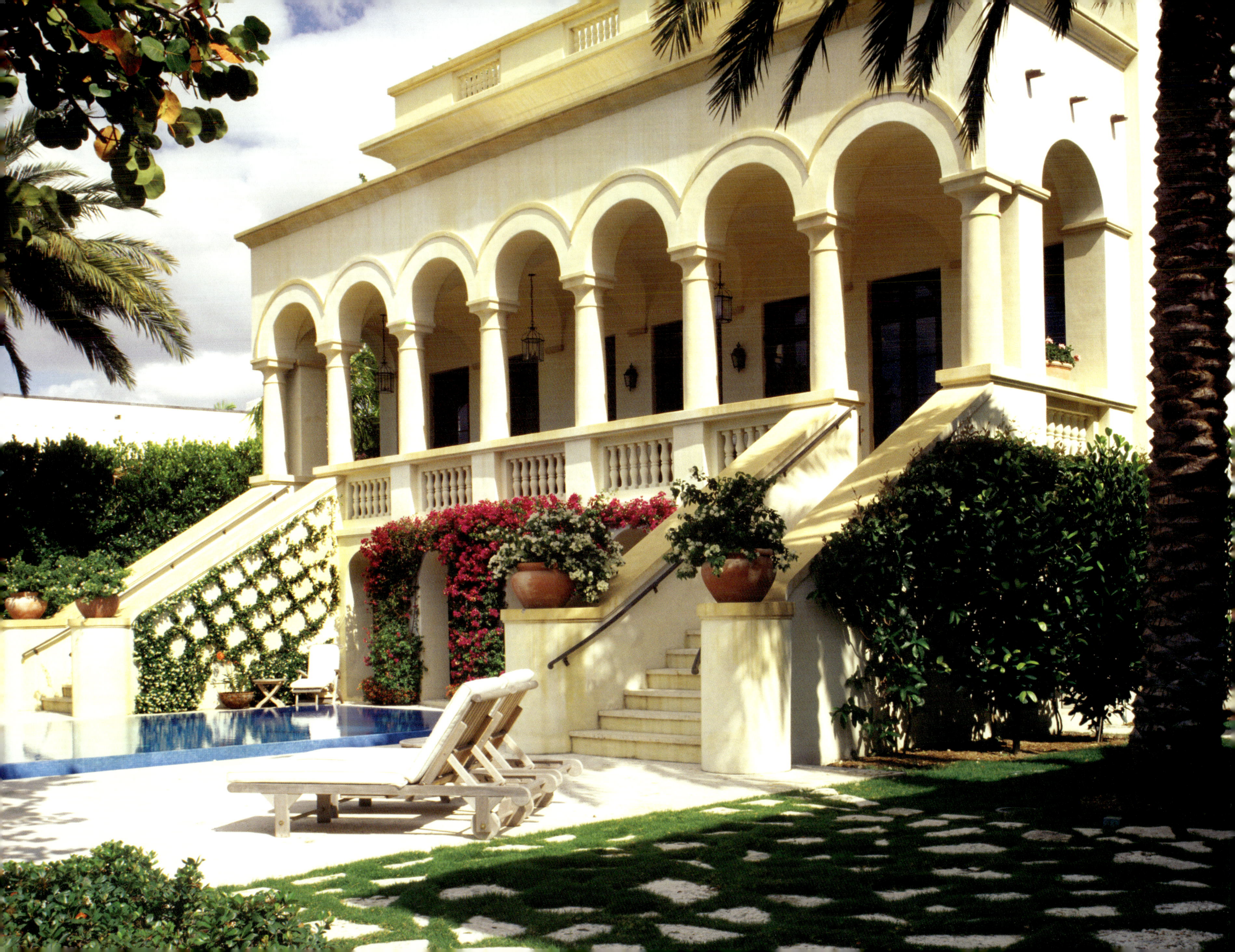

RAFAEL PORTUONDO & JOSE LUIS GONZALEZ-PEROTTI

Portuondo Perotti Architects

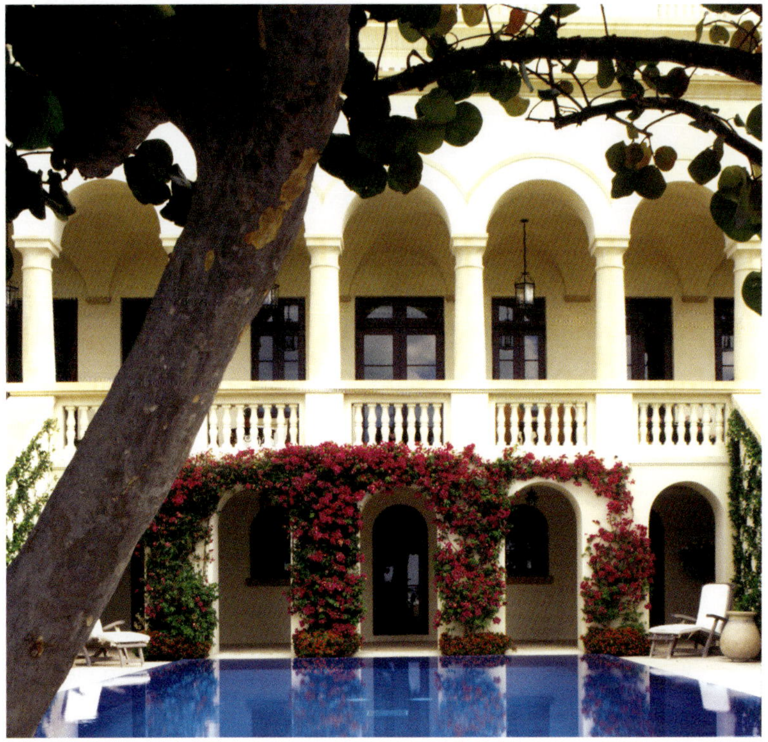

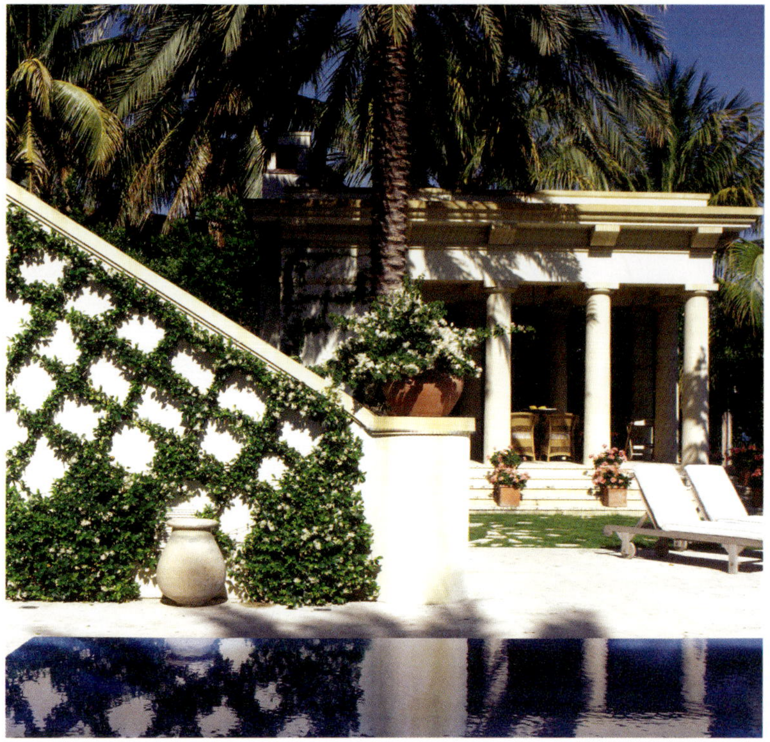

ABOVE LEFT: This view illustrates the center axis, which in classical architecture is an important moment creating an opportunity for the balance and alignment of interior and exterior spaces throughout the design.
Photograph by Carlos Domenech

ABOVE RIGHT: The rear stair and pavilion display the dialogue between structures often emblematic of the classical architectural style, while creating a picturesque setting surrounding the pool and rear yard.
Photograph by Carlos Domenech

LEFT: The stairs in the rear façade book-end both lower and upper loggias, affording the rooms in the rear of the home with views of the public waterway, while at the same time creating an intimate space for the owners.
Photograph by Carlos Domenech

Portuondo Perotti Architects is a hugely successful architectural studio known for their distinctive, serious, timeless commercial and residential designs. Founding partners Jose Perotti and Rafael Portuondo recognize they are a distinct part of the Floridian architectural scene and have set the aesthetic standards for others to follow.

The duo has a different design approach than most. They try and realize how they'll impact their neighbors and the surrounding environment when envisioning a solution to a design problem. "We approach design much more urbanisticly," Rafael said. "We see ourselves as part of a collective whole, which is a much more traditional way of approaching architecture. We're part of an urban fabric. And we approach projects that way."

The two met 20 years ago while working at the same architectural firm. They were friends and had similar goals. When the time was right the two joined forces and started their own studio. They say they complement each other and make a dynamic team. While Jose focuses on design, construction documents, and running the office, Rafael's focus is on design and client presentations.

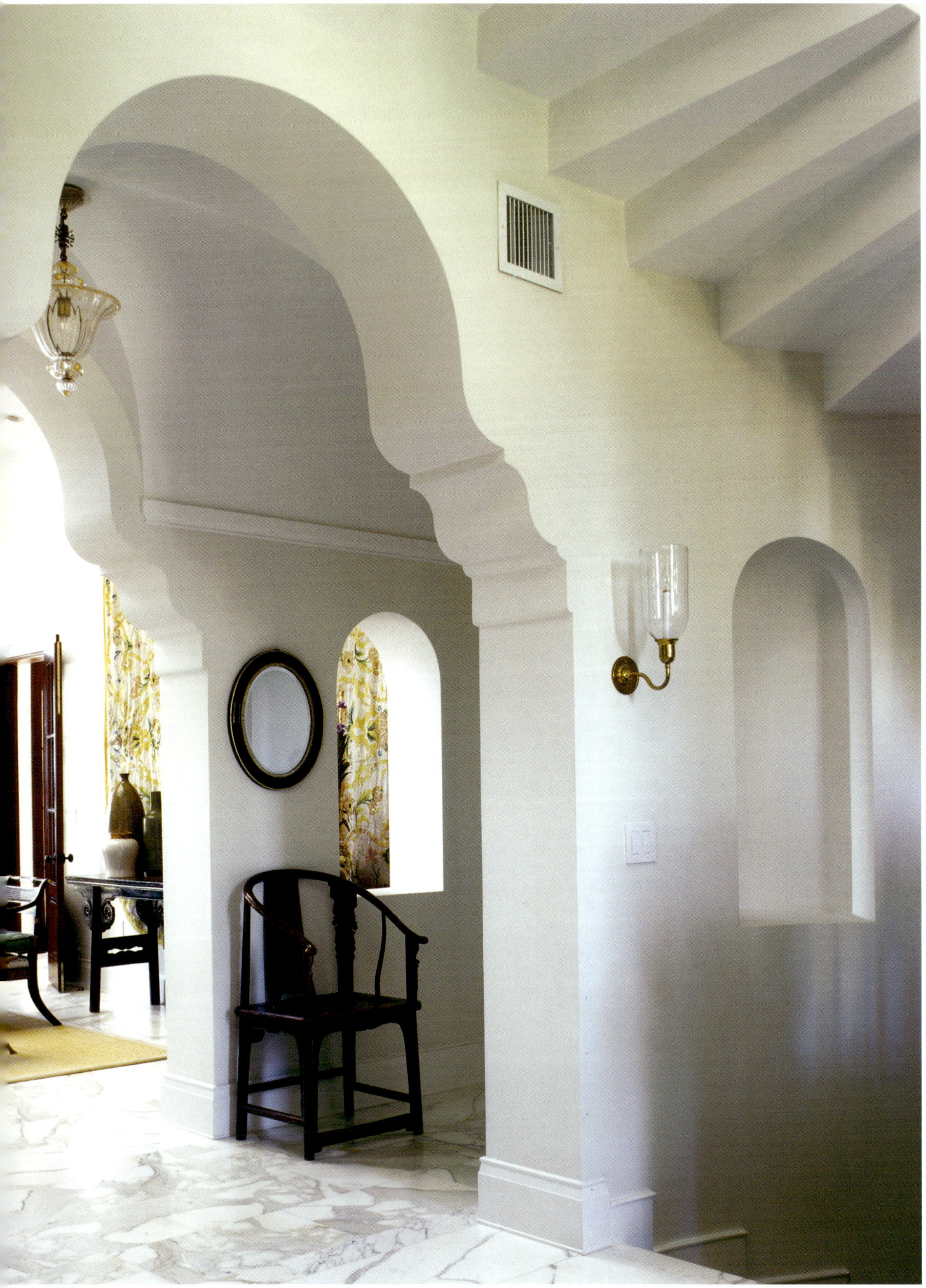

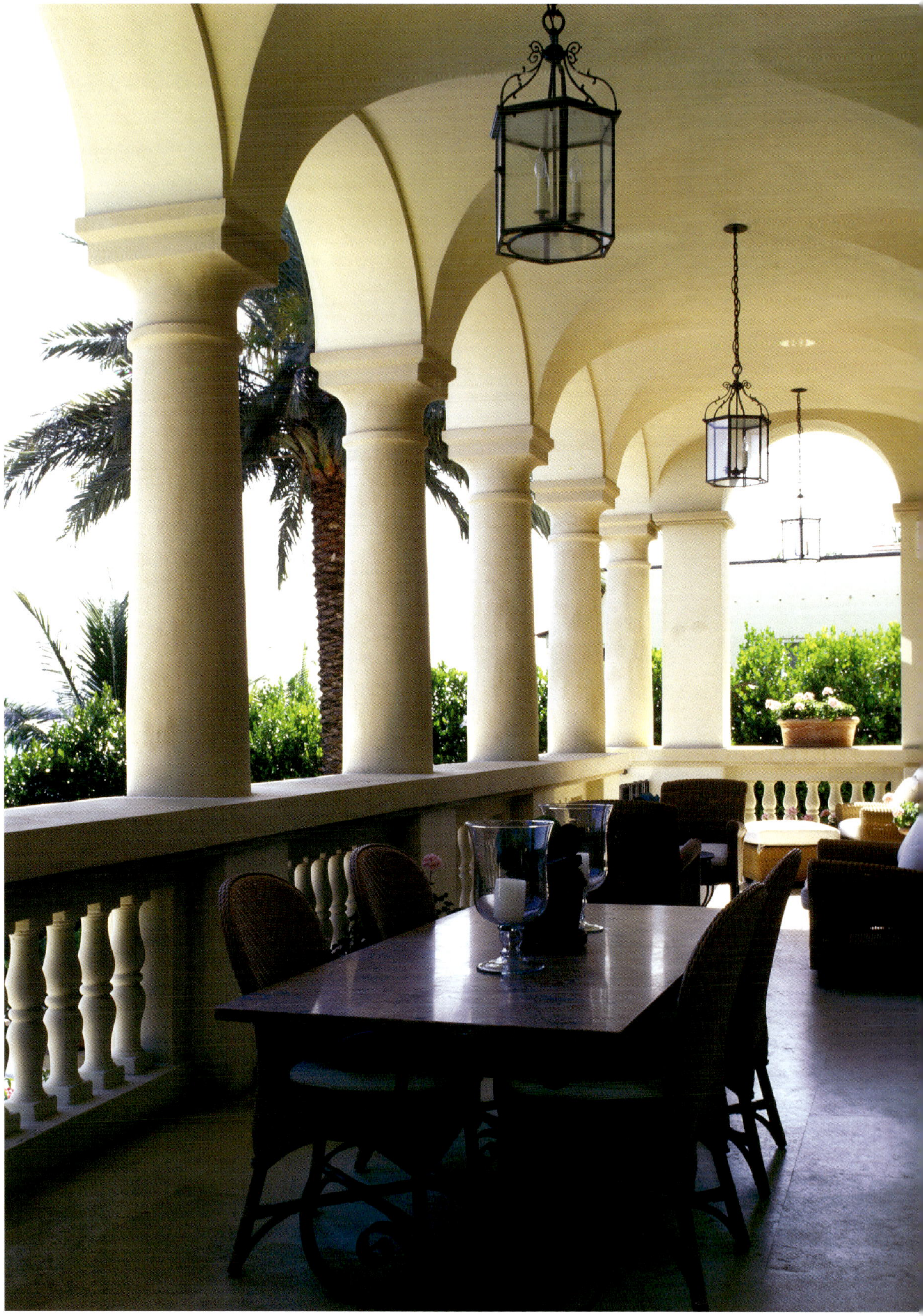

A major goal for Jose and Rafael is to achieve well proportioned structural designs creating an everlasting appeal through a sense of timelessness. They say many times a client will dictate the style wanted in their homes and then the duo personalize it and make it their own, all the while maintaining the client's original wishes.

They believe good design doesn't have to cost a lot of money. Rafael says that their business is divided up 80 percent high-end residential and 20 percent commercial. They have worked on smaller 3,500-square-foot homes and larger grand estate homes that are as much as 25,000 square feet. "We take a lot of care in doing both big and small structures," Rafael says. In the end he puts as much effort into the smaller budgeted projects as he does the larger.

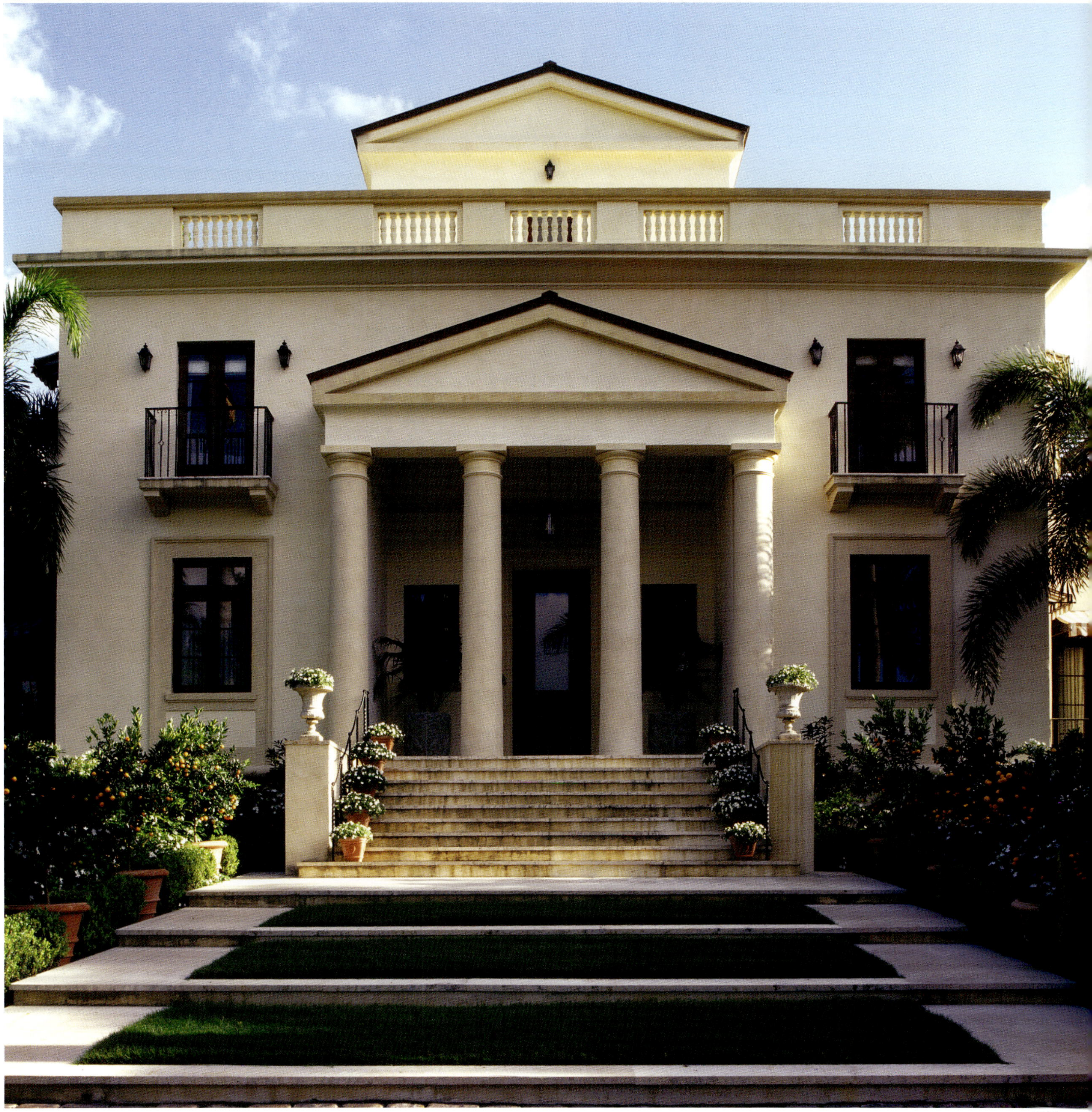

RIGHT: In a site where the rear yard is the dominant space, the front façade must give a sense of presence on the street it fronts. The façade creates a foreground space and expresses the central axis displayed in the entry portico and roof pavilion.
Photograph by Carlos Domenech

FACING PAGE LEFT: Caribbean style elements often create a powerful complement to the strength of classical architecture, in dictating details by way of designing profiles as opposed to building out stucco and plaster details in three dimensions.
Photograph by Carlos Domenech

FACING PAGE RIGHT: The upper loggia is intended to act as an exterior living room. The goal was that through the design of the elements within the loggia the room would give a sense of timelessness.
Photograph by Carlos Domenech

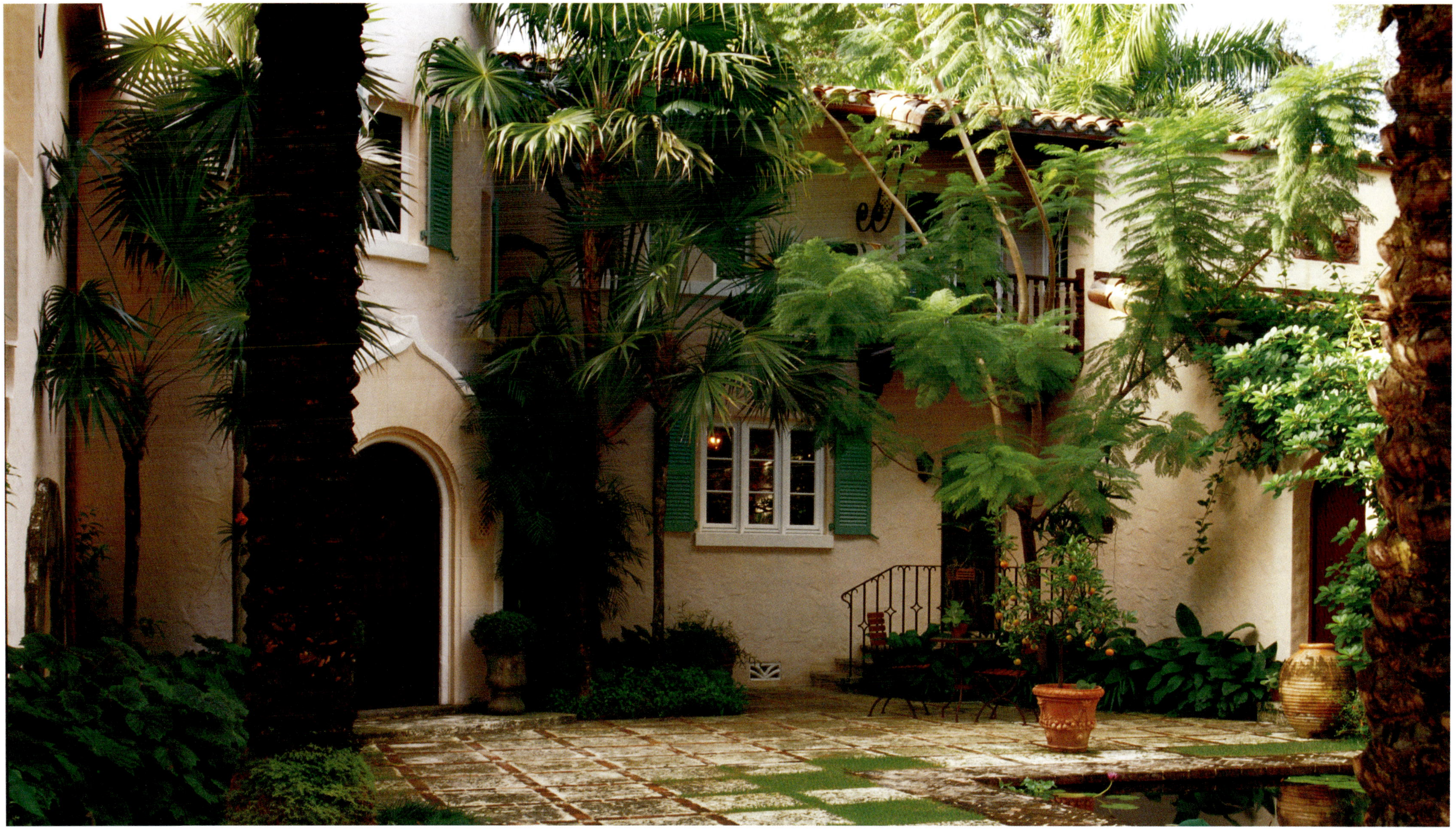

Some of their commercial work has included the gateway to the Miami River, the Brickell Bridge, a commission that they received won in an international competition and the Second Avenue Bridge, in which Jose and Rafael were selected out of 25 different firms. They also won a Golden Palm award for a 30,000-square-foot office building the designed in Palm Beach for the Palm Beach Community Foundation.

Ninety percent of their design work is in the Southern Florida area including Coral Gables and the famous Coconut Grove. And much of their inspiration and influence has come from Southern Florida architects and the abundance of examples of their work in the area. Jose and Rafael also look at other areas with similar climates for inspiration and direction with their own projects. Some of these areas of similarity and architectural influence include South Africa, Cuba, the Caribbean, Spain, Guatemala and other tropical areas. They study the elements of the architectural structures and then rethink them to figure out how to integrate these elements within the Floridian aesthetic.

The design works that Jose and Rafael are most proud of are the projects currently under construction. "We really do engage the proportions of our homes, including the materials, the gardens and even the auxiliary structures," Rafael said. "We have been blessed because we've had the opportunity to design structures that have been really special to our clients and to ourselves."

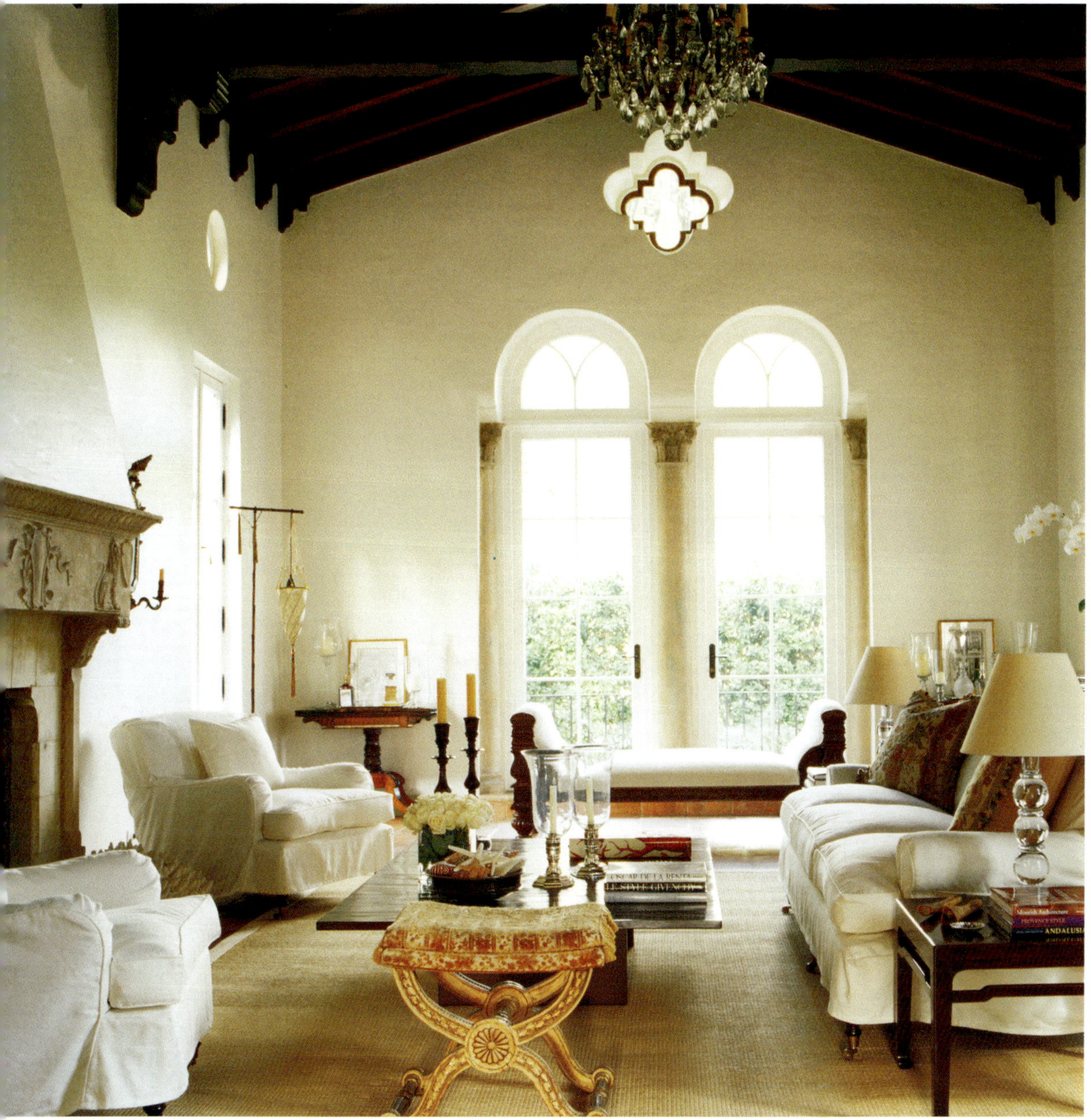

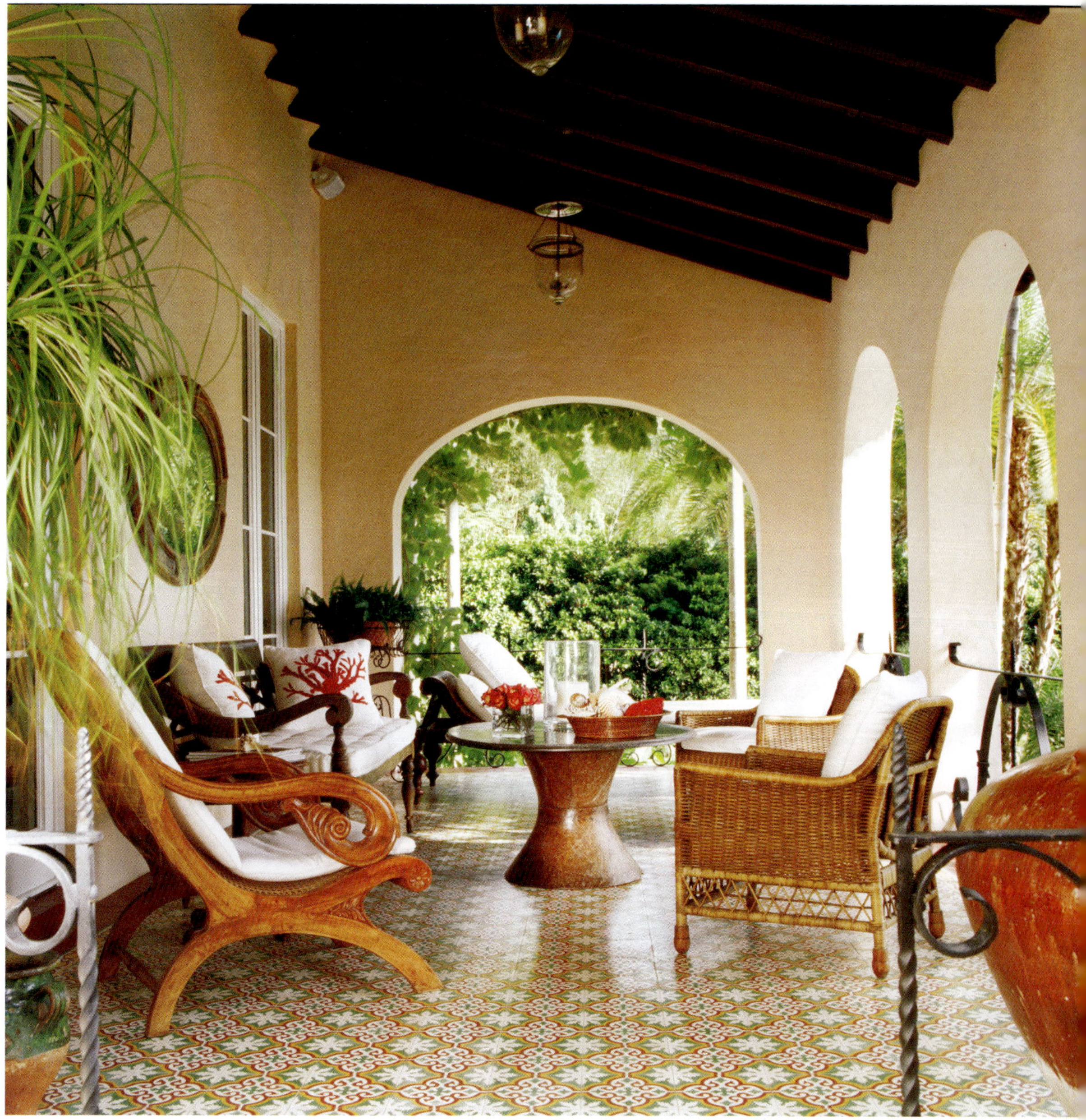

ABOVE LEFT: Elements in this space including the double-door and quatrefoil, mahogany ceiling, terracotta floors, and white walls create a room which provides a sense of grandeur and intimacy at the same time.
Photograph by Tria Giovan

ABOVE RIGHT: This loggia was inspired by Cuban and Caribbean styles, displayed in the bright Cuban-tile floor and arrangement of elements. The colors in the space tie in the landscaping to the home providing a tranquil yet elegant space.
Photograph by Tria Giovan

FACING PAGE: This home is about the understated elegance it possesses by way of the elements it displays. The landscaping complements the informality and transforms the setting to a picturesque surrounding for the home.
Photograph by Tria Giovan

ADDITIONAL CREDITS: *Pages 152-155*—Project Manager, Mike Sardiñas; M.E.P. Engineer, RPJ, Inc. Engineers; Structural Engineer, De Los Reyes Engineers; Landscape Architect, Sanchez & Maddux; General Contractor, Fountainhead Group. *Pages 156-157*—Project Manager, Jordi Esteban; M.E.P. Engineer, RPJ, Inc. Engineers; Structural Engineer, De Los Reyes Engineers; Landscape Architect, Sanchez & Maddux; General Contractor, Renaissance Group.

PORTUONDO PEROTTI ARCHITECTS
Rafael Portuondo, AIA, President
Jose Luis Gonzalez-Perotti AIA, Vice President
5717 Southwest 8th Street
Miami, FL 33139
305.442.1262
Fax 305.442.1511
www.portuondo-perotti.com

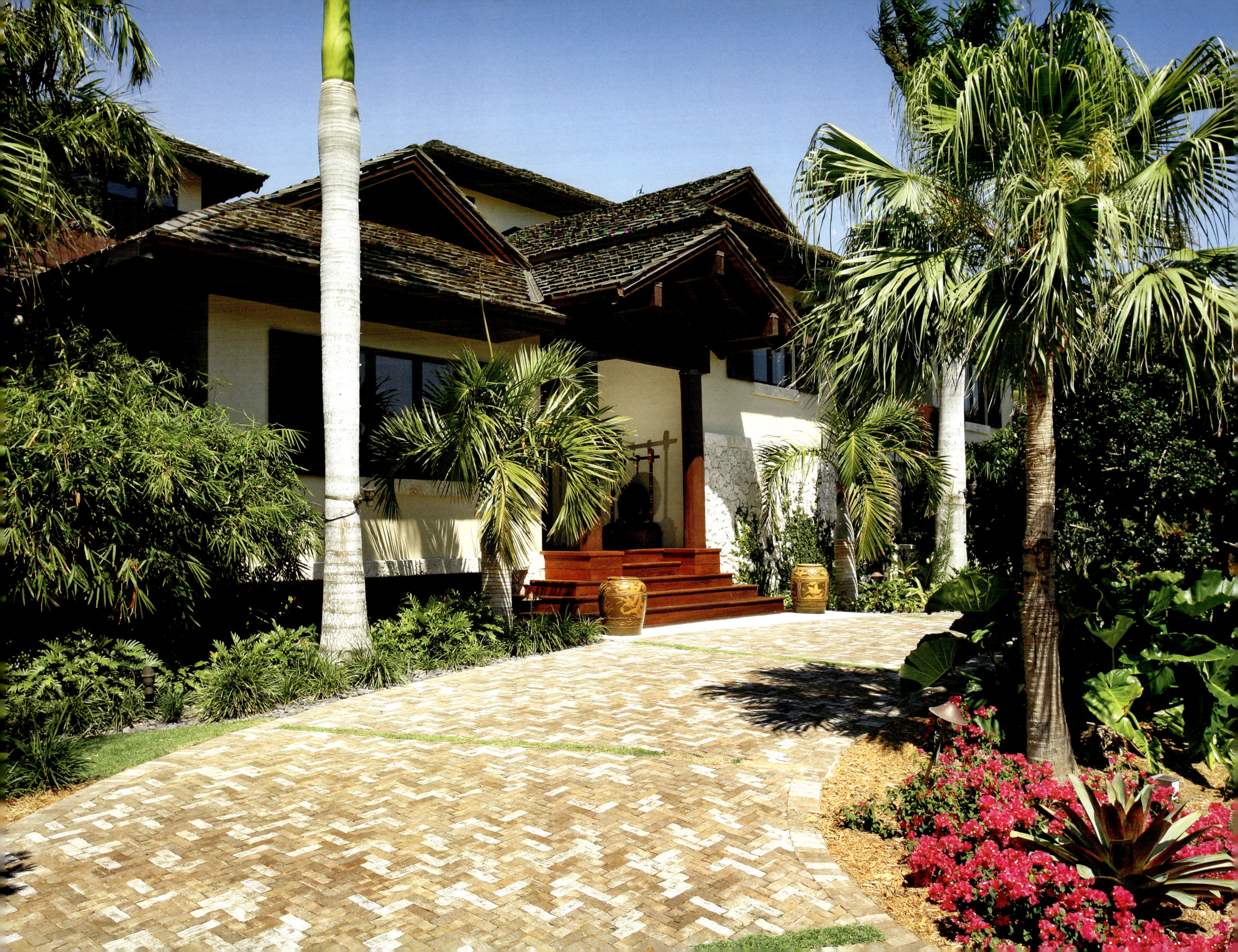

TIMOTHY SLAWSON

Timothy James Slawson, P. A.

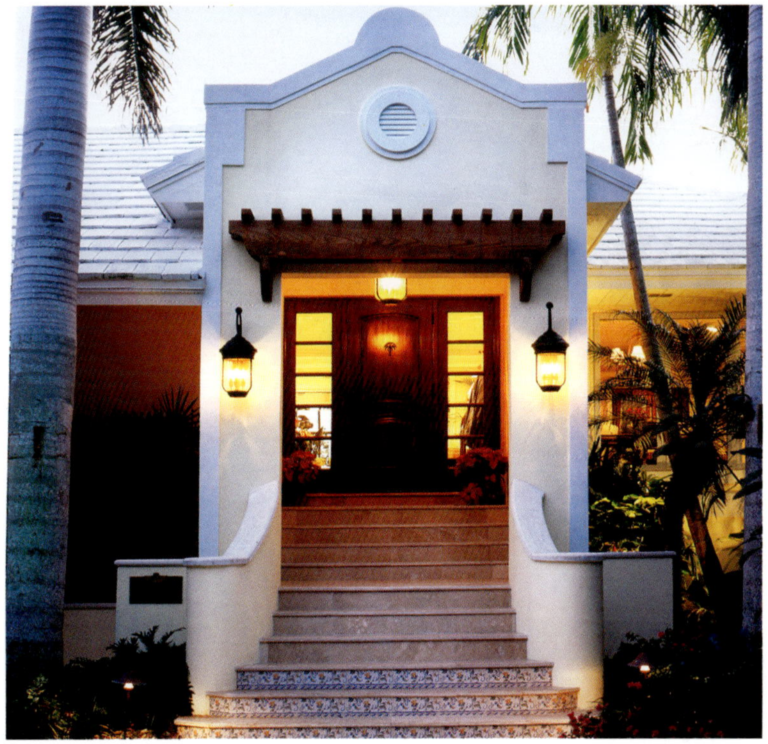

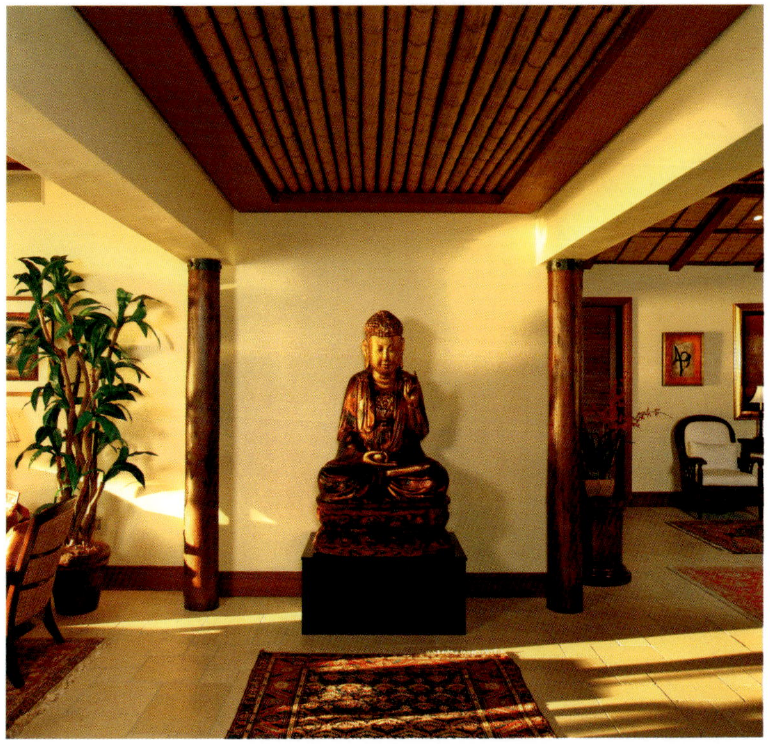

Timothy James Slawson knew at the age of 13 that he wanted to be an architect when he grew up. His love of drawing and the influence of his uncle, a contractor, steered Timothy toward his destined career.

Timothy's uncle was working on projects that the young architect-to-be found amazing as he saw the projects transform from blueprints to finished structures. However, his uncle wasn't the only influence on the young man's career choice; it was also his fascination with clean lines and how things are connected.

Today, those pure lines dominate his architectural aesthetics. Timothy works by the principle of "Keep it simple." He incorporates understated elements to achieve a sense of flow in his residential firm's projects. He allows the architecture to make the statement of beauty, and upon entering the homes he has designed, one notices not just one element of the architecture, but the whole picture.

After graduating from the University of Miami, Timothy worked in the residential related market for some time, but with no great consequences. Through a stroke of good fortune, he was able to get his foot in the door with a very influential firm (Fergis & Selck Architects) and it was truly a dream job

ABOVE LEFT: The remodeling of this home transformed a wood cladded house into a Bermuda wonder. The new elegance was really a welcome site for the entry.
Photograph by Doug Thomson & Tom Harper

ABOVE RIGHT: The location of Buddha was carefully located so that there is not one time of the day where "Buddha" has the same reflection.
Photograph by Tom Harper

LEFT: The Bali-style architecture was created using a variety of building materials. Keystone, clay, cedar, cypress, and Ipé are all integrated together.
Photograph by Tom Harper

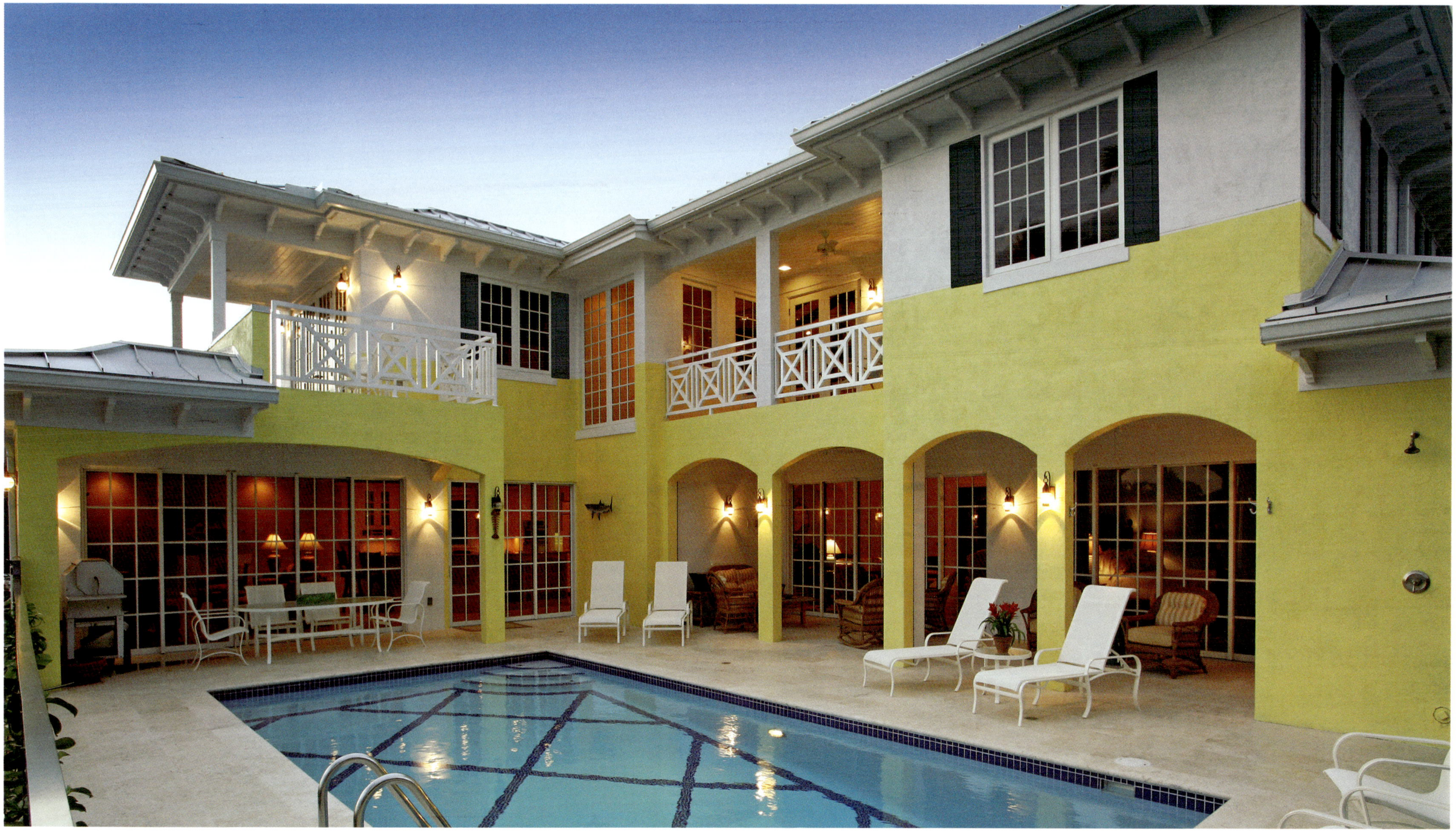

for the young architect. Working with the firm allowed him to break into the high-end residential market and taught him the old-school architectural mentality of pencils and paper combined with new computer generated techniques, which Timothy whole-heartedly adopted and implemented.

When working with a client, he lets the designs of his projects be governed by what his client wants. He says that he doesn't design these homes for himself; instead, he acquires his vision from information he gains from carefully listening to his clients' desires. That's why he doesn't have a particular style per se, because each client dictates their own tastes and he never wants to force an aesthetic. "I listen to my clients," Timothy says. "I let them keep designing their house, which doesn't allow me to force anything on them. I give them my interpretation, but I won't push a style or aesthetic that they don't want."

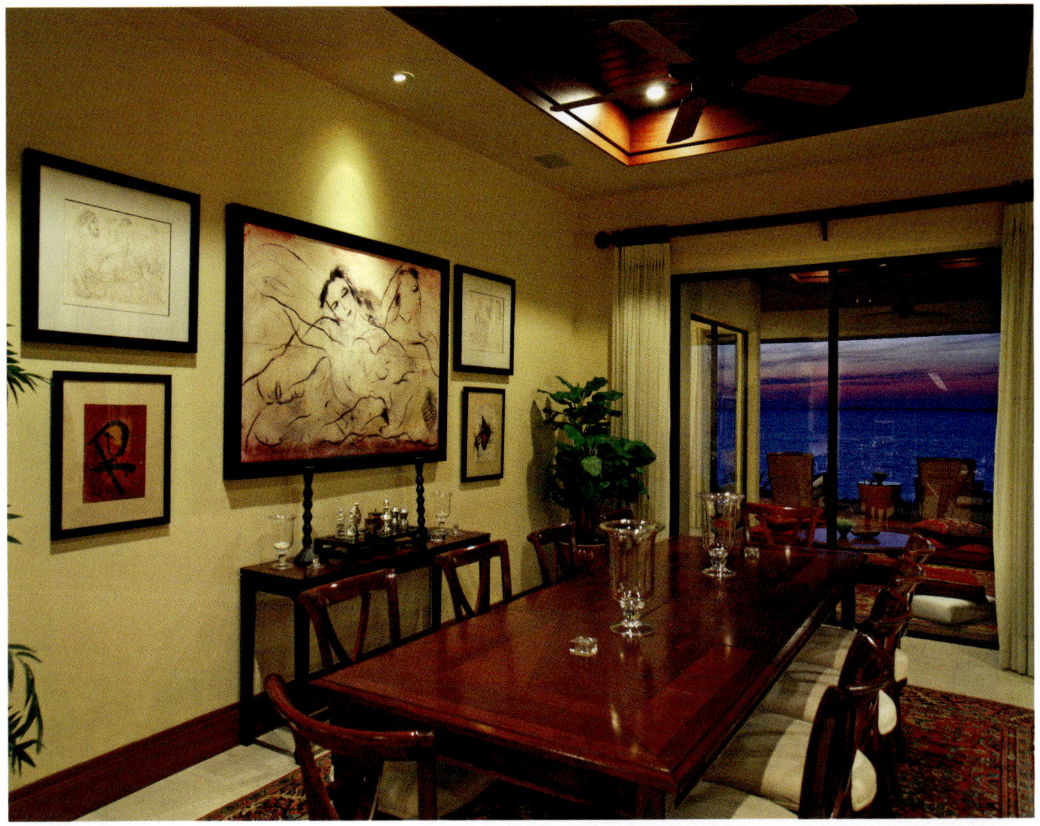

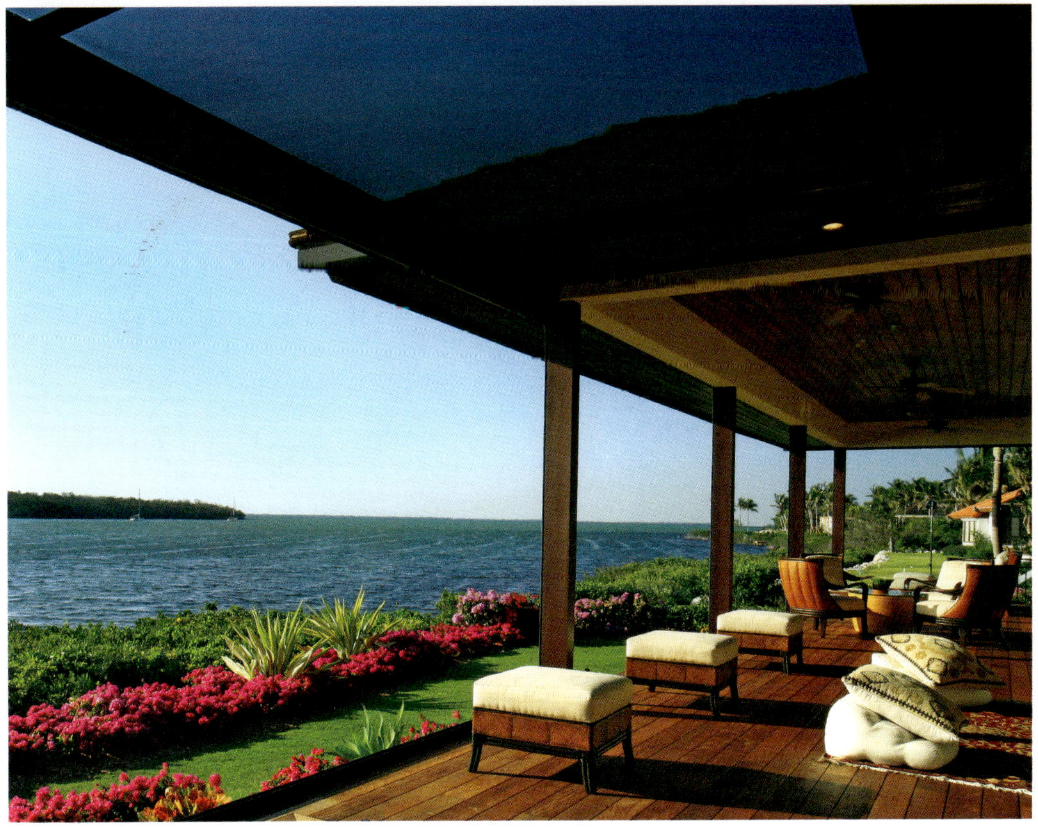

Q&A

more about timothy...

WHAT PERSONAL INDULGENCE DO YOU SPEND THE MOST MONEY ON?

If I have time, I love to travel with my wife, Maria, and our children.

WHAT IS THE MOST UNUSUAL DESIGN YOU'VE USED ON A PROJECT?

We incorporated 200-year-old Chinese gates as entry doors. The original door pegs were kept with custom-designed bearing casings to support the doors. There are no hinges and the doors swing with a finger's touch.

WHAT SEPARATES YOU FROM YOUR COMPETITION?

There is no secret that great service will lead to continued success. I also have to understand that I am designing a home for my clients and not for myself.

DESCRIBE YOUR STYLE?

I don't really have a specific style, but whatever style I design I try to use clean lines, open spaces, and tropical elements to complement our regional location.

TIMOTHY JAMES SLAWSON, PA
Timothy Slawson, AIA
27 Northeast 10th Street
Homestead, FL 33030
786.293.6000
Fax 786.293.6001

TOP: This dining room has great internal design features as well as a beautiful sunset every day of the year.
Photograph by Tom Harper

BOTTOM: All the major rooms of the house have access to this porch. There are concealed roll down bug screens in the soffits if needed.
Photograph by Tom Harper

FACING PAGE: The house was designed for the best view outward. The pool was located for the best sun exposure, and also complements the view.
Photograph by Tom Harper

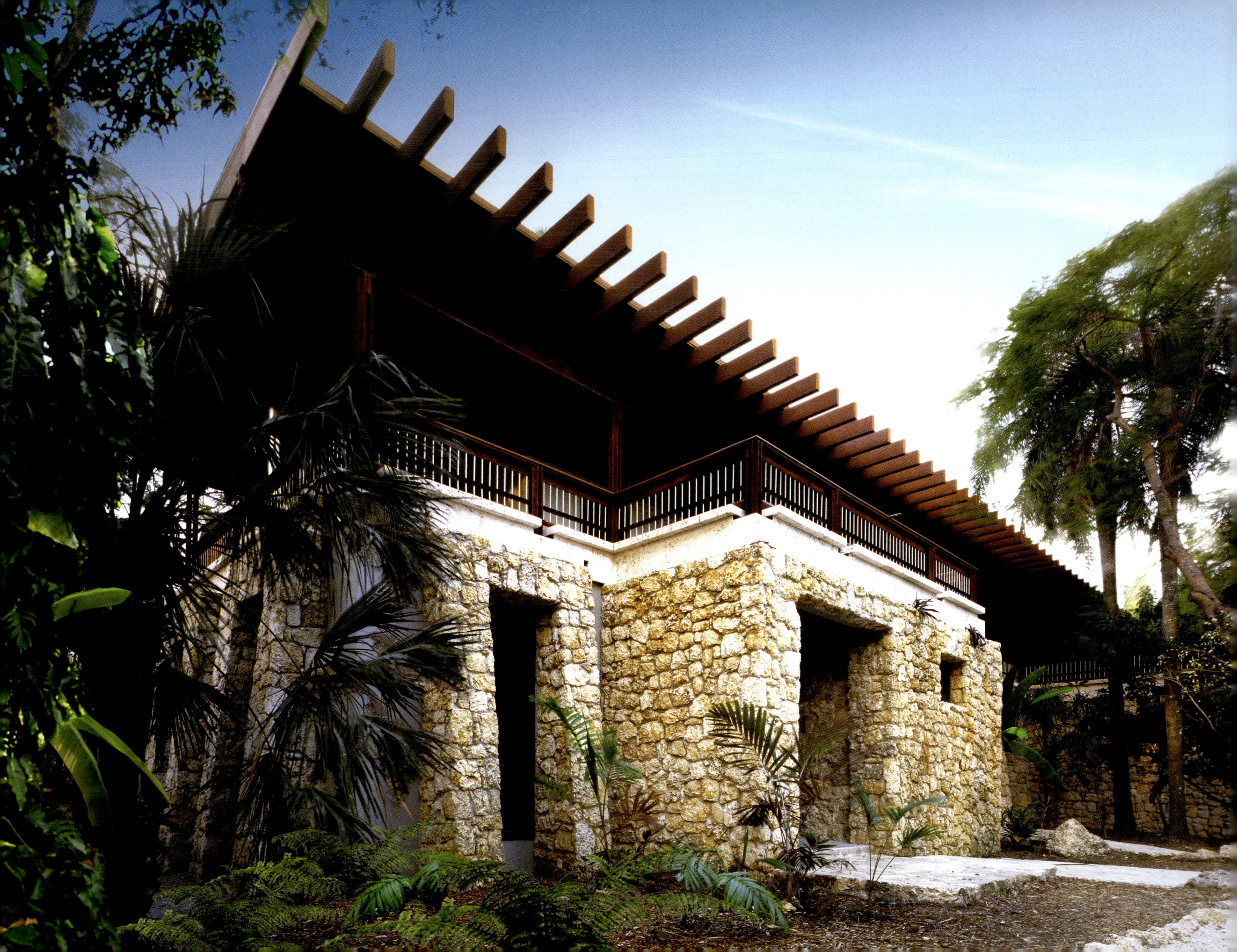

MAX STRANG

Max Strang Architecture

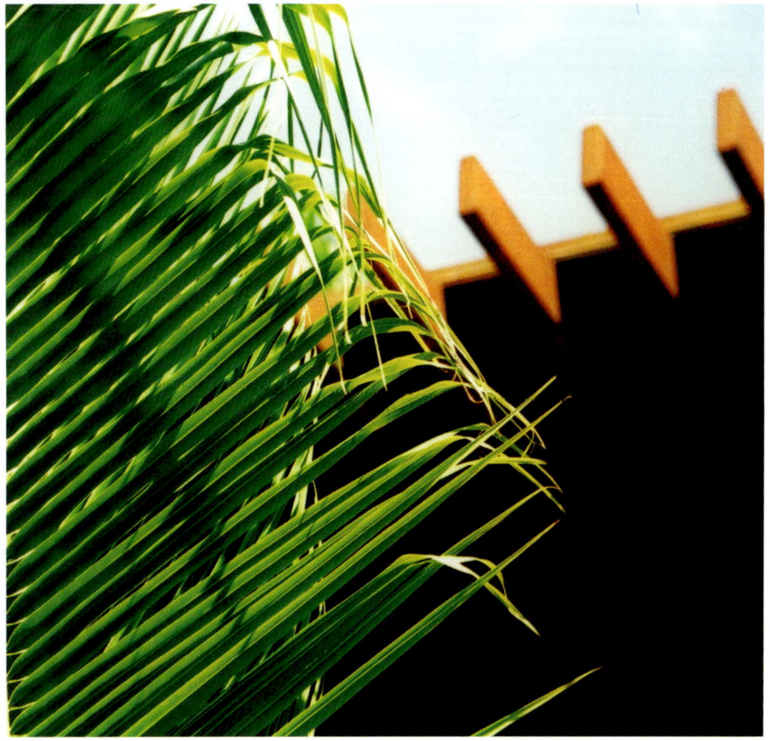

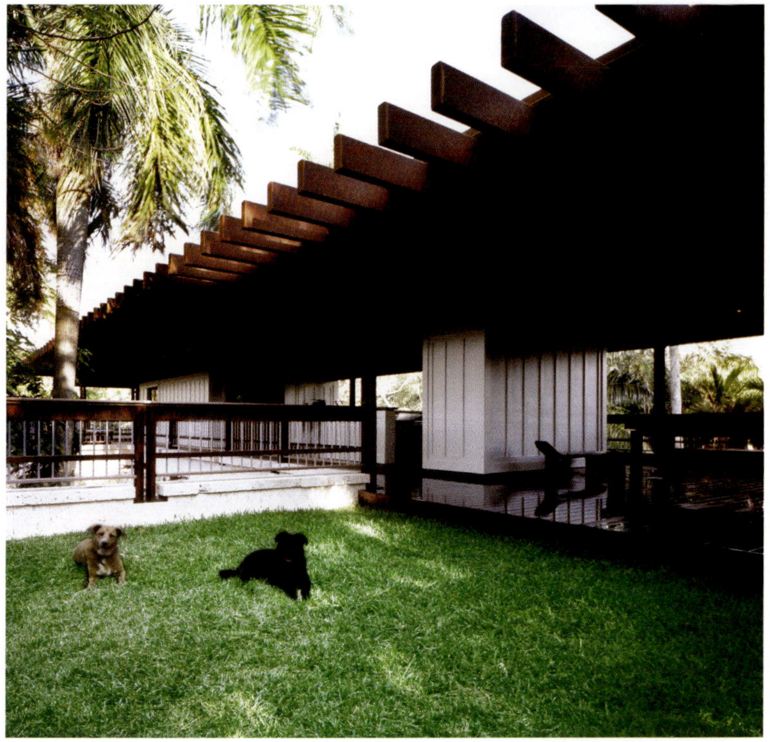

Max Strang has rapidly developed a name for himself in South Florida as an architect sensitive to site, place, and the environment. His own house has recently won recognition from the American Institute of Architects at both the local and state level. In 2003, he was named by AIA Miami as the "Young Architect of the Year."

When asked to define his style of architecture, Max gives it a new moniker: environmental modernism. "Our landscape, culture and climate carry within them an opportunity to enhance the character of a home or building. Using this as a basis for inspiration, environmental modernism emphasizes a timeless approach to design," he says.

How did he develop this vision? A bit of fate initially spurred Max toward architecture. He grew up in a modern house in Winter Haven, Florida, designed by the prominent architect, Gene Leedy, among the founders of the Bauhaus-inspired Sarasota School of Architecture. "These architects were known for their modern designs in the '50s and '60s that fit the Florida climate," Max says. As a result of his strong attachment to the Strang family home, Max set a goal for himself: become an architect and work for Leedy.

ABOVE LEFT: Nature's rhythms are echoed in the designs of Max Strang Architecture.
Photograph by Max Strang Architecture

ABOVE RIGHT: Industrial steel beams hover above a "green sodded roof" on the second floor of this Miami residence.
Photograph by Max Strang Architecture

LEFT: This residence demonstrates how the designs of Max Strang Architecture can be daring and sensitive at the same time.
Photograph by Max Strang Architecture

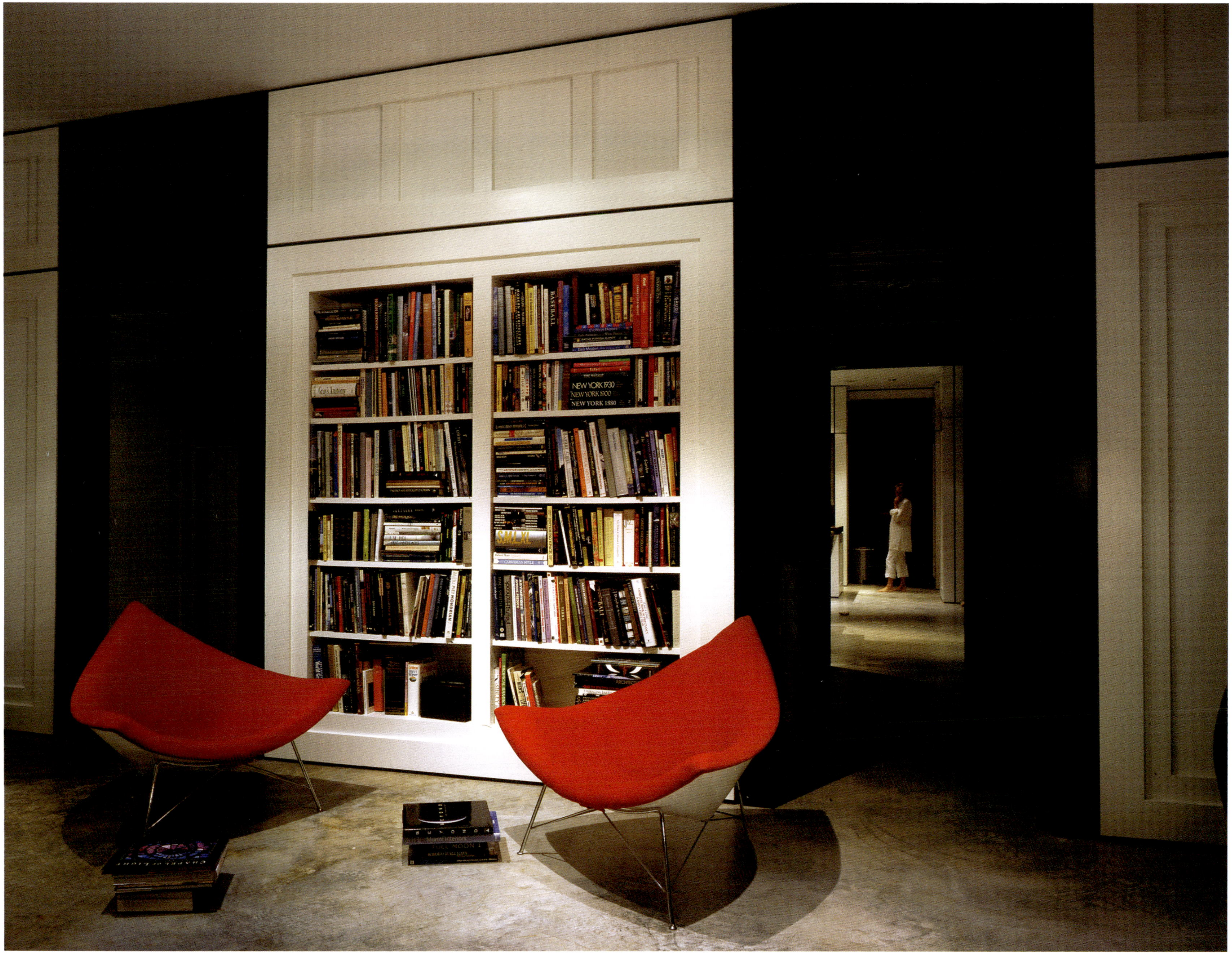

BASEBALL
NEW YORK 1930
NEW YORK 1900
NEW YORK 1880
Gray's Anatomy
S,M,L,XL

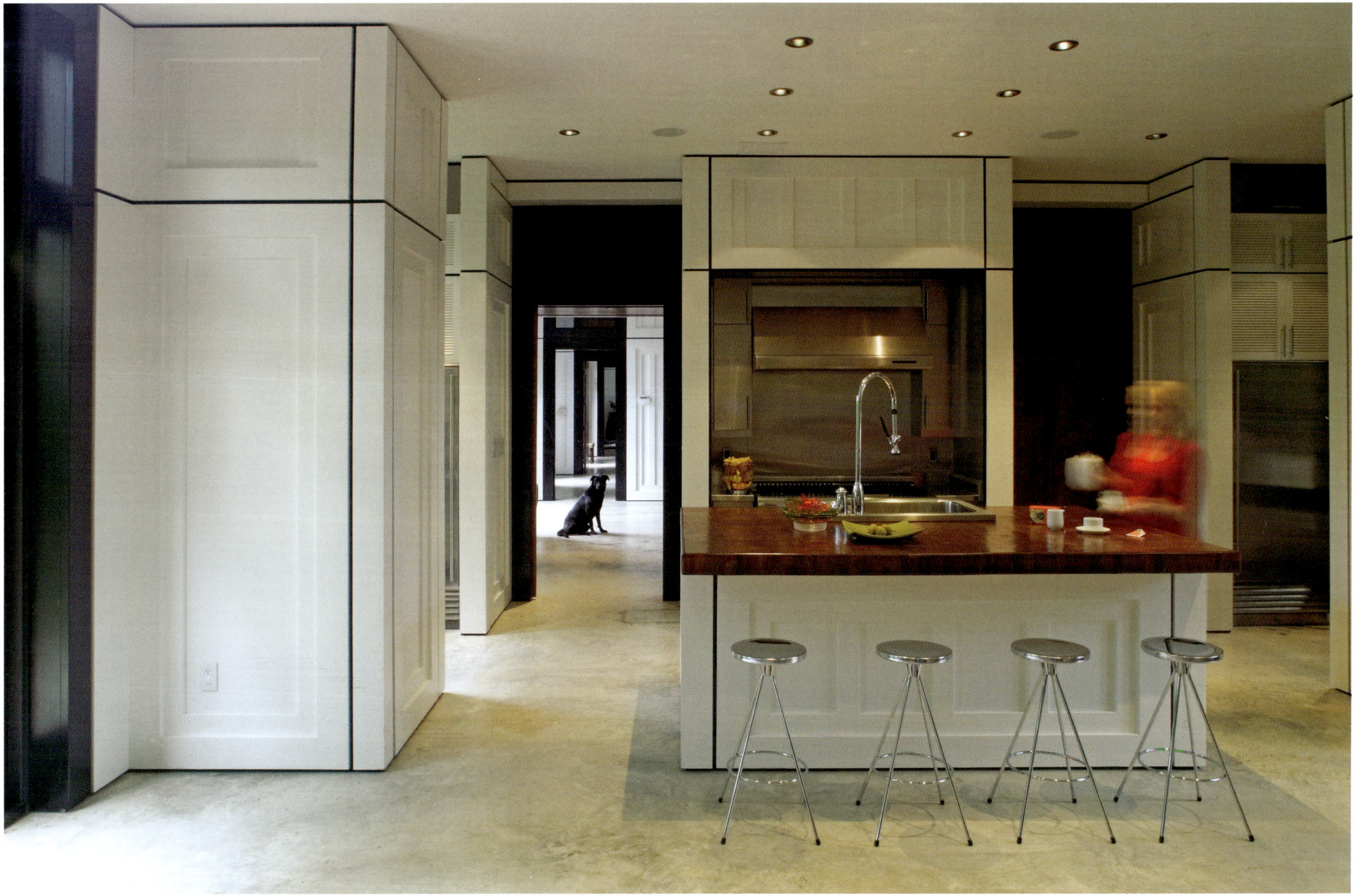

ABOVE: This minimalistic kitchen was designed around an island made of recycled Dade County Pine.
Photograph by Claudia Uribe Touri

FACING PAGE: A polished concrete floor provides a sophisticated aesthetic.
Photograph by Max Strang Architecture

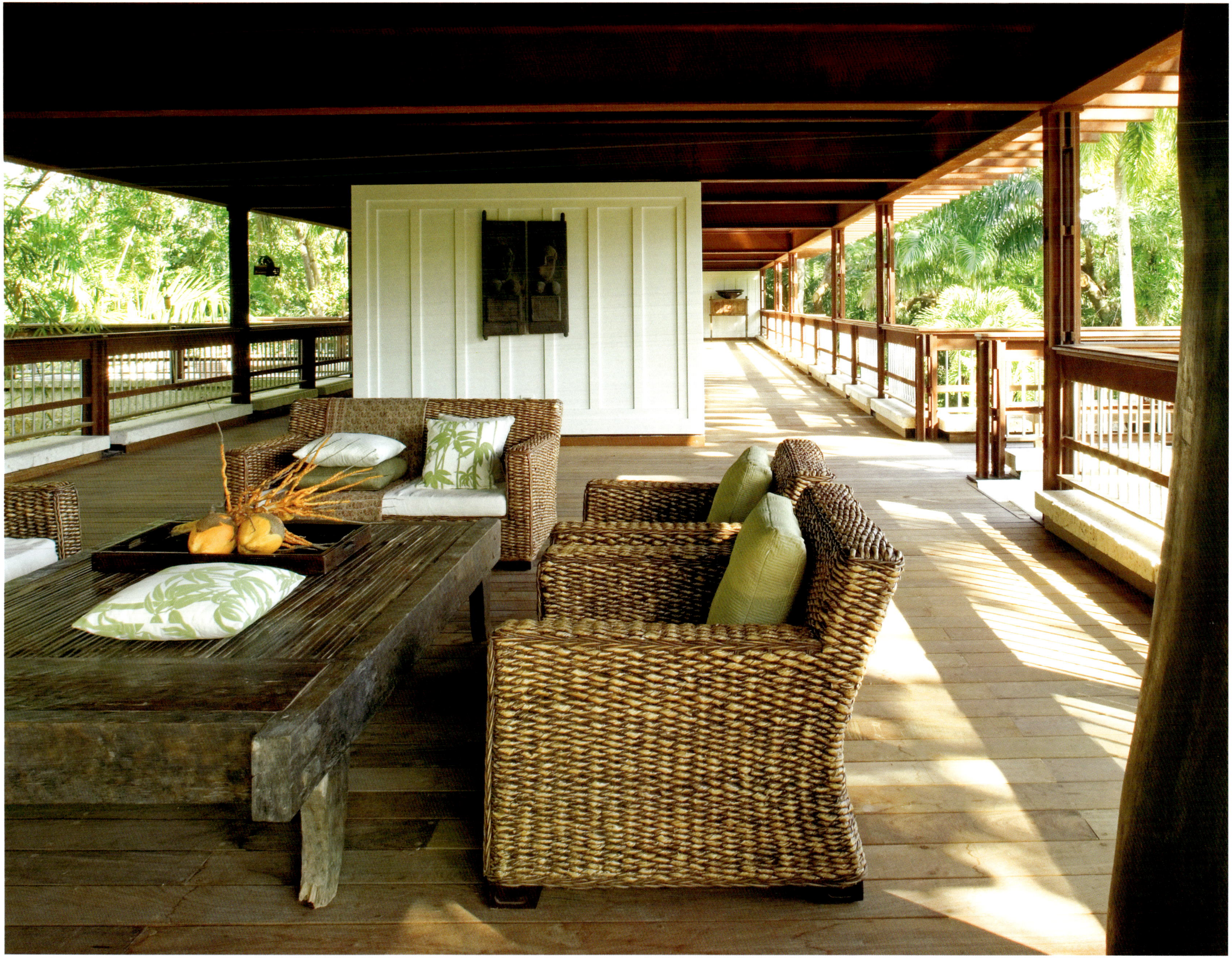

He achieved both, earning his undergraduate degree at the University of Florida School of Architecture in 1994 and joining Leedy's firm, where he gained practical experience. He later decided to further his education, enrolling in the Graduate School of Architecture at Columbia University, one of the most prestigious programs in the country.

Living in New York exposed him not only to a world of design and architectural experiences, but also to the availability of important contacts. He was hired by the New York-based SHoP Architects, where he worked on MOSEX (the Museum of Sex), and interned briefly in London for star architect Zaha Hadid, who designed the celebrated Cincinnati Museum of Contemporary Art. Max moved to South Florida because it offered a sophisticated urban environment in close proximity to the Caribbean, where he wanted to design projects. Although he still commuted to New York on a routine basis, he eventually established his own firm in Miami and immediately began to receive respectable commissions.

From the start, he has demonstrated the ability to produce and succeed. For example, a dormitory for visiting scholars at The Kampong of the National Tropical Botanical Garden in Coconut Grove, combines limestone exteriors—a traditional South Florida material—with another local necessity—solar panels and a rain-water collection system. Another commission, low-cost housing for a local developer, combined a design inspired by Bahamian "shotgun" shacks, with a modern metal roof. It was his own home, however, that put Max on the Miami architecture and design map. The design featured exposed structural steel, local limestone and a soaring 4,000-square-foot Ipe wood terrace. Occupying the entire second level, the terrace is sheltered by industrial steel I-beams, and offers seating found on a trip to Indonesia. The house is surrounded by lush plantings of royal palms, bamboo and tropical fruit trees, along with passion flower and bleeding heart vines. The interior is just as magical and daring. The floors are concrete, while many of the walls are white or stained a dark ebony or mahogany hue for contrast, with stainless steel accents acting

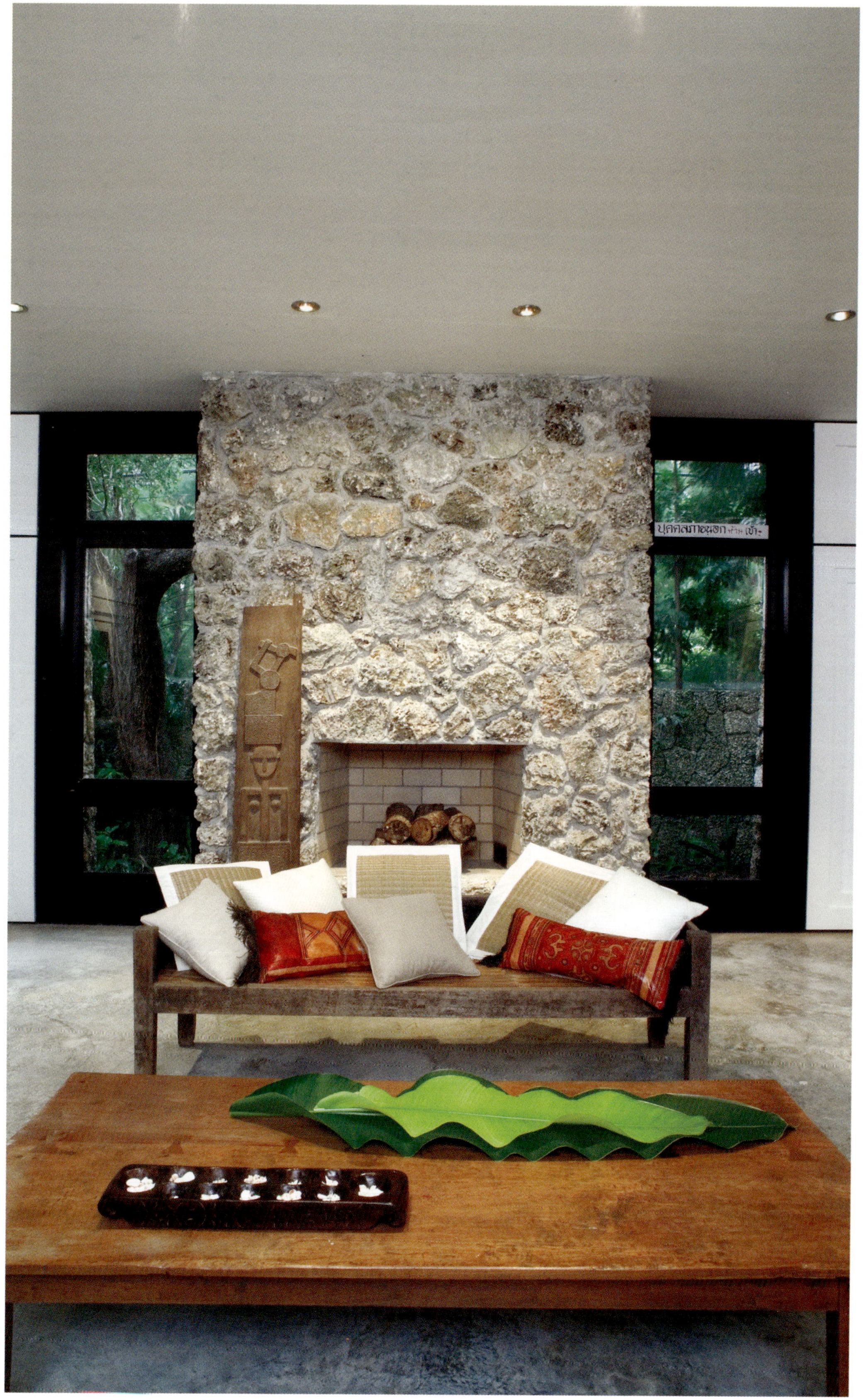

RIGHT: A native limestone, called "oolite," is also used as an interior finish material.
Photograph by Claudia Uribe Touri

FACING PAGE: Color, texture, light and shadow play off each other on the long second-floor veranda.
Photograph by Claudia Uribe Touri

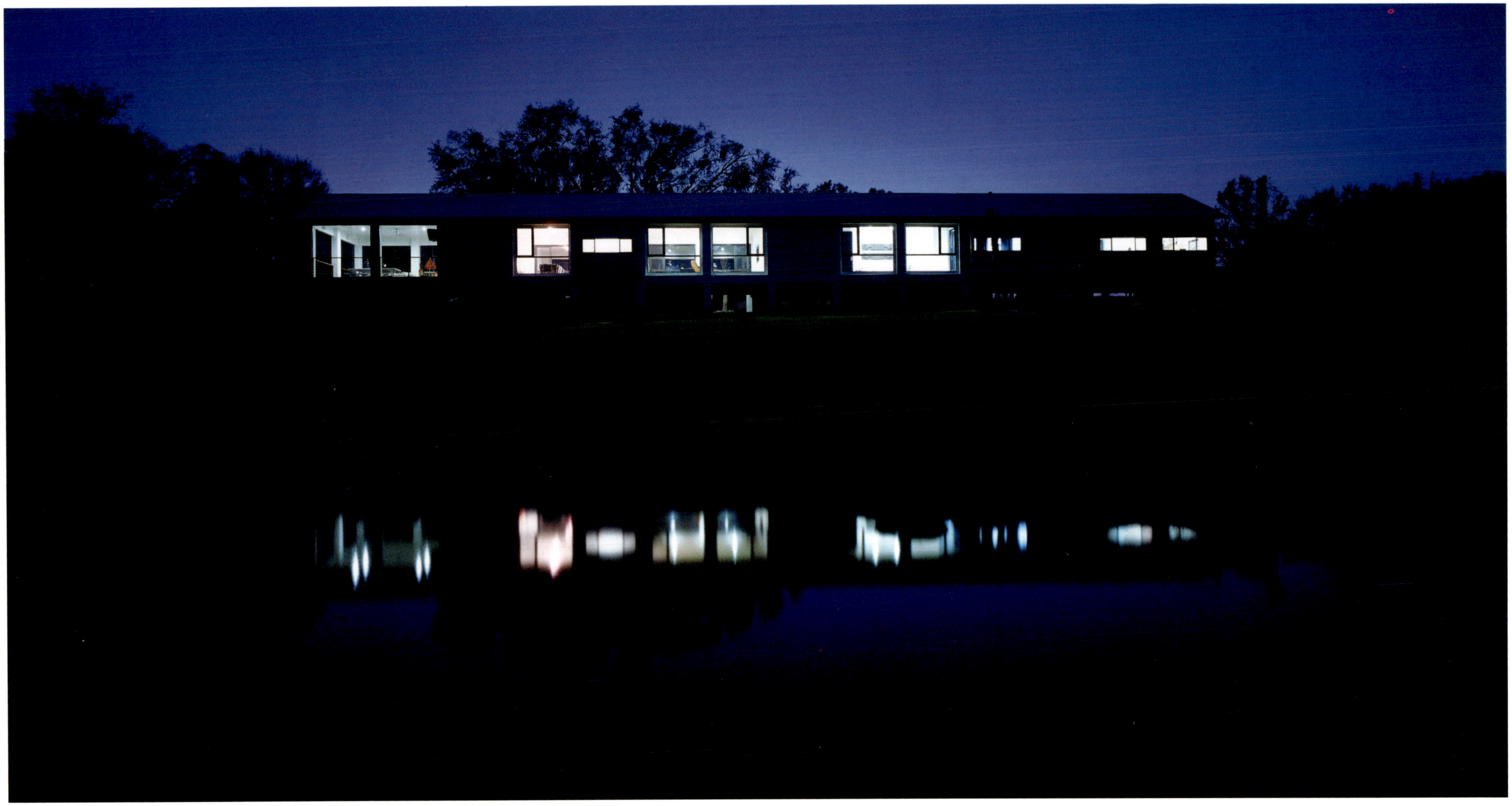

as punctuation marks. Rooms are minimally furnished. In the master bedroom, there is only a bed; in the bathroom, the white freestanding tub looks both stark and serene. Recently, the director of "Miami Vice" selected the Strang residence for critical scenes in the film, released in summer 2006.

Max's dream of working in the Caribbean has come true. He is currently working on several homes in the Bahamas and an eco-resort in Costa Rica. He has also turned his attention to several commercial projects, including innovative and environmentally-friendly solutions for The Home Depot in Coconut Grove and a BP gas station on Biscayne Boulevard in downtown Miami. Both of these high-profile commissions incorporate a "living-wall" system as a major design feature. Environmental Modernism is indeed alive and well in South Florida, with Max in the forefront.

Max incorporates a range of textures in his work that reflect his love of nature, an interest his shares with his wife, Tamara, who volunteers at Fairchild Tropical Botanical Gardens in nearby Coral Gables.

With each assignment it is obvious that this architect pushes himself, as he explains, "not to be repetitive and predictable, but to be edgy and experimental." Yet at the same time he is adamant that his designs be timeless. Those who have watched his climb and noticed the many professional accolades, are convinced that Max Strang will continue to make his indelible mark in the years to come throughout South Florida and the Caribbean.

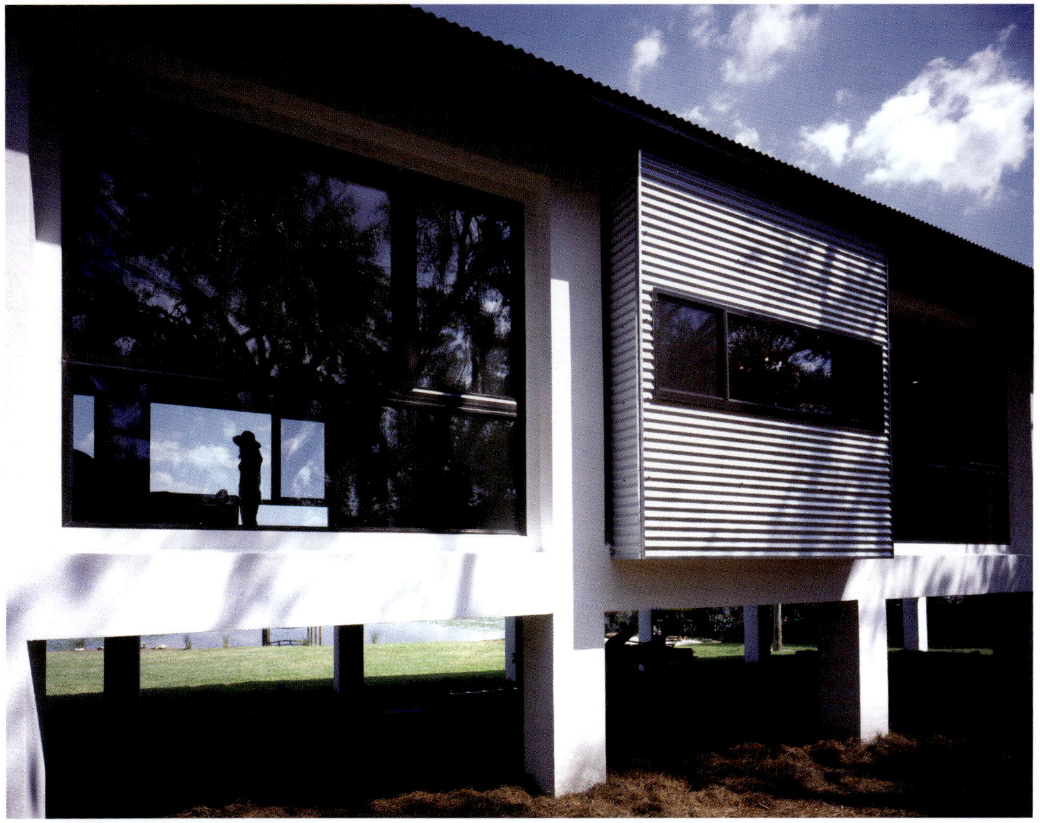

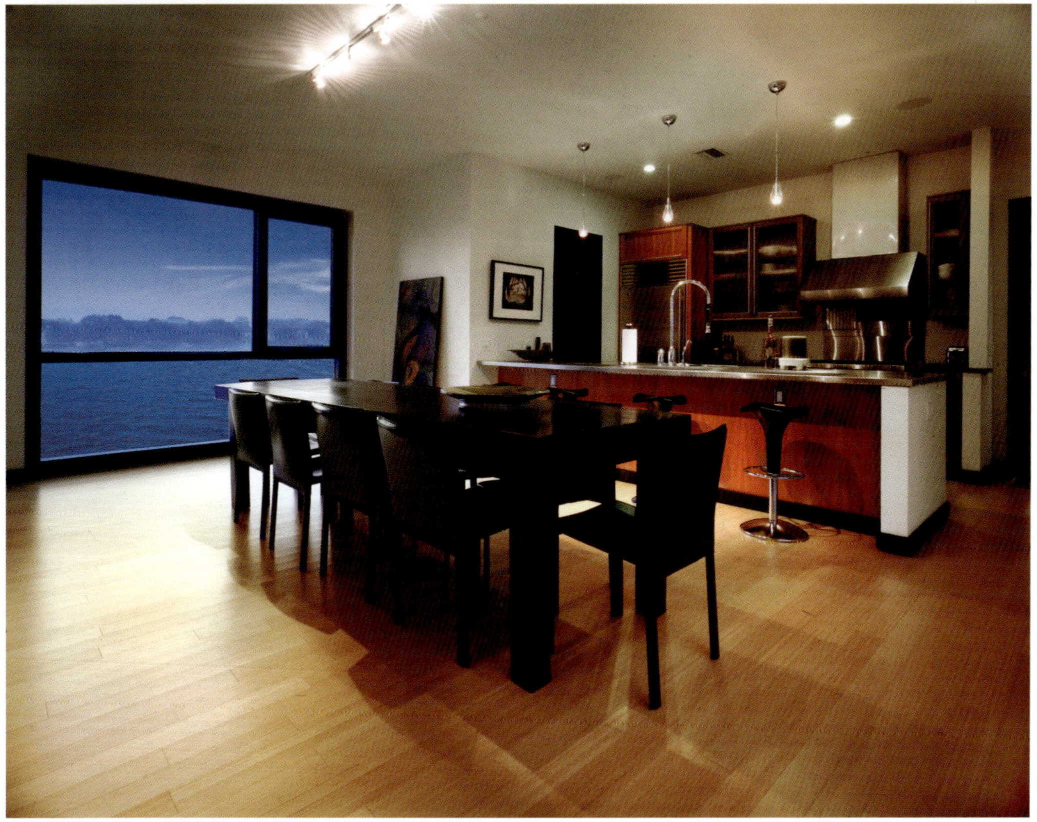

Q&A

more about max...

WHAT ACCREDITATIONS AND ASSOCIATION MEMBERSHIPS DO YOU POSSESS?

Young Architect of the Year, Miami, A.I.A., 2003; "Sexiest House in Miami," *Ocean Drive* magazine; Merit Award of Excellence, A.I.A. 2005.

DESCRIBE YOUR STYLE OR DESIGN PREFERENCES?

Architecture that is simultaneously daring and sensitive.

WHAT IS THE BEST PART OF BEING AN ARCHITECT?

It is a magical process to take a project from a conceptual idea to an inhabitable structure.

WHO HAS HAD THE BIGGEST INFLUENCE ON YOUR CAREER?

My wife; she reintroduced me to nature, which profoundly influences my architectural design.

WHAT IS A SINGLE THING YOU WOULD DO TO BRING A DULL HOUSE TO LIFE?

Strip the walls bare and expose the structure.

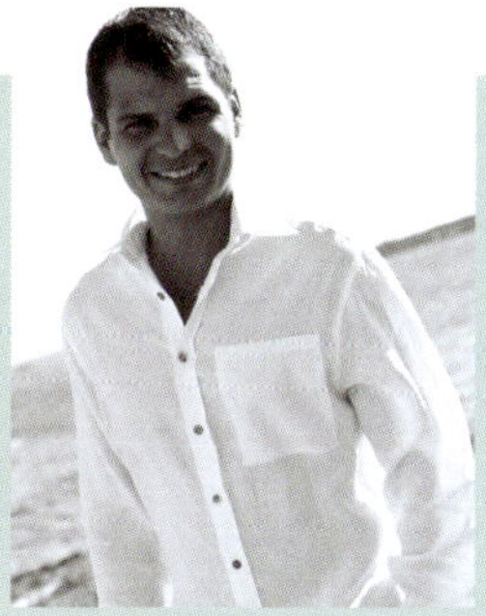

MAX STRANG ARCHITECTURE
Max Strang
125 Grand Avenue
Coconut Grove, FL 33133
305.569.0068
www.strangarchitecture.com

TOP: A modular approach was utilized in the construction of this modern home. Pre-cast concrete elements create a flexible framework.
Photograph by Max Strang Architecture

BOTTOM: The dining room of this lakeside home uses large windows to capitalize on the dramatic view.
Photograph by Max Strang Architecture

FACING PAGE: This nighttime image captures the harmony of modern living in a natural environment.
Photograph by Max Strang Architecture

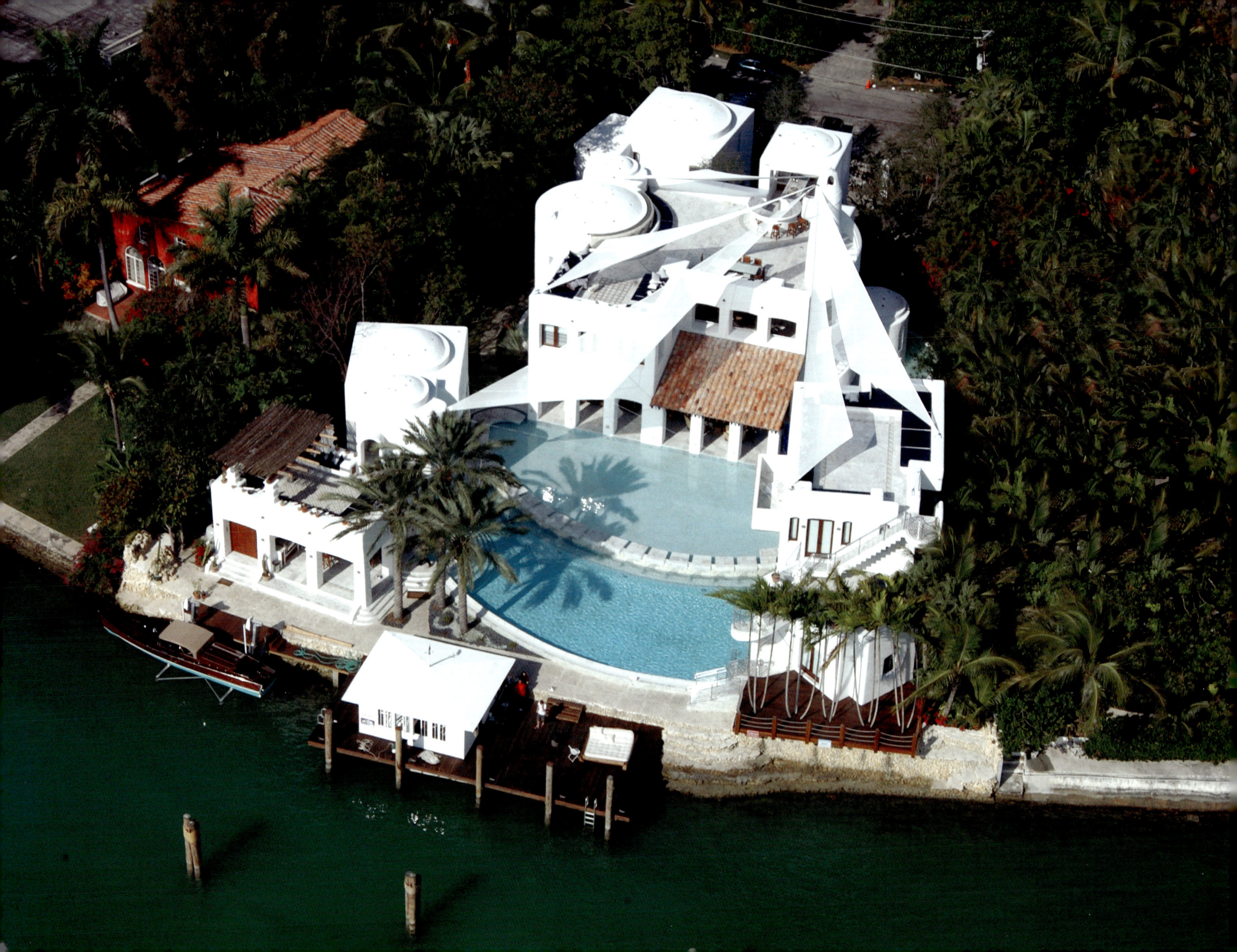

JOHN TURCHIN

John Turchin Companies

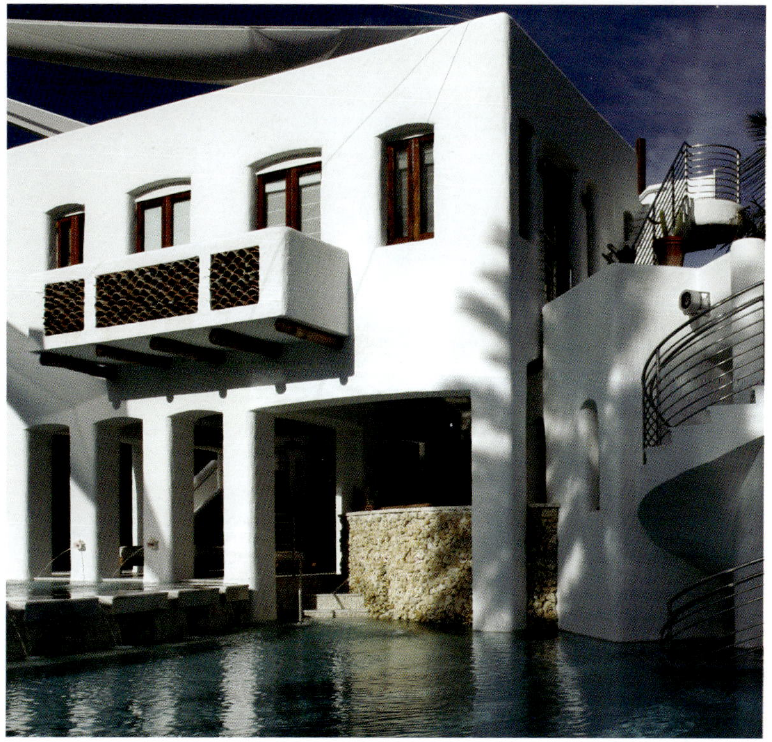

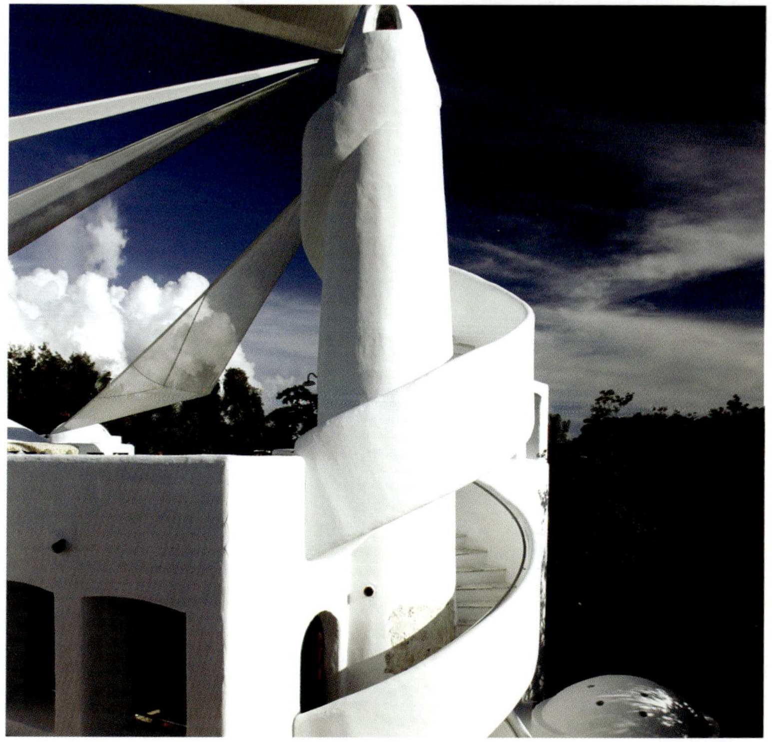

ABOVE LEFT: The cabana houses three guest bedroom suites and its polished railings accentuate the outdoor spiral staircase leading directly down into the pool. The loggia and rooftop terraces provide plenty of space for lounging and entertaining.
Photograph by Mark Roskams

ABOVE RIGHT: A 50-foot-tall spiral observation tower on the rooftop of the main house fans out soaring authentic white boat sails.
Photograph by Mark Roskams

LEFT: "Casa Blanca" A modernist interpretation of Greek Mediterranean style. "Florida's BEST Awards 2005" awarded by the Builders Association of South Florida. Striking architecture combines angular and rounded style; domed and flat rooflines complement arched windows and doorways. This home is a favorite for music awards shows and video shoots, innumerable fashion spreads and a favorite for movie productions.
Photograph by Aerial Photography, Inc.

John Turchin learned the construction trade as the third generation of his family to enter the profession. His grandfather, Ben, started the family business in 1927 and built some of Miami's most prestigious Art Deco hotels. His father, Robert, dazzled the city with chic vertical high-rises.

John took his passion for building to an even more luxurious, unique level. He not only constructs houses and communities, but fashions lifestyle architecture in the most picturesque settings—from waterfront property in Miami Beach, the rustic North Carolina mountains to the sandy white beaches of the Bahamas. "Live in one of our houses and you never need to take a vacation," John says.

When John joined the family business in 1979, he and two brothers initially focused on building spec homes in Palm Beach. They took on commercial projects and in the go-go '80s became known for creating sizzle with the biggest night clubs in Miami Beach such as Club Nu. After Hurricane Andrew devastated the area in 1992, John formed John Turchin Construction with his brother, Robert, to renovate and build custom waterfront houses unlike any competitors.

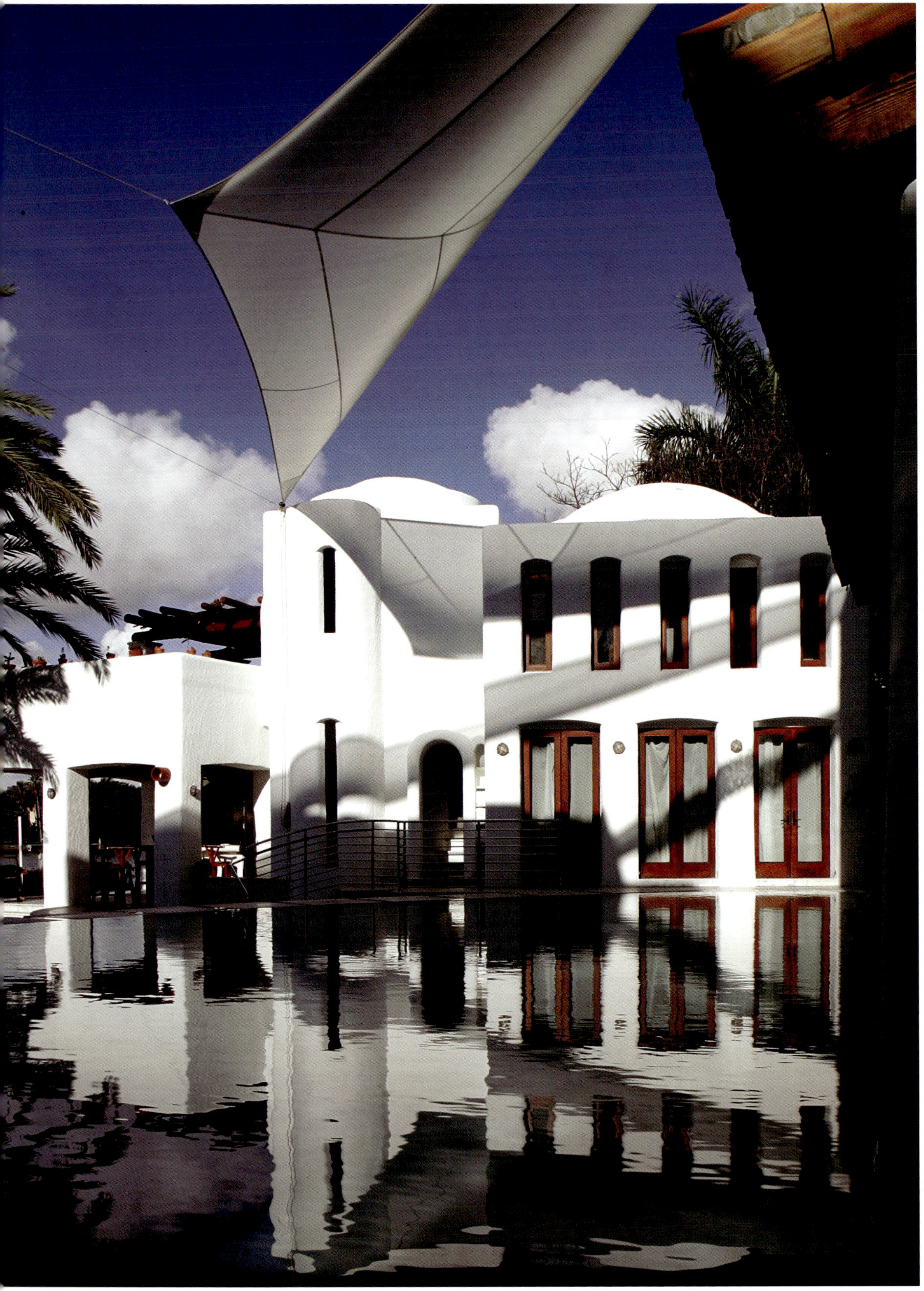

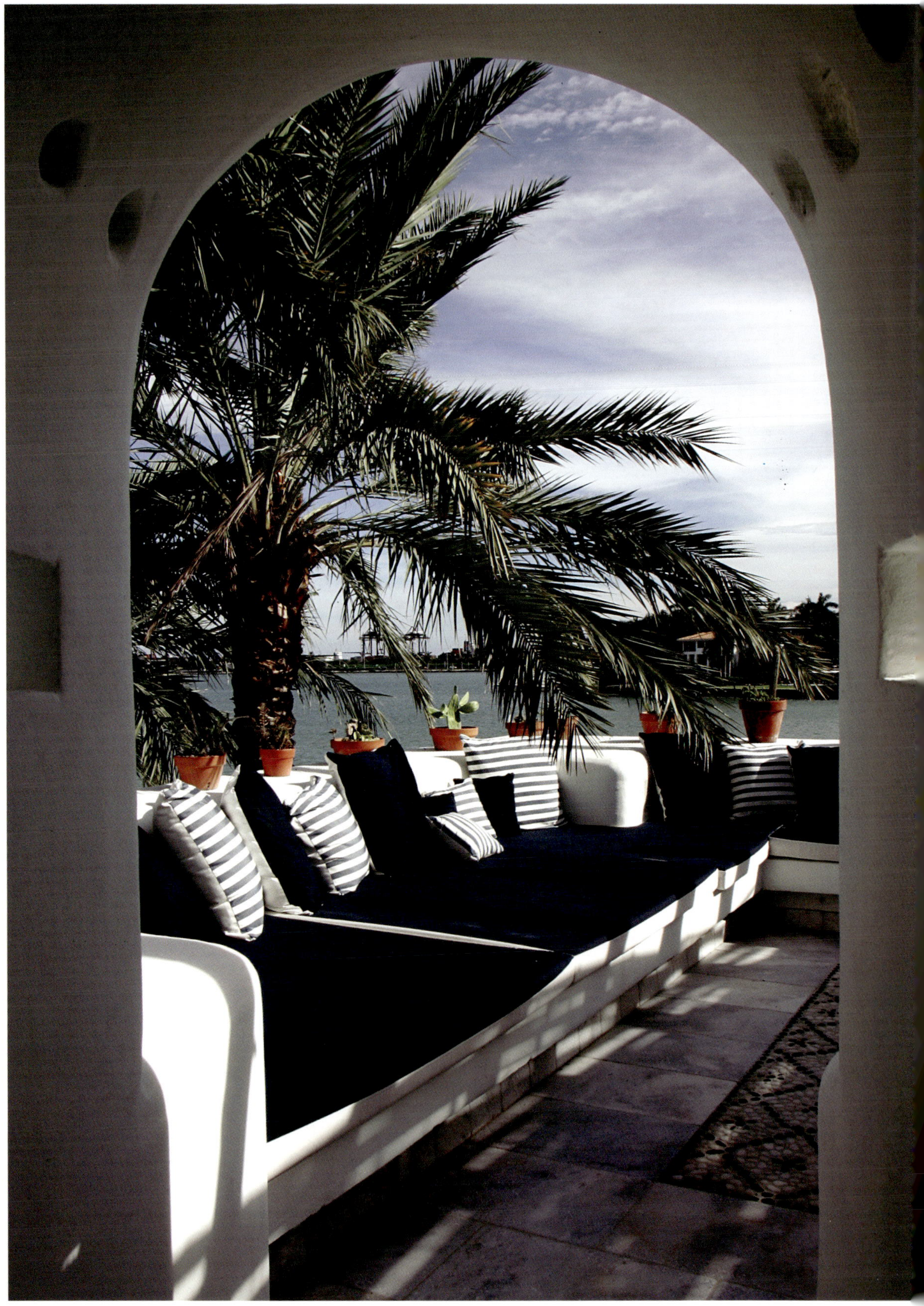

The brothers and partners soon tired of building enormous "ego" houses for others and switched to spec houses that better reflected their desire for luxury with a twist. The concept still guides their boutique firm, which builds fewer than 10 homes a year. Each brings to life an instantly recognizable, glamorous design with distinct architecture and state-of-the-art facilities. The homes cater to affluent owners' discriminating tastes and allow them to play out their fabulous lifestyles.

John's design for his family's home on Hibiscus Island in Florida serves as the perfect prototype with its "Mykonos in Miami" theme. The all-white exterior structure, constructed from solid concrete to withstand hurricanes, brings to mind sun-kissed homes on the Greek islands with soaring white sails, as well as those along the rugged Mexican coastline and deep within this country's Southwest. Its unique plan features separate units that appear to be built into a giant swimming pool and open to the environment.

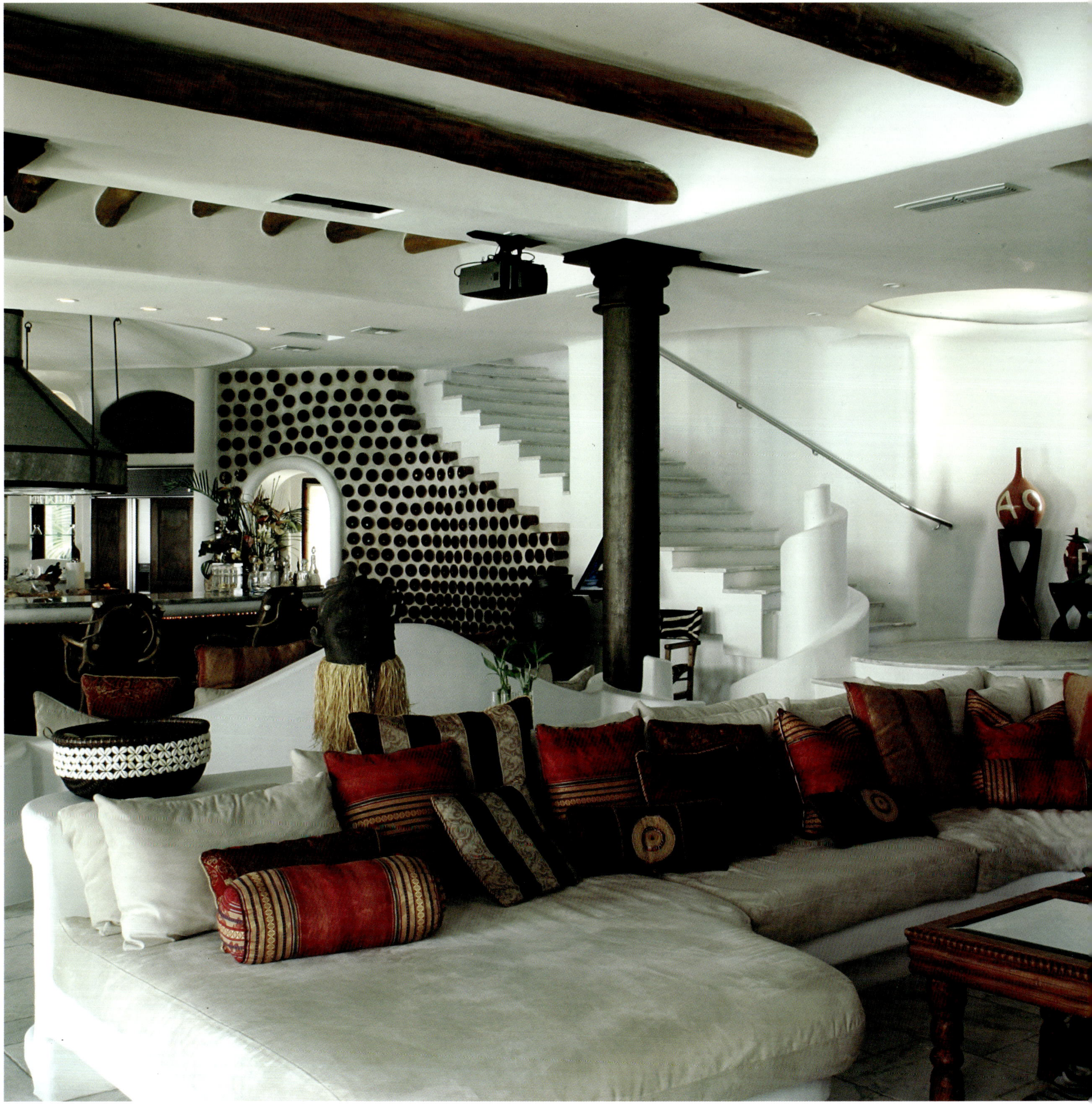

RIGHT: A large, rectangular living room flows into a circular kitchen creating geometric visual interest. Wine cellar walls are created with terracotta tiles. Open-beamed ceilings create the feel of indoor and outdoor spaces flowing together.
Photograph by Mark Roskams

FACING PAGE LEFT: The entertainment pavilion hosts a studio complete with arched windows and doorways. Also featured is a barbeque and wet bar on the first floor, as well as a roof top terrace, gym, and office/library with a private dock and boathouse.
Photograph by Mark Roskams

FACING PAGE RIGHT: Views of Star Island off this entertainment terrace make it perfect for hosting intimate private parties.
Photograph by Mark Roskams

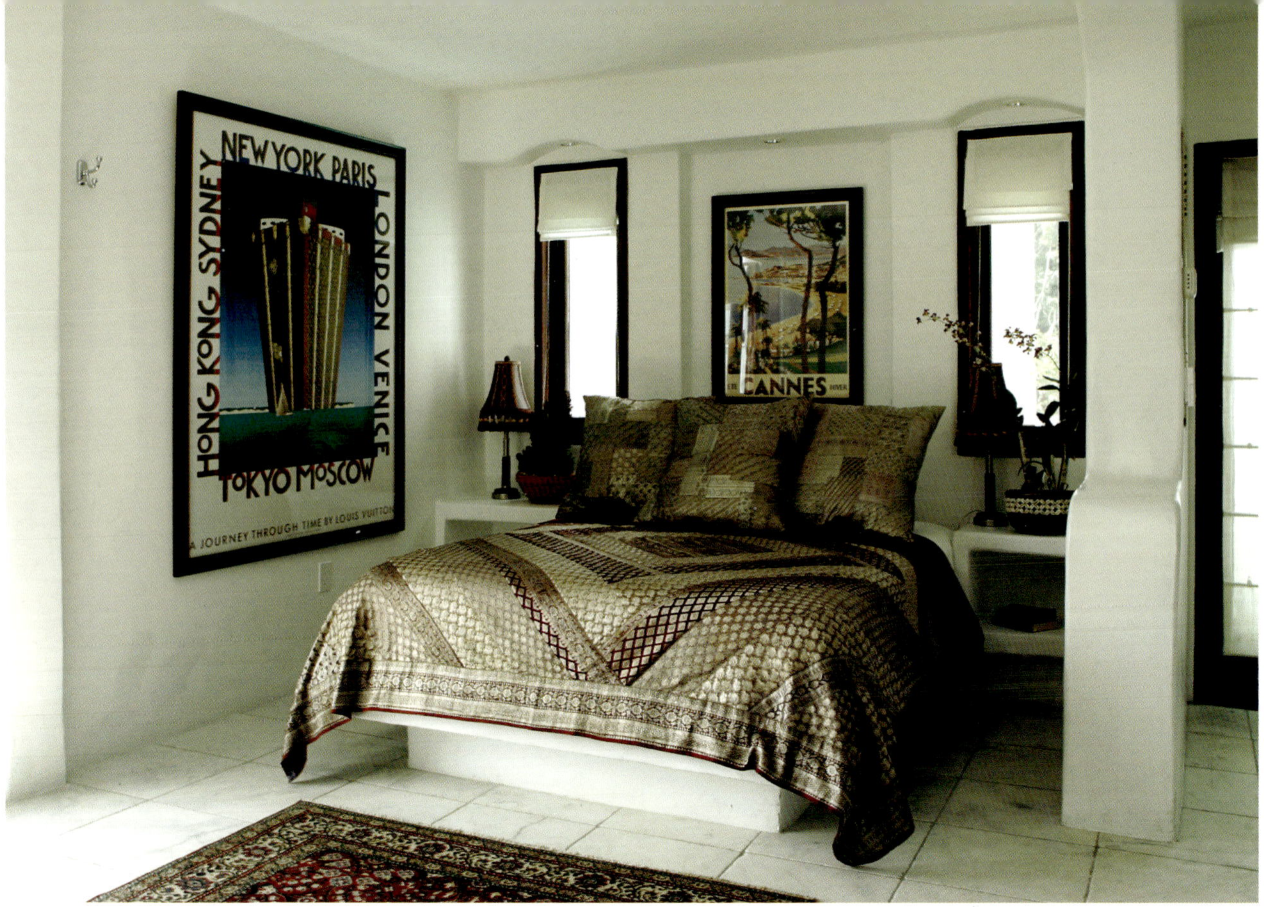

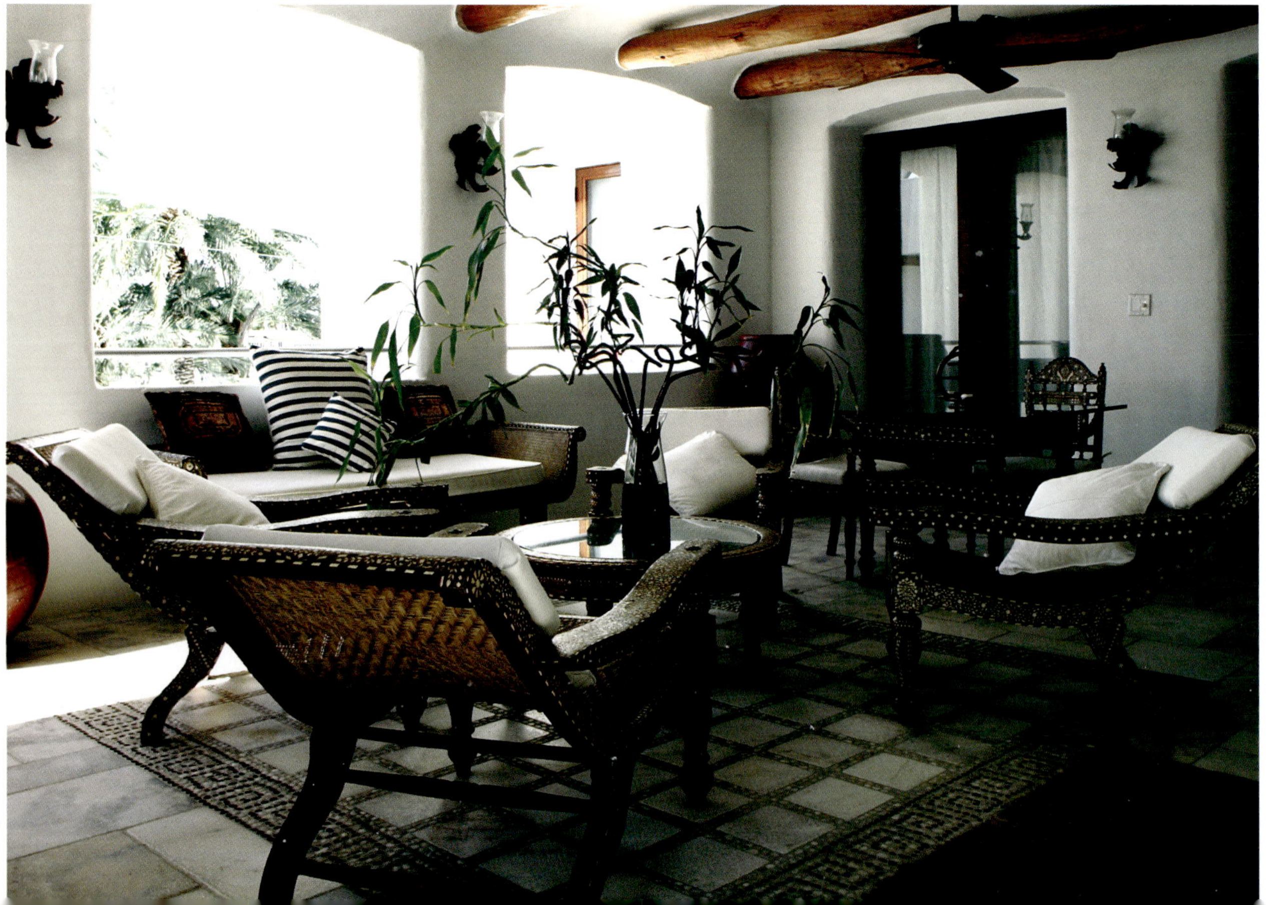

Not all of the company's construction is confined to Florida. The Lodges at Eagles Nests in Banner Elk, North Carolina, allows grown-ups to recall their happy days as campers, while living in a privileged style suited to their success as adults. Set high in the Blue Ridge Mountains on 1,300 acres, the Lodge features elegant "cabins" with logs brought in from Canada or the Adirondacks. Activities range from playing baseball to sport shooting, hiking, fly-fishing, roasting s'mores outdoors, horseback riding on miles of bucolic trails and pursuing art projects in a complete art center, enjoying winter sports on private ski slopes and racing on a motorcross track. After playing hard in the rugged outdoors, owners can rejuvenate their spirits at a pampering spa.

John's Bora-Bora-style village on the drawing board for the Bahamas will bring together owners who love to boat in a haven that leads to the Caribbean, considered the world's boating capital. Besides fulfilling their fantasy of living in thatched Bora-Bora-style huts, they can surf, fish, bird-watch, scuba dive, walk along pristine white sandy beaches or swim in iridescent turquoise waters.

For John there's never an end to translating dreams into realities, so his clients can enjoy unparalleled pleasure, nature and beauty. Many of his ideas are inspired by his love of art. His canvases just happen to be multi million-dollar homes.

His own dream is that his two children will join him in business in the not too distant future. The odds of bringing in a fourth generation may be tough, but if anyone can do it most think John will be the one.

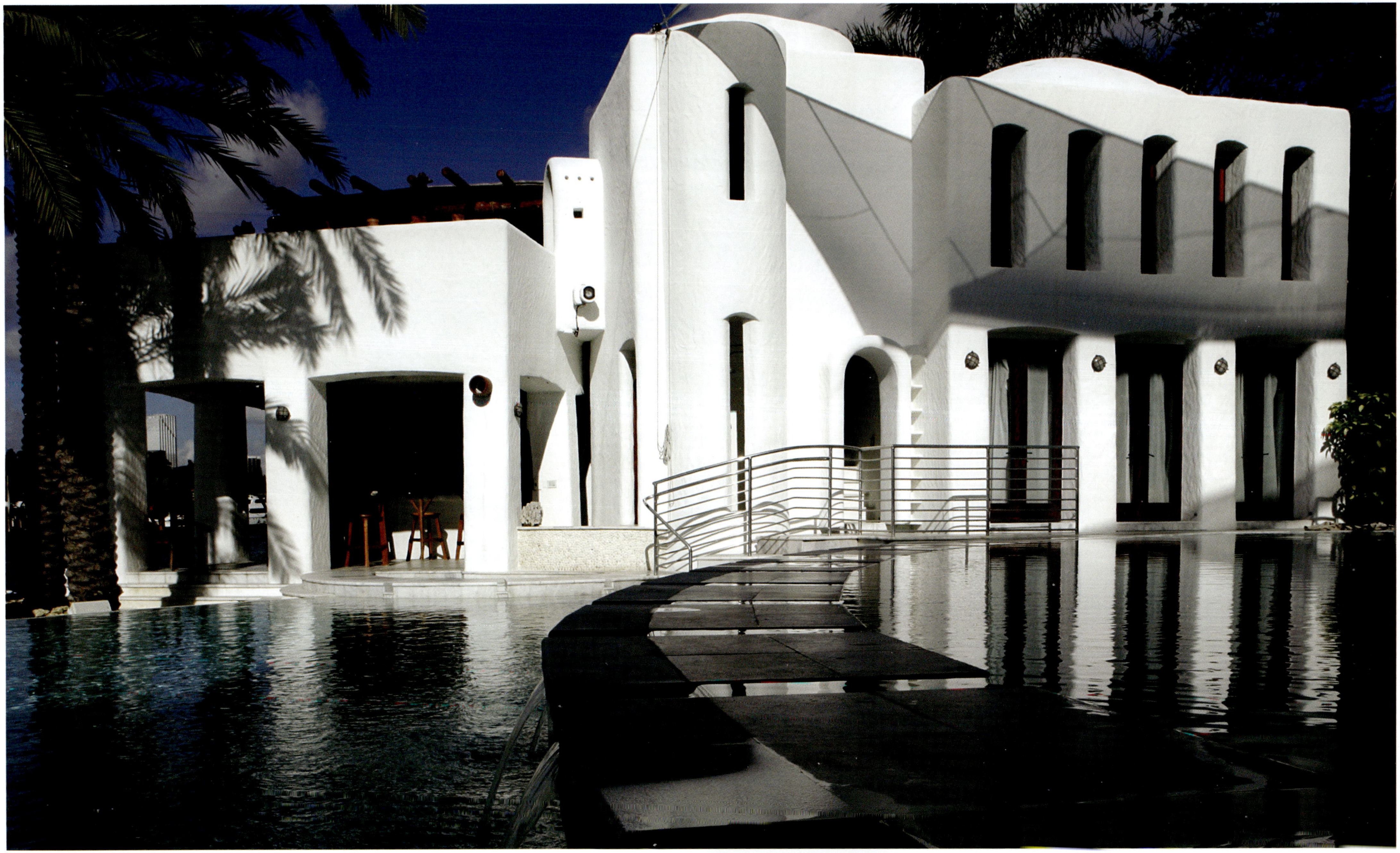

ABOVE: The home boasts a multi-level, Grecian-style pool that overlooks breathtaking views of Biscayne Bay. A stepping stone bridge provides a pathway across the pool, and a large, rounded fountain brings the soothing sound and look of running water. French doors open to 150 feet of water frontage—ample space for dockage of a large yacht, and everything, lends itself to entertaining on a grand scale!
Photograph by Mark Roskams

FACING PAGE TOP: This guest bedroom suite is designed in the Mediterranean style of casual elegance.
Photograph by Mark Roskams

FACING PAGE BOTTOM. This relaxing sitting area is located outside the master suite terrace. The area features Indonesian style woven-cane plantation furniture with mother-of-pearl inlays.
Photograph by Mark Roskams

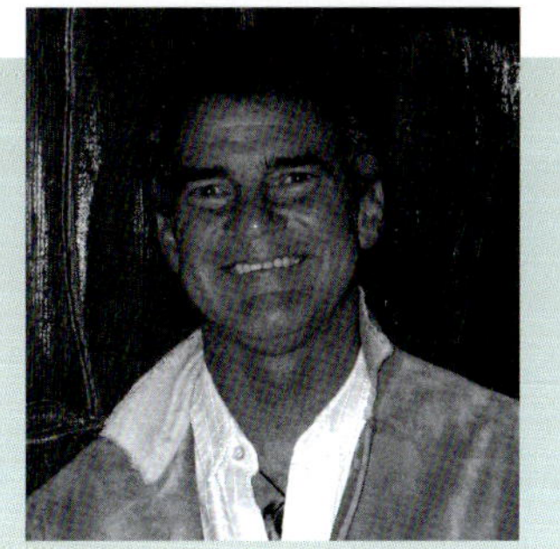

JOHN TURCHIN COMPANIES
John Turchin, Developer
1900 Sunset Harbour Drive, Suite 1
Miami Beach, FL 33139
305.672.0702
www.turchinproperties.com

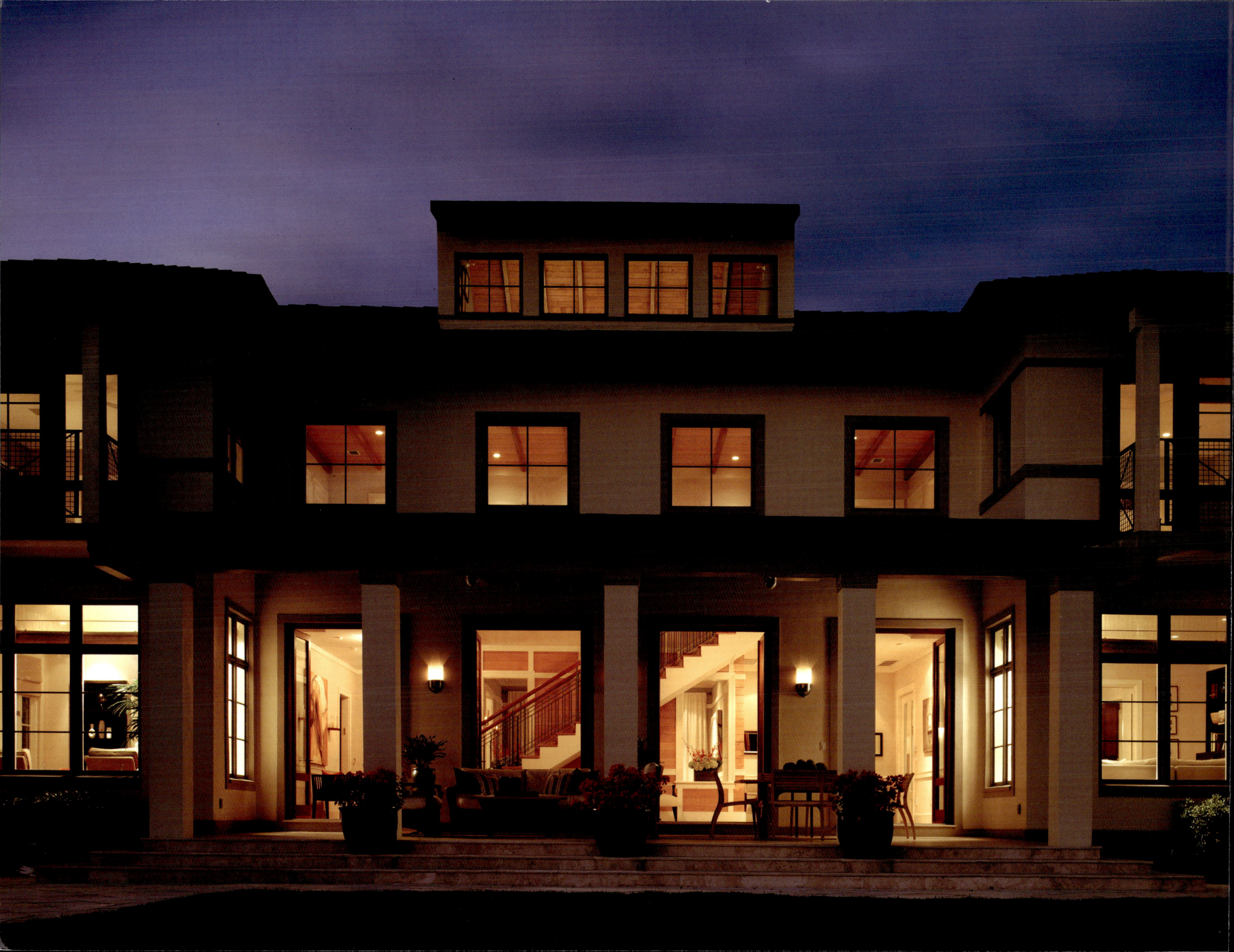

JAYA KADER ZEBEDE

KZ ARCHITECTURE

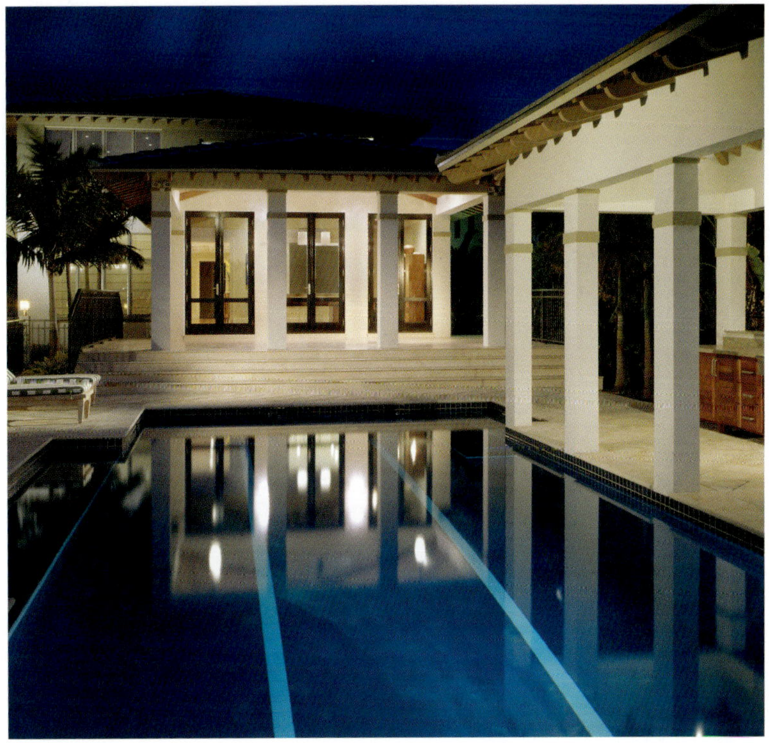

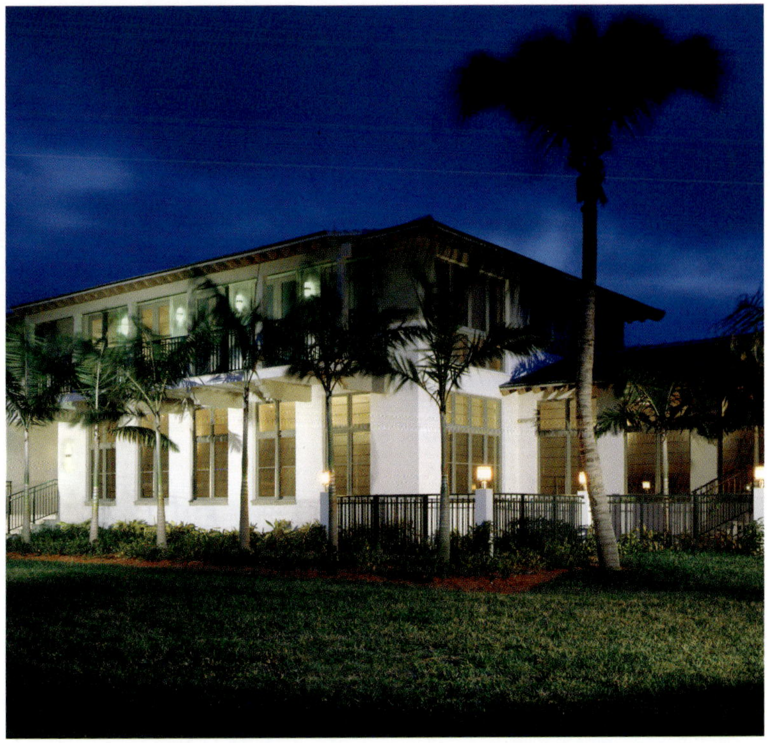

"I do not believe that one style is appropriate for every building; instead I strive to respond to the specific conditions of a site and to the owner's program and desires," says Jaya Kader Zebede. Jaya's designs, forceful and classically modern, strongly reflect her architectural philosophy which emphasizes respect for purpose and context. Jaya stresses a collaborative approach to the design process, where dialogue with clients and consultants from complementary disciplines contribute to a project's success.

Jaya's approach reflects the eclectic cultures among which she has worked. After growing up in Costa Rica, she spent 15 years in the Boston area. She studied art and architectural history at Brandeis University where she earned a Bachelor of Arts. She also spent a semester in Italy studying Renaissance Art and Architecture. In 1988 she earned a Master of Architecture at the Harvard University Graduate School of Design. After graduation, Jaya worked for several prominent architects in the Boston area: Moshe Safdie, Peter Forbes and Graham Gund.

Upon moving to South Florida, Jaya participated in numerous projects that attest to her commitment to professional collaboration. She was instrumental in the development of a team which included Borrelli and Associates and Robert A.M. Stern from New York to participate in an international competition for the Miami Beach Library and Cultural Center in South Beach. Her team was awarded the project in 1998. In addition, Jaya participated in two competitions with Maryann Thompson Architects, a Cambridge, Massachusetts-based firm. These were a competition for Temple Beth Am in 1999 and a competition for a Municipal Center in Islamorada in 2004.

ABOVE LEFT: In this waterfront residence, the pool area is integrated with a generous covered porch and a barbeque pavilion, providing ample outdoor entertaining space.
Photograph by Troy Campbell

ABOVE RIGHT: By breaking up the plan into three different sections, this residence on a long and narrow waterfront site maximizes views from every main room in the house, including the living room, dining room, family room and master bedroom.
Photograph by Troy Campbell

LEFT: This waterfront residence strives to integrate the living structure with the striking beauty of the surrounding landscape. With the main living spaces enjoying water views on both sides of the H plan, the central portion of the house is a two-story gallery that serves as the organizing element of the house. The intent is to allow the occupants to feel the landscape as they move through the residence.
Photograph by George Cott

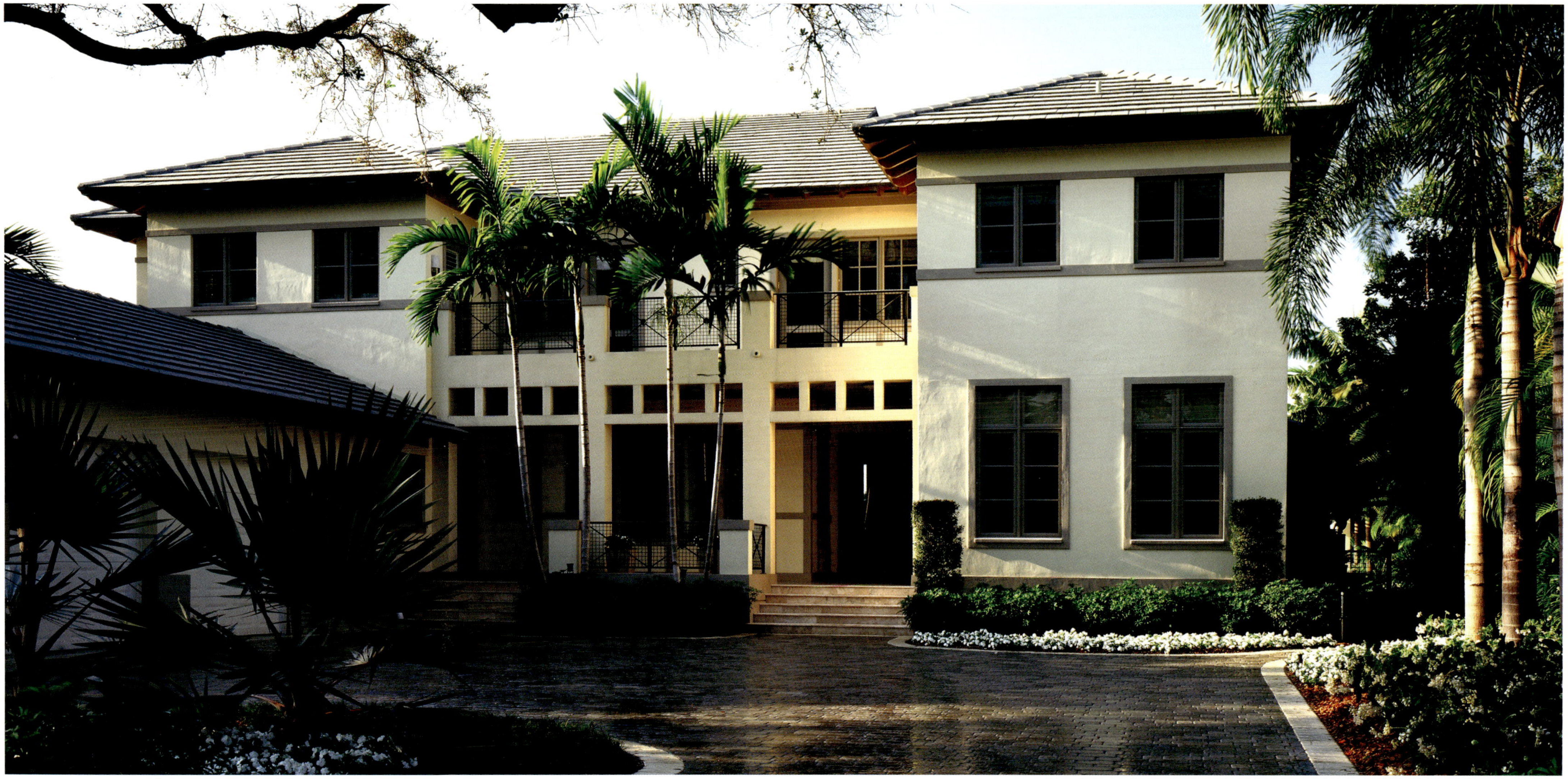

KZ Architecture was founded in 2002 in Bay Harbor Islands, Florida. Its projects, some built and many underway, reflect a deep respect for the local climate and the area's design history. Standing on striking waterfront sites, her homes embody a language that weave together the traditional and the modern, as well as the indoors and the outdoors. The landscape is made to permeate the structures through large windows, doorways, balconies and porches. Large overhangs and dormers provide environmentally sensitive solutions to the tropical settings.

Jaya's practice also concentrates on issues of functionality, materiality and constructability. Choosing the right material is essential to any design's successful execution. Building in South Florida—an area highly vulnerable to climate concerns including hurricanes, termites, and mold—Jaya chooses plaster and stucco for her Florida Cracker-inspired homes instead of the original wood framing prototypes. These traditional wood elements get reinterpreted and abstracted into masonry.

Jaya also expresses her creativity by making playful designs as she toys with the conventional notions of indoors and outdoors. In her home, a large rounded balcony at the top of the stairs whimsically imitates an exterior porch as it serves as an interior hall to bedrooms as well as a perch from which to view the outdoors. The dining room is clad in materials usually reserved for exterior surfaces. In addition, she has commissioned art marrying the house to the landscape which it reflects.

How does Jaya arrive at such a complex mix? "You keep drawing and exploring alternatives until you're satisfied. Eventually, like in music, the process leads you to a composition that is resolved."

One client's letter of praise echoes her approach and further explains her success. "Slowly, patiently, laden with deep questions, [Jaya] probed our minds to determine our needs, our expectations, and our life style…It was [her] professionalism, dedication to excellence, tenacity, and meticulous attention to detail that made it all possible."

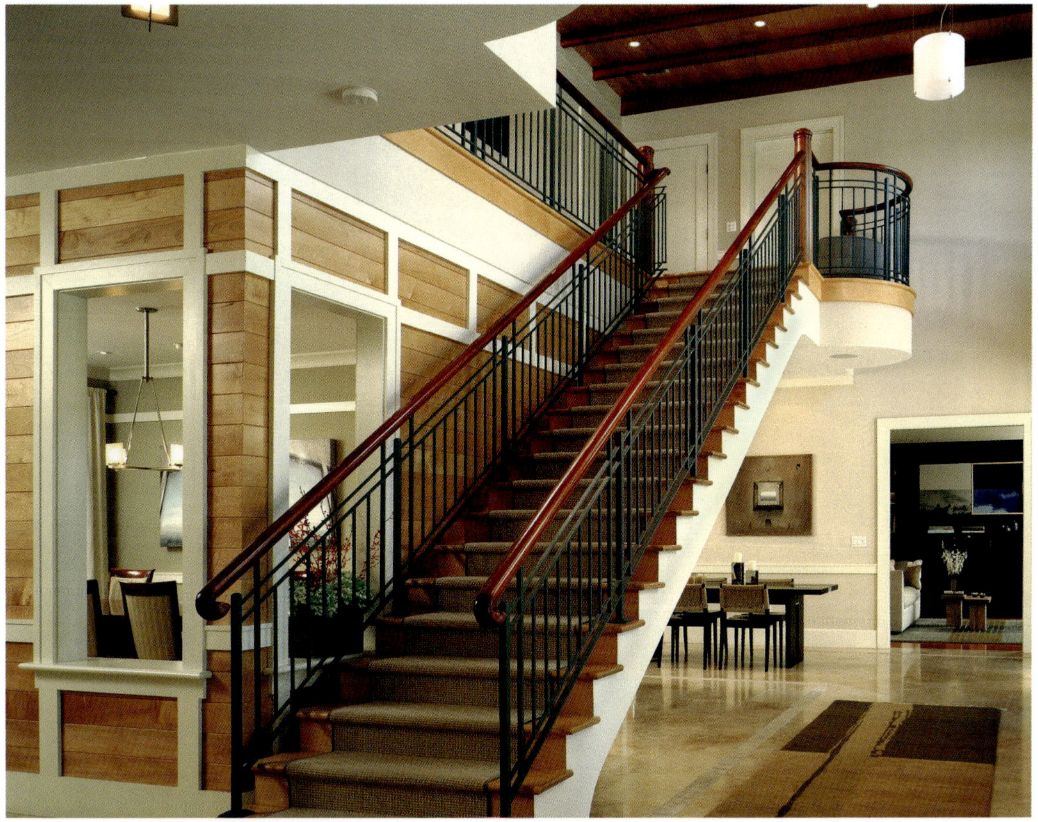

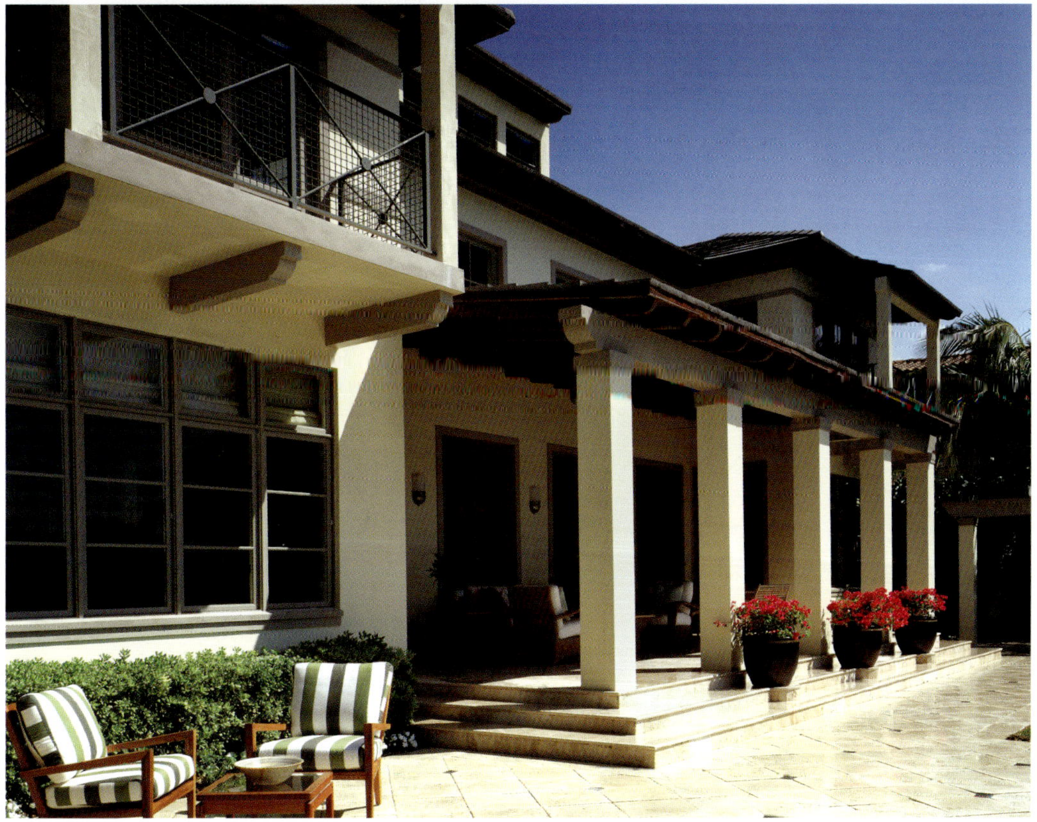

Q&A more about jaya...

WHAT ONE ELEMENT OF STYLE OR PHILOSOPHY HAVE YOU STUCK WITH THAT STILL WORKS FOR YOU TODAY?

Contextual, i.e. respect for the aesthetic and cultural values of the context in which you build.

WHO HAS HAD THE BIGGEST INFLUENCE ON YOUR CAREER?

I believe architecture is a collaborative discipline. I have been fortunate throughout my development as a professional to have had great mentors, school professors, friends and colleagues that have nourished my understanding of architecture and its process.

HOW LONG HAVE YOU BEEN AN ARCHITECT?

An architect since 1988; I founded KZ Architecture in 2002.

DESCRIBE YOUR STYLE OR DESIGN PREFERENCES.

I do not believe that architecture is about heroic stylistic gestures. It's about sensitivity to site, to beauty, to proportions, to materials, to the building's functionality and to the people that will dwell in it.

KZ ARCHITECTURE
Jaya Kader Zebede, AIA
9424 West Broadview Drive
Bay Harbor Islands, FL 33154
305.865.9911
Fax 305.865.0572
www.kzarchitecture.com

TOP: A two-story hallway connects this waterfront residence to the exterior living spaces and is articulated as an indoor-outdoor space. Situated within the great space of the hall, the stair and the dining room are conceived as outdoor-like objects that reinforce the inside-outside interplay of the architecture. The single run stair leads to a porch-like second floor. The articulation of the dining room walls evoke the wood board siding of old Cracker houses. Inverting the traditional courtyard plan, this "indoor pavilion" becomes the heart of the house.
Photograph by George Cott

BOTTOM: Borrowing from the language of the Florida vernacular, this residence has large overhangs, generous porches and covered balconies. These provide environmentally sensitive solutions for a home in a tropical climate.
Photograph by George Cott

FACING PAGE: In this traditional H plan residence, one of the legs of the H gets shifted to receive the volume of the garage. Large balconies and porches reflect motifs of traditional Florida vernacular homes.
Photograph by George Cott

PUBLISHING TEAM

Brian G. Carabet, Publisher

John A. Shand, Publisher

Phil Reavis, Executive Publisher

Beth Benton, Senior Associate Publisher

Mary Elizabeth Acree, Graphic Designer

Michele Cunningham-Scott, Graphic Designer

Emily Kattan, Graphic Designer

Elizabeth Gionta, Editor

Aaron Barker, Editor

Rosalie Wilson, Editor

Lori Capullo, Editor

Kristy Randall, Production Coordinator

Laura Greenwood, Production Coordinator

Jennifer Lenhart, Traffic Coordinator

Carol Kendall, Project Management

Beverly Smith, Project Management

Troy Campbell, Contributing Photographer

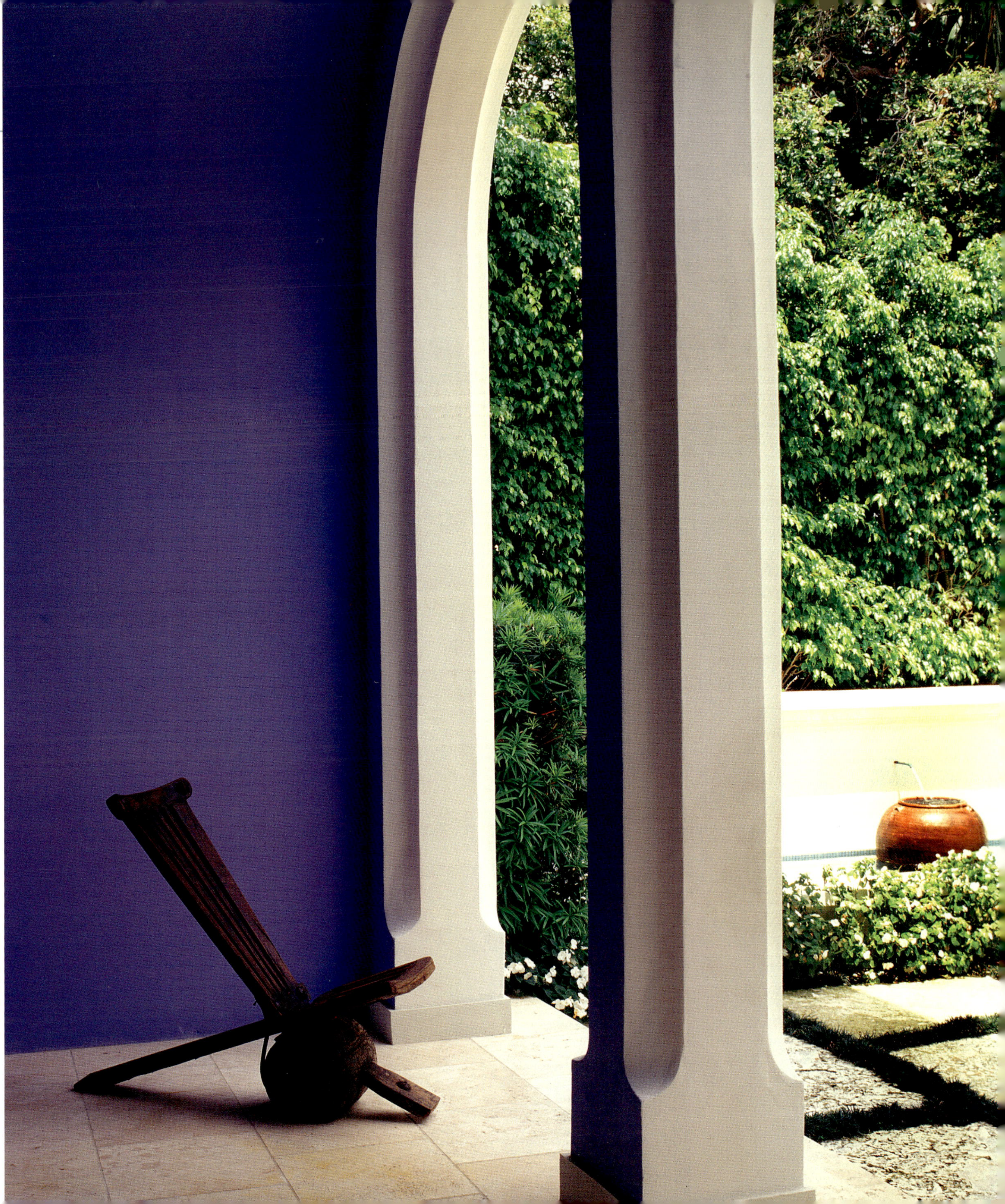

Jose Luis Hernandez, photo by Carlos Domenech

The PANACHE Portfolio

The catalog of fine books in the areas of interior design and architecture and design continues to grow for Panache Partners, LLC. With more than 30 books published or in production, look for one or more of these keepsake books in a market near you.

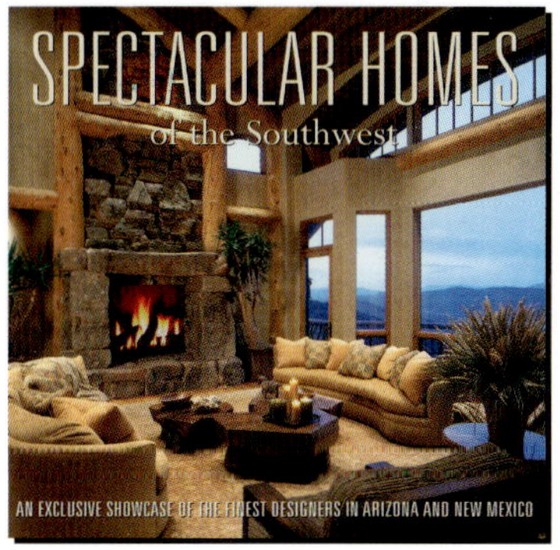

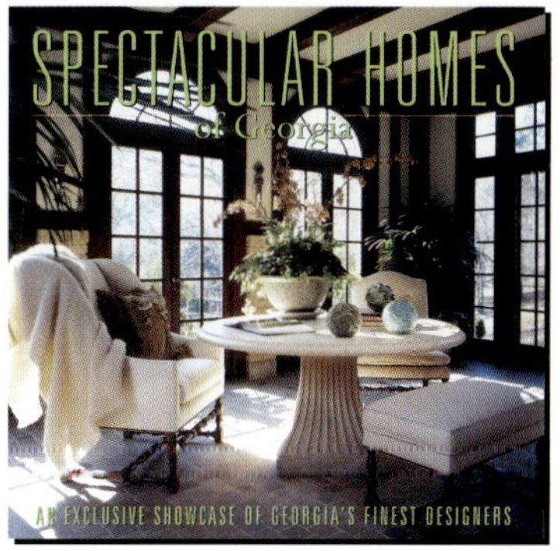

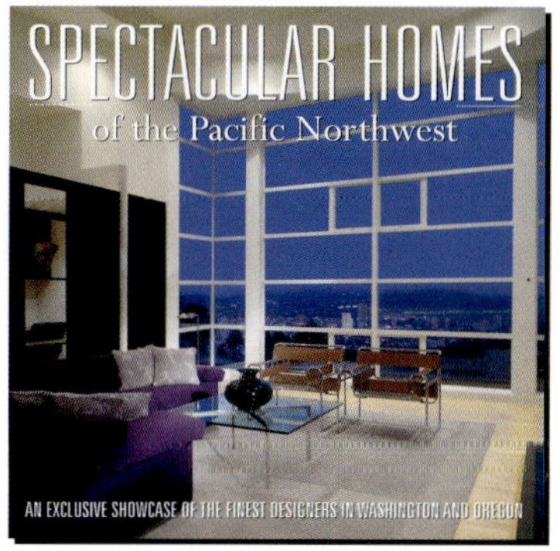

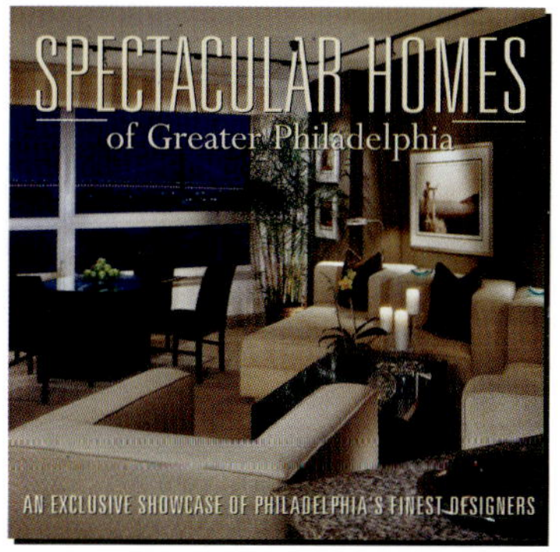

Spectacular Homes Series

Published in 2005

Spectacular Homes of Georgia
Spectacular Homes of South Florida
Spectacular Homes of Tennessee
Spectacular Homes of Texas

Published or Publishing in 2006

Spectacular Homes of California
Spectacular Homes of the Carolinas
Spectacular Homes of Chicago
Spectacular Homes of Colorado
Spectacular Homes of Florida
Spectacular Homes of Michigan
Spectacular Homes of the Pacific Northwest
Spectacular Homes of Greater Philadelphia
Spectacular Homes of the Southwest
Spectacular Homes of Washington DC

Other titles available from Panache Partners

Spectacular Hotels
Texans and Their Pets
Spectacular Restaurants of Texas

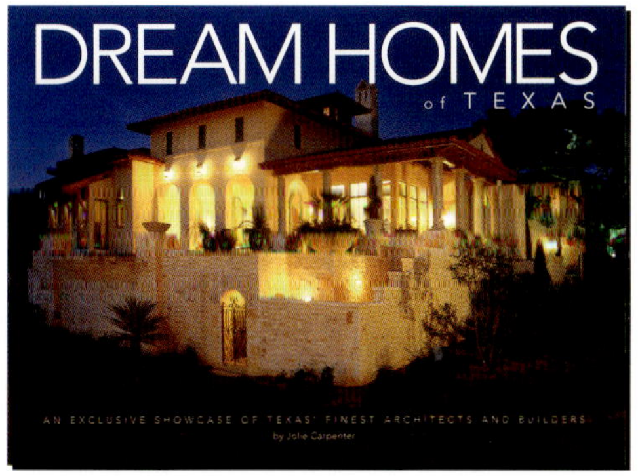

Dream Homes Series

Published in 2005

Dream Homes of Texas

Published or Publishing in 2006

Dream Homes of Colorado
Dream Homes of South Florida
Dream Homes of New Jersey
Dream Homes of New York
Dream Homes of Greater Philadelphia
Dream Homes of the Western Deserts

Order two or more copies today and we'll pay the shipping.

To order visit www.panache.com
or call 972.661.9884.

PANACHE PARTNERS LLC

Creating Spectacular Publications for Discerning Readers

INDEX OF DESIGNERS

Tim Slawson, photo by Tom Harper

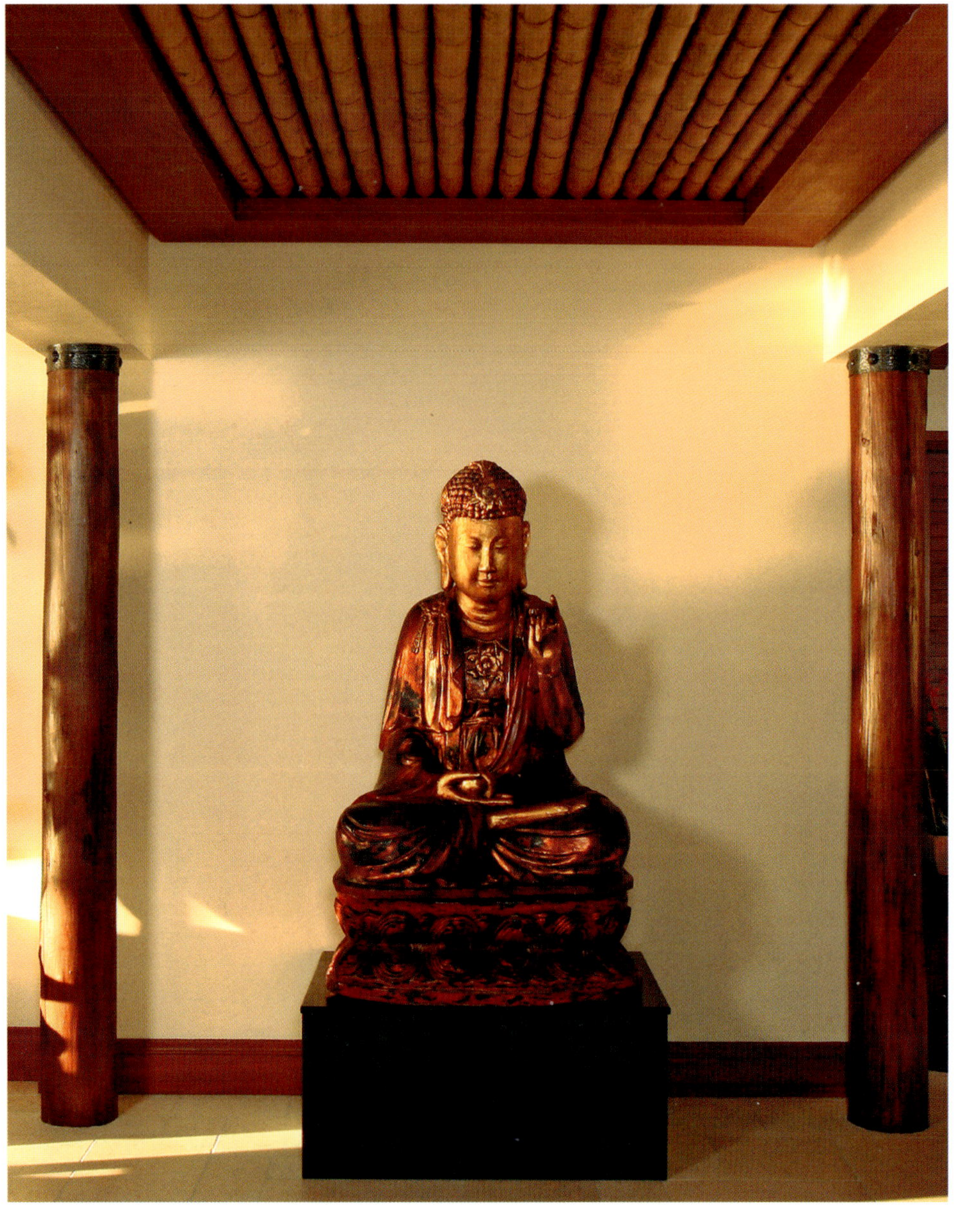